Elements of Demography

(With Demographic Profile of India and the World)

Elements of Demography

(With Demographic Profile of India and the World)

V.C. SINHA

M.A., M.Com., Ph. D., D. Litt.
Head, Department of Business Economics
A.P.S. University
Rewa, M.P.

E. ZACHARIA

M.A., Ph. D.
Professor and Head
Department of Economics
Govt. P.G., T.R.S. College
Rewa, M.P.

ALLIED PUBLISHERS PRIVATE LIMITED

NEW DELHI MUMBAI KOLKATA LUCKNOW CHENNAI
NAGPUR BANGALORE HYDERABAD AHMEDABAD

ALLIED PUBLISHERS PRIVATE LIMITED

1/13-14 Asaf Ali Road, **New Delhi**–110002
Ph.: 011-23239001 • E-mail: delhi.books@alliedpublishers.com

47/9 Prag Narain Road, Near Kalyan Bhawan, **Lucknow**–226001
Ph.: 0522-2209942 • E-mail: lko.books@alliedpublishers.com

17 Chittaranjan Avenue, **Kolkata**–700072
Ph.: 033-22129618 • E-mail: cal.books@alliedpublishers.com

15 J.N. Heredia Marg, Ballard Estate, **Mumbai**–400001
Ph.: 022-42126969 • E-mail: mumbai.books@alliedpublishers.com

60 Shiv Sunder Apartments (Ground Floor), Central Bazar Road,
Bajaj Nagar, **Nagpur**–440010
Ph.: 0712-2234210 • E-mail: ngp.books@alliedpublishers.com

F-1 Sun House (First Floor), C.G. Road, Navrangpura,
Ellisbridge P.O., **Ahmedabad**–380006
Ph.: 079-26465916 • E-mail: ahmbd.books@alliedpublishers.com

751 Anna Salai, **Chennai**–600002
Ph.: 044-28523938 • E-mail: chennai.books@alliedpublishers.com

5th Main Road, Gandhinagar, **Bangalore**–560009
Ph.: 080-22262081 • E-mail: bngl.books@alliedpublishers.com

3-2-844/6 & 7 Kachiguda Station Road, **Hyderabad**–500027
Ph.: 040-24619079 • E-mail: hyd.books@alliedpublishers.com

Website: www.alliedpublishers.com

First Edition, 1984

Second Edition, 1986

Edition, 2018

ISBN : 81-7764-044-5

Published by Sunil Sachdev and printed by Ravi Sachdev at Allied Publishers Private Limited, Printing Division, A-104 Mayapuri Phase II, New Delhi - 110064

To
My Reverend Teacher
Dr. J.S. MATHUR
Professor of Commerce and
Business Administration
Allahabad University

V.C. SINHA

PREFACE TO THE SECOND EDITION

We place on record our sense of gratitude to the students and the teachers for their appreciation of our work. It has afforded us an opportunity to bring out the second edition of the book within a year. The second edition has been thoroughly revised, enlarged and updated. Various new topics and new sections have been introduced. The coverage of the book has been made more comprehensive.

A few of the salient features of this edition are:

- The book attempts to cover the entire topical issues and aspects of Indian population within its ambit.
- The subject matter has been presented in simple and legible style to project the new emerging trends in demographic tendencies.
- The study seeks to present the various aspects of India's population not only from the historical perspective but also from the analytical angle.
- The facts and figures in the earlier edition have been updated by drawing liberally from the 1981 Census data for inclusion in the present edition.
- Adequate care has been taken to provide all the relevant materials in a brief and precise way without neglecting any of the essential aspects of demography.

We are deeply thankful to Dr. Mrs. Pushpa Sinha and Mrs. Mariamma Zacharia, M.A. for the meticulous way, in which they helped us in revising the book.

We owe special debt of gratitude to Shri Sunil Sachdev, Director of Allied Publishers Ltd., for taking pains to get the book published in time.

I acknowledge with thanks the suggestions and advice received from various quarters for the improvement of the book. I am confident that the book would prove more useful to the teachers and the students of the subject. We shall welcome constructive criticisms and suggestions from the professors and students alike to make this book more useful in future.

–Authors

CONTENTS

PART I–INTRODUCTORY 1–220

Chapters

1. Definition, Nature, Scope and Importance of Demography ... 1
2. Demography and Other Social Sciences ... 13
3. Origin and Development of Demography ... 20
4. Some Basic Concepts of Demographic Analysis ... 36
5. Nature of Demographic Data ... 45
6. Population Census ... 53
7. Vital Statistics ... 65
8. Mortality and Mortality Measurement ... 70
9. Morbidity ... 99
10. Fertility and Measurement of Fertility ... 103
11. Measurement, Projection and Estimation of Population ... 131
12. The Life Table ... 166
13. Migration ... 182
14. Population and Economic Development ... 211

PART II–POPULATION THEORIES 221–281

15. Malthusian Theory of Population ... 224
16. Neo-Malthusianism ... 238
17. The Optimum Theory of Population ... 241
18. Social and Economic Theories of Population ... 254
19. Biological and Natural Theories of Population ... 270
20. Theory of Demographic Transition ... 283

PART III—INDIA'S POPULATION 289–522

21. Trends in Indian Population Growth ... 289
22. Trends and Differentials in Fertility (Birth Rates) in India ... 302
23. Age at Marriage in India ... 320
24. Widow Remarriage in India ... 336
25. Mortality (Death Rates), Trends and Differentials in India ... 340
26. The Composition of Population ... 359
27. Migration in India ... 384
28. Urbanisation in India ... 396
29. Occupational Structure of Indian Population ... 425
30. Qualitative Aspects of Indian Population ... 442
31. Impact of Population Growth on Economic Development of India ... 463
32. Sources of Demographic Data in India ... 472
33. Population Policy in India ... 491

PART IV–WORLD POPULATION 523–592

34. Population of World ... 523
35. Population of Japan ... 540
36. Population of China ... 549
37. Population of Sri Lanka ... 557
38. Population of U.S.S.R. ... 567
39. Population of United States of America ... 575
40. Population of Great Britain ... 588

1

Definition, Nature, Scope and Importance of Demography

The term 'demography' is derived from two Greek words, 'Demas', the people and 'Grapho', to draw or write. Thus its meaning is to draw or write about people.

The credit for fusing together the two Greek words and coining the term demography goes to Achille Guillard, who in 1855 wrote his book 'Elements de statistique humaine en demographic camparee'. In fact John Graunt is the real founder of demography, who in 1762 wrote the book "Natural and political observation made upon the bills of Mortality".

Definition of Demography

As regard definition of this term, the economists, geographers, social scientists and others have defined it in their own way that suits their convenience and view point. Obviously some definitions have adopted a narrow outlook on the subject while some have made its scope very wide. Some of the important definitions which have been given in this regard are discussed below.

The Multilingual Demographic Dictionary defines demography as the "Scientific study of human populations, primarily with respect to their size, their structure and their development." (U.N. 1958: 3)

The Multilingual Demographic Dictionary, however, differentiates between various aspects of demography by defining separately demographic statistics, economic demography and social demography; the latter two imply the "study of relations between demographic phenomena on the one hand and economic and social phenomena on the other".

Another limited view of demography is taken by Wrong who defines it as the statistical description and analysis of human populations.

According to Peter R. Cox: "Demography is the study of statistical methods of human population involving primarily the measurements of the size, growth and diminution of the numbers of the people, the rate, death rate, population growth, sex ratio and health condition, etc.

Many economic issues like unemployment, income condition of the masses, standard of living, labour conditions and living standard, production, consumption, saving-habits, correlation between population and economic development are all part of Macro Demography Study.

Social problems like marital status, composition of the family, growing trend about caste, religion, education, etc., form part of macro demography. Geography can also be studied with the help of macro demography. For example problems of migration, urbanisation, etc. form part of macro demograpy.

Micro Demography

According to the narrow view, we study demography as small units like individual, family, group etc. In fact these units constitute the primary elements of macro analysis. For instance if we study the fertility rate of women in Rewa or Bhopal, it forms part of micro demography. On the other hand, if we study the fertility of women for the whole of India or Madhya Pradesh, and Rewa and Bhopal divisions are included as units of the same, then the study will fall within the macro analysis. According to Prof. Bogue "Micro Demography is the study of the growth, distribution and redistribution of the population within community, state, economic area or other local area. This included both numerical and composition aspects and is performed by using meaningful subdivision of community of local areas."

BALANCED VIEW OF DEMOGRAPHY

This school of thought have presented a balanced view of the nature and scope of demography. According to Thompson and Lewis "under demography we can develop the understanding of population variables like fertility, mortality, information about female population, their health condition, marital status, distribution of population according to villages and their classification according to their occupation, and also to collect and study information about social and economic condition."

These days it is accepted that demography is the study of human society and has very little to do with individualistic human problems. It takes the use of figures and arithmatics. In the World Population Conferences held by the United Nations Organisation in

1954 and 1968 the following topics were discussed: (1) Fertility, (2) Mortality, (3) Migration, (4) Genetic composition, (5) Future prospects, (6) Population and resources, (7) Techniques of measurement, (8) Training of demographers, (9) Distribution of population, (10) Family planning, (11) Population projection, (12) Demographic aspects of housing, education, saving and investment.

According to Whipple the subject matter of demography comprises of :

(1) Geneology, Ancestory and their records.
(2) Human Eugenics.
(3) Registration of vital events.
(4) Census of Population.
(5) Biometrics dealing with the study of structure, growth and strength of human body.
(6) Pathometrics dealing with the knowledge of disease and anatomy.

In short, in the subject matter of Demography we study the following:

(1) Size

The number of people living in a given place at a given time, its comparison with previous period and the future projection are important elements of size of population. Facts like these are sought by industrial concerns, schools, universities, hospitals as well as by demographers and other social scientists. More complex issues like the rate of change and the trends shown by these rates are also part of this aspect. The causes of change like natality, mortality and migration are analysed with the use of biological, social, economic and cultural variables.

(2) Composition of Population

Composition of population covers all the measurable characteristics of the people who form a given population. The most widely used characteristics are age and sex. If other things remain the same, the population with a long proportion of men and women in the early reproductive years of 18 to 35 years of age would have high crude birth rates. Productive man power will be high in a community tha t has a large proportion of total population between the ages of 15 and 65. Rural and urban residence, marital status, occupation, education, religion, etc., are some other characteristics in the composition of population. According to Thompson and Lewis "The student of population is interested not only in the composition of population at a given moment of time but also in the changes taking place in the composition, the causes of these changes and their effect on community life."

(3) Distribution of Population

Under it we study how are people distributed in the world in the categories labelled advanced urban industrial regions. The changes taking place in the numbers and proportions in different categories and their causes are also important.

Issues of internal distribution of population like rural farm and rural non-farm communities and different kinds of urban communities are also dealt under the caption distribution. Basically changes are taking place in the distribution of population by the cumulative effect of differences in mortality, birth and net migration rates. To understand the size, composition and distribution of population, demographers must study natality, mortality and migration and finally he must search the social significance of statistics he has studied under these headings.

(4) Labour Force

Labour force constitutes an important field of economic study. Labour force falls into two classes, viz., economically active labour force and economically dependent or inactive labour force. Under the category of economically active labour force falls employed as well as involuntarily unemployed labour force. In economically inactive labour force comes housewives, students, fixed income recipients, etc. Labour force study consists of gainful worker concept, status of labour, time reference, duration period, etc.

The principle measures of labour force analysis or economic activity include crude activity rate or crude labour force participation rate, the age, sex, labour force participation rates, the general labour force participation rate, the standardised labour force participation rates, etc. The labour force participation rates are studied separately for male workers as well as female workers. In addition, demographers undertake national as well as international studies concerning employment and different kinds of unemployment like under-employment, disguised unemployment, rural unemployment, frictional unemployment, structural unemployment, etc.

(5) Population Policy

The need of proper population policy has come to occupy an indispensable adjunct of population planning. Population growth impinges on the socio-economic development of the country. Population policy studies embrace items like the philosophy and guiding principles of population policy, the magnitudes of the problem, organisational structure of policy frame, services and supplies, education and motivation, family planning targets, family planning progress and achievements, family planning expenditure, births averted and effect on birth rate, etc.

Family planning programmes are evolved according to the local requirements. Suggestions are offered by world organisations from time to time.

NATURE OF DEMOGRAPHY

A science is a systematic body of knowledge dealing with cause and effect. Many definitions of science are given, of which some are given here.

According to Green: "Science is a way of investigating." According to Karl Pearson: "The unity of science consists alone in its method, not in its nature." As Beisanz, G. and Beisanz. M. put it "It is approach rather than content that is the test of science."

Scientific Method

Scientific method is a systematic study of a subject matter within a given scope. The problem to be dealt with should be clearly defined before starting work on a scientific system. Scientific method consists of well defined steps which are as follows:

(1) *Observation*: The starting point of scientific system is to minutely observe the subject matter under study. This study is conducted with the help of exact instrument of observation.

(2) *Recording*: The next step in scientific system is to make a careful record of the observation without any personal bias.

(3) *Classification*: This is the most important step of the scientific method. Under it the collected materials are properly classified and organised. As Karl Pearson states: "The classification of facts, the recognition of their sequence and relative significance is the function of science." Classification should show the mutual relation of the elements.

(4) *Generalisation*: The next step in scientific system is to generalise or to find a common rule on the basis of semblance in the classified matter. The common rule is called a scientific principle. In the words of MacIver "Such a law is simply another name for a carefully described and uniformly recurring sequence of conditions."

(5) *Verification*: A scientific system is incomplete without verification of the generalisations. Verification of the scientific principles is necessary to preserve the scientific nature of the study.

Basic Requisites of Science

The special features of science are enumerated below:

(1) *Scientific method*: Scientific method is the basic ingredient to enable a subject to be called a science.

(2) *Representing facts*: Science studies facts. Its subject matter is based on these facts.

(3) *Universal*: Scientific principles can be applied at all places. They are invariably true in all countries and at all times.

(4) *Possibility to verify*: Scientific rules can be examined at any time and their veracity could be established.

(5) *Cause and effect relation*: Science tries to discover cause and effect relations of the subject matter under study.

(6) *Prediction*: Scientific analysis can be used to predict on the subject matter. Science knows that 'what will be', can be decided on the basis of 'what is', on account of the immutable and universal nature of cause and effect law.

Demography as a Science

Application of scientific yardsticks to demography reveals that it possesses all the basic elements of a science. This truth can be shown as under:

(1) *Demography employs scientific method*: All methods of social demography are scientific. To begin with facts are assembled through observation. Afterwards they are presented systematically and then classified and finally common principles are made on the basis of accepted facts.

(2) *Demography makes factual study*: Demography comprises of factual studies concerning population with census as the principle method of study. Census study is based on factual enumeration of the people.

(3) *Demographic principles are universal*: The rules of demography are proved in all countries so long as the circumstances are the same.

(4) *Demographic principles can be verified*: Demographic principles are true even if they are subjected to repeated scrutiny. Their veracity can be confirmed at all times.

(5) *Demography defines cause and effect relations*: Social demography discovers cause and effect relationship in events, social reactions

and in social facts. It seeks to explain what and why of events.

(6) *Demography can predict*: Cause-effect relationship helps the demographer to make guess work of the future and predict about social relations, events, etc. He can decide 'what will be' on the basis 'what is', i.e. on basis of cause and effect relationship.

John. V. Gramman said: "Demography is both an abstract science and applied science and applied technology."

The scientific nature of demography was also emphasised by Irene Taeuber who stated: "With improved data, new techniques and the precise measurement of the demographic transition that is occurring, demography has become a science rather than literature." Demography employs scientific methods, the foremost of which is analysis. S.N. Agarwala righty said: "Demography deals with population statistics. Population studies deal with analytical interpretation of population dynamics and composition which covers a wider area. . . . We are shifting from demography to population studies."

The scientific nature of demography is revealed through its aims. The major aims of demography are as under:

(1) Achievement of knowledge of the size, organisation and distribution of population related to the field of study.

(2) Description of past evolution of population in a given area and its distribution in different fields.

(3) Enquiry into trends of population and its relationship with the different aspects of social organisation in an area.

(4) Advance projection and prediction of future demographic trends and evolution and its possible consequences.

It is crystal clear that demography performs all functions characteristic of a science such as cause and effect relation and predict about future. It employs scientific methods of observation and analysis. It is factual as well as universal. It is veridical. It establishes cause and effect relationship. Its laws are verifiable generalisations.

IMPORTANCE OF DEMOGRAPHY

The opinion could be ventured that the study of population was one of the milestones in the development of social sciences. Demography presents population data in a systematic manner. Its importance could be gauged from the growing application of population figures in several disciplines of study. Its significance to the individual and society hardly requires any emphasis.

In the recent decades population is multiplying by leaps and bounds. This phenomenon is having its impact in every sphere of human life, more particularly in the social and economic life of the society. Population policy constitutes the main plank of the global programme to salvage mankind from the spectre of hunger which hangs like the sword of Democles.

Significance of demography in different fields could be treated as under:

(1) *Political*: In the political field the authorities would be able to know with the help of factual demographic data about the rate at which the number of voters, both male and female, are increasing and how the generation gap is gradually influencing national and international politics. Besides data on population can help in identifying pockets of high concentration, what types of arrangements will be needed for conducting elections, which are the areas from where influx of population takes place, establishment of international peace and prosperity, etc.

(2) *Economic*: The importance of demographic studies in the economic field compasses a wide spectrum. It aids in framing economic programmes which can contribute to economic development. With the help of population studies we can know how far economic development is keeping pace with the rate of growth in population, which helps in taking appropriate measures to overcome imbalance between the two, if any.

Population figures furnish information in occupational pattern which helps in assessing the growth and modernisation of the economy. As pointed out by Kathrine Organski and A.F.K. Organski: "If you wish to know how fast a nation is progressing in its economic modernisation, look at the figures on occupations, at the percentage of population engaged in agriculture, in industry and in service."

Employment is a basic human need. Population studies can help in focusing attention on the dimension of unemployment and employment which can be of use in evolving remedial measures. Information about per capita income of the people, consumption habits, per capita consumption and production, etc., can be obtained as a result of population study.

(3) *Economic planning*: Economic planning for development is gaining universal acceptance, more particularly in the less developed nations as a 'sine qua non' of the country's progress and prosperity. Planning involves the optimum use of human and material resources to subserve the best interest of the nation. Planning without precise data about population growth rates and its regional distribution would be like putting the cart before the horse. With the help of

population figures alone the planning authorities would be able to allocate resources to the various sectors of the economy with a view to overcome regional imbalances. Food production targets and determination of the priorities of development cannot be undertaken without population figures. Population and food supply are mutually bound up. Without proper population studies, the whole edifice of plan will fall like a frail house of cards.

(4) *Social*: Demography is that part of human knowledge which is most closely concerned with the systematic and organised study of society. It is here that the society will come to know what social needs are essential for the growing population. The children of today are the leaders of tomorrow, and to realise this aim it requires that programmes of child development are initiated and implemented. Demographic study assumes importance because child development programmes are included in the study. It is population factor which makes it necessary for making improvised provision of electricity, road, water, housing, school, hospital needs of the society on the one hand and shopping centres, hygienic facilities, etc., on the other. The state would be in a position to know with the help of population data about the law and order problem which growing population will create and how to solve these problems so that the people feel secure.

Discussing the importance of demography Kingslay Davis stated that population figures constitute the main source of understanding the foundation of human society. He puts the following fields of study under demography:

(1) Population information of a particular region.
(2) Study of population increase rates and decrease rates.
(3) Research into the optimum rates of population change.
(4) Projection of future trends in population.

Population problem is one of the basic problems of the society which gives rise to many other problems leading to social disorganisation and disequilibrium. Demographic studies can aid in the process of evolving better relations. Demography determines the rate of social change and helps in social organisation, stability and balance.

(5) *Administrative*: Administrators find population studies immensely useful. An administrator will have to give due consideration to the population factor in gearing the administrative machinery to fulfil the needs of the people.

To conclude, Hauser and Duncan have rightly said: "It will undoubtedly follow that population studies will, in turn also help to improve predictability and explanation in the related disciplines."

SELECT REFERENCES

1. Bogue, Donald, J.: *Principles of Demography*, New York, John Wiley and Sons Inc., 1969.
2. Bernard, B.: *Demographic Analysis.*
3. Cox, Peter R.: *Demography*, (Fourth edition), Cambridge, Institute of Actuaries and the Faculty of Actuaries at the University Press, 1970.
4. Ford, Thomas R. and Gordon F. De Jong: *Social Demography*, Englewood Cliffs, Prentice Hall Inc., 1970.
5. Hauser, Philip M. and Otis Dudley Duncan: *The Study of Population : An Inventory and Appraisal*, Chicago, The University of Chicago Press, 1959.
6. Lynnsmith, T.: *Fundamentals of Population Study*, Chicago, 1960.
7. Lorimer, F.: "The Development of Demography" in the Study of Population, Chicago, 1959.
8. Spiegelman, M.: *Introduction to Demography*, Harvard University Press, Cambridge, Mass., 1968.

EXAMINATION QUESTIONS

1. **Discuss the scope and importance of demography.**
2. **'It is difficult to define demography.' Elucidate.**
3. **What are the main elements of demography? Discuss the scope of demography with this reference.**
4. **Discuss the scope and importance of demography in a developing country like India.**
5. **'With improved data, new technique and the precise measurement of the demographic transition that is occurring, demography has become science rather than literature." Explain this statement.**
6. **Distinguish between demographic analysis and population study.**

2

Demography and Other Social Sciences

Demography opens up an original approach in studying human society. Its significance is increasing in recent years, with the use of new techniques in presenting demographic data and its practical application. It has come to occupy an important and independent status in the comity of social sciences. Very few subjects can boast of having such wide application in other social sciences as demography. It has percolated into other disciplines, notably the acturial science, agronomy, economics, economic geography, history, human biology, social policy and sociology. In all of these it is useful to have knowledge of one or more aspects of demography.

(1) DEMOGRAPHY AND SOCIOLOGY

Demography is generally regarded as a branch of other fields like sociology, economics or geography. In America in the dictionary of occupational titles demographer is listed and briefly described under the general heading sociologist. Sociology believes that man is a social animal. Similarly demography also accepts man as a unit of society and a group in which man is born and in which he dies. The group remains the same, though it changes its size. Sociologists treat demography as a subject most needed for understanding social reactions and pressures. This is perhaps the reason and also provides an important link between the two subjects.

Relations: (1) Demography deals with the population and sociology studies society. Both are bound together and the study of population will be incomplete and misleading without sufficient knowledge of society.

(2) MacIvar and Page defined sociology as a science of social relations. Society is said to be a cob web of social relations which revolvc around the individual in the society. Demography is a treatment of group of individuals.

(3) Demographer analyses the nature and composition of population for which knowledge of the nature and character of society is indispensable, because society provides the canvas to draw demographic paintings.

(4) Birth rates and death rates are essential components of demography. Social institutions and social conditions have direct bearing on birth rates and death rates. For example birth rate depends, inter alia, on child marriage and joint family. We know that population grows not only due to biological reasons but also on account of social outlook which the people have about the birth of their children. Change in fertility rates and cross sectional fertility differentials have raised the whole question of fertility as a social phenomenon.

(5) Similarly death rate is a vital demographic variable. A number of variables of sociological origin like social habits, environments, living conditions, etc., influences death rate. Mortality is a subject of deliberate controls and the often unintended consequences of other features of social systems. Every society exhibits types of action deliberately directed at restoring and maintaining health and preventing death.

(6) Public health is studied under demography while chalking out schemes of public health the social perspective is not lost sight of.

(7) Demography studies population enumeration. Population census exhaustively covers extensive fields like nature and composition of population, sex, marriage, age, occupation, etc. Social conditions vary from country to country and consequently the treatment of population census also differs from country to country. Socials issues are fundamental problems of sociology which clearly shows the close links between sociology and demography.

(8) Population policy is chalked out on the basis of expert opinion of scholars. Population, policy is a demographic issue which differs from country to country depending on the social circumstances available. This is an indication of the effect of sociological factors in demographic study.

(9) A population is clearly limited by the means of subsistence. The simplified formula

$$\frac{\text{Resources}}{\text{Population}} = \text{Level of consumption}$$

or the sophisticated formula

$$\frac{\text{Product}}{\text{Population}} = \text{Level of consumption.}$$

are inviting. Many social conditions determine the equilibrium between the numerator and denominator, which differ widely from country to country. These factors are analysed in both sociology and demography. No theory claiming to be scientific, however, can well avoid the interplay between demographic and social phenomena.

(10) The theory of demographic transition provides avenues for wider empirical generalisation and integration with the help of sociological theory. Feldman pointed out that demographic transition is a result of multiple causation and contemporary social conditions have relevance in its determination.

(11) Social stratification, one of Broom and Selznicks Principal elements of social system has demographic aspects. Social status on the one hand and fertility and mortality on the other clearly stand in reciprocal relation. Class position affects fertility position and life expectancy.

In the words of Wilbert E. Moore: "Treating demographic variables as exogenous to social systems involves a mode of abstraction that runs grave risk of errors of fact and interpretation."

Differences: (1) Demography entails a clear emphasis on quantitative variables and measurement. Sociology comprises predominantly of qualitative descriptions and generalisations about social patterns and structures not amenable to quantification

(2) Demographers deal with distributive characteristics of a society while sociology deals with unifying concepts like social structure, culture, etc.

(3) Much of demographic measurement deals with rates and trend in rates which are not found in sociology.

(4) Sociology is much wider in scope and the study of 'what is' whereas, demography is narrower in field and deals with 'what ought to be'.

(5) Sociology is a general social science while demography is a specialised field of social study.

(6) Sociology treats the general social relationship, whereas demography handles those social relations which have population orientation.

(2) DEMOGRAPHY AND ANTHROPOLOGY

Oxford Universal Dictionary defines demography as 'that branch of anthropology which treats of the statistics of birth, deaths, diseases, etc.' Traditionally physical anthropology has been concerned with three major problems: The evolution of man and the primares, the *entogenetic* development of man after birth and the classification of living varieties of man. Demography presents quantitative treatment of four principal topics—fertility, mortality, marriage and migration.

Similarities between the two are as under:

(1) During the last thirty years demography and anthropology have come to overlap each other. Population theory underwent substantial modification to understand the combination of rapid growth in population and widespread poverty in the anthropological areas of the world and in understanding the nonlogistic or unlawful growth in population.

(2) Both disciplines of study treats the original structure of human evolution, blood group, classification and geographical distribution, etc. Evolution of man and classification of living varieties of man have been modified by the rise of population genetics.

(3) Contemporary physical anthropology has interest in the demographic topics like fertility, mortality, mating, migration, population number and composition as they are of fundamental importance in the study of changes in gene frequency.

(4) Cultural anthropology is also related to demography. Lorimer developed the relationship between culture and human fertility.

The foregoing assessment reflects the mutual relation between demography and anthropology.

(3) DEMOGRAPHY AND HUMAN ECOLOGY

Both demography and human ecology are closely inter-related. Human ecology is concerned with birth which is a logical concomitant of the population base. Besides ecology also deals with environment, relationship, etc. From the ecological point of view population can be seen in terms of the extent to which people share in exploiting and developing the same environmental resources. According to Hutchinson and Dewey: "Ecology is nothing else but bio-demography."

Adams characterised human ecology as "that general subject which deals with the relations and inter-relations between nature in general and human nature in particular."

Similarities: (1) Dewey designated human ecology as bio-demography.

(2) Human ecologist is concerned with a number of demographic problems, uses demographic data and employ demographic

technique.

(3) Life tables are studied both by ecologists and demographers. In the words of Otis Duncan: "Human ecology provides a general perspective, heuristic principles and concepts and specific hypothesis of first rate significance to the demographer."

(4) Demographic variables are used in ecological research as independent variable or dependable variable or as indicators. For example a small dispersed population cannot have an elaborate social organisation as a large concentrated one. The suburbs of metropolitan centres in the United States have higher level of fertility than central city population.

Difference: Human ecology is merely concerned with territorial demography whereas demography covers many other fields of population study. Cultural and social institutions connected with demography are outside the periphery of human ecology.

(4) DEMOGRAPHY AND ECONOMICS

Economics and demography are closely intertwined. The points at which the subject matter of economics converge may be indicated in terms of economic and demographic variables.

Today demography is considered as a branch of economics.

Relation: (1) Population is a source of labour supply and change in population influence labour supply. Production is partially a function of labour supply. Human beings are ends in themselves and instruments of production. The welfare of the mass is a basic concern of economics.

(2) Increase in population will call for measures to provide employments and pool resources to augment production.

(3) Economic planning and development are influenced to great extent by the population factor. Low population and more production can provide high per capita income and rising standard of living.

(4) Population explosion will require the recasting of investment priorities to meet the consumption and non-consumable products which will be needed by the children.

(5) Population growth figures will guide economists to draw up schemes to meet the basic needs programme of the people in terms of schools, hospitals, roads, sanitation, etc. Statistics on diseases will help in identifying the diseases in different regions and in initiating remedial measures.

(6) Population figures can assist in determining the technique of

production. If the labour supply is superabundant, then labour intensive scheme of production will be more economical.

(7) Economic variables like capital stock and per capita capital stock, land resources, functional and personal distribution of income, terms of trade, annual volume of saving, investment, consumption, qualitative composition of investment, occupational composition of people, etc., are determined by the population factor.

(8) Economic factors influence demographic variables like mortality, fertility, natural increases, emigration, immigration, internal migration, density of population, distribution of population, age and sex composition, qualitative composition, etc.

Difference: In spite of the close relations the two fields cannot merge in each other and should maintain their separate identity and existence. Economics has escalated and branched into a vast subject with wide scope. Field of demographic study is much limited in scope. It is concerned with collection of data. Thus the demographer furnishes the foundation for the economist to construct the superstructure.

To quote Dr. B.N. Ganguli: "Unless demography, economics and sociology join hands in an interdisciplinary sweep of course, content and perspective, the teaching of economics cannot be concrete and meaningful as one would wish."

(5) DEMOGRAPHY AND GEOGRAPAY

Geography is one of the oldest of the sciences. It is concerned with the content of space and it treats the distributive relations of objects in space. Geography studies the distributional aspects of population, which brings it very close to demography.

Relation : (1) Geography deals with natural environment like climate, rain, temperature, etc. which have direct bearing on human life on the earth. This indicates the mutual relationship of demography and geography.

(2) Population is the main theme of demography and human geography. According to Trewartha G.T.: "Population is the point of reference from which all other elements are observed and from which they all singly and collectively derive significance and meaning."

(3) In modern times geography treats birth rate, death rate, migration, etc., which are also demographic components.

(4) Population census enumeration must be conducted within a geographic framework. Geographers have assisted in the design of

every decennial United States' census since Gannetts time.

(5) Geographers have studied the areawise differentiation of population on the basis of census enumeration data.

(6) Population provides the essential background for all geography.

(7) Geography research and settlement planning will be taken into account in any evaluation of population dynamics.

Difference: Geography is essentially concerned with climate, natural resources, rivers, forest, mountain, etc., over which man has no control. On the other hand demographer is concerned with facts, figures and details of population over which he has full control.

SELECT REFERENCES

Note: As in Chapter 1.

EXAMINATION QUESTIONS

1. Define demography. Establish the relationship of demography with other sciences.

therefore, less conscious about the problems of limitation of population growth and more alert to its advantages for military and similar other purposes.

Roman writers were more concerned with the practical problem of encouraging population growth, unlike the Greeks who dealt with the population theory. They viewed celibacy with disfavour, defended marriage and procreation and enacted legislation for promoting marriage and birth. Cicero decried polygamy and community ownership of wives and recommended monogamy to give a fillip to birth rate. Cicero did not approve of out migration to regulate population increase. Pliny supported immigration to overcome stagnation in population.

(2) WESTERN DEMOGRAPHIC THOUGHT OF THE MIDDLE AGES

Population ideas of the people of middle Europe falls into two periods, i.e. the period from A.D. 400-1200 and A.D. 1200-1500 The christian writers of medieval Europe considered the question of population entirely from moral and ethical angles. Roman philosophy was viewed with disfavour. Materialistic philosopy of life was relegated to the background, and spiritualism and thought of the other world ruled supreme. Divorce, child killing, abortion, etc., were opposed tooth and nail. Biblical tenets were the guidelines for daily life. The people believed that natural and social calamities could reduce the population and consequently, to keep the population at a particular level, birth rate should be high. The biblical advice be fruitful and multiply aided this view.

In fact two prominent thinkers gave their views on demography in middle ages.

(1) *Ibna Khaldun* (*1342-1406*): He was the leading Muslim social scientist, who in his book "Universal History" tried to explain population transition.

(2) *Givanni Botero*: He held the view that whatever be the size of population, birth rate will remain high. Countries with deficient resources to support its population will have to face terrible consequences unless the population is controlled.

Mercantilist's Thought

During the 17th and 18th centuries the mercantilist school of political economy flourished in Europe. Their slogan was more gold, more power and more wealth. Their aim was not to increase per capita income but to raise the natural income over the wage cost of production. The excess was viewed as a potential source of tax revenue for the state. Mercantilists believed that growth in population will create increased demand for finished goods and consequently consumption will go up. Manpower will also be available to produce more and more. Samuel Forrey stated: "People and plenty are commonly the begetters, the one of the other, if rightly ordered." Prof. Child maintained that increasing population alone could make the people happy and prosperous. These writers equated the growth of population with the augumentation of economic, political and military strength of the state. Cantillon suggested "if agriculture of a country would not be expanded in proportion to the population or if such an expansion would involve diminishing returns, additional agricultural products could be obtained from abroad in exchange for manufactured goods."

Physiocratic philosophy: In France the physiocrats believed that any attempt to check population was only an hindrance on the way of God's will and as such population growth was in the interest of society as a whole. They also believed that "As it is in the physical order that men thus united in society multiply promptly, by natural and necessary parallel to the multiplication they are reduced due to lack of means of subsistence if they do not, at the same time, multiply those means of cultivation."

(3) MODERN DEMOGRAPHIC THOUGHT

The founding fathers of demography: More realistically demography as a science of population analysis developed during the 17th century. The first of the writers whose name deserves mention in this context was Johan Graunt.

Johan Graunt (1620-1644): Rightly, John Graunt could be disignated the father of demography. John Graunt set forth his findings in a pamphlet published in London in 1662 named 'Natural and Political observation made upon the Bills of Mortality'. John Graunt was the exponent of the analysis approach. According to Willcox he discovered "the uniformity and predictability of many important biological phenomena taken in the mass." Graunt stressed the importance of measuring the logistics of population by simple indices which were easily calculable. Thus he, more than any other man was the founder of modern vital statistics.

Sir William Patty (1623-1687): If Graunt was the founder of the new science, Petty was its godfather, giving it the name .political arithmetic and enhancing its social position. His main publications were:

(1) Political Arithmetic.

(2) Observations upon the Dublin Bills of Mortality, 1683.

(3) Political Anatomy of Ireland.

Petty emphasised the establishment of a central statistical office. He helped in the development of Graunts Life Table with the help of 'arbitrary proportions'. Petty stressed the analysis of the following factors:

(1) Structure, composition and projection of population.

(2) Expansion of population.

(3) Urbanisation.

(4) Problems of less developed nations.

(5) Unemployment and national income and

(6) Man Power.

Edmund Halley (1656 to 1742): Edmund Halley who achieved immortality by charting a comet, constructed the first empirical life table with the Church records of Breslan, Silesia. He used his data with great ingenuity and obtained estimates of expected numbers of persons in a stationary population by single years of age through eighty four years.

Richard Price: He prepared estimates of the population of England and Wales in 1695. It was the most substantial finding on this subject between the Norman conquest and first Census of England and Wales in 1801. He defended his results with considerable sophistication by evidence and inferences.

Johan Peter Susmilch: Johan Susmilch, a Lutheran clergymen, became the leading exponent of demography in the middle decades of the eighteenth century. His publication "The Principles of Divine Order' appeared in 1741, which he later revised in 1761-62 and in 1765. He rejected the physio-theology by Derham, and emphasised the law of numbers. He noted that

(i) Men are more prone to accept a new spouse if a first marriage is dissolved by death than are women. There is a tendency among men towards successive polygamy. He concluded that God, in his infinite wisdom, had provided for this propensity.

(ii) In most nations there is normally a moderate excess of births over deaths, giving a gradual increase in population.

(iii) Death is more frequent in the first week of life and declines to a low level in the vicinity of fifteen years.

(iv) It is the duty of Government to preserve this tendency.

(v) In rural districts decline in the rates of marriage was generally due to compete occupancy on the land and in cities it is chiefly due to luxury and high prices.

PHASES OF HISTORY OF DEMOGRAPHY

History of demography falls into Four phases.

(*i*) *First Phase*: *Thomas Robert Malthus* (*1766-1834*): In 1798, T. R. Malthus, a young clergyman, published his famous brochure. At this time he had not carried out any empirical investigations. Thereafter, convinced of the validity of his thesis and finding himself in the midst of a lively controversy, he eagerly explored all the aspects of population changes. The principle of population, according to Malthus, is that the increase of population, which constantly tends to exceed increase of the means of subsistence. It is checked by the resultant intensification of misery and vice unless a preventive check restraint from marriage intervenes. His assumptions about the necessary relations between demographic and economic changes was challenged. Karl Marx who criticised Malthus, developed his attack on Malthus' doctrine with only slight and casual reference to any actual demographic phenomena.

Malthus was first to evolve the problem approach in demography.

He had awaken tremendous interest in the population question but only a few of the scholars who engaged in this discussion during the following century undertook empirical studies. The immediate impact and influence was that population problems began to be analysed, studied and critically approached in all parts of the world. In this way it can be said Malthus' efforts constituted the first phase of population study.

When Malthus was expounding his population thesis, a Chinese Philospher Hungliang Chi was also engaged in studying the population problem. It is a matter of chance that he too reached identical conclusions to which Malthus reached.

(*ii*) *Second Phase*: Second phase of demographic studies started with the beginning of 19th century.

Joshia Milne: Joshia Milne started improving the studies related to figures.

William Far: He was the leading English vital statistician during the middle decades of the nineteeth century. He prepared report about population of Victorian era, so that it was possible to undertake social legislation.

Johan Finlaison: He came to the conclusion that for realistic estimation, proper registration of birth, death and marriage was necessary.

Achille Guilliard: He coined the term demography to designate the science of population studies.

The greatest progress in demography during the 19th century came through investigation of mortality and related topics.

(*iii*) *Third Phase*: The third phase about population studies started in the beginning of the 20th century.

Carr Saunders: He brought out his volume entitled "The Population Problem: A Study in Human Evolution". It was an important empirical attempt to present demography as a new branch of knowledge. He also developed the optimum theory of population. Thompson and Lewis stated: "In brief, Carr Saunders may be said to sponser the theory that man's growth in numbers has been largely determined by his denotions of economically desirable numbers under his conditions of life. But since Carr Saunders regards man's growth as wholly within his control and as conditioned by the attitudes of mind that he has developed under his institutions and particular physical conditions of his life, his theory stands in sharp contrast to those who were based on natural law."

It was during this period that Enxer Ludwig Moser, Alfred Lotka, Bockh, etc. developed quantitative theories of population.

(*iv*) *Fourth Phase*: It is also known as the modern phase of demographic studies. Demography as a discipline has been developed with a rigorous but limited core of analytical theory and well defined statistical techniques. These are subjected to revision and new experimentation.

Use of mathematical approach is taking place on a wide scale. Verhulest developed Logistic curve theory for population studies, Organisations like U.N.O. and individuals like Cannan, Bowley, Whelpton, Pearl, Simon Kuznets, Dorothy Thomas, Coale, etc. have done commendable work in enlarging the frontiers of demographic studies. Emphasis on the inter-disciplinary nature of population studies in place of pure demography is gaining currency. In the words of Dr. B.N.Ganguli: "It is a field where biologists and sociologists have joined hand to correct the follies of a civilisation caught up in the bold advances of modern science towards specialisation of nature and the eventual exhaustion of natural resources. Economists, demographers and sociologists can no longer afford to ignore the ecological dimensions of both population and development."

DEVELOPMENT OF DEMOGRAPHY IN INDIA

Development of demography in India can be studied under two

broad headings: (a) Development of demography in pre-independent India and (b) Development of demography in post-independent India.

(a) *Development of demography in pre-Independent India*: The Indians know the value of population studies since ancient time. The Arthashastra of Kautilya gives a detailed description of how to conduct a population, economic and agricultural census. During the reign of Akbar; The Great, Abul Fazal compiled the *Ain-e-Akbari* containing comprehensive data on population, industry, wealth and traits of population. During the British period the system of decennial census started with the first census in 1872. An important contribution to the growth of demography in India has been made in Imperial Gazetteers. The first Imperial Gazetteer was published in 1881 in 9 volumes at the instance of W.W. Hunter in 1882 a companion volume entitled 'The Indian Empire: Its History, People and Products', was published. Revised versions of the Imperial Gazetteers were published in 26 volumes during the period 1907 and 1909.

The first Indian Population Conference was held in 1936 under the auspices of the University of Lucknow. At this conference a paper entitled "Future Growth of India's Population" was presented. The second All India Conference on population and the First Family Hygiene Conference was held in Bombay in 1938 and a paper on differential fertility based on field experience in Cochin State was presented. The second All-India Conference on Population and the first Family Hygiene Conference were jointly held in Bombay in 1938.

We shall now take up population studies in pre-independent India. The earliest study on India's Population based on an analysis of Census data that we have come across is a book by M. Subraya Kamath entitled "The Census of India: An Analysis and Criticism." published by the Theosophical Publishing House, Madras in 1914, with an introduction by Annie Besant. Kamath based his study on the Censuses in India from 1881 to 1911 and draws special attention to infanticide, infant marriages, and child widows in India.

The other important contribution to populations studies were as follows:

(1) P.K. Wattal:	The Population Problem in India (1916)
(2) Brij Narain:	The Population of India (1925)
(3) D.G. Karve:	Poverty and Population in India (1936)

(4) B.T. Banadive: The Population Problem in India (1936)
(5) B.K. Sarkar: The Sociology of Population (1936)
(6) Radhakamal Mukerjee: Food Planning for 400 Millions (1938)
(7) B.N. Ganguli: Trends of Agriculture and Population in the Ganges Valley (1938)
(8) Gyan Chand: India's Teeming Millions (1939)
(9) N.V. Sovani: The Population Problem of India—a Regional Approach
(10) Radhakamal Mukerjee: Political Economy of Population (1943)
(11) S. Chandrasekhar: India's Population—Fact and Policy. (1946)
(12) D. Ghosh: The Pressure of Population and Economic Efficiency in India (1946)

During the period 1940 to 1956 the Government of India started taking interest in population studies. In 1944, the then Department of Education, Health and Lands set up the Population Data Committee under the Chairmanship of W.M. Yeats "to advise the Government of India on the available data relating to growth of population." The Family Planning Association of India was founded in Bombay in 1949 and it started propagating population control. In 1946, the Government of India appointed the Health Survey and Development Committee (Popularly known as the Bhore Committee) to study health conditions in India and to make recommendations for their improvement.

The Institute collected data on fertility through field enquiries. In 1945, the All India Institute of Hygiene and Public Health, Calcutta conducted several field studies under the guidance of Dr. C. Chandrasekharan. In 1942, Prof. N.V. Sovani of the Gokhale Institute of Politics and Economics, Pune, published a study entitled "The Population Problem in India: A Regional Approach".

The importance of teaching formal and technical demography in colleges and universities was first emphasised by a Committee set up by the U.N. Secretary General in December 1953 and the matter came up for consideration in the Population Commission in March 1955. The Government of India established its Demographic Advisory Committee in 1958. The founding of the Demographic Advisory Committee in 1958, preceded by the establishment of the DTRC at Chembur, Bombay in 1957, led to the official support of six other Centres of Demographic Research at Delhi, Calcutta, Poona, Trivandrum, Dharwar and Madras.

(*b*) *Post-independent developmeut of demography*: The following are important land marks in post-independence growth of demography in India.

(1) *The Indian Census, the Vital Registration System and the National Sample Survey*: The Indian Census and the Vital Registration System are almost the only source not only of historical demography but also of the study of specific regions and spaces over time. These two sources and, for the last two decades, the National Survey provide the best reservoirs of information. The Indian census was primarily designed to give the administrator a working knowedge of the people he had to deal with. The vital statistics system was similarly designed to keep a rough tab on mortality, morbidity and natality by defined geographical spaces. The NSS alone of all the three was conceived and designed by P.C. Mahalanobis to generate systematic data for planning purposes and for the organisation of societies.

(2) *Indian Association for the Study of Population*: A significant forward step in the development of demography in India was taken in 1972 with the establishment of the Indian Association for the study of population. The Indian Association for the Study of Population (IASP) started publication of a journal, *Demography India*, in 1972, with financial support from the Family Planning Foundation of India. The demand for demographers is gradually increasing in this country.

(3) *Teaching in Demography*: The subject of teaching of demography in the universities was taken up earnestly at the First Asian Population Conference in the fall of 1963 and between 1963 and 1966. The Universities of Aligarh, Allahabad, Banaras, Baroda, Gorakhpur, Lucknow, Jaipur and Saugar instituted post-graduate teaching in demography as an optional paper in M.A. Economics. Poona introduced demography as a compulsory paper in M.Sc. Statistics.

At the post-graduate level demography was taught leading to M.Sc. degree in the university of Kerala for the first time in India. In 1973 a Population Studies Centre was established at Shri Venkateshwara University, Tirupati. Since 1974 demography is being taught at J.N.U. Besides it forms a part of the syllabi as an optional paper in Economics at Agra, Aligarh, Allahabad, Banaras, Baroda, Bombay, Calcutta, Gorakhpur, Gujarat, Lucknow, Meerut, Rajasthan, Rewa, Saugar and other Universities. It is a part of the post-graduate courses in sociology at Annamalai, Gorakhpur, Lucknow, Punjab, Vikram and Indore Universities. Provision has been made for lectures on demography, population problems and vital statistics in post-graduate teaching in Economics, Statistics and Sociology at some 20 universities.

The University of Madras, one of the oldest universities in India, has established a Centre for Population Studies, promoting and teaching and research in the field of population. To start with the Centre is offering two diploma courses in Population Studies: (a) a Post-Graduate Diploma in Population Studies and (b) a Post-M.A., M.Sc. Diploma in Population Studies. Appropriate steps are also being taken to establish a full-fledged independent Department of Population Studies. The Post-Graduate Degree Course in Population Studies is started from the academic year 1984.

(4) *Demographic Training and Research in India*: Another major development in the last decade has been the creation of the infrastructure for demographic training and research in India through the establishment of the Demographic Training and Research Centre at Bombay (sponsored with assistance from the United Nations to serve as a "regional" training centre for the countries in Asia), and the setting up of a chain of demographic Research Centres at several universities, research institutes and Government Departments. A co-ordinating Central Family Planning Institute has also been established in New Delhi. Thus the foundations have been laid for continuous training of demographers and long-term research in demogarphy.

A list of institutions engaged in demographic research and family planning communication action research centres in India is given in Tables 1 and 2.

TABLE 1 : Institutions engaged in Demographic Research in India

Name of the Centre/Institution	*Areas of researsh activities*
1. International Institute for Population Studies, Bombay.	Fertilty, nuptiality migration family planning attitude, communication and evaluation, mortality and population simulation model.
2. Economics Department, Bombay University, Bombay	Migration, Economic activity anaysis, sex ratio
3. Central Statistical Organization, New Delhi.	Population projections, fertility.
4. Demographic Research Centre, Institute of Economic growth, Delhi.	Migration, urbanisation, fertility changes.

Name of the Centre/Institution	*Areas of Reseach Activities*
5. Institute of Manpower Research, New Delhi.	Area manpower surveys, manpower studies.
6. National Council of Applied Economic Research, New Delhi	Population projections, city surveys.
7. National Sample Survey, New Delhi.	Fertility, employment and unemployment, births and deaths.
8. Office of the Registrar General of India, New Delhi	Census operations, mortality, fertility birth registration.
9. Planning and Evaluation Division, Ministry of Health and Family Planning, New Delhi.	Family Planning programme evaluation.
10. Demographic Research Centre, Gokhale Institute of Politics and Economics, Poona.	Fertility, family planning, demographic surveys, interdistrict migration.
11. Demographic Research Centre, Bureau of Economics and Statistics, Trivandrum.	Family planning, fertility, migration.
12. Administrative Staff College, Hyderabad.	Family planning management, health management and information system.
13. Demographic Research Centre, Institute of Economic Research, Dharwar.	Fertility, demographic surveys of cities.
14. Department of Statistics, University of Kerala, Kerala.	Fertility, fertility surveys, family growth study, population models.
15. Indian Institute of Management, Ahmedabad	Family planning management, management information and evaluation system.
16. Indian Institute of Management, Calcutta	Family planning.
17. Demographic Research Centre, Indian Statistical Institute, Calcutta.	Fertility, family planning, mortality, nuptiality.
18. Indian Institute of Management Banglore.	Health statistics.
19. Operations Research Group, Baroda.	Family planning and fertility surveys.
20. Population Studies Centre, Sri Venkateshwara University, Tirupati.	Population, education, cost-benefit studies.
21. Demographic Research Centre, Banaras Hindu University Varanasi.	Mathematical models, small-scale sample surveys.
22. Demographic Research Centre, Lucknow University, Lucknow.	Fertility, demographic surveys population projections.
23. PopulationCentre, India Population Project, Lucknow.	Benchmark surveys, family planning management studies, nutrition and

	family planning evaluation, family planning training, management information and evaluation system.
24. Population Centre, India Population project, Banglore.	Surveys, evaluation, management studies.
25. Demographic Research Centre, Patna University, Patna	Demographic surveys, biostatistical studies, mathematical models.
26. Demographic Research Unit, Jadavpur University, Jadavpur.	Mathematical models, metropolitan area studies.
27. Demographic Research Centre, Patna University, Patna.	Fertility, family planning, demographic surveys.

TABLE 2: Family Planning Communication Action Research Centres in Ind'a

Name of the Centre/Institution	*Areas of Research Activities*
1. Demographic Communication, Action Research Centre, Institute for Social and Economic Change, Bangalore.	KAP, evaluation, city surveys.
2. Council for Social Development, India International Centre. New Delhi.	Infant and child mortality, fertility. and marriage.
3. All India Institute of Hygiene and Public Health, Calcutta.	KAP, evaluation communication.
4. Department of Psychology, University of Patna, Patna.	Attitude scale.
5. Department of Sociology, University of Kerala, Trivandrum.	KAP, evaluation, communication.
6. Department of Rural Economics and Sociology, Utkal University, Bhubaneswar.	Family planning communication.
7. Institute for Economic and Social Change, Bangalore.	Migration, regional activities.
8. International Institute for Population Studies, Bombay.	KAP, family planning evaluation, family planning communication, cost-benefit analysis, target setting.
9. Institute of Rural Health and Family Planning, Gandhigram.	Family Planning training, family planning and health evaluation studies and fertilility and mortality.
10. Indian Institute of Technology, Kanpur.	Family planning attitude studies.
11. Gokhale Institute of Polices and Economics, Poona.	KAP, organisational aspects, evaluation communication.
12. Family Planning Research Unit, Indian Statistical Institute, Calcutta.	Evaluation motivation, communication.
13. Population Centre, India	Family planning, nutrition.

Name of the Cedtre/Institution	*Areas of Research Activities*
Population Project, Bangalore	
14. Population Centre, India, Population Project, Lucknow	Family planning, nutrition
15. National Institute of Family Planning, New Delhi	KAP, family planning evaluation, family planning communication.
16. Shri V.T. Krishnamachari Institute of Rural Health, Baroda.	Training, evaluation, KAP, organization aspects.

Suggestions regarding Teaching, Training and Research in the field of Demography in India.

It is an accepted fact that so long as the unbridled growth of population growth is not effectively curbed, to dream about socio-economic growth is to build castles in the air. Our planners are aware of this bitter truth and have started giving due importance to population statistics in the plans of socio-economic development. It can be stated that the study of demographic problems, collection of data, their tabulation and interpretation etc. should be undertaken on a regular footing. This calls for the need of specialised demographers who can conduct research in this field on a permanent basis.

Besides, qualified experts in demography should be appointed in the departments of economics and sociology of the different universities. They should also conduct research in the population field.

Demography should be taught in the degree classes as a compulsory subject in each and every university of India. This will help the students to realise the significance of the mutual relations of population and economic development. Similarly, an extensive syllabii should he chalked out for the teaching of demography at the post-graduate level, which should include related subjects like economics, sociology, psychology, statistics, research methodology etc. Presentation of a dissertation on any demographic aspect should be made compulsory for the students in the final year of M.A. course. Liberal grants should be provided by the Government to the universities for purchase of books, calculating machines, and for miscellaneous purposes.

Once the subject is introduced in the university, it will create an environment in which the teachers and students will automatically take interest in the field of research. Dr. S.N. Agarwala, the noted Demographist, has given the following suggestions:

Under the present conditions it may not be possible to appoint additional teaching staff in the universities and colleges as it will increase the financial burden. To tide over this problem it would be advisable for the university to depute one or two professors to undergo training in demography in specialised institutions. This calls for the launching of a specialised training programme in demography, which can assist the university and college teachers to gain specialised training.

Since the need of trained demographers is high, short term training courses in demography should be organised in places like Population Research Institute, Bombay, etc. The staff of statistical, public health and other government departments can also be trained in these institutes.

In the States a third type of training programme in demography and family planning should be introduced. Training centres for short term training courses be set up for this purpose. In these centres the employees working in the Family Planning Bureau and family welfare centres of states who are involved in collecting statistics should be trained.

Besides, in the demographic research centres and Family Planning Bureaus short period training programmes should be undertaken to orient the social reformers, women workers, nurses, doctors and surpanchs with the new techniques, problems and solutions of family planning.

In order to popularise population education and family planning, knowledge about communication and publicity should be imparted to these staff.

One important shortcoming about demographic study is that it is included in the curriculum of post-graduate courses straightaway. The students being unfamiliar with the subject fight shy to offer this subject. Hence it should be introduced in the curriculum at the undergraduate level stage.

At present the future prospects of the students of demography do not appear to be bright. Hence so long as the post of demographer is not created in the departments of family welfare, census, planning and other social organisations it is difficult to motivate students to offer this subject. There is no association at the national level to promote the study of demography.

SELECT REFERENCES

1. Agrawal, S.N. (ed.): *India's Population: Sone Problems in Perspective Planning*, Bombay, Asia Publishing House, 1960.
2. Bose, Ashish, Desai, P.B. and Jain, S.P.: *Studies in]Demography*, George Allen and Uwin Ltd., 1970.
3. Chandrasekhar: *India's Population: Fact and Policy*, New York, The John Day Company, 1946, p. 75.
4. Kamat, A.R.: Presidential address delivered to the Section of Statistics at Fifty-sixth Session of the Indian Science Congress, Bombay, 1969, p. 8.
5. Asok Mitra: "Population Studies in Population Policy", Paper for National Conference on Population Policy and Programmes, New Delhi, December 1923, 1926, Special Committee, Paper I (Session I). See also: Asok Mitra, *Demographic Aspects of Development Planning*, 1961 (unpublished).
6. Philip, P.J.: A note on courses in demography offered by Policy and Programmes, New Delhi, 19-23 December, 1969. See also: B.L. Raina: Universities and Studies in the Field of Population, CFPI Technical Paper No. 5, New Delhi, Central Family Planning Institute, May 1969.

EXAMINATION QUESTIONS

1. **Write a short essay on the evolution of demography.**
2. **Trace the development of demography in India.**
3. **Give constructive suggestions regarding teaching, training and research in the field of demography in India.**

4

Some Basic Concepts of Demographic Analysis

1. Observation

Demographic facts and figures are assembled on the basis of the observation of individuals and groups. Observations are conducted with naked eye on the course of events which are opened to conflicting influences acting concurrently. Observation can be of different types.

Human beings are the objects of observation on whom controlled experiment is not possible as in physical sciences. The sense in which experiment is possible in demographic study is that different populations can be studied at the same time and the same population can be studied at different times. Observation requires sufficient skill, knowledge, expertise and judgement. Slight neglect or biased view can result in misleading conclusions. Demographic facts cannot have mathematical precision because of the intervention of exogenous factors. Changes taking place with time and group cannot be properly observed and quantified.

2. Relative Number

Students of population will be interested in collecting facts and establishing relations between sets of data and find out ratios and rates. Both ratios and rates are relative figures and express a relation between two or more numbers. It is commonly felt that relative numbers are more useful or better than absolute numbers. But this opinion is not correct for all times and in all cases.

In certain cases absolute numbers can be more useful than relative numbers. Absolute numbers are raw data of population. Where comparison is indispensable or useful, relative numbers are needed, or else absolute numbers can serve the purpose.

3. Rates

Rates are used to observe demographic figures in a meaningful way. Birth rates, death rates, marriage rates, etc., are used in demographic studies. Some of the important demographic rates are as follows:

1. *Crude birth rate*: The number of live births in the year, per 1,000 population at mid-year.

2. *Crude death rates*: The number of deaths in the year, per 1,000 population at mid-year.

3. *Crude marriage rate*: The number of marriages (not persons marrying) in the year, per 1,000 population at mid-year.

4. *Crude divorce rate*: The number of divorces (not persons divorcing) in the year, per 1,000 population at mid-year.

5. *Crude rate of natural increase*: Difference between the crude birth and death rates.

6. *Abortion Rate*: The estimated number of abortions per 1,000 women aged 15-44 years in a given year.

7. *Age-specific rate*: Rate obtained for specific age groups (for example, age-specific fertility rate, death rate, marriage rate, illiteracy rate, school enrolment rate, etc.).

8. *General fertility rate*: The number of live births per 1,000 women aged 15-44 years in a g ven year.

9. *Gross Reproduction Rate (GRR)*: The average number of daughters that would be born alive to a woman (or group of women) during her life time if she passed through her child-earing years conforming to the age-specific fertility rates of a given year. See net reproduction rate and total fertility rate.

10. *Growth rate*: The rate at which a population is increasing (or decreasing) in a given year due to natural increase and net migration, expressed as a percentagh of the base population.

11. *Infant mortality rate*: The number of deaths of infants under one year of age in a given year per 1,000 live births in that year.

12. *Maternal mortality rate*: The number of deaths to women due to pregnancy and child-birth complications pcr 100,000 live births in a given ycar.

13. *Marriage rate* (or crude marriage rate): The number of marriages per 1,000 populatjon in a given year.

14. *Martial fertility rate*: The number of legtimate live births per 1,000 married women aged 15-44 years in a given year.

15. *Net migration rate*: The net effect of immigration and emigration on an arca's population, expressed as increase or decrease per 1,000 population of the area in a given year.

16. *Net reproduction rate (NRR)*: The average number of daughters that would be born to a women (or group of women) if she

passed through her lifetime from birth conforming to the age-specific fertility and mortality rates of a given year. This rate is similar to the gross reproduction rate, but takes into account that some women will die before completing their child-bearing years. An NRR of 1.00 means each generation of mothers is having exactly enough daughters to replace itself in the population. See gross reproduction rate, total fertility rate, and replacement level fertility.

17. *Perinatal mortality rate*: The number of foetal deaths after 28 weeks of pregnancy (late foetal death) plus the number of deaths to infants under 7 days of age per 1,000 live births.

18. *Postneonatal mortality rate*: The annual number of infant deaths at 28 days to one year of age per 1,000 live births in a given year.

19. *Survival rate*: The proportion of persons in a specified group (age, sex, health status, etc.) alive at the beginning of an interval (e.g., a 5-year period) who survive to the end of the interval.

20. *Total Fertility Rate* (*TFR*). The average number of children that would be born alive to a woman (or group of women) during her lifetime if she were to pass through her child-bearing years conforming to the age-specific fertility rates of a given year. See also gross reproduction rate and net reproduction rate.

4. Ratio

Ratios differ from rates. A rate counts the number of events in a restricted time period, for example, one year and would be only half that value for a half year. A ratio prevails at a particular point in time, and in this sense it is a prevalence concept rather than the incidence concept underlying a rate.

1. *Abortion ratio*: The estimated number of abortions per 1,000 live births in a given year.

2. *Age dependency ratio*: The ratio of persons in the ages defined as dependent (under 15 and over 64 years) to those in the ages defined as economically productive (15-64 years) in a population.

3. *Child-woman ratio*: The number of children under 5 years old per 1,000 women aged 15-44 years in a population. This crude fertility measure, based on basic census data, is sometimes used when more specific fertility information is not available.

4. *Dependency ratio*: The ratio of the economically dependent part of the population to the productive part; arbitrarily defined as the ratio of the elderly (those 65 years and over) plus the young (those under 15 years of age) to the population in the "working ages" (those 15-64 years of age).

(5) *Sex ratio*: the number of males per 100 females in a population.

(6) *Age-sex structure*: The composition of population as determined by the number of proportion of males and females in each age category. The age-sex structure of a population is the cumulative result of past trends in fertility, mortality, and migration. Information on age-sex composition is an essential prerequisite for the description and analysis of many other types of demographic data.

(7) *Census*: A canvas of a given area, resulting in an enumeration of the entire population, and the compilation of demographic, social, and economic information pertaining to that population at a specific time. (See also survey).

(8) *Child-bearing years*: The reproductive age span of women, arbitrarily assumed for statistical purposes to be 15-44 years in the U.S. In other countries, the range is often set at 15-49 years.

(9) *Cohort*: A group of people sharing a common temporal demographic experience who are observed through time. For example, the birth cohort of 1980 would be the people born in that year. There are also marriage cohorts, school class cohorts, etc.

(10) *Exponential growth*: A constant rate of growth applied to a continuously growing base over a period of time; for example, a savings account increasing at compound interest; a snowball gathering mass; a population growing at 3.0 per cent annually.

(11) *Family planning*: The conscious effort of couples to regulate the number and spacing of births. Family planning usually connotes the use of birth control to avoid pregnancy, but also includes efforts of couples to induce pregnancy.

(12) *Fecundity*: The physiological capacity of a woman, man, or couple to produce a live child.

(13) *Fertility*: The actual reproductive performance of an individual, a couple, a group, or a population.

(14) *Growth rate*: The rate at which a population is increasing (or decreasing) in a given year due to natural increase and net migration, expressed as a percentage of the base population.

(15) *In-migration*: The process of entering one administrative subdivision of a country (e.g., country or state) from another subdivision to take up residence.

(16) *Life expectancy*: The average number of additional years a person would live if current mortality trends were to continue. Most commonly cited as life expectancy at birth.

(17) *Life table*: A tabular display of life expectancy and the probability of dying at each age for a given population according

to the age-specific death rates prevailing at that time. The life table gives an organised, complete picture of a population's mortality.

(18) *Median age*: The age which divides a population into two numerically equal groups; that is, half the people are younger than this age and half are older.

(19) *Mean Age*: The average age of all the members of a population.

(20) *Migration*: The movement of people across a specified boundary for the purpose of establishing a new permanent residence. Divided into international migration (migration between countries) and internal migration (migration within a country).

(21) *Neonatal mortality rate*: The number of deaths to infant under 28 days of age in a given year per 1,000 live births in that year.

(22) *Nuptiality*: The frequency, characteristics, and dissolution of marriages in a population.

(23) *Population density*: Population per unit of land area; for example persons per square mile, or persons per square kilometre of arable land.

(24) *Population distribution*: The pattern of settlement and dispersal of a population.

(25) *Population projection*: Computation of future changes in population numbers, given certain assumptions aboul future trends in the rates of fertility, mortality and migration. Demographers often issue low, medium and high projections of the same population, based on different assumptions of how these rates will change in the future.

(26) *Population Pyramid*: A special type of bar chart that shows the distribution of a population by age and sex.

(27) *Urbanization*: Growth in the proportion of a population living in urban areas.

(28) *Vital statistics*: Demographic data on births, deaths, fetal deaths, marriages, and divorces.

SOME PRACTICAL ILLUSTRATIONS

1. From the following informations, calculate Dependency Ratio, Sex Ratio, Density Ratio and Literacy Ratio:

Total Population	3,00,000	
Male Population	1,53,000	
Area of the City	7,500	Square Km.
Aged Population	24,000	
Child Population	1,26,000	
Literate Population	1,08,000	

Solution:

1. Dependency Ratio $= \frac{D}{W} \times K$

$$= \frac{24,000 + 1,26,000}{1,50,000} \times 1 = 1$$

2. Sex Ratio $= \frac{F}{M} \times K$

$$= \frac{1,47,000}{1,53,000} \times 1,000 = 961 \text{ Per 1,000 Males}$$

3. Density Ratio $= \frac{P}{A} \times K$

$$= \frac{3,00,000}{7,500} \times 1 = 40 \text{ Per Square Km.}$$

4. Literacy Ratio $= \frac{L}{P} \times K$

$$= \frac{1,08,000}{3,00,000} \times 100 = 36\%$$

2. From the following statistics, compute Literacy ratio, Dependency ratio and Density ratio:

Total Population of City	1,00,000
Literate Population	30,700
Aged Population	24,000
Child Population	20,000
Area of the City (Sq. Km.)	2,000

Solution:

1. Literacy Ratio $= \frac{L}{P} \times K = \frac{30{,}700}{1{,}00{,}000} \times 100 = 307$

2. Dependency Ratio $= \frac{D}{W} \times K = \frac{24{,}000 \times 20{,}000}{56{,}000} \times 1 = 0.785$

3. Density Ratio $= \frac{P}{A} \times K = \frac{1{,}00{,}000}{2{,}000} \times 1 = 50$ Per Square Km.

3. Compute Sex ratios from the following table:

Age	Males (000)	Females (000)
0—9	712	695
10—19	605	600
20—29	508	498
30—39	409	400
40—49	320	299
50—59	230	240
60—69	152	170
70—79	70	95
80 and above	20	30

Solution:

Age	*Males (000)*	*Females (000)*	*Computation*	*Sex Ratio*
0—9	712	695	$\frac{Fi}{Mi} K = \frac{6{,}95{,}000}{7{,}12{,}000} \times 1{,}000$	976
10—19	605	600	,, $\frac{6{,}00{,}000}{6{,}05{,}000} \times 1{,}000$	991
20—29	508	498	,, $\frac{4{,}98{,}000}{5{,}08{,}000} \times 1{,}000$	980
30—39	409	400	,, $\frac{4{,}00{,}000}{4{,}09{,}000} \times 1{,}000$	978
40—49	320	299	,, $\frac{2{,}99{,}000}{3{,}20{,}000} \times 1{,}000$	934
50—59	230	240	,, $\frac{2{,}40{,}000}{2{,}30{,}000} \times 1{,}000$	1,043
60—69	152	170	,, $\frac{1{,}70{,}000}{1{,}52{,}000} \times 1{,}000$	1,118
70—79	70	95	,, $\frac{95{,}000}{70\ 000} \times 1{,}000$	1,357
80 and above	20	30	,, $\frac{30{,}000}{20{,}000} \times 1{,}000$	1,500
Total	3,026	3,027	$\frac{F}{M} K = \frac{30{,}27{,}000}{30{,}26{,}000} \times 1{,}000$	1,000

Here K is taken as 1,000.

4. Construct an age sex pyramid on percentage scale from the following table:

Age	Males (in lakhs)	Females (in lakhs)
0—9	75	72
10—19	45	42
20—29	30	36
30—39	27	30
40—49	18	15
50—59	15	18
60—69	9	9
70 and above	6	3

Solution:

Age	*Male*	*Female*	*Computation*	*Sex Ratio*
0—9	75	72	$\frac{Fi}{Mi}K=\frac{72,000}{75,000}\times 1,000$	960
10—19	45	42	,, $\frac{42,040}{45,000}\times 1,000$	933
20—29	30	36	,, $\frac{36,000}{30,000}\times 1,000$	1,200
30—39	27	30	,, $\frac{30,000}{27,000}\times 1,000$	1,111
40—49	18	15	,, $\frac{15,000}{18,000}\times 1,000$	833
50—59	15	18	,, $\frac{18,000}{15,000}\times 1,000$	1,200
60—69	9	9	,, $\frac{9,000}{9,000}\times 1,000$	1,000
70 and above	6	3	,, $\frac{3,000}{6,000}\times 1,000$	500
Total	225	225	$\frac{F}{M}K=\frac{2,25,000}{2,25,000}\times 1,000$	1,000

EXAMINATION QUESTIONS

1. Write short notes on the following:

(*a*) Sex Ratio, (*b*) Dependency Ratio, (*c*) Density Ratio, (*d*) Literacy Ratio, (*e*) Exponential Growth, (*f*) Cohort, and (*g*) Life Expectancy.

2. From the following statistics, compute literacy ratio, dependency ratio and density ratio:

1. Total population of the town	1,50,000
2. Literate population	45,960
3. Aged population	24,000
4. Child population	29,000
5. Area of the town (sq. km.)	3,000

3. Compute sex ratios from the following table:

Age	Males (in lakhs)	Females (in lakhs)
0-9	25	24
10-19	15	14
20-29	10	12
30-39	9	10
40-49	6	5
50-59	5	
60-69	3	
70 and over	2	

5

Nature of Demographic Data

Demographers use two kinds of data: (1) Information about persons, i.e. characteristics of age, sex, residence, and (2) Information about events. Information about rates of birth and deaths are called vital rates. Migration, marriage and divorce are also treated under vital events. Different methods are employed in obtaining demographic data. Normally three methods are used in studying the universe, namely census method, sampling method and registration method.

I. CENSUS METHOD

Census is the enumeration of the total population as of a given moment of time. It is also defined as the "total process of collecting, compiling and publishing demographic, economic and social data pertaining, at a specified time or times to all persons in a country or delimited territory." (U.N.O.)

It helps not only in collecting figures but also provide information about the economy of the nation. Census is normally conducted at fixed intervals, as for instance, after every 10 years in India.

There are different methods by which census is conducted viz., direct enumeration, indirect enumeration, real enumeration and legal enumeration. Under the direct enumeration the official enumerators themselves elicit information by direct inquiry and enter them in pretested schedules, tables and questionnaires. Under indirect enumeration, the schedules are send through post to the informants, who in turn, returns them after filling the necessary information, This method was employed by Japan in 1955, while in U.S., Russia and India the direct method is favoured. Real and legal enumerations are based on the locality of enumeration. Where a person is enumerated at any place where he is present during the time of enumeration, it is known as real enumeration. When the enumeration of a person takes place at his place of normal residence, it is called legal enumeration.

Main Features of Census

(1) Census is a national stock taking process collecting detailed information about migration of the people, about their age, sex, occupations, etc., on people living in a country at a point of time.

(2) The State is responsible for organising and conducting census.

(3) During census operations every effort is made to collect first hand information about every person. Individual or family is treated as a unit.

(4) The entire census operation should be completed within a given span of time.

(5) The schedules are collected, examined and analysed statistically. Most of the census operations are conducted once in a decade.

(6) Census data is published after due verification of the assembled data.

(7) Census operations are preceded by preliminary steps, like choice of area, preparation of advance list of dwellings in each area, training of enumerators, preparation of forms for enumeration, etc.

Census and Registration

Census and registration are often confused and figures collected by way of registration are treated as population figures. During census direct contacts are established whereas in registration only names are registered and as such no direct contact is established. In addition, whereas registration process continues throughout the year, census operations are carried out at specific time and are completed within a specified period. Besides, census operations are repeated after regular intervals, while registrations are made according to the exigencies of the occasion and is a continuing process.

Barclay in his "Techniques of Population Analysis" observed the following shortcoming of census: "In practice, some people are always missing. It is unpracticable to include all cases which belong to the universe. Some cases which ought to be covered according to rule are always omitted. On the other hand, some may be recorded more than once."

(For details see chapter on population census)

II. REGISTRATION

Life statistics are sources of population data. The following demographic events are registered, viz. (1) Birth, (2) Death, (3) Marriage,

(4) Divorce, (5) Separation, (6) Annulment, (7) Re-marriage, etc.

Registration is essentially a product of the 19th century when lists of baptism, burials and wedding were kept by ecclesiastical authorities from much earlier times. In France it originated in 1308. Bills of mortility were registration statement issued by parish clerks in times of plague showing the number of deaths and their causes. This classification of cases was originallv crude in nature. Civil-registration was first introduced in England and Wales in 1836, but since the original introduction, there have been considerable developments. Thus penalties for failure to register birth were introduced in England in 1874 and compulsory registration of still birth was introduced from 1926. Sweden could really claim the honour of the pioneer in the field of vital statistics. A law was enacted in Sweden in 1748 to maintain tabular records of population. Thus schedules were prepared every year for parish showing particulars of births, death, marital status, etc. These schedules were systematically drawn up and they may be regarded as a beginning of the advanced methods of continuous registration. In striking contrast, the natural system of vital registration in U.S.A. had a very slow beginning because it was a State subject. In 1946 the natural office of vital statistics was set up to undertake registration.

Usually registration covers events like birth, death, marriage, divorce, separation, etc. Registration, unlike census continues throughout the year, as such shortage of enumerators is not felt. Registration has legal connotation, because it provides information about citizenship, marital status, succession rights and settlement of disputes about birth and death.

Registration as Secondary Data Source

Registration data are utilised as secondary data source by demographers. Three sources are:

(1) Vital registration.

(2) Population register.

(3) Government records.

(1) *Vital registration*: Every country has made it obligatory for its citizens to register births, death, marriage, etc. Such figures make it possible to make comparisons after suitable intervals. It is called comparative static analysis which assists in collecting information on fertility, mortality, etc. Registration figures are incomplete on account of the insufficient public response in reporting vital events, more particularly marriages, separation, divorces, etc., are not properly registered. In India where fertility data collected

amounts to perhaps only 50 to 90 per cent of actual occurrences and therefore they are untrustworthy for measuring long-term trends. Even where the coverage is complete, age and cccupation are incorrectly reported.

Registration involved the filling up of schedules.

(a) *Birth certificate*: (1) Name, (2) Father's Name, (3) Age of mother, (4) Legitimacy, (5) Order of birth, (6) Occupation of husband, (7) Place of birth, (8) Place of residence.

(b) *Death certificate*: (1) Name of the deceased, (2) Sex. (3) Race/Caste, (4) Age of deceased, (5) Place of death, (6) Occupation, (7) Permanent residence, (8) Place of birth, (9) Cause of death.

(c) *Marriage Certificate*: (1) Name of the bride, (2) Father's name, (3) Name of the bridegroom, (4) Name of the husband/wife, (5) Race of bride, (6) Age of bride. (7) Place of birth of bride/bridegroom, (8) Occupation of bridegroom.

Reliability of the registration data depends upon the accuracy of information supplied to the registrar office. Usually, correct and factual information is obtained because it is simple and non-confiden tial in nature. Difficulty arises when one person like a village guard is required to supply the information for the entire village and he does not furnish correct information. In U.S.A. people get themselves registered, as such registration certificates are needed to obtain citizenship rights, employment and social security.

(2) *Population register*: Permanent population register is maintained in European countries for administrative and legal purposes. It helps to verify the correctness of population census figures. Population trends could be observed with its help. Sweden is maintaining such a register.

(3) *Government records*: Secondary data about population is collected from other records. Life Insurance Corporation maintains record of birth, death and population trends in some countries. Population records are maintaind in almost every civilised country to meet social obligations like the unemployment, insurance, old age pension, employment, etc. Other purposes include provision of ration to the people, maintaining electoral lists, Income-tax lists, lists of telephone subscribers, about people associated with social and other organisations, etc. "Even when the data provided by administrative operations are limited, they may provide an ideal sampling frame for carrying out special surveys. For example, it is very costly to find by routine interviewing of randomly selected households, representative samples of migrants, divorced persons, members of particular ethnic or religions groups or couples with two children. The records kept

for administrative purposes may provide a compratively complete or representative set of homes and addresses which can then be sampled for intensive interviewing."

III. SAMPLE SURVEY

Sample survey is an important method of collecting demographic data. It is based on a sample drawn from an indefinitely large ideal population. The sample so chosen is surveyed with the help of a limited group of skilled staff and the collected data are tabulated, analysed and published. This method is quick and less expensive. Sample surveys can be held often and the questions asked can be varied. Although there will be a wide margin of statistical error in the information collected, this margin can be measured and by verifying the size of the sample, it can be satisfactorily controlled. Samples are like medicines. They can be harmful when they are taken carelessly.

Use of sampling in demography: The uses of sampling in demography falls into three groups: (1) *Gaining information independently without complete enumeration*: The results obtained on the basis of the sample survey are applied for the entire country and estimates could be obtained with reasonable accuracy. However, sampling cannot take the place of complete count because of two reasons.

(i) If a census or registration is compulsory it can be applied to every one and not only to a certain section of the people.

(ii) Sampling to be effective requires stratification of the universe and this can be achieved only if there is a suitable reference framework based on a recent census.

(2) Sampling can be used to update the results of a complete census taken some times before.

(3) Sampling is used to supplement a current census and find out the accuracy of the count.

Examples of sampling being used to aid complete census can be found in every phase of the work of census, from planning, enumeration, processing, tabulating, devaluation of the quality, etc. The questionnaires of census are pretested and their efficiency could be observed with the help of sampling. The schedules of personal information can be designed in such a way that some questions are asked of every one but others are asked only of a sample. This method helps the census to provide a framework for sampling. It can also minimise the trouble caused to the public. It will help in including more questions on the schedule and reduce the labour of tabulation.

Tabulation of a sample size from a complete set of schedules helps in publishing the results of the census much earlier than otherwise would be the case. It helps in getting an immediate appraisal of the data urgently needed for planning and research.

Sampling may be used to check the accuracy of the census data. If the response of the householders is suspect, renumeration can be made. Census data can be checked in the light of the source of data like vital register with the sampling technique.

Errors in Sampling

Usually there are coverage, classification, and sampling errors in sampling method for population figures. It calls for the help of qualified and competent persons to handle the data and reduce errors. When unqualified and inexperienced people are in charge of the work, errors creep in. Paucity of resources and staff presents further problems. The non-representative character of the sample is another fly in the ointment.

The manner in which the sample is chosen is of great importance. If there is bias in it, the data obtained will not be representative of the whole population. Difficulties arise on account of the non-cooperation by the informants. Therefore, it is essential that this method should be very carefully and consciously used.

Importance of population statistics: A pertinent question raised regarding the population statistics concerns their social importance. Some of the benefits may be discussed as under:

Social benefits: (1) We can get information about trends in child marriage, widow marriage, Sati and other social evils and improvements made in our social life.

(2) We can find rates of child mortality, causes of deaths of men and women due to causes like family discord, love frustration, etc.

(3) Progress of language and linguistic behaviour of the people can be found out.

(4) It helps in providing social infrastructure like schools, hospitals, colleges, cinema houses, sanitary facilities, etc.

Political benefits (1) We can know the number of voters and make arrangements for the ballot-papers and polling booths on its basis.

(2) The number of seats in Lok Sabha and State legislative assemblies is linked with the population. Statistics of population helps in making suitable alteration in the number of seats.

(3) Similarly, seats reservation could be made in elected bodies to members of scheduled castes and tribes on the basis of population figures.

(4) Population statistics forms the basis of delimitation of constituency for conducting elections.

Economic benefits: (1) Population statistics can provide information about the progress in the industrial field, which the nation is making.

(2) We can find out the standard of living of the people with the help of population figures as also the distribution of income in the society.

(3) With their help we can find out the regional imbalance and invite the attention of the Government towards their removal.

(4) By observing in trend in population, it becomes possible to find out the consumption needs of the people of the country and adopt measures to meet the situation.

(5) Budget estimates are made on the basis of the population data. Information when available in this regard helps in providing transport, communication and other facilities to thickly populated areas.

(6) It aids in evolving suitable employment and labour policies.

(7) Density of population is measured with the help of population data. Information when available in this regard helps in providing transport, communication and other facilities to thickly populated areas.

(8) Budget estimates are made on the basis of the population figures. Tax structure is drawn upon the basis of the population data.

Other benefits: Figures are extensively employed in every sphere of human activity. The statistics and figures are needed for opening schools, hospitals, employment centres, introduction of new trades in technical and non-technical institution and also in striking a balance between population and food needs. So many problems which growth of population creates can only be solved when the state is fully conscious of the magnitude of the problem, which comes only with the help of population figures. Population figures are also needed by sociologists, economists, traders, trading institution and organisations. There is close link between population and price of commodities, population and local consumption and exports. Even the insurance companies decide about their business on the basis of birth and death figures on the one hand and the rate at which people die on the other. U.N.O. in one of its report said: "The development of statistics are causing history to be written. . . . Now statistical inquiry leads him (historian) into hovels, homes, workshops, mines, fields, hospitals and all other places where human nature displays his weakness and strength. In these explorations he discovers the seeds of natural growth and decay and thus becomes the prophet of his generation."

SELECT REFERENCES

1. Bogue, D.J.: "The Pros and Cons of 'Self-Enumeration', "*Demography*, (2), 1965.
2. Barclay, G.W.: *Techniques of Population Analysis*, Wiley, New York, 1958.
3. Bose, Ashish: *Urbanization in India : An Inventory of Source Materials*. Academic Books Limited, New Delhi, 1970.
4. Census of India 1971: Census Centenary Publication No. 5, Office of the Registrar General, India, Ministry of Home Affairs, New Delhi, 1972.
5. Census of India 1961: A Guide to the 1961; Census Publication Programme, Office of the Registrar General, India, Ministry of Home Affairs, New Delhi, 1964.
6. Mitra, A. : *The Census of India in India—Census, 1872-1951*. A check-list and Index, Basic Collections in Micro-Edition, Inter Documentation Company, A.G. Zug-Switzerland, 1966.
7. Saxena, G.B.: *Indian Population in Transition*, Commercial Publication Bureau, New Delhi, 1971.
8. U.N.: Hand Book of Vital Statistical Methods, 1955.
9. U.N.: Hand Book of Population Census Methods, 3 Vols. 1965.
10. U.N.: The Determinants and Consequences of Population Trends.
11. Willcox, W.F.: "Census", *Encyclopaedia of the Social Sciences*, 3 Mac-Millan, New York, 1930.
12. Yates. F.: Sampling Methods for Census and Surveys, 1959.
13. Zachariah, K.C.: *Historical Study of Internal Migration in the Indian Sub-Continent 1900-1931*, Asia Publishing House, 1965.

EXAMINATION QUESTIONS

1. What are the important sources of demographic data?

6

Population Census

For any country population data has a vital bearing from the economic and social points of view. Demographic materials are assembled with the aid of census. Continuous supply of population data is essential for the successful implementation of plans in an underdeveloped country. It is well nigh impossible to make an assesement of the requirements of a country without adequate demographic data.

Census of population is not merely the counting of heads but it also includes detailed information on the human capital and its characteristics. Literally census is the combination of two words—Public + Counting.

Public means the people of the country and counting involves collection of information about them.

A census of population may be defined "as the total process of collecting, compiling and publishing demographic, economic and social data pertaining at a specified time or times to all persons in a country of delimited territory." To put it in another way, census is the collection of information about birth, death, occupational, social and economic conditions of the people of the country at a given time.

HISTORY OF CENSUS

History of census of a comprehensive nature is roughly 150 years old. Initially the number of countries were few and far between where systematic census took place after regular intervals. Systematic collection of census data had begun from 1895. Recorded figures of census indicate that between 1895 and 1944 nearly 42 to 49 countries collected census data. The number of countries collecting regular census rose to 65 by the year 1954.

Comprehensive census operations were conducted in 1961. Today throughout the globe systematic collection of census data has become a regular feature.

The census conducted in the 19th century and modern times differed widely in their scope and nature. In olden days census data pertained to the number of soldiers, enumeration of tax payers or collection of information of socio-political nature. Today the range of information covers a wider field and the methodology employed is very scientific.

Problems Connected with Census

Census operations entail heavy cost in terms of men, money and materials. It is time consuming as well as patience consuming. Therefore the maximum possible information should be collected. Some of the problems are:

(1) The terms used in the proformas for collection of information are interpreted in different ways.

(2) There is shortage of trained personnel which makes the collection and processing difficult.

(3) Census operations require field work which is extremely tedious. Dishonest field workers dish out cooked figures which vitiates the results.

(4) Basic terms are not uniformally applied during enumeration. Replies to question vary widely in spite of detailed instructions. For instance, education is differently interpreted by different enumerations. In rural areas a person who knows three R's may be called educated, whereas in urban areas even high school student may be considered uneducated.

(5) Due to personal reasons many people do not give correct information or on account of the failure of the investigator to establish proper rapport with the persons from whom the information is to be collected.

(6) Wide gaps are left while finalising the proformas because of the difficulty involved in filling them. For instance while eliciting information on age, people are divided into age groups like 1-5. 6-10, etc. In this way a gap of 5 years is allowed.

CENSUS TECHNIQUES

(1) De facto Method
(2) De jure Method

(1) De facto Method

Under it, a date is fixed for the census of the whole country. Usually such an operation is conducted during night, which is called the census night. Usually it is a moon-lit night and the people are exhorted not to leave their home.

Enumerators count people on this night wherever they are found. When the people actually present are counted at the same moment in a census, it is called de facto census of population. Since the enumeration is rounded off in day's time, it is also called date system or one night enumeration system. Both in India as well as in England this was the system followed up to 1931, which was however discontinued later on.

Merits and Demerits

De facto method has its own merits and demerits.

Merits: (1) It is very clear and simple.

(2) International comparisons can be made easily.

(3) Time taken for the whole operation is very little.

(4) Information collected is reliable and dependable.

Disadvantages: (1) There is a natural tendency to underestimate the population. The method of de facto census is not fool proof. Normally the floating population is not counted and so the data is not representative and turn out to be incorrect.

(2) This method calls for a large number of well qualified and trained field workers.

Shortage of such people results in the employment of incompetent people and the results become biased.

(3) Due to paucity of time very few questions are put in the questionnaire. Census is conducted once in ten years and so it is necessary to frame questionnaire in such a way as to elicit maximum information.

(4) The rapid and fast nature of this method leaves room for errors and mistakes to creep in.

(2) De jure Method

Under the dejure method every individual in a particular area is personally counted and the requisite information obtained. Temporary residents are excluded from its purview. A temporary resident is enumerated at his permanent place of residence. The enumeration work is prolonged for two to three weeks which is known as enumeration period.

Merits and Demerits

Merits: (1) One advantage of this system is that since the period of enumeration is quite sufficient, chances of inaccuracies are reduced to the minimum.

(2) Similarly the number of questions inserted can be increased.

(3) The work can be successfully done even if trained personnel are few in number.

(4) The data collected through this method is dependable and can be used for purposes such as transfer of property, dispute about successor, formulation of government policy on education, etc.

Disadvantages: (1) Proper definition of household, permanent residence, etc., poses problem.

(2) The period of enumeration is staggered long. Meanwhile birth, death and migration take place which cannot be properly accounted for.

(3) It is difficult to count persons who have no permanent residence.

(4) Correct and accurate information in respect of persons who have more than one temporary residence also presents difficulties.

Both the systems have their merits and defects. As Barclay says: "Hence we cannot say there is any perfect or correct scheme for counting the population. The selection of either one of these standards or more commonly some mixture of the two has an effect which is present in every figure of the census. Obviously more people in the questionable categories, the greater the effect of choosing one standard or the other."

PLANNING OF CENSUS AND ITS SCOPE

The method of census operation is neither uniform throughout the world nor is it necessary to be uniform. Even in a country the method of census employed varies from time to time. A single model is not suitable for a country for all times. Census method has to be modified in the light of changes in the social, cultural and educational levels.

It is essential that the census operation should be planned. Otherwise the information will probably turn out to be untrust worthy, inadequate, irregular and unscientific. For ensuring regularity, continuity and objectivity proper thought and planning of census is essential.

Time schedule: Census operation involves wide field and complex work and its utility is great. Adequate preliminary planning is a prerequisite for its success, more particularly for a country where the census is being conducted for the first time. The operation follows a given time schedule. Census calendar can be divided into three parts:

(1) Pre-enumeration.

(2) Enumeration.

(3) Post-enumeration.

Thus the process of census work is broken up in the time segments as indicated above and performed.

Scope of Census

Area of census coverage is designed according to the necessity of the country. The first step is to draw up questionnaire. Adequate knowledge and expertise is called for in the preparation of the questionnaire.

The questions should be plain, clear and unambiguous. Question should be so worded that answer to one question can provide information on more than one point. The question should be pretested and chained in such a manner that answer to one question becomes a link to another question. No such question should be included which invites any sharp reaction or put the respondent in an embarrassing position. The language of the question should not include any academic jargon. The questionnaire should enlist information in the following ways:

(1) Location at the time of census.

(2) Usual place of residence.

(3) Total members in the house, and relation with the head.

(4) Sex, age and marital status.

(5) Place of birth.

(6) Occupation and other economic information.

(7) Nationality.

(8) Cultural information like religion, caste, language, education.

(9) Information on the composition of population like birth rate, death rate, rural and urban residence, etc.

Census Laws

It is the sacred obligation of the people to furnish correct and reliable information of census. However census laws are also enacted to ensure proper conduct of the census. These statutory provisions make it binding on the citizens to supply the information through the census statistics, are not however rigid in nature. The law provides adequate safeguards to maintain the secrecy of the information to ward off doubts, fears and suspicion from the minds of respondents. Law also provides the machinery for census operation, fixes the year of census and provides punishment for non-cooperation, supply of false information, etc.

For example it is very costly to find by routine interviewing of randomly selected households representing samples of migrants, divorced persons, members of particular ethnic or religious groups or couples with two children. The records kept for administrative purposes may provide a comparatively complete or representative sets of homes and addresses which can then be sampled for intensive interviewing.

(1) *Vital registration*: Today in most of countries people have started registration about births, deaths, marriage, divorce, remarriage, etc. In France such registration started from 1803. But civil registration of population was first started in Sweden in 1748. Accuracy of vital registration depends on the accuracy of information which is supplied to the registration office. Usually the information given is correct because it is simple and non-confidential in nature. Moreover it is a kind of information which is known to every person in the family. Difficulty can however, arise only in cases where one person like chowkidar, etc., is required to supply information for the whole village and he does not realise its significance. In the advanced countries people compulsorily register themselves simply because registration certificates are needed for obtaining citizenship rights, employment and social securities, etc.

(2) *Population registration*: This type of registration includes besides vital information about births and deaths, information on migration, etc. In many European countries maintenance of permanent population register for certain administrative and legal reasons is considered absolutely necessary. The figures collected at the time of census are verified by it and the gaps filled in. This system also gives population trends.

CENSUS METHOD

Census is performed with the aid of two methods viz. canvassor method and householder method.

Under canvassor method the government enumerators visit every household and collect the required information from the head of the household. This method is profitably employed to collect the information from illiterate respondents. The householder method is used to obtain information from literate respondents. Then schedules are distributed to every family and the head of the family fills them up and return. In every census both the methods are adopted simultaneously.

DATE AND MOMENT

Census operations are held throughout the country at one unit of time. Every precaution is taken to avoid double counting. Deaths taking place on or before the date of enumeration are left out of the counting.

All the informations are collected from the head of the household with occasionally other family members are also questioned to verify the facts.

Census operation is a complicated task. The situation becomes complex when the population does not remain stationary or when people are not available at their place of residence or when the population is spread over a wide area.

Sample method: Under the sampling method, instead of taking a complete census, representative samples of population are counted and the results obtained are used to estimate the population of the whole country. The crux of the problem is the selection of representative samples. It is rather convenient to select a sample when the population is more or less homogeneous. But difficulty arises when the nature of the population is heterogeneous, which makes the selection of a representative sample extremely difficult.

Today sampling method is an indispensable adjunct of the census operation. In fact sampling can result in a lot of saving in terms of time, money and energy, though it cannot be substituted in place of complete census. This method is simple, convenient and economical. Normally, it is used to ascertain the margin of error in a complete count.

POST-CENSUS WORK

This work devolves into the following operations:

(*i*) *Editing*: Editing involves the correction and proper presentation of data collected under the census. Entries are properly made and missing entries are collected again. All the facts are closely scrutinised and anomalies and contradictions are corrected.

(*ii*) *Coding and punching*: This task involves the conversion of information in the questionnaires into quantitative codes and placed at appropriate places. This makes the further processing easy and scientific punches made at the card at different places give separate identities. Somes operations like the identification of sex, etc., are easy while assessment of economic condition presents difficulties.

(*iii*) *Sorting, compilation and tabulation*: Punched cards are used to prepare tables with the aid of the following operation:

(*i*) Classification of cards into separate groups.

(*ii*) Counting of individual in each group and present the data.

(*iii*) Prepare tables out of the data obtained.

BUDGETARY PROVISION FOR CENSUS

Census operation is based on adequate budgetary provision. The entire census operation is covered within the budget provided for. Since the whole operation involves heavy financial commitment to the government, so the budgetary provisions are indispensable for the successful conduct of the census operation.

ORGANISATION OF CENSUS

Census organisation calls for network of establishments from regional to national level. At the apex is a central office which gives the necessary directions concerning the census. Below the central office a number of offices function at the provincial and regional levels. The staff working in these establishments are required to be well trained permanent workers. They should be trained in the sophisticated technique from time to time. Of late, census departments are equipped with adequate number of sophisticated machines like computers.

The organisation set up of the census work is as under:

I

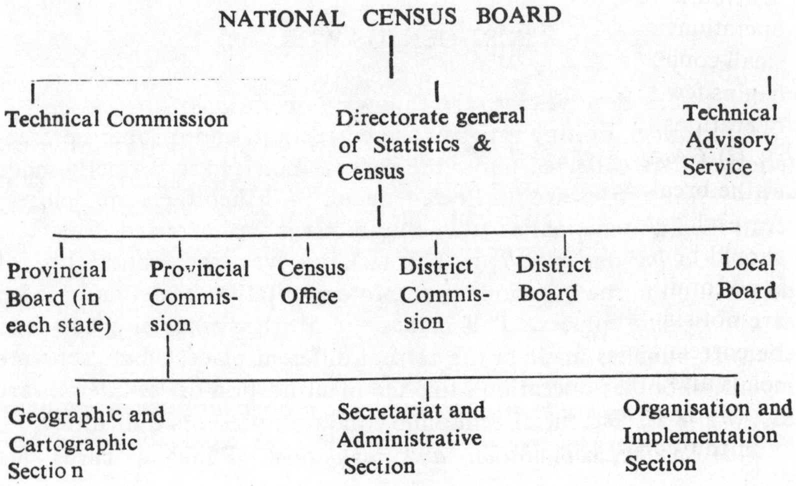

II

CENSUS ORGANISATION

Geographic and Cartographic Section	Secretariat and Administration	Collection Coding Tabulation

III

AFTER ENUMERATION

Technical Commission	Directorate General of Statistics and Census	Analysis and Publication

The three main divisions of census work can be divided into the following three parts:

(1) Pre-enumeration work (Organisation)

(2) Enumeration work (Organisation)

(3) Post-enumeration work (Organisation)

(1) **Pre-enumeration Work**

As the census work is very comprehensive it can be efficiently handled only with the help of specified time-table. Pre-enumeration work includes different kinds of preparations which are to be done before the census work starts. There are no universal norms regarding the period from where the preliminary pre-census begin. The period varies depending on the geographical area and the geographic distribution of the population in a particular country. Preliminary operations begin years before the census in a big country while in a small country with low density of population the preliminary work begins few months earlier. Pre-census work breaks up in to following operations :

(*i*) *Geographical and cartographical works*: Map prepration involves the breaking up of the country into different census zones and for each zone maps are separately prepared. Adequate safeguards should be made to ensure that even the smallest part of the country is not omitted or a particular village or group of villages or segment are not simultaneously included in two separate regions. Map should be correct and complete in every respect. In certain areas mohalla, roads and homes should be properly entered in the map.

(*ii*) *Determination of the enumeration area*: For census enumeration the borders of every region should be fixed in advance. An enumeration area is delimited at the minimum possible level to facilitate the enumerator to perform the work in a convenient way. As far as possible the population of the different areas of enumeration should be more or less the same. Each enumeration area should come within a single political unit, i.e. one unit should not fall within two states or two districts.

(*iii*) *Preparation of the questionnaires and instructions*: Questionnaire preparation is the main part of the pre-enumeration work. Questions should be drawn scientifically. The language of the questions should be simple and understandable. No such question should be included which invites any sharp reaction or puts the respondent in an embarrassing position.

Regarding the number of questions, it must be adequate in number to collect the required information. The number should not be too much as it will make the tabulation cost prohibitive.

The number as well as the nature of questions depends on the literacy level of the respondents. If the people are educated and are aware of their responsibilities it becomes easier to enlist the necessary information. Questionnaire can be divided into 3 categories.

(*i*) Single individual questionnaire which is meant to collect information from a single individual.

(*ii*) Single household questionnaire which is used to collect information from each and every household.

(*iii*) Multiple household questionnaire which aids the collection of information on a group of households.

Usually the second and third kinds of questionnaires are used.

Briefly questionnaire includes the following questions:

(*i*) Name of the head of the household and the relationship of the rest of the household members.

(*ii*) Persons living in the house but not related to the head. (*a*) Nationality (*b*) Religion (*c*) Schedule Caste, Tribe and Anglo-Indian etc.

(*iii*) Marital status.

(*a*) For unmarried (*b*) For married (*c*) Widow (*d*) Divorced.

(*iv*) Age approximate (write 0 for those below one year).

(*v*) Place of birth, district, state, etc. If foreigner, information regarding nationality, etc.

(*vi*) If displaced person, the date of arrival in India in the first column and in the second column the district to which the person belonged at the time of displacement.

(*vii*) Mother tongue.

(*viii*) Other languages known.

(*ix*) Economic status—earning member or dependent. In the first part employed, in the second part self-employed, nature of work, etc.

(*x*) Detailed information regarding occupation.

(*xi*) Income from other sources.

(*xii*) Literacy.

(*xiii*) Other particulars.

(*xiv*) Sex.

(4) *Census test*: The prepared schedules and questionnaires are pre-tested through field trial and experimental census, with a view to overcome the shortcomings, if any. Modifications are made in the schedules in the light of preliminary survey.

(5) *Pre-Planning the Data Processing Department*: It is an important department with offices at the central, state, regional and district level. This department is equipped with trained workers and machines like computers, electronic machines, etc.

(6) *Training of personnel and publicity*: To perform the work efficiently proper training will have to be given to the personnel employed in fields like computer operation, cartography, punch card operators, etc. Similarly the significance of census should be publicised through documentary, film, poster, pamphlet, mobile vehicles, press, etc. In underdeveloped countries field publicity is important to overcome the apathy of the villagers who are illiterate and to enlist their cooperation in collecting facts and figures.

(2) Census Operation

Record System. Population estimation can be made with the use of registers of records, which are of three kinds:

(a) Aministrative records.

(b) Vital registers.

(c) Population registers.

(a) Administrative Records

Administrative records of taxpayers, land tax records etc. are used to estimate the population. In some countries life insurance corporations and companies keep records about population trends and birth and death rates. Even when the data provided by administrative operation are limited, they may provide an ideal sampling frame for carrying out special surveys.

3. Post-Census Checking

After completing the tests the census figures are compared with the vital registers and population registers. Thereafter the census results are verified with the help of balancing equation with the results of earlier census.

The birth and immigration figures are added to the previous census figures while death and emigration figures are deleted from it:

The formula used is:

$$P_1=P_0+B+I-D-E$$

Index. ∴ P_1= Current population

P_0= Previous population

B = Birth

I = Immigration

D=Death

E=Emigration

EVALUATION OF POPULATION RESULTS

To find out mistakes in the census, sampling method is used a second time. In the light of experience and post-census sampling results the shortcomings in the census operation can be detected. This will help in overcoming defects in any future census.

Publication: It is the last unit in the chain of census operations. The results of the census are published for the knowledge of every body. A brief report of the census results is published immediately after the enumeration. Subsequently the detailed results are published within one or two years.

SELECT REFERENCES

As in Previous Chapter.

EXAMINATION QUESTIONS

1. Define Population census. Discuss the problems connected with census.
2. Distinguish between De-facto and De-jure Methods of cencus techinque.

7

Vital Statistics

We live in the age of science in which along with scientific development, the importance of statistics is also growing enormously. Vital statistics deals with birth, death, divorce and remarriage, etc.

Population statistics falls into three broad categories:

(1) Population census,
(2) Ad hoc demographic survey,
(3) Registration of vital events.

(1) *Population census*: It is the primary duty of every country to collect demographic data and interpret them. Census constitutes the backbone of the demographic data. From the sociological angle, census enumeration involves in addition to the counting of heads, the collection of a host of materials which display the demographic peculiarities of the country. Census operation presupposes a well organised central authority, usually the state. It also requires considerable allocation of economic resources, for statistics are a costly commodity. The completeness and accuracy of census data are in considerable degree functions of the attitudes and intellectual level of the population under observation. Census deals with the collection, classification and publications of numerical data relating to the size and economic and social life of the entire population of a country during a given time.

(2) *Ad hoc demographic survey*: Normally complete population census is undertaken once in 10 years. During the inter-census period, population estimates are projected with the help of ad hoc surveys on small samples of population in different regions. Such studies are called ad hoc demographic studies.

(3) *Vital statistics*: By vital statistics we mean the statistical explanation of live birth, death, foetal death, marriage, termination of marriage, adoption, legitimation, recognition, annulment and legal separation.

N.B. Ryder stated: "The registration system may provide cumulative summaries for successive time periods of population movements like birth, death, migration, marriage and marital dissolution, as well as demographic and other relevant characteristics of the individuals involved in these events."

The above definition is fairly wide and scientific. However under the conditions prevalent in underdeveloped countries, its application is of limited validity on account of insufficient registration of vital events like births, deaths, marriage, etc. Besides in India marriage is partly a function which is generally registered. Bengarium stated: "Traditionally vital statistics deal with quantitative estimate of birth, death, marriage and disease which can be used to study the health and development of human beings."

In the narrow sense vital statistics is concerned only with the figures of fertility and mortality.

Difference between Vital Statistics and Population Statistics

(1) Normally population census is conducted once in 10 years whereas vital events registration continues for all times without any time gap.

(2) In fact population census is the records of the population of a country while vital statistics are related to the events taking place in the life of individuals of the country.

(3) Census enumeration provides the population statistics at a particular point of time while vital statistics give information on the trend of population changes through birth, death, etc. Vital statistics is a process of continuous evaluation of population.

(4) Respondents are legally bound to furnish the information sought under the census operations, while registration of vital events is still not compulsory in many countries. Many people in India even do not bother to register events like birth, death, marriage, etc., with the authorities.

Though vital statistics and census have some differences, yet both are closely related to each other. Vital statistics could be obtained with the census data and the size of population and its composition could be estimated from time to time with the aid of registration of vital events. In fact John Graunt who made an appraisal of the population of England did so with the help of vital statistics because census was not held in those days in England.

COMPUTATION OF RATES OF VITAL EVENTS

To estimate the size of population at a given time, the following formula may be used:

$$P(t) = (o) + B(t) - D(t) + I(t) - E(t)$$

in this formula:

$P(t)$ = Total population at a point of time
$P(o)$ = Total population at a point of time taken as base
$B(t)$ = Total number of birth during the given period
$D(t)$ = Total number of death during the given period
$I(t)$ = Total number of immigrants
$E(t)$ = Total number of emigrants.

It is clear from the formula that there are four variables determining the size of population, viz., birth, death, immigration and emigration. They constitute the major basic vital events. However in many countries only birth and death rates are given due cognizance under vital statistics. Therefore our present study embraces only mortality and fertility under the vital statistics. These have been dealt in separate chapters under the heads "Fertility and fertility measurement" and "Mortality and mortality measurement."

Use of Vital Statistics

Vital statistics have very deep and profound significance in the life of the people and for the nation.

(1) Vital statistics help us in analysing demographic trends in the country. The following facts could be obtained with its help:

(*i*) They aid in the population projection of a country without taking recourse to census operation.

(*ii*) Vital statistics help us to make an appraisal of population at any given point of time while census enumerations are held after an interval of 10 years. Thus vital statistics fill the gap in the census method and supplement it.

(*iii*) The main constituents of vital statistics like birth, death, marriage, separation, remarriage, disease statistics are analysed and the trends in the composition size and distribution of population are studied systematically with the help of vital statistics.

(*iv*) Birth rate, death rate, reproduction rate, etc., enable us to assess the growth rate in population and replacement rate from time to time.

(*v*) Knowledge of vital events makes it easy to know the future trends in population and make precise projection of future population.

(2) *Use of vital statistics in health services*: (*i*) The nature and magnitude of health service requirements could be assessed on the basis of vital statistics. Facts and figures obtained through the registration of vital events give us an idea of the requirements in the fields of hospital, maternity centre, child welfare centres, etc.

(*ii*) In the field of family planning the vital statistics can be employed to evolve appropriate population policies and also assess the impact of the policies which help in making corrective measures.

(*iii*) Vital statistics are useful in diseases eradication programmes. Suitable measures to check diseases depend very much on the causes of such diseases. Mortality figures by census are useful in not only getting information on mortality but also they give information on death specific cause.

(3) *Legal importance of vital statistics*: Vital statistics have legal significance because they help to give statutory validity to birth date, death date, place and cause of death etc. Certificates obtained from the Office of Vital Statistics are useful in establishing the right of inheritance and help in identifying the nominees for claims of property, insurance fund, etc.

(4) *Vital statistics are beneficial in studying the social situation*: Social and family condition could be properly studied with the aid of vital figures. Data on marriage, legal separation, divorce, remarriage, widowhood, etc., give us insight into the laws, customs and traditions, etc. prevalent in the society. Vital statistics presents facts on all these events which provide the necessary information about the social customs and conventions. Because of their growing importance in the social field, vital statistics is called the mirror of the society.

(5) *Use in the area of planning*: Modern age is the age of planning. Data furnished by vital statistics could provide the background to frame suitable programmes to benefit the masses.

(6) *Other uses of vital statistics*: (*i*) Vital statistics are useful in different walks of life. They help in framing policies of social security. They are useful in evolving immigration and emigration rules.

(*ii*) Age statistics can be used to analyse the efficiency of working population.

(*iii*) Food requirements of the country, adequate distribution, rationing, etc., can be based on the data obtained through registration of vital events.

(*iv*) They are useful in updating the electoral rolls, in military service, etc.

Vital statistics are also useful from the international viewpoint. Only by a sufficiently wide survey of human facts can the required norms of all sorts be established, norms which represent the characters of the great unit constituted by the aggregation of all the nations.

However, it should be noted that vital statistics, like all statistics and multiple vital records, are not ends in themselves but tools for the study and understanding of other phenomena.

SELECT REFERENCES

1. Berent, J.: "Fertility and Social Mobility", *Population Studies*, Vol. 5, No. 3, 1950.
2. Barclay, G.W.: *Techniques of Population Analysis*, Wiley, New York, 1966.
3. Carlsson, G.: "The Decline of Fertility: Innovation or Adjustment Process" *Population Studies*, (20), 1966.

4. Kuczynski, R.R.: *The Measurement of Population Growth, Methods and Results*, Sidgerick and Jackson, London, 1935.

5. Moriyama, T.M. and Guralnick, L.: "Occupational and Social Class Differences in Mortality", in *Milbank Memorial Fund Quarterly*, Trends and Differentials in Mortality, New York, 1956.

6. Madigan, F.C.: "Are Sex Mortality Differentials Biologically Caused?", *Milbank Memorial Fund Quarterly*, (35), 1957.

7. Myers, R.J.: "The Impact of Med Care on Demography", *Demography* (3), 1966.

8. Petersen, W.: *Population*, The Macmillan Co., London, 1969.

9. Whelpton, P.K. and Kiser, C.V. (eds.): "Social and Psychological Factors affecting Fertility", *Milbank Memorial Fund Quarterly*, New York, 5.

EXAMINATION QUESTIONS

1. What is vital statistics? State the importance of vital statistics.
2. Distinguish between vital statistics and population statistics.

8

Mortality and Mortality Measurement

From biological view mortality implies the end of that body which had a live birth. However from the demographic viewpoint mortality denotes the fall in the size of population on account of death. Population growth can be due to a fall in death rate in addition to an increase in birth rate.

Importance of Mortality Data

Study of phenomenon of death and its measurement is not only significant from the demographic analysis, but also from the point of health standard to achieve better health and medical facilities. As observed by David M. Heer, death cycle not only influences the size of population but also its composition nature and its ethos. Its important effects are delineated as under.

(1) *Disruption of mental equilibrium*

The tradition of mourning and other institutional rites have rapidly declined on account of a fall in death rate. This has forced people to behave as if no death has taken place in the family soon after bereavement in the family. Such external appearance creates a lot of mental tension which results in diseases originating out of mental disequilibrium. Thus it can be seen that the institution of mourning after death can positively help in maintaining the mental balance.

(2) *Setback of self-confidence*

The incident of death inflicts a blow to the self-confidence of an individual. Frequent deaths in the family drive a person to desperation and make him depressed. He may hold God responsible for his misery which may eventually turn him into an atheist.

(3) *Size of the family*

The frequency of death also determines the size of the family. In societies where joint family system prevails the death rate is noticed to be generally high. In a society where nuclear family system is in vogue the mortality rate is comparatively less.

(4) *Outlook towards the future*

The outlook of an individual towards the future will be pessimistic in a society where the mortality rate is quite high. They will fight shy to incur sufficient expenditure even towards the education of their children as they are unable to enjoy the fruits of their sacrifice in the future. They wish to put their children to gainful employment to supplement the family income. The motivation of save and invest is also conspicuous by its absence in a society afflicted with the bane of high mortality.

(5) *Lack of enthusiasm towards children*

If the death rate is high, then the parents do not shower much affection on their children and also do not tend to be much ambitious or optimistic towards their children. Consequently, the upbringing of the children is neglected.

(6) *Type of marriage*

Prof. Heer is of the view that in general marriage is arranged by the parents in a society faced with the prospect of high mortality rate. Two reasons are adduced to explain this tendency.

(*a*) Children's fear that if they disobey their parent's wish then it may prove to be a cause of death and (*b*) the sorrow at the time of death will be less, if the marriage is an arranged one rather than a love marriage. That is why in underdeveloped countries with high death rates arranged marriages are high.

(7) *Life expectancy*

The incidence of mortality affects the life expectancy. The life expectancy today reflects the past trends in mortality rates and they provide the necessary factual data for future projection of population on the basis of probable death rate in future.

(8) *Health services*

Mortality statistics can help in throwing light on the achievements of health care and services in the society. The causes of death are also registered.

(9) *Probability of widowhood*

Data concerning mortality can provide us a mechanism to forecast the probability of widowhood in the society.

Various Causes of Mortality

Many different causes are responsible for death, viz., disease, weakness, accident etc.

The United Nations has categorised the various causes of mortality. Some of them are given as under:

(1) *First category*—Epidemic, parasitic and lung diseases.
(2) *Second category*—Cancer.
(3) *Third category*—Diseases of communicative type.
(4) *Fourth category*—Death due to violence.
(5) *Fifth category*—Other diseases like diabetes, diseases of new born babies in the first week of infancy etc.

The first category of diseases includes diseases like contagious, parasitic and lung infection. The developed countries of the world have successfully conquered contagious diseases like malaria, small-pox, cholera, typhoid, tuberculosis etc. Nevertheless the underdeveloped countries have not been able to contain these diseases in a satisfactory way. In fact as economic development takes place the knowledge of health and laws governing general physique also increases. The environment tends to undergo radical transformation. Consequently the dread and wide stranglehold of these diseases tend to loosen. Prof. Bogue has expressed the view that the control over epidemic diseases has been perhaps the main single reason for the rapid decline in mortality rate in developed countries.

The second category includes cancer, which accounts for nearly 18 per cent of the total deaths. Medical science is conducting continuous research into the causes and cure of cancer, but the results have not been satisfactory so far. The pressure of cancer is felt apparently less in developping countries where the population is composed mainly of young people; while the incidence of cancer is more common among those who are in the evening of their life.

In the third category comes those diseases that are associated with blood vessels, respiratory tracts, pulse etc. With advancing age the pressure on these will increase. These diseases originate out of the disorganisation of the various organs of the body. Therefore they cannot be completely rooted out, but their intensity can be reduced to some extent and prolong the hour of reckoning.

In the fourth group we can include such deaths which result from violence. Among the many reasons for unnatural deaths, we can include suicide, accident, attack with sharp weapons like knife, bullet injury etc. It is an irony of fate that the progress in education failed to make any decline in death due to violence. But on the other hand it has given rise to new forms of crime and violence.

In the last category we can include all other factors causing death connected with liver, intestine, appendicitis, ulcer, paediatrics, etc. Diseases belonging to this category are also curable and the death rate from this category is on the decline. The United Nations has sought to link life expectancy and age composition with the five categories of death enunciated above and indicated three main tendencies:

(*a*) When the life span increases from 40 years to 60 years, then the pressure of death resulting from the first category of diseases ceases. On the other hand diseases in the second, third and fifth categories start going up.

(*b*) As life expectancy rises from 60 to 70 years death from the first category continues to fall, while death due to second and third category diseases remains stationary.

(*c*) When life expectancy exceeds 70 years the incidence of death due to first, second and third categories causes tends to decline while death due to fifth category factors decreases rapidly.

Empirical Study of the Causes of Mortality

Empirical studies into causes of mortality have shown that three factors are mainly responsible for it:

(*i*) Hereditary factors influence mortality.

(*ii*) Body structure of an individual like physical and mental characteristics influence mortality.

(*iii*) Environmental factors like the size of the community, tradition, climate, locality like rural or urban origin, occupation, wide vision, overcrowding etc. influence mortality.

The variables included in the three categories may be interrelated and to that extent their effects are complex and confusing.

Practical experience shows that the effect of environment exercises a preponderant influence on mortality in underdeveloped countries while the environmental factors are not so significant in the case of developed countries. In fact, the developed countries have been able to regulate the environment to a great extent. Thus hereditary and psychological factors are the important determinants of mortality in developed countries. Of late, growing pollution of air, water, vegetables etc. in developed countries once again catapulted the environmental factors to the foreground as agents of death. Some experts have expressed gloomy forebodings about the survival of mankind unless the environmental pollution is effectively checked. However at present the mortality rate is very low in developed countries. Four reasons are attributed to this phenomenon:

(*a*) Regulation of epidemics and diseases in a big way; (*b*) mechanisation of agriculture; (*c*) development of trade and international trade in particular and (*d*) opening of the continents and colonies for economic use.

In fact, the mortality rate has declined in developed countries in three stages:

(1) *In the first stage* the standard of living improved to some extent with economic development. People have access to balanced diet which reduced death rate by 10 points.

(2) *In the second stage* improved public health services and control over epidemics and diseases resulted in a fall in death rate by another 10 points. Fall in age specific death rate is also discernible and more particularly the child mortality rate has fallen sharply.

(3) *In the third stage* the development of bio-chemistry has resulted in the rapid development of medical science which helped in bringing down mortality rate substantially. At present the developed countries have death rates in the range of 7 to 9 per thousand. Probably it would not be practicable to bring down the death rate below this limit.

Factors Affecting Mortality

(*i*) *Income*: It is an important variable affecting mortality. Studies have established the differences in mortality in different income classes in the overall economic conditions. It is reflected in the per capita income and the level of consumption in these communities. It has been observed that after attaining a minimum level of consumption and income, differences in income have a negligible effect on death rate.

(*ii*) *Occupation*: As compared to skilled labourers and workers engaged in different agricultural pursuits the death rate among unskilled and non-agricultural labourers is more.

Lillian Guralink has worked out the standardised death rate among 25-51 age group according to occupation. The findings are as given below:

Occupation	*Standard death rate*
All occupations	100
Technical, administrative and managerial class	83
Businessmen	79
Skilled workers like clerks etc.	94
Semi-skilled worker	101
Non-agricultural labour	167
Agricultural labour	96

The effect of occupational difference on mortality is narrowing down in western countries. It is being said that variations in mortality associated with diverse occupations are not due to the nature of occupations as such but rather due to the standards of living which the various occupations can give effect to. This line of reasoning is reinforced by the fact that the ratio of mortality of husband and wife is the same.

(*iii*) *Heredity*. Mortality is also influenced by hereditary factors. Studies conducted by Beetonce, Pearson, Holmes, Bell, Wilson, Doeering, etc. have yielded the conclusion that there is positive correlation between the life span of parents and their children. Raymond Pearl regards this as the most important factor determining mortality.

(*iv*) *Marital status*. It has been seen that the mortality rate is high among unmarried widowers, widows, and divorcees, as compared to married people. This difference is observed in every age group. Prof. Shirtleaf has conducted separate studies of the death rates in males and females and concluded that death rate is high among unmarried as compared to married in every age group. However, this difference is less as between married and unmarried women.

The reason for this difference in mortality can be explained by the fact that generally married people get better care of their health. They also lead a regular life. Their mutual concern for each other, nourishing food, etc. keep them conscious of maintaining their health. On the other hand a person living single leads a careless life and becomes a drug addict, resulting in early death.

(*v*) *Male-female*. In developed countries normally the death rate among the male population is more than the female population. A likely reason for this is that men are exposed to industrial and professional risks. In western countries the ways of life and values of life differ as between men and women on account of which death rate is more among men.

(*vi*) *Geographical factor*. In developed countries death rate is affected by geographical features, more particularly among those in the same income and professional class. Of late, the tremendous strides in the western countries in scientific field has helped man to learn the art of controlling nature which has reduced the effect of geographical factors on mortality.

(*vii*) *Urban-rural difference*. History is replete with examples that mortality rate in the village is less than the death rate in town. However during the last few years this gulf in death rate is narrowing down. However Prof. Darn believes that it is difficult to classify death rate into urban and rural as most of the village people seek admission in hospitals in a city when they fall seriously ill and generally die in the city. This tendency creates the impression that death rate is falling in village while it is going up in the cities.

(*viii*) *Poverty*. Another factor promoting death rate is poverty. In affluent areas the living standards are high and more attention is given to health on account of which death rate will be less there. Among the poor death rate is high as compared to rich due to poverty.

(*ix*) *Industrial environment*. Prof. Guralink has estimated the mortality rate according to industry. He has reached the conclusion that the incidence of suicide is very common among those engaged in business activities. Tuberculosis is common among miners, accidents are frequent in construction and transport activities. Liver troubles are common in transport workers. Prof. Guralink has worked out the standardised death rate industrywise as under:

Industry	*Standardised death rate*
Agriculture, forest and fisheries	97
Mining	125
Construction	119
Manufacture	92
Transport and communication	124
Wholesale and retail trade	99
Finance, Insurance Banking	94
Trade and maintenance industry	110
Personal services	122
Entertainment	135
Entrepreneur class	135
Public service	93

(x) *Health services.* In those places where health service facilities are available death rate is observed to be less. Spread of health services enables the control of diseases before they assume alarming proportions.

Causes of Infant Mortality

We can study the causes of high infant mortality under the following heads:

(1) *Birth related causes*

Under this head we can include those causes which are responsible for neonatal death like death due to birth before maturity period of pregnancy, deformity, birth wounds, suffocation, lack of timely medical car etc.

(2) *Standard of living*

Infant mortality and standard of living are mutually dependent. Parents with higher income can bring up their children in a better way. In other words, as the level of economic condition improves infant mortality decreases. A survey conducted in Stockholm shows that there is negative correlation between the living standard and infant mortality as indicated in the following table:

Infant mortality rate	*Father's income below 4,000 Kr.*	*Father's income above 10,000 Kr.*
1. Infant mortality rate	48.9	14.3
2. Neonatal rate	24.0	11.4
3. Death rate from the second to 12th month	24.9	2.9

The data reveals that infant mortality is more among the poor as compared to the rich.

(3) *Lack of education*

In fact, mortality rate also depends on the educational level of parents. Educated parents provide nourishing diet to their children, give them the best available medical care during illness and immunize them against diseases through control devices.

(4) *Medical treatment facilities*

Death rate is less in those places where medical facilities are available without much difficulty. Medical care can check the spread of child diseases and timely medical care can control the disease in the initial period. That is why infant mortality rate is less in cities as compared to rural areas.

(5) *High birth rate*

In countries with high birth rate the death rate too will be high. Every decrease in birth will be followed by a corresponding fall in death rate.

(6) *Ligitimacy*

Infant mortality is high in illegitimate children not born out of wedlock. Death rate is comparatively less in children born of legitimate birth. Society looks down with contempt on illegitimately born children and their mothers. The tendency to do away with such illegitimate children is another reason for the high infant mortality.

Limitations of Mortality Data

Mortality data by causes are not easily available. Besides, it is not easy to find out the real causes of death. The constraints in this respect are as under:

(*i*) Major portion of deaths takes place in the absence of doctors which makes it difficult to diagonise the precise causes of death.

(*ii*) The person who registers the death has also a role in providing the correct cause of death. If he does not understand the real cause of death the result can be erroneous.

(*iii*) At times the dead person might have been a patient suffering from more than one disease. Therefore it is difficult to fix the precise disease which caused death.

(*iv*) All cases of death are not registered which makes the data incomplete.

Professor Hauser has stated that the entire causes of the shortcomings of mortality data can be arranged under the following captions:

(i) Not accepting uniform definitions.
(ii) Not exercising caution while collecting data.
(iii) Supply of biased information by informants.
(iv) Changes in the methods of tabulation, classification and editing of data.
(v) Rigidity of the registration procedure and reluctance to accept international norms or inability to make timely changes in the registration rules.

In spite of these defects the mortality is of immense utility.

MEASUREMENT OF MORTALITY

The study of mortality conditions pertaining to a given population revolves around the following measures of death rates:

1. General or crude death rates.
2. Specific death rates.
3. Standardised death rates.

1. General or Crude Death Rates

General or crude death rate is a measure of the fall in population which takes place as a result of death. It is based on the following process:

(a) Death rate of every age group is worked out per 1000 numbers.

(b) The total population in every age group is assumed to be the weight for that group.

(c) The death rate in each group is multiplied with the corresponding weight of that group and the products for different age groups are added.

(d) The sum obtained is divided by the total population.

The quotient will be the general or crude death rate. According to David Heer: "Crude death rate may be defined as the ratio of the number of deaths which occur within a population during a specified year to the size of that population at mid-year."

The following formula is used to estimate the crude death rate:

$$CDR = \frac{\Sigma D}{\Sigma P} \times 1000$$

where CDR=Crude death rate.

ΣD=Total death in region at a given time.

ΣP=Total population of the same region during that year (Middle of the year).

Illustration: 1

From the following data calculate the Crude Death Rate:

Age group in years	0-10	10-30	30-50	50-70	70 and above
Population	10,000	20,000	30,000	20,000	4,000
Deaths	250	60	60	400	2,000

Solution:

$$CDR=\frac{\Sigma P}{\Sigma P}\times 1000$$

$$\Sigma D=250+60+60+400+2{,}000=2{,}770$$

$$\Sigma P=10{,}000+20{,}000+30{,}000+20{,}000+4{,}000=84{,}000$$

$$CDR=\frac{2{,}770}{84{,}000}\times 1{,}000=32.98 \text{ per thousand}$$

Broadly crude death rate indicates the probability of death within a given population. It is widely used to assess the proportion of death. It is a simple measure as it requires only the figures of total death and the total population at the mid-point of the same year. Crude death rate suffers from some lacuna as for instance it is unsuitable to make inter-regional comparisons. Mortality varies from age to age. If the age distribution differs from place to place any comparison of crude death will lead to misleading conclusions. In those places where the proportion of old people is high, the crude death rate is bound to be high as compared to a locality where the youngsters constitute the major portion of the population.

2. Specific Death Rate

This is yet another measure of death rate. There are two types of specific death rates: (1) Age specific death rate, (2) Death rates by causes. Infant mortality among infants is usually on the high side and gradually the frequency of death declines with every increase in age. To work out the age specific death rate, the population is classified under different categories according to age groups. Afterwards age specific death rate of the population is classified under different categories according to age groups. Afterwards age specific death rate is worked out on the following basis:

$$\text{Age specific death rate}=\frac{\text{No. of deaths in a specific age group of population of an area in a given period}}{\text{Total population in that age group in the same area}}\times 1000$$

$$ASDR=\left(\frac{D_i}{P_i}\times k\right)$$

This formula can be employed to work out the death rate among different age groups with the help of age specific death rate. We can find out crude death rate as well. Age specific death deals with the deaths throughout the given year and it does not say whether the death took place during the beginning or end of the year.

With the help of age specific death rates, crude death rates can be calculated with the following formula:

$$CDR=\frac{\Sigma(P_x D_x)}{\Sigma P_x}$$

Illustration: 2

On the basis of the figures given below, calculate Age Specific Death Rate for all age-groups. On the basis of Age Specific Death Rate, also calculate the Crude Death Rate.

Age groups in years	0-10	10-30	30-50	50-70	70 and above
Population	5,000	10,000	15,000	10,000	2,000
Deaths	125	30	30	200	1,000

Solution:

Calculation of CDR and Age Specific Death Rates:

Age Group	Population	Deaths	Age Specific Death Rates
Years	P_x	D	$(D \div P_x) \times 1000 = D_x$
0-10	5,000	125	$(125 \div 5{,}000) \times 1{,}000 = 25$
10-30	10,000	30	$(30 \div 10{,}000) \times 1{,}000 = 3$
30-50	15,000	30	$(30 \div 15{,}000) \times 1{,}000 = 2$
50-70	10,000	200	$(200 \div 10{,}000) \times 1{,}000 = 20$
70 and above	2,000	1,000	$(1{,}000 \div 2{,}000) \times 1{,}000 = 500$
Total	42,00	1,385	

$$CDR=\frac{\Sigma(P_x D_x)}{\Sigma P_x}$$

$$=\frac{(5{,}000\times 25)+(10{,}000\times 3)+(15{,}000\times 2)+(10{,}000\times 20)+(2{,}000\times 500)}{42{,}000}$$

$$=\frac{(1{,}25{,}000+30{,}000+30{,}000+2{,}00{,}000+10{,}00{,}000)}{42{,}000}$$

$$=\frac{13{,}85{,}000}{42{,}000}+32.98 \text{ per thousand}$$

Some important specific death rates:

(*i*) *Cause specific death rate*: In cause specific death rate we classify death according to causes of death. Depending on requirement it can be worked out along with age specific death rate.

(*ii*) ***Infant mortalily rate***: Under this category efforts are made to find out the death rate of infants below one year. Normally the risk of infant mortality rate is more in the beginning of life as a result of which infant mortality rates are fairly higher than crude death rates.

$$\text{Annual Infant Mortality Rate} = \frac{\text{Death rate among infants}}{\text{Number of children born in that year}} \times 1000$$

Similarly we can work out annual maternal mortality rate also.

3. Standardised Death Rate

Standardised death rate is a relative measure of death rate which provides the comparative death rates of two places or two different periods.

Thompson and Lewis put it as under: "The standardised death rate based on age specific death rates supplies a simple and accurate basis for comparing the death rate of different populations."

Barclay compared crude death rates and standardised death rates and said: "An age standard death rate fills either of the two needs. One is simply to summarise a set of age specific rates independently of the age composition of the population. The other is to show the probable influence of a population's age composition on its crude death rate when its actual age specific death rates are not known.

Standardisation can be of two types: (*i*) Direct standardisation. (*ii*) Indirect standardisation.

(*i*) *Direct Standardisation*

In direct standardisation, different age specific rates are applied to standard population. As Barclay puts it: "Thus there are two common types of procedures for computing standard rates. One consists of applying different age specific rates to standard population. This is called in English and American usage as direct standardisation." In this method the population distribution of any given locality is taken as the standard. Thereafter the age specific death rates are multiplied with the standard population and the following formula applied:

$$SDR = \frac{\Sigma(P_s \times D_l)}{\Sigma P_s}$$

where SDR = Standardised death rate
P_s = Standard population
D_l = Age specific death rates of local population.

(*ii*) *Indirect Standardisation*

Indirect standardised death rate consists of applying a standard set of rates to different population by age.

Under this method the age specific death rate of a given locality is taken as the standard. Afterwards the following formula is used to find out index of death rate:

$$\text{Index of Death Rate (Local population)} = \frac{\Sigma P_l \times D_s}{\Sigma P_l}$$

where P_l=Local population

D_s=Standardised age specific death rates.

Thereafter the crude death rate of the standard place is obtained with the following formula:

$$CDR=\frac{\Sigma(P_s \times D_s)}{\Sigma P_s}$$

Crude death rate of the standard locality is divided by the index death rate to arrive at the correction factor:

$$\text{Correction factor}=\frac{CDR \text{ of standard population}}{\text{Index } DR \text{ (Local population)}}$$

$$F=\frac{\Sigma(P_s \times D_l)}{P_s} : \frac{\Sigma(P_l \times D_s)}{P_l}$$

Finally death rate of the local population is multiplied with the correction factor to obtain death rate.

$SDR_l=CDR_l \times F$ in which CDR_l means crude death of the local population and F means correction factor:

Illustration : 3

Compute the crude and standardised death rates of the two populations A and B from the following data:

Age group (Year)	*Town A*		*Town B*	
	Population	*Deaths*	*Population*	*Deaths*
Below 5	15,000	360	40,000	1,000
5-30	20,000	400	52,000	1,040
Above 30	10,000	280	8,000	240
Total	45,000	1,040	1,00,000	2,280

Solution :

$$\text{Crude Death Rate}=\frac{N}{P} \times 1000$$

where N=No. of deaths, P=Population

$$\text{CDR for town A}=\frac{1,040}{45,000} \times 1,000=23.11$$

$$\text{CDR for town B}=\frac{2,280}{1,00,000} \times 1,000=22.80$$

Standardised death rate taking population of town *A* as standard population:

Age-group (years)	*Town A*			*Town B*		
	Population	*Deaths*	*Death rate per thousand*	*Population*	*Deaths*	*Death rate per thousand*
Below 5	15,000	360	24	40,000	1000	25
5-30	20,000	400	20	52,000	1040	20
Above 30	10,000	280	28	8,000	240	30
Total	45,000	1040		1,00,000	2280	

Standardised Death Rate (town *A*)

$$= \frac{(15{,}000 \times 24) + (20{,}000 \times 20) + (10{,}000 \times 28)}{15{,}000 + 20{,}000 + 10{,}000}$$

$$= \frac{3{,}60{,}000 + 4{,}00{,}000 + 2{,}80{,}000}{45{,}000} = \frac{10{,}40{,}000}{45{,}000} = 23.11$$

Standardised Death Rate (town *B*)

$$= \frac{(15{,}000 \times 25) + (20{,}000 \times 20) + (10{,}000 \times 30)}{15{,}000 + 20{,}000 + 10{,}000}$$

$$= \frac{3{,}75{,}000 + 4{,}00{,}000 + 3{,}00{,}000}{45{,}000} = \frac{7{,}15{,}000}{45{,}000} = 15.89$$

We can now say that the death rate in town B is higher than town A.

Another method of computing standardized death rate is to take some assumed population (that is the population of neither town A nor B) as standard. But this method is not so popular.

Illustration: 4

From the following data which of the two towns *A* and *B* would you consider to be more healthy (assume town B as standard):

Age	*Town A*		*Town B*	
	Population	*Deaths*	*Population*	*Deaths*
0-15	10,000	200	15,000	370
15-50	18,000	500	20,000	600
50 and above	2,000	50	5,000	100

Solution:

Calculation of Standardised Death Rate

Age	*Town A*			*Town B*		
	Population	*Deaths*	*Death rate per thousand*	*Population*	*Deaths*	*Death rate per thousand*
0-15	10,000	200	20.0	15,000	370	24
15-50	18,000	500	27.8	20,000	600	30
50 and above	2,000	50	25.0	5,000	100	20
Total	30,000	750		40,000	1,070	

$$\text{SDR of town B} = \frac{N}{P} \times 1000$$

$$= \frac{1,070}{30,000} \times 1000 = 35.67$$

This is also the standardised death rate of town B because town B is taken as standard.

$$\text{SDR of town A} = \frac{(15,000 \times 20) + (20,000 \times 27.8) + (5,000 \times 25)}{15,000 + 20,000 + 5,000}$$

$$= \frac{3,00,000 + 5,56,000 + 1,25,000}{40,000} = \frac{9,81,000}{40,000} = 24.5$$

Since the SDR of town A is less than that of town B, hence town A is more healthy.

Illustration: 5

From the following figures calculate CDR and SDR.

Age group	*Population*	*Death rate per thousand*	*Standard age distribution*
0-10	400	40	600
10-20	1,500	4	1,000
20-60	2,400	10	3,000
60 and above	700	30	400

Solution:

Calculation of CDR and SDR

$$\text{CDR} = \frac{(400 \times 40) + (1,500 \times 4) + (2,400 \times 10) + (700 \times 30)}{400 + 1,500 + 2,400 + 700}$$

$$= \frac{16,000 + 6,000 + 24,000 + 21,000}{5,000}$$

$$=\frac{6,7000}{5,000}=13.40 \text{ per thousand}$$

$$SDR=\frac{\Sigma P_s \times D}{\Sigma P_s}$$

$$=\frac{(600\times 40)+(1,000\times 4)+(3,000\times 10)+(400+30)}{600+1,000+3,000+400}$$

$$=\frac{24,000+4,000+30,000+12,000}{5,000}$$

$$=\frac{70,000}{5,000}=14.00 \text{ per thousand}$$

Ans. 14.00 per thousand SDR =
13.4 per thousand CDR

Practical Problems and Solutions

1. Calculate the Crude Death Rate; Age Specific Death Rate and Standard Death Rate (using direct method) from the following data:

Age Group	*Town A*		*Town B*	
	Population	*Deaths*	*Population*	*Deaths*
Under 5	5,000	25	7,000	49
5-20	25,000	175	33,000	330
20-55	15,000	150	40,000	280
55 and above	5,000	100	20,000	400
	50,000	450	1,00,000	1,059

Solution:

Age Group	*Town A*			*Town B*		
	Popu-lation P×L	*Deaths D*	*Age Specific Death Rates D×S*	*Population P×L*	*Deaths D*	*Age Specific Death Rates D×L*
Under 5	5,000	25	$\frac{25}{5,000}\times 1,000=5$	7,000	49	$\frac{49}{7,000}\times 1,000=7$
5-20	25,000	175	$\frac{175}{25,000}\times 1,000=7$	33,000	330	$\frac{330}{34,000}\times 1,000=10$
20-55	15,000	150	$\frac{150}{15,000}\times 1,000=10$	40,000	280	$\frac{280}{40,000}\times 1,000=7$
55 and Above	5,000	100	$\frac{100}{5,000}\times 1,000=20$	20,000	400	$\frac{400}{20,000}\times 1,000=20$
Total	50,000	450		1,00,000	1,059	

$$\text{CDR 'A'} = \frac{\text{Total Deaths}}{\text{Total Population}} \times 1{,}000$$

$$= \frac{\Sigma D}{\Sigma P} \times 1{,}000 = \frac{450}{50{,}000} \times 1{,}000 = 9.00 \text{ per thousand}$$

$$\text{CDR 'B'} = \frac{\Sigma D}{\Sigma P} \times 1{,}000 = \frac{1{,}059}{1{,}000} \times 1000 = 10.59 \text{ per thousand}$$

D_s has been calculated from the above table.

$$\text{SDR 'B'} = \frac{\Sigma P_s D_1}{\Sigma P_s}$$

$$= \frac{(5{,}000 \times 7) + (25{,}000 \times 10) + (15{,}000 \times 7) + (5{,}000 \times 20)}{5{,}000 + 25{,}000 + 15{,}000 + 5{,}000}$$

$$= \frac{4{,}90{,}000}{50{,}000} = 9.8 \text{ per thousand}$$

Note: Town A's crude death rate and standard death rate will be the same.

2 Given below are the figures of population and number of deaths in town 'A' and town 'B'. Calculate Crude and Standardised Death Rates using both the direct and indirect methods of standardisation.

Age Group	*Town 'A'*		*Town 'B'*	
	Population	*Deaths*	*Population*	*Deaths*
0-10	20,000	400	40,000	400
10-35	50,000	500	1,20,000	240
35-55	90,000	450	1,60,000	800
Above 55	40,000	800	80,000	2,560

Solution:

Age Group	*Town A*			*Town B*		
	Population P_x	*Deaths D*	*Age Specific Death Rates D × S*	*Population P_x*	*Deaths D*	*Age Specific Death Rates D × L*
0-10	20,000	400	$\frac{400}{20{,}000} \times 1{,}000 = 20$	40,000	400	$\frac{400}{40{,}000} \times 1{,}000 = 10$
10-35	50,000	500	$\frac{500}{50{,}000} \times 1{,}000 = 10$	1,20,000	240	$\frac{240}{1{,}20{,}000} \times 1{,}000 = 2$
35-55	90,000	450	$\frac{450}{90{,}000} \times 1{,}000 = 5$	1,60,000	800	$\frac{800}{1{,}60{,}000} \times 1{,}000 = 5$
Above 55	40,000	800	$\frac{800}{40{,}000} \times 1{,}000 = 20$	80,000	2,560	$\frac{2{,}560}{80{,}000} \times 1{,}000 = 32$
	2,00,000	2,150		4,00,000	4,000	

$$\text{CDR 'A'} = \frac{\Sigma D}{\Sigma P} \times 1{,}000$$

$$= \frac{2{,}150}{2{,}00{,}000} \times 1{,}000 = 10.75 \text{ per thousand}$$

$$\text{CDR 'B'} = \frac{\Sigma D}{\Sigma P} \times 1{,}000$$

$$= \frac{4{,}000}{4{,}00{,}000} \times 1{,}000 = 10 \text{ per thousand}$$

Calculation of SDR by Direct Method:

$$\text{SDR 'A'} = \frac{\Sigma P_s . D_1}{\Sigma P_s}$$

$$= \frac{(20{,}000 \times 20) + (50{,}000 \times 10) + (90{,}000 \times 5) + (40{,}000 \times 20)}{20{,}000 + 50{,}000 + 90{,}000 + 40{,}000}$$

$$= \frac{21{,}50{,}000}{2{,}00{,}000} = 10.75 \text{ per thousand}$$

Thus there in no difference of Town A between CDR and SDR

$$\text{SDR 'B'} = \frac{\Sigma P_s . D_1}{\Sigma P_s}$$

$$= \frac{(20{,}000 \times 10) + (50{,}000 \times 2) + (90{,}000 \times 5) + (40{,}000 \times 32)}{20{,}000 + 50{,}000 + 90{,}000 + 40{,}000}$$

$$= \frac{20{,}30{,}000}{2{,}00{,}000} = 10.15 \text{ per thousand}$$

Calculation of SDR by Indirect Method:

SDR 'A'=10.15 per thousand as Standard Town's CDR will be equal to Standard Town's SDR.

SDR 'B'

$$\text{IDR (Local Town)} = \frac{\Sigma P_s \times D_l}{\Sigma P_s}$$

$$= \frac{(40{,}000 \times 20) + (1{,}20{,}000 \times 10) + (1{,}60{,}000 \times 5) + (80{,}000 \times 20)}{40{,}00{,}000 + 1{,}20{,}000 + 1{,}60{,}000 + 80{,}000}$$

$$= \frac{44{,}00{,}000}{4{,}00{,}000} = 11$$

$$\text{C.F.} = \frac{\text{CDR of Standard Population}}{\text{IDR of Local Population}}$$

$$= \frac{10.75}{11.00} = 977$$

$$\text{SDR 'B'} = \text{CDR 'B'} \times \text{CF}$$

$$= 10 \times .977 = 9.77 \text{ per thousand.}$$

3. Given the following data:

Age Group	*Standard Population Composition*	*Town 'A' Death Rate per 1000*	*Town 'B' Death Rate per 1000*
0-5	75	25	30
5-15	250	5	6
15-65	600	7	8
65 and over	75	65	70
	1,000		

Crude Death Rate of both towns is 12.2%. Do you agree both towns are equally healthy?

Solution:

As per problem the crude death rate in both the towns is 12.2% but crude death rate is unsuitable for live studies. The standardised death rate is suitable for comparison which is calculated as follows:

Age Group	*Standard Population Composition P×S*	*Death Rate per town 1,000*		*D×A (2×3)*	*S×B (2×4)*
		Town 'A' D×A	*Town B D×B*		
(1)	*(2)*	*(3)*	*(4)*	*(5)*	*(6)*
0-5	75	25	30	1,875	2,250
5-15	250	5	6	1,250	1,500
15-65	600	7	8	4,000	4,800
65 and over	75	65	70	4,875	5,250
	1,000			12,200	13,800

$$\text{SDR 'A'} = \frac{12{,}200}{1{,}000} = 12.2 \text{ per thousand}$$

$$\text{SDR 'B'} = \frac{13{,}800}{1{,}000} = 13.8 \text{ per thousand}$$

From the above standardised death rate, it is clear that the standardised death rate in town A is 12.2 per thousand while it is 13.8 per thousand in town B. Thus, the SDR in town A is less which proves that town A has more healthy population as compared to town B. Hence the assumption that both the towns are equally healthy is wrong.

4. From the following data compute specific death rates for all groups and from these values calculate Crude Death Rates also:

Age Group	: Below 5	5-15	15-35	35-55	Above 55
Population (000)	: 7	22	14	5	2
No. of Deaths	: 200	350	100	50	100

Solution:

Computation of Age Specific Death Rate.

Age Group (year)	*Population* P_x	*Death Rate* D	*Age Specific Rate* $(D \div P_x) \times 1000 = D_x$	$P_x \times D_x$
Below 5	7,000	200	28.6.	2,00,200
5-15	22,000	350	16.0	3,52,000
15-35	14,000	100	7.1	99,400
35-55	5,000	50	10.0	50,000
Above 55	2,000	100	50.0	1,00,000
	50,000	800		8,01,600

I. $CDR = \frac{\Sigma(P_x \times D_x)}{\Sigma P_x} = \frac{8,01,600}{50,000} = 16.0\%$

II. $CDR = \frac{\Sigma D}{\Sigma P} \times 1,000 = \frac{800}{50,000} \times 1,000 = 16.0\%$

5. The deaths of two towns A and B are given according to age groups and you are asked to compare the health conditions of two towns; which of them would you consider to be more healthy and why?

Age Group	*Town A*		*Town B*	
	Population	*Deaths*	*Population*	*Deaths*
0-10	20,000	500	10,000	250
10-30	50,000	400	15,000	120
30-60	60,000	900	20,000	300
60 and over	20,000	800	5,000	500
Total	1,50,000		50,000	

Solution:

Calculation of Crude and Standard Death Rate—

Age Group	*Town 'A'*		*Rate per thousand*	*Town 'B'*		*Rate per thousand* R_2
	Population P_t	*Deaths*		*Population*	*Deaths*	
0-10	20,000	500	25	10,000	250	25
10-30	50,000	400	8	15,000	120	8
30-60	60,000	900	15	20,000	300	15
60 & over	20,000	800	40	5,000	200	40
Total	1,50,000	2,600		50,000	870	

Crude Death Rate

A Town	B Town
$CDR = \frac{\Sigma D}{\Sigma P} \times 1,000$	$CDR = \frac{\Sigma D}{\Sigma P} \times 1,000$
$= \frac{2.600}{1,50,000} \times 1,000 = 17.33$	$= \frac{870}{5,000} \times 1,000 = 17.4$

By comparing the crude death rate in both the towns it is evident that death rate is higher in town B as compared to town A and as such town A is apparently more healthy. However, such a conclusion is misleading as the population in different age groups is different in the two towns. Hence the standardised death rate of town B is worked out by assuming the population of town A as the standard. This helps in drawing correct conclusions by placing both the cities on the same footing.

$$\text{Standard Death Rate of 'B' Town} = \frac{\Sigma(P_s \times D_s)}{\Sigma P_s}$$

$$= \frac{(20,000 \times 25) + (50,000 \times 8) + (60,000 \times 15) + (20,000 \times 40)}{1,50,000}$$

$$= \frac{5,00.000 + 4,00.000 + 9,00,000 + 8,00,000}{1,50,000}$$

$$= \frac{26,00,000}{1,50,000} = 17.33 \text{ per thousand}$$

The CDR death rate of town A is found to be identical with the SDR of B, which means that both towns have the same health status.

6. From the following data find (a) crude death rates (b) specific death rates for each age group. for towns A and B separately and comment on the results:

Age group (years)	*Town A*		*Town B*	
	Population	*Number of deaths*	*Population*	*Number of deaths*
Under 5	25,000	550	10,000	220
5-15	40.000	280	15,000	105
15-35	60,000	720	20.000	240
Over 35	15,000	525	15,000	525
Total	1,40.000	2,075	60,000	1.090

Solution:

Crude death rate for Town 'A'

$$= \frac{2,075}{1,40,000} \times 1,000$$

$$= 14.82$$

Crude death rate for Town 'B'

$$= \frac{1,090}{60,000} \times 1,000$$

$$= 18,166$$

Computation of Specific Death Rates

Age group (years)	Town A Population ('000)	Town A Deaths	Town A Specific Death Rate	Town B Population ('000)	Town B Deaths	Town B Specific Death Rate
Under 5	25	550	22	10	220	22
5-15	40	280	7	15	105	7
15-35	60	720	12	20	240	12
Over 35	15	525	35	15	525	35
Total	140	2,075		60	1,090	

Thus specific death rates for towns A and B at each age group are the same. Yet crude death rate for town A is the higher. This shows that CDR is highly unreliable for comparing the overall mortality situation between the two places.

7. The distribution of population according to different age groups and the annual death rate specific to the age groups of two towns A and B are as follows:

Age Group	Town A Population ('000)	Town A Death rate per 1,000	Town B Population in thousand	Town B Death Rate
0-5	30	100	50	101
5-15	35	25	60	26
15-40	65	10	160	11
Above 40	20	30	30	31

Find:

(i) Crude death rates of A and B.

(ii) The death rate of B taking A as a Standard Population.

Solution:

Computation of CDR

Age Group (Years)	Town A Population in ('000)	Town A Specific death rate per 1,000	Town B Population in 1,000	Town B Specific death rate	$P_x M_x$
0-5	30	100	50	101	3,030
5-15	35	25	60	26	910
15-40	65	10	160	11	715
Above 40	20	30	30	31	620
Total	150		300		5,275

$$\text{CDR of Town A}=\frac{30\times100+35\times25+65\times10+20\times30}{30+35+65+20}$$

$$=\frac{3,000+875+650+600}{150}$$

$$=\frac{5,125}{150}=34.17$$

$$\text{CDR of town B}=\frac{50\times101+60\times26+160\times11+30\times31}{50+60+160+30}$$

$$=\frac{5.050+1,560+1,760+930}{300}$$

$$=\frac{9,300}{300}=31$$

$$\text{SDR of town B}=\frac{\Sigma P_x M_x}{\Sigma P_x}=\frac{4,2'4}{150}=28.5$$

Since SDR of town B is less than that of town A, population of town B is healthier than that of town A.

8. Which of the two localities A and B is healthier?

Age Group	*Locality 'A'*		*Locality 'B'*	
	Population	*Deaths per 1,000*	*Population*	*Deaths per 1,000*
0-10	600	30	600	40
10-20	1,000	5	1,000	4
20-60	3,000	8	3,000	10
60 and Above	400	50	400	30

Solution:

Standardised Death Rate of locality A is:

$$=\frac{600\times30+1,000\times5+3.000\times8+400\times50}{600+1,000+3,000+400}$$

$$=\frac{6,70,00}{5,000}=13.4$$

Standardised Death Rate of locality B is:

$$=\frac{600\times40+1,000\times4+3,000\times10+400\times30}{5,000}$$

$$=\frac{70,000}{5,000}=14$$

Since the SDR of the locality A is less than of the locality B, the locality A is healthier.

9. From the following information calculate the Crude Death Rate with the help of age specific death rates as:

Age Group :	Less than 5	5-15	15-35	35-55	55 and above
Population ('000):	8	20	15	4	3
No. of Deaths :	208	340	105	90	117

Solution:

Age Group *Year*	*Population* P_x	*No. of Deaths* *D*	*Age Specific Death Rate* $D \div P_x \times 1{,}000 = D_x$	$P_x \times D_x$
Less than 5	8,000	208	$(208 \div 8{,}000) \times 1{,}000 = 26$	20,08,000
5-15	20,000	340	$(340 \div 20{,}000) \times 1{,}000 = 17$	3,40,000
15-25	15,000	105	$(105 \div 15{,}000) \times 1{,}000 = 7$	1,05,000
35-55	4,000	90	$(90 \div 4{,}000) \times 1{,}000 = 22.5$	90,000
55 and above	3,000	117	$(117 \div 3{,}000) \times 1{,}000 = 39$	1,17,000
Total	50,000	860		26,60,000

$$\text{CDR} = \frac{\Sigma(P_x \times D_x)}{\Sigma P_x}$$

$$= \frac{26{,}60{,}000}{50{,}000}$$

$$= 53.2$$

10. Given below are the figures of population and number of deaths in Standard town and Local town. Calculate crude and standardised death rates using both the direct and indirect methods of standardisation.

Age Group	*Standard Town*		*Local Town*	
	Population	*No. of Deaths*	*Population*	*No. of Deaths*
Less than 5	5,000	150	7,500	135
5-25	25,000	500	20,000	500
25-55	15,000	225	20,000	400
55 and above	5,000	300	2,500	125
Total	50,000	1,175	50,000	1,160

Solution:

Calculation of Age Specific Rate

Age Group	*Standard Town*			*Local Town*			
Year	*Population* P_s	*No. of Deaths*	*Death Rate* D_s	*Population*	*No. of Deaths*	*Death Rate* D_t	$P_s \times D_t$
Less than 5	5,000	150	30	7,500	135	18	90,000
5-25	25,000	500	20	20,000	500	25	6,25,000
25-55	15,000	225	15	20,000	400	20	3,00,000
55 and above	5,000	300	60	2,500	125	50	2,50,000
Total	50,000	1,175		50,000	1,160		12,65,000

Crude Death Rate:

Standard Town

$$CDR = \frac{\Sigma D}{\Sigma P} \times 1{,}000$$

$$= \frac{1{,}175}{50{,}000} \times 1{,}000 = 23.5\%$$

Local Town

$$CDR = \frac{1{,}160}{50{,}000} \times 1{,}000$$

$$= 23.2\%$$

By Alternative Formula

$$CDR = \frac{\Sigma(P_s \times D_s)}{\Sigma P_s}$$

$$= \frac{11{,}75{,}000}{50{,}000}$$

$$= 23.5\%$$

$$CDR = \frac{\Sigma(P_t \times D_t)}{\Sigma P_t}$$

$$= \frac{11{,}60{,}000}{50{,}000}$$

$$= 23.2\%$$

Direct Standardisation:

$$SDR = \frac{\Sigma(P_s \times D_t)}{\Sigma P_s} = \frac{12{,}65{,}000}{50{,}000} = 25.3\%$$

CDR of Standard Town = 23.5%

SDR of Local Town = 25.3%

Indirect Standardisation:

$$\text{Index Death Rate (Local)} = \frac{\Sigma(P_t \times D_s)}{\Sigma P_t}$$

$$= \frac{(7{,}500 \times 30) + (20{,}000 \times 20) + (20{,}000 \times 15) + (2{,}500 \times 60)}{50{,}000}$$

$$= \frac{10{,}75{,}000}{50{,}000} = 21.5\%$$

CDR (Standard Town) = 23.5%

$$\frac{\text{CDR (Standard)}}{\text{Index DR (Local)}}$$

$$CF = \frac{\Sigma(P_s \times D_s)}{\Sigma P_s} \div \frac{\Sigma(P_t \times D_s)}{\Sigma P_t} = \frac{23.5}{21.5} = 1.093$$

11. From the following information calculate Standard Death Rate of country A and B.

Age Group Year	*Death Rate per thousand*		*Standard Population (in L..khs)*
	Country A	*Country B*	
0-4	18.870	4.348	120
5-14	0.759	0.465	207
15-24	1.385	0.767	183
25-34	2.048	1.075	148
35-44	3.326	1.882	120
45-54	7.006	4.669	94
55-64	18.111	12.477	71
65-74	45.795	34.060	41
75 and above	124.258	116.443	16
Total			1,000

Solution:

Calculation of Standard Death Rate

Age Group	*Death Rate % D_x*		*Standard Population (in Lakhs)*	*Country 'A' $D_x \times P_s$*	*Country 'B' $D_x \times P_s$*
	Country A	*Country B*			
0- 4	18.870	4.348	120	2264.400	521.760
5-14	0.759	0.465	207	157.113	96.255
15-24	1.385	0.767	183	253.455	140.361
25-34	2.048	1.075	148	303.104	159.100
35-44	3.326	1.882	120	399.120	225.840
45-54	7.006	4.669	94	658.564	438.886
55-64	18.111	12.467	71	1285.881	885.867
65-74	45.795	34.660	41	1877.595	1396.460
75 and above	124.258	116.443	16	1988.128	1862.928
Total			1000 ΣP_s	9187.360 $\Sigma(D_x \times P_s)$	5727.457 $\Sigma(D_x \times P_s)$

Age in year	*Standard Population*		*Local Population*	
	Population	*Deaths*	*Population*	*Deaths*
0-10	600	18	400	16
10-20	1000	5	1500	6
20-60	3000	24	2400	24
60 and above	400	20	700	21

EXAMINATION QUESTIONS

1. Explain in detail the social and cultural factors influencing death rate.
2. Clearly explain the various methods of mortality measurement. Give in detail the merits and demerits of standardised death rate.
3. What do you mean by crude death rate? Is it a correct measure of the population growth of a particular place? If not, what modifications will you suggest to get better results?
4. (*a*) What are the drawbacks of the use of crude death rate to measure the mortality in a given period and place? How can these defects be removed with the help of revised death rates? Explain the process of estimating the death rate in a life table.

   (*b*) Explain the crude and standardised death rates. Explain in brief the direct and indirect methods of finding out standardised death rate?

   (*c*) Distinguish between crude and standardised death rate and between gross and net reproductive rates. Why this distinction is necessary?

PRACTICAL QUESTIONS

1. Estimate the standard death rate for the following two countries:

Age group in year	*Death Rate per 1000*		*Standardised population in lakhs*
	Country I	*Country II*	
0-4	10.0	5.0	100
5-14	1.0	2.0	200
15-24	1.4	1.0	190
25-34	2.0	1.0	180
35-44	3.3	2.0	120
45-54	7.0	5.0	100
55-64	15.0	12.0	70
65-74	40.0	35.0	30
75 and above	120.0	110.0	10

[SDR_I=6.372 $STDR_{II}$=5.1]

2. (*a*) Distinguish between 'Crude' and 'Standardised' Death rates.

   (b) Calculate crude death rates and standardised death rates of the local population from the following data. Compare them with crude rates of standard population.

Age in year	*Standard Population*		*Local Population*	
	Population	*Deaths*	*Population*	*Deaths*
0-10	600	18	400	16
10-20	1000	5	1500	6
20-60	3000	24	2400	24
60 and above	400	20	700	21

[CDR=13.4 STDR=14]

3. Calculate the crude and standardised death rates for the following data:

Age Group	*Population ('000)*	*Number of (deaths)*	*Standard age distributions per 1,000*
0-9	21	350	221
10-24	30	102	298
25-44	37	229	285
45-64	17	354	149
65 and over	5	415	47

4. Calculate the crude and standardised death rate.

Age Group	*Population*	*Death Rate per 1,000*	*Standard Age Distribution*
0-10	400	40	600
10-20	1500	4	1000
20-60	2400	10	3000
61 and over	700	30	400

[CDR=13.4%; SDR=14%]

5.

Age Group	*No. of Women '000*	*No. of Children born*
15-19	20	600
20-24	18	1200
25-29	14	80
30-45	8	96

Calculate GFR and TFR

[GFR=32.933 TFR=571.9]

6. Calcutate the CDR and SDR from the following data:

Age Group	*Population ('000)*	*Deaths*	*Standard Age Distribution per 1,000*
0-9	21	350	221
10-24	30	102	298
25-44	37	229	285
45-65	17	354	149
65 and over	5	415	47

[CDR 13.18% SDR=13.09%]

7. The following table gives the population and mortality data of Town A and Town B. State which town is more healthy.

Age Groups (years)	*Town A*		*Town B*	
	Population	*Deaths*	*Population*	*Deaths*
0-15	15,000	360	20,000	500
15-30	20,000	400	52.000	1,040
50 above	5,000	140	8,000	240
Total	40,000	9C0	80,000	1,780

[CDR (Town A)=22.5%; CDR (Town B)=22.25%; SDR (Town B)=23.15%; Town A is more healthy]

8. Given below are the figures of population and number of deaths in towns A and B. Calculate Standardised Death Rate of town 'B' using direct method of standardisation.

Age Group	Town A		Town B	
	Population ('000)	Death Rate per thousand	Population ('000)	Death Rate per thousand
0-15	14	15	25	20
15-25	26	12	35	10
25-45	40	5	70	4
Above 45	20	20	20	20

[SDR 'B' (Direct Method) 11.00 per thousand; SDR 'B' (Indirect Method) 11.12 per thousand]

9. The information below relates to age, population and per thousand deaths of three towns A, B and C. Assuming population of town C as standard, determine which town is most healthy.

Age Group	Town A		Town B		Town C	
	Population ('000)	Death Rate	Population ('000)	Death Rate	Population ('000)	Death Rate
0-10	80	100	35	100	15	100
10-25	120	30	65	40	35	20
25-50	60	20	60	120	30	100
Over 50	40	200	40	400	20	300

[Town 'A' is most healthy. SDR: A=71.50 per thousand; B=145.00 per thousand and C=112.00 per thousand]

9

Morbidity

Morbidity is a state of affair in which an individual is undergoing physical, mental or social sufferings. According to the U.N., Health does not mean the absence of disease and weakness, but it is that state when a person is perfectly sound both physically and socially.

Morbidity conditions can be classified as under:

(1) Affected by disease or trouble.

(2) Disease or debility which does not result in immediate incapacity as for instance problems of sight, some special handicaps or old diseases.

(3) Diseases which could not be diagnosed and about which the patient is not aware.

(4) Diseased persons who are not feeling well physically.

Importance of the Study of Morbidity

If a person is morbid and incapable to work properly, its adverse repercussions will affect the whole society. Hence the study of morbidity is important from the following counts:

(1) A person who is indisposed cannot perform his duties adequately. Consequently it will not only result in economic loss to the individual but the national income will also go down.

(2) Study of morbidity helps in creating an awareness about the various diseases and their magnitude. This can help in giving proper direction to public health programmes.

(3) Morbidity affects not only the person who suffers but other people too have to face its ill effects as in the case of contagious diseases.

(4) Study of morbidity helps the firms engaged in manufacturing drugs and medicines to make decisious regarding the quantity of the product and the nature of the medicines.

(5) Life Insurance Company can easily fix the premium rates.

Sources of Morbidity Statistics

There are three main sources of collecting data relating to morbidity. They are as under:

(*i*) Patient or the person who presents his case.
(*ii*) Doctor.
(*iii*) Special survey.

The following methods are used to collect data from the above sources:

(1) Survey method.
(2) Recording method.

(1) *Survey Method*

Under this method the survey work is undertaken from time to time at a predetermined place wherein the data pertaining to types of morbidity, medical facilities, diseases etc. are collected. The surveys can be of different types. In single visit survey, the interviewer visits the place of survey and contacts the head of the household and collects the data on morbidity. Generally, such surveys provide the morbidity rate due to seasonal diseases during the survey period. In periodic visit survey the heads of the households are contacted after regular intervals and extensive data are collected. In long term survey information is collected on gradually spreading diseases. Under it the person and the household are kept under observation for a long period. In case finding survey efforts are made to identify those individuals who suffer from the disease under investigation.

(2) *Recording Method*

Under the recording method the morbidity figures are collected from administrative records. Hospitals, Life Insurance Corporations, physicians, firms, schools, government offices etc. provide information regarding morbidity. However great care should be exercised before these data are employed for further use.

Measurement of Morbidity

Depending on the duration of diseases morbid persons can be placed in any of the following categories:

(*i*) Morbid persons who have been cured of their disease during the period under consideration.

(*ii*) Persons who have fallen ill and have been cured during the period, under survey.

(*iii*) Morbidity before the reference period, but cured after the expiry of the reference period.

(*iv*) Falling ill during the reference period but cured after the reference period.

Morbidity is measured with the following main rates:

(1) *Incidence rate*

Incidence rate means the number of morbid persons out of every 1000 persons during the reference period. Symbolically:

$$\text{Incidence rate} = \frac{\text{No. of persons becoming morbid during the given period}}{\text{Average number of existing persons}} \times 1000$$

The numerator can be obtained by adding (*ii*) and (*iv*). Age specific or injury specific incidence rate can also be used to find out incidence rates.

(2) *Prevalence rate*

To find out prevalence rate it is necessary to obtain the aggregate of the persons in all the above four categories. To work out this rate the number of morbid persons is divided by the average population of that specific area and the quotient is multiplied by 1000. Symbolically:

$$\text{Prevalence rate} = \frac{\text{Total morbid persons during the given period}}{\text{Average population of the concerned place}} \times 1000$$

By making a comparative study of the prevalence rate during different periods we shall be able to know the incidence, growth and control over morbidity.

(3) *Case fatality rate*

Within this we study the ratio of persons dying from particular disease and the number of people suffering from the same disease during a given period. Symbolically:

$$\text{Case fatality rate} = \frac{\text{Number of deaths due to given disease during a given period}}{\text{Number of suffering people from the same disease during the given period}} \times 1000$$

This rate gives us the death rate due to a given disease.

Similarly we can find out occupational injury rate, rate of physical handicap etc. All these rates are worked out on age, sex and disease by cause basis.

EXAMINATION QUESTIONS

1. What do you mean by morbidity? State the importance of the study of morbidity.
2. State the various methods of measuring morbidity.

10

Fertility and Measurement of Fertility

'Fertility' in demography refers to the actual birth performance of the group of women or to the relative frequency with which the births occur in total population or in the population exposed to it. It is a result of 'fecundity', the physiological capacity to reproduce. Fertility can exist only among fecund women and therefore we can classify women into two categories, viz. (*a*) those possessing fecundity and (*b*) those who do not possess fecundity. Only women of the latter category could be termed fertile. It is also likely that a fecund woman may not release her potential fecundity into actual reproduction. This is because the child-bearing process depends on the fertility of both male and female. Only when the male and female have the child-bearing capacity will it be possible to have actual reproduction. Deficiency in one normally affects the other which results in sterility to the one capable of reproduction. In fact, it is an established fact that women capable of reproducing are also fecund while such authentic proof is not available in the case of those who do not bear any child.

Study of fertility relates to a definite period on account of which it raises two important questions (1) what are the factors determining fertility? (2) How is fertility measured for different periods i.e. what are the different rates of fertility measurements?

FACTORS AFFECTING FERTILITY

Fertility differences are observed for different groups of people in the society. Similarly definite differences in fertility rates are also observed between developed and developing countries. Comparative variations in fertility are also noticed in social, economic, caste related, religions, religious and cultural groups. In some cases the fertility rates are higher than the national average while the rates are lower than the national average in some others. Fertility differences emanate out of many causes which can be studied under the following broad outlines:

(1) Indirect Social Factors,
(2) Direct Social Factors,
(3) Other Social Factors.

(1) Indirect Social Factors

The indirect social factors affecting fertility are as follows:

(i) Age of marriage

Marriage is a social institution binding a man and woman to fulfil their sexual urge, which has close relation to the process of procreation. In this context fertility depends on the period of fecundity which marriage provides to the eligible couple, or in other words, what is the age of marriage? Provided the marriage takes place at an early age, the fertility duration will be correspondingly high. In fact marriage at a low age is an indication of low level of education, which at the same time reflects the traditional social and value system which keeps the birth rate high. On the other hand, early marriage and child bearing at a very low age will result in high incidence of infant mortality as well as deterioration of the mother's health. It is on account of this that the probability of enforced self-restraint and celibacy is high.

Joginder Kumar has estimated that if we adopt the pattern of marriage level of Sweden in our country the birth rate in India (41 in 1961) will come down to 17.8. Similarly if the age at marriage is fixed at 25 years, the birth rate can be brought down by 50%.

(ii) Polygamy

This is a rare phenomenon in the world. Generally it is noticed that in polygamy the fertility rate per woman is comparatively lower than monogamy. Some demographers do not subscribe to the view that fertility is low under polygamy.

(iii) Separation and divorce

The effect of separation and divorce on fertility can be studied with the help of the following information:

(*a*) Frequency of separation and divorce
(*b*) Age at the time of divorce or separation
(*c*) Frequency of remarriage after divorce or separation
(*d*) Duration between divorce and remarriage

As a general rule the fertility will be less the longer is the period of divorce or separation. Prof. Robberts concluded on the basis of his studies on Jamaica (1954) that the fertility is high among those couples who live continuously together, average among those who normally stay together and for those who occasionally stay together it is very low.

In 1961 Prof. Ardener succeeded in establishing correlation between low fertility and instability of marriage

(iv) Widowhood

Widow or widower is a normal phenomenon among old agers whereas it is misfortune in the case of youngsters. A woman loses her fertility at the very time when she becomes a widow. The influence of widowhood on fertility depends on the custom regarding widow remarriage in the society. If a woman remarries immediately after the death of her spouse, there will be no adverse affect on her fertility. Widow marriage depends on the social customs. Besides post-natal restrictions, frequency of union, celibacy, polygamy etc. influence the birth rate.

(2) **Direct Social Factors**

Direct social factors influencing fertility include the following:

(A) *Preventive measures*

During ancient times restrain as well as celibacy were accepted as effective means to check fertility. However, modernity relegated these methods to the background and introduced other means of birth control like abortion, pills, loop etc. The supporters of artificial checks of fertility argue that celibacy, moral restraint etc. impose a lot of suffering on the person which is injurious to health. The modern means of family planning imposes no such burden on the individual, besides acting as a powerful means of fertility control.

(B) *Mortality trends*

In underdeveloped countries mortality rate or trend is an important factor influencing fertility. It influences the procreation process at three states.

High death incidence reduces the survival rate of infants and children, which prevents children from reaching the stage of doing economically productive activity. Consequently child bearing at the latter part of the married life becomes a necessity to act as an insurance against old age. Higher rate of fertility does not mean ability to procreate is also high. On the other hand it means that like inefficient methods of production child bearing is also carried out inefficiently.

By the constellation of various related factors like weak health, poor nourishment, high death rate, the compulsion of having more children so that atleast a few may survive during old age of the parents, etc. may ultimately reduce the child-bearing capacity and child-bearing rate.

Thus a necessary condition to reduce birth rate is a fall in the death rate.

(C) *Abortion*

Abortion is the accepted way of family planning in progressive societies. Abortion has been legalised in all the developed countries. In India, too, abortion had been legalised. Its objective is to save the child from the jaws of death which awaits him in the absence of security, service and food in a poor country.

(D) *Infanticide*

Even in olden times Greek philosophers have advocated infanticide for a healthy population. In primitive societies infanticide was practised extensively and India is no exeption to it. In many cases deformed children and infants born at inauspicious time were done to death. However now this custom is on the wane on account of which its effect of fertility is negligible.

(*i*) *Socio-economic status*

Socio-economic status of individuals influences fertility. It has been normally observed that people belonging to the higher income bracket have lower fertility while people belonging to low socio-economic group have high fertility rates. If we analyse the fertility of different socio-economic groups as different steps of a ladder, its shape will be like a pyramid with a broad base and a tapering top. The highest socio-economic group will have the lowest population. High fertility in the lower socio economic ladder is on account of the following factors like (*a*) lack of foresight, (*b*) viewing children as assets, (*c*) considering children as props during old age, (*d*) union is looked upon as a form of recreation etc. Besides the poor has to face the problems of earning their means of livelihood and the child is not regarded as a burden but as a potential bread winner right from a very early age. The cost of feeding children is also low. Consequently fertility is high among the low socio-economic class.

(*ii*) *Social status of females*

Fertility hinges on the social status of women also. In a society where the women's role is regarded merely to bear and rear children the fertility rate will be high. In a society where women are involved in national activities on a equal footing with men, they do not like to be fettered with the home burden. They would naturally prefer to have a small family. That is why educated and employed women have low fertility as compared to illiterate women and others engaged only household chores.

(*iii*) *Outlook regarding children*

The number of children is mainly a personal issue. To maintain the family status children in the family are considered essential in almost every society. In some societies, that family is regarded as prosperous which has large number of children. Even today boys are given more importance in the family and the size of the family keeps on increasing till a male child is born. Women having children are viewed with esteem in the society. Therefore till such time desire for children and particularly the craze for son persists, fertility will continue to remain high.

(*iv*) *Social and cultural values*

Social and cultural values influence fertility through direct or economic factors. In underdeveloped countries the fertility rate is high due to traditional value system. The following chart presents a comparative study of the values and attitudes in developed and developing countries:

Basic question	*Traditional high birth pattern*	*Modern low birth pattern*
1. What is the relationship between individual and nature?	Man is a slave of both God and nature. Man has no control over his fate. Fatalism.	Man can control nature. God works through man. Optimism.
2. What is the relationship between man and time?	Present oriented (lives in today). Less Planning.	Future oriented. Planned.
3. Nature of sex relation.	Basically sinful sex relation is defined as an act of duty for satisfaction. Sex relation is to propagate the race.	Basically good sex relation is for mutual satisfaction. Sex relation for propagation of race as well as for recreation.
4. What is the nature of human activities and functions?	Living and work is for earning livelihood.	Work oriented.
5. Nature of human relationship.	Family oriented. Based on near and dear ones. No participation in social organisations.	Individualism. Based on relations outside near and dear ones. Participation in non-family social activities.

Note: The chart is based on the article, 'Modern and traditional value orientations and fertility behaviour: A social demographic study' in his book on Demography, page 38. W.B. CLIFFORD.

The above chart reveals that in traditional societies social system and cultural values are not conducive to economic growth and therefore they are incapable of assisting in reducing fertility.

In these countries non-economic factors basically neutralise the favourable effects of economic factors which maintain the fertility rate high.

(v) Education

Education makes radical change in outlook which enables one to know the importance of factors influencing individual and family. Other things remaining the same, education, more particularly women's education has a negative correlation with fertility. Studies conducted in the U.S. with the help of data provided by 1940 population census reveal that if other variables are regulated, father's education has 20 per cent effect on fertility while mother's education has more than double the effect of father's on fertility. One reason for this is the late marriage age in the case of educated women which reduced the fertility period. In addition it is not liked by educated women to be burdened by too much child bearing since they are also employed outside. Besides an educated person is also concerned with the maintenance of standard of living which makes him adopt family planning devices.

Colin Clark has concluded on the basis of data pertaining to underdeveloped countries that in urban and rural surroundings, education has a definite positive impact on fertility rate. Studies conducted in Poona and Mysore have shown among educated women the number of children at the age of 45 years is 5.3 for those who are literate, 4.5 for those women who have studied upto class 7th and 3.4 for those who have studied upto class 10th.

Surveys conducted by the National Sample Survey in 1960-61 show that the number of children per illiterate woman was 6.6, between 5-4.6 for women with 7-11 years of education and 2 for women with university education.

Dandekar worked out the coefficient of correlation between education and fertility rate at 0.67 which proves the above hypothesis.

(vi) Type and composition of family

It is generally presumed that joint family system raises the rate of birth. That cultural set up with emphasis on large family contributes to the rise in fertility rate. It is only natural for joint family to be related to high birth rate as the age of marriage is very low in this set up and the burden of bringing up the children is not an individual responsibility but a joint responsibility. Joint family can also bring down the rate of fertility on account of reasons like less opportunity to the couple for frequent sex union, control of traditions, etc. Therefore in older age groups fertility is low in less developed countries.

(*vii*) *Employment and profession*

As a general rule fertility is high among those engaged in physical labour as contrasted to people engaged in mental work. Persons engaged in business activities have less fertility as they are generally preoccupied with their routine work which affects little time to think about sexual diversions.

Thompson has come to the conclusion that birth rate is high among those engaged in physical labour as compared to white collar workers and it is also high among farmers as compared to service class.

(*viii*) *Income*

In general it has been noticed that there is negative relationship between income and fertility rate. One reason for this is there is high correlation between high income with education, favourable occupation, balanced diet, etc. on account of which death rate falls. It is also assumed that the higher the protein intake the lesser will be the fertility rate. There is positive correlation between the rate of protein intake and the level of per capita income.

Prof. Leibenstein studied the increase in income and its effect on fertility on the basis of the cost of upbringing children in relation to the utility derived from children. He stated that the people in poor countries have to spend comparatively much less in bringing up their children. Thus the cost of rearing the children is relatively less than the corresponding utility derived from putting their children to gainful employment.

Leibenstein cited three main advantages which parents derive out of children:

(1) A child is a consumption good on account of the love and pleasure which the parents get from their issues.

(2) The children are also agents of production because they start earning from early childhood and feed their parents.

(3) A child is a prop to his parents in old age as the parents depend on his earning when they themselves are unable to earn. Thus a child is a source of security.

In developed countries the birth rate is based on supply and demand. It also depends on the cost of upbringing of the child and the facilities provided for health, education, sanitation, medical and similar other facilities (Fig. 1).

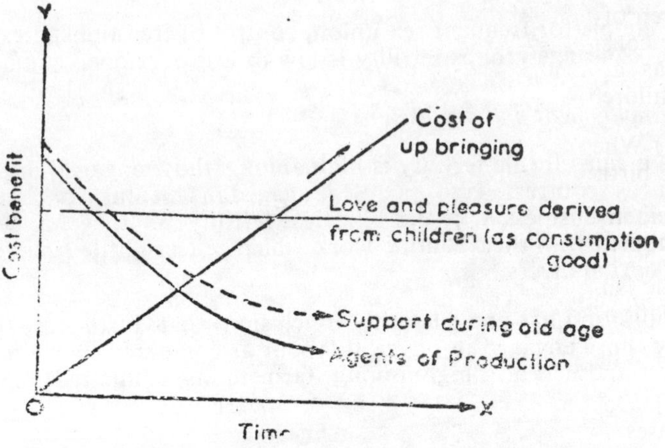

Fig. 1.

Every child provides equal pleasure and it has nothing to do with the income which will come out of him. Leibenstein concluded that birth rate is initimately associated with an increase in income per head which in turn is the outcome of economic development. Development calls for putting in "Critical minimum efforts" by the Nation. To quote Leibenstein: "In order to achieve the transition from the state of backwardness to the more developed state where we can expect steady social growth, it is necessary, though not always sufficient, condition that at some point during some period, the economy should receive stimulus to growth that is greater than certain critical minimum size."

Increase in income. Views of Leibenstein on decline in birth rate, death rate and population increase run as follows:

(1) Fall in income per head is accompanied by high death rate. This will tend to increase the aforesaid three types of utilities. High death rate will bring about a scaling down of the cost of upbringing the offspring which provides sufficient incentive to increase birth rate.

(2) When the per capita income is high death rate tends to decelerate but birth rate does not react quickly and fail to shrink. The fall in birth is a gradual process because the utility derived out of the children tends to go down very slowly and as a result the temptation to reduce the number of children does not manifest immediately in all families.

(3) However as and when the income of the family shows significant rise and the death rate ebbs, the utility derived out of children begins to fall appreciably. The parents at this stage become economically well off to sustain themselves in old age and the need to depend on children during old age loses much of its significance. On the other hand the cost of upbringing the children, their education, health, clothing and similar other expenditures tend to increase. The

children of rich also do not start earning at an early age. The cost factor considerably outweighs the relative benefits anticipated which acts as a disincentive to increase the birth rate. The desire to have less children gets stronger, every child is considered a burden.

(4) When the income grows very high, then the death rate as well as the birth rate tend to fall perceptibly.

Leibenstein held the view that at the initial stages increase in income leads to slight rise.

The sum and substance of his doctrine points to four stages of population growth:

(1) When both death rate and birth rate are high.

(2) Death rate is low but birth rate is high and population increases.

(3) Death rate is low, birth rate also is low but slightly higher leading to slow increase in population.

(4) Birth rate is less, death rate also falls and the country is faced with very low increase in population and the country is poised for high growth and progress.

Leibenstein observed: "The less the fertility lag, the less the critical minimum efforts necessary for growth. The point at which fertility decline sets in will determine the height of critical minimum income level.

In developed countries it has been observed that after a stage has been reached, birth rate can increase with an increase in per capita income. In this way the functional relation between fertility rate and income is like the English letter "J".

Studies conducted in India and other countries yielded contradictory results. Citing the incidence of different countries Prof. Colin Clark observed that in the early years income and fertility rate are positively correlated.

(*ix*) *Urbanisation*

Surveys conducted in the urban and rural areas clearly reveals that in general fertility is high in rural domain as compared to urban areas. As population from rural areas migrate to urban complex their fertility rates show distinct fall. Affluence, luxury living, keen competition for progress and spread of education are normal features of urban life. These promote logical, materialistic and individualistic attitude among urban population which reffects in planned way of family life. The paternal responsibilities and higher cost of living in cities compound this tendency. These features are responsible for the low level of fertility in urban locations as against rural areas.

It does not mean that urban fertility remains invariably low for all times. For example a study conductd by Adna Ferrin Weber does not provide any conclusive evidence of high fertility among rural folks. Her conclusion is that if we leave out some of the metropolitan cities, the fertility rate in rest of the urban complexes runs counter to the general conclusion Similarly a study conducted by D.V. Glass into the fertility variations in England during 1851-1931 period also gives no proof to support the hypothesis that maximum fertility is found in predominantly rural areas.

(*x*) *Fertility and food supply*

Ever since Malthus wrote his celebrated essays on population attention was focussed on the problem of population and food supply. Malthus stated that nature will restore the balance population and food supply but this relationship was not simple and clear. Though it is said that in a society where food supply is short fertility too will be low, it is not a truism. It is wrong to conclude that only food requirement is the only variable determining fertility since other factors like social status, local customs etc. also influence fertility.

(*xi*) *Social mobility*

Social mobility too plays an important role in determining the fertility process. Normally social mobility and fertility are inversely related as with every increase in social mobility, fertility tends to go down.

(*xii*) *Ethnic factor, class and religion and fertility*

Caste culture, class and religion do not have much influence on fertility in a direct way, but they exercise some effect on fertility during the different stages of fertility process through intermediate factors. In Western countries the fertility rate among the Protestants have been noticed to be lower than among Roman Catholics. Persons born in foreign countries have higher fertility than persons born in their motherland and likewise fertility among the whites is higher than fertility among the blacks.

In India it is presumed that fertility is low among Hindus whereas it is high among Muslims. The 18th round of NSS data show that in the urban and rural areas the fertility among Christians is the least, it is somewhat higher among the Sikhs and it is the highest among Muslims. This difference is more due to income and education. J.R. Rele in his book Fertility Differentials in India, observed that the average size of family is 5.9 among Brahmin and Kshatriya castes, 7.3 among intermediate castes, 7.0 among lower class and 7.4 among Muslims.

Many social scientists have opined that among religious minority groups the fertility rate is higher than other groups. This hypothesis is correct in the case of Muslims and Sikhs in India, but it is not valid in the case of Parsis who have a lower birth rate.

(xiii) Height, climate and birth rate

A study conducted by W. James on 'The effects of altitudes on fertility and Andean countries population studies' reveals that the coefficient of correlation between altitude and fertility rate is between —.728 to —.825, which is significant from the statistical viewpoint. It can be due to the following reasons:

(*a*) It is a scientific truism that if animals are taken to high altitude they experience a decline in fertility and therefore it is likely that a person moving to the high ranges from the planes may experience a fall in fertility.

(*b*) It is also likely that infant and child mortality may be more in high altitudes. In 51 American states the child mortality during milking period and altitude was observed to be correlated with a coefficient of .29 which is significant with a 5% degree of freedom.

(*c*) Though no concrete evidence is available, it has been noticed that the incidence of sudden abortion is more in hilly tracts.

In general it can be said that before pronouncing any conclusion on climate and fertility it would be worthwhile to pay attention to the correlation between climate and socio-economic variables. Normally it can be stated that fertility and birth rates are high in tropical regions and it is only natural to expect a flood of children in tropics. However, facts do not support this statement. Colin Clark has adduced facts and figures to prove that in those regions and among these people in European countries where family planning is not adopted, birth rate is more as compared to the population in Asia. Thus the correlation between fertility and tropical climate is only an unscientific generalisation and not a scientific truth.

Professor Donald Bogue considers the following factors as more important in determining fertility:

(1) *Marital status*

Age at marriage, status as married, unmarried, widowhood, widower separation, percentage of divorce in society, etc. influence fertility.

(2) *Educational attainment*

Higher level of education leads to a fall in fertility. Throughout the world there appears to be a strong inverse correlation between the amount of educational attainment and the level of fertility. Maximum fertility is noticed in those women who are illiterate while fertility is low among educated women.

(3) *Urban and rural residence*

Urbanisation and fertility are negatively correlated. Statistics relating to urban and rural fertility have shown that the fertility of women in every age group is higer in rural areas as compared to urban areas.

(4) *Region of residence*

Fertility is also affected by the climate of the place of residence. Normally fertility is higher in tropical regions as compared to temperate zones. That is why the population is high in places where the climate is comparatively hot.

(5) *Occupation of husband*

The occupation of the husband and fertility are closely related. Where the husband enjoys high social status, the fertility will also be less in that family. In people of lower income strata the birth rate is high. Even then this relation is not so simple and clear. As a general rule people belonging to the lower middle class families have low fertility while the upper middle class families have higher fertility.

(6) *Income of husband*

Prof. Bogue feels that the relation between fertility and income level can be represented by 'U' curve. Among lower income groups the fertility will be high, for middle income group the fertility will be the least and it will again show further increase among high income group.

Classical economists believed that there is direct correlation between poverty and fertility in that in poor families the fertility is very high while it is low in rich families. However since 1945 this thesis has undergone a complete reversal.

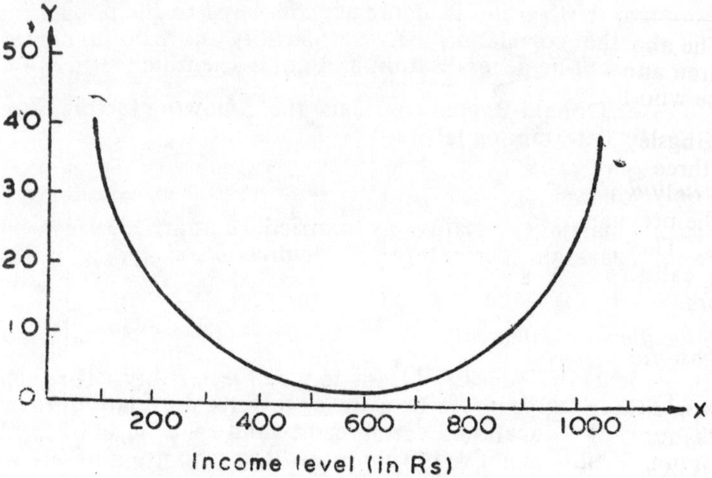

(7) *Occupation of employed women*

Fertility in general is less among working women, social scientists, accountants, auditors, designers, draughtsmen, college teachers, advocates. Prof. Bogue is of the view that women engaged in mental work have less than average fertility.

(8) *Use of contraceptives*

Contraceptives have a direct influence on fertility. As the use of contraceptives becomes popular, the fertility rate decreases.

(9) *Attitude towards the size of family*

Helpton conducted studies on the attitude regarding size of family for America in 1860 and arrived at some important conclusions. They are listed below:

Number of children	*White*	*Non-white*
0	0	0
1	0	1
2	18	22
3	28	19
4	43	39
5	5	7
6 or more	6	13
Average	3.5	3.8

The above data yield the inference that everybody likes to have children and the majority of people would prefer 2, 3 or 4 children. Those who like to have 5 or more children are very few in number.

Kingsley Davis and J. Blake have put the factors affecting fertility into three categories. They are of the view that a new issue can be born only when (1) there is union, (2) union leads to conception and (3) the pregnancy period is completed without any untoward incidents. These three stages encompass all the factors of fertility. They call these stages as 'intermediate variables' which include 11 factors.

I. *Those factors leading to union of male and female couple*

(A) Factors affecting union or separation during reproductive period:

(*i*) Age at the time of sexual intercourse

(*ii*) Permanent virginity—proportion of women who can never establish conjugal relation.

(*iii*) That period of reproductive age during which contact was possible:

(*a*) Time when the causes leading to divorce, separation etc. surfaced.

(*b*) Time when the death of husband caused the snapping of union.

(B) Factors affecting sex union while living together:

(*iv*) Voluntary abstinence.

(*v*) Forced abstinence (sickness, short period, separation due to compelling circumstances, impotency etc.

(*vi*) Frequency of sex union.

II. *Those factors affecting conception*

(*vii*) Effect of involuntary factors responsible for incapacity or inability.

(*viii*) Use of contraceptives or non-use of such devices:

(*a*) chemical or medicinal or mechanical devices.

(*b*) other techniques.

(*ix*) Effect of voluntary factors leading to sterility (family planning operation like vasectomy, tubectomy etc.).

III. *Factors affecting the completion of pregnancy*

(*x*) Infanticide—due to involuntary reasons.

(*xi*) Infanticide—due to voluntary reasons.

Difference between birth rate and fertility rate

Basis of Difference	*Fertility rate*	*Birth rate*
1. Basis of calculation	Fertility rate is obtained on the basis of the number of children to women of fertility age (15.49).	Birth rate is worked out on the basis of the number of infants born in a given place and the total number of infants.
2. Kinds	Fertility rates are of three kinds, viz. general, age specific and total.	Birth rates are of two kinds, viz., standardised and non-standardised.

3. Basis of rate	Fertility rate is worked out on the basis of 1000 women of the fertility age.	Birth rate is known on the basis of population per thousand.
4. Rate enumerated	Generally fertility rate is comparatively more than birth rate.	Generally birth rate is less than fertility rate.
5. Use	Fertility rate is used to measure the sex ratio as also to study the female fertility.	Birth rate is employed to study the infants born at a given place as well as to study the rate of increase in population.
6. Time	Total fertility rate (TFR) which is one measurement of fertility related to the entire fertility period of women (15.49).	Birth rate relates to the births taking place at a fixed time.

Measurement of Fertility

Fertility is a concept which is primarily concerned with the number of live children born.

Some important fertility rates are as under:

(1) *Crude birth rate*. The crude birth rate for any given population is obtained by dividing the number of births recorded in that population during a specified year by its total numbers, which gives a fraction of birth per person. When this fraction is multiplied by 1000, the result is the number of births per thousand of population. This rate is called crude because all the differences in the composition between population are ignored in calculating it.

Its formula is: $CBR = \frac{\Sigma B}{\Sigma P} \times 1000$

where

CBR = Crude birth rate

B = Total live children born in a locality during one year.

ΣP = Total population of the same area during the same year (Middle of the year)

Illustration: 1

Age Group	*Female Population*	*No. of Live Births to Mothers*
15-19	34,000	680
20-24	36,000	3,960
25-29	40,000	5,800
30-34	30,000	3,000
35-39	24,000	1,680
40-44	20,000	800
45-49	16,000	80
Total	2,00,000	16,000

The total population of the city in 1980 was 8,00,000. With the help of the above information, determine the crude birth rate.

Solution:

Crude Birth Rate or

$$CBR = \frac{\Sigma B}{\Sigma P} \times 1000$$

$$= \frac{16,000}{8,00,000} \times 1000$$

$$= 20 \text{ per thousand} \quad \text{Ans.}$$

Crude birth rate suffers from all the defects which are associated with crude death rate. Under it the ratio of total number of child birth is worked out in relation to total population which includes men and women above 49 years and children below 15 years. In fact fertility should be studied in respect of population between 15-49 years of age. Crude birth rate is not a true measure of fertility.

(2) *General fertility rate.* The general fertility rate according to Thompson and Lewis: "Uses the number of women of a child bearing age (15-44 or 15-49) in a population as a base for the calculation of birth rate than the total population. This rate is the number of birth per 1000 women of these ages." This rate is more refined than the crude birth rates because in addition to eliminating the influence of difference in size between population, it also eliminates the effect of certain compositional differences which might exist in the population being compared. Fertility rate is always represented in 1000.

$$GFR = \frac{\Sigma B}{\Sigma P_f} \times 1000$$

$$\text{General fertility rate} = \frac{\text{Total No. of children born in the year}}{\text{Total No. of women between 15 to 49 years}} \times 1000$$

where ΣB=Number of live children born in the year.

ΣP_f=Eligible mothers between the age group of 15-49 years.

Illustration: 2

From the following data given below calculate GFR.

Age Group	*Female Population*	*No. of Live Births*
15-19	21,000	420
20-24	24,000	2,400
25-29	27,000	4,050
30-34	30,000	3,000
35-39	24,000	1,680
40-44	18,000	900
45-49	6,000	60
Total	1,50,000	12,510

Solution:

Calculation of *GFR*:

$$GFR = \frac{\Sigma B}{\Sigma P_f} \times 1000, \quad \frac{12,510}{1,50,000} \times 1000 = 83.4 \text{ per thousand}$$

(3) *Specific fertility rate.* Specific fertility rates for any year are obtained by dividing the number of births to mother of each age in that year by the number of women of this age in the population at that date and multiplying the figure by 1000. Women of different fertility period are grouped according to age 15-19, 20-24, 25-29, 30-34, 35-39, 40-44, 45-49 age groups.

Specific fertility rate of women between 20-24 age group:

$$SFR = \frac{BX}{P_f X} \times 1000$$

where SFR=Age specific rate

BX=Number of live children born to women of the specific age

$P_f X$=Number of women of the specific age group.

Illustration: 3

On the basis of figures in Illustration 2, calculate Age-Specific Fertility Rates.

Solution:

Calculation of SFR

Age Group	*Female Population*	*No. of Live Births*	*Age Specific Fertility Rate* $=\frac{BX}{PfX}\times 1{,}000$
15-19	21,000	420	$\frac{420}{21{,}000}\times 1{,}000=20$
20-24	24,000	2,400	$\frac{24{,}00}{24{,}000}\times 1{,}000=100$
25-29	27,000	4,050	$\frac{4{,}050}{27{,}000}\times 1{,}000=150$
30-34	30,000	3,000	$\frac{3{,}000}{30{,}000}\times 1{,}000=100$
35-39	24,000	1,680	$\frac{1{,}680}{24{,}000}\times 1{,}000=70$
40-44	18,000	900	$\frac{900}{18{,}000}\times 1{,}000=50$
45-49	6,000	60	$\frac{60}{6{,}000}\times 1{,}000=10$
Total	1,50,000	12,510	$\Sigma SFR=500$

$$SFR=\frac{BX}{PfX}\times 1000 \text{ (Age group 15-19 years)}$$

$$\frac{420}{21{,}000}\times 1000=20 \text{ Per thousand}$$

Similarly the SFR for other age groups is calculated.

(4) *Total fertility rate.* The total fertility rate for all women aged 15-49 may be calculated by adding the age specific fertility rate of seven five years groups and multiplying this total by 5. This rate explains the possible number of children per 1000 fertile women on the assumption that no death occurs among the women.

The Formula

$TFR=\Sigma SFR\times i$ is used to present total fertility rate.

where TFR=Total fertility rate

ΣSFR=Specific fertility rate

i=Magnitude of the age group

or

Total fertility rate=Specific birth rate × Magnitude of the age group

Illustration: 4

On the basis of figures given in Illustration 3, calculate TFR.

Solution:

Calculation of TFR—

$TFR=\Sigma SFR\times i$

$=500\times 5=2{,}500$ per thousand

Illustration: 5

Age group	*No. of women in 1000*	*Children born in 1000*
15-19	55	20
20-24	70	180
25-29	65	200
30-34	64	170
35-39	60	120
40 44	58	60
45-49	50	10

From the figures given below find out the (*a*) General fertility rate (*b*) Specific fertility rate and (*c*) Total fertility rate.

Solution:

Estimation of fertility rate

Age group	*No. of women*	*No. of children*	*Specific fertility rate*
1	*2*	*3*	*4*
15-19	55	20	$\frac{20}{55}\times1000=363.6$
20-24	70	180	$\frac{180}{70}\times1000=2571.4$
25-29	65	200	$\frac{200}{65}\times1000=3076.9$
30-34	64	170	$\frac{170}{60}\times1000=2833.3$
35-39	60	120	$\frac{120}{60}\times1000=2000.00$
40-44	58	60	$\frac{60}{58}\times1000=1034.5$
45-49	50	10	$\frac{10}{50}\times1000=200.00$
	422	760	12079.7

(1) General fertility rate $=\dfrac{\text{Total No. of children born}}{\text{Number of women 15-49 age group}}\times1000$

$$=\frac{760}{422}\times1000=1800.$$

(2) Age specific fertility rate=(Method is shown in column No. 4 of the table)

(3) Total fertility rate$=12079.7\times5=60398.5$

It means given the per thousand fertility period of women other things remaining the same, 1000 women would probably produce 59513 children.

Total fertility per woman obtained by dividing the total fertility rate by 1000. Her total fertility rate per woman

$$=\frac{60398.5}{1000}=60.399$$

TYPICAL PROBLEMS AND SOLUTIONS

1. From the following information find out (*i*) CBR (*ii*) GFR (*iii*) TFR.

Age Group	*Female Population (in thousands)*	*No. of Live Births*
15-19	17	340
20-24	18	1,980
25-29	20	2,900
30-34	15	1,500
35-39	12	840
40-44	10	400
45-49	8	40
Total	100	8,000

Total Population is 4,00,000.

Solution:

Age Group	*Female Population (in '000)*	*No. of Live Births*	*SFR*
15-19	17	340	340/17000 × 1000=20
20-24	18	1,980	1980/18000 × 1000=110
25-29	20	2,900	2900/20000 × 1000=145
30-34	15	1,500	1500/15000 × 1000=100
35-39	12	840	840/12000 × 1000= 70
40-44	10	400	400/10000 × 1000= 40
45-49	8	40	40/8000 × 1000= 5
Total	100	8,000	490

(*i*) $\text{CBR} = \dfrac{\text{Total Live Births}}{\text{Total Population}} \times 1000 = \dfrac{8000}{4{,}00{,}000} \times 1000 = 20$ Per thousand

(*ii*) $\text{GFR} = \dfrac{\Sigma B_X}{\Sigma P f_X} \times 1000 = \dfrac{8000}{1{,}00{,}000} \times 1000 = 80$ Per thousand

(*iii*) $\text{TFR} = \Sigma \text{SFR} \times i = 490 \times 5 = 2450$ Per thousand.

2. Calculate G.F.R., T.F.R. and G.R.R. from the following information. You may assume female births at 600 for the calculation of G.R.R.

Age Group Years	*No. of Women (000)*	*No. of Live Births*	*S.F.R. %*
15-19	20	160	30.0
20-24	18	1200	66.7
25-29	14	800	57.1
30-45	8	96	12.0
Total	60	2256	165.8

Solution:

$$\text{G.F.R.} = \frac{\Sigma Bx}{\Sigma Pf} \times 100 \quad \text{or} \quad \frac{2256}{60{,}000} \times 1000 = 37.6$$

$$\text{T.F.R.} = \Sigma \text{SFR} \times i$$

$$= \Sigma[(30 \times 5) + (66.7 \times 5) + (57.1 \times 5) + (12 \times 15)]$$

$$= 150 + 333.5 + 285.5 + 180 = 949.0\%$$

$$\text{T.F.R. Per woman} = 5 \times \Sigma\text{SFR} \div 1000 = 949 \div 1000 = 0.95$$

$$\text{G.R.R.} = \frac{\text{No. of Female Birth}}{\text{No. of Births}} \times \text{Total fertility rate}$$

$$= \frac{1600}{2596} \times 0.95 = 0.564$$

3. Compute the General Specific and Total Fertility Rate from the following data:

Age Group (years)	*No. of Women*	*No. of Live Births*
15-19	25,0C0	800
20-24	20,000	2,400
25-29	18,000	2,000
30-34	15,000	1,500
35-39	12,000	500
40-44	6,000	120
45-49	4,000	10
Total	1,C0,000	7,330

Solution:

(1) $\text{G.F.R.} = \frac{7330}{100000} \times 1000 = 73.30\%$

(2) $\text{S.F.R.} = \frac{Bx}{Px} \times 1000 = \frac{800}{25000} \times 1000$

$= 32\%$

20-24 Fertility Rate $=\frac{2400}{20000}\times 1000=120$

25-29 ,, ,, $=\frac{2000}{18000}\times 1000=111.1$

30-34 ,, ,, $=\frac{1500}{15000}\times 1000=100$

35-39 ,, ,, $=\frac{500}{12000}\times 1000=41.7$

40-44 ,, ,, $=\frac{120}{6000}\times 1000=20$

45-49 ,, ,, $=\frac{10}{4000}\times 1000=2.5$

(3) T.F.R. $=(32+120+111.1+100+41.7+20+2.5)\times 5=427.3\times 5$

$=2136.5\%$

4. Compute the crude birth rate, general fertility rate, specific fertility rate and total fertility rate from the following data:

Age Group :	15-19	20-24	25-29	30-34	35-39	40-44	45-49	
No. of Women (000):	25	20	18	15	12	6	4	=100
No. of Live Births :	800	2400	2000	1400	480	110	10	=7200

Solution:

1. C.B.R. $=\frac{\Sigma B}{\Sigma P}\times 100$ or $\frac{7.200}{4,00,000}\times 1000=18\%$

2. G.B.R. $=\frac{\Sigma B}{\Sigma Pf}\times 1000$ or $\frac{7,200}{1,00,000}\times 1000=72\%$

3. S.F.R.

Age Group	*No. of Women*	*Live Birth*	*S.F.R.*
13-19	25,000	800	800÷25,000×1,000=32.0
20-24	20,000	2,400	2,400÷20,000×1,000=120.0
25-29	18,000	2,000	2,000÷18,000×1,000=111.1
30-34	15,000	1,400	1,400÷15,000×1,000= 93.3
35-39	12,000	480	480÷12,000×1,000= 40.9
40-44	6,000	110	110÷ 6,000×1,000= 18.3
45-49	4,000	10	10÷ 4,000×1,000= 2.5
	1,00,000	7,200	417.2

T.F.R. $=\Sigma SFR\times i=417.2\times 520=86.0\%$

T.F.R. per woman $=5\times \Sigma S.F.R.\div 1000$

$=2086\div 10000=2.086$ Ans.

5.

Age Group	*No. of Women in '000*	*No. of Live Births in '000*
15-19	55	20
20-24	70	180
25-29	65	200
30-34	64	170
35-39	60	120
40-44	58	60
45-49	50	10

Calculate (*i*) G.F.R. (*ii*) S.F.R. (*iii*) T.F.R.

Solution:

Age Group	*No. of Women in ('000)*	*No. of Live Births*	*S.F.R.*
15-19	55	20	$\frac{20}{55}\times 1000=363.6$
20-24	70	180	$\frac{180}{70}\times 1000=2571.4$
25-29	65	200	$\frac{200}{65}\times 1000=3076.9$
30-34	64	170	$\frac{170}{64}\times 1000=2656.3$
35-39	60	120	$\frac{120}{60}\times 1000=2000.0$
40-44	58	60	$\frac{60}{58}\times 1000=1034.5$
45-49	50	10	$\frac{10}{50}\times 1000=200.0$
	422	760	11902.7

(1) G.F.R. $=\frac{760}{422}\times 1000=1800$

(2) S.F.R.=As shown in column four of the table.

(3) T.F.R.$=\Sigma SFR\times i=11902.7\times 5=59513.5$ per thousand.

6. From the following table calculate G.F.R. & T.F.R. if the sex ratio is M:F=52 : 48; also calculate G.R.R.

Age	*Female Population in Thousands*	*S.F.R. Per Thousand*
15-19	88	120
20-24	86	2,400
25-29	83	3,000
30-34	82	2,000
35-39	78	1,000
40-44	76	500

Solution:

Calculation of G.F.R., T.F.R. and G.R.R.

Age Group	*Female Population in thousands*	*S.F.R. per thousand*	*Total Number of Children born*
15-19	88	120	120 × 88=10,560
20-24	86	2400	2400 × 86=2,06,400
25-29	83	3000	3000 × 83=2,49,000
30-34	82	2000	2000 × 82=1,64,000
35-39	78	1000	1000 × 78=78,000
40-44	76	500	500 × 76=38,000
Total	493	ΣS.F.R.=9020	7,45,960

$$\text{G.F.R.} = \frac{\text{Total No. of Children born}}{\text{Total No. of Females}} \times 1000$$

$$= \frac{7,45,960}{4,93,000} \times 1000 = 1,513 \text{ Thousands}$$

$$\text{T.F.R.} = \Sigma\text{S.F.R.} \times i$$

$$= 9,020 \times 5 = 45,100 \text{ per thousand}$$

$$\text{G.R.R.} = \frac{\text{T.F.R.} \times \frac{\Sigma Bf}{\Sigma B}}{1,000}$$

$$= \frac{45,100 \times \frac{48}{100}}{1,000} = \frac{21,648}{1,000}$$

$$= 21.68 \text{ per woman.}$$

7. The number of lives occurring in a city in certain year is shown below classified according to age of mother, along with the female population in each quinquennial age group of the child bearing period:

Age-group years	*Female Population (in '000)*	*No. of Live Births in a Year*
15-19	16	400
20-24	15	1,700
25-29	14	2,100
30-34	13	1,430
35-39	12	960
40-44	11	330
45-49	9	36

The total population of the city was 3,00,000.

Solution:

Calculations for Fertility Rate

Age Group 1	*Female Population* 2	*No. of Live Births* 3	*S.F.R* =[(3)÷2] ×1000 4
15-19	16,000	400	25
20-24	15,000	1,710	114
25-29	14,000	2,100	150
30-34	13,000	1,433	110
35-39	12,000	960	80
40-44	11,000	330	30
45-49	9,000	36	4
Total	90,000	6,969	513

(i) Crude Birth Rate:

$$\text{C.B.R.} = \frac{6,969}{3,00,000} \times 1,000 = 23.23$$

(ii) General Fertility Rate:

$$\text{G.F.R.} = \frac{6,969}{90,000} \times 1,000 = 77.43$$

(iii) Specific Fertility Rate:

$$\text{S.F.R.} = \frac{\text{No. of live births}}{\text{No. of women (for a particular age-group)}}$$

Thus S.F.R. The age group 15-19 is 25 etc.

(iv) Total Fertility Rate:

T.F.R. = 513 × 5 = 2565

T.F.R. per woman will be $\frac{2565}{1,000} = 2.565$

SELECT REFERENCES

1. Berent, J.: "Fertility and Social Mobility", *Population Studies*, Vol. 5, No. 3, 1950.
2. Barclay, G.W.: *Techniques of Population Analysis*, Wiley, New York, 1966.
3. Carlsson, G. : "The Decline of Fertility: Innovation or Adjustment Process", *Population Studies*, (20), 1966.
4. Kuczynski, R.R.: *The Measurement of Population Growth, Methods and Results*, Sidgerick and Jackson, London, 1935.

Moriyama, T.M. and Guralnick, L.: "Occupational and Social Class Differences in Mortality ", in *Milbank Memorial Fund Quarterly*, Trends and Differentials in Mortality, New York, 1956.

6. Madigan, F.C.: "Are Sex Mortality Differentials Biologically Caused ?", *Milbank Memorial Fund Quarterly*, (35), 1957.

7. Myers, R.J.; "The Impact of Med care on Demography", *Demography* (3), 1966.
8. Petersen, W.: *Population*, The Macmillan Co., London, 1969.
9. Whelpton, P.K. and Kiser, C.V. (eds.): "Social and Psychological Factors affecting Fertility", *Milbank Memorial Fund Quarterly*, New York, 5.

EXAMINATION QUESTIONS

1. What do you understand by fertility? Differentiate between Fertility and Fecundity.
2. Describe factors which affect fertility. Distinguish between birth rate and fertility rate.
3. Describe in brief the various rates of fertility measurement.
4. From the following data, calculate the General Fertility Rate, Specific Fertility Rate and Total Fertility Rate.

Age Group	*Female Population*	*No. of Live Births*
15-19	20,000	400
20-24	24,000	2,400
25-29	40,000	6,000
30-34	44,000	4,400
35-39	32,000	2,240
40-44	30,000	1,500
45-49	10,000	100

[**Answer**: G.F.R.=85.20 Per thousand.
S.F.R.=20, 100, 150, 100, 70, 50 and 10 per thousand for respective age group.
T.F.R.=2.500 Per thousand].

5. From the following data, calculate the General Fertility Rate and the Total Fertility Rate.

Age Group	*Fertility Rate* (*Per 1000*)
15-19	30
20-24	240
25-29	300
30-34	210
35-39	180
40-44	60
45-49	30

[**Answer**: G.F.R.=50 per thousand, T.F.R.=1750 per thousand].

6. From the following data calculate GFR and TFR.

Age Group	*Female Population*	*Age Specific Fertility Rate* (*Per 1,000*)
15-19	15,000	100
20-29	35,000	200
30-36	20,000	150
37-44	25,000	50
45-49	5,000	20

[**Answer**: GFR 128.50 per thousand, TFR 40.50 per thousand].

7. From the following information, calculate GFR and TFR.

Age Group	*SFR or Annual Fertility Rate (per 1,000)*
15-19	20
20-29	37
30-36	30
37-44	25
45-49	10

[Answer: GFR=26.57 per thousand, TFR=930 per thousand].

8. From the following information, calculate GFR and TFR.

Age Group	*Female Population*	*SFR*
15-19	500	60
20-26	1,000	100
27-35	1,500	300
36-40	1,000	200
41-44	600	90
45-49	400	50
Total	5,000	800

[Answer: CFR=170.8 per thousand, TFR=5,310 per thousand].

9. Calculate (*i*) General Fertility Rate (*ii*) Specific Fertility Rate (*iii*) Total Fertility Rate from the following data. It is given that out of 9,000 births, the number of females is 4,300.

Age-group (years)	16—20	21—25	26—30	31—35	36—40	41—45	46—50
No. of women ('000)	25	24	20	16	15	12	8
No. of live births in a year	1140	3000	2740	1360	600	150	10

[.075, 2.23].

10. The following table shows the number of women of child bearing ages and yearly births by quinquennial age group for a city in (Rewa) Madhya Pradesh.

Age Group	*Female Population in thousands*	*No. of Births*
15-19	16	400
20-24	15	1,710
25-29	14	2,100
30-34	13	1,430
35-39	12	960
40-44	11	330
45-49	9	36

Calculate the General Fertility Rate, Total Fertility Rate and Gross Reproductien Rate. You may assume that the ratio of male to female children is 13 : 12.

11. The age specific fertility rates (A.S.F.R.) and the female population in the reproductive age in a village together with the female population in the same age groups for the whole district are given below.

Age groups	*A.S.F.R. per 1,000 in the village*	*Female population (in '000) in the village*	*Female population (in '000) in the district*
15-19	61	16	2,136
20-24	285	26	2,304
25-29	322	21	1,920
30-34	260	18	1,621
35-39	125	11	1,305
40-44	51	10	906

Calculate the general fertility rate for the village. Also compute a standardised rate for the village using the district female population as a standard population.

11

Measurement, Projection and Estimation of Population

The following methods are in vogue to measure the increase in population:

(1) Crude Rate of Natural Increase.
(2) Vital Index of Population.
(3) Gross Reproduction Rate.
(4) Net Reproduction Rate.

1. Crude Rate of Natural Increase

This rate is derived by subtracting crude death rate from crude birth rate.

Crude Rate of Natural Increase=Crude birth rate—Crude death rate.

If the total births and deaths of a given year are available, the crude rate of natural increase in population can be obtained with the use of the following equation:

Crude Rate of Natural Increase$=\frac{B-D}{P}\times 100$ where B = Births, D=Deaths, P=Mid-year Population.

For example suppose the population of India in 1968 was 50 crores while the number of births is 2.2 crores and the total number of deaths is 0.7 crore, then the crude rate of natural increase for the year under review will be 30 per thousand

i.e. crude rate of natural increase for 1968$=\frac{2.2-0.7}{50}\times 1000$

$=30/\text{T}$ per thousand

2. Vital Index of Population

This device was employed by Dr. Raymond Pearl to measure the population increase. According to this method the proportion of birth figures over death figures is worked out and the product is multiplied by 100. In the form of equation:

$$\text{Vital Index of Population}=\frac{\text{Number of births}}{\text{Number of deaths}}\times 100$$

In case this proportion exceeds 100, it indicates an increase in population whereas if the proportion falls below 100, then it results in a fall in population. In the example cited above the vital index of population for 1968 will be

$$\frac{2.2}{7}\times 100=314.3$$

Both the methods discussed above are imperfect as they do not take into account the child bearing age of women, maternity deaths and number of infants born. Since these factors also influence estimation of population.

3. Gross Reproduction Rate

Since the population increases mainly through female births, it will be obviously more logical if we restrict ourselves to female births only. The gross reproductive rate may be defined as the number of females expected to be born to 1,000 newly born girls, if none of these girls dies without having passed through the child-bearing age. The gross reproductive rate may be calculated from total fertility rate, if the male-female ratio at birth is known and may be obtained from the formula:

$$\text{GRR}=\frac{\text{Number of female births}}{\text{Total number of births}}\times \text{Total fertility rate}$$

Also $$\text{GRR}=\frac{\text{No. of female children born to 1,000 women}}{1{,}000}$$

Or

$$\text{GRR}=\frac{\Sigma Bf}{1{,}000}$$

The GRR is used as a measure of the fertility in a population. It is useful for comparing fertility in different areas or in the same area at different time periods. The GRR could in theory range from 0 to about 5.

Thus if the number of live-births during a year be 2776000 of which 1300000 are female live-births then to obtain gross reproduction rate, the total fertility rate must be reduced in the proportion $\frac{1300000}{2776000}=0.46$ and hence if 7696 is the number of births to 2000 women during the period, the rate $\frac{7696}{2000}\times 0.48=1.84704$ would be called the gross reproduction rate.

The gross reproduction rate may also be calculated from general fertility rate.

Illustration: 1

Calculate **GRR** from the information given below:

Age Group	*No. of female children born to 1,000 women passing through each age group*
15-19	300
20-24	2,100
25-29	2,400
30-34	1,800
35-39	1,200
40-44	300
45-49	150
	8,250

Solution:

Total number of female children born per 1000 women during their entire fertility period=(300+200+2400×1800+1200+300+150)=8250 females.

$$\text{GRR}=\frac{\Sigma \text{Bf}}{1000}=\frac{8250}{1000}=8.25 \text{ per woman}$$

ΣBf=Total number of female children born to 1000 women.

II Equation:

When the number of women according to age groups and the female children born to them are known then gross reproductive rate can be obtained with the following formula:

$$\text{GRR}=\Sigma\left[\frac{(\text{BF})}{\text{Pf}}\times \text{i}\right]$$

where BF=number of female children born in specific age group.

Pf =women's population in specific age group.

i =age class interval.

Illustration: 2

Calculate **GRR** from the information given below:

Age Group	*Female population*	*No. of female children born*
15-19	20,000	4,000
20-24	40,000	12,000
25-29	80,000	24,000
30-34	60,000	12,000
35-39	40,000	16,000
40-44	20,000	4,000
45-49	4,000	400

Solution:

$$GRR = \Sigma\left[\left(\frac{Bf}{Pf}\right)\times i\right]$$

In the following table $\frac{Bf}{Pf}\times i$ has been calculated in col. iv.

Calculation of GRR

Age Group (*i*)	*Female population* (*ii*)	*No. of Female Children Born* (*iii*)	*Bf/Pf × i* (*iv*)
15-19	20,000	4,000	4,000/20,000 × 5=1.0
20-24	40,000	12,000	12,000/40,000 × 5=1.5
25-29	80,000	32,000	32,000/80,000 × 5=2.0
30-34	60,000	12,000	12,000/60,000 × 5=1.0
35-39	40,000	16,000	16,000/40,000 × 5=2.0
40-44	20,000	4,000	4,000/20,000 × 5=1.0
45-49	4,000	400	400/ 4,000 × 5=0.5
Total	2,64,000	80,400	9.0

The sum of col. iv will give GRR. Hence GRR=9 per woman.

III Equation:

$$GRR = \frac{TFR\times\frac{\Sigma Bf}{\Sigma B}}{1000}$$

Since TFR is related to women per thousand but GRR is worked out on per woman basis, hence here the numerator is divided by 1000.

In the above formula

GRR=Gross reproductive rate.

TFR=Total fertility rate.

BF=Number of female children born per 1000 women belonging to each reproductive age group.

Pf=Women's population in each specific age group.

ΣB=Total number of births.

Illustration: 3

Given :

TFR=5000 per thousand

M : F Ratio=60 : 40

Find out GRR.

Solution:

$$GRR = \frac{TFR \times \frac{\Sigma Bf}{\Sigma B}}{1000}$$. In this equation $\frac{\Sigma Bf}{\Sigma B}$ =Women's ratio. *i.e.* the ratio at which the total number of female births took place. In the above example M : F=60 : 40. Hence if the total number of births is 100 the ratio of female children will be $\frac{40}{100}$.

By substituting the values in the above equation

$$GRR = \frac{5000 \times \frac{40}{100}}{1000} = \frac{2000}{1000} = 20 \text{ per woman.}$$

Illustration: 4

From the information given below calculate Gross Reproduction Rate (GRR) if the sex ratio is MF=60 : 40.

Age Group	*No. of children born to 1000 women passing through each Age Group*
15-19	200
20-24	280
25-29	360
30-34	320
35-39	200
40-44	120
45-49	40

Solution:

On the basis of sex ratio the proportion of female children will be $\frac{40}{100}$.

Calculation of GRR

Age Group	*No. of children born to 1000 women passing through each Age Group*	*No. of female children born to 100 women passing through each Age Group*
15-19	200	$200 \times \frac{40}{100} = 80$
20-24	280	$280 \times \frac{40}{100} = 112$
25-29	360	$360 \times \frac{40}{100} = 144$
30-34	320	$320 \times \frac{40}{100} = 128$
35-39	200	$200 \times \frac{40}{100} = 80$
40-44	120	$120 \times \frac{40}{100} = 48$
45-49	40	$40 \times \frac{40}{100} = 16$
Total	1520	$\Sigma Bf = 608$

$$GRR = \frac{\Sigma Bf}{1000} = \frac{608}{1000} = .608 \text{ per woman.}$$

Difference between net reproductive rate and gross reproductive rate

Basis of comparison	*Gross reproductive rate*	*Net reproductive rate*
1. Basis of calculation	Gross reproductive rate is based on the expected number of female births per thousand new born female children. This does not take into account the death rate.	Net reproductive rate is based on the number of live female births expected from every new born one thousand girl children. This is estimated after adjustment of death rate.
2. Rate of measurement	This rate is generally more than the net reproductive rate.	Generally this rate does not exceed the gross reproductive rate.
3. Use	By definition it cannot provide an accurate measurement of the growth of population.	By definition it can provide an accurate measurement of the growth of population.
4. Comparability	Comparison of the population of two different places on the basis of this rate will not be feasible.	This can provide a correct basis for a comparative study of the population growth in two different places.
5. Division	This is not amenable to any sort of sub-division for measuring population growth.	This can be used to measure population growth by dividing it into three viz. one more than one and less than one.

4. Net Reproduction Rate

The net reproduction rate is the rate at which the female population replaces itself. It is an index for the self-replacement potentiality of a population with given age-specific rates of fertility and mortality. It means that if we want to calculate the rate of population growth, we must ask, "What is the total number of daughters that will have been born to 1000 new born girl babies by the time the latter have all completed their life span." If the total number of girls being born to 1000 women at the child-bearing age (15 to 45 or 50 years) is 1000 the NRR will be 1. This shows that the present generation of females will on death have been fully replaced by the new born babies (girls) and the population will be constant. If only 800 (girls) babies are born to such 1000 women of child-bearing age, the NRR will be 0.8 and if in the long run, it continues the population will definitely decrease. If 2000 (girls) babies are born, the NRR will be 2 and if that persists for some years, the ultimate rate of population growth per generation will be 100 per cent. The 2000 (girls) babies will have left 4000 daughters behind them during their child-bearing age. In short, if 1000 girls of child-bearing age survive per 1000 girls born, then the population is stationary; if larger than 1000 survive, then the population is increasing; otherwise it is decreasing. Thus the rate at which the female population is replacing itself is the net reproduction rate. It indicates how rapidly the population would ultimately grow, if the risks of death and the fertility of each age group remained unchanged and there were no migrations.

Thus, the First Equation or Formula would be as under:

$$\text{Female net reproduction rate} = \frac{\text{Number of female children expected to be born to 1000 newly born females on the basis of current fertility and mortality rates}}{1000}$$

Or

$$NRR = \frac{\Sigma Bf \times S}{1000}$$

However, even the net reproduction rate as a measure of replacement of population cannot be much relied upon because of the following two reasons:

1. The population of a country may become depleted more by migration than by falling birth rate or the country may receive fresh stock of immigrants who might be more virile.

2. It assumes constant rates of fertility and mortality over a generation. In actual life both these rates go on changing.

***Illustration*: 5**

Calculatc the net production rate from the following data:

Age group of child-bearing females	*No. of female children born to 1000 women passing through each age group*	*No. of survivors out of each 100 female children*	*Age group of child-bearing females*	*No. of female children born to 1000 women passing through each age group*	*No. of survivors out of each 1000 female children*
15-20	50	850	35-40	300	650
20-25	180	800	40-45	100	600
25-30	450	750	45-50	40	500
30-35	500	700			

Solution:

Calculation of Net Reproduction Rate

Age group	*No. of female children born to 1000 women*	*No. of survivors*	*No. of survivors which replaced present women*
15-20	50	850	$\frac{50\times850}{1000}=42.5$
20-25	180	800	$\frac{180\times800}{1000}=144.0$
25-30	450	750	$\frac{450\times750}{1000}=337.5$
30-35	500	700	$\frac{500\times700}{1000}=350.0$
35-40	300	650	$\frac{300\times650}{1000}=195.0$
40-45	100	600	$\frac{100\times600}{1000}=60.0$
45-50	40	500	$\frac{40\times500}{1000}=20.0$
	1620		$=1{,}149.0$

$$\text{NRR}=\frac{(\text{No. of female births}\times\text{Survival rate})}{1000}$$

$$=\frac{1149}{1000}=1.149$$

ΣBf=Total Number of Female Births expected to 1,000 newly born Female Children

S=Survival Rate.

Illustration: 6

From the following data calculate gross Net Reproduction Rate (NRR):

Age Group	*No. of female born to per 1000 women passing through each age group*	*Survival Rate*
15-19	40	800
20-24	1,000	700
25-29	1,200	650
30-34	800	600
35-39	500	500
40-44	200	450
45-49	100	400

Note: Survival rate indicates the number of survival of women belonging to different age groups out of 1000 wcmen, i.e. if we deduct the survival rate from 1000 we can derive the mortality rate per thousand women in every age group. Thus on the basis of survival rate we shall know the number of surviving women during fertility period.

Solution:

Calculation of No. of female children survived and NRR

Age Group	*No. of female children born to per 1,000 women*	*Survival Rate*	*No. of female children survived*
15-19	40	800	$40\times\frac{800}{1000}=32$
20-24	1,000	700	$1000\times\frac{700}{1000}=700$
25-29	1,200	650	$1200\times\frac{650}{1000}=780$
30-34	800	600	$800\times\frac{600}{1000}=480$
35-39	500	500	$500\times\frac{500}{1000}=250$
40-44	200	450	$200\times\frac{450}{1000}=90$
45-49	100	400	$100\times\frac{400}{1000}=40$
	3,840		2,372

$$NRR=\frac{\Sigma Bf\times S}{1000}=\frac{2,372}{1,000}=2.372 \text{ per woman}$$

Second Equation: (A) To begin with the age specific female fertility rate will be derived on the basis of the number of female birth to women of child bearing age on the basis of the following formula:

$$F = \frac{Bf}{Pf}$$

where F = Age specific fertility rate based on female birth only.

(B) The female fertility rate based on female birth is multiplied by the survival rate of women of different age groups and the range of age group and added and the sum obtained is the net reproductive rate.

$$NRR = \Sigma\left[\left(\frac{\Sigma Bf}{Pf} \times S\right) \times i\right]$$

Or

$$NRR = [(F \times S) \times i]$$

where,

S = Survival Rate

$$F = \frac{Bf}{Pf}$$

i = Interval of age groups.

Illustration: 7

On the basis of following information calculate NRR

Age Group	*Female Population*	*Female Birth*	*Survival Rate*
15-19	3,000	150	700
20-24	15,000	300	900
25-29	30,000	750	700
30-34	22,500	900	500
35-39	15,000	150	900
40-44	7,500	75	400
45-49	1,500	15	0 (zero)

Solution:

Age Group	Female population (*Pf*)	Female Birth (*Bf*)	Survival Rate (*S*)	$F=\frac{Bf}{Pf}$	$(F\times S)\times i$
(1)	(2)	(3)	(4)	(5)	(6)
15-19	3,000	150	700	$\frac{150}{3,000}=0.050$	$.050\times\frac{700}{1000}\times 5=0.175$
20-24	15,000	300	900	$\frac{300}{15,000}=0.020$	$.020\times\frac{900}{1000}\times 5=0.090$
25-29	30,000	750	700	$\frac{750}{30,000}=0.025$	$.025\times\frac{700}{1000}\times 5=0.087$
30-34	22,500	900	500	$\frac{900}{22,500}=0.040$	$.040\times\frac{500}{1000}\times 5=0.100$
35-39	15,000	150	900	$\frac{150}{15,000}=0.010$	$.010\times\frac{900}{1000}\times 5=0.045$
40-44	7,500	75	400	$\frac{75}{7,500}=0.010$	$0.010\times\frac{400}{1000}\times 5=0.02$
45-49	1,500	15	0 (zero)	$\frac{15}{1,500}=0.010$	$0.010\times\frac{0}{1000}\times 5=0.000$
					$\Sigma[(F\times S)\times i]=(0.517)$

The sum of the above column 6, *i.e.*, $\Sigma[(F\times S)\times i]$ will be the NRR=0.517 per woman.

Illustration: 8

From the following data calculate Gross Reproduction Rate and Net Reproduction Rate of females in a rural area of Gwalior—

Age Group	*Female Population*	*Female Birth*	*Survival Rate*
15-19	10,000	300	0.90
20-24	9,000	630	0.89
25-29	8,000	480	0.88
30-34	7,000	280	0.87
35-39	6,000	150	0·85
40-44	5,000	35	0.83
45-49	3,000	12	0.80

Solution:

Yx	*Pf*	*Bf*	*F=Bf÷Pf*	*S*	*F×S*
15-19	10,000	300	0.030	0.90	0.0270
20-24	9,000	630	0.070	0.89	0.0623
25-29	8,000	480	0.060	0.88	0.0528
30-34	7,000	280	0.040	0.87	0.0348
35-39	6,000	150	0.025	0.85	0.0212
40-44	5,000	35	0.007	0.83	0.0058
45-49	3,000	12	0.004	0.80	0.0032
Total	48,000	1,887	0.236	6.02	0.2071

Gross Reproduction Rate

$$GRR=\Sigma\left(\frac{Bf}{Pf}\right)\times 5=\Sigma F\times 5$$

$$=0.236\times 5=1.180$$

Net Reproduction Rate

$$NRR=\Sigma(F\times S)\times 5$$

$$=0.2071\times 5=1.0355$$

It is clear that the population is growing.

Practical Problems and Solutions

1. Calculate GRR and NRR from the information given below : The M : F=50 : 50

Age Group	*Female Population*	*No. of Live Births*	*Mortality Rate*
15-20	10,000	1,600	100
20-30	15,000	3,000	0
30-37	20,000	3,000	50
37-43	15,000	600	200
43-50	4,000	80	1,000

Solution:

Calculation of GRR and NRR

Age Group	*Female Population*	*No. of Live Births*	*Mortality Rate*	*No. of Live Female Births*	$\frac{Bfx}{Pfx}=F$	*Fxi*	$(F\times i)\times(S)$
1	*2*	*3*	*4*	*5*	*6*	*7*	*8*
15-20	10,000	1,600	100	$\frac{50}{100}\times 1,600=800$	$\frac{800}{10,000}=.08$	$.08\times 5=.400$	$.40\times\frac{900}{1.000}=.360$
20-30	15,000	3,000	0	$\frac{50}{100}\times 3,000=1,500$	$\frac{1,500}{15,000}=.10$	$.10\times 10=1.000$	$1.00\times\frac{1,000}{1,000}=1.000$
30-37	20,000	3,000	50	$\frac{50}{100}\times 3,000=1,500$	$\frac{1,500}{20,000}=.075$	$.075\times 7=.525$	$.525\times\frac{950}{1,000}=.499$
37-43	15,000	600	200	$\frac{50}{100}\times 600=300$	$\frac{300}{15,000}=.02$	$.02\times 6=.120$	$.12\times\frac{800}{1,000}=.096$
43-50	4,000	80	1,000	$\frac{50}{100}\times 80=40$	$\frac{40}{4,000}=.01$	$.01\times 7=.070$	$.07\times\frac{0}{1,000}=.00$
Total	64,000	8,280		4,140		2.115	1.955

$$GRR=\sum_{19}^{50}\left[\left(\frac{Bf}{Pf}\right)\times i\right]=2.115 \text{ per woman}$$

(As calculated in columns six and seven)

$$NRR=\sum_{15}^{50}\left[\left(\frac{Bf}{Pf}\times S\right)\times i\right]=\Sigma[(F\times S)\times i]=1.955 \text{ per woman}$$

(As calculated in column eight)

2. Compute (*i*) GFR (*ii*) SFR (*iii*) TFR, and (*iv*) the gross reproduction rate from the data given below:

Age group of child bearing female :	15—19	20—24	25—29	30—34	35—39	40—44	45—49
Number of women ('000) :	16.0	16.4	15.8	15.2	14.8	15.0	14.5
Total Births	260	2,244	1,894	1,320	916	280	145

Assume that the proportion of female births is 46.2 per cent.

Solution:

Calculation for Fertility Rates

Age (year)	*Number of Women*	*Number of Births*	*Age-specific fertility rate*$=[(3)\div(2)]\times 1000$
(1)	(2)	(3)	(4)
15-19	16.0	260	15
20-24	16.4	2,244	137
25-29	15.8	1,894	116
30-34	15.2	1,320	86
35-39	14.8	916	62
40-44	15.0	280	19
45-49	14.5	145	10
Total	107.7	7,059	445

$$\text{GFR}=\frac{7{,}059}{1{,}07{,}700}\times 1{,}000=65.54 \text{ per thousand}$$

$$\text{TFR}=\Sigma(\text{SFR})\times 5=2225 \text{ per thousand}$$

The only difference in calculation of the Gross Reproduction Rate (GRR) from TFR is that we take into account only female births (not all births). Assuming that the sex ratio of children is the same for all age-group of mothers the total number of female children expected to be born by a woman throughout the child-bearing period (assuming no death) gives the GRR.

$$\text{GRR}=\frac{\text{No. of female births}}{\text{Total births}}\times\text{TFR}$$

$$=\frac{46.2}{100}\times 2{,}230=1{,}030 \text{ per thousand.}$$

3. Compute (*i*) the gross reproduction rate and (*ii*) the net reproduction rate from the data given below:

Age (year)	*Number of Women* ('000)	*Number of female births*	*Number of total births*	*Survival Rate*
15-19	16.0	140	260	0.969
20-24	16.4	1,130	2,244	0.967
25-29	15.8	980	1,894	0.963
30-34	15.2	670	1,320	0.958
35-39	14.8	460	916	0.952
40-44	15.0	150	280	0.942
45-49	14.5	80	145	0.928

Solution:

Calculations for GRR and NRR

Age group (year)	*No. of women ('000)*	*No. of Female births*	*Female births per 100 women*	*Survival Rate*	*Female Children Survival per 1000*
(1)	(2)	(3)	(4)=$\frac{3}{2}$	(5)	(6)=(4)×(5)
15-19	16.0	140	8.75	0.969	8.48
20-24	16.4	1,130	68.90	0.967	66.63
25-29	15.8	980	62.03	0.963	59.73
30-34	15.2	670	44.08	0.958	42.23
35-39	14.8	460	31.08	0.952	29.59
40-44	15.0	150	10.00	0.942	9.42
45-49	14.5	80	5.52	0.928	5.12
Total			230.36		221.20

$$\text{Gross Reproduction Rate} = \frac{\Sigma Bf}{1{,}000}$$

$$= \frac{230.36}{1000} = 0.2306$$

$$\text{Net Reproduction Rate} = \frac{\Sigma \text{ Female Birth Survived per 1000}}{1000}$$

$$= \frac{212.2}{1000} = 0.212$$

4. From the data given below, calculate the gross reproduction rate and net reproduction rate.

Age group	*Number of children born to 1000 women passing through the age group*	*Mortality Rate*
16-20	150	120
21-25	1,500	180
26-30	2,000	150
31-35	800	200
36-40	500	220
41-45	200	330
46-50	100	250

Sex ratio being Males : Females=52 : 48

Solution:

Calculations for GRR and NRR

Age group	*Number of children born to 1000 women passing through the agegroup*	*Number of Female Children =48% of (2)*	*Survival rate =1—(Mortality rate per woman)*	*Number of Female children survived*
(1)	(2)	(3)	(4)	(5)
16-20	150	$\frac{150\times48}{100}=72$	1—0.12=0.88	$\frac{72\times0.88}{1000}=63.36$
21-25	1,500	$\frac{1,500\times48}{100}=720$	1—0.18=0.82	$\frac{720\times0.82}{1000}=604.80$
26-30	2,000	$\frac{2,000\times48}{100}=960$	1—0.15=0.85	$\frac{960\times0.85}{1000}=816.00$
31-35	800	$\frac{800\times48}{100}=384$	1—0.20=0.80	$\frac{384\times0.80}{1000}=307.20$
36-40	500	$\frac{500\times48}{100}=240$	1—0.22=0.78	$\frac{240\times0.78}{1000}=187.20$
41-45	200	$\frac{200\times48}{100}=96$	1—0.23=0.77	$\frac{96\times0.77}{1000}=73.92$
46-50	100	$\frac{100\times48}{100}=48$	1—0.25=0.75	$\frac{48\times0.75}{1000}=36.00$
Total		2,520		2088

$$\therefore \text{Gross Reproduction Rate} = \frac{\Sigma Bf}{1,000}$$

$$= \frac{2,520}{1,000} = 2.52$$

$$\text{NRR} = \frac{2088}{1000} = 2.088$$

5. Calculate GRR and NRR from the following data.

Age Group (year)	*Specific Fertility Rate per woman*	*Per year per Female Child Birth*
15-20	.0236	4.482
20-25	.1149	4.426
25-30	.1451	4.359
30-35	.1226	4.288
35-40	.0796	4.202
40-45	.0359	4.100
45-50	.0033	3.979

Sex ratio being Males : Females=48 : 52

Solution:

Age group	*Specific fertility rate per woman*	*Per year per female child birth*	*Per woman expected births (mortality adjusted)*
15-20	.0236	4.482	.10578
20-25	.1149	4.426	.50855
25-30	.1451	4.359	.63249
30-35	.1226	4.288	.52571
35-40	.0796	4.202	.03345
40-45	.0359	4.100	.14719
45-50	.0033	3.979	.01313
Total	.5250		1.96631

$$GRR = TFR \times \frac{Bf}{Bf+Bm}$$

$$= 0.525 \times 6 \times \frac{48}{48+52}$$

$$= 2.625 \times .48 = 1.26$$

$$NRR = \Sigma Bx\left(\frac{Lx}{Lo}\right) \times \frac{Bf}{B}$$

$NRR = \sum_{15}^{50} Bx\left(\frac{Lx}{Lo}\right)$ but bx denotes the number of female children born per woman while in the problem only the number of children (both male and female) born is known, which makes its necessary to multiply with sex ratio $\frac{48}{100}$.

$\therefore$ NRR$=1.96630 \times .48 = .9438$

6. From the following information calculate female gross reproduction rate.

Age group (year)	*No. of females born to per 1,000 women passing through each age group*
16-20	180
21-25	1,800
26-30	2,200
31-35	1,000
36-40	600
41-45	100
46-50	80

Sex ratio being M : F=52 : 48

Solution:

Age group (year)	*No. of female children born to per 1,000 women*	*No. of female births per 1,000 women (48%)*
16-20	180	180 × .48 = 86.4
21-25	1,800	1800 × .48 = 864.0
26-30	2,200	2200 × .48 = 1056.0
31-35	1,000	1000 × .48 = 480.0
36-40	600	600 × .48 = 288.0
41-45	100	100 × .48 = 48.0
46-50	80	80 × .48 = 38.4
Total		ΣSFR = 2860.8

$$\text{GRR} = \frac{2860.8}{1000} = 2.8608$$

Illustration: 9

From the following information calculate GFR and TFR.

Age Group	*SFR or Annual Fertility Rate (per thousand)*
15-19	75
20-24	105
25-29	120
30-34	150
35-39	120
40-44	30
45-49	30
Total	630

Solution:

Age Group	*Female Population (Assumed)*	*Fertility Rate*	*No. of Live Births*
15-19	1,000	75	$\frac{75}{1,000} \times 1,000 = 75$
20-24	1,000	105	$\frac{105}{1,000} \times 1,000 = 105$
25-29	1,000	120	$\frac{120}{1,000} \times 1,000 = 120$
30-34	1,000	150	$\frac{150}{1,000} = 1,000 = 150$
35-39	1,000	120	$\frac{120}{1,000} \times 1,000 = 120$
40-44	1,000	30	$\frac{30}{1,000} \times 1,000 = 30$
45-49	1,000	30	$\frac{30}{1,000} \times 1,000 = 30$
Total	7,000	630	630

$$\text{GFR} = \frac{\Sigma B}{\Sigma Pf} \times 1,000 = \frac{630}{7,000} \times 1,000 = 90 \text{ per thousand}$$

$$\text{TFR} = \Sigma \text{SFR} \times i = 630 \times 5 = 3,150$$

To derive GFR it is necessary to know the total number of infants born in each age group and the total number of women in the reproductive age. However, in this problem both the above factors are not known. Hence we have to assume the number of women in every age group, as with the help of this we can find the number of infants born with the help of specific fertility rate. Thus we have assumed here that the number of women in each age group is 1000. The total number of women in the 7 age groups adds up to 7000. Sum of SFR will provide the aggregate number of children born.

Illustration: 10

From the data given below, calculate GFR, SFR and TFR.

Age Group	*Female Population*	*No. of Live Births*
15-19	4,000	400
20-29	12,000	1,800
30-36	16,000	3,200
37-44	6,000	600
45-49	2,000	40
Total	40,000	6,040

Solution:

Age Group	*Female Population*	*No. of Live Births*	*Age Specific Fertility Rate* $= \frac{B}{Pf} \times 1000$
15-19	4,000	4	$\frac{400}{4,000} \times 1,000 = 100$
20-29	12,000	1,800	$\frac{1,800}{12,000} \times 1,000 = 150$
30-36	16,000	3,200	$\frac{3,200}{16,000} \times 1,000 = 200$
37-44	6,000	600	$\frac{600}{6,000} \times 1,000 = 100$
45-49	2,000	40	$\frac{40}{2,000} \times 1,000 = 20$
Total	40,000	6,040	$= 570$

(*i*) $\text{GFR} = \frac{\Sigma B}{\Sigma Pf} \times 1,000 \times \frac{6,040}{40,000} \times 1,000 = 151$ per thousand

(*ii*) $\text{SFR} = \frac{Bx}{Pfx} \times 1,000$ (15-19 age group)

$\frac{400}{4,000} \times 1000 = 100$ per thousand

Similarly the SFR of other age groups is computed.

(*iii*) $TFR = \Sigma SFR \times i$

Since in this question class-intervals are not equal, TFR will be calculated as shown in the table.

Age Group	*SFR*	*Age Class Internal*	*SFR × i*
15-19	100	5	500
20-29	150	10	1,500
30-36	200	7	1,400
37-44	100	8	800
45-49	20	5	100
			Σ(SFR × i) = 4,300

Hence TFR = 4,300 per thousand.

Illustration: 11

Calculate GRR and NRR from the following data:

Age Group	*No. of female children born to 1,000 women passing each Age Group*	*Survival Rate*
15-19	30	850
20-24	100	800
25-29	300	750
30-34	250	700
35-39	230	600
40-44	85	500
45-49	10	400
Total	1,005	

Solution:

Calculation of GRR and NRR

Age Group	*No. of Female Children*	*Survival Rate*	*No. of female births per 1,000 women*
15-19	30	850	30 × (850 ÷ 1000) = 25.5
20-24	100	800	100 × (800 ÷ 1000) = 80.00
25-29	300	750	300 × (750 ÷ 1000) = 225.00
30-34	250	700	250 × (700 ÷ 1000) = 175.00
35-39	230	600	230 × (600 ÷ 1000) = 138.00
40-44	85	500	85 × (500 ÷ 1000) = 42.5
45-49	10	400	10 × (400 ÷ 1000) = 4
	1,005		690.0

$$GRR = \frac{\Sigma Bf}{1000} = \frac{1,005}{1,000} = 1.005$$

$$NRR = \frac{\Sigma Bf \times 5}{1,000} = \frac{690}{1,000} = 0.69$$

POPULATION PROJECTION

Population projections are calculation of future demographic quantities and trends obtained by using accumulated substantiative knowledge and applying the most recent methodology. The desire to predict the future of populations has been an important stimulus to the evolution of demographic methods, which in turn has been the principal prerequisite to refining population projections.

Population projections have assumed significance in recent times in day to day life. Through it we look into the future demographic picture. On the basis of certain assumptions it tries to expound the possible size of population immigration and emigration position, birth and death rates, etc. at some future date.

Information obtained through projection is important for planners, politicians, sociologists, economists and Government. Projections of population have vital bearing on the social and economic life of the nation. If we bear the limitation of projection in mind and adopt adequate methods of projection, it can yield valuable results. In short population projections are among the basic ingredients for social and economic planning. They illustrate possible trends in human resources, indicate the needs of a population, and provide a basis for judging whether attempts should be made to alter demographic trends.

Population projection is not very simple but is not proper to think that this forecasting technique is cumbersome. In fact, so far several projections have been held in the population field many of which are nearest approximation to truth.

Projections into the future can be predictions if the system of facts is sufficiently comprehensive. Projections are neither estimates, nor forecasts but in between forecasts and predictions. Projections are less precise than scientific quantities. It is also wrong to think that projection is only guess work.

Many countries have national projections prepared by a government office, usually by the principal statistical institution. The Population Division of the United Nations produces a comprehensive set of national, regional, and global estimates and projections, revised every five years. The current edition, 'World Population Trends and Prospects by Country, 1950-2000'; Summary Report of the 1978 Assessment (1979), includes projections for 210 countries.

TYPES AND METHODS OF POPULATION PROJECTIONS

There are two main types of population projections:

1. Mathematical method of curve fitting method.
2. Component method.

1. Mathematical Method

In some countries there is no system of registration of birth and death but census operations are conducted from time to time. Mathematical method is employed in such countries for projection. In 1835 Mr. Quetulet presented a theory which states: "The resistance or the sum of the obstacles opposed to the unlimited growth of population increases in proportion to the square of the velocity with which the population tends to increase."

Mathematical method uses formulae and equations to forecast future population. Interpolation and extrapolation of the population figures are done to obtain the desired information. This method is more useful for making back projection.

(*i*) *Linear interpolation*. On the assumption that the annual change in population remains the same, population projection for years falling within two census years can be made with the use of the formula $Pe = P_1 + \frac{n}{N} P_2 - P_1)$

where,

Pe = Population projection for any middle year.

P_1 & P_2 = Size of population during the census years succeeding and preceding the projection year.

N = Total number of years or months between the two census periods.

n = Number of years or months between the projection year and the preceding census.

This method is simple as well as easy to understand but it has limited utility because of its unrealistic nature.

Illustration: 1

Population of a country in 1941 was 30 crores and 55 crores in 1971. Estimate the population of the city in 1956.

Solution:

$$Pe = P_1 + \frac{n}{N}\left(P_2 - P_1 \right)$$

$$= 30 + \frac{15}{30}\left(55 - 30 \right)$$

$$= 30 + \tfrac{1}{2}\,(25) = 42.5 \text{ crores.}$$

Illustration: 2

Population of a city in 1951 was 12 lakhs and 21 lakhs in 1981. Estimate population of the city in 1960.

Solution:

$$Pe = P_1 + \frac{n}{N}\left(P_2 - P_1\right)$$

$$= 12 + \frac{9}{30}\left(21 - 12\right)$$

$$= 12 + \frac{9}{30}\left(9\right)$$

$$= 12 + 2.7$$

$$= 14.7$$

(*ii*) *Geometric mean.* According to this method projections are made when the following variables are available:

(*a*) When the population of two census years is available.

(*b*) When it is desired to estimate the population of any mid-census year.

(*c*) The geometric mean of the population figures of the two census years will be the estimated population of the year for which the estimate are desired:

Formula: $Pm = \sqrt{P_1 \times P_2}$

Where

P_1 and P_2 = Census figures of population of the preceding and succeedings years of the year of projection.

Pm = Estimated population of the desired year.

Illustration: 3

If the population of a country in 1961 and 1971 was 40 crores and 50 crores respectively, estimate the population for the year 1966.

Solution:

$$Pm = \sqrt{40 \times 50}$$

$$= \sqrt{2{,}000}$$

$$= 44.72 \text{ crores}$$

(*iii*) *Logistic curves.* In 1838 Mr. Verhulst gave logistic curve, which was subsequently presented by Pearl and Reed. They experimented on the flies and came to the conclusion that up to a certain stage the population grows rapidly and thereafter it ceases to grow and becomes stationary.

It is of 'S' shape logistic curve which is said to be very useful in making projections.

Its formula is as under:

$$Yx = \frac{K}{1 + 10a + bx}$$

where,

$$K=\frac{2Y_0Y_1Y_2-Y_1^2(Y^0+Y_1)}{Y^0Y_2-Y_1^2}$$

$$a=\log\frac{(K-y_0)}{y_0},\quad b=\frac{1}{n}\log\left\{\frac{Y^0(k-Y_1)}{Y_1(k-y_0)}\right\}$$

in which y_0, y_1 and y_2 are the respective geometric mean of the beginning, middle and last years of the time series. This method is not very popular because of the complicated mathematical calculation involved.

(*iv*) *Compound interest base*. In this method we assume that the population is continuously growing, which means that it is growing according to compound interest principle. The annual growth rate according to this method can be found out with the help of the following formula—

$$\frac{P_2}{P_1}=e^{rn}$$

where e=Base of natural logarithms which is equal to 2.7183.

P_2 and P_1=Population according to second and first censuses respectively.

This formula is more logical.

Unless otherwise specified, this formula should be employed.

Merits:

This observed change method of population growth has many advantages:

(*i*) It is logical.

(*ii*) This method requires the use of limited data.

(*iii*) In this method both the data are available from the same universe.

Demerits:

(*i*) This is a crude method and it has clubbed together the effects of all the changes from all sources.

(*ii*) This method cannot be applied if the data pertaining to a single census is available or if the figures of two censuses are not comparable.

Illustration: 4

Measure and comment on the rate of growth of India's population over the last decades from the following data:

Year	*Population (in millions)*
1931	279
1941	318
1951	361
1961	439
1971	548
1981	684

Solution:

$$\frac{P_2}{P_1}=e^{rn}$$

Substituting the values:

For decade 1931-41

$$\frac{318}{279}=2.7183^{r\times 10}$$

or Log 318−Log 279=$r\times 10\times$ Log 2.7183

or $r\times 10\times 0.4343=2.5024-2.4456$

or $r\times 4.343=0.0568$

$$\therefore \quad r=\frac{0.0568}{4.363}$$

$$=0.01308$$

For decade 1941-1951

$$\frac{361}{318}=2.7183^{r\times 10}$$

or Log 361−Log 318=$r\times 10\times$ Log 2.7183

or $r\times 10\times 0.4343=2.5575-2.5024$

or $r\times 4.343=0.0551$

$$\therefore \quad r=\frac{0.0551}{4.343}$$

$$=0.01269$$

For decade 1951-61

$$\frac{439}{361}=2.7183^{r\times 10}$$

or Log 439−Log 361=$r\times 10\times$ Log 2.7183

or $r\times 10\times 0.4343=2.6425-2.5575$

or $r\times 4.343=0.0850$

$$\therefore \quad r=\frac{0.0850}{4.343}$$

$$=0.01957$$

For decade 1961-71

$$\frac{548}{439} = 2.7183^{r \times 10}$$

or $\text{Log } 548 - \text{Log } 439 = r \times 10 \times \text{Log } 2.7183$

or $r \times 10 \times 0.4343 = 2.7388 - 2.6425$

or $r \times 4.343 = 0.0963$

$$\therefore \quad r = \frac{0.0963}{4.343}$$

$$= 0.02217$$

For decade 1971-81

$$\frac{684}{548} = 2.7183^{r \times 10}$$

$\text{Log } 684 - \text{Log } 548 = r \times 10 \times \text{Log } 2.7183$

$2.835 - 2.73878 = r \times 10 \times 0.4343$

$4.343\, r = 0.0962194.$

$$r = \frac{0.0962194}{4.343}$$

$$= 0.022155$$

Illustration: 5

Comment on the rate of population growth from the following table:

Year	*Population*	*(in millions)*
1951	361	63
1961	439	74
1971	548	88
1981	684	110

Solution:

INDIA'S POPULATION

Substituting the value

For decade 1951-61

$$\frac{439}{361} = 2.7183^{r \times 10}$$

or $\text{Log } 439 - \text{Log } 361 = r \times 10 \times \text{Log } 2.7183$

or $r \times 10 \times 0.4343 = 2.6425 - 2.5575$

or $r \times 4.343 = 0.0850$

$$\therefore \quad r = \frac{0.0850}{4.343}$$

$$= 0.01957.$$

For decade 1961-71

$$\frac{548}{439} = 2.7183^{r \times 10}$$

or Log 548—Log 439$=r \times 10 \times$ Log 2.7183

or $r \times 10 \times 0.4343 = 2.7388 - 2.6425$

or $r \times 4.343 = 0.0963$

$$\therefore \quad r = \frac{0.0963}{4.343}$$

$$= 0.02217$$

For decade 1971-81

$$\frac{684}{548} = 2.7183^{r \times 10}$$

Log 684—Log 548$=r \times 10 \times$ Log 2.7183

$2.853 - 2.73878 = r \times 10 \times 0.4343$

$$4.343 = \frac{0.0962184}{4.343} = 0.02215$$

U.P.'s POPULATION

$$\frac{P_2}{P_1} = e^{rn}$$

Substituting the value

For decade 1951-61

$$\frac{74}{63} = 2.7183^{r \times 10}$$

or Log 74—Log 63$=r \times 10 \times$ Log 2.7183

or $r \times 10 \times 0.4343 = 1.8692 - 1.7993$

or $r \times 4.343 = 0.0699$

$$\therefore \; r = \frac{0.0699}{4.343}$$

$$= 0.0161$$

For decade 1961-71

$$\frac{88}{74} = 2.7183^{r \times 10}$$

or Log 88$-$Log 74$=r \times 10 \times$ Log 2.7183

or $r \times 10 \times 0.4343 = 1.9445 - 1.8692$

or $r \times 4.343 = 0.0753$

$$\therefore \; = \frac{0.0753}{4.343}$$

$$r = 0.01734$$

For decade 1971-81

$$\frac{110}{88}=2.7183^{r\times 10}$$

or Log 110—Log 88 $=r\times 10\times$ Log 2.7183

or $r\times 10\times 0.4343=2.0413927-1.94448$

$$\therefore\quad r=\frac{0.09691}{0.4343\times 10}=0.022314$$

Limitations of Mathematical Method

The mathematical device of projection is not satisfactory. For realistic projections, it is essential that correct and dependable information about death and birth rates and migration of population should be collected. United Nations population studies has observed the following defects of the mathematical method:

(1) This method of projection is not a real index of the future trends.

(2) It does not correctly reflect the past trends.

(3) It is not imperative that the logistic curve should be as 'S' shape.

(4) In fact curve fitting does not take into consideration the past and future socio-economic changes. Besides, this method is inadequate as it assumes birth rate, death rate and migration, etc., to remain the same.

2. Component Method

This method is widely employed to make population projections. Component method takes into account the dynamic nature of variables like birth rate, death rate and migration.

As regards birth rate it should be clear as to what will be the expected number of women and girls during the projected period and how many of them will be likely mothers. There should also be information about such problems as divorce rate, the rate at which widows will get themselves remarried and also about the marriage rate. There should also be some idea about percentage age of women who will not be in a position to give birth to children and also the percentage of sterile men. Some couples may not be in a position to produce children due to various reasons. The percentage age of people who will be expected to accept family planning devices and who will not like to adopt these devices should also be well estimated. The spacing of children should also be estimated. Social and economic changes and their influence on birth, death and divorce should also be assessed.

Death rate. Economists, sociologists, etc., are found to underestimate the death rate. In practice death rate does not fall as anticipated. Death rate is related to birth rate. It is also linked with composition and nature of population. It should thus be estimated as to the extent to which society can check infant mortality and to which extent people at old age will die.

Migration. On the basis of past data on migration, estimation on future migration can be made.

Formula. These days the formula adopted to project population is as under:

$$Pt+a=Pt-Bxa^t-Dxa^t+Ixat-Oxa^t$$

where

at=Time interval.

Pt=Population at a time.

Bxa^t=Number of birth during the time interval.

Dxa^t=Number of deaths during the time interval.

Ixa^t=Number of immigrants during the time interval.

Oxa^t=Number of out-migrants during the time interval.

Correct estimation of birth and death rates will help in making accurate projections.

TYPES OF PROJECTIONS

1. Total Projection and Regional Projection

Projection can be total if it is for the whole country. But when the projection is made for a province, regional or ethnic group, it is called regional or sectoral projection.

Regional projection is pretty difficult as compared to total projection because there are no impediments to internal mobility from one region to other. It is difficult to regulate inter-regional migration while external migration can be easily recorded and regulated.

2. Forward Projection and Backward Projection

Forward projections in the future are made from data in the past. Backward projections or reversed projections into the past aids in a variety of estimating procedures. Back projections can be used to find population of the past particularly in countries where census operation has been started recently. Sometimes back projections are made to check the correctness of past records also.

3. High, Medium and Low Projections of Population

Population projections are made on certain basic assumption. If the assumptions are true, the projections will also be accurate. Projections made on wrong premises will yield results at variance with reality. Normally the following assumption can be made with regard to the four basic determinants of population.

Assumptions on the Factors Influencing Population

Sl. No.	*Factor birth rate*	*High increasing rate*	*Moderate rate of increase*	*Low rate of increase*
1.	Death rate	High increasing rate	Moderate increasing rate	Low rate of increase
2.	Migration	High rate	Moderate rate	Low rate
3.	Immigration	High rate	Moderate rate	Low rate

On the basis of assumptions given above, three kinds of projections are possible:

(*i*) *High projection of population.* This is based on the assumptions of (*i*) High birth rate; (*ii*) Low mortality rate; (*iii*) High immigration; and (*iv*) Low emigration.

High projection is suitable for less developed countries passing through the transition stage. In such countries population doubles itself in 25 years and projections are made on this basis.

(*ii*) *Medium projection of population.* It is based on the assumptions of (*i*) Medium increase in birth rate; (*ii*) Medium increase in death rate; (*iii*) Medium increase in immigration; and (*iv*) Medium emigration.

These variables will register increase, but the rate of increase will be neither rapid nor very slow but at a moderate rate. Medium population projection is useful and correct for those countries where population doubles itself in 35 to 45 years. This type of projection is useful for those countries in which health services are improved and family planning schemes are successfully implemented.

(*iii*) *Low projection of population.* Low population projections are made on the assumptions of:

(*i*) If birth rate is high, death rate is also high.

(*ii*) Where birth rate is low, death rate too is low.

(*iii*) If emigration is high then immigration is also high.

(*iv*) If emigration rate is low, immigration rate too will be low.

Projection of this kind is useful for those countries where population doubles in 45 to 55 years. High birth rates and high death rates are valid for backward poor countries where both birth and mortality rates are high while for developed countries the assumption of low birth rate and low death rate holds good.

Precautions and Conditions for Projections

Population projection is closely related to the development efforts and consequently every precaution should be taken in making projections. Precautions can be studied as under:

1. Area of projection should not be very narrow but sufficiently wide.

2. Projection is not merely a mathematical calculation. Accurate projection calls for accurate figures on birth, death and migration. Reliable figures of birth rate can be obtained only on the basis of authentic figures on the attitude of people towards family planning. Similarly clear information should be available as to how far medical facilities will be available to control death rate. The main precondition, therefore, is to obtain realistic information on death and birth rates.

3. The researcher should not allow personal bias to enter into his projection. Otherwise the whole effort will be an exercise in futility.

4. The researcher should be prepared to publish his findings no matter whether the results obtained by him are to his satisfaction or not.

5. Projection should not be for long periods as far as possible, because under such circumstances chances of errors creeping in are high.

6. The researcher should adopt a flexible attitude and thus as the occasion demands he should be prepared to repeat his projections.

7. Researcher should enjoy sufficient freedom to make his study without interference to reach at correct conclusions.

8. Technical knowledge is also important. The researcher should have adequate grounding in projection. Otherwise the projection is likely to be misleading.

Importance. What is the need of projection and what are its benefits to society? Some of the important advantages are:

(*i*) Census operations are conducted after fairly long intervals, generally 10 years apart. It is with the help of projections that population growth during the intervening years can be found.

(*ii*) Population projections help in planning for the future for all walks of life, including social, economic, and political.

(*iii*) In countries where census operations started late, back projections are useful to find out the past trends in population.

(*iv*) We are living in an age of planning in which long period planning is very essential. For future planning, knowledge of trends in future population is important. Hence projections are very useful for planning.

(*v*) *Hajnal* maintained that it is probable that projections may not be completely true, but it is better to have some data rather than no data at all.

LIMITATIONS OF PROJECTIONS

Today in all civilised societies projection has come to stay. Many institutions are engaged in this task. But usually projections are not correct as is evident from the fact that demographers and institutions have given different projections. J.J. Spengler said that the economists "artificially mechanise, artificially simplify, artificially generalise, artificially systematise, artificially fixate, artificially factorise, artificially close, artificially isolate. ... They assume the heterogeneous to be homogeneous, the complex to be simple, the open to be close, the connected to be isolated...unavoidably therefore predictions about economic reality which are produced with the aid of these techniques are quite undependable.

In social sciences projections are undependable as the variables themselves do not behave as anticipated. Ian Bowen said: "Projections are made of hypothesis and many a time turn out to be incorrect. Still the economists and statisticians stake their reputation for the pressure of necessity is too great. Many writers distinguish between projections and predictions A projection is therefore a prediction with an extra danger sign attached."

1. From the point of subject matters population projection has the following two defects: (*a*) Lack of uniformity of population data, and (*b*) Mobility of population.

2. Another defect of projection is that long period projections are practically of little use.

3. Projections may turn out to be false as errors may creep in because population changes are not within control.

4. Population projections may turn out to be incorrect like weather forecast.

5. Projection is possible within static and closed economy which poses difficulties in modern open economics.

Population Growth and Age Structure

The vital statistics are not of uniform rates on account of which they cannot provide sufficient information on age structure. The age composition is based on the population growth rates in the past years. In fact, the age composition of the current population determines the prospects of population growth rate in future. The future population growth coefficient can be estimated on the basis of the ratio of the population of reproductive age group to the total population. If the population in this age group is more it is conducive to natural growth rate of population.

The age composition of current population provides us with the estimate regarding the efficiency of replacement of population at a future date. A higher proportion of women in the reproductive age group is conducive to the natural growth rate of population. When we represent the age and sex composition of population on a geometric graph it gives the shape of a pyramid. The graphic presentation of age and sex composition of a population is called age-sex pyramid or population pyramid.

Age-sex pyramid includes the population of both males and females. At times one year class interval age groups are employed but generally five year age group is normally adequate. It also reduces the workload.

Age-sex pyramids are of two types:

(*i*) Absolute age-sex pyramid.

(*ii*) Relative age-sex pyramid.

In absolute age-sex pyramid the real population statistics are displayed. Hence any change in its shape makes it unsuitable for purposes of comparison. Unless specified otherwise, the absolute age-sex pyramid is prepaid.

Relative age-sex pyramid adopts a common scale which makes comparison easy. Generally it is represented in percentage. Even if the population size varies the areas covered by these pyramids remain identical. In case the population figures of two separate places are given it is essential to construct relative age-sex pyramid.

Construction of Age-Sex Pyramids

The following particulars must be borne in mind while constructing an age-sex pyramid:

1. It has become a convention to represent age on the vertical axis and the population of different age groups on the horizontal axis.
2. A vertical line is drawn from the centre of the base line OX—the left of this line shows male population and the right of this line shows female population.
3. The point of intersection of vertical line with the horizontal line indicates zero.
4. The scale of measurement of vertical and horizontal lines should be mentioned clearly.

SELECT REFERENCES

1. Cassen, Robert and Tim Dyson: "New Populations for India", *Population and Development Review*, Vol. 2, No. 1, 1976, pp. 101-136.
2. Glass, David V.: "Demographic Prediction", *Proceedings of the Royal Society*, Series B, 168 (1011), pp. 119-139, 15 August 1967.
3. Grauman, John V.: "Success and Failure in Population Forecasts of the 1950s : A General Appraisal", In *Proceedings of the World Population Conference, 1965*, Vol. 3, pp. 10-14, New York, United Nations, 1967.
4. Keyfitz, Nathan: "On Future Population", *Journal of the American Statistical Association*, 67 (338), pp. 347-363, June 1972.
5. Raghavachari, S.: "Population Projections, 1976-2001", in Ashish Bose, P.B. Desai, Ashok Mitra and J.N. Sharma (eds.), *Population in India's Development, 1947-2000*, Vikas, Delhi, 1975, pp. 431-444.
6. Ramachandran, K.V.: "Population projections and their uses in social, economic and regional planning and policy making", Projections of Populations of Sub-National Areas: Report of a working group, Bankok, 1969, pp. 1-39 (mimeo).
7. Shryock, Henry, S., Jacob, S. Siegel *et al.*: *The Methods and Materials of Demography*. Vol. II, U.S. Government Printing Office, Washington, 1973, Chapters 23 and 24, pp. 725-809.

EXAMINATION QUESTIONS

1. What do you understand by population growth? Describe its characteristics. Discuss the various measurements of population growth.
2. How Population Projections are made? Explain fully their importance and point out its limitations.
3. Construct an age-sex pyramid on percentage scale with the help of hypothetical figures.
4. Population of India in 1971 was 54.81 crores and in 1981 was 68.38 crores. Estimate India's population in 1985.
5. Population of U.P. in 1971 is 8 crores and in 1981 is 11 crores. Estimate U.P.'s population in 1986.
6. Comment on the rate of population growth from the following table:

Population (in millions)

Years	*India*	*Bihar*
1961	439.3	46.5
1971	548.1	56.4
1981	683.8	69.8

7. Construct age-sex pyramid from the following table:

Population (in lakhs)

Age group	Country X *Males*	Country X *Females*	Country Y *Males*	Country Y *Females*
0-9	10	12	110	100
10-19	15	16	120	110
20-29	18	20	90	85
30-39	20	22	80	75
40-49	18	18	75	72
50-59	15	16	60	60
60-69	12	13	45	47
70 and above	10	10	30	35

12

The Life Table

The life table is an effective tool for analysing the forces of mortality in a population. Life table has been defined by Keyfitz as "...a scheme for expressing the form of mortality in terms of probabilities. It is also a population model, covering the simplest case which is worth discussing; a cohort or group of people born at the same moment, closed to migration and followed through successive ages until they die. Like other successful models, the life table has given its shape to the natural world; we are incapable of thinking of population change and mortality from any other starting point." According to Donald Bogue "the life table is a mathematical model that portrays mortality condition at a particular time among a population and provides a basis for measuring longevity. It is based on age specific mortality rates observed for a population for a particular year." It shows how many would die at each age and how many would survive to each age if they were exposed to the probability of death at each are observed. In other words, a life table would answer the question, "suppose 1,00,000 infants were born at the same time, how many would reach 1, 5, 10, 15, 20, etc. years of age on the supposition that a given schedule of age-specific death rates would apply throughout their lifetime?" Thus a life table shows the number of survivors from birth to successive ages and the average length of life on the supposition of age specific death rates applying throughout an entire generation.

Ulpian's life table tried to explain the chain of declining figures of survivals but the methodology employed by him was not scientific. No systematic endeavour was made till the end of 17th century to make statistical study of life table. The concept of life table was probably introduced in a table by Graunt in his book "Natural and Political Observation" made upon the bills of mortality in 1662. Petty is another individual who has made important contribution to the evolution of life table. By the end of 18th century proper and revised life tables have been prepared for meeting life insurance objectives. Evler and Sussmilch revised the original form of the life table. It is Mr. Halley who gave the life table its modern pattern. Knapp and Kuezynski also made vital contribution in finalising the structure of life table.

The life tables are of two types: (*a*) cross-sectional or time specific and (*b*) longitudinal or generation. The first type employs data for a single cross-section of time to represent an entire generation while the longitudinal life table takes a real cohort group of people that began life during a specified interval and follows them in subsequent years, until all have died. Furthermore, a life table could be complete or abridged. In a complete life table single years of ages are taken while in an abridged life table ages are grouped in 5 or 10 years of interval, except in the initial years.

Life tables can be constructed for countries, group of countries, particular areas, as well as for groups selected by sex, race, occupation or other specified characteristics, thus giving a comparative mortality picture. This technique is also used to determine the utility age, duration of marriage period, fertility analysis, etc.

Assumptions

In the construction of life table for a particular hypothetical cohort the following assumptions are made:

(1) There is no change in mortality rates over time, which means that the given schedule of risks remains constant.

(2) The cohort is closed which means that there is no out-migration or in-migration and changes take place only due to mortality.

(3) A hypothetical cohort or radix is usually set at 1000 or 10,000 persons to simplify the comparability of survivors in the life table. This is also useful to study two life tables for different times and place.

(4) Life tables are generally prepared for homogeneous sexes because there is difference in age-specific death rates for men and women.

In addition to the above assumptions, two more axioms help to present a complete history of life.

(5) The death rate is related to age-specific death rate.

(6) A synthetic cohort can be prepared on the basis of death rate.

Nature of Life Table

Life table has got eight columns as is evident from the proforma given in the succeeding page.

Structure of Life Table

The eight columns of the life table are constructed on the following basis:

(*1*) *First Column* (x)

In the first column the age is entered in serial order from zero to maximum, probable age (99) in whole numbers.

(*2*) *Second Column* (l_x)

This column shows the number of persons living at x age in which the initial figure will be those of new born babies who begin the first year of their life together. This figure will generally be presented in the simplified form of a whole number like 1,000 or 1,00,000.

(*3*) *Third Column* (d_x)

Third column reveals the number of dead persons between each age x and the succeeding year of age $(x+1)$. In the table 1710 infants die before completing the first year of their life which means that only 1,00,000—1,700=98,290 infants reach the first year of their age. The aggregate death figure between age 1 year and 2 years is 1,592. Therefore, only 98,290−1,592=96,698 children could reach the age of 2 years. Thus, $d_x=l_x-l_x+1$.

This column of the life table is of strategic importance because if all the entries in this column are known and the original cohort or base index is also known, the entire life table can be constructed.

(*4*) *IVth Column* (q_x)

This column presents the probable mortality rate between every age and the succeeding age $(x+1)$. The mortaility rate is obtained by dividing the number of dying persons (d_x) at each age by the number of people surviving at that age, *i.e.*,

$$q_x=\frac{d_x}{l_x}$$

In the above life table the probability of mortality is 1710÷1,00,000=.01710.

q_x can be represented per thousand form also *i.e.*

$$\frac{d}{l_x}\times 1000$$

(*5*) *Vth Column* (P_x)

P_x indicates the probability of survival between the year x and $x+1$. The relative P_x can be obtained by subtracting q_x from 1, *i.e.* $P_x=1-q_x$.

In the table the probability of survival upto 1 year is 1—.01710 =.98290.

(6) *VIth Column* (L_x)

This column portrays the average number of survivals between age x and $x+1$, *i.e.*

$$L_x=\frac{l_x+(l_x+1)}{2}$$

or $$L_x=l_x-\tfrac{1}{2}d_x$$

In the table $L_0=\frac{l_0+l_1}{2}=\frac{100000+98290}{2}=99145$

Similarly, $L_1=\frac{l_1+l_2}{2}=\frac{98290+96698}{2}=97494$

(7) *VIIth Column* (T_x)

This column shows the number of surviving people at L_x age who are likely to live for some more years. This can be worked out by adding the values in the preceding column from bottom to top.

Hence, $T_x=L_x+L+1+L_x+2+L_x+3$ ... upto the end of the table.

$$T_x=T_x+1+L_x$$

In the table T98=T99+L98=2+5=7

$$T_0=T_1+L_0+3987275+99145=4086420$$

(8) *VIIIth Column* (e_x^0)

The last column gives the average life expectancy of the population of x years of age. In the form of equation:

$$e_x^0=\frac{T_w}{l_x}$$

In the table, for age of zero year,

$$e_x^0=\frac{4086420}{100000}=40.86$$

From the above analysis it is clear that column q_x is basic in the table. On the basis of which the values of other columns of a life table can be filled up. An example of life table is given below:

Life Table

Age	*Living at age X*	*Dying betweeu ages X and X+1*	*Mortality rate*	*Survivance rate*	*Living between ages X and X+1*	*Living above age X*	*Mean after life time at age X*
X	l_x	d_x	q_x	p_x	L_x	T_x	e^0_x
0	1,00,000	1,710	.01710	.98290	99,145	4,086,420	40.86
1	98,290	1,592	.01620	.98380	97,494	3,987,275	40.57
2	96,698	1,483	.01534	.98466	95,957	3,889,781	40.23
3	95,215	1,383	.01452	.98548	94,523	3,793,824	39.84
4	93,832	1,293	.01378	.98622	93,186	3,699,301	39.42
—	—	—	—	—	—	—	—
—	—	—	—	—	—	—	—
—	—	—	—	—	—	—	—
95	21	9	.40957	.59043	16	32	1.52
96	12	6	.42932	.57068	9	16	1.34
97	6	3	.44964	.55036	5	7	1.17
98	3	2	.47046	.52954	2	2	0.67
99	1	1	.49176	.50824	—	—	—

Adopted from Life Table (1941-50) from the Paper No. 2 of Census of India 1951

Illustration: 1

Fill up the blanks which are marked with a question-mark in the skeleton life table:

Age X	l_x	d_x	p_x	q_x	L_x	T_x	e^0_x	m_x
30	76227	?	?	?	?	27296732	?	?
31	758580					?		

(*Agra, B. Sc., 1958*)

Solution:

Assuming age of 30 years as x and 31 years as $x+1$, the value of unknown quantities with their notations take the following equation:

$d_{30}=l_{30}-l_{31}=762227-758580=3647$

$q_{30}=d_{30}/l_{30}=3647\div762227=0.005$

$p_{30}=l-q_{30}=1-0.005=0.995$

$$L_{30}=\frac{l_{30}+l_{31}}{2}=\frac{762227+758580}{2}=760404$$

$T_1=T_{30}-L_{30}=27296732-760404=26536328$

$$e^0_x=\frac{T_{30}}{L_{30}}=\frac{27296732}{762227}=35.80$$

Hence the table will have the following form after filling the blanks:

X	*l*	*d*	*p*	*q*	L	T	e^0_x
30	762227	3647	0.995	.005	760404	27296732	35.80
31	758580	—	—	—	—	26536328	—

Illustration: 2

Fill up the blanks in the portion of a life table given below:

Age in years	l_x	d_x	p_x	q_x	L_x	T_x	e^0_x
7	90000	500	?	?	?	4850000	?
8	?	400	?	?	?	?	?

Solution:

In the usual notations, we have

$l_8=l_7-d_7=90000-500=8950\ 0$

$$p_7=\frac{l_8}{l_7}=\frac{89500}{90000}=0.9943$$

$$q_7 = l - p_7 = 1 - 0.9943 = 0.0057$$

$$l_9 = l_8 = 89500 -- 400 = 89100$$

$$p_8 = \frac{l_8}{l_7} = \frac{89100}{89500} - 0.9955$$

$$q_8 = l - p_8 = 1 - 0.9955 = 0.0045$$

$$L_7 = \frac{l_7 + l_8}{2} = \frac{90000 + 89500}{2} = 89750$$

$$L_8 = \frac{l_8 + l_9}{2} = \frac{89500 + 89100}{2} = 89300$$

$$e^0_7 = \frac{T_7}{l_7} = \frac{4850000}{90000} = 53.89$$

$$T_8 = T_7 - L_7 = 4850000 - 89750 = 4760250$$

$$e_8{}^0 = \frac{T_8}{l_8} = \frac{4760250}{89500} = 53.19$$

Illustration: 3

Fill in the blanks in the following skeleton life table which are marked with question marks:

Age	l_x	d_x	q_x	p_x	L_x	T_x	e^0_x
20	693435	?	.?	?	?	35081126	?
21	690673	—	—	—	—	—	?

Solution:

$$d_x = l_x - l_{x+1} = 693435 - 690673 = 2762$$

$$q_x = \frac{d_x}{l_x} = \frac{2762}{693435} = 00398;\ p_x = l - q_x = 1 - .00398 = .99602$$

$$L_x = \frac{l_x = l_{x+1}}{2} = \frac{693435 + 690673}{2} = \frac{1384138}{2} = 692054$$

$$T_{x+1} = T_x - L_x = 35081126 - 692054 = 34389072$$

$$e^0_x = \frac{T_x}{l_x} = e^0_{20} = \frac{T_{20}}{l_{20}} = \frac{35081126}{693435} = 50.59$$

$$e^0_{21} = \frac{T_{21}}{l_{21}} = \frac{34389072}{690673} = 49.79$$

Illustration: 4

Fill the missing entries in the following extract form of a life table:

x	l_x	d_x	p_x	q_x	L_x	T_x	e^0_x
20	71167						
21	70768						
22	70367	403			70166	2394139	....

Solution:

x	l_x	$d_x=l_x-l_{x+1}$	$p_x=\frac{l_{x+1}}{l_x}$	$q_x=l-p_x$	$L_x=\frac{l_x+l_{x+1}}{2}$	$T_x=T_{x-1}-l_{x-1}$	$e^0_x=\frac{T_x}{l_x}$
20	71167	71167—70768=399	$\frac{70768}{71167}=0.994$	1—0.994 =0.006	$\frac{71167+70768}{2}$ =70967.5	2464907+71167 =2536074	$\frac{2536074}{71167}$
21	70768	70768—70367=401	$\frac{70367}{70768}=0.993$	—0.993 =0.007	$\frac{70768+70367}{2}$ =70567.5	2394139+70768 =2464907	$\frac{2464907}{70768}$
22	70367	403	$\frac{69964}{70367}=0.994$	—0.994 =0.006	70166	2394139	$\frac{2394139}{70367}$
23	70367—403=69964						

Illustration: 5

Complete the following part of a life table:

Age (in years) x	l_x	d_x	q_x	p_x	L_x	T_x	e^0_x
11	12,000	?	?	?	?	?	?
12	8,000	?	?	?	?	?	?
13	6,000	?	?	?	?	?	?
14	4,000						

Solution:

(*i*) $d_x = l_x - l_{x+1}$ by relation

$d_{11} = 12{,}000 - 8{,}000 = 4{,}000$

$d_{12} = 8{,}000 - 6{,}000 = 2{,}000$

$d_{13} = 6{,}000 - 4{,}000 = 2{,}000$

(*ii*) $q_x = \dfrac{d_x}{l_x}$ by relation

$q_{11} = \dfrac{4{,}000}{12{,}000}\ 0.333$

$q_{12} = \dfrac{2{,}000}{8{,}000} = 0.2500$

$q_{13} = \dfrac{2{,}000}{6{,}000} = 0.3333$

(*iii*) $P_x = l - q_x$ by relation

$P_{11} = 1 - 0.3333 = 0.6667$

$P_{12} = 1 - 0.2500 = 0.7500$

$P_{13} = 1 - 0.3333 = 0.6667$

(*iv*) $L_x = \dfrac{l_x + l_{x+1}}{2}$ by relation

$L_{11} = \dfrac{12{,}000 + 8{,}000}{2} = 10{,}000$

$L_{12} = \dfrac{8{,}000 + 6{,}000}{2} = 7{,}000$

$L_{13} = \dfrac{6{,}000 + 4{,}000}{2} = 5{,}000$

(*v*) $T_x = L_x + L_{x+1} + \ldots\ldots\ldots$ by relation

$T_{11} = L_{11} + L_{12} + L_{13} + L_{14}$

$= 10{,}000 + 7{,}000 + 5{,}000 + 3{,}000 = 25{,}000$

$T_{12} = L_{12} + L_{13} + L_{14}$

$= 7{,}000 + 5{,}000 + 3{,}000 = 15{,}000$

$T_{13} = L_{13} + L_{14} = 5{,}000 + 3{,}000 = 8{,}000$

$T_{14} = L_{14} = 3{,}000$

(*vi*) $e^0{}_x — \frac{T_x}{L_x}$ by relation

$$e^0{}_{11} = \frac{25,000}{12,000} = 2.0833$$

$$e^0{}_{12} = \frac{15,000}{8,000} — 1.8750$$

$$e^0{}_{13} — \frac{8,000}{6,000} = 1.3333$$

$$e^0{}_{14} = \frac{3,000}{4,000} = 0.7500$$

Hence complete life table will be as below:

Age (*in years*)	l_x	d_x	q_x	p_x	L_x	T_x	$e^0{}_x$
11	12,000	4,000	0.3333	0.6667	10,000	25,000	2.0833
12	8,000	2,000	0.2500	0.7500	7,000	15,000	1.8750
13	6,000	2,000	0.3333	0.6667	5,000	8,000	1.3333
14	4,000				3,000	3,000	1.7500

Multiple Decrement Table

Most of the life tables group all deaths due to single cause. However multiple decrement tables also can be calculated. It is worked out by showing separate columns for the major causes of death. Similarly, a table can contain two columns, to show the diminution of an original group. For example the state of maidenhood of girl at a given age can be changed by either marriage or death. This type of life table which includes both or several decrements can be prepared on the basis of decrement rate. This can be analysed through table given below.

Multiple decrement analysis

Age	*No. of maidens* b.x	*Deaths* bd.dx	*Marriages* bm.dx
1	—	—	—
20	961	4	35
21	922	4	46
22	872	—	—
23	—	—	—
24	—	—	—

In like manner there can be several tables of similar kind. The above table is a double decrement table as there are two sources of decrements shown in the table.

There may be decrement in the state of worker at a particular age by death, retirement, migration, leaves, etc. This can be illustrated with the help of a multiple decrement table as under:

Multiple decrement table

Age	*Numbers according to work*	*Deaths*	*Resignations*	*Retirement*
16	1000	4	108	—
17	888	5	85	1
18	797	5	70	1
19	721	6	57	1
20	657	5	42	1
21	609	5	34	2
22	509	5	28	2
23	534	4	21	2
24	507	4	17	3

Cause Deleted Tables

Many refinements have been introduced in the life table method. Tables can be, for instance, constructed with mortality rate adjusted in downward direction to eliminate particular causes of death. This enables to measure the relative importance of a given cause of death in a population according to the increase in average life expectancy and survival probabilities that would occur if that cause was eliminated. The gains in life expectancy will, however, be modest even when major illnesses are removed. For example if all cancers are eliminated from the 1969-71 mortality rates of American white males the gain would be only 2.31 years in expectation of life at birth. Eliminating all kinds of heart diseases would add only 6.14 years to the average life expectation span. These gains are limited as people freed from the specified cause are then exposed to death from all other causes in sufficient number.

Cause deleted tables are constructed on the assumption that the various causes of death are independent. Therefore, the elimination of one cause does not influence the occurrence of any other. This device is useful to make a comparative study of the relative impact of diseases on current mortality patterns.

Besides, to adjust a set of q_x values to eliminate a particular cause of death, accurate data by cause are needed. Unfortunately such data are not reliable even in developed countries. Thus only broad generalisation of pattern is possible in cause deleted analysis of factors influencing death.

Model Lif Tables

Model life tables can be constricted by examining the structure of many empirical life tables. The purpose of model life table is to show the typical mortality picture across a range of different age patterns and age expectations. Model life tables are useful when data of mortality and life expectation are not either available or are of doubtful quality. Model life table involves considerable guess work, yet the probable error involved in it may be considerably less than the error encountered by using the empirical data directly.

The first major model life table was published by the United Nations population division in 1955 which was based on 158 sex-specific actual life tables. This work was followed by the publication of a large series of model life tables by Ansley Coale and Parl Demeny in 1966. These tables were based on 300 actual life tables pertaining to different populations and different time periods.

Willam Brass in 1975 used a logit system to transform a standard table based on two parameters. As additional knowledge about actual mortality patterns has accumulated, the necessity to revise model life tables has been keenly felt so that they can accommodate patterns containing high mortality among young and old ages.

Uses of Life Tables

The life table has been applied to a wide range of topics. Demographers like Graunt, Makeham and Benjamin Grompertz, etc., have used it for estimation study and marriage analysis.

(1) *Life expectancy (at birth)*. Determination of average life expectancy on the basis of present age specific mortality trend is an important field wherein life tables are useful. It is used for making comparison at national and international levels.

(2) *Projection of population*. By using present mortality rate, it becomes easy to project population for a future date. Registered death does not meet this requirement The precision of projection depends on the realities of hypothetical group of population. These projections help in making decisions and testing the accuracy of statistical sources. Life table is also useful in making hypothetical model of population and studying crude death and migration rates.

(3) *Estimation of migration*. Life table survival rates can be used for estimation of net migration by age in a population. Given the age distribution of population at two dates (say 5 or 10 years

apart) and life table survival rates, one can easily estimate the number of survivors at various ages at a later date. The difference of the estimate of survivors and the actual enumerated population can be attributed to migration.

(4) *Hypothetical stationary population.* Life table gives hypothetical stationary population with deaths and births in a cohort assumed to be the same and is equal to 1,00,000.

(5) *Analysis of cause of death statistics.* Analogous to the life table described here life tables can also be constructed showing the

Life table and actual proportions ever married, by age, 1974 Sri Lanka fertility survey

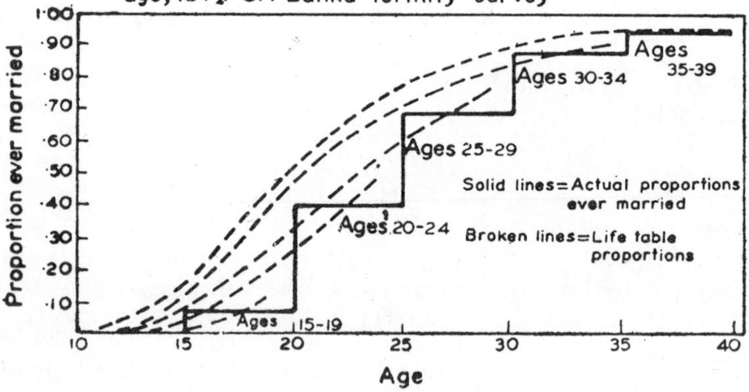

number of deaths at various ages by cause and the probabilities of death by various causes at each age. Such a life table with two or more factors of decrement is called a multiple decrement life table.

(6) *Comparison of mortality.* Two or more populations can be compared with greater accuracy by the values obtained from life table, as doubts related to mortality are closely related to the age structure which is a dynamic aspect of population composition. Such comparison is possible only when we are considering the same places and times as mortality is invariably related to a particular base period.

(7) *Marriage patterns.* Using age-at-marriage information, the life table can show that marriage patterns have been changing and that these changes have been relatively steady over quite a number of years. For younger age groups, the proportion married at each age is consistenly lower.

Other Uses

1. The appraisal of the accuracy of census enumerations and vital registration data.

2. Study of trends in age distribution of a population.

3. Estimation of the size of future labour force.

4. Forecast of the school-going population in connection with school building programmes.

5. Computation of the probable number of future widows.

6. Estimation of the probable number of future orphans in a community.

7. Use in family planning—life table and life table principles have been widely used in the evaluation of family planning programmes.

8. Multiple decrement life tables for socio-economic data. Multiple decrement life tables can also be prepared to analyse the various types of socio-economic data.

Stationary and Stable Population

Stationary and stable models of population are based on the fundamental assumption of definite and fixed mortality and fertility rates. Migration is totally non-existent in these models. They are constructed on the basis of age structure. Though the models are more or less similar, there are few dissimilarities.

Stationary Population

Provided the age specific fertility and mortality rates are constant and migration effect is neutralised, then the population will become stationary. Thus, average presence of persons in different age groups will be more or less, equal to the cohort in the beginning. The population will remain the same at each age group as in the beginning.

Thus a stationary population is a hypothetical model of population based on perpetually unchanging conditions of fertility, mortality and total size. It can be constructed for both men and women simultaneously. If Lx represents survivor at exact age x, dx number of deaths between age x and $x+1$, Lx years lived between age x and $x+1$, Tx total years lived after exact age x and

$T_x = T_0$, then birth rate and death rate are equal to $\frac{L_0}{T_0}k$, since

life expectancy at birth is $e^0 = \frac{T_0}{L_0}$,

Then birth rate=death rate= $\frac{1}{e_0}k$.

The assumption of equality of birth rate and death rate at every age level is not realistic. The model has very little use in practical life.

Stable Population

The stable population represents the permanent structure that a hypothetical population would finally have, if the assumed age specific birth and death rates remain unchanged. It is derived completely from these death and birth rates. It is closed against migration. The stable population succeeds in bringing together fertility and mortality rates in a single self-sufficient scheme. Unlike stationary population, new cohort does not have any definite size, because it is constructed on the basis of birth rate and population of reproductive age. In this way, though the assumptions are the same as for stationary population, yet population can vary. Stable population has its own age structure, which is based on stationary birth and death rates. Thus it is useful in understanding the different forms of development and age structure in given conditions. Just like net reproductive rate, the concept of stable population is unreal. This hypothetical model can shed some light on the composition of population under definite and specific conditions.

MULTI-STATE APPROACHES

Ander Rogers and associates have in 1975 brought many demographic analyses under a single approach. In this approach, individuals are free to move within a matrix, among several states or conditions. Transitions are permitted from one state to another state in either direction. For example in geographic transition, the movement can be among all states. Statistically speaking movement can be from employment to unemployment and *vice versa* or from non-marriage to marriage. In these cases movements may not be completely free. For example in working life one can move from employment to death but it is not possible to move the other way. Similarly in tables of married life one can move from the currently married to the divorced state but not to the single state. Matrix mathematics adopt readily to these simplifications as well as to complex conditions. As John Rose puts it: "Thus the new methods make traditional analyses easier, permit more realistic assumptions, enlarge the scope of what can be investigated, and yield insights not previously attainable."

SELECT REFERENCES

1. Barclay, G.W.: *Techniques of Population Analysis*, Wiley, New York, 1966.
2. Benjamin, B.: *Demographic Analysis*, 1958.
3. Bose, A.: *Urbanization in India: An Inventory Source of Materials*, Academic Book Ltd., New Delhi, 1970.
4. Cox, P.R.: *Demography*.
5. Census of India: Census Centenary Publication No. 5, O.R.G., Ministry of Home Affairs, New Delhi, 1972.

6. Desai, P.B.: *A Survey of Research in Demography*, I.C.S.R., India, 1975.
7. Ross, A. John: *International Encyclopedia of Population.*
8. Thompson, W.S. and Lewis, D.T.: *Population Problems*, McGraw Hill Book Company, New York.
9. U.N.: *Handbook of Vital Statistics Methods*, 1955.

EXAMINATION QUESTIONS

1. What is a life table? Give the various components of life table.
2. What do you mean by life table? What are its assumptions?
3. (*a*) In a certain life table $l_{10}=8{,}000$, $q_{10}=0.0125$, $d_{11}=80$ and $T_{11}=3{,}16{,}790$. Calculate the value for l_x, d_x, p_x, q_x, L_x, T_x, and e^0_x for the ages 10 and 11 years.

   (M. Com., Delhi, 1976)

   (*b*) From the life table up to age 3 starting with radix $l_0=1{,}00{,}000$ on the basis of the following values:

   (Figures in thousands)

$l_0=90$	$d_0=10$
$l_1=80$	$d_1=8$
$l_2=60$	$d_2=6$
$l_3=50$	$d_3=5$

(B. Com., Karnataka, 1971)

4. (*a*) Explain the symbols l_x, d_x, q_x, and e_x of the mortality table. Obtain a formula for e_x.

   (*b*) Calculate e_{80} from the following extract of a mortality table:

Age x	80	81	82	83	84	85	86	87	88	89	90	91
l_x	185	145	110	81	57	39	25	15	9	5	2	1

(B Com., Karnataka, 1973)

5. A part of a life table is given below with most of the entries missing. Supply the missing entries explaining the meaning of each symbol.

Age	10	11	12	13	14	15	16	17	18	19
l_x	93102	—	—	—	—	—	—	—	—	—
$1000q_x$	0.62	0.66	0.72	0.80	0.90	1.00	1.12	1.23	1.33	1.40
L_x	—	—	—	—	—	—	—	—	—	—
T_x	—	—	—	—	—	—	—	—	—	48,42,446
e_x	—	—	—	—	—	—	—	—	—	—

6. In the following table fill in the blanks which are marked with a query (?):

Age (x)	l_x	d_x	p_x	q_x	L_x	T_x	e^0_x
10	74600	?	?	?	?	32,66,067	?
11	74340	—	—	—	—	?	?

Ans. :

x	l_x	d_x	p_x	q_x	L_x	T_x	e^0_x
10	74600	260	0.99651	0.00349	74,470	3266067	43.78
11	74340	—	—	—	—	3191597	42.93

13

Migration

THE CONCEPT OF MIGRATION

Migration is a vague concept and different definitions and concepts of migration are used in different parts of the world. Thus migration statistics are not comparable across countries. Generally it is defined as geographic mobility that involves a change of usual residence between defined political or statistical areas, or between residence areas of different types. In short a person who crosses an administrative boundary is considered to be a migrant.

According to Concise Oxford Dictionary, "'Migrate means to move from one place, country or town to another. Thus migration is the movement from one place to another within the country or outside it."

United Nations Multilingual Demographic Dictionary, defines Migration as "a form of geographical mobility or spatial mobility between one geographical unit and another, generally involving a change in residence from the place of origin or place of departure to the place of destination or place or arrival."

The migration defined here is parmanent migration. It is distinguished from the 'temporary' and the 'short distance moves.' All such temporary movements begin and ultimately terminate in the same place or community but, being studied from many disciplinary positions, are identified by a confusing variety of terms: 'return migration', 'circular migration', 'wage-labour migration', 'seasonal mobility', 'sojourner movements', 'transhumance', 'commuting'.

These terms refer to circuits of movement by individuals and small groups between points of origin and destination and lack any declared intention of a permanent or semi-permanent change in residence. Figure 1 illustrates the difference between 'circulation' and 'migration'.

Thus, "*a migrant is a person who has changed his residence from one geographically well defined area to another area with the intention of permanently or semi-permanently settling at the new place.*"

The two broad classifications of migration are international and internal migration. International migration refers to the movement across national boundaries and therefore, it has a political significance and is dramatic also as it involves the crossing of the more formidable cultural and political barriers. On the other hand internal migration signifies the movement within the boundaries of a given nation. In total it constitutes all changes of residence within

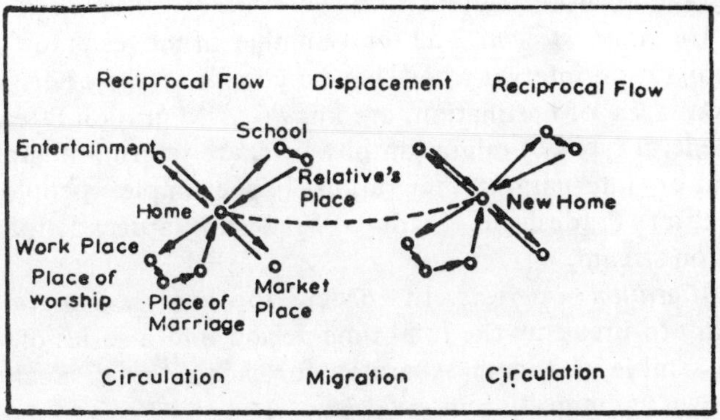

Reciprocal flow and displacement of people

Fig. 1.

the national territory and as such involves not only the exchange of population between the communities but also within the communities. Although internal migration is not so easily measurable and defined as international migration, but certainly it touches a far greater number of people.

Definition of Certain Terms Associated with Migration

1. *Place of origin and place of destination.* The place which the migrant leaves is called 'place of origin' and, for that place, the person is an 'out-migrant'. The place where the migrant arrives is known as 'place of destination' and the person is called an 'in-migrant'.

2. *In-migration and out-migration.* A migrant who travels from the area of origin to the area of destination is in-migrant with respect to the area of destination and outmigrant with respect to the area of origin. However, both these terms are applicable to internal or within the country migration only, for example the migration of rural people to urban areas in India everywhere.

3. *Immigration and emigration.* These terms are used in the context of international migration from one country to another, for

example immigration of Hindus from Bangladesh to India and emigration of Indians to United States.

4. *Gross and net migration*. The gross migration is the sum of in-migration (or immigration) and out-migration (emigration). When we say that Madhya Pradesh had a net addition in its population through migration, it means that the number of inmigrants over a specified time period in Madhya Pradesh exceeded the number of outmigrants from the state.

5. *Migration stream*. The total number of moves made during a given migration interval which have a common area of origin and a common area of destination, are known as Migration Streams. The most general types of migration however, are internal migration and external or international migration. For example, people moving from Uttar Pradesh to Madhya Pradesh in a decade form such a migration stream.

6. *Migration intervals*. In order to analyse migration it is necessary to break up the total time period into a series of intervals and assemble the data separately for each interval. Such intervals are known as 'migration intervals'.

MEASUREMENT OF MIGRATION

The measurement of migration is very complex. There are many problems of measuring migration. The reasons for this are obvious. Migration is purely a socio-economic phenomenon which is a result of a complex mechanism involving social, psychological, political, economic, institutional and other determinants. Another problem is of specifying time-interval. If it is too short, it will be impossible to distinguish between visitors and migrants. If it is too large then it will be difficult to identify and count frequent inter-period changes of residence.

Measurement of migration involves the clear definition and understanding of terms like usual place of residence, place of origin, place of destination, etc. Besides distinction between internal and international migration, as well as between migrants and movers will have to be made. All these problems create hurdles in the precise quantification of migration.

Measurement of population can be both direct and indirect.

(1) Direct Measures for Estimating Migration

These include place of birth (POB), duration of residence, place of last residence and place of residence at a fix prior data.

1. *Place of birth method.* This is based on the statistics collected from direct questions asked during a census on the mobility of persons. These questions are asked about the place of birth. Migrants are the persons enumerated in a place which is not their place of birth. Non-migrants are the persons enumerated in the place where they are born.

The migration data obtained from the place of birth question relate to the life time migration. It can be used to estimate the net migration for an area between two survey dates or for the intercensal period. The formula for the estimation of net migration in the intercensal period is:

$$\text{Net migration } (NM) = (I_{t+n} - O_{t+n}) - S_i I_t - S_o O_t)$$
$$= (I_{t+n} - S_i I_t) + (S_o O_t - O_{t+n})$$
$$= M_1 + M_2$$

Where I and O refer to the number of immigrants and outmigrants, S to the survival ratio (i.e., proportion surviving), and the subscripts t, $t+n$, o and t to the time t, time $t+n$, outmigrants and immigrants, respectively. M_1 and M_2 are the respective net immigration among persons born outside the area and that among the persons born inside the area.[1]

The following are the advantages of using place of birth for measurement of life-time internal migration in a country:

(*i*) The question on the place of birth is simple and easy to ask. It is also easily understood.

(*ii*) It can also be used to measure rural urban migration.

(*iii*) The information obtained through this question is generally correct and complete since it is expected that a normal person would easily remember his or her place of birth.

However, the place of birth as a measure of lifetime internal migration suffers from the following disadvantages:

(*i*) Since answers to the census questionnaires are generally given by the head of the family or some important members of the household, the possibilities of errors are there.

(*ii*) It cannot be possible to know by this that via how many stay in different places a person finally reached the destination.

(*iii*) There may be a tendency to report a better known place as the place of birth instead of the actual place of birth.

(*iv*) There is no time reference of migration; migration does not include return migration, and the subsequent moves of the migrants

1. U.N. Methods of Measuring Internal Migration Manual VI, ST/SOA/ Series A/47, New York, 1970.

are not taken into consideration.

(*v*) Another source of error is the frequently changing boundaries of a state due to political reasons of which the respondent may be unaware.

(*vi*) Sometimes special conditions may lead to unsatisfactory data; in India customarily, women go to their parents house for delivery (at least for the first delivery) and it may cause spurious migration.

(*vii*) The respondent may not be aware of the boundary changes of geographic or administrative units and may report the birth place inaccurately.

(*viii*) The birth place data do not convey any idea about the time of movement which may be from 4 days to 50 years, before the date of enumeration.

2. *Place of last residence.* The question concerning place of last residence fills up the gaps of place of birth data. This information may be classified into two categories: (*i*) Migrants whose place of last residence and the place of present residence are different, (*ii*) Non-migrants whose place of last residence and the place of enumeration are the same. The migrants therefore include all lifetime migrants plus the return migrants. This question provides a slightly better estimate of migration flows than the question on 'place of birth'. Since a person who returns to his birth place after living a number of years at another place will be counted as non-migrant in the latter case, but in the former case, he will be taken as migrant. However, place of last residence, too, lacks a definite time reference of migration.

This data may be used to measure migration in exactly the same way as data on the place of birth are used. It reflects a direct movement from the place of origin to the place of destination.

3. *Duration of residence.* Along with the question concerning place of birth and place of enumeration, sometimes a question about duration of residence at the place of enumeration is asked in a census. This question added for the first time in the 1961 Census in India and was repeated in 1971 and 1981.

According to this question a person whose age is more than the duration of residence at the place of enumeration is a migrant; and non-migrant otherwise. Migrants by the duration of residence definition include the persons born outside the place of enumeration and the return migrants.

The advantages of duration of residence as a direct measure for estimating migrant are as follows:

(*i*) The most significant advantage of duration of residence approach lies in inclusion of return migrants, which can be used for the indication of past migration trends.

(*ii*) It gives an idea about the category of migrants according to the trends in past migration.

This measurement suffers from the following problems or limitations:

(*i*) Usually the head of the family gives the information. It can not be authentically said that the respondent knows about duration of every member of his family. It concludes that the data is not necessarily complete.

(*ii*) The question of duration does not differentiate between internal migrants and does not provide the data on the place of origin of migrants and does not provide the data on the place of origin of migrants. This makes the study of outmigration, net migration and place of origin of migrants impossible.

(*iii*) The data on duration of residence are also affected by the digit preference tendency of the respondants. For example, the persons telling their residence about 10, 15, 20, 25, etc., years are more than the persons telling their residence as 3, 7, 11, 13, etc. The data also become inaccurate due to the recall laps by the respondants.

(*iv*) A category of 'unknown duration' reported, which may be of considerable size may create another problem.

4. *Place of residence at a fixed prior date*. In some census questionnaires a question is asked about the place of residence at a fixed prior date or on a specified date. According to this question a person is a migrant if his place of residence at fixed prior date differs from his place of enumeration and non-migrant otherwise. This provides enough information on both the timing of migration as well as the origin of migrants. According to U.N. Manual VI, the data on this are useful in any study of migration as "migration interval is clear cut, migration status is determined by a comparison of residence at two definite points of time, and a migrant is defined as a person whose residence at the census date differs from his residence at the specified prior date."[2]

Though the measurement of migration on the basis of residence at a fixed prior date is simple and satisfactory, it suffers from the following disadvantages:

(*i*) The possibility of inaccuracy in data due to recall lapse is more in this method than in other methods of measurement of

2. U.N. Manual VI: Methods of measuring internal migration.

migration.

(*ii*) This data cannot be used for estimating the components of intercensal population growth in the case of the reference period for the question on the place of residence at a fixed prior date being not the same.

(*iii*) This method does not consider the possibilities of multiple moves during the X-year period prior to the survey date.

(*iv*) The data generated by this question relate to the migration experience of only those migrants who have survived to the date of survey (census or sample), and not of all migrants.

(2) Indirect Measures of Estimation of Net-migration

In indirect measures of estimation of net-migration, population data of two successive censuses are used. Under this approach three techniques can be adopted for migration estimation:

(*a*) The Vital Statistics Method.

(*b*) The Survival Ratio Method.

(*c*) The Migration Rate Method.

1. *The vital statistics method.* The vital statistics method for estimation uses census counts at two points in time with statistics of births and deaths, to calculate net migration. If data on the size of population are obtained at two different dates one can easily calculate the change (increase or decrease) of population in the interval. Further, if records of births and deaths are available (or can be estimated) for the corresponding interval, they can provide the estimate of natural increase. By subtracting the natural increase from the total population change, the estimate of net migration can be achieved.

This can be illustrated in the following way:

$$\text{Net Migration} = (P_1 - P_0) - (B - D)$$
$$= P_1 - E_0 - B + D$$

where P_1 is the population at the later census, P_0 is the population at the earlier census, B is the total of births, and D is the total of deaths in the period between the census. It is clear that this method needs accurate estimates of births and deaths from the vital registration system. It is because of this reason that sometimes this method is also called a vital statistics method.

The following is an example of the use of the Vital Statistics Method for the estimates of net migration:

Though this is the simplest method of indirect estimation of migration, but no calculation of in- or out-migration or migration streams can be made by it.

Estimates of Net Migration to *X* City by the Vital Statistics Methods, 1961-1971

1. Population of *X* city, 1961 = P_0	=	1,416,056
2. Population of *X*-city, 1971 = P_1	=	1,729,141
3. Increase in Population 1971 − 1961 = (2)−(1)	=	313,085
4. Number of Births in *X*-city, 1961-1971 = *B*	=	653,190
5. Deaths during 1961-71 (*D*)	=	371,286
6. Natural increase in *X*-city, 1961-71 = (4)−(5)	=	281,904
7. Net Migration to *X*-city 1961-71 = (3)−(6)	=	31,181

Erroneous records of births and/or deaths or any error in the total population size can cause error in the estimate of migration.

This method cannot be much useful in developing countries. It is assumed in this method that there must be complete uniformity and perfect homogeneity in census methods classifications and its precision, which is not possible in the case of developing countries. This causes error in this procedure. Besides, the data obtained in these countries are not adequate due to errors in the reporting of births and deaths.

2. *The survival ratio method.* A second approach estimates net migration for the period between two censuses by survivorship probabilities (obtained from existing life table). A set of life table survival rates is applied to the population at the first census in order to derive an estimate of the number of persons expected to be living at the time of the second census. The difference between the expected population and the enumerated population is the estimate of net migration.

Also, the net migration can be had by knowing the survival ratios of two consecutive census operations, in the lack of appropriate Life Table or where its use is banned for any unknown reason.

The estimation of net migration for children born between two censuses cannot be estimated neither by census survival ratio method, nor by life table survival ratio method.

The advantages of survival ratio method are: (*a*) it does not require accurate statistics of births and deaths, and (*b*) it provides the estimate of migration by age and sex. In principle the method is simple.

3. *The migration rate method.* Migration rates are designed to relate numbers of migrants to the size of population of the regions of countries of origin or destination. The basic rates are:

(*i*) In-migration or immigration rate: $\frac{I}{P} \times 1000$

(*ii*) Out migration or emigration rate: $\frac{O}{P} \times 1000$

(*iii*) Net Migration rate: $\frac{I - O}{P} \times 1000$

(*iv*) Cross Migration Rate: $\frac{I + O}{P} \times 1000$

where I is the number of migrants into a region or a country, O is the number of migrants out of a region or a country, P is an appropriate measure of the population in the region or country of destination or origin. It may be noted that the concept of a rate as involving a population "at risk" does not strictly apply in the case of in-migration, immigration or net migration. Nevertheless, the measures may be of use for substantive analysis.

We can have migration rates specific of certain characteristics of the population if the relevant data to determine the number of migrants possessing specific characteristics are available. Thus

$$m_1 = \frac{M_1}{P_1} \times 1000$$

Where m_1 = The rate of migration for population of a specified geographical area characterised by trait 1. (e.g. sex, age, marital status, etc.)

M_1 = Number of migrants characterised by same trait 1.

P_1 = Total population of the area possessing the same trait 1.

THEORIES AND MODELS OF MIGRATION

From the available literature, it seems that demographers have not so far evolved any comprehensive theory of human migration that fits well with the demographic processes. Most theoretical formulations on migration represent attempting at generalising empirical results. Some of the important theories of migration are discussed below:

1. Ravenstein's Law of Migration

Ravenstein was the first to develop a theoretical basis to human migration. The following summarises the major points of the law:

(*a*) Migrants move from areas of low economic opportunity to those of high economic opportunity.

(*b*) The decision to move and the selection of destination are influenced by distance, with migrants from the rural areas often showing a tendency to move first towards nearby towns, and then towards large cities.

(*c*) Migration accelerates with development of the means of transport and communication and expansion of trade and industry.

(*d*) Each stream of rural-urban migration produces a counter-stream of urban-rural migration, although the former tends to dominate the latter.

(*e*) The urban residents are less migratory than the rural.

Ravenstein's theory can be described as showing uniformities observed in empirical situations and cannot be considered as laws in the strict sense. However, early models of internal migration were influenced by Earnest George Ravenstein's pioneering work in the nineteenth century, relating migration to the size of the population at two geographic points and to the distance between them.

2. Zipf's Gravity Model

After Ravenstein, there was no attempt at formulating theories for a long interval of over 50 years. Zipf in 1946, and Stewart in 1942 attempted to draw upon physical settings to explain the movement of individuals. Their theories are labelled as gravitational as they treat human beings and their movement as individuals. According to this model, people move as if drawn by a gravitational force that diminishes with distance; the number of persons who moved between any two areas is directly proportional to the product of the two populations and inversely proportional to the distance between them.

Despite the simplicity of Zipf's model, several objections have found it unsatisfactory. This model is unrealistic as it is symmetrical, assuming equal flow in both directions. It does not specify why there is such an interaction and it does not take into account characteristics of places of origin and destination, or of migrants, that could influence both the volume and direction of movements.

3. Stouffer's Model

Zipf's gravity model was modified by Samuel A. Stouffer, who came out with the theory of intervening opportunities in 1940. 'Intervening opportunities' being a relative concept it was later replaced by 'Intervening obstacles' by Stouffer himself.

According to Stouffer's model, migrants are attracted by a set of positive factors at their place of destination while they are repulsed by negative factors in their place of origin. The greater the net attraction, the more likely migrants are to overcome intervening difficulties. The degree of migration would be inversely related to the distance between the two places as also the extent of intervening opportunities but directly related to the opportunities in the two places. To move towards the attractive forces, migrants must overcome a series of intervening obstacles. Intervening obstacles include cost or lack of transport, lack of integration with the national road system, closer acceptable destinations, limited information about potential destinations, no urban kin or other contacts to assist the migrant upon arrival, no linkage to urban areas through governmental services, and familial constraints on the movement of a household member. Personnel characteristics of the potential migrant affect his ability to overcome intervening obstacles. In general migrants tend to be positively selected with respect to youth, education and household income relative to non-migrants in the place of origin. Over time, it is assumed that there would be less difference between sending and receiving areas, more kin in the place of destination, and greater ease of access, thereby reducing intervening obstacles and resulting in less selectivity of migrants.

Galle and Tacuber replicated this model with the migration data of the 1960 Census of the USA for cities with 100,000 or more population and found that the model was an extremely good fit. But this model may not hold good in a developing country like India because of the excessive disguised unemployment and ignorance of intervening opportunities. Besides, this model is based on the assumption of the availability of and a general knowledge of job opportunities in almost all the cities, which would not be found in the developing countries in general and in India in particular.

4. Lee's Theory of Migration

According to Everett Lee the decision to migrate and the process of migration is determined by the following four factors:

(*i*) *Factors associated with the area of origin.* In each area there are several factors which motivate migration to outside area.

(*ii*) *Factors associated with the area of destination.* More attractive forces at the destination increase migrant selectivity: conversely, stronger influence of repulsive forces at the destination reduces selectivity. Generally, the places, with the most attractive forces have been a nation's metropolitan areas; therefore, these areas should also have the highest proportion of selectivity migrants.

(*iii*) *Intervening obstacles.* Increased difficulty of intervening obstacles raises migrant selectivity. The most important intervening obstacles are distance and transportation. These have been considerably reduced in modern times due to technological advance.

(*iv*) *Personal factors.* Everett S. Lee's model focuses attention on individual behaviour and on the perceptions and decision-making process of the migrant. He developed "a general scheme into which a variety of special movements can be placed." He catagorises forces exerting influence on migrant perception into "pluses" and "minuses". The former pull individuals towards them, the latter tend to drive them away. There are 'zeros' also, in which the competing forces are, more or less evenly balanced.

Lee proposed a category of personal elements that includes age, education, sex, and race, added to factors that the associated with the area of origin, the area of destination, and intervening obstacles.

In Fig. 2, pluses represent factors that hold and draw people, minuses factors that repel or push people from the area, and zeros characteristics towards which people are indifferent. The effects of these forces vary according to personal qualities of the potential migrant.

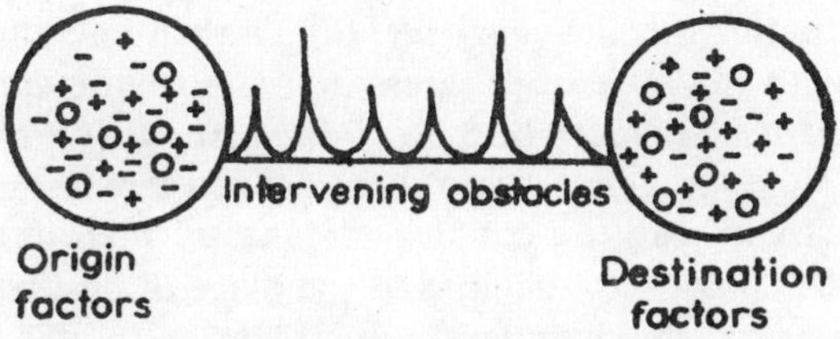

Source:- Lee Everett S. "A Theory of Migration." Demography 3(1): 47–57, 1966.

Fig. 2.

In short, in the theory of migration, Lee has emphasised the role of pull factors or those associated with the destination areas, push factors or those associated with the areas of origin, intervening obstacles such as ethnic barriers, distance and cost, and personal factors.

Conceptual Framework for Migration Analysis

Lee has fomulated several hypotheses within the conceptual framework of the above mentioned 4 types of factors. These hypotheses are as follows:

(*I*) *Characteristics of migrants.* (1) Migrants responding primarily to minus factors at origin tend to be negatively selective; or where the minus factors are overwhelming for the entire population group, they may not be selected at all for migration; (2) Migration is selective; (3) Migrants responding primarily to plus factors at destination tends to be positively selective; (5) The degree of positive selection increases with the difficulties posed by the intervening obstacles; (5) When all migrants are considered together, selection for migration tends to be bi-model; (6) The characteristics of migrants tend to be intermediate between the characteristics of the population of the place of origin and of the population of the place of destination; (7) The heightened propensity to migrate at certain stages of the life-cycle is important in the selection of migrants.

(*II*) *Volume of migration.* (1) The volume of migration within a given territory varies with the degree of areas included in that territory; (2) The volume of migration is related to the difficulty of surmounting the intervening variables; (3) Unless severe checks are imposed, both the volume and rate of migration tend to increase with time; (4) The volume of migration is related to the difficulty of surmounting the intervening variables; (5) The volume of migration varies with fluctuations in the economy; (6) The volume and rate of migration vary with the state of progress in a country or area.

(*III*) *Streams and counter-streams of migration.* (1) Migration tends to take place largely within well-defined streams; (2) The efficiency of the stream and the counter stream of migration tends to be low if the place of origin and the place of destination are similar; (3) For every major migration stream, a counter-stream also develops; (4) The efficiency of migration streams will be high if the intervening obstacles are great; (5) The efficiency of the stream (ratio of stream to counter-stream or the net redistribution of population affected by the opposite flow) is high if the major factors in the development of a migration stream are minus factors at origin; (6) The efficiency of a migration stream varies with economic conditions, being high in prosperous times and low in time of depression.

Lee analysis based on 'pluses' and 'minuses' factors tend to be an over-simplification. These 'pluses' and 'minuses' factors must be interpreted in the overall demographic context. Under conditions of high rate of natural increase, not only in the rural areas, but in the urban areas as well (as a result of high birth rates and rapidly declining death rates) the push or 'minuses' factors operate in urban areas also. However, Lee's theory is reflected in a broad range of studies, particularly those dealing with migrant selectivity and push-pull factors. Probably, the pull factors continue to be dominant rather than push factors in almost all the big cities and metropolises.

5. Todaro's Model

Michael P. Todaro (1976) has put forward the theory of perceived income and employment opportunities to explain migration. Other things remaining the same, prospects of higher income in the urban areas promote migration towards the cities. This is how he sums up four major features of his model:

(*i*) Migration is stimulated primarily by rational economic considerations of relative benefits and costs, mostly financial, but also psychological.

(*ii*) Rural-urban migration depends on the probability what an urban labourer can successfully find a modern-sector job as well as on the urban-rural income differential. Migration is then a response to expected rather than actual earnings.

(*iii*) The probability of rural-urban migration is directly related to the perceived rural-urban income differential and the probability of obtaining a job in the city. Costs of moving reduce the probability of migration.

(*iv*) Migration rates in excess of urban job opportunity growth rates are not only possible but also rational and probable in the face of continued positive urban-rural expected income differentials. High rates of urban unemployment are therefore inevitable outcomes of the serious imbalances of economic opportunities between urban and rural areas of most underdeveloped countries.

John Harris and Todaro extended this model to incorporate a two-sector internal trade model of migration and unemployment. The Harris-Todaro extension gives explicit attention to the impact of migration on rural incomes, urban and rural output, and social welfare.

Todaro conceptualises the process of rural-urban migration in two steps. In the first step the migrant arrives in the urban area, and, in many cases, remains either unemployed or are underemployed in the traditional, or informal sector. In the second step he often succeeds in getting a job in the modern sector which generally carries higher earnings. If we see from the life-span income point of view, the modern sector earnings during the second step would be sufficiently high so as to neutralize the zero or low traditional sector earnings of the first step. Thus, even if the migrant initially experienced a loss of income as a result of migration, he could still be acting rationally as long as the present value of the life-span urban income exceeds the present value of the rural income plus the costs of relocation.

Though the model has been empirically tested in a number of countries, and it performs fairly well with both aggregate census and survey data, it suffers from the following weaknesses:

(a) It is based on the wrong assumption that all potential migrants have equal information about the urban labour market and have equal access to urban jobs.

(b) This model has overlooked the possibility of migrants acquiring skills in the urban areas.

(c) This model is partial because it does not emphasise the role of non-economic factors in the mobility decisions.

(d) It is also wrong to assume that potential migrants are homogeneous in respect of skills and attitudes.

6. L-F-R Model of Migration

The first comprehensive model of economic development which gave due consideration to the process of rural-urban labour transfer was evolved by Prof. W. Arthur Lewis (1954), and later extended by Rains and Fei (1961). The combined structure is now known as the L-F-R-model.

This model believes that due to the increasing growth of population, most of the under-developed countries have unlimited supply of labour, which is available at the subsistence wage rate. The large reservoir of such labour force is generally found in the subsistence sector of the economy and the withdrawal of this labour force from the "subsistence sector" to the "capitalist sector" results in capital formation and thus economic development takes place. Thus this model is based on a concept of dual economy comprising a subsistence sector and capitalist sector. Subsistence or agriculture sector is characterised by unemployment and underemployment and a capitalist sector or a modern sector is characterised by full employment. In subsistence sector the people are generally backward, illiterate, simple and unskilled. In contrast, the people are advanced, literate, sophisticated and skilled in the capital sector. In subsistence sector, the average productivity of worker is lower than that in the capitalist sector and so the average wage in the subsistence sector is comparatively lower than that in the capitalist sector. Generally the marginal productivity of such workers in the agricultural sector is negligible or zero or even negative. Thus in this sector, wages exceed marginal productivity. In the capitalist sector, wages are maintained at levels much higher than the average agricultural wage. In this dual economy, migration from the subsistence sector to the modern sector augments industrial production and the capitalists' profit. Since this profit is ploughed back in the industrial sector, it further increases the demand for labour from the subsistence sector. This process continues as long as the reserve army of disguised unemployed, whose supply to the urban industrial sector is assumed to be elastic at the given urban wage, exists in the rural subsistence sector. This process comes to an end eventually when the rate of expansion of demand for labour outstrips the growth rate of population in the rural areas.

Thus, this model considers migration as an equilibrating mechanism which, through transfer of labour from the labour-surplus sector to the labour-deficit sector, brings about equality between the two sectors.

Despite the simplicity, Lewis' model suffers from the following weaknesses:

(*i*) Migration is not induced solely by unemployment and underemployment in the rural areas, although there is no doubt that this is an important factor in the decision to migrate.

(*ii*) The migration of labour force from the subsistence to the capitalist sector is not an easy task as visualised by Lewis in his model. The case of migrant labour force poses special problems that cannot be analysed adequately in the Lewis model.

(*iii*) Lewis model overstates the capacity of the modern sector to absorb surplus labour from the subsistence sector. Industrialisation in many underdeveloped countries has not provided sufficient pull in the industrial sector to draw surplus labour from the primary sector. Myrdal shows that the whole idea of labour transfer is unrealistic in backward countries.

(*iv*) The assumption of near-zero marginal productivity in agriculture has not been confirmed empirically. On the contrary, the available evidence from several developing countries, shows that under given conditions of production, the allocation of labour usually tends to be optimal, and any withdrawal of labour would lead to a fall in output unless the yield-increasing innovations are simultaneously introduced.

Microanalytic and Macroanalytic Models

One summary classification distinguishes two types of models, terming one group 'microanalytic' and the other 'macroanalytic'. The microanalytic models throw light on individual behaviour and social and psychological determinants of immobility as well as of mobility. On the other hand, the macroanalytic models focus on the ecological determinants of population flows, like size and distance. It remains now to integrate the two in models that allow for the interaction of those influences in a context of economic development and social change.

THE DETERMINANTS OF MIGRATION

The theories of migration forwarded by Ravenstein, Lee, Lewis and Ranisand Fei, and Todaro attempt to explain the factors in deciding the migration processes. Weiner has rightly pointed out, "if it is the assessment of the consequences of migration that leads policy-makers to intervene, it is the assessment of determinants of migration that leads policy to choose particular instruments for intervention. Thus the study of determinants of migration assumes important place in policy related studies.

It would be useful to give a brief review of the studies done on the determinants of migration. Prof. Berg has listed the major migration determination factors as (*i*) the intensity of preference for money income against 'leisure' in the village, (*ii*) the level of his income from village production, (*iii*) the effort price of income earnable in the village, and (*iv*) the effort price of earnings outside the village.

D'Souza in his study of migrants to Dandeli and its environs found that given economic opportunities, migrants did not lag behind. He concluded that depending on the nature of economic opportunities, only persons with certain distinctive socio-cultural background migrate.

Connell *et al.* sought to find the determinants at the village level. They identified a set of push factors (such as land shortage, poor quality of land and unequal distribution of land) along with a set of 'pull' factors (commercialization of agriculture and access to towns and roads) and hybrid factors (literacy, extent of cash cropping in the village) which are associated with migration propensities. At the individual level, they could not trace such simple relationship between those who suffer from land scarcity and their propensity to migrate.

H.V. Sovani lists the main causes of migration as follows, (*a*) unemployment at home, (*b*) meagre income, and (*c*) insufficient land. I. Desmukh studied the migration from a few villages to Delhi, and found perfect rank correlation between unemployment rates and migration rates. Similarly John Parr has found out-migration as a means of easing the difficulties faced by depressed areas, particularly the difficulties created by unemployment.

According to Richard W. Wilkie the process of migration is influenced by a variety of factors such as (*a*) proximity to the city (to minimise moving and visit costs); (*b*) presence of kin in alternative destinations; (*c*) information about alternative destinations; (*d*) city amenities or quality of life; (*e*) specific types of employment available; (*f*) duration of migration (seasonal, circular, permanent); (*g*) cultural similarities.

Many of the studies on the determinants of migration can be subsumed under the 'rural-push and urban-pull' theory. But this aspect should not lead one to conclude that some sort of economic determinism operates this 'push and pull' in migration. While the economic factors contribute to a large extent in the decision to migrate, other social and cultural factors also operate in this decision-making. In fact movements of people from one area to another are determined by a variety of factors—demographic, cultural, political, geographical, social and economic. Pressure of population, marriage, employment or occupation, achievement, education of children, cultural affinity or contracts, conscious government policies, unfavourable topographical or climatic conditions are some of the numerous factors that have motivated people to migrate from one place to another. It is always not possible to identify one single factor that has been the cause of a person's migration; very often migration is motivated by the combined operation of two or more factors. Some of the important factors may briefly be discussed as under:

1. *Economic factors*. The most important determinant of migration is economic. It has been established in several studies that the low agricultural incomes and agricultural unemployment and underemployment in developing countries, are the major factors pushing migrants towards areas with greater job opportunities. In short people move from areas of low economic opportunity to those of high economic opportunity. We find people going from East to West in search of better economic prospects. West is more industrialised and needs manpower of all kinds. In the words of Thompson and Lewis, "It is merely a recognition of the fact that far and away the most important cause of migration during the great emigration from Europe was the desire to improve economic status." In short, migrants are attracted to areas of new industrial development and regions of higher per capita income.

2. *Demographic factors*. The pressure of population, resulting in a high man-land ratio, has been widely regarded as one of the

important causes of rural out-migration. With a given mode of production, in many developing countries, particularly in India, only a part of the labour force can be absorbed by agriculture. Hence surplus population must move to the urban centres to be gainfully employed. But the pressure of population is certainly not the only cause of increasing rural unemployment and underemployment. Equally important causes seem to be the low rate of investment in agriculture, fragmentation of land ownership, inequalities in the distribution of land and other productive assets, allocative mechanisms which discriminate in favour of the owners of wealth, and a pattern of investment and technological change which is *biassed* against labour. The main reason for this bias is the fact that much of the farm technology is imported from labour-scarce countries, and favours the use of capital against the use of labour.

The other biological determinants of demographic processes—birth rate and death rate—bears a positive relationship with the migration. People migrate to the area where male specific birth rate is high, and vice-versa. In countries where death rate is high, as compared with the birth rate, obviously male population will be tempted to migrate as chances of employment are bound to be there. Similarly, in the countries of low population growth-rate, emigration is discouraged and immigration is encouraged.

3. *Geographical factors*. People migrate to places where there is better climate or where minerals are found in abundance. In India. Massorrie, Simla, Darjeeling, etc., are the places where people move for climatic changes. Similarly, Switzerland is a place where migrants from all parts of the world may be seen. Similarly people move out to places proved to be flood affected or earthquakes are quite frequent. In short, people prefer to migrate to places which are comparatively safe and where the climate is salubrious.

4. *Social factors*. Social factors are also responsible for migration. People quit their place or country of origin where social barriers are rigid which do not afford the development of the individual. The people also migrate to be away from family feuds and disputed family life. The girls are migrant for ever after marriage and have to move to the places where they are asked or accompanied by their husbands.

5. *Political factors*. These days political factors are becoming important for migration. People migrate to other countries when they find that political systems and institutions of their country are not suited to them. Some people do not tolerate totalitarian regimes or dictatorship and leave their country. In may cases fear of war or

likely breakout of disturbances, inflation, etc., prompt many to leave their country. Racial or regional discrimination also result in migration.

Policies of the state also exercise a powerful influence on the migrants. Important among them are: policies which foster a concentrated growth of industrial infrastructure in the cities, a pattern of investment and technological change which is biased against labour, social investments which are preponderantly urban. As a result of such state policies, the income differential between urban and rural sector has been widening, and has encouraged further migration for rural to urban areas. Similarly, Government's policy of discrimination towards a particular community can result in the migration of the people belonging to that community.

6. *Religious factors.* The migration is also caused by the religious motives or religious conflicts. The people migrate to religious places where they find religion of their taste prevails. Similarly, the people migrate to new places when there is religious intoleration and conflicts. Today, Iran and Iraq and many other countries are facing home-war owing to the religious reasons.

Consequences of or Impact of Migration on Society

The migration process has tended to have a profound effect on both the areas from which the migrants come (i.e. Places of Origin) and the areas in which they finally settle. The effect of internal migration on the migrants and on the rural communities they leave behind vary according to the type of migrant, the volume of migration, and the nature of the places involved.

Consequences for Rural Areas

The effects of migration at the place of origin can be conveniently divided into following categories:

(*a*) *Effect on population.* Out-migration from a rural area reduces its population and may be effective in alleviating overcrowding. Migration of young adult male members of the village can be expected to influence the rate of natural increase as has been observed in India, New Guinea, and parts of West Africa. But if young men leave but return frequently for visits, the birth rate may not drop because the return visits allow couples to maintain sexual relations. Even if birth rates are unaltered by migration, average family size will decline. There would be fewer adolescents or adults in each household.

The other significant demographic consequences due to migration are as follows:

(*i*) Migration through augmented contacts with the more modernised sectors may influence the value system of the rural communities, and rural inhabitants may internalise lower fertility norms.

(*ii*) Returning migrants may also spread new values and information about family planning and may introduce new family size concepts.

(*iii*) Migration of unmarried males of young, working age might result in severe imbalances of the sex ratio in rural areas and influence the proportion of persons able to find marriage partners.

(*iv*) Young persons dominate among the rural out-migrants. When young working persons leave an area, the ratio of dependents to workers rises, particularly if there is no accompanying drop in birth rates.

(*v*) Migration affects the level and distribution of income in rural areas, and income distribution is considered to be a significant determinant of fertility and aggregate population growth.

(*vi*) Out-migration from an area creates scarcity of labour supply with the consequence that marginal workers, i.e. numbers of female work force, and juveniles and senile dependants tend to join the rank of workers. This is a more marked phenomenon in the labour intensive agricultural areas.

(*b*) *Economic Effects.* The economic effects of migration on the rural areas can be studied under following points:

(*i*) *Effects on rural employment and income.* If the migrant is unemployed prior to leaving the village, unemployment rates may fall; but if the migrant is a student or is not in the labour force, there would be no observable change in unemployment levels. Similarly, changes in per capita income or productivity levels depend on the contributions of the migrant before and after moving and on the households' immediate and long-term responses to migration. In short, the net effect of migration on rural employment and income cannot be determined a priori.

The optimistic views that rural out-migration leads to agricultural expansion are due to two reasons: Firstly, a declining labour/land ratio provides a new environment conducive to changing rural production technique. Second, the reduced supply of labour is also likely to push up agricultural wage rates and stimulate the adoption of labour-saving technology. Remittances from urban areas are also likely to raise rural incomes, and may not only increase levels of consumption, but also encourage technological change that further raises rural incomes.

On the other hand, many observers have argued that rural-urban migration may lead to the lowering of rural incomes. This is largely because, as several studies have shown, that is generally the young, the better educated and the ambitious who are motivated to leave the rural areas. Their movement involves a sizeable transfer of human capital out of the rural sector which might adversely affect agricultural productivity and incomes, and thus encourage more migration. (*see* Hathway, 1964). Besides, though rural communities may have surplus labour when considered on an annual basis, out-migration which results in shortage of labour at times of peak labour demand is likely to reduce the total agricultural output.

The empirical evidence available on the effects of migration on rural incomes and employment is both limited and inconclusive. However, we can conclude that in the long run, rural out-migration can reduce population pressure and enhance labour productivity, incomes and rural welfare. But in the short run these changes seldom have been observed. Incomes and productivity generally have failed to rise, and in some instances they have fallen. Income inequality and class differentiation have been exacerbated.

(*ii*) *Effects on rural capital formation and technological change.* An important economic consequence of migration is the remittances sent by the migrants. Studies show that remittances can constitute a fairly large share of the income of the family in the migrant's place of origin. Remittances ranging from 25 to 50 per cent of the migrant's earnings have been found in Kenya, Uganda, Nepal, Pakistan, and Mexico. The number of households affected is fairly substantial. Surveys in Nepal and India show that one half to two-thirds of all rural households receive remittances.

In a study of the village data collected by Delhi Agro-economic Research Centre, the percentage of remittances fluctuated between 26 and 69 with migrants from 3 villages contributing more than half of their income. Evidence suggests that over a long time period (of the migrants' stay) the amount and regularity of remittances fall.

The net effect of remittances on the rural economy is difficult to determine a priori. They may add to productive investment for the development and diversification of agriculture or of non-agricultural activities in the rural areas, or be spent on housing and education, or be used to relieve the poverty of those who remain behind. On the other hand, they may be used unproductively for conspicuous consumption. Remittances may even erode work habits, since they increase resources without the need for any effort on the part of recipient, thus reducing the pressure for economic and social change.

In addition, the full effects of remittances on capital formation in rural areas will depend on their size and frequency. Intermittant or uncertain remittances may not be invested.

A number of studies show that very little of the money that is remitted is used directly as investment in agriculture. Connell *et al.* in their survey of literature quote a large number of studies which indicate that a major proportion of remittances is consumed in everyday household needs or in conspicuous consumption, and that investment in agriculture is not evident.

Longer-term remittances, especially those from international migrants, may be used to purchase land, farm-machinery, land and other agricultural equipments (Stark, 1977). This is illustrated by the widespread use of international remittance income for purchase of tubewells in Pakistan. It should be noted that only rich households have enough income to divert some of the remittances to major investment. In such a case remittances may merely strengthen the position of rich farmers who could increase their control of the rural economy. This could reduce competitive pressures. on them to innovate. We can conclude that remittances do not have a significant impact on rural productivity levels.

(*c*) *Social and cultural effects.* When people leave a community, the social fabric of the community inevitably changes. The social impact of migration at the village of origin can be seen in terms of the breakdown of formal relationships even though the extended family is becoming more important. S. Srivastava found in a U.P. village that traditional economic and social ties between castes involved in the 'jajmani' relationships are breaking down and economic and social relationships are becoming more important.

Out-migration tends to result in a greater integration of the village with outside communities. The remaining villagers will know more about urban ways and will be more likely to adopt selected urban behaviours, specially the purchase of urban consumption goods and the desire for formal education.

There is evidence that migration exacerbates socio-economic inequalities. If migration is concentrated among the fairly rich and the fairly poor, then income inequality may tend to grow. Attendent on this increasing economic inequality is greater social and political inequality. Among the Riff in Morocco (Amersfoort, 1978) and Tzintzuntzanos in Mexico, (Kemper and Foster, 1975), migration has resulted in increasingly visible social and economic differentiation between the 'haves' and 'have nots'.

Other social impact of migration would be in inducing changes in the role of children and women. Studies in many countries confirm the increase in farm or wage-earning responsibilities undertaken by wives of absent husbands. These changes are most pronounced among the poorer women for whom migrants remittances may be extremely limited. As the mother takes on more farm of off-farm work, her children are asked to undertake more of the household responsibilities. Hence children get less time to devote to school. Migration also induced changes to village family structure or social networks suggest substantial modification of traditional patterns. Women left behind by male migrants in Columbia, Kenya, Mexico, and Jambia assume responsibility for many decisions previously reserved exclusively for men.

There is also the effect of return-migration on culture. The migrant brings with him his own norms, values and attitudes and, over a course of time, learns those of the place of destination. If he visits his home (town or village) quite frequently, he carries back many of the ideas from the new place. He thus becomes an instrument of cultural diffusion. Where families have members living in both urban and rural areas, their social networks expand to include persons in both areas. This bridging facilitates cultural diffusion from city to countryside. The resulting diversity may enhance family's flexibility in coping with the ups and downs of life.

CONSEQUENCES FOR URBAN AREAS

The consequences of migration on the urban areas or on the place of destination are more difficult to discern. However, we shall try to analyse these consequences under following points:

Effect on the Demographic Structure of Urban Population

In addition to its effect on urban growth, migration can have other demographic impacts.

In urban areas migration, being strongly adult male selective, tends to swell the workforce and change the existing occupational structure. At places where industrial development is in progress such migration has a favourable impact as it provides cheap labour which, when absorbed in the industry, tends to change the occupational structure of the area in favour of industry and in the long run also helps diversify the economic activities. However, in areas of labour saturation, such migrants have an impact in favour of services. They are generally engaged in petty trade, transport, household services, etc.

Migration will also affect population growth since fertility in urban areas is often lower than in rural areas due to a number of factors such as higher costs of rearing children, improved communications, and greater access to improved child health care and family planning services. Costs in terms of demands on the time of parents and education and maintenance expenditure are higher in urban areas. Also, generally, parents have a target number of children, and lower fertility may be a response to lower infant mortality rates due to improved health standards, increased medical care and better nutrition in urban areas. It is expected, therefore, that migration itself and exposure to a milieu of lower fertility will bring about lower fertility among migrants.

Empirical evidences suggest that migrant women will desire or have smaller families after moving if they (*i*) are young at time of migration; (*ii*) delay marriage or first union, (*iii*) experience lower infant and child mortality in conjunction with continued lactation and abstinence or use of birth control methods, (*iv*) have or obtain literary skills, (*v*) have aspirations for themselves or children, (*vi*) interact with reference groups supportive of small families, (*vii*) are committed to work outside the home and in a non-housewife career, (*viii*) are less reliant on children for help and plan more investment in children's education and support, (*ix*) are part of a culture with an openness to modernisation and change, and (*x*) are aware of and can obtain contraceptives.

Effect on Wages and Unemployment

A priori, it is difficult to state unequivocally whether migration worsens or improves unemployment level and income level in the urban areas. In Chile, Colombia, India, Indonesia, Mexico, and other countries many migrants claim to have improved their real income and employment status as a result of migration, although usually not as much as they had expected (Findley, 1977). Similarly, in Chile it was found that before moving to Santiago, 35 per cent of the migrants were unemployed or unpaid family workers, but only 3 per cent were unemployed shortly after arriving. In fact, there are many ways by which migrants can increase the level of employment; for example, they may lower wage rates in urban areas, and this may lead to an expansion of employment. The increased supply of labour may stimulate investment and bring about a higher rate of industrialisation. The consumption patterns of migrants may be oriented towards 'basic needs' goods and services produced by relatively labour-intensive technologies. Besides, the migrants may stimulate employment in informal sector by providing dynamic components to economic growth like, entrepreneurial skill and small-scale working capital, which may catalyse development; and finally they may sustain a higher rate of growth because of their relatively higher propensity to save, a lower rate of absenteeism, and greater work intensity.

While precise figures are difficult to find out on the proportion of migrants who make little or no real economic gain, available figures suggest that about one-fourth of all migrants fail to improve themselves.

Effect on Urban Income Distribution

According to Rodgers, the impact of migration on urban income distribution will depend on the relative propensities of different groups of migrants to enter the various segments of the urban labour market as well as on their mobility potential among these segments. If the majority of migrants enter low-status, low-income jobs, the direct and immediate effect of their migration would be the worsening of the over-all distribution of urban income. However, the long run effect of migration on income distribution in the urban areas will depend partly on the opportunities available to migrants to move into the more modern sectors of the urban economy, and thereby raise their income.

Effect on Labour Force Participation

The most widely discussed effect on rural-urban migration for the urban areas is the effect on labour force participation. A priori, it is not possible to conclude anything on this vital issue. Some observers have advocated that, other things being equal, migrants to the urban areas are likely to have a lower propensity to participate in the labour force than natives (Peek and Antolinez 1977). They give three reasons for the same. First, migrants may be 'target workers'—those who move to the urban areas for a specific time period with the purpose of, say, saving enough money to buy land or capital equipment for farming back in the village—and they are unlikely to have the same degree of commitment to work as natives and may, therefore, be less preferred by the employers. Secondly, if the urban labour market is segmented and migrants are pushed into low-wage, less secure, and low-status jobs, with a reduced prospect of upward mobility, this may reduce their incentive to participate in the labour force. Thirdly, migrants are not likely to have contracts to the same extent as natives which may reduce their chances of finding suitable employment, and, thus place them at disadvantage in searching for work.

On the contrary, a number of studies suggest that migrants are likely to participate in the labour force to a greater extent than natives (Standing, 1978). They give two main reasons for this. First, migrants are generally having a greater urgency for immediate income, and are, therefore, less able than natives to remain openly unemployed. Second, migrants often have lower aspirations and expectations and are, therefore, likely to take up whatever jobs are available (Herrick, 1965). Third, migrants are an achievement-oriented group and usually take greater risks in order to advance themselves. They should, therefore, have a higher participation rate. Finally, many of the migrants are likely to be single persons who generally tend to have higher participation rates except where such migrants are students or retired persons.

On balance, there seems to be a greater weight in the argument that migrants tend to have a higher participation rate than natives.

Effects on Availability of Urban Amenities and Migrant's Adujstment, Assimilation and Integration

Although migration can serve as an adjustment mechanism for the economic and social system, this quick pace of massive movement, at the same time, creates serious shortages of basic service in these cities. They chronically suffer from water and power shortages. Their transportation systems are worked beyond their capacities. The position in regard to public latrines, parks, schools and gardens is most unsatisfactory. Along with these shortages, there emerged another problem of rising slums and squater settlements. In these 'shanty towns' migrants live 'without public services, unsanitary, and in many respects almost intolerably insecure'. This is the culture of 'poverty' as described by Oscar Lewis, they acquired in these congested and frustrating cities. In this culture, the people will 'produce little wealth and receive little in return'.

At the place of destination, the problems of migrant's adjustment, assimilation and integration also arises. The words adjustment, assimilation and integration are often used interchangeably in migration literature. Although these words are closely related, their meanings are not necessarily the same and needed to be specified. Graphic presentation of the concepts of adjustment, assimilation and integration is shown in Fig. 3.

Gordon (1964) suggested that assimilation has seven basic sub-processes. These include (1) the cultural or behavioural stage of assimilation; (2) structural assimilation; (3) intermarriage; (4) identification of peoplehood or ethnicity; (5) and (6) lack of discriminatory behaviour and attitudes by the hosts to the new group; (7) lack

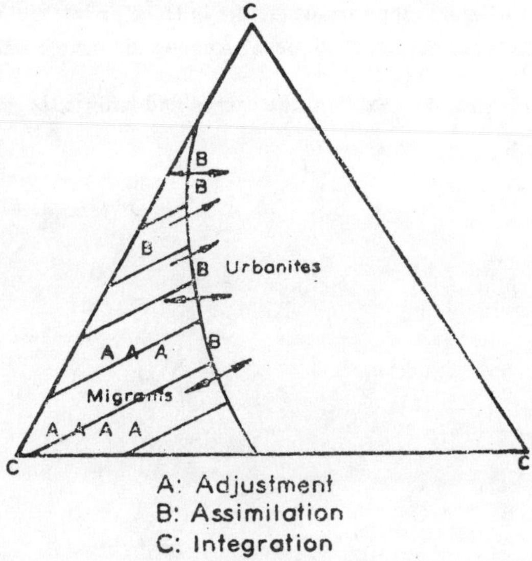

Fig. 3.

of conflict in public and civic aspects. Gordon hypothesised that cultural assimilation (acculturation) is likely to occur first and once structural assimilation has occurred all other types will follow (Jansen, 1969).

Empirical studies reveal that whether or not movers succeed in adjusting themselves to the urban way of life depends heavily on the pre-selectivity of migrants at the sending areas (Abu-Lughod, 1961; Zachariah, 1966; Green, 1978). However, at the place of destination, the adjustment process is also facilitated by familiar contacts. The location of friends and relatives is well recognised as an important factor in destination selection of migrants. On the whole migrants seem to be able to adjust satisfactorily to the urban life, especially with longer duration of residence.

EXAMINATION QUESTIONS

1. Define the term migration. State the various methods of measuring migration.
2. Explain the relation between migration and socio-economic change. State the various factors promoting migration. What are the main obstacles to migration?
3. Distinguish clearly between internal migration and international migration. Explain the various factors influencing internal migration.
4. What does internal migration mean? Analyse the factors affecting internal migration.
5. Define urbanisation. Explain the causes and effects of migration from villages to cities.

14

Population and Economic Development

There are various ways of defining and measuring economic growth.* An increase in total real national income over a long period is one ('real' and 'long period' because changes in the value of money due to inflation or deflation and cyclical swings in output must be allowed for). But an increase in real national income might be accompanied by even faster growth in population, so we would be faced with the paradox of a situation in which there might be growing national income accompanied by declining per capita income. A second measure of growth is, therefore, to divide the increase in national income by the increase in population, so that the indicator of economic growth becomes the increase in income per head. But difficulties remain.

If all the increase in national income went to a small and relatively well-off section of the population, and the share of income going to the rest remained the same while their numbers grow; most of the population would be both relatively and absolutely worse off than before. If economic growth is to be regarded as a process which raises the real standard of living of a community as a whole, a third indicator of economic growth is income per head supplemented by

*There is a tendency to use the terms economic development, economic growth, economic progress and secular change interchangeably. Although it is possible to make some distinction among these terms, they are in essence synonymous.

Lady U.K. Hicks has characterised the problem of the under-developed countries as that of economic development as distinguished from that of economic growth of advanced countries. She has pointed out that the problems of under-developed countries are related to development of unused resources, though their uses are well known while the problems of advanced countries are connected with growth most of their resources being already known and developed to a great extent.[1]

J.A. Schumpeter defines economic development is a discontinuous and spontaneous change in the stationary state which forever alters and displaces the equilibrium state previously existing; while growth is a gradual and steady change in the long run which comes about a general increase in the rate of savings and population.[2]

information on the distribution of income and the extent to which national resources are were being used to satisfy the preferences of consumers as a whole.

This meaning of economic growth requires value judgements on what is desirable or undesirable change in the distribution of income. The main objective of economic growth, to raise standards of living, is generally a very long-term objective that may require living standards to be depressed in the short run, e.g. by saving to accumulate capital or to build national defences. To avoid the necessity for 'welfare' judgements, and for simplicity, many economists use the figure of real national income as the measure of economic growth. If required, adjustments for increase in population can then be made separately.

Economic growth may be viewed, in brief, as a process whereby an economy's real income increase over a long period of time.[3]

Economic growth involves (*a*) a better allocation of resources on the basis of given supplies of factors and production functions, (*b*) an increase in factor supplies, and (*c*) a change in production functions.

The above processes are influenced by labour, capital and technology. Of these the first is the active agent and provides the motive force.

HUMAN RESOURCES OR LABOUR

The size, composition and socio-cultural characteristics of a population are some of the important determinants of the pace and level of economic development. Not only do demographic forces influence the nature and quantity of all factors of production; they also determine the kind of economic climate within which all activities take place. The constant interaction between man and his environment has an effect on the size and quality of the natural base. The quality of the human resources also plays an important role in determining the type of technology, the modes of organisation, and the targets of production. It is not surprising, therefore, that much attention has been devoted in the literature of economic growth to problems of population and human resources.

Human resources are germane to the building up of an economy and they have a two-pronged relationship with economic growth. Population is both most dynamic agent of production and the beneficiary of the entire process of development. In other words, on the one side, population has production aspect and on the other a consumption aspect. As an agent of production man contributes his labour, which acting on the natural resources produce the goods and services needed for satisfying human needs. Man's role as a consumer is also of great importance.

But the extent to which growth in the number of people, contributes to output depends not only on the extent of increase in the number, but also on pattern of the population increases, the availability of complementary resources, the technique of production adopted and on the context in which it occurs.

It is on this account that increase in population has different impacts in different types of economy.

In the Case of Advanced Economies

Increase in population may or may not be accompanied by a rise in per capita income. Much depends on the rate of capital formation and the availability of unutilised natural resources. In most of the advanced economies, economic growth and increase in population have gone hand and hand, because in these economies capital formation was fast, and in some of them (as in the U.S.A.) vast natural resources were available. From the estimates made by Prof. Kuznets it is evident that during the first half of the 19th century the rate of growth of population in the United States was 2 per cent per year while in U.K. the rate of increase in working population during 1850-1875 was 1 per cent. This increase in population brought about an increase in productivity, and per capita income increase the savings of the economy and thereby increases capital formation.

It has been witnessed that in advanced economies increase in population has an advantageous bent as:

(*i*) It led to fuller utilisation of resources. In the newly settled countries, as in the U.S.A., in spite of plenty of resources, economic development was held back by the paucity of population. William Petty attributed the prosperity of Netherlands in the nineteenth century to the rapid growth of population. Similarly, Industrial Revolution in U.K. took place at the period of rapid population growth.

(*ii*) An excess of cheap labour enables a country to compete successfully with the goods produced by expensive machinery.

(*iii*) Population growth becomes very helpful especially at the late stage of economic development by increasing the effective demand and extending the market. When market is extended, division of labour can also be extended and the marginal efficiency of capital can be maintained. This can prevent the onslaught of secular stagnation.

Lord J.M. Keynes favoured a growth of population to meet the challenge of deficiency of effective demand and his disciple A.H. Hansen believes that a faster rate of growth of population is highly desirable if 'secular-stagnation' is to be avoided. They point out that if the rate of growth of population is faster, there would be greater effective demand for goods and services. This results in an increase in the Marginal Efficiency of Capital, which brings about an increase in investment, output which in its turn, creates further employment, output and income. It also enables a fuller utilisation of the installed capacity of industries.

(*iv*) Population growth leads to higher social mobility by shifting labour gradually from agriculture to industry, or from one type of industry to another. It is a powerful force, according to Colin Clark, to bring a change in the traditional methods and to transform the economy to much more advanced and productive stages. Clark observes that people work for their children and with increasing number of children, the incentive for work would be higher. Similarly, Hirschman contends that population pressure on living standard would lead to a counter-pressure i.e., to activity to restore the traditional standard and in doing this, environment has to be controlled, works will increase and development efforts will be organised. Hirschman says that if certain slacks are present in the economy, population growth can provide stimulus to sustained development.

Thus in an advanced economy, an increase in population is a boon—unless it becomes unmanageably large during a depression. Actually, it has been witnessed that in Western European countries increase in population has been very helpful to bring about rapid industrialisation. Since the means to produce wealth are always available in an increasing scale, therefore, an increasing population is always helpful in helping economic growth. We must repeat the basic fact that in these economies capital increased much faster than population. Consequently, increase in population proved a helpful factor for growth.

The Case of Underdeveloped Economies

The effect of increasing population is different in underdeveloped countries from what is experienced in an advanced economy because the initial conditions are different and generally there is an unlimited supply of labour, and low rate of capital formation. In such a setting, an increasing population is only deterrent; an injury inflicted upon the people. The thesis that a man has not only a stomach but also two hands for production, and therefore, a large population is desirable for development is absurd in context of underdeveloped countries. Before the pair of hands can start producing, investment is needed not only for housing, education health, etc. but also for obtaining the means of production-tools, etc. The important question is to relate the size and growth of population to the resources and the levels of technology for their utilisation.

In the Keynesian model of under-employment equilibrium where the problem is one of a full utilisation of the available resources, a rise in effective demand brought about by a faster population growth will have a stimulating effect on the growth of income. In short, Keynesian economists believe that a faster rate of growth of population is highly desirable if "secular stagnation" is to be avoided. The condition under which a declining population tends to lead to secular stagnation are however different from those found in backward countries. The stagnation-problem of a 'mature' economy, in so far as it is real, is a problem of population, natural resources and technology failing to keep pace with, or utilise fully, capital accumulation. But the low level stagnation of a backward economy is due to capital accumulation and the supply of resources failing to keep pace with population growth.* The underdeveloped country suffers not from a deficiency of effective demand but primarily from a deficiency of the supply of capital.

It should also be noted that increase in population in advanced countries of Europe and North America occurred along with industrialisation and was really part and parcel of a more general process of rising living standards, industrialisation, and technological progress. But underdeveloped countries have shown very little economic growth, yet their population are expanding rapidly. This may be so on account of these countries having 'imported' certain by-products of development from the economically advanced countries but not the growth process itself. More specifically, the spread of Western technique of public health, sanitation, and medicine to the

*There may be some basis for the belief that in fact deficiencies of effective demand are often a problem in low income economies as well as in high income economies. . . . But even if deficiencies of effective demand as a barrier to economic growth are accepted as a possibility in low income economies; it does not follow that a more rapid population growth will under these circumstances serve as a major stimulus, since there is no apparent way in low income economy for greater numbers to be translated into very much higher consumption expenditure or higher prospective returns to capital. Coales and Hoover, Population growth and Economic Development in Low Income Countries, p. 21.

underdeveloped countries are causing sharply falling death rates and rapid population growth even in the absence of rising living standards and the other accompaniments of economic progress. As it is sometimes put, these countries are having a "public health revolution" prior to and independently of an "industrial revolution".

Prof. Horace Belshaw has studied the effects of the interactions of these variables with the help of the famous Cobb-Douglas equation which is expressed as:

$$P = bL^kC^j$$

Where P, L and C are output, labour and capital, b is a constant, different for different economies, and k and j are exponents of labour and capital, respectively and indicate the proportionate change in output (P), for a given proportionate change in the factor (L or C).

His analysis of the effects of the interactions of the above variables on economic growth has led him to the conclusion that a rise in levels of consumption in a growing population would require one of more of the following conditions:

(*a*) A rate of increase in capital stock (i.e. rate of investment) exceeding both the rate of increase in population and that in national income.

(*b*) Economies of scale large enough to offset such diminishing factor returns as might occur if the rate of growth of population exceeded that of capital stock.

(*c*) An improvement in the ratio of labour to population.

(*d*) Improvements in the efficiency of labour and/or capital.

It is profoundly clear that none of these conditions exist in developing economies of today. Although most underdeveloped countries are seriously inclined to achieve rapid economic growth, their determination is best by such problems as excessive rate of population growth, unfavourable age structure, unbalanced distribution of population, immobility of manpower, inadequacy of trained manpower, low physical efficiency, under-employment, institutional resistance and cultural inertia. Hence, on the face of it, it does not appear that an enormous or sizeable increase in population would stimulate economic growth. There are, however, certain positive considerations as well which substantiate the notion that population growth in underdeveloped countries acts like a drag on economic progress and slows down the pace of economic growth. The impact of rising population as drag on economic resources is felt in a variety of ways. It would be of interest to examine the problem in this setting.

1. POPULATION GROWTH AND CAPITAL FORMATION

Due to the heavy burden on the natural resource of low-income countries brought about by a high rate of population growth, the requirements of initial capital are likely to be very large. The investment outlay of such countries gets diverted towards providing essential consumer goods and social overhead like education, health housing etc. to the increased number of persons, so that the proportion of investment resources left for providing roads, power, machinery gets reduced. Hence the volume of capital formation suffers. According to J.J. Spengler a population increase of one per cent per annum necessitates four per cent of community's national income as investment that would just maintain the living standards intact. Colin Clark has also supported Spengler's criterion. He says: " . . . yo cover an increase in the labour force of 1 per cent, a capital investment equal to 4 per cent of the national income will be necessary, we thus get a very simple rule. Take the expected rate of population increases and multiply it by four. This gives us the percentage of National Income which has to be invested in order to provide employment, of the same average kind as now exists, for the increasing population."

It may noted that the above tests have been propounded for what Sauvy has called a 'demographic investment' which would imply an investment sufficient to maintain a constant living standard of the growing population. He distinguishes from it the 'economic investment' which relates to investments for bringing about a rate of growth of national income higher than the rate of growth of population so that per capita income rises and a higher standard of living is attained. The pace and volume of the latter have naturally to be faster and greater than the simple 'demographic investment'. Thus if an economy is just embarking on 'demographic investment' it cannot achieve an improvement in living standards. This would imply that the fruits of planned economic growth have more than been eaten away by the explosive growth of population.

According to detailed recent study, a representative sample of less developed countries shows that over 65 per cent of their total investments are devoted to maintaining the level of per capita income at a constant level, whereas the corresponding figure for a sample of developed countries was less than 25 per cent.

To assess the contribution of population to national income we must measure the addition made by it to output and deduct therefrom the amount of this output consumed by population. The measure of the net contribution made by rising population to nation income would depend upon the amount of income producing equipment per worker and the state of technology; the qualitative composition of the labour force and the size of the labour force. In low income countries the inadequacy of capital equipment available to labour reduces its productivity in addition to the fact that insufficient advance has been made in skills and technology. As such, population serves as an obstacle to economic growth chiefly because it hinders the rate of capital formation.

2. POPULATION AND THE BURDEN OF UNPRODUCTIVE CONSUMERS

The existence of a relatively larger proportion of population in the lower age group and low life expectancy in underdeveloped countries as compared with developed countries constitutes a drag on the productive effort of the economy. A high fertility rate in underdeveloped countries has saddled their economy with a large number of children who have to be fed without making any contribution to production. The greater the increase in population, the greater is the dependency ratio of non-workers to workers. Its consumption requirements would naturally increase and they would effect the flow of savings adversely. In Asia, Africa and Latin America population below 15 years of age constitutes 40 per cent of the total population, while in the United States of America and the United Kingdom, it ranges between 23-25 per cent of the total population.

The dependency load of a population is calculated on the basis of its contribution to production and consumption. For example, if the consumption needs are counted in terms of one unit for each adult working persons, one-half for each aged person and one-third for each child then for a population comprising 42 per cent children, 3 per cent aged and 55 per cent adults of productive age the dependency load per 100 adults of productive age would be 128 consumers equivalents. In an advanced country where the age composition is more favourable to production (23 per cent children, 67 per cent adults and 10 per cent aged) the corresponding ratio is 119 per 100.

A preponderance of children in the population is harmful for several reasons. Firstly it leads to a diversion of recources from capital formation to population maintenance. A high and increasing population of children increases the burden of the care of the young through nutrition, medical care, public health and education. But since mortality rate among children in low income countries is much higher than in industrial countries it means not only a diversion of resources but a wastage of resources as well. It has been estimated that the cost of rearing children who die before the age of 15 years is 22.5 per cent of national income in India as compared with 6.5 per cent in U.K. "Economically speaking, the under-developed countries suffer a considerable loss of investment-material and immaterial in up-bringing and educational efforts in respect of substantial number of young people who never reach the prime of life. Even if the amount invested per capita is below the equivalent of the cost of education, clothing and food customary in Western countries, the outlay lost in the aggregate is staggering." Besides the loss entailed by the economy on account of maintenance of children who die before reaching a productive age, the survivors 'productive period' is shorter in poor countries than in the advanced countries. It reduces the ratio of the labour force to the total population. Thus the 'bottom heavy' age structure of population reinforced by a shorter life expectancy leaves an adverse impact on total and per capita output. Secondly, the dependence load represented by the larger proportion of children is sought to be relieved by employing them at an early age and making them contribute what little they can to the family income. It amounts to a wasteful exploitation of children workers who may be forced into work at under-developed level of skill and stamina and may cause under-employment. The U.N. study on population makes the telling remark: "The position is rather like that of peasants compelled by hunger to harvest their wheat every year before it has ripend."

In short, the low percentage of persons in the 'productive age' bracket in poor countries hampers their rates of economic growth. As argued by Coale and Hoover, "When mortality risks are reduced, high fertility becomes a burden by increasing the dependency ratio, by diverting capital from uses that would raise per capita output, and in the long run by overwhelming any finite resources." Their studies of Mexico and India disclose that continued high fertility for the next three decades would result in very little addition to the labour force but would add appreciately to the population under 15 years of age. As the pace of economic development depends on conserving consumption to maximise investments, less of a given output can be devoted to investment when the ratio of dependents to producers is high. Thus high fertility promotes consumption at the expense of investment and economic growth. In contrast, with fewer dependents, more could be invested and more produced. Then, with fewer people to divide the output, investment could be maintained while adding to economic welfare and building up those forces that improves physical and psychological capacity to produce.

3. POPULATION AND UNEMPLOYMENT

An important consequence of rapid rate of population growth without a corresponding increase in the level of economic development is that there is a large-scale unemployment in urban areas and disguised unemployment in rural areas. An increasing population adds to the labour force. But labour has to work with capital. No one can really be employed with oneself. Employment, that way, means not only simply the use of labour but capital as well. Since employment is connected with capital, it follows that potential for employment will be conditioned by capital availability. Jobs do not widen in under-developed economies because as the labour force is increasing, the complementary resources particularly capital are not available. Low incomes, reduced savings, retarded investment (as per cent of national income) hamper capital formation and increasing job avenues for the rising population are not available. Problems facing such economies for providing new employment opportunities are essentially problems of capital accumulation and growth. This would generate a high level of economic activity, and create new employment potential. Since the backlog of unemployment and a steadily increasing population throwing in the stream of workforce ever-increasing job seekers are mounting, the rate of investment has to be large enough to overtake the rate of population growth. This is Herculean task for a low-income country to achieve if it is left to its own resources. "Thus the existence of population pressures makes it extremely difficult for an underdeveloped country like India to absorb the increase in labour force in gainful employment. Actually employment is a part of the growth process it is not something separate it is not possible to have only employment without growth, or for matter of that growth without, in general, increasing employment. Step by step, with growth and development the country has to be taken from the low level of employment to a higher level.

4. POPULATION PRESSURE ON MEANS OF SUBSISTENCE

Burgeoning population also dislocates the land-man ratio. Pressure on existing productive resources mounts up. Land is subjected to these pressures with greater severity because its supply is inelastic, and it cannot be increased even if the best of determination is there. For example, we are already using about 40 per cent of our geographical area and have exhausted most our cultivable land. It is necessary to recognise an important fact, viz., that the land-man ratio is continuously declining because of increase in population. This is but natural as the increase in population is very much more than the increase in cultivated land.

The pressure of population on land is also reflected in a steady increase in the number of agricultural labourers. As the family increases, sub-division of holding leaves each member with a smaller holding which is much below the subsistence level and he accordingly turns into a labourer.

The consequence of a rising pressure of population on land are serious indeed. Overcrowding increases the number of dependents, adds to under-employment and reduces per capita productivity. The saving capacity is reduced since the net contribution to the economy is unfavourable (more consumers and less producers). Land improvement, adoption of improved techniques and capital formation in the farm sector continues to exert its downward pull on an economy which is undeavouring hard to attain a 'self generating' status.

5. POPULATION GROWTH AND FOOD SHORTAGE

Ever since Malthus wrote his celebrated essays on population, attention was focused on the problem of population versus food supply. He said broadly that population increased in geometrical progression and food production increases in arithmetical progression. Therefore, population will always tend to outrun available subsistence. Checks to population growth might be those of 'vice, misery or moral restraint'. But it was not clearly explained by Malthus why the balance is not restored between population and food production. David Ricardo, writing a few years later, made the underlying idea clearer and more plausible, adding successive units of labour to a fixed supply of land would lead to diminishing increments of output. This is one aspect of the famous 'law of diminishing returns'. So as population rises, average output per man would fall. But the views of the classical economists on population and food supply turned out to have been widely over-pessimistic as they did not forsee the great increases in food output due to improved agricultural techniques and the opening up of land to commercial production. This was a development largely made possible by revolutionary change advances in transport. There are instances where both the density of population and the rate of population growth is high but food production is also very high (e.g., in Japan). The main reason is that there the development of science and technology enabled the people to raise food output commensurate with the increase in their own numbers. But the increases in agricultural productivity have not, however, been world-wide. The problem of food shortage is being faced by underdeveloped countries which have failed to respond to the challenge of rapidly growing populations by improving agricultural technology fast enough. In short, food production per capita in the underdeveloped countries, as a group has not risen as fast as population. Consumption levels have been maintained by a reduction of food exports or an increases of imports. The failure of food production in underdeveloped countries were typically more than half the labour force is engaged in agriculture, to keep pace with population growth reflects the very low level of productivity that still remains. Much of the growth of output that has taken place can be attributed to growth in cultivated areas rather than to increases in yield. The possibilities for such increases in the future are much smaller than in the past. If food production is to rise as fast as population growth in the future, the rate of increase of yield will have to be very much greater than in the past. "The main difficulty for an underdeveloped country is how to close the food gap. Even though agricultural production may be increasing, the majority of people are inadequately fed. India, too, has been experiencing a disturbing food economy. It has been called a 'high food drain economy'. We are importing food from other countries which has been a constant strain on our slender foreign exchange resource base. Rising population of India over the last thirty years has kept the per capita availability of cereals almost stable, imports of foodgrains have increased sizeably, and productivity indices present a sad tale.

The foregoing discussion clearly reveals that the problem of population is of much more concern to the emerging underdeveloped and developing economies of Asia, Africa and Latin America. It cripples the drive for economic development because it demands that resources which could be invested to raise the incomes in the future must instead be consumed now, simply to maintain existing standards of living. Even if bold efforts at mobilising resources for intensifying both the production and productivity drive are made, the gaps between 'growth of population' and 'growth of investment' are not covered. This calls for a suitable population policy to be pursued in underdeveloped countries so as to unleash greater resources for real economic development; rather than fritter away the nations' wealth and output to feed the additional population. In an illuminating address to the Board of Governors, the President of the World Bank, Mr. Robert McNamara, observed: "Without a slowing down and control of population explosion, the life awaiting millions upon millions of this planet's future inhabitants will be stunted, miserable and tragic, if you prefer the hackneyed but fitting phrase, of the philosopher Hobbeanasty, brutish and short." In the words of Pearson Commission, "There can be no serious social and economic planning unless the ominous implication of uncontrolled population growth are understood and acted upon." The report further adds: "No other phenomenon casts a darker shadow over the prospects of international development than the staggering growth of population." The Commission stresses that the population problem will not just fade away. It will be resolved either by a sensible solution or untold suffering. Let India take the warning.

SELECT REFERENCES

1. Bose, Ashish: *Environment and Population : Some Ecological and Demographic Implications for Development Planning in Asia,* Paper presented in the Second Asian Population Conference, Tokyo, Nov. 1972, Published in APSS, No. 28, pp. 363-375.
2. Bright Shingh, D: *Economics of Development*, Asia Publishing House, Bombay, 1962.
3. Coale, A.J.: *Population Dilemma*, pp. 50-69.
4. Gunnar, Myrdal: *Asian Drama*, Vol. II, pp. 1464-1470.
5. Hauser, P.M.: *The Population Dilemma*, p. 51.
6. Jain, S.P.: *Indian Population and Development*, New Delhi, NCERT, 1977, p. 180.
7. Kuznets, S.: "Demographic Aspect of Modern Economic Growth", World Population Conference, 1965, Background Papers, Belgrade, WPC/WP/380, p. 1.
8. Scrimshaw, N.S.: Arch, Environ., Health, 1969,

EXAMINATION QUESTIONS

1. Examine the relation between economic growth and population increase.
2. Illustrate with examples how population growth retards economic development.

15

Malthusian Theory of Population

The theory of population as enunciated by T.R. Malthus, a clergyman, may be regarded as the starting point of all modern speculation on the subject. Malthus expressed his views in his book, "An Essay on the Principles of population as it affects the future improvements of society" (1st edn., 1798) which went through several editions. The essay is still a living influence and has been engaging the attention of people in all ages. Close on the heels of this essay on population followed his other books:

(1) Observation on the effects of the Corn law, 1814.
(2) Nature are progress of rent, 1815.
(3) The poor law, 1817.
(4) Measure of value, 1825.
(5) Definitions in political economy, 1827.

Malthus* and His Time

In order to appreciate the writings of Malthus we should have a general idea of the intellectual, social, political and economic conditions in which he lived.

(1) *Industrial revolution.* Malthus witnessed the upsurge of industrial revolutions where industries prospered at the expenses of agriculture leading to lopsided development. Beside the evils of the capitalism like economic inequality, widespread unemployment, stark poverty, starvation, exploitation, business fluctuations, etc. reared their ugly heads. The resulting poverty enveloped the whole country. The entire nation suffered from acute poverty on account of the imbalance between population and food supply, though reliable statistic on population was not available.

(2) *Deterioration of the economic condition.* When Malthus lived the British economy was passing through the worst form of economic

*Thomas Robert Malthus was born in England in 1766 and died in 1834. He had a distinguished under-graduate career at Cambridge University and entered the Church of England as a Minister in 1979. He was Professor of History and Economics from 1806 until his death in 1834.

crisis. Widespread famine, disease, poverty, squalor and unemployment prevailed all around. Agriculture was passing through a lean period especially towards the latter half of the eighteenth century in contrast to the prosperity of the initial period of the 18th century. Agricultural slide down put a heavy burden on the society.

(3) *Views of Mercantialists and Physiocrats.* Mercantialism and Physiocracy were the main prevailing systems of West Europe in the 18th century. Mercantialists regarded that a nation's strength depended on the extent to which it was economically self-sufficient and upon the numbers of its people. Thompson and Lewis put the mercantialists view thus: "Numbers were believed to ensure both economic and military strength." Similarly physiocrats believed it unwise and harmful to put artificial curb on population, according to them is to violate the natural order.

(4) *Influence of William Godwin.* Malthus was profoundly influenced by William Godwin. Godwin's book "Enquiry concerning political justice and its influence on morals and happiness" appeared in 1793. Godwin attributed the root of all human misery to administrative inefficiency, bad laws, corrupt rulers, greedy employers and so forth. Thus if some of the man's institutions were abolished and some reformed, suffering would disappear. As a result man's very nature would undergo a radical organic change so that he would no longer be his worst enemy. Godwin emphasised that thus man's passions would be subdued, his vices would disappear, his thoughts would become exalted and he would be establishing an earthly paradise.

The French thinker Condereet also subscribed to the utopian views projected by Godwin, Malthus opposed the utopian views. He did not believe that man was likely to undergo any significant biological change. He believed that man's sexual passion and his basic impulses were likely to remain what they had been always. The structure created by the utopians seemed to Malthus extremely flimsy.

(5) *The idea of human progress.* The concept of purely static order, in which man was a play thing of destiny, was slowly changing during Malthus time. The French revolution had made thoughtful men to sit and ponder on man's future. This breeze of dynamic order inspired Malthus to visualise the change in a dynamic pattern.

(6) *The Discovery of Natural Laws.* Some men believed in the productive efficiency of man and his nature due to the discovery of natural laws. It was also felt by some that these natural laws might also operate to determine human behaviour. On the other hand,

some philosophers held that man himself was not subject to any natural law of growth. Malthus did not believe in the rapid perfectibility of human nature which prompted him to propound his principle of population.

(7) *Influence of contemporary thinkers.* Among the contemporary thinkers who inspired Malthus, mention must be made of Sir Mathew Helay, David Hume, Joseph Townshend, Sir Walter Raliey and Robert Wilas. They all accepted the fact that birth rate tends to outstrip death rate which if unchecked will spell disaster to mankind. Sir Walter Railey felt that population increase will invariably exceed the ideal number and the surplus population will die of disease, hunger and war. Sir Mathew Haley in his 'primitive organisation of mankind' shed light on the geometric ratio and concluded that every couple is capable of producing 20 issues in their life span but on an average they produce only 6 children. Their views have helped Malthus in giving concrete shape to his views.

The immediate inspiration was the daily argument between Malthus and his father at breakfast. His father held the perfectionist view that the human race was getting better every day. Finally the younger Malthus become so agitated that he wrote a book that was an instantaneous best seller.

Some scholars treat Malthus' work as a reply to Adam Smith. James Voner felt that the book of Malthus should have been captioned 'An Essay on the Poverty of Nations' as a rejoinder to Smith's book 'The Wealth of Nations'.

MALTHUS POPULATION THEORY

Malthus principle of population is as follows:

(1) Assumptions

(*i*) Food is necessary to the existence of man.

(*ii*) Passion between the sexes is necessary and will remain nearly in its present state.

(*iii*) There is direct relation between standard of living and child bearing.

(*iv*) Law of diminishing returns operates in agriculture.

STATEMENT OF THE THEORY

Malthus states, "population, when unchecked increases in a geometrical ratio. Subsistence increases only in an arithematic ratio."

According to him the power of population is indefinitely greater than the power in the earth to produce subsistence for man. A slight acquaintance with numbers will show the immensity of the first power in comparison to the second.

Population Increase at Geometric Progression

Malthus first took the observation of Benjamin Franklin that in American colonies where resources were abundant population tended to double every 25 years or so. Thus starting from 1 population in successive period of 25 years will be 1, 2, 4, 8, 16, 32, 64, 128, 256. The increase becomes so large that there is no space in the world for all the people to stand. *OX* axis depicts the period in years and *OY* axis shows population increases. The population curve rises from the left to the right as indicated in the (Fig. 1) through *P* curve. Malthus did not say that population would increase at these rates. This was only its tendency if unchecked.

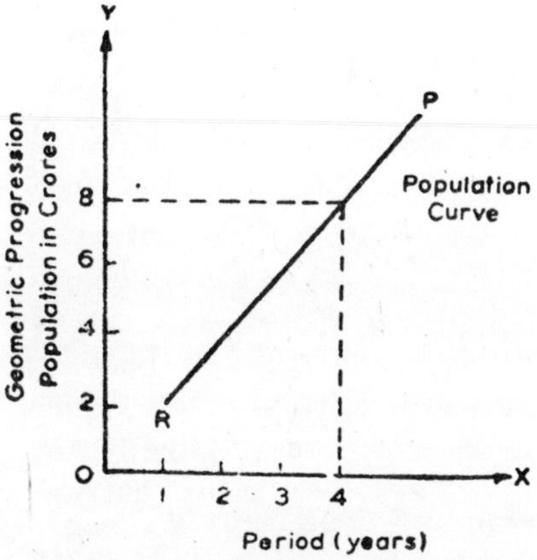

Fig. 1.

The geometric progression (G.P.) is a sequence of terms (g^1, g^2, g^t+1) in which each term is the same multiple of its predecessor.

$$g^2/g^1 = g^3/g^2 = g^t + 1/g^t = \beta$$

If, $\beta = 1 + 1 > 1$ the term grows like compound interest.

Food Supply Increases in Arithmetical Progression

Food supply increases in a slow arithmetical progression (A.P.) due to the operation of the law of diminishing returns. Thus the supply in successive similar periods will be 1, 2, 3, 4, 5, 6, 7, 8, 9 (after 200 years.)

Food supply is presented (Fig. 2) on *OY* axis and period of time in years on the *OX* axis. The 45 per cent angle (*OF*) line shows the directly proportionate relation between food supply and the period of time. An arithmatic progression is a sequence (a, a^2, a^3, a^e, a^t+1) in which the difference between each term and its predecessor is the same constant ($a^1 - a^2 = a^t + 1 - a^t = X$).

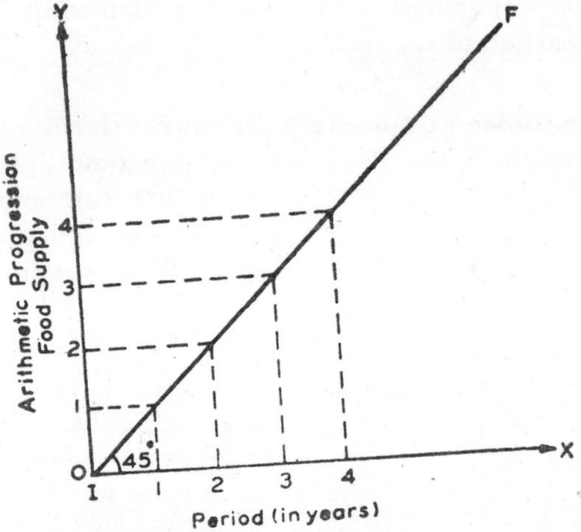

Fig. 2. Diagrammatic presentation of food supply increases.

Disequilibrium between Population and Food Supply

Since population increases in geometrical progression and the food supply in arithmetical progression, population tends to outrun food supply. As Malthus wrote "A perfectly happy and virtuous community will double every twenty-five years, but there can be no similar increases in their food. The best lands are taken up first,

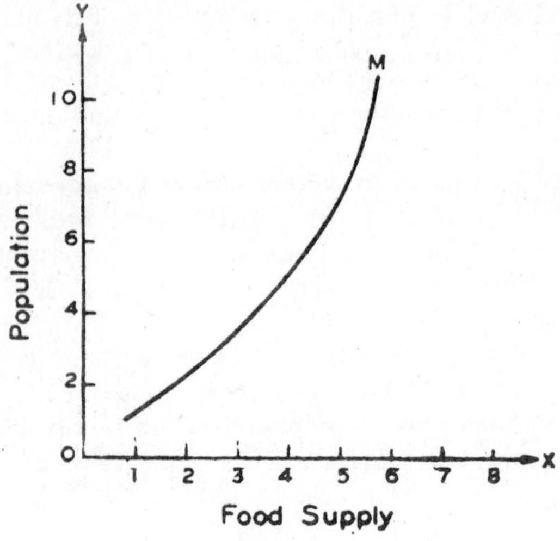

Fig. 3.

then the next best, then the inferior, at last the worst, at each stage the amount of food increases in a slow arithmetical ratio, man himself increases in a quick geometrical ratio, unless want and vice stop him."

Thus an imbalance is created which leads to over population. This is depicted in Fig. 3.

Control of Population

Malthus pointed out that there are two kinds of checks to correct the imbalance between population and food supply. He suggested the positive and preventive checks.

(*a*) *Positive checks.* In his first edition Malthus puts emphasis on positive checks that acts to increase the death rate like pestilence, femine, diseases, war, natural calamities, vicious customs with regard to women, great cities, unwholesome manufactures, luxury, etc. Malthus felt that, "The table of nature is laid for limited number of guests and those who come uninvited must starve." He believed that the positive checks resulted basically from the pressure of population on subsistence. Positive checks bring in its train extreme misery. It brings about a short period equilibrium between population and food supply which is disturbed sooner or later leading to the Malthusian cycle: Over population→Positive checks→High birth rates→Over population→Positive checks→Over population.

(*b*) *Preventive checks.* The second kind of check to the growth of population Malthus called the preventive or prudential check, because it operated to bring down the birth rate. In Malthus' words: "The preventive checks include late marriages, chastity and other similar measures aimed at checking population growth deliberately." Preventive checks fall into two parts:

(*i*) *Moral restraint.* Clergyman Malthus advocated moral restraint with prudential postponement of early marriage until a family could be supported. According to Malthus the struggle for existence is an illustration of the wisdom of Nature, which keeps poor people from becoming soft and lazy. He felt that celibacy is the only way out to escape the fury of positive checks. He advised women to remain unmarried till the age of 28.

(*ii*) *Artificial restraints.* It includes all modern devices of birth control. Neo-Malthusians emphasised its use on a wide scale, while Malthus treated them as vice or sin.

According to Malthus the two checks are the true causes of the slow increase of population in all the states of modern Europe. According to him preventive checks are always in operation in a civilized society, for positive checks are crude. He believed that preventive checks would never be sufficiently strong to eliminate the operation of the positive checks arising mainly from the pressure of population on subsistence. Man's sex passions and his material needs were in essential conflict.

Subsistence Level of Wages

Malthus believed that population always tended to grow to a size which could yield just barely subsistence level of wages. Vice and misery would prevent population from increasing beyond subsistence. Moral restraint can result in restraining the population from growing more rapidly than wages.

Reliance on Diminishing Returns

Malthus preached that while population increased as in G.P., means of subsistence grew as in A.P. The reason for slow growth of means of subsistence was the application of the law of diminishing returns. Provided that the arts of agriculture do not change, when capital and labour is successively increased by equal amounts, total output increases at a diminishing rate. The marginal return to successive doses of labour and capital goes on declining. Gide and Rist make a significant observation: "It means as if the law of diminishing returns were the real basis of the Malthusian laws, although Malthus himself makes no express mention of it."

The theory can be illustrated with the help of a chart.

Malthusian Theory of Population

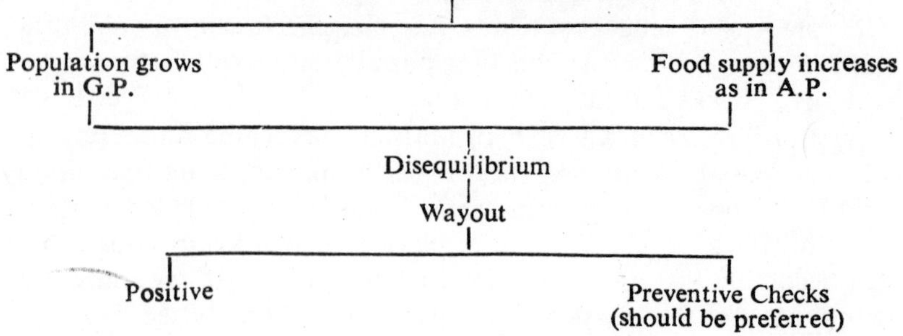

The theory of population can be summarised into three propositions: (1) population is necessarily limited by the means of subsistence; (2) population invariably increases where the means of subsistence increase unless prevented by some very powerful checks and (3) those checks which keep population on a level with means of subsistence are all resolvable into moral restraint, vice and misery.

Criticism of the Malthusian Doctrine

The Malthusian thesis was an unwarranted, hasty generalisation which was logically unsound. Naturally Malthus has been the target of scathing criticism by both friends and foes. Among those who joined the fray, the names of Godwin, Cannan, Nicholson, Membort figure prominantly. Godwin observed about it as "That black and terrible demon which is always ready to stifle the hopes of humanity." Malthus himself regarded his first essay as an unsatisfactory statement of the principle of population. Therefore he revised and rewrote the first edition. It seems strange, therefore, that many of his critics have written as though they were unaware that the 1st edition of the essay had ever been revised, expanded and modified. Despite the statistics covering many countries incorporated in his later editions, it is felt that his views were over-simplifications. The theory is criticised on the following grounds:

(1) *The basic assumptions of the Malthusian theory are not correct.* (*a*) The operations of the law of diminishing returns can be postponed indefinitely. Malthusian notion on food supply is based on a static economic law, i.e., the law of diminishing returns. Malthus could not foresee the miracles technical progress over a period of time which have stayed the law of diminishing returns. As a resuit of which food supply has increased much faster than the arithmetic progression.

(*b*) There is no direct relationship between sexual instinct and child bearing: In fact the desire to have children is a noble objective based on social, religious and geographical conditions, while the sex instinct is a base natural desire.

(*c*) The postulation that an improvement in standard of living leads to an increase in population is not borne out by facts. The choice before an educated couple is to have a 'baby' or a 'baby Austin' and very often it is the car that wins. The greater the malnutrition the more the fecundity and frenzy for breeding.

(*d*) It is not correct to presume that sexual urge remains the same in human beings. It changed according to circumstances and the spread of education nutrition, entertainment, etc. Improved standard of living have resulted in a decline in sexual instinct.

(2) *The mathematical form of the theory is not correct.* Emperical evidences do not corroborate the rate of increase in food supply and population in 25 years as visualised by Malthus. Rather, the

food supply has increased more than in the arithmetical progression. This criticism looses much of its sting as Malthus used it in the first edition to make his principle clear and deleted it in his second edition.

(3) *Malthus could not foresee the opening up of new area.* He failed to perceive the opening up of new areas of America. New Zealand, Australia, Argentina, etc., where extensive farming of virgin land led to increased production of food. Consequently, countries like England, France, etc. have been provided with plenty of supply of cheep food. Rapid improvement in the means of transport acted as a catalyst in the process; a factor overlooked by Malthus. No wonder the spectre of famine has become a thing of the past.

(4) *History does not support the fears of Malthus.* Malthus has proved to be a false prophet as his worst predictions were believed by subsequent events. In some countries like France the rate of increase in population was very slow. In other countries the increase in population was not a problem because growth in popution was accompanied by increased national income. His pessimistic prophesy that misery will stalk these countries if they fail to check the growth of population through preventive checks proved wrong.

(5) *Positive checks are not due to over-populution.* National calamities are not peculiar to over-populated countries. They visit even thinly populated countries such as France, Japan, etc.

(6) *Every increase in population is not harmful.* Malthus belief that every increase in population is harmful is not correct. Up to the optimum level an increase in population should be welcomed as it will benefit the country to increase its per capita income rapidly.

(7) *Population is not related to food supply but to total wealth.* Malthusian theory is based on a weak relationship between population and food supply. As a matter of fact the right relationship is between population and total wealth. If a country is materially rich it can feed its millions well by importing food stuffs in exchange for its products or money. Britain is a typical example as it imports all its food requirement from Holland, Denmark, Belgium and Argentina in exchange for its products.

(8) *Increase in population is the result of a decline in birth.* The Malthusian theory is one-sided. It takes the increase in population as the result of a rising birth rate, whereas population has grown considerably the world over due to decline in death rate. Malthus could not foresee the tremendous advancement of medical sciences which have controlled fatal diseases and made human life longer. This is true more particularly in the case of India where Malthusian

theory is said to operate.

(9) *Preventive checks do not mean moral restraint.* Malthus suggested moral restraint, celibacy, etc. to contain population. He could not imagine the modern devices of contraceptives which are being extensively employed in checking population. Moral restraint alone cannot help control the increase in population, which Malthus suggested.

(10) *Malthus failed to recognise the manpower aspect in population.* Malthus thought that every baby coming to the world is a burden on society. According to Cannan, "A baby comes to the world not only with a mouth and a stomach but also with a pair of hands. It means that an increase in population means an increase in manpower which may tend to augement production.

Population should be viewed in relation to production. As pointed out by Seligmen: "The problem of population is not merely one of mere size but of efficient production and equitable distribution.

(11) *Malthus held the poor people responsible for their misery.* Malthus felt that the poor people tried to increase their number faster. Malthus said that "The poor are themselves the cause of their poverty." Karl Marx and other socialist writers took strong exception to this view and held exploitation of labour, unequal distribution, defective Government policies, etc., responsible for the poverty of the mass.

(12) *Malthus adopted the inductive method in his principle.* Malthus extensively employed statistical data pertaining to few countries to evolve his thesis. The inductive method which he has used cannot be of universal application.

(13) *Malthus has taken one point of time into consideration.* Malthus has forgotten that times can change and when it takes place food production can also increase.

(14) *Other criticisms.* (*a*) Professor Haney observed that Malthus expounded the theory under the influence of his surroundings. "He knew what had happened, he show that was happening, but influenced by his surroundings his vision as to what was to happen was unduly obscured," stated Haney.

(*b*) Malthus has taken it for granted that the human beings are invariably vegetarians. The reality is that large number of people are non-vegetarians who subsist on fish, meat, etc.

(*c*) Marx accused Malthus of being a plagiarist by profession. He observed: "He borrowed non-sense from earlier writers (Theory of Population from Rev. Townshed). His geometric and arithmetic progressions were purely chimerical hypotheses. He copied and para-phrased Rev. Townshed like a slavish plagiarist."

(*d*) Winston Churchill and Henry Villard were of the view that a stage is bound to come when growth of population growth will automatically be checked and will not follow the geometric progression.

(*e*) Malthus thought that every child born in a family will survive. But in communities where birth rate is high death rate is also very high. Prof. Gide said: "Germs are extraordinarily prolific but their undue multiplication is pitilessly retarded by a law which demands the death of certain proportion so that the life like a well regulated reservoir always remains at a mean level, the terrible gaps made by death is being replenished by a new flow."

Evaluation. According to Samuelson: "Nevertheless the Germs of truth of his doctrines are still important for understanding the population behaviour of India, Haite, China and other parts of the Globe." Malthusian doctrine may not be applicable to West European countries, but it is useful in understanding the population problems of underdeveloped countries including Asia, Africa and South America. Besides, the people of Europe were made wiser by Malthus who warned them of the evils of over-population and they used measures to check it.

The widespread use of contraceptive is an indication of its vitality. Samuelson viewed: "Going through several editions, the book influences the thinking of the people of all over the world." It is still a living influence today. Malthus' views depend directly on the law of diminishing returns and continue to have relevance.

J.B. Clark says that "The Malthusian theory of population has been so often refuted as to prove its vitality." Marshal and Pigon incorporated his views in their theories. Keynes was forced to write about, "Some Economic consequences of the Doctrine of population." The Malthusian thesis was the main factor behind the problem of declining population in France. Malthus' conclusion was used so widely by the conservatives in the political controversy over the poor laws. In short the truth in the views of Malthus can be summarised as below:

(1) The forecast of Malthus is an approximation to truth in the less-developed countries. The rising population of India is a concrete proof of his influence. India's population increased at the rate of 1.33 per cent per year in the Nineteen-sixties and 2.28 per cent in the seventies.

(2) Opinions also bolstered the argument that trade unions could

not improve the welfare of workers.

(3) In the affluent countries like England, France and America the extensive use of methods of birth control and abortion indicates the influence of Malthus. Even today the computers make head lines when it spells out the limits of growth by a more elaborate simulation of Malthus geometric and arithmetic progressions.

(4) Edward East in his book 'Mankind at the cross roads' expressed the view that if the present trend in population continued the available arable land throughout the world will be insufficient to meet the food requirement of the teeming millions.

Walker worte that "The Malthusian theory is applicable to all communities without consideration of colour and place. Malthusianism has stood unshattered and impregnable amid all the controversy that has raged around it."

According to Thompson and Lewis: "Malthus deserves great credit for bringing this problem to the attention of people as well as for the calm and objective manner in which he analysed the facts available to him and thus increased our understanding of an extremely important element affecting human welfare."

MALTHUSIAN THEORY AND ITS APPLICATION IN INDIA

It has already been stated above that the Malthusian theory of population applies in India. This view is supported by a number of considerations.

(1) *High rate of population growth*. Population increase rate is outstripping the growth in food supply in India. Every year a new Australia is added to our conutry or in other words 1 crore 30 lakhs more people are added to the existing population. Population is increasing at a rate of 2.42 per cent an year while food production was 8 crores tonnes in 1960-61, 10 crores tonnes in 1973-74, 12 crores tonnes in 1979-80 and 14 crores tonnes in 1983-84.

(2) *Low level of food production in the country*. A brief study of last few years food production reveals that the position is none too rosy. We have been forced on several occasions in the past to depend on food imports though at present we could build up sufficient buffer.

(3) *Positive checks are in operation*. The disequilibrium between food supply and birth rate alone does not prove the operation of Malthus' doctrine. Recurring floods, disease, etc., also lends credence to his thesis.

(4) *Growing emphasis on family planning*. Under the family plan-

ning schemes intense efforts are made to popularise the methods of birth control. This is positive proof of the influence of Malthusian doctrine.

(5) *Enactment of law.* Statutory provision of minimum age of marriage and family size. is an acceptance of the need to keep the Malthusian ghost at bay.

(6) *Law of diminishing returns.* The traditional way of cultivation and the operation of the law of diminishing returns in many parts of the country are facts supporting the operation of Malthusian devil in India.

(7) *Mounting unemployment.* Rising tide of unemployment, low standard of living, high incidence of birth and death rates proves the validity of Malthus in India. In the light of the above facts it can be concluded that the Malthusian theory applies to India to a great extent. During the last few years especially after 1975 as a result of the adoption of Smt. Indira Gandhi's 20-point programme substantial improvement took place in production, distribution, wage rates, land distribution, etc. If the trend continues the Malthusian spectre of excess population could be held in check.

(8) India has a very low per capita income. At the end of the Third Plan, the per capita income was the same as at the beginning of the plan. The reason was that the slow growth in national income was eaten up entirely by the increase in numbers over the plan period.

Thus we are forced to regretfully conclude that the Malthus doctrine is valid in India and the Damocles' sword of rapidly increasing population will be a drag on our progress for a number of years to come.

SELECT REFERENCES

1. Bonar, James: *Malthus and His Work*, The Macmillan Co., New York, 1924, Field, James A.: *Essays on Population and Other Papers*, The University of Chicago Press, Chicago, 1931.
2. Glass, D.V. (ed.): *Introduction to Malthus*, John Wiley & Sons Inc., New York, 1950.
3. Godwin, William: "Of Population : An Euquiry Concerning the Power of Increase in the Numbers of Mankind". Being an Answer to Mr. Malthus's Essay on that subject, Longman, Hurst, Rees, Orme, and Brown, London, 1820.
4. Griffith, Grosvenor Talbot: *Population Problems of the Age of Malthus*, Cambridge University Press, London, 1926.
5. Malthus, Thomas Robert: *An Essay on Population*, 2 Vols., J.M. Dent &

Sons Ltd., Publishers, London; E.P. Dutton & Co. Ltd., London, 1926 A Facsimile reprint.
6. Meek, Ronald L.: *Marx and Engels on Malthus*, London, Lawrence and Wishart, 1953.
7. Place, Francis: Illustrations and Proofs of the Principle of Population, Including an Examination of the Proposed Remedies of Mr. Malthus, and a Reply to the Objections of Mr. Godwin and others, ed. by Norman E. Himes, Houghton Mifflin Company, Boston, 1930.
8. Spiegel, Henry W.: *The Development of Economic Thought: Great Economists in Perspective*, John Wiley & Sons Inc., New York, 1952.
9. Stangeland, Charles Emil: *Pre-Malthusian Doctrines of Population: A Study in the History of Economic Theory*, Columbia University Press, The Macmillan Company (agents), New York, 1904.
10. Thompson, Warren S. & David T. Lewis: *Population Problems* (Fifth edition), New York: McGraw Hill Book Company, 1976, Chapters 2 and 3.

EXAMINATION QUESTIONS

1. Examine critically the population theory of Malthus.
2. 'The Malthusian theory has lost much of its strength for the present society'. Explain the reasons.
3. Explain the Malthusian theory of population. How far is it applicable to an underdeveloped country lie India?
4. 'The Malthusian theory has been so often refuted as to prove its vitality'. Examine the statement.
5. 'The Malthusian theory of population was a product of contemporary situation'. Explain this statement and bring out the salient features of the Malthusian theory of population.

16

Neo-Malthusianism

Neo-Malthusians belong to that group of economists and demographers who have blind faith in whatsoever Malthus said about growth of population. Neo-Malthusianism is a cult or movement started by the followers of Malthus' views. They believed in checking the growth of population without any restraint on unfettered sexual pleasures. The leading exponent of this view was Francis Place, who popularised foetal killing in 1920. New Malthusianism originated in 1854 when Dr. Drysdale brought out his famous book: 'Elements of Social Science'. He established the Malthusian Society in 1877, which gave further impetus to neo-Malthusian movement in England and America. Supporters of this movement regarded themselves descendents of Malthus and propagated their views with spiritual zeal. Marie Stopes of Britain and Margret Stanger of America were prominant among the neo-Malthusians.

In recent times doctors, social scientists, political scientists, economists, etc. have shown keen interest to the neo-Malthusian views.

Malthus was a clergy man, belonging to the Roman Catholic Church, who shunned the use of artificial means of birth control which he treated as sin. He was obsessed by the impending economic hell, but the measures of control which he suggested were within the religious codes. He stood against the use of contraceptives. Neo-Malthusians ushered in quite radical views of birth control without, in any way supressing sensuous pleasures. They stood for the use of artificial methods of birth control including chemical, physical and other modern family planning techniques. To them any price will not be too much if it could reduce birth rates.

They did not believe that the desire for sex pleasure and the desire for offspring were one and the same. They have adopted the stand that the social, religious and cultural attitudes of the people are rapidly changing and the desire to reduce the number of children is gaining approval every where. The following factors have been cited to buttress their view.

(1) Women would like to escape the pangs of births.

(2) Many women have come to regard marriage and child bearing and rearing as a hindrance to their freedom.

(3) Ladies would not like to have children because it will deform their body shape and make them unattractive.

(4) The growing individualistic and happiness seeking attitude militated against regimentation and family life.

(5) The growing importance of State social security measures has provided sufficient gurantee against old age which prompted many to remain unmarried and lead a carefree life.

(6) The declining of faith in religion is a positive factor which reduced the importance of marriage and family life.

Gide observed, "were Malthus now alive, he would not be a neo-Malthusian He would not have pardoned his disciples the perpetration of sexual frauds, which enable man to be freed from the responsibilities which Nature intended him to bear."

Points of difference between Malthus and Neo-Malthusians may be discussed as under:

(1) Malthus did not see any difference between the desire for sex and the desire for children, where as neo-Malthusians attach differences to them. To them sex desire is natural whereas desire to procreate is based on religious, social and cultural consideration. As stated by Gide. The first is mere animal instinct which arouse the most impetus of passions and is common to all man. The second is frequently social and religious in origin assuming different form according to exigencies of time and place." The Hindus want to have children because a childless person is condemned for hell. The poor views every child as a potential bread winner. The Muslims want to increase their tribe.

(2) Malthus accepted that sex urge is a fundamental human nature, but he has advocated moral restraint etc., and self-control. Neo-Malthusians believed that the urge of sex is natural which should not be suppressed. Any attempt to check the sex desire will create mental agony to the people. This will force people to adopt evil practices. Malthus firmly believed that artificial means of birth control were wrong and it amounted to sin. He observed: "The restraints which I have recommended are quite of a different character. They are not only pointed out by religion but tend in the most marked manner to stimulate industry.

(3) Neo-Malthusians encouraged the use of contraceptives because with their use the human beings can satisfy their sexual desire without the risk of child birth. They felt that all sections of the societv -equire birth control. They argued that birth of children by

unmarried mothers should be checked as it will otherwise create evil consequence to society. A married woman can maintain her health if she is not exposed to frequent child bearing. Population growth rate will be checked automatically and the nation will move towards prosperity.

(4) Malthus believed that the tendency of population growth to outstrip food supply is a natural phenomenon. Neo-Malthusians held that with the use of modern scientific means and methods it is possible to check population growth and increase food production in comparison to population growth.

Criticism of Neo-Malthusian Views

Critics felt that the use of contraceptives will lead to degeneration of women and create mental, physical and moral suffering. It will have deleterious social consequences. Womanhood will be spoiled at the very source and result in many diseases among women. Extensive use of birth control may lead to the extermination of human race itself. As pertinently observed by Bertrand Russel: "What is regrettable at present is not the decline of birth rate in itself, but the fact that the decline is the greatest in the best elements of the population."

SELECT REFERENCES

As in Previous Chapter.

EXAMINATION QUESTIONS

1. Malthus is dead, Malthusianism is immortal'. In the light of this statement bring out the main thoughts of neo-Malthusians.
2. 'If Malthus were alive he would not have been a neo-Malthusian'. Explain this statement.

17

The Optimum Theory of Population

The optimum theory of population is the product of reaction to the Malthusian theory of population. The theory taken into consideration the entire economic aspects related to population, economic conditions, etc., and tries to lay down desirable norms regarding population. Optimum population refers to a State where the population is neither more nor less than the socially desirable level.

Origin and Development of the Theory

Prof. Edward West in his 'Essay on the application of capital to land' discussed the relation between population and manpower. Prof. Henry Sidgewick in his book 'The principles of political economy' appears to have given the idea of optimum population a new orientation. He pointed out that just as a firm maximises its production when the factors of production are combined in ideal proportions, similarly the whole economy will be maximising production by the judicious combination of productive factors. The idea of optimum is implicit in the views of Sidgewick, though he does not explicitly state the word.

The credit for having introduced the term 'optimum' in the field of population and presenting the theory goes to Prof. Edwin Cannan, who published his 'Wealth' in 1924. The idea was popularised by Robbins, Dalton and Carr Saunders.

Unlike the Malthusian theory, the optimum theory does not establish relationship between population and food supply. Rather it is concerned with the relation between the size of population and wealth production. The Malthusian theory is a general one applicable to every country irrespective of its economic conditions. On the other hand, optimum theory is a particular theory which studies the population problem in the light of economic condition.

For every region it is essential to have some minimum population to maintain and run essential services. Maximum population should be viewed separately for each section of society. In primitive society death rate and birth rate remain high. If both are equal then the population will remain in temporary equilibrium. But such a balance is less favourable than one attained by population planning. It is accepted that every country must conceive an optimum population and should try to hold it.

Assumption of the Theory

1. When the population grows the ratio between total population and working population remains the same.

2. Production per head of working population and the hours of work remain constant.

3. When at a point of time, the population of a country increases with that of natural resources, technical know-how and capital do not change. So the law of diminishing returns begins to operate after some time. When the factors are not combined in suitable proportion, it would not be possible to maximise production.

The exponents of the theory believed that from the national point of view, population should be treated as labour force and every increase in the labour force affords an opportunity to exploit the material resources available in the country.

Definition

1. *Boulding K.E.* "The population at which the standard of life is a maximum is called the optimum population."

2. *Prof. Dalton.* "Optimum population is that which gives the maximum income per head."

3. *Robbins.* "Optimum population is that which makes the maximum returns possible."

4. *Hicks.* "The optimum population is that level of population which would make output per head a maximum."

5. *Carr Saunders.* "The optimum population is that which produces maximum economic welfare. Maximum economic welfare is not necessarily the same as maximum real income per head but for all practical purposes they may be taken as equivalent."

6. *Prof. Cannan.* "At any given time (in a country) there is what may be called a point of maximum return when the amount of labour is such that both an increase or decrease in it would diminish proportionate returns. If population is not large enough to bring all industry up to this point, returns will be less than they might be and remedy is increase of population; if on the other hand population is so great that the point has been passed, returns are again less than they might be and remedy is decrease in population."

7. *Imre Ferenezi.* "Quantitatively, it implies a set of economic and social conditions which will allow each citizen an opportunity to

satisfy his fundamental needs according to certain minimum standards. Qualitatively, it means a population programme which, while guaranteeing the continued maintenance of a people, takes into account the eugenic as well as ethnic improvement of the population. Obviously a fixed optimum is an impossibility."

If we were to examine these views, we find that their emphasis was on different aspects of the optimum size. Cannan, Robbins, Eric Roll, etc. view the optimum population from the maximisation of production. Robbin's definition takes into consideration the entire productive activity of the economy in relation to population. Both Cannan and Robbins neglect the distributional aspects of the problem. Maximisation of production is not enough for the optimum level of population, in addition what is required is its equitable distribution.

Dalton's view is more scientific and realistic. Dalton's definition of maximisation of income per head fulfils both the requirements of an ideal population.

Carr Saunders' definition in terms of maximisation of economic welfare presupposes the making of value judgements regarding incomé distribution and composition of output.

INTERPRETATION OF THE OPTIMUM POPULATION

Population is to be seen as the manpower required for exploitation of the natural resources and promote economic growth. As long as the optimum point is not reached the nation shall not be able to exploit the natural resources properly and fully. On the other hand when the population crosses that point, then the nation would not get maximum return because the burden on other resources will tend to be heavy and become disproportionate. At the optimum point the resources are fully utilised which gives the ideal combination of factors of production. It also helps in suitable specialisation and division of labour. Consequently the national gross production and income per capita become highest. It is the point at which the external economics are fully utilised and the diseconomics have not set in.

The gist of optimum theory as an empirical theory is very scientific. Given a criterion, the theory asserts that the function $y(p)$ increases over a range of low value of P, reaches the maximum and decreases as P increases.

$$Y = y(P)$$

Where y = per capita real income

P = Population.

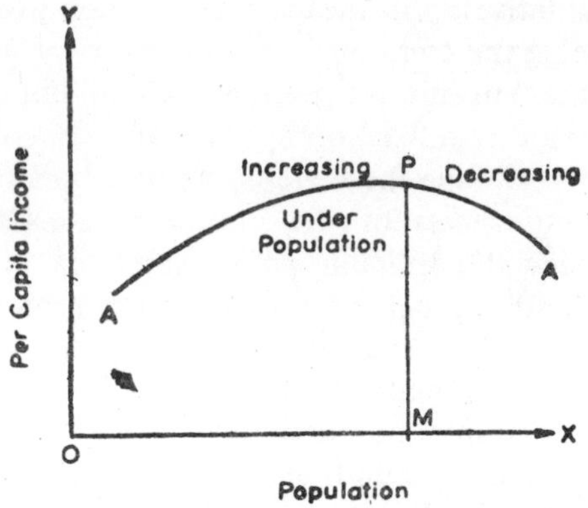

Fig. 1.

The optimum population function shown above could be represented as a simple curve concave to X axis with a single hump. The Point P shows the optimum point at which the per capita income is highest. Up to the point 'P' growth in population is accompanied by a corresponding increase in per capita income. However beyond the point OM, further increase in population results in a decline in per capita income.

This could be explained with reference to the laws of production. To begin with the law of increasing returns operate under which as the population increases marginal and average productivity too increase. At the point of optimum population the law of constant returns take over and with further increase in population, the law of diminishing returns tends to overtake the economy.

Prof. Dalton's Formula

Prof. Dalton is of the view that the theory is not static. His analysis is based on the volatility of population in consonance with the changing times and circumstances. For numerical measurement of the maladjustment between the actual and optimum population at a point of time Dalton has given the following formula:

$$M = \frac{A-O}{O}$$

Where, M=Maladjustment in population
A=Actual Population.
O=Optimum population.

If M is positive then it is an indication of over-population. On the contrary if M is negative it is to be concluded that the population is below optimum. If M is zero, it shows the optimum or ideal state.

For example if the actual population of a country is 60 crores, optimum population is 50 crores, then maladjustment:

$$M = \frac{60-50}{50} = \frac{10}{50} = +0.2$$

It means that 'M' is positive which requires corrective measures.

Comparison of the Views of Dalton and Robbins

Dalton holds the view that the optimum population is that ideal size population which provides maximum income per head. Any expansion or dimunition in the size of the population above or below the optimum level will pull down income per capita. Given the state of natural resources, techniques of production and the available volume of capital stock, there is a definite size of population corresponding the highest per capita income. Other things remaining the same, any shift in the population from this norm will bring about a fall in per capita income. When the per capita income rises with an increase in population it is a sign of under-population. If the per capita income falls it is a sign of over-population.

Prof. Robbins holds somewhat different views about optimum size of population. According to him the population which just makes the maximum returns possible is the optimum population. According to him increase in population is desirable to the extent to which there is increase in production. Robbins has laid more emphasis on the maximisation of total income while Dalton's emphasis was on per capita income. As long as the people get enough to meet their day to day requirement it should be deemed to be within the desirable optimum population. Every increase in population is welcome according to Robbins as long as the people are engaged in some productive work.

Prof. Robbins viewed the whole question of population from the national income point, whereas Dalton adopted a stance in which the emphasis was on per capita income. Prof. Robbins adopted a subjective outlook while Dalton approached the whole issue from an objective angle.

The optimum population as conceived by Robbins is some what higher than the optimum number on which Prof. Dalton has focussed his attention. Robbins tried to establish a causative nexus between production and consumption while Dalton on the contrary took pains to forge a link between production and distribution.

Optimum Level is not a Static Concept

The optimum level is not a fixed point "if changes with change in any of the factors assumed to the constant. For example if the technique of production undergoes improvement, the output per head will increase resulting in a shifting up of the optimum population. With the tapping of additional sources of natural resources, it is likely that the optimum point will be higher in future than today. Thus optimum is a volatile moving point. According to Cannan: "At any given time increase of labour up to a certain point is attended by increasing proportionate returns and beyond that point further increase of labour is attended by diminishing proportionate returns." The point of maximum returns is the point of optimum. This is illustrated in Fig. 2.

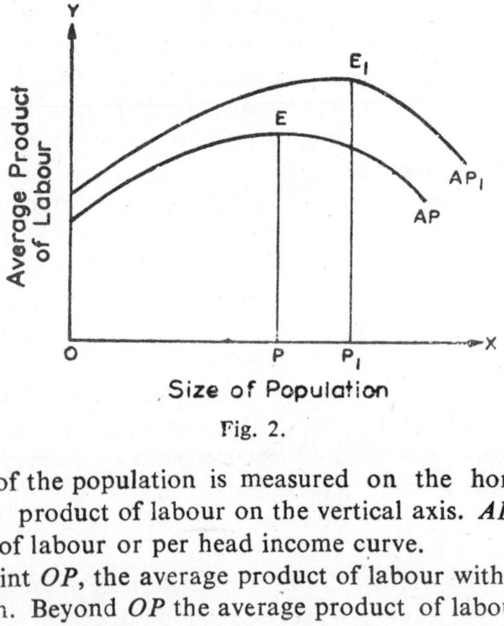

Fig. 2.

The size of the population is measured on the horizontal axis and average product of labour on the vertical axis. *AP* is the average product of labour or per head income curve.

Up to point *OP*, the average product of labour with an increase in population. Beyond *OP* the average product of labour starts falling. Hence at a population *OP* average product or income per capita (*IP*) is the highest which makes it the optimum population. To the left of *OP*, it is overpopulated.

Due to the introduction of improved techniques of production the average product of labour might increase and push the level of per capita income upward so that the optimum point rises. This is shown with the help of *AP*, curve. It represents higher average production and per head income and point *E*, shows the maximum per capita income at the new optimum level of population *OP*.

It has been observed by Prof. Clark: "In the actual dynamic world of abrupt kaliedoscopic change the quest for the optimum population is likely to prove to be a fruitless search after a will of the wisp that always eludes our grasp."

Views of Carr Saunders

Carr Saunders maintained that man has always striven to attain an optimum number. This optimum is not fixed for all times. He observed: "On the contrary it is constantly varying as the condition referred to vary and as skill has tended to increase throughout history so has the number economically desirable tended to increase." He regards man's growth as wholly within his control. With population growth, specialisation and division of labour will get impetus which increase the income per head. Where the per head income starts falling the optimum point gets disturbed. His treatment of the problem is purely from the economic point of view. He has introduced welfare criteria into his analysis.

CRITICISM OF THE OPTIMUM THEORY

The theory has serious weakness which should not be lost sight of. This has considerably reduced the practical utility and value of the theory.

1. *There is no evidence of optimum level.* It is difficult to say whether there is anything like an optimum population. There is no evidence about the optimum population level in any country. In fact, it is impossible to measure it. Optimum population implies a quantitative and qualitative ideal population for the country. The quantitative aspect implies in addition to age composition other factor like physique, knowledge, intelligence, etc. These variables are subject to change and are related to environment.

2. *Choice of criteria.* The choice of criteria involves considerations other than scientific also. However scientific methods are used to clarify them which is not practical.

3. *Per capita income cannot be correctly measured.* Per capita income is a variable which cannot be measured easily. To find out variation in per head income bristles with insurmountable difficulties. The data on per capita income are often inadequate, misleading and unreliable which make the concept of optimum of doubtful validity.

4. *The theory ignores the distributional aspect of increase in per capita income.* It is not certain that increase in population accompanied by increase in per capita income would usher in an era of

prosperity to the country. On the contrary an increase in wealth often leads to concentration of income in the hands of few rich which will create widespread disparity in income distribution, which may prove harmful to the economy. Thus the optimum theory of population ignores the distributional aspect of increase in per capita income.

5. *The optimum population is a moving point.* The theory is static. The theory assumes that the stock of capital, natural resources, technique of production, etc. are constant. Therefore what is optimum at a point of time may remain so far a period of time. But it is not correct to presume so. When population varies in the real world there is also concomitant variation in technology and organisation. As a result what may be optimum at a point of time might become less or more than the optimum over a period of time. This is illustrated in Fig. 3.

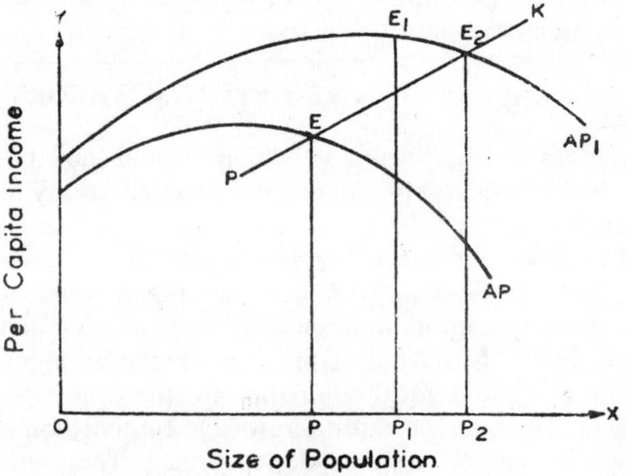

Fig. 3.

Population size is presented on *X* axis and per capita income an *Y* axis.

AP curve is the average product of labour or per capita income curve. Suppose the technique of production improves which shifts the per capita income to AP_1. Consequently, optimum point shifts from *E* to E_2 showing an increase in optimum population from *OP* to OP_2, per capita income rises from *EP* to E_2P_2. The *AP* and AP_1 curves can also shift upward or downward, as a result of rise or fall of productivity. If the locus of all such points like *E*, E_2, etc. are joined by a line, we have the *PK* curve which represents the path of the movement of the optimum theory of population as a result of changes in economic factors. However, if the actual level of population is assumed to be OP_1 and the optimum level OP the country is over populated. If OP_2 is the optimum population, then the country is underpopulated.

6. *This theory has no place in state policies.* The concept of optimum population has no place in State Policies. Employment, output, etc., are sought to be increased with the help of fiscal and monetary policies, but optimum population was not referred to for policy use. Thus the theory has little practical utility.

7. *It is difficult to achieve in practice.* Achieving an optimum population through the exercise of available population policies as well as ascertaining the optimum present formidable difficulties.

8. *Theory neglects social and institutional conditions.* The theory takes into consideration economic factors while social and institutional conditions in a country also influence the level of population. What is optimum from economic view may not may be so from defence consideration of the country. Thus the theory is one sided.

9. *The theory fails to explain the dynamics of population.* The theory merely helps in finding out the population at a point of time. But the theory does not tell us as to why and how the population of the country increased or decreased. So it is not even desirable to call it a population theory.

10. *The theory is purely materialistic.* The theory adopts a purely materialistic outlook in which progress of society is measured in terms of per capita income. Wealth is not an end in itself, but it is only a means to an end.

Prof. Wipple said "A nations true wealth lies not in land and water, not in its forest and mines, not in its flocks and herds, not in its dollars, but in its healthy and happy men, women and children."

11. *The theory is impractical and un-scientific.* The view of optimum population has been criticised by Hicks as of little practical value. Prof. B.K. Sarkar said that it is essentially un-scientific. Paul Mombor says that the theory is of abstract value. G.E.B. Reuter said that it is one of the most sterile idea that ever grew out of our science. Brinley Thomas is of the view that the whole concept is shadowy and elusive.

12. *The concept of optimum has been used in different sense.* Manuel Cottlieb wrote: "Various writers have proposed definitions of optimum in different terms of 'Economic Welfare', 'standard of living', 'real income', constant output, and the total realised desirability. There is also controversy as to whether the optimum should be conceived as 'Economic optimum' or 'Social or spiritual

optimum".

Importance of the Optimum Population Theory

Like the Malthusian theory, critics have pronounced the optimum theory dead from time to time. Nevertheless, there continues to be steady stream of writings on the subject, though it no longer appears to be at the centre of interest. As stated by Gottlieb: "Despite the difficulties in ascertaining a unique value of the optimum at any given time, the theory is asserted to have value in directing attention to the phenomenon of depressing effect of population growth on per capita income and the desirability of investigating the status of various industries in respect to increase or decreasing returns."

The theory is important on the following counts:

1. It stresses the need to control the population and therefore it is useful to support the family planning programmes.

2. It emphasises the need to increase income per head which can contribute to the welfare of the citizens of a country.

3. Equally important is its emphasis on changing the environment according to time and changing conditions to maintain the equilibrium of society and nation.

4. The theory tries to establish earnest connection between population and economic progress.

5. The theory views population as agent of production and points out neither over population nor under population will be beneficial for the country.

6. Its exponents have discussed the whole concept of optimum population on the basis of income per head, which is scientific theorising.

7. It has successfully countered the psycosis that man is a slave of his environment and showed that through judicious combination of factors of production, we can conquer our surroundings.

8. The approach is optimistic. Humanity does not have a future which is black, devoid of hope and full of misery. In fact, man becomes master of his destiny since he can change the 'optimum' by changing his own efficiency, techniques of production and stock of capital.

9. The optimum theory has a leaning towards welfare economics because when determining the optimum number for a country welfare consideration have to be kept in view. This is especially clear from the explanation given by Carr Saunders.

10. There is stress on proper exploitation of natural resources

and this approach is growth-oriented. A country which makes proper use of all that the nature has given to it free of charge, can support a larger population.

11. The optimum theory is based on a forward-looking approach. Suppose there is over-population. What does the theory prescribe? Production should be increased by increasing the efficiency of the workers and a proper investment programme based on sound planning.

12. The optimum theory is dynamic. As we have noted above the optimum number goes on changing.

13. The Malthusian Theory has significance only in the context of over-population. The optimum theory can describe either type of mal-adjustment—over-population or under-population.

Is Optimum Theory an Improvement Over the Malthusian Theory?

After an examination of both the Malthusian theory and the optimum theory of population we can observe the following superiority of the optimum theory over the Malthusian theory.

1. Prof. Malthus has linked population growth with the availability of food or food supplies, whereas the authors of optimum theory linked population growth with natural resources, capital and production techniques and ultimately with total production.

2. Malthus considered every increase in population harmful whereas the optimum theory considers the population harmful only if it exceeds the optimum limit.

3. Prof. Gide has pointed out that Malthus was a pessimist with a negative approch. Optimum theory of population exudes optimism. Malthus was obsessed by the possibility of an impending economic hell, while the supporters of optimum theory of population were elated by the hope of a coming paradise.

4. Malthus has concluded that the visitations of natural calamities like floods, earthquakes, etc. are harbingers of excess population. Optimum theory has adopted a realistic stand in this matter. It does not give much significance to these natural calamities but considers the question exclusively from the angle of income per head. The country will be over populated only if the population increase results in a fall in per capita income.

5. Optimum criteria has laid down the economically feasible population, in the context of natural resources, capital stock, technique of production, etc. Malthus failed to give a scientific assessment of the socially desirable quantities of population.

6. **Malthusian** theory finds ready application in backward and over-populated countries, whereas the optimum theory could be applied to all types of countries whatever be the size of its population.

7. Malthus viewed population from the consumption angle, whereas the optimum theory considers the whole issue from the productive point of view. Every child born was treated as a burden on the available supply of the food. Optimum theory considers the population as addition to labour supply. Malthus theory is considered as a static equilibrium theory whereas the optimum theory is more dynamic and volatile.

8. Malthus harps on the theme of moral and religious codes in population theory while the optimum theory is free from these ethical concepts and adopts a more rationalistic approach.

9. The optimum theory is more realistic. By taking decline in per capita income as the index of over-population it recognises that over-population can exist even, when it is not accompanied by the operation of positive checks like wars, epidemics, etc.

Conclusion

Thus the optimum theory has contributed in its own way to the discussion of population problems in our times. According to Hauser and Duncan: "One is led to the conclusion that the potential contributions of optimum theory, whatever they may be, have been prejudiced by the combination of normative and empirical considerations in the frame of a single doctrine and that, partly as a result of this, there has been vigorous persecution of the kind of emperical-research suggested by optimum theory."

SELECT REFERENCES

1. Coontz, S.E.: *Population Theories and their Economic Interpretation*, 1957.
2. Hauser, P.M. & Duncan, O.D.: *The Study of Population*, Chicago, 1959.
3. Petersen, W.: *Population*, New York, 1961.
4. Carr Saunders, A.M.: *World Population: Past Growth and Present Trends*, London, 1964.
5. U.N.: "World Population: Challenge to Development". Summary of the Highlights of the World Population Conference, Belgrade, Yugoslavia, 1965, New York, 1966.

EXAMINATION QUESTIONS

1. Discuss the optimum theory of population. Is it possible to achieve the optimum level of population?
2. Examine in detail the optimum theory of population. How far is it an improvement over the Malthusian theory of population?
3. The problem of population is not only a problem of size but it is a problem of efficient production and equitable distribution. Explain critically.
4. Malthusian theory of population is pessimistic while optimum theory of population is optimistic; but none of them is a perfect theory of population. Discuss.
5. What do you mean by over-population? Explain the concept of optimum population.

18

Social and Economic Theories of Population

Many thinkers in the field of sociology and economics have contributed their views about population growth. Some of the important theories are:

(1) Population and Social Maladjustment Theory of Henry George.

(2) Social Capillarity Theory by Dumont.

(3) Voluntarism Theory of Fetter.

(4) Principle of Individuality by Nitti.

(5) Brento's Theory of Increasing Prosperity.

(6) Karl Marx's Theory of Surplus Population.

(7) Theory of Rationalism by U. Stenberg.

(8) Carr Saunders' Optimum Theory.

(9) Leibenstein's Theory of Population and Economic Growth.

1. HENRY GEORGE'S THEORY OF SOCIAL MALADJUSTMENT

Henry George (1839-1897) was an American economist and social reformer. His book 'Progress and Prosperity' was published in 1879. He ruled out any natural enemity between men's natural tendency to increase in numbers and his ability to provide subsistence for them. He pointed out: "The law of population accords with and is subordinate to the law of intellectual developments, and any danger that human beings may be brought into a world where they cannot be provided for, arises not from the ordinances of nature, but from social maladjustments that in the midst of wealth condemn men to want."

He agreed with Spencer that fecundity will decrease with an improvement of the intellect. With intellectual development, birth rate will come down.

He advocated the thesis of a single tax on land as a solution to the population problem. If the rent which people pay for the use of land is siphoned off in the form of a tax on further tax is required. He believed private ownership detrimental to production. He suggested socialisation of land to yield more yield which will overcome over-population or scarcity of subsistence. Thus he provided a social panacea to solve the population problem.

It is reasonable to assume that he believed in contraceptives as a means to reduce population.

Critical estimate. Henry George could not explain how the population will come down with the development of the intellect. Whether it is through family planning methods or through reduction in fertility was not adequately explained.

2. SOCIAL CAPILLARITY THEORY OF DUMONT

Arsene Dumont (1849-1902) was a professor in the University of Strasbourg. He studied the population growth in France during the latter part of 19th century and evolved his theory of social capillarity. Thompson and Lewis stated his thesis thus: "Briefly stated His belief was that the individual tends to mount to higher levels in his social environment by a process similar to physical capillarity. In this process of climbing upwards he becomes less and less likely to reproduce himself; he is drawn out of the milieu and away from the family."

Consequently his interest in family and race welfare recede to the background. His sole motivation will be to climb up in the social ladder. Dumont says: "What gravity is to the physical world, capillarity is to the social order."

Dumont regarded the movement from one class to other is the 'raisonne de etre' of decline in birth rate. He concluded that, "The development of numbers in a nation is an inverse ratio to the development of the individual." He did not toe the line of Spencer that change in population was a biological feature.

Dumont regarded social capillarity to be more effective in a country where obstacles to the movement from class to class are weak and hindrances few. Citing the example of France, he explains the rapid deceleration of population to social capillarity opportunities in a democratic set up. Stating the views of Dumont, Thompson and Lewis said: "People at a distance from centre of attraction and in occupation where individual has little opportunity to develop are not drawn into the capillary movement so rapidly and hence are not likely to reduce their birth rate to the same degree. They will continue to increase and thereby, to supply new candidates for capillary action; these in turn, will become ambitious social climbers and will soon die out."

Dumont felt that in a country like India, on account of caste system, social capillarity is relatively weak and consequently birth rates continue to rule high. Rigidity of social structure is a constraint on social upward movement. Individual development will not be engrossing under such circumstances.

Dumont's theory and Spencer's theory of antagonism between individual and genesis have much in common. However, Dumont's theory permits much larger personal choice in determining reproductive behaviour than does Spencer's.

Dumont did not fully subscribe to the views given by Malthus. Increase of wealth does not increase population but it increases family prestige. However, Dumont admits that Joseph Garnier has proved the correctness of Malthusian geometric progression. In fact, among uncivilised people, the prosperity to reproduce is more. With an improvement in standard of living, everybody would strive to improve their social standing. This could be possible only through a reduction in the number of children and therefore with an increase in wealth, birth rate declines.

Dumont classified population theories into three categories.

(*a*) *Malthusian theory.* This theory is applicable in uncivilised animal like societies. In such society, the population will increase in geometric proportion.

(*b*) *Quillar's principle of population.* He did not agree with the opinion of Quillar. Dumont said that when an uncivilised society goes little ahead, it begins to believe that where there is food, there are people to eat as well.

In such a society population increase according to food production, and positive checks do not operate.

(*c*) *Social capillarity.* Dumont feels that with the complete development of society an individual would like to secure prestige in every sphere of activity. However this goal could be achieved only through rational thinking and commitment towards certain ideals. Where a person starts mounting the social ladder, birth rate shrinks. In fact no society can climb the social ladder with a heavy burden of children on its back. Dumont considers his population thesis directly related to the social development. He believes that the social capillarity is inversely related to birth rate. In progressive society, the ambition to ascend the social ladder is more intense. These people who migrate to cities have less children. Dumont observed: "Just as a column of liquid must be thin in order to rise under the force of capillarity, so must a family be small to rise in the social scale."

The time and energy of the poor are burned up in producing more children. If they divert their resources including time and money to the production of wealth they can pass through social capillarity. Production of one or two children could help in achieving this status.

Explaining the cases of the difference in fertility in cities and villages, Dumont observed that city dwellers are more eager to rise in the social ladder. In cities people have the capacity to think and improve knowledge and act rationally. Birth rate in cities is also low due to the high cost of bringing up the children and the desire to go up speedily and quickly.

Liberal environment, desire for social vertical mobility, effort and desire of middle class to rise, improved standard, etc., have also contributed to decline in birth rate in cities.

Birth rate in villagers remains high due to the rigidity of caste system, orthodoxy, poverty, illiteracy, lack of vigour, etc. Poverty by itself is not the cause of high birth rate but it is because of ignorance and lack of vigour.

Dumont was against the socialistic socio-economic system; as it does not provide sufficient opportunity for social capillarity. He observed: "The socialist principle of equality of function, if entirely applied would necessarily imply the destruction of social capillarity and cause high birth rate."

Dumont was also against the system of cut-throat competitive system since it frustrates the aspirations of the poor and the average individual to rise in social status.

Critical Evaluation. Dumont has definitely given an intelligent explanation of the population growth concept. However, it has been criticised on the following grounds:

(1) It cannot be accepted as a law of population.

(2) The conclusion that birth rate is low in cities as compared to villages cannot be accepted as a universal principle governing population.

In India, the labourers keep their families in villages and live alone in cities. That is why the birth rate is low in cities.

(3) To rise in the social life is remotely related to the number of children. If it were true then ladies without children should have arisen to the very top.

(4) To grow in social stature in the outcome of the combination of many factors like social, political, economic condition, etc.

(5) Many people have improved their social standing in spite of

their having many children and continue to produce children even after attaining social esteem. Many with few children still remain at the lower rung of the social ladder.

(6) To establish fertility with social capillarity is to view the population theory in isolation. Other factors also deserve careful consideration.

To quote Thompson and Lewis: "On the whole this statement of relation between individuation and genesis seems a decided improvement over Spencer's. It has the merit of directing more attention to the actual conditions under which people live as important factors in developing preventive checks to population growth, checks which could render the subsistence checks less operative. Malthus hoped for this result although he did not approve of contraception as Dumont clearly did."

3. FRANK FETTER'S THEORY OF VOLUNTARISM

Frank Fetter was an economic and social thinker who propounded the theory of voluntarism towards the end of the 19th century. He disagreed with the Malthusian law of population, which he considered one sided. The main drawback of the Malthusian doctrine was that it gave undue importance to the sexual propensity and sex act in determining the birth rate, while ignoring other factors. Similarly Malthus held the shortage food the principal reason for death rate. He said that many societies in the world, where children or the aged were killed not on account of food deficiency but on account of orthodoxy or they wanted to have beautiful or healthy offspring. Fetter tried to point out many other factors influencing death rate. The salient features of Fetter's theory could be shown as under:

Birth Rate among the Rich

The rich voluntarily restrict the birth rate through judicious exercise of their intellect and common sense. The reason of low birth rate among the rich are:

(1) The affluent section of society would like to enjoy maximum material happiness which will be jeopardised in case the children are many.

(2) Rich people believe in accumulating wealth and property. More birth means that the property will have to be subdivided which is a proposition which they try to avoid.

(3) The rich people spent very heavily in rearing up their

children which creates undue strain on resources. The expenditure starts from the very birth itself. On the other hand the children being to give return at a much later stage on account of which the rich try to keep the birth rate low.

Birth Rate among the Poor

Fetter believed that the individual voluntarily through his own desire produce children under the influence of socio-economic pressures. Birth rate among the poor is high on account of the following reasons:

(1) Poor people employ their children in remunerative productive work at a very early age which acts as an incentive to birth rate.

(2) Poor people spent very little in upbringing their progene. Consequently they are very less concerned about the number of children.

(3) The poor are less intelligent and lack common sense. They do not think rationally about the number of children, which keeps the birth rate fairly high.

(4) The poor are less ambitious and do not have the problem of inheritence and division of property because they have only poverty to divide. Naturally the birth rate is high.

Critical evaluation. The contention that the rich produce less and the poor produce more children is not borne out by facts. Many rich people have more children than the poor. Fetter assumed that birth rate is the outcome of free choice of individual. The fact is that even today birth is regarded as a natural normal phenomenon.

4. FRANCISCO S. NITTI'S THEORY OF INDIVISUALITY

Francisco Nitti was an Italian economist and social reformer. In his book "Population and the Social System", Nitti expounded his theory of individuality. He dealt at length on the theories of population advanced by Malthus, Mark, Spencer, Dumont, etc. He disagreed with the opinion of Malthus that the population invariably outstrip food supply. He agreed with the views expressed by Spencer that increase in population was not always harmful for the society. In fact in several instances it assisted in human progress and civilisation. Nitti's population thought runs as follows:

(1) Nitti claimed that the mighty citadel of Malthusian thesis will crumble down to pieces under the onslaught of his criticism.

Population cannot get ahead of the food supply.

(2) Nitti attacked the gloomy predictions of Malthus that the persistent increase in population will create serious problems before society. He believed that population increase will have beneficial effect in the social and cultural progress.

(3) Nitti subscribed to the view that population growth is due partly to ethical, moral, social, economic and political factors; but economic factors are by far the most important. He said: "The influence of physical moral order and the influence of political order are but slight compared to influence of an economic kind.

(4) Nitti attached considerable significance to biological factors as determinant of the fertility rates. He observed: "The solution of problems of population, which has been scarced anything better than darkness to economist is to be found in biological theory, which has revealed new horizons to demographic science."

(5) He maintained that when the individuality grows economic disparity will decrease considerably. Social cooperation will be strengthened. Food production will maintain parity with population and the demand of population will not haunt mankind.

5. L. BRENTO'S THEORY OF INCREASING PROSPERITY

Brento has advanced the theory of increasing prosperity and pleasure. His approach was based on the conception that pleasure seeking is the paramount aim of human life. His thesis is:

(1) Every man has a definite aim in his life to the fulfilment of which he directs his endeavours.

(2) Fundamental principle of all human endeavour is to maximise happiness in society.

(3) Birth rate is determined by the availability of the means of pleasure and happiness in society.

(4) Poor people have less avenues of pleasure and happiness. They toil very hard and lead an unhygenic life in slums where the sources of enjoyment and pleasure are limited. Therefore they have more children.

(5) Brento feels that the rich have considerable sources of pleasure and enjoyment. Even the women in the rich class can remain unmarried for sufficient length of time. Naturally the birth rate among the rich is less.

(6) Marriage is looked upon as a problem for the poor. Consequently they try to get over this problem as quickly as they can, which results in child marriage.

(7) Marriage has never been looked upon as a problem among the rich and as such they marry much late in life. So the birth rate is also less among the rich.

Evaluation. The theory has been criticised on several grounds:

(1) Population and birth rate cannot be explained in terms of pleasure calculus alone.

(2) High birth rate among the poor is not only due to lack of diversion but also due to other and more important factors.

(3) Serious reflection on the issue will show that housing problem, shortage of space in the house, too many members in the family gives less occasion to poor couples to meet together.

(4) The assumption that the frenzy for breading is high among the poor is not correct. On the contrary sex instinct is more among rich due to favourable environment, good food and other considerations.

(5) This theory is not universal like other similar theories on the subject.

6. KARL MARX'S THEORY OF SURPLUS POPULATION

Karl Marx (1818-1893) was a scientific socialist of repute. His socialistic theory of population was christianed as the theory of surplus population. Marx made scathing attack on the Malthusian theory of population as figment of imagination and utter falsehood. He ascribed the tendency of man to press on the means of subsistence to evils of capitalism which would disappear with the emergence of communism. When communism is in operation, there can be no poverty and hardship whatever be the rate of population increase.

Marx stated his view thus: "It is the working population which, while effecting the accumulation of capital also produces the means whereby it is itself rendered relatively superfluous, is turned into a relatively surplus population, and it does so to an ever increasing extent. This is a law of population peculiar to the capitalist method; and in fact every method of production that rises in the course of history has its own peculiar, historical valid law of population."

Marx's Views

(1) Marx held that surplus population and employment are the consequence of capitalist system which fails to provide jobs for all:

(a) The capitalist epoch is a system under which the wealth and capital are concentrated in the hands of few individuals. The demand for labourers fails to keep up with the increase in the number of workers; which creates a vast reserve army of unemployed.

(*b*) The dominant motive behind the capitalist system in profit on account of which the labour is paid less than the value of labour power, and the surplus value is pocketed by the capitalist.

(*c*) The capitalist introduces labour saving machines and rationalisation, etc. to increase the surplus value. With accumulation of capital, unemployment spreads, wages decline and poverty increases. The cumulative effect of the poverty and unemployment creates the surplus population.

(2) Marx dismissed as rubbish the argument that the population increase is due to improvidence and biological factors.

(3) Marx ascribed low food production to inequality in land distribution, zamindari system, shortage of land with the real tiller and uncertainty in land tenure.

(4) Marx believed that the proletariat help the wheels of production move and increase the profit of the capitalist while they are subject to exploitation. The capitalist is a vampire that thrives on the blood of the poor labourer and gets richer and fatter the more blood it sucks.

(5) It is difficult, according to Marx to give a universal population theory valid for all times. The mode of production undergoes changes from time to time which necessitates new approach to the problem from time to time. Under capitalism the principle of surplus population alone is applicable.

(6) Unemployment is a distinguishing feature of capitalism. As the decay of capitalism snowballs, the conditions will become favourable for collective method of production to give full employment and a good living to able bodied worker no matter how fastly or greatly their numbers increased. It will also bring down death rate considerably.

Marx refuted Malthus. Commenting on Malthus, Marx said: "I should like to remind him that this work, in its first form, was nothing more than a school boyish, superficial, and parsonic declamatory plagiarism from Defoe, Sir James Stuart, Townsend, Franklin, Wallace and others, and did not contain a single sentence thought out by Malthus himself."

He accused Malthus of having stuffed into the framework of his first essay a lot of self-digested material gathered from different sources with new matter borrowed from others.

Criticism

(1) Marx sought to criticise Malthus with the use of personal abuse and invective. Thompson and Lewis observed: "There can be no question of sincerity of Marx's belief in the evils of capitalism as the sole basis of poverty but he should have confined his efforts to discredit Malthus views to personal ridicule and vilification. Apparently Marx must have had deep seated doubts that Malthus' views could be sufficiently disposed of by an appeal to facts and reasons." In fact the attack on Malthus was made without making thorough study of the principles of population of Malthus.

(2) It is not correct to presume that under communism, there will be no need to check the population growth at any stage. Even in communist countries population is sought to be restricted on ground of mother's health. Russia and China are veering round to the opinion of planned parenthood.

(3) Marx's chief purpose was to discredit capitalism, for which he sought to put the blame of surplus population on the capitalist set up.

(4) Marx found in communism the panacea for the ills of the society, but he failed to elaborate on the fertility behaviour, propensity of population growth etc., in his set up.

(5) To state that population is no problem in a socialistic set up, whatever be the rate of population growth is wishful thinking.

(6) The opinion may be ventured that the Marxian philosophy was torn in between deep seated hatred towards capitalism and blind support towards communism, and gone astray from the path of realism.

7. THEORY OF RATIONALISM BY U. STRENBERG

U. Strenberg has expounded his "Theory of Rationalism as the cause of the fertility decline" within the European sphere of civilisation. According to him the population theory should in addition to explaining the causes of fall (or rise) in population of the rich should also explain the causes of the declining (or increasing) population among the poor. He attributed the fall in birth rate to logic and intelligence. According to him, natural and biological factors are less important in the determination of birth as compared to mental factors. Strenberg was the first demographer to have realised that birth rate among the poor can be less. He showed that in countries like Norway and Finland birth rate is low in spite of grinding poverty.

Strenberg's views are summarised as follows:

(1) Birth rate is basically the result of thinking and has nothing to do with biological or natural factors.

(2) Birth rate among the rich does not decline automatically. Similarly birth rate among the poor does not go up automatically.

(3) It is on account of the thinking of the people that the birth rate will go up or goes down depend, and it is remotely related to urban or rural setting.

(4) Strenberg came down heavily on the capitalist. He held the view that low fertility originated out of capitalist mentality. Capitalist is guided by the desire to secure power in political, social and economic fields. He thinks about the pros and cons of a given action in meeting his objects. Selfishness and self-sufficiency are the life's main aim which guide his actions. Surprisingly, in addition to menfolk women too are guided by these aims and this phenomenon rules their thinking about child-bearing. He said: "The women too become musculinised (when infected by the capitalist mentality, in their search for equality). Love relations become business-like and matter of fact."

(5) Economic development leads to a fall in the birth rate. When the birth rate tends to fall, the condition will become favourable for rapid economic development. He said: "An unbiased observation might tempt us to suppose that rising welfare is not the cause of the decreasing birth but its result. In other words, one limits the number of births in order to be able to obtain prosperity. Prosperity therefore is not the cause but the goal and birth control, the means for attainment of this goal."

(6) Strenberg concluded that the urban psychology gradually comes to influence the thinking of village people also. The villagers too think in terms of economic development, as a result of which they try to restrict their birth rate. They rearrange their priorities and values of life and develop habits more akin to the city folks and try to bring down the birth rate as quickly as possible.

(7) Strenberg's analysis represents a balanced approach which gives due cognizance to psychological, social and economic factors influencing birth rates.

8. OPTIMUM THEORY OF POPULATION BY CARRSAUNDERS

(See Chapter on Optimum Population)

9. LEIBENSTEIN'S THEORY OF POPULATION AND ECONOMIC GROWTH

Leibenstein has come forward with an economie explanation of population problem or otherwise known as the population theory of economic development. His views can be presented as under:

(1) *Size and living standard.* The more the population of a country it will have to make strenuous efforts to come out of the mesh of low living standards.

(2) *Density of population.* Leibenstein maintained that high density is not a constraint to economic development nor can we say that low density is stimulant to economic growth. Economic growth hinges on factors like quantity and quality of the raw materials available, size and availability of capital, state of technology, laws of production, etc.

(3) *Birth rate and economic growth.* Leibenstein believed that the decline in birth rate follows economic development. Naturally primary attention should be given to programmes of economic development. Simultaneously measures to control birth rate should also be implemented. So long as economic development does not take place, the citizens do not act rationally as they would not be aware of the means and the methods of birth control.

Leibenstein's Theory of Critical Minimum Effort

Leibenstein closely studied the views of the thinkers who held that birth rate tends to get weakened with socio-economic control and technical progress. Prominent among such thinkers are C.P. Blake, W.S. Thompson, etc. He conducted studies into the demographic stages of underdeveloped and backward economics and reached the following conclusions:

(1) In fact the inhabitants of developing poor countries are relatively less rational or irrational in comparison to the residents of developed countries. They do not have access to the means of contraceptives nor are they familiar with the methods to control population and tends to ignore its importance. They treat sex act and procreation on the same footing.

(2) Poor countries have to pass through the traumatic experience of high incidence of death rates. Consequently birth rates, too are also very high since otherwise it is likely that a person can be without any child in his old age.

(*a*) The people in poor countries have to spend comparatively much less in bringing up their children. Thus the cost of rearing the children is relatively less than the corresponding utility derived from putting their children to gainful employment.

(*b*) Leibenstein cited three main advantages which parents derive out of children:

(1) A child is a consumption good on account of the love and pleasure which the parents get from their issues.

(2) The children are also agents of production because they start earning from early childhood and feed their parents.

(3) A child is a prop to his parents in old age as the parents depend on his earning when they themselves are unable to earn. Thus a child is a source of security.

In developed countries the birth rate is based on supply and demand. It also depends on the cost of upbringing of the child and the facilities provided for health, education, sanitation, medical and similar other facilities. (Fig. 1)

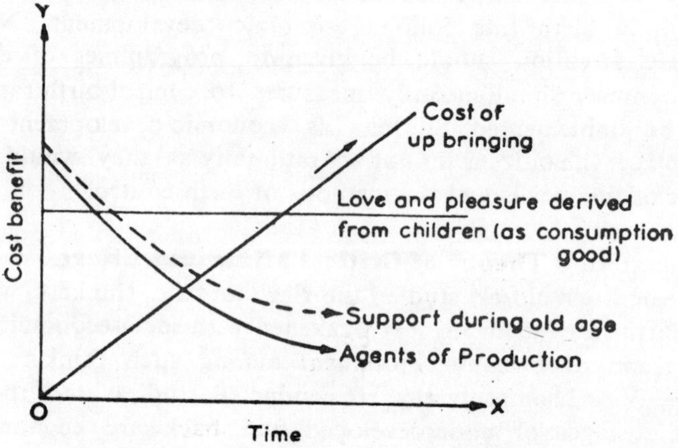

Fig. 1

Every child provides equal pleasure and it has nothing to do with the income which will come out of him. Leibenstein concluded that birth rate is intimately associated with an increase in income per head which in turn in the outcome of economic development. Development calls for putting in 'Critical minimum efforts" by the Nation. To quote Leibenstein: "In order to achieve the transition from the state of backwardness to the more developed state where we can expect steady social growth, it is necessary, though not always sufficient, condition that at some point during some period, the economy should receive stimulus to growth that is greater than certain critical minimum size."

Increase in income. Views of Leibenstein on decline in birth rate, death rate and population increase run as follows:

(1) Fall in income per head is accompanied by high death rate. This will tend to increase the aforesaid three types of utilities. High death rate will bring about a scaling down of the cost of up-bringing the offspring which provides sufficient incentive to increase birth rate.

(2) When the per capita income is high death rate tends to decelerate but birth rate does not react quickly and fail to shrink. The fall in birth is a gradual process because the utility derived out of the children tends to go down very slowly and as a result the temptation to reduce the number of children does not manifest immediately in all families.

(3) However as and when the income of the family shows significant rise and the death rate ebbs, the utility derived out of children begins to fall appreciably. The parents at this stage become economically well off to sustain themselves in old age and the need to depend on children during old age loses much of its significance. On the other hand the cost of upbringing the children, their education, health, clothing and similar other expenditures tend to increase. The children of rich also do not start earning at an early age. The cost factor considerably outweigh the relative benefits anticipated which acts as a disincentive to increase the birth rate. The desire to have less children get stronger, every child is considered a burden.

(4) When the income grows very high, then the death rate as well as the birth rate tend to fall perceptibly.

Leibenstein held the view that when at the initial stages increase in income leads to slight rise.

The sum and substance of his doctrine points to four stages of population growth:

(1) When both death rate and birth rate are high.

(2) Death rate is low but birth rate is high and population increases.

(3) Death rate is low, birth rate also is low but slightly higher leading to slow increase in population.

(4) Birth rate is less, death rate also falls and the country is faced with very low increase in population and the country is poised for high growth and progress.

Leibenstein observed: "The less the fertility lag, the less the critical minimum efforts necessary for growth. The point at which fertility decline sets in will determine the height of critical minimum income level.

The requirement of critical minimum effort is needed in less developed countries because in developed countries with every increase in income birth rate declines substantially. On this basis 'Threshold Hypothesis' of fertility decline operates, which means that so long as a given economic standard is not achieved attempt to bring down birth rate will be a wild goose chase. All efforts made till then will be wasteful and after that useless.

Criticism

1. Leibenstein assumes that population increases as the income rises above the subsistence level. But after a certain level of income, the population declines. This assumption implies that the rise in income has a direct bearing on the growth of population. But in reality, this relation is not so simple as has been assumed by Leibenstein.

2. Leibenstein ignores the role of state in checking the growth of population. No government can afford to wait for the per capita income to rise above the critical minimum level so that population growth may decline, because it is a very long term affair.

The "motivation theory" of population growth, propounded by Leibenstein, explains that rate of population growth is an increasing function of per capita income up to a certain level of income, after that it is a decreasing function of income because of high cost of rearing a large family. The relationship between population growth and per capita income is illustrated by the diagram given below.

In Fig. 2, the curve *P* indicates the rate of population growth at each per capita income level, which is measured by the curve *N*. At the level of subsistence equilibrium, a growth of population and income is absent. If the per capita income is raised to *Yb*, the rate of growth of population and income is at 1 per cent in both the cases. At *Ye* the rate of growth of population (2%) is higher than the rate of growth of national income (1%). At *Ye*, the rate of growth of population declines. This has been possible because of higher level of per capita income (*Ye*) here. This critical minimum per capita income level, by reducing the rate of population

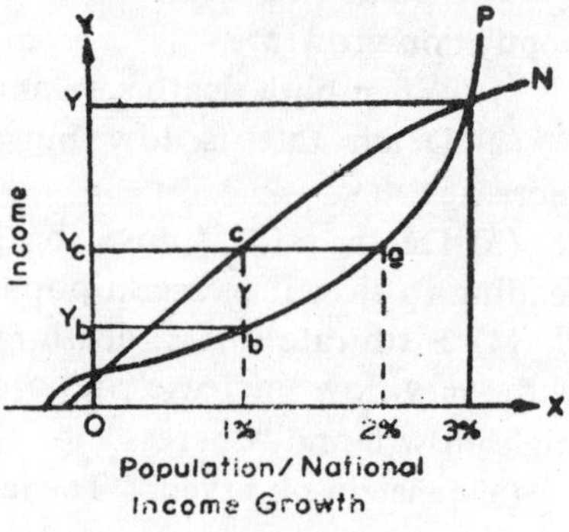

Fig. 2

growth, helps the process of economic development. The rate of population growth acts as an income depressing factor, while the rate of increase in per capita income acts as an income increasing factor.

Thus *Ye* level of per capita income is critical minimum per capita income which can sustain itself or which can generate the process of self-sustained growth. According to Leibenstein, the less developed countries must raise their per capita income to this level, if they want to achieve the sustained growth.

EXAMINATION QUESTIONS

1. Critically examine Karl Marx's theory of population.
2. Evaluate the social capillaries theory of Dumont.
3. Examine Nitti's theory of individuality.
4. Discuss the Frank Fetter's theory of volunteerism.
5. Explain the population theory of Henry George.
6. Critically analyse the theory of population and economic growth propounded by Leibenstein.
7. Explain Brento's theory of increasing prosperity.
8. Examine the population theory of U. Stenberg.

19

Biological and Natural Theories of Population

In our modern times biological theories of population have made significant contribution to the study of demography. These theories are based on the principle that human beings are like animal and plant species and undergo the same process of origin, growth and decay. Some of the important theories are:

(1) Sadler's Theory of Destiny.
(2) Doubleday's Theory of Diet.
(3) Jouse-De-Castro's Theory of Protein Consumption.
(4) Pearl and Reed's Logistic Curve Theory.
(5) Herbert Spencer's Biological Theory.
(6) Carrado Gini's Theory of Population.

1. SADLER'S THEORY OF DESTINY

Michael Thomas Sadler (1780-1835) was an English Social reformer and was a contemporary of Malthus. He believed that the natural law of population was contrary to the theories expounded by Malthus. His book 'The Law of Population' was divided into two volumes. According to him Malthus was a dishonest plagiarist.

His statement of the natural law of population was as follows: "The fecundity of human beings is, *ceteris paribus* in the inverse ratio of the condensation of their numbers; and, still in direct contradiction to the theory now maintained (Malthus'), the variation in that fecundity is effectuated not by the wretchedness and misery but by happiness and prosperity of the species." His conclusions are:

(1) With increasing density of population, the fertility would diminish naturally and the population will cease to grow at the exact point where the number of people will enjoy the greatest happiness. He explained with illustration the increase relation between density and fertility.

(2) He projected an optimistic view of population increase. He repudiated the geometric growth rate enunciated by Malthus.

(3) He tried to establish a directly proportionate link between

population and food supply. The means of subsistence will be augmented with every growth in population. If the population will grow, the masses will produce what they require.

(4) He concluded that high death rate will lead to a corresponding increase in birth rate and *vice versa*. He observed: "The prolificness of an equal number of individuals, other circumstances being similar, is greater when the mortality is greater, and on the contrary smaller, when the mortality is less.

Criticism

Sadler has provided a natural principle of population growth that furnished a rational basis for faith in the rapid perfectibility of man's lot. But if suffers from certain shortcomings.

(1) Sadler failed to give clear distribution between fertility and fecundity. As Thompson and Lewis puts it: "He did not distinguish clearly between fecundity and fertility and he believed that there was no anlagorism between man's natural capacity to produce, which he never defined, and his capacity to produce adequate subsistence for all who would be born."

(2) His argument suffers from circular reasoning:

To say that high density of population will bring in its train low fertility rate and high mortality rate and at the same time high mortality rate will lead to high birth rate is a paradox.

(3) The statement that without any genuine human effort population will automatically be reduced appears to be wishful thinking. It calls for concerted efforts to hold the population in check.

(4) Sadler's contention that when capital grows, population will come down is based on wrong premises. For instance, in a country like India capital accumulation is taking place at a fast pace, but the population growth has not abated.

In spite of the criticisms, the theory could breathe some fresh air of optimism to the whole issue of population.

2. DOUBLEDAY'S THEORY OF DIET

Thomas Doubleday like Sadler was an English economist and social philosopher. Writing 20 years after Sadler, he enunciated a different natural law governing population. He held that population increase is inversely related to his food supply. In other words the greater the quantity of food supply, the less will be the rate of population increase. Doubleday observed: "Amongst those in a state of affluence, and well supplied with luxuries, a constant decrease goes on. Amongst those who form the mean and median between two opposite states, that is to say, those who are tolerably well supplied with good food and not overworked, nor yet idle, population is stationary. Hence it follows that it is upon the numerical proportion which these three states bear to each other in any society that increase or decrease on the whole depends."

Doubleday has mentioned two states of food supply.

(1) *Plethoric stage.* In this stage one can get good food. Fertility is low in this stage.

(2) *Deplethoric stage.* In this stage there is a diminution of proper nourishment due to food shortage. This stage is favourable to fertility.

Doubleday maintained that the fertility of all living beings depends on their being bulky or thin. Experience has shown that fat animals and birds give birth to less children, while thin give birth to more. "An overfed plant can be revived only if depletion of plant, i.e. ringing the bark, extreme lopping and the trending the roots is done."

Doubleday has divided the society into three groups.

(1) In the first category falls the affluent people who are rolling in luxury. Their number is on the decline. To reverse this process they should engage in mental and physical activities and lead a busy life in place of lazy life.

(2) Poor people have less food supply and they increase and multiply their number very fast. As Doubleday puts it: "There is in all societies a constant increase going on amongst that portion of it which is worst supplied with food, in short among the poor."

(3) In the middle ladder comes the average income group which gets a normal diet. They are neither overworked nor idle and their number stays stationary.

Doubleday concluded: "Hence it follows that it is upon the numerical proportion which these three states bear to each other in society that increase or decrease upon the whole depends."

Recently a variant of this theory has been enumerated by Castro which is known as the theory of protein consumption. This view maintains that a high protein content in food reduces fecundity and *vice versa.* Raising the protein content in the diet is offered as a panacea to overcome the growth in population.

Criticism

(1) Thompson and Lewis felt that there is no scientific basis for the belief that intake of caloric or proportion of protein in the diet

has noticeable effect upon fecundity.

(2) The fertility of a population may be affected substantially by the use of contraceptives, while fecundity remains unchanged.

(3) The belief of Doubleday that with the reduction in fertility rate, the inequality in the distribution will be ironed out is purely false optimism.

(4) Spencer has attacked the concept that the rich person is invariably fat and that fatness brings down fertility. He felt that bad disgestion is the root cause of fatness. He stated "The cases Doubleday cites of infertility accompanied by fatness are not cases of high nutrition properly so called, but cases of such deceptive absorption or assimilation as constitute low nutrition."

(5) His contention that the rich have few children and the poor have far too many is far from truth. In real life several instances are there where the rich have more issues than the poor.

3. JOUSE-DE-CASTRO'S THEORY OF PROTEIN CONSUMPTION

In his book "The Geography of Hunger" Castro has linked birth rate with the consumption of protein. In 1920 Mr. R.J. Slonakar conducted experiments on rats and made certain findings, which have been accepted by Castro. Castro maintained that a high protein content in the diet reduces fecundity while a low protein content raises it. Castro supported the thesis adduced by Doubleday that birth rate is influenced by food supply. Experiments on rats conducted by Slonakar yielded the result that with the administration of protein rich food, the rats have grown fatty and fecundity declined. Basing his conclusion on this, Castro averred that protein rich diet tends to make a person fat and reduced fecundity.

According to him the poor have no balanced food and are always short of protein in food with the result that their liver become sluggish. Consequently Oestrogens in the women's body get neutralised and increase in number and the fecundity also registers an upward momentum.

The root cause of population increase in poor countries is the protein deficiency in food. The rich nation are to be blamed for the growth of population in poor countries. The imperial and colonial powers have never tried to improve the living standard of the colonies. In place of improving the diet quality of their people, they have been subjected to exploitation. Low wage and grinding poverty increased the frenzy for breeding which led to increase in population by leaps and bounds. This resulted in further reduction in the protein contents in food and increased the capacity to produce still more children which become a vicious cycle.

Castro was pained to observe that the capitalists, wealthy class, imperialists, scientists, etc., failed to give adeqaute attention to the problem of deficiency in food. The producers, traders, etc., treated production, exchange, distribution, consumption, etc., as purely economic activities of commercial nature and ignored the social aspects of poverty. Castro tried to quantify the magnitude of starvation from protein deficiency and puts it at $\frac{2}{3}$ of the world population who become victims of malnutrition, disease or early death. According to Castro we do not pay much attention to the problem of human erosion on account of food deficiency, while we are very much alert to the problem of soil erosion.

Writing in the context of India, Castro reflected that nearly one half of the children born in this country subsist only on starvation diet and die before they are able to produce any children. He said, "Chronic hunger increases sexual activity. Thus primary need is emphasised to compensate for the dimunition of the other. But sexual activity goes down with acute hunger."

Castro suggested that the question of balanced food should be tackled on a priority basis to eradicate malnutrition. He emphasised the use of extensive cultivation and improved methods of farming. Economic development can bring about the much-needed reduction in birth rate. As Castro puts it: "When deserts of ice and impenetrable jungles are being turned to gardens and orchards, when the lands we farm and the plants we grow are being made to multiply their field, and while we are barely learning how to tap the great food reservoirs of waters, the wild flora, and of artificial synthesis, the Malthusians go on setting up their sinister scare crows. It is nothing to us, since we have no reasons to fear them."

Critical Estimation

Castro took pains to explain with illustrations the correlation between fertility and food value. But his explanation suffers from serious shortcomings.

(1) It may be true that the nature of food can influence the fertility rate, but this fact cannot be accepted as an axiom. The relationship between food and fertility cannot be expressed in terms of any law.

(2) Many rich countries experienced high birth rate with an improvement in the diet habits.

(3) Decline in population in many countries could be attributed not only to protein content in food, but also to other factors like, education, recreation and the use of contraceptives and other means of family planning.

(4) Similarly high birth rate in poor countries could be attributed, in addition to deficient food to other factors like education, entertainment, religio-cultural conventions, child marriage, joint family system, agriculture-oriented economy, etc.

(5) Preventive checks also can control birth rate. Thompson and Lewis said: "We now know that the fertility of any population i.e., the actual bearing of living children, may be affected substantially by preventive checks of various kinds, while fecundity remains unchanged."

(6) Leibenstein criticised Castro when he says: "The reason why this approach is fallacious is that the economy might not have experienced sustained development if fertility rates had not declined at some crucial stage during the expansion. One need not impute the absence of a barrier simply because the race is of such a nature that the barrier cannot be seen when it is successfully overcome."

(7) Coontz feels that we cannot take it for granted that human fertility is conditioned by food. Fluctuation in fertility during trade cycle cannot be explained in the context of food. According to Coontz: "It is possible to accept Castro's thesis that poverty is mainly traceable to socio-economic conditions and should not be attributed to the holding assent to the proposition that human fertility is related to diet. It does not follow that capacity means utilisation of fertility function of diet."

4. PEARL AND REED'S LOGISTIC CURVE THEORY

In 1835 Queteled advanced the theory that with increasing density of population, the growth of population tends to slow down. In 1835 Verhulst put it in the form of a mathematical curve which he named the logistic. However, it was forgotten and the logistic curve was not used in population theory again until 1920 when it was independently discovered by Pearl and Reed. Initially, the theory was based on experiments with yeast, fruitflies and chickens. The conditions of the experiments were : (1) the initial population was small in relation to the space which was provided for it, (2) ample food was provided, (3) the experimenter provided the food externally, (4) space limit of the environment was held constant.

Under these conditions, Pearl found that each of the species tended to multiply at a fast pace initially, which was maintained until a very high density was reached. Then the rate of increase decelerated and ultimately all growth ceased. Pearl concluded: "Population wanes and waxes, rises and falls and increases rapidly and slowly and on the whole it is ever increasing."

Briefly the theory can be presented under the following heads:

(1) Population does not grow in geometric progression, but it moves in an irregular path at times growing fast and retarding afterwards. This cycle repeats itself. The assumptions of the theory are:

(*a*) The land regularised available is scarce which constitutes a constraint in population increase.

(*b*) Rate of population can neither rise to infinity nor decline to zero.

(*c*) Rise and fall of population assume the form of a cycle: "To determine the cycle by changes in the growth of population is obviously circular.

(*d*) The point of maximum rate of growth is the point of inflection of the population growth curve. After that point is passed the rate of growth becomes progressively slower, till finally the curve stretches along nearly horizontal, in close approach to the upper asymptote which belongs to the particular cultural epoch and the area involved.

In Fig. 1 the size of population is taken on the *x*-axis and the time period on the *y*-axis. The big *S* is the logistic curve where population starts increasing at point *P* and continues to grow up to point *E*.

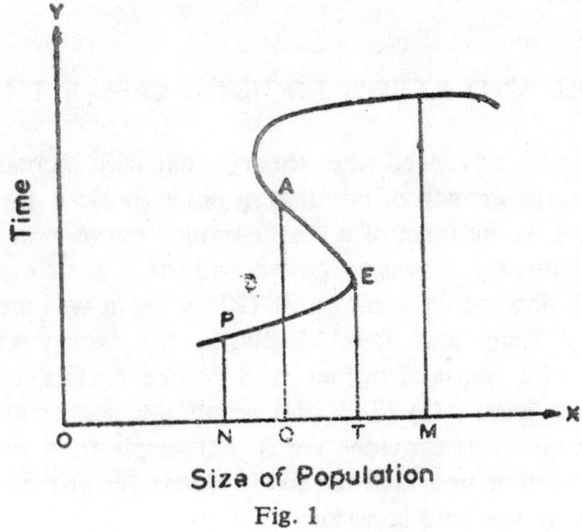

Fig. 1

The growth of population is very steady from point *ON* to *OT*. From *E* onwards, population starts declining. For instance, at point *A* it declines to *OQ* from *OT*. The decline goes on till the point *R* after which the population again begins to grow. At point *L* the overall size of population increases to *OM* over time.

Even after the fall, the population stays at a higher plateau.

(2) Pearl and Reed analysed the population of many countries and cities and found that the growth in population is more or less like economic growth.

(3) It is difficult to give a precise time span for a country to move from one stage of growth to reach the other stage.

(4) Poor couples like to come close to each other frequently with the result that they have more children than the rich.

Pearl could not carry out his experiments with human beings as he had to face formidable hurdles in his attempts.

Comparison with Malthus

The theory gives a good account of the nature of population growth to show that central tendency of population is to maintain its upward momentum. It is superior to the Malthusian theory on the following counts:

(1) Malthus said that the population always keeps on increasing. But this theory states that the increase in population will come down after some time and finally falls to zero rate or even declines.

(2) Malthus believed that the population keeps on increasing at a geometric progression, but Pearl thinks that it is not necessary for population to increase according to given rates.

(3) Malthus maintained that population tends to grow fast with economic and cultural development, while the supporters of logistic theory believe that with development the population will either become stationary or even decline.

Criticism

(1) Pearl based his conclusions on the study made on fruitflies. It is well-known that the analogy is far-fetched and cannot be a true statement of facts.

(2) Pearl's conclusions and his basic assumptions are mutually contradictory. On the one side he says that when the density goes up, the fertility rate will come down. On the other hand he tried to explain the high birth rate in labour colonies, where the density too is high, to the frequent contact of couples.

(3) The theory is one-sided as it fails to take cognizance of reli-

gious, socio-cultural and economic aspects of population.

(4) The theory fails to take into account the effect of environmental changes on the human character, aspiration, conduct and thinking.

(5) The theory's practical validity has not been conclusively proved. Forecasting by means of the logistic curve would be attended with considerable hazards.

(6) The logistic was not always the type of curve that best described the past population growth of a given country or region.

(7) Even where a logistic described the past growth of population more precisely than other curves, it did not follow that the population would continue to follow the curve.

(8) It had not been established that, because of the inherent nature of the growth process, a population must pursue the path of a logistic even when there were strong reasons for supposing that an 'S' shaped curve would be traced.

The population division of U.N. states: "Critics of the logistic law therefore looked upon it primarily as an empirical formula which sometimes described the past course of population growth and might well represent the future tendency under certain conditions."

5. HERBERT SPENCER'S BIOLOGICAL THEORY

Herbert Spencer (1820-1903) was a famous English philosopher who was concerned chiefly with explaining social and biological development by natural forces. His book 'The Principles of Biology" contains his exposition of the natural law of population growth. His theory is also known as the Biological Theory of Population. There were much similarity in the views of Spencer, Sadler and Doubleday. His theory runs thus:

(1) Spencer thought that there was a natural law that would absolve man from any responsibility from the control of his increase in numbers. This aim is achieved through a weakening of man's interest in reproduction and diverting his time and effort to personal, scientific and economic development. According to him in nature there is hostility between genesis and individuation. The more hard work the individual does for his advancement in his specialised field of work, the reproductive desire will be weakened.

(2) Spencer took recourse to the evolutionary theory in the field of population. This growth is fundamentally from the simple form to the complex. With increasing development of society, life tends to be complex which brings about a reduction in fertility.

(*a*) Societies where life is more complex, birth rate is correspondingly less.

(*b*) On the contrary where life is not so complex, fertility rate is fairly high.

(3) Spencer visualised a natural reduction in the reproductive capacity, more particularly among women as more time and energy is devoted to personal development. This reproductive deficiency is attributed to the overtaxing of the brain by women. Women belonging to rich families are relatively more sterile due to their mental exertion in comparison to women belonging to poor families. They also suffer from inability to suckle their infants. Spencer observed: "In its full sense, the reproductive power means the power to bear a well developed infant, and to supply that infant with the natural food for the natural period. Most of the flat chested girls who survive their high pressure education are incompetent to do this. Were their fertility measured by the number of children they could rear without artificial aid, they would prove relatively very infertile."

(4) Spencer has tried to establish a correlation between size and fertility rate. Those human beings who are small have more and higher fertility rate. He commented, "the minutest organisms multiply asexually in their millions." The small compound like cells are produced in thousands, whereas more compound in hundreds and still bigger lose their productive capacity.

(5) Spencer considered longivity as a factor determining birth rate and death rate. As the life and timing become complex, life expectancy become more and death rate comes down. In poverty individuation is less and genesis is more. Quite often men of unusual mental ability leave no offspring.

(6) Where the fertility rate is high the following consequences ensue:

(*a*) Death rate will also increase because there will be less individuation.

(*b*) Life expectancy will also go down due to lack of individuation.

(7) Spencer never considered population increase harmful or unwelcome. He felt more population will create more manpower which resulted in the exploitation of natural resources. This process has helped in social, economic and cultural advancement of the people. Revolutionary changes have also taken place on account of the progress in the above fields.

(8) Spencer suggested that if birth rate is to be reduced, it could be achieved by an increase in life expectancy. To quote him: "When population growth tends to become excessive and thereby the extinction

of species, individuation steps in and resolves all differences."

Critical Estimation

Spencer's theory throws valuable light into the reproductive capacity. Even then, it is not free from defects.

(1) Spencer's theory cannot be designated as the real theory of population.

(2) It is not correct to treat population as a purely biological phenomenon.

(3) Spencer's thesis that with a natural evolution process of individuation, fertility will be low cannot be established conclusively.

(4) Empirical evidence do not lend support to the argument that fertility rate is less among the rich.

(5) It is also not realistic to hold that fertility among girls belonging to poor class is more. Educated women also are equally endowed with reproduction capacity.

(6) During the days when Spencer wrote his thesis the birth rate in western countries was not low, nor is it low today.

6. CORRADO GINNI'S THEORY OF POPULATION

Corrado Gini (1884) was a Social Scientist of Italy. He became interested in population changes as they affected the evolution of society and, in particular, the evolution of nations. He subscribed to the view that every nation at the primary stage has almost the same sort of composition and simplicity of growth. Fertility is fairly high during this period. With the growth of population economic and social problems crop up which make the society complex. New industrial and trade problems are superimposed on the already complex state to compound the difficulties. Fertility starts going down at this point. Thompson and Lewis states: "He thought that the evolution of a nation or of any society was closely linked to the changes in their rates of population growth and to the varying proportion of the growth coming from the different social classes." Gini's theory is treated here as a natural law theory because he believed that biological factors are responsible for population growth. The reasons for varying rates of population in different societies should be sought in the differences in their biological traits.

Gini showed with the use of statistics based on several countries that a comparative small proportion of one generation produces the majority of people in subsequent generation. He described the process of the growth of nations as the cyclical rise and fall of population "

Cyclical Growth

The growth in population is akin to the life cycle of an individual. The first stage is marked by rapid growth. The second period is one of slower growth and mature achievement. The third period is known as the senescene period during which the number of people decline and the quality of civilization undergoes deterioration. As observed by Thompson and Lewis: "Every nation in its youth is simple and undifferentiated in structure and has a high rate of fertility, because each generation springs from the people who are hereditarily most prolific, i.e. highly fecund." As a result such a nation grows rapidly in numbers, this growth is followed by growing complexity. This period is marked by industrial and commercial activity and development of social classes. Pressure of population will be felt, which is being siphoned off through colonisation or war or both.

In the next stage social and economic complexities become more acute, which is followed by a decrease in the rate of population growth. This phenomena is partly due to loss of energetic people through war and colonisation. The increase in proportion of the upper class people whose number increases at a slow rate also create a decline in population.

According to Gini the chief cause of population growth is biological. As quoted by Thompson and Lewis: "Gini believed that the biological factor in declining fertility was the fundamental factor, that it really underlays the influence of economic and social factors, which only apparently determined the decline in fertility."

The decline in fertility is due to the decline in ability to bear children. Initially this decline in fertility is manifested in the upper class and sooner than later it spreads to other classes. As the energetic and prolific members of the lower class are imbibed in the higher class, they too become less fertile. The fertility of the entire upper class suffers decline. As quoted by Thompson and Lewis, "According to Professor Gini, even the sterility of these climbers is not a consequence of the social conditions surrounding this climbing; it is, rather, a result of the weakening of the reproductive instinct and is an inevitable phase of the cycle of population growth."

SELECT REFERENCES

1. Doubleday, T.: *The True Law of Population shown to be connected with the Food of the People*, 2nd edn., George Pierce, London, 1847.
2. Harris Foundations: *Population*, Lectures on the Harris Foundation, 1929, by Carrdo Gini, Shiroshi Hashu, Robert R. Kuezynshi, Oliver

Edwin Baker, The University of Chicago Press, Chicago, 1930.
3. Sadler, M.T.: *Ireland: Its Evils and Their Remedies*, John Murray (Publishers) Ltd., London, 1829.
4. Spencer, H.: *The Principles of Biology*, 2 Vols., D. Appleton & Co., Inc., New York, 1867-68.
5. Meek, Ronald L.: *Marx and Engels on Malthus*, London: Lawrence and Wishart, 1953.
6. Thompson, Warren S. and David T. Lewis: *Population Problem* (Fifth edition), New York: McGraw Hill Book Company, 1976, Chapters 2 and 3.
7. United Nations, *Determinants and Consequences of Population Trends*, Volume I, New York: United Nations, 1973, Chapter II.

EXAMINATION QUESTIONS

1. Explain in brief the following theories:
   a—Sadler's theory of destiny.
   b—Doubleday's theory of diet.
   c—Jouse De Castro's theory
   d—Logistic curve of Pearl and Reed.
   e—Biological theory of Herbert Spencer.
   f—Corrado Gini's theory of population.

20

Theory of Demographic Transition

(The Population Cycle-stages of Population Growth)

It has been suggested that there are a number of distinct stages in demographic growth through which population passes, the stages being collectively known as the population cycle or the theory of 'demographic transition'. The demographic transition is the relationship between fertility and mortality, i.e., between the birth rate and the death rate. The theory pinpoints the changes in these rates which occur as a consequence of economic development. Sax had identified four stages involved in this demographic transition that has historically accompanied modern economic development:

The first stage. Sometimes called the high fluctuating stage, is marked by high fertility and mortality rates (about 35 per thousand) and by slow or intermittent population growth. The first phase occurs in those economies which are characterised by low productivity, low standard of living, heavy agricultural dependence, primitive means of production and underdeveloped means of transport. In such economies death rates are high due to widespread prevalence of illiteracy, universality of marriage, early marriage, absence of desire to

Four Stages of Demographic Transition

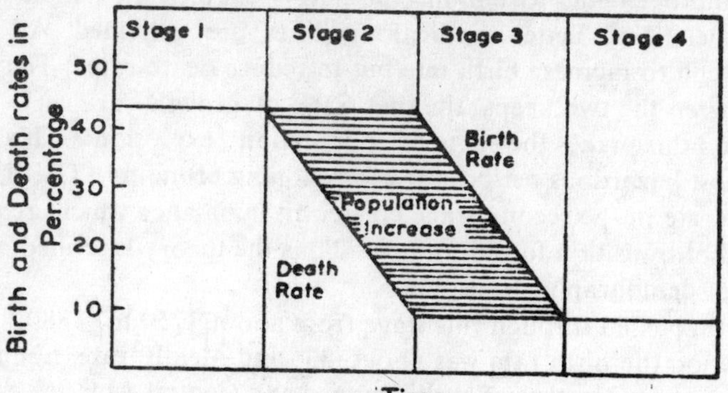

Fig. 1

plan families, and last but not the least, as a consequence of deep-rooted social beliefs and customs about the size of the family, attitude towards children, etc. Moreover, in a primitive society, there are economic advantages of large family in the form of low cost of children and their earnings. "Children contribute at an early age and are the traditional sources of security in the old age of parents. The prevalent high death rates, especially in infancy, imply that such security can be attained only when many children are born." In such a society, since the high birth rate is balanced by the high death rate. regular increase in population is very low. This stage is usually referred to as the stage of "high potential growth" but of low actual growth. This term is a tacit acknowledgement of the variability of the death rate and of its suspectibility to control or reduction, under modern conditions.

Britain passed through this stage prior to the Industrial Revolution. Countries of Central, Western and Eastern Africa and South-East Asia are included in this stage where the increase in population is conditioned by the frequent occurrences of famines, pestilence, floods and droughts.

The second stage. This stage is also known as the early expanding or youthful demographic stage, when death rate begins to decline but birth rate lags considerably behind. This accelerates the growth of population. High growth potential of the first stage is realised in the high actual growth in the second stage as a consequence of decline in death rate. In countries belonging to this phase, agriculture techniques are improved by various scientific devices so that food supply becomes more abundant. The improvement in transport makes the supply of food regular. Increasing industrialisation brings about all-round improvement. Rise in income levels enables the people to improve their diet. Better medical facilities are provided. All these factors tend to increase birth rate but to reduce death rate. The wide gap between the two keeps the net rate of growth at very high levels and this makes the stage of 'population explosion'. This stage is the most hazardous period for a developing economy. The decline in death rate in the second stage creates an imbalance which requires a period of transition for adjustment. Thus the theory is termed as the theory of demographic transition.

Britain passed through this stage from about 1750 to 1880, in the latter period the birth rate was about 33 and death rate about 20. Many countries Northern South America and Central America as well as China and parts of South East Asia belong to this stage. Abrupt declines in death and birth rate over 40 per thousand have produced some startling natural increase: Costa Rica (1962) 42.0, Brunei (1960) 38.0, Mexico (1962) 34.3, and Malaya (1960) 31.4. A number of countries with birth rate of 30-40 per thousand and natural increase rates of 20-30 per thousand should also be included in this stage; Mauritius (1961) 29.9, Hong Kong (1961) 28.3, Singapore (1962) 28.2, Ceylon (1960) 28.0, India 24.7, Trinidad and Tobago (1961) 22.8.

It may be noted here that if it was appropriate to call the demographic change in Europe over the last two centuries "the Demographic Transition"; it is certainly not appropriate to use the same term for what is happening in the developing countries today. The reason is that the condition in the developing countries since World War II definitely is not similar to the experiences of the European countries on which the transition theory was based. Whereas it took European countries 150 to 200 years to reduce their death rate below 15, this is being done in developing countries now in 15 or 20 years. A one per cent rate of increase of population in European countries is definitely different from a three per cent rate of increase in developing countries. What is happening in the developing countries is not a "Transition" it is, as Kingsley Davis has said, an "Explosion".

The third or late expanding stage of population: This stage is characterised by declining fertility (about 20 per thousand) and with mortality declining more rapidly (to about 12 per thousand). Natural increase rates tend to lie between 10 and 20 per thousand. Spain and Yugoslavia, the Netherlands and the United States, Australia, Portugal, U.S.S.R., Canada, Argentina, Israel and New Zealand belong to this phase. The economy of these countries is based relatively on advanced agriculture and modern industry. With the growth of industrialisation, population tends to shift away from rural areas towards industrial and commercial centres.

The fourth stage: This stage also known as low fluctuating stage is characterised by low fertility (birth rates between 10 and 20 per thousand) balanced equally by low mortality rates (death rates of 8 to 13 per thousand). The result is very low natural increase of population. Many European countries and one Asian country, Japan, may be classified in a fourth stage of population growth. The countries coming under this phase are Hungary, Sweden, Belgium, Luxembourg, Czechoslovakia, Austria, England and Wales, Denmark, Scotland, France, West Germany, Norway, Finland, Rumania, Switzerland, Italy, Bulgaria and Japan. The economy of these countries is characterised by highly developed industries, mechanised agriculture and the excess of urban population. Growth of urban population and with the development of economic roles for women outside the home, tends to increase the possibility of economic mobility that can better be achieved with small families and tends to decrease the economic advantages of a large family. One of the features of economic development is typically increasing urbanisation and children are usually more of a burden and less of an asset in an urban than in a rural setting. Thus the fourth stage is characterised by low birth rate, low death rate, small family size and low growth rate of population. This is the stage of incipient decline of population.

Thus these four stages reveal the transformation of a primitive high birth and high death rate and low-income economy into a low birth and low death rate and high-income economy. This shift is caused by the development of new technology and accumulation of capital. Figure 1 depicts the four stages involved in this demographic transition which are set out above. In this figure the first stage is characterised by high and fluctuating birth and death rates, which, on the average, nearly cancel out. In the second stage, death rates start declining while birth rates remain high. Stages two and three are the periods of explosion, when there is a large differential between birth and death rates due to declining death rates and constant birth rates. Finally, in stage four death rates and birth rates are both again near balance, but this time at lower rates than in stage one.

In most European countries a decline in fertility did not begin until the second half of the nineteenth century. It has continued, with minor interruptions, until the present. In the mid-1700 European birth rates were high (35-40 per thousand in most countries) but not as high in many of today's developing countries (often 40-50). The sharpest decline in fertility occurred between 1870 and 1930, when they levelled out at around 20, and most European countries today have rates between 15 and 20.

Prior to World War II, the developing countries also were characterised by 'high birth and death rates' and thus had low rates of natural increase. The demographic transition began with a rapid post-war decline in death rates unaccompanied by a corresponding decline in birth rates.

Most of the developing countries today are in the second stage, and are experiencing population explosions. To answer the question whether the population explosion can continue indefinitely, we first must ask whether these countries will also experience the same type of demographic transition.

Relevance of the demographic transition theory to developing countries: Will a developing country such as India follow a similar population cycle on its own? Many population experts do not think so. They cite separate factors which they feel hinder the application of the transitional theory to the presently over-populated developing countries. They base their arguments on the contrasts they observe between the economic conditions and demographic situation in the developing countries today with those prevailing in the developed countries at the corresponding stage of development. They emphasize the following differences:[1]

1. The decline in the death rate in the developing countries has been sudden and rapid and it has not been accompanied by any economic development. On the other hand, the decline in the death rate in the developed countries was slow and gradual, and was the result of overall economic development.

2. The birth rates in the developing countries today range between 40 per thousand and 60 per thousand. Further we have not observed any significant decline in their birth rates even though the death rates have declined considerably. On the other hand the developed countries never experienced birth rates above 40 per thousand during their development period. Moreover, after a time lag, these countries registered a decline in their birth rates.

3 Thus, the magnitude of the population explosion being experienced by the developing countries today is much more severe. Such high rates of population growth were never experienced by the developed countries.

4. The developing countries today are at a much lower level of economic development than was the case for the developed countries at the time of their development.

5. The opportunities for large-scale international migration as existed during the eighteenth and nineteenth centuries do not exist any more.

6. The developing countries today are relatively more densely populated than was the case with the developed countries during their period of development.

7. Unlike most developed countries, the developing countries today have no colonies to exploit.

SELECT REFERENCES

1. Bose, Ashish, "The Population Puzzle in India", *Economic Development and Cultural Change*, Vol. 7, No. 3, April 1959, pp. 245-246. The article contains a useful summary of these differences.

---

1. Cowgil, Donaldo: "Transition Theory as General Population Theory", *Social Force*, 1963.

2. Clark, C.: *Population Growth and Land Use*, 1967.
3. Hoover, E.M.: *Population Growth and Economic Development in Low Income Countries*, Princeton, 1958.
4. Coontz, S.E.: *Population Theories and their Economic Interpretation*, 1957.
5. Ryder, N.B.: "The Conceptualization of the Transition in Fertility", Cold Spring Harbor Symposium on Quantitative Biology (22), 1957.
6. Sinha, V.C.: *Dynamics of India's Population Growth*, 1975.
7. Van, N.L.: "Demographic Transition Re-examined", *American Sociological Review* (20) 1955.
8. Vance, R.B.: "Is Theory for Demographers?" *Social Force*, (31), 1952.

EXAMINATION QUESTIONS

1. Describe the theory of 'Demographic Transition' on the basis of various growth cycles of population.
2. Describe critically the demographic transition theory of population. In which stage of population transition in India is passing at present?

21

Trends in Indian Population Growth

India today possesses about 2.4 per cent of the total land area of the world but she has to support about 15.2 per cent of the world population. The world's present estimated population is about 4492 million and India's population constitutes about one-eighth of the world's population. According to the estimates of the census of 1981 the population of India is 68.4 crores. India's population is larger than the combined population of Bangladesh, Indonesia, Burma, Malaysia, Pakistan, Philippines, Republic of Vietnam, Thailand and Sri Lanka. The Mainland China is the only country whose population exceeds that of India.

At the present rate of growth, estimated to be 2.2 per cent a year, India's population is increasing at the rate of 14 million a year. It is as though the entire population of a country such as Australia is added every year. What does the addition of nearly 14 million people mean to India's economy? It means making available every year, among other things, "tonnes of food, 2.5 million houses, 4 million jobs, 126,500 schools, 372,500 teachers and 188 million metres of cloth." Thus, such a massive annual increase in population imposes a heavy burden on an already overburdened economy and almost completely wipes out the progress which the country makes.

Growth of India's Population before 1891

Let us examine the pattern of India's population growth from an historical perspective. We have no information about the size of population in ancient or medieval India. Of course some estimates have been provided by more enthusiastic scholars. Moreland estimated that the population of India in 1605 was 10 crores. According to Dr. Pradha Kumar Mukerjee, the population of India was 10.50 crores at the beginning of 19th century. Estimates made by Kingsley Davis are considered realistic. In his book population of India and Pakistan, Kingsley Davis gives the population as under in Table 1:

Table 1. India's Population*

Year	*Population in Crores*
300 B.C.	10.14
A.D. 1600	10
A.D. 1800	12
1885	17.5
1871	21.5

The above figures are also based on estimates. The figures reveal the continuous increase in population in India. However, the rate of increase in the olden days was not significant. There was constant shift in the areas where population was concentrated. Census enumeration started only after this period in India.

Growth of Population since 1901

Our knowledge of the population trends in India comes mainly from the Indian Census. It is a matter of great satisfaction that records are available for the last 100 years which provide fairly reliable estimates of the population and the growth rate. A study of absolute population and percentage growth rates of population in India can be made from the following table (Table 2):

Table 2. Growth of Population in India

Census year	*Population (in crores)*	*Decennial increase or decrease (in crores)*	*Percentage increase or decrease during the decades*	*Annual rate of growth*
1901	23.6	0.0	0.0	—
1911	25.2	1.6	5.7	0.57
1921	25.1	—0.1	—0.3	—0.03
		The year of the great divide		
1931	27.9	2.8	11.0	1.10
1941	31.9	4.0	14.2	1.42
1951	36.1	5.2	13.3	1.33
1961	43.9	7.8	21.5	2.15
1971	54.8	10.9	24.6	2.40
1981	68.4	13.6	24.7	2.21

Table 2 shows the growth of our population since 1901 and its highly significant acceleration since 1921 much more so since 1951. Up to the year 1921, the year of the 'great divide', the population of India increased at a very low rate. In between 1891 and 1901, the growth rate was zero. Between 1901 and 1911 the population rose at a very slow rate of 0.57 per cent per annum. Of the seven decades, 1911-21 was the only one decade which registered an annual decrease of population. This was caused by severe famines and epidemics of the years preceding the census, of which the most devastating was the nation-wide influenza epidemic of 1918-19. During the 20-year period covered by the first phase, the annual rate of growth averaged 0.26 per cent and a mere 13 million was added to the country's population.

The second phase covers the period 1921-1951 when the population grew steadily each decade although at a modest annual rate of 1.05 per cent during 1921-1931; 1.34 per cent between 1931 and 1941; and 1.26 per cent between 1941 and 1951. Between 1921 and 1951, the annual rate of increase averaged about 1.2 per cent and another 1.10 crore persons were added to the country's population during this 30-year period. No wonder, therefore, the year 1921 is aptly styled as the 'Great Divide' in Indian demographic literature. The main factors responsible for relative stability in the rate of growth of population were the Bengal famine of 1942-43 which took a heavy toll of lives and the dislocation caused by the partition of the country. The population of India which was 43.92 crores in 1961 registered a rise and stood at 54.7 crores in 1971.

The third phase covers the period since 1951 when there were further substantial increases in population by 21.5 per cent or at the rate of 1.98 per cent per annum in the decade 1951-1961; by 24.8 per cent or at an average annual rate of 2.24 per cent during 1961-1971; and by 24.75 per cent or an yearly average rate 2.25 per cent during 1971-1981. During each successive decade since 1951 there appears to have been an increase in the average annual rate of growth of the population.

The 1981 census of India disclosed a population of 684 million with an addition of 136 million during the decade 1971-81 and a decadal growth rate of 24.75 per cent or 2.21 per cent annually which shows little change from 24.80 and 2.22, respectively in the previous decade. Thus the population increased by 15 million during the three decades of 1891 to 1921, but during the next three decades of 1921-51, it increased by 110 million which is seven times the increase of the previous period. During the next two decades (1951-1961 and 1961-1971), the population increased by 78 million and 109 million, respectively. These increases are phenomenal. It took India hundreds of years to attain a population of 250 million in 1921 but it took only 45 years to double it. And, at the current rate of growth, the population will double every 32 years. Such an accelerating growth was not foreseen by the Indian planners. The analysis thus leads us to conclude that while there was no impact of the family planning programme at all during 1951-71, it was very little, almost insignificant during 1971-81. According to demographers, even if India were to take drastic measures to reduce its birth rate to the replacement level by 1985, its population would still reach the billion mark by A.D. 2000. This is the inevitable consequence of having an age structure which is heavily skewed towards the younger age group. Nearly 40 per cent of the present population is below 15 years of age.

The skyrocketing of India's population has seriously aggravated the problems of economic development. Demographers call it a period of population explosion to dramatise the severity of the situation. Figure 1 portrays the "vertical" nature of the demographic explosion.

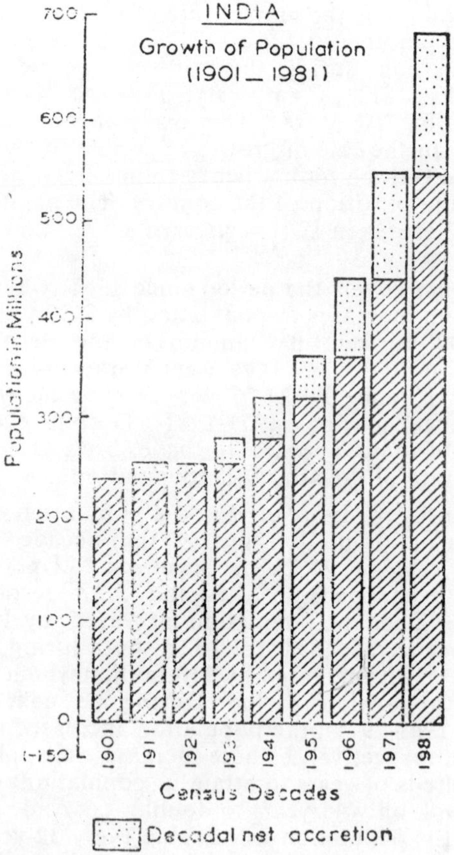

Fig. 1.

Why Exploding Population

Leaving aside the question of migration, the rate of growth of population is the function of birth rate and death rate, so an explanation to the acceleration of the population growth can be obtained from an analysis of India's past birth and death rates which reveal that in the three decades from 1921 to 1951 the death rates were markedly below the levels recorded prior to 1921 while the birth rates have remained practically stationary all through. The death rate declined from 47 per thousand in 1911-20 to 14.8 per thousand in 1981 while the birth rate fell from 48 per thousand to only 36 per thousand during the same period. It is the imbalance between these two rates, brought about mainly by the sudden and rapid decline in the death rate, which is responsible for the explosive growth of India's population. The trends in India's birth and death rates are given in Table 3.

Table 3. India's Birth and Death Rates, 1901-81

Year	*Estimated birth rate*	*Estimated death rate*	*Increase in population*
1901-10	49.2	42.6	6.6
1911-20	48.1	47.2	0.9
1921-30	46.4	36.3	10.1
1931-40	45.2	31.2	14.0
1941-50	39.9	27.4	12.5
1951-60	41.7	22.8	18.9
1961-70	39.0	17.0	22.0
1981 (census)	36.0	14.8	21.2

Source: S.P. Jain, "Some Aspects of Mortality", in Population in India's Development, 1947-2000, Ashish Bose, *et al.* (ed.) Delhi, Vikas, 1974, p. 320.

There have been several factors responsible for this dramatic decline in the dath rate, viz. control of famine through improved

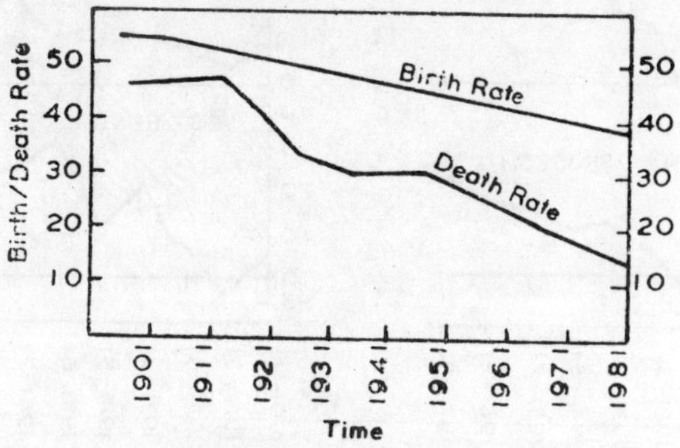

Fig. 2.

means of transport, reduction in the incidence of epidemics, improvement in sanitation, public health and greater regularity of

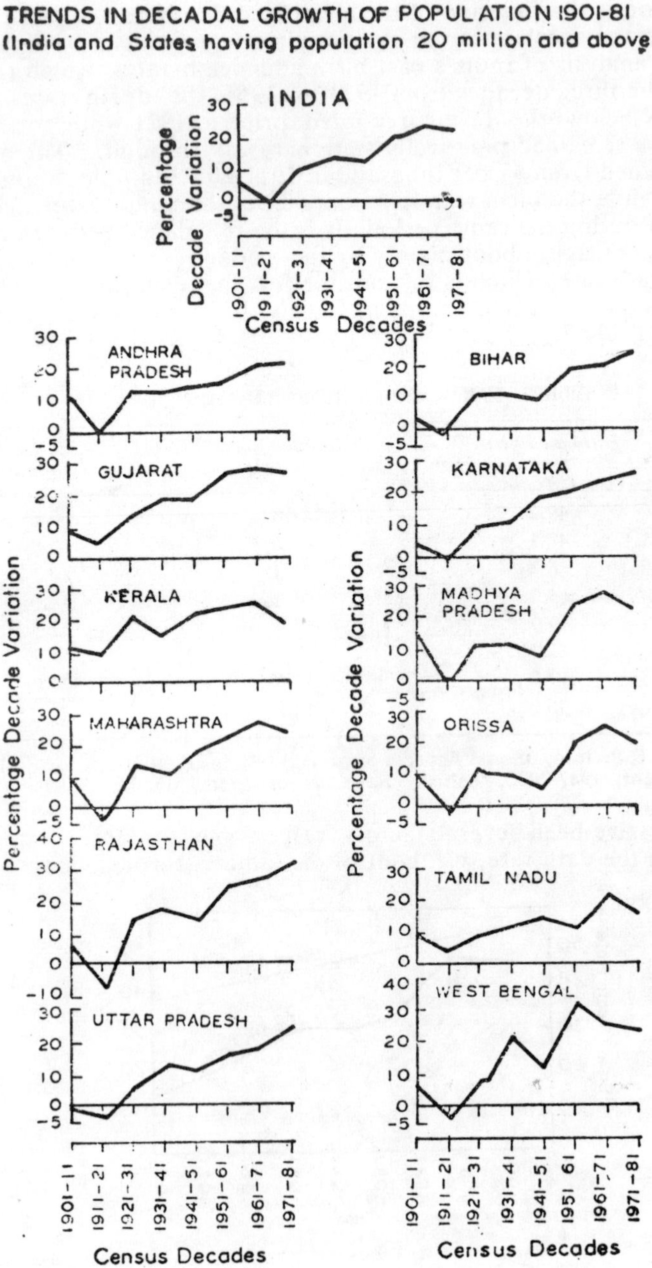
TRENDS IN DECADAL GROWTH OF POPULATION 1901-81
(India and States having population 20 million and above)
INDIA
ANDHRA PRADESH
BIHAR
GUJARAT
KARNATAKA
KERALA
MADHYA PRADESH
MAHARASHTRA
ORISSA
RAJASTHAN
TAMIL NADU
UTTAR PRADESH
WEST BENGAL
Percentage Decade Variation
Census Decades
1901-11
1911-21
1921-31
1931-41
1941-51
1951-61
1961-71
1971-81

Fig. 3.

food supply, higher incomes deployed to reduce suffering and greater political stability. India has achieved a remarkable result in public health work since 1950. The successful attack on the factors causing high mortality is reflected in an increased life expectancy at birth and also in a sharp reduction in the infant mortality rate. The latter has dropped from 232 per thousand in 1901 to 125 in 1981. Although this rate is still considerably high when compared to the rates in West, the decline is dramatic and represents considerable progress. Life-span of mean expectation has increased from 23.6 years in 1901 to 54.0 years in 1981. This is a significant achievement.

An important feature of the decline in the death rate is that it has been accomplished without any significant development in the economic front. The reduction in mortality has been achieved by the use of quick and inexpensive methods of fighting diseases. Whereas the western countries took 70 years to 80 years to achieve a similar decline in mortality it took India hardly 20 years.

Since 1971, there have been further reductions in fertility as well as mortality. Although there have been fluctuations in the death rate since 1971, the estimated crude death rate in 1975 was 15.9. It is expected that crude death rates will decline further over the years. The trend of a declining fertility is also more firm and definite during recent years, especially since 1961 and could largely be attributed to the more vigorous family planning drive. Though in the past, social scientists and demographers were pessimistic regarding possibilities of substantial reduction in Indian fertility, recent developments indicate that India is on a near take-off stage in fertility decline. As noted by Rele, "..... the initial stage of the onset of declining fertility seems well on its way. This is normally the crucial stage. Once, this is achieved, the next stage of more rapid decline in fertility may be expected, provided it is supported by programme inputs as well as simulteneous social and economic development."

Inter-State Variation in Population in India

While there is a cross section of opinions about the national growth, an important feature brought out by the 1981 census is that the problem of rapid population growth in India is essentialty a regional problem. The growth rates among the 15 major States (those with a population above 10 million) has varied from 17.23 in Tamil Nadu to 32.36 in Rajasthan. Also in 7 States (with a total population of 340 million) the growth rate has increased imparting a higher momentum to population growth.

A study of the quantitative population growth differentials in various States will reveal that the extent of variation is very wide. We have twenty-two States and also nine union territories. The union territories are comparatively very small units, altogether they account for only about 3 per cent of the total population of the

Table 4. Decennial Growth Rate of Population, 1901-81

State	Size of Population (in million) 1901	Size of Population (in million) 1981	% increase between 1901 and 1981	Decennial Variation of Population in Percentage 1901-1911	1911-1921	1921-1931	1931-1941	1941-1951	1951-1961	1961-1971	1971-1981	% Variation of growth rate of population of 1971-81 over 1961-71
	(1)	(2)	(3)	(4)	(5)	(6)	(7)	(8)	(9)	(10)	(11)	(12)
Andhra Pradesh	19.1	53.4	+180.10	+12.49	− 0.13	+12.99	+12.75	+14.02	+15.65	+20.65	+22.76	+ 8.90
Assam	3.7	19.9	+505.01	+16.85	+20.17	+20.13	+20.49	+20.10	+35.06	+34.37	+36.09	+ 3.26
Bihar	27.3	69.8	+155.65	+3.67	− 0.66	+11.45	+12.20	+10.27	+19.77	+21.36	+23.90	+12.05
Gujarat	9.1	33.9	+273.41	+7.79	+ 3.79	+12.92	+19.25	+18.69	+26.88	+29:34	+27.21	— 7.42
Haryana	4.6	12.8	+177.97	+ 9.70	+ 1.95	+ 7.14	+15.63	+ 7.60	+33.79	+31.36	+28.04	−13.00
Himachal Pradesh	1.9	4.2	+120.67	− 1.22	+ 1.65	+ 5.23	+11.54	+ 5.42	+17.87	+21.76	+22.46	— 2.52
Jammu & Kashmir	2.1	5.9	+179.60	+ 7.16	+ 5.75	+10.14	+10.36	+10.42	+ 9.44	+29.60	+29.57	— 0.27
Kerala	6.4	24.4	+297.16	+11.75	+ 9.16	+21.85	+16.04	+22.82	+24.75	+25.89	+19.00	—27.73
Madhya Padesh	16.9	52.1	+209.19	+15.30	— 1.38	+11.39	+12.34	+ 8.67	+24.17	+28.66	+25.15	—12.26
Maharashtra	19.4	62.6	+223.30	*10.74	— 2.91	*14.91	+11.94	+19.27	*23.60	+27.26	+24.36	—11.26
Mysore	13.0	37.0	+183.75	+ 3.60	— 1.09	+ 9.38	+11.09	+19.36	+21.57	+24.07	+26.43	+ 9.12
Nagaland	0.1	0.7	+661.48	+46.76	+ 6.55	+12.62	+ 6.04	+ 8.60	+14.07	+39.64	+49.73	+24.70
Orissa	10.3	26.2	+155.00	−10.44	— 1.94	+11.94	+10.22	+ 6.38	+19.82	+24.99	+19.72	−21.28
Punjab	7.5	16.6	+120.00	+10.78	— 6.26	+12.07	+19.32	— 4.58	+21.56	+21.00	+23.01	+ 6.04
Rajasthan	10.3	34.1	+231.29	+ 6.70	— 6.29	+14.14	+18.01	+15.20	+26.20	+27.63	+32.36	+16.28
Tamil Nadu	19.2	48.2	+150.86	+ 8.57	3.47	+ 8.52	+11.91	+14.66	+11.85	+22.01	+17.23	−22.74
Uttar Pradesh	48.6	110.8	+227.97	— 0.97	— 3.08	+ 6.66	+13.57	+11.82	+16.66	+19.82	+25.49	+28.87
West Bengal	16.9	54.4	+221.64	+ 6.25	— 2.91	+18.14	+22.93	+13.22	+32.80	+27.24	+22.96	−14.55
All India	238.4	683.8	+186.84	+ 5.73	− 0.30	+111.00	+14.23	+13.31	+21.69	+24.66	+24.75	— 0.20

Union. We will consider here only the eighteen States. Meghalaya, Tripura, Manipur and Sikkim are not included. In Table 3 differences in the rates of growth of population in different States are brought out.

An analysis of Table 4 would reveal the following interesting facts.

Column 1 of Table 4 gives the population size of each State according to the 1981 census. It is seen that Uttar Pradesh makes for 1/6, Bihar 1/10 with Maharashtra accounting for the another 1/11th of national population. West Bengal, Andhra Pradesh, and Tamil Nadu has each a population of 48 million. Karnataka and Madhya Pradesh are practically of the same size with population a little over 50 million in each. Gujarat and Rajasthan each has a population of about 35 million. Orissa and Kerala from another group each having a population around 25 million. Assam and Punjab form another band. Each has a population of about 19 million. At lowest level are Haryana with 13 million population, Jammu and Kashmir 6 million, Himachal Pradesh 4 million and Nagaland 0.71 million population. Thus in terms of population size, Uttar Pradesh, Bihar and Maharashtra are predominantly on the top of the scale, while others like Jammu and Kashmir, Himachal Pradesh and Nagaland have little significance in the all-India scene. This is indicative of the fact that the organisation of the country into the States and union territories has not been done on the basis of population, but on some other basis, namely, language, cultural and political considerations.

The rate of population growth varied from State to State in each of the 8 decades of the period as shown in Table 4. The second decade, 1911-21, witnessed the influenza epidemic, so the population of eleven States declined. The maximum decrease being 6.29 per cent for Rajasthan among these eleven States. The remaining seven States registered an increase in population which was 20.17 per cent, at the maximum, for Assam. Of the remaining seven decades witnessing growth of population, the first one, 1901-11 recorded the smallest rate of increase. The increase was shared by 15 States, while Haryana, Himachal Pradesh and Uttar Pradesh suffered a reduction in their population. Each of the remaining six decades, from 1921 to 1981, registered an increase in population which was shared by all the States.

The States can be grouped on the basis of the decadal growth rates in relation to the all-India average for each of the decades from 1901-11 to 1971-81, on the basis of Table 4, the States can be grouped in the following manner.

(A) Growth rate during each of the decades in 1901 to 1981 was always above all-India growth rate:

1. Assam, 2. Gujarat.

(B) Growth rate always below all-India growth rate:
Nil.

(C) Growth rate above all-India growth rate except in the decades mentioned in brackets:

(1) Haryana (1901-11, 1921-31, 1941-51)
(2) Kerala (1971-1981)
(3) Madhya Pradesh (1911-21, 1931-41, 1941-51)
(4) Maharashtra (1911-21, 1931-41, 1971-81)
(5) Nagaland (1931-41, 1941-51, 1951-61)
(6) Rajasthan (1911-21).

(D) Growth rate below the all-India growth rate except in the decades mentioned in brackets:

(1) Bihar (1921-31)
(2) Himachal Pradesh (1911-21)
(3) Karnataka (1941-51, 1961-71, 1971-81)
(4) Orissa (1901-11, 1921-31, 1961-71)
(5) Tamil Nadu (1901-11, 1911-21, 1941-51)
(6) Uttar Pradesh (1971-81).

(E) Growth rate above in 4 decades and below in 4 decades than the all-India growth rate—decades indicated in brackets are those where the growth rate was above the all-India figures:

(1) Andhra Pradesh (1901-11, 1911-21, 1921-31, 1941-51)
(2) Jammu & Kashmir (1901-11, 1911-21, 1961-71, 1971-81)
(3) Punjab (1911-21, 1921-31, 1931-41, 1951-61)
(4) West Bengal (1901-11, 1931-41, 1951-61, 1961-71).

While there is doubtless an absolute increase in most cases, it will be noticed from columns 10 and 11 of Table 2 that in quite a few States the percentage decadal growth rate in the decade 1971-81 has been lower than that in the decade 1961-71. This is so in the case of Gujarat, Haryana, Himachal Pradesh, Kerala, Madhya Pradesh, Maharashtra, Manipur, Meghalaya, Orissa, Tamil Nadu, Tripura, West Bengal and in the Union Territories of Andaman and Nicobar Islands, Arunachal Pradesh, Chandigarh, Delhi, Goa, Daman & Diu and Lakshadweep. However in the case of Himachal Pradesh, Meghalaya, Delhi and Pondicherry the decadal growth rates in these two decades are almost equal, the difference being of the order of plus/minus one point. The decadal growth rate in the decade 1971-81 has been higher than the corresponding rate of the previous decade 1961-71 only in the States of Andhra Pradesh, Bihar, Karnataka, Nagaland, Punjab, Rajasthan, Sikkim, Uttar Pradesh and in the Union Territories of Dadra and Nagar Haveli and Mizoram.

As for the decadal growth rates in the districts are concerned there are a few pockets which have high rates of growth in the decade 1971-81 even above 45 per cent. These are in the districts of Bangalore in Karnataka, Thana in Maharashtra, Bikaner in Rajasthan, Bhopal in Madhya Pradesh and in certain districts of Sikkim, Arunachal Pradesh, and Mizoram. Areas of fairly high growth rates are fairly concentrated in Rajasthan and in particular, the high growth rates of Ganganagar district and Jaipur are noticeable.

The growth rate in the country and in the states can be considered from the point of view of the percentage variation of the growth rates in the decades 1961-71 and 1971-81. The per cent decadal variation of growth rate, which can be considered as the rate of change of the growth rate itself during the decade, is negative in the case of A States and positive in the case of B States. The decadal variation of growth rate also has a wide range.

Among the major States those with slowing growth rates are Kerala, Tamil Nadu and Orissa. As against these States, the others which have negative per cent decadal variation of growth rate fall within two other ranges. In the major States of Assam, Bihar, Punjab, Andhra Pradesh, Karnataka, Rajasthan and Uttar Pradesh one notices an increase in the per cent decadal variation of growth rate itself.

The study of the regional population growth trends reveals that the extent of inter-State variations is very wide. What is more significant in some States of high population pressure is that it has been increasing faster than the States in which the pressure is, relatively speaking, less severe. This implies that in spite of the heavy population pressure, to which these States are being subjected their rate of population growth has become faster. Though emigration from States of high pressure of population is higher but the outflow of population will not substantially reduce this pressure and the difference in intensity of pressure will only marginally be affected by the transfer of population to other states. Variations in the rate of population growth in different parts of each State are also as wide as among the States. More cannot be said about these variations here, all that need be stressed is that these wide ranges of variations in the rates of population growth of various States are the most cardinal features of the population situation in India, and the policy makers, who do not give their due consideration to these variations, must necessarily invite the charge of formulating their policies and plans in very unreal terms. This great diversity in the rates of population growth call for intensive examination of the whole population situation in relation to the problems of development and social change. These inter-State variations in population need to be investigated as parts of regional and sub-regional plans of development. It is unfortunate that regional and sub-regional aspects of planning have been so far neglected; but as they have to be given their due place in future in the more earnestly undertaken schemes of development in terms of real planning, the variations in the rates of population growth within the States will necessarily have to be fully examined and evaluated.

Population Change vis-a-vis Demographic Transition

Attempts have been made by several scholars like Kingsley Davis, Dudley Kirt, Gunnar Myrdal etc. to apply transition theory to the analysis of demographic situation in India and other underdeveloped countries. It has been argued that the population growth trend in India is very much in tune with the established theory of demographic transition. Before 1921 both birth and death rates were high. Afterwards death rate decelerated rapidly with birth rate trailing behind which created the phenomenon of population explosion. Since 1961 fertility too has declined in India.

However, a closer scrutiny exposes the fallacies involved in fitting the Indian case within the strait jacket of the transition theory.

(I) *Death rate*

The sequence and tempo of population change in India deviates significantly from the transition theory. For instance the period between 1871-1921 witnessed an increase of 20% in population which invalidates the zero growth hypothesis. Similarly, the early transitional stage too, did not fructify in the Indian case as birth rate also declined along with death rate. Thus India in fact stripped the early transitional stage.

India and other developing countries accomplished the decline in death rate in a relatively short span of at the most 20 years whereas it was protracted over a period of over 100 years in the Western countries to experience sizeable fall in death rate.

(II) *Fertility reduction*

India could draw on the experience of other countries to bring about a quick fertility reduction. Besides, new methods of birth contraceptions, unknown to the Western world, are developed cheaply. In addition mass communication media like Radio, TV etc. imparted the necessary information regarding family planning. Over and above, the family planning programmes and policies have been evolved and implemented by the Governments on a war footing.

The Transition Theory has Malthusian Overtones

The Western writers made pessimistic conclusions of population explosion in India based on the concept of irrational behaviour of Indian masses. They failed to understand that the high fertility of the Indian villager is rational in the sense of optimization of his economic welfare in the present circumstances and family structure. It safeguards against risks like old age, unemployment, infirmities etc. as the intergenerational wealth flow is from children to parents. Institutional changes like nuclear family, education etc. rather than industrialisation alone can inculcate the rationality of low fertility among Indians. This would turn the tide which reverses the flow of wealth from parents to children. When the child is looked upon as a potential factor of production requiring investment in terms of nutrition, education etc. the parents would be motivated to have less children. When this attitudinal change takes place India would require fertility reduction techniques on a large scale.

Thus the theory of demographic transition is an insufficient guide to interpret Indian demographic situation. Democracy has successfully worked in India and in similar way the future population trends may provide a fitting reply to the neo-Malthusianists and supporters of the theory of demographic transition.

EXAMINATION QUESTIONS

1. Write an essay on the population growth in India.
2. The year 1921 marks a watershed in the population growth of India. Explain this statement and throw light on the growth rate of the population in India.
3. The population growth in India between 1891 and 1921 was negative. Explain the reasons for this.
4. The distribution of population among the different states in India is unequal. What significance has it?

22

Trends and Differentials in Fertility (Birth Rates) in India

In India before Independence, the problem which drew greater concern was that of abnormally high mortality and morbidity, and the study of fertility did not receive as much attention. The reason was that prior to 1921, the population in the subcontinent recorded a chequered growth because of the high and fluctuating death rates. The 1931 Census referred to the high fertility in India as a 'devastating torrent of babies' and suggested that the influx of babies should be stopped if progress was to be made. However, these warnings failed to elicit needed attention and the study of human fertility in India remained a neglected field. However, since Independence, the way of thinking of the planners and administrators has undergone sharp change. It was realized that if reduction in fertility was to be effected, it would be necessary to have adequate knowledge of the fertility behaviour of the people in the proper cultural context. Hence the number of fertility and KAP studies carried out in India during the past two decades has been very impressive.

Pioneering efforts to estimate the crude birth rate in the subcontinent were made by Kingsley Davis, who has provided estimates for the period 1891 to 1941. For the decade 1951-61, the available estimates include those by the Registrar General, Saxena, Visaria, Rele and Sinha, and the United Nations. For 1961-1971, estimates of birth rates have been given by the Registrar General, Rele and Sinha, Adlakha and Kirk and Raghavachari. From 1970 onwards the estimates of the Sample Registration System (SRS) in India are available. Table 1 furnishes the various estimates of the national birth rate.

It is obvious from Table 1 that:

(*i*) The birth rate in India during the first half of the twentieth century was very high.

(*ii*) Although the official estimate of the birth rate for 1951-61 was 41.7, various other estimates indicate that the birth rate at that time was still high, around 45 per thousand of the population.

(*iii*) The real decline in fertility occurred during 1966-1977, with the intensification of the national family planning programme.

(*iv*) Estimates based on SRS indicate that the Indian birth rate has been slowly but consistently declining from 36.8 in 1970 to 33.2 in 1979.

Table 1. Levels and trends in estimated birth rates in India, 1901—1979

Source	*Year*	*Birth Rate*
1. Kingsley Devis	1901-11	49.2
	1911-21	48.1
	1921-31	46.4
	1931-41	45.2
2. Registrar General	1941-51	39.9
3. Registrar General	1951-61	41.7
4. G.B. Saxena	1951-61	46.0
5. P.M. Visaria	1951-61	44.9
6. Rele and Sinha	1951-61	45.0
7. United Nations	1951-61	45.1
8. Registrar General	1961-71	41.1
9. Rele and Sinha	1961-71	41.0
10. Adlakha and Kirk	1961-71	40.5-42.0
11. S. Raghavachari Reverse Survival Method from age (i) 0-9	1961-71	41.1
(ii) 5-9	1961-66	41.6
(iii) 0-4	1966-70	40.2
12. Sample Registration System (SRS)	1970	36.8
	1971	36.9
	1972	36.6
	1973	34.6
	1974	34.5
	1975	35.2
	1976	34.4
	1977	33.0
	1978	33.3
	1979	33.2

Apart from the studies and estimations of fertility at the national level, there are several studies available in India at sub-national levels. They also confirm that much desired downward movement of fertility has set it. Kumudini Dandekar and Vaijayanti Bhate observe that there has been a 10 per cent decline in fertility in six villages of Maharashtra during the three five year plan periods, that is, from 1954 to 1966. The results of the Standard Fertility Surveys sponsored by the Government of India are also revealing in this context. They were conducted in the Family Planning Communication Action Research Projects of Calcutta, Delhi, (Mehrauli Block), Gandhigram and Shadnagar, and covered the period ranging from 1964 to 1971. The estimates based on these studies indicate overall trends of declining birth rate during the study periods of five to seven years (see Table 2). The computations on the number of births saved due to the acceptance of birth control methods in India indicate that there has been a 15.1 per cent decline in the birth rate during the period from 1960-61 to 1973-74.

Table 2. Trends in birth rates as revealed by family planning communication action research projects

Year	*Gandhi-gram*	*Year*	*Calcutta Centre I*	*Calcutta Centre II*	*Year*	*Mehrauli Delhi*	*Year*	*Shad-nagar*
1964	35.5	1963/64	24.7	26.0	1962/63	49.6	1966/67	47.4
1965	36.1	1964/65	22.6	21.8	1963/64	52.3	1967/68	43.6
1966	31.6	1965/66	21.3	17.8	1964/65	50·4	1968/69	38.2
1967	33.8	1966/67	19.8	15.5	1965/66	47.8	1969/70	40.6
1968	31.2	1967/68	17.6	17.8	1966/67	50.6	1970/71	42.6
1969	29.4				1967/68	46.9		
					1968/69	45.9		

Statewise Birth Rates

There are large variations in the birth rates among the states and union territories. The national birth rate has varied from 36.9 in

Table 3. Crude birth rates by rural and urban areas: India and States, 1970-79

State	*1970*	*1975*	*1978*	*1979*
1. Andhra Pradesh	35.4	34.9	33.6	31.9
2. Assam	38.8	30.1	30.8	32.4
3. Bihar	32.0	27.7	31.2	32.0
4. Gujarat	41.0	37.0	35.8	35.7
5. Haryana	36.2	38.0	33.5	36.4
6. Himachal Pradesh	32.7	32.7	27.3	31.8
7. Jammu & Kashmir	33.0	31.9	31.8	31.1
8. Karnataka	33.0	27.7	29.2	28.9
9. Kerala	31.6	28.0	25.2	26.1
10. Madhya Pradesh	39.3	40.3	37.2	37.8
11. Maharashtra	31.5	29.7	26.9	27.1
12. Manipur	34.1	24.5	32.3	30.0
13. Orissa	38.1	33.6	32.9	32.4
14. Punjab	33.8	31.8	29.4	29.3
15. Rajasthan	38.5	36.9	35.5	35.2
16. Tamil Nadu	30.0	30.7	28.8	28.1
17. Uttar Pradesh	45.4	43.1	40.4	39.6
18. West Bengal	27.8	28.7	28.7	NA
India	36.8	35.2	33.3	33.2

1971 to 33.0 in 1979. States like Gujarat, Madhya Pradesh, Rajasthan and Uttar Pradesh have had birth rates mostly above the national average. In contrast, the birth rate in Kerala, Karnataka, Tamil Nadu, Andhra Pradesh and Maharashtra has been below the national average for most part of the time span. Among the major States, Kerala is the only State which has been able to achieve a birth rate of about 25 in 1978.

Causes for High Birth Rate in India

There are various reasons why India's birth rate continues to be high. More important reasons may be noted:

1. *The social and religious customs.* In India, as in some of the south European countries, the birth rate is very largely influenced by social conditions and customs associated with marriage. In India, marriage is universal. Everyone in India sooner or later, usually sooner gets married. Unmarried persons are looked down by the society. Marriage is not merely a necessary social institution but a quasi-religious duty. Among the Hindus, everybody must have at least one son otherwise the parents are supposed to be deprived of certain benefits in the other world after death. Marriage in India is sacramental. To have a big family is considered to be a blessing of the God. As a result of such attitudes, we generally do not find unmarried men and women, and married people without children.

Age at marriage. Besides universality of marriage in India, marriage age of both males and females is low. Eight out of 10 girls in India are married in most fertile period (*i.e.* between 15 to 20 years of age). It has been calculated by Kuczynaky that the probability of the chance of married women below 20 in having a child within a year is 1/2 and the probability diminishes as the age advances.

Table 4 shows the proportion marrying in the different age groups and the median age.

Table 4. Proportion marrying in different age groups

Age Group	*1901*	*1911*	*1921*	*1931*	*1941*	*1961*
10-14	45.7	44.5	30.9	40.8	24.5	19.5
15-19	38.7	39.2	41.3	46.5	50.3	51.3
20-24	11.4	11.9	13.6	8.0	21.1	23.2
25	4.2	4.4	5.2	4.7	4.1	6.0
Median marriage age	15.6	15.7	16.2	16.0	17.5	18.0

The above table strikingly shows (*i*) that the proportion that marries after the age of 24 is low and has remained steady around

5% over the last sixty years. Thus the terminal marriage age by which bulk of girls married has remained unchanged at 25. There is the gradual decline of marriages below age 15. The pace of decline was larger during 1931-41. A proportion of the marriages postponed at ages 10-14 was performed at ages 15-19 but a greater proportion took place at ages 20-24. *(ii)* The median marriage age increased from 15.6 years to 16.2 years during 1901-21. It increased to 17.5 years in 1951. There was a little increase to 18 years by 1961. Thus the main gain was realised between 1941 and 1951. Compared to 1941, 1961 showed only small improvement.

To summarise, it may be said that though a remarkable decline in the proportion of marrying at ages below 15 took place, it was still higher. The fact that about 20 per cent of the females in 1961 and 12 per cent of the females in 1971 in the age group 10-14 had been married, shows the failure of these legislations. The current move to raise the minimum age at marriage to 18-21 years by legislation is unlikely to be successful since it cannot be effectively implemented. A rise in the age at marriage can occur only with high motivation among women for a better life for themselves.

2. *High mean duration.* As marriage takes place early in India, there is high mean duration of fertile union. By the duration of fertile union, we mean the time spent by a woman between the age of her effective marriage (nuptials) and her age at the time of her widowhood, separation death or the maximum fertile age (presumed to be 45 in the case of Indian women.

3. *Environmental cause.* India has a hot climate and in comparison to the colder countries of Europe, puberty is reached here earlier. So the marriage age and the period of child-bearing age in the female tends to grow longer with the result that the number of children per marriage is larger. There seems to be some positive correlation between hot climate and fertility. Really speaking, even in the animal and the vegetable kingdoms hotter areas are more prolific than the colder ones and the same seems to hold good even of the human beings. It is widely established that menstruation begins earlier in tropical countries than among the population of European stock and that people in the tropics have more frequent sexual intercourse. At least one influential writer even argues that sex plays a kind of "national sport in India".

It is found that about 80% of the Indian girls get their menstruation between ages of 12 and 15, about 50% of them get married before they complete 15th year. This is due to the fact that a Hindu woman, umarried at puberty, is a source of social disgrace to her family. But with the spread of education, this way of thinking is on the decline.

4. *Economic factor.* It has been pointed out that the people of humble means tend to have larger families than the well-to-do,

because the arrival of an additional child is considered as a source of additional income. In poor families, the children are put to work at an early age and as such they supplement the meagre resources of family. Again, because of the lack of saving, these children, when they grow up, provide security to their parents in old age. In this sense, they act like insurance for their parents. In the rural areas, the prosperity of a cultivator is largely judged by the number of his children, especially sons. In the case of joint families, every one gets a share in the income of the family; hence on one really cares as to how many children are born in the family.

Poverty itself is a potent cause for higher birth rate. There is no limit below that of starvation and starving parents never seriously bother about the number of children they have. The size of the family hardly makes any difference for one who is already starving. The basal poverty of the people in India not only makes them oblivious of the importance of the standard of living but it also makes them indifferent to the number of children they have.

5. *Low level of literacy*. Majority of people in India are illiterate. Low literacy turns old beliefs into obduracy and makes adaptation to new values, particularly with regard to small sized families and family limitation ideas, extremely difficult. In consequence, the addition to the human resource streams continues unabated. The relation between fertility and education has been the subject of investigation of a number of studies in India. Invariably, all the studies have supported the view that the average fertility of the women who are quantitatively well educated is lower than that of those who are modestly educated or uneducated.

6. *Age structure*. The distribution of population according to age has vital bearings in so far as it affects the population through marriage and fecundity. Since 1901, the proportion of children in our population has been about 40% varying from 39% in 1901 to nearly 42% in 1981. If high birth rate is maintained and rate of infant mortality is improved, as it most likely will, the proportion of children in population would probably rise still higher. This implies that 'young and more fecund' people dominate our population, so that with the prevailing universality of marriage, the marriage rate must be high and the birth rate must also correspond to it.

7. *Sex structure*. The sex-ratio, *i.e.*, number of women per thousand males, which in its own turn, may be affected by past fertility, mortality and migration, plays a significant role in determining birth and death rates in a country. India has got an adverse sex-ratio, *i.e.*, the number of males is greater than the number of females and this has got its own repercussions on the birth rate. With falling proportion of females in the total population and disproportion between males and females increasing in the States, the effect of increase in the proportionate married persons will be, on

the theoretical assumption, partly neutralised by increasing imbalance in sex-ratios. As no study has so far been undertaken on regional imbalance of population growth and regional disproportion in sex ratios, it cannot be stated what will be the net result of these mutually offsetting changes of fertility of our people on the growth of population.

The current fertility in India is also high due to the higher average number of children desired due to son preference. In so far as son preference is a cause for high birth rate in India, nothing can be done except to allow the socio-economic processes to act on the cultural attitudes of the population.

8. *Low level of family planning practice.* The most important reason for high birth rate in India is the lack of knowledge about birth control methods. Until recently there has been complete absence of conscious family planning in India, and the use of contraceptive has been practically unknown. It cannot be said that even now a substantial number of people have adequate and proper knowledge about the ABC of family planning. Many of those who know equate family planning with contraceptive or abortion etc., few regard it as equivalent to a planned family. The ORG survey found that nearly 78 per cent of the couples interviewed were aware of at least one method of birth control but only half as many had the knowledge of its use, leaving condoms out of account. The actual practice of any method was by only 13.6%. It was also found that those having three or more children have higher levels of awareness and knowledge than those having none or less than three. But, even in the group having three or more children and not wanting any more, the ever user percentage was barely 28. This shows the gap that exists between the need and the actual practice, and this gap is certainly not due to lack of awareness but could be, to some extent, due to the lack of knowledge. The wide gap that exists between knowledge and practice in this group is due to the lack of strong motivation for family planning.

World Pattern of Fertility

Additional observation on current fertility levels may be made by examining the extremes of fertility for countries around the world. In Table 5 for example, the 20 countries with the lowest and highest crude birth rate for 1980-85 are presented. Of the 156 countries considered, Switzerland ranks as the lowest, close behind Switzerland are other Western European countries, as well as Northern European countries.

The 20 countries with the highest crude birth rate are dominated by African and Arab Middle Eastern countries. The highest fertility among the 156 countries occurs in Kenya for which crude birth rate is 55 per thousand. Currently, there are 13 countries in the world with total fertility rates of 7.0 or more and 59 countries with total fertility rates of 6.0 or more.

Table 5. Twenty countries with lowest and highest crude birth rate, 1980-85

Country	*Crude death rate per 1000 population*	*Country*	*Crude birth rate per 1000 population*
Lowest		**Highest**	
1. Switzerland	8	137. Upper Volta	48
2. Germany Federal Republic of	10	138. Senegal	48
3. Luxembourg	10	139. Gambia	48
4. Denmark	11	140. East Timor	48
5. Sweden	11	141. Democratic Yemen	48
6. Austria	12	142. Burundi	48
7. Belgium	12	143. Liberia	49
8. Japan	12	144. Ethiopia	49
9. Netherlands	12	145. United Republic of Tanzania	50
10. Norway	12	146. Uganda	50
11. Finland	13	147. Nigeria	50
12. German Democratic Republic	13	148. Mauritania	50
13. Italy	13	149. Mali	50
14. United Kingdom of Great Britain and Northern Ireland	13	150. Botswana	50
15. France	14	151. Afghanistan	50
16. Hungary	14	152. Rwanda	51
17. Bulgaria	15	153. Niger	51
18. Australia	16	154. Benin	51
19. Canada	16	155. Malawi	52
20. Czechoslovakia	16	156. Kenya	55

Source: United Nations, World Population Prospects: Estimates and Projections as assessed in 1982, p. 21.

DIFFERENTIAL FERTILITY

Whereas in Western countries much attention has been devoted to study the difference between the fertility of various groups of the population of a country but unfortunately in India not only the statistics on overall fertility are lacking but differential fertility rates are also rare. In India differentials are not yet greatly affected by such variables as caste, education, occupation or economic status. There are, however, indications that the Western pattern will also be repeated in India in course of time.

1. Age Pattern of Fertility

Birth rate is the most common index of fertility but it does not give any idea of the pattern of fertility schedule. Crude birth rate suffers from a great limitation in as much as it does not take into account the age structure of the population. To have a better idea of the fertility situation, it is essential to compute the age pattern of fertility.

The study of the age pattern of fertility is an important addition and throws light on several aspects of reproduction in the community. It provides clues to questions such as (*i*) what is the tempo of child-bearing, (*ii*) what age do women start participating in reproduction, (*iii*) until what age do the women continue to bear children, (*iv*) what is the average family size, (*v*) has there been any shift in the pattern of child-bearing in the community over a period of time, if so, how and why, (*vi*) how is the age specific schedule affected by the use of diverse forms of birth control methods.

The age pattern of fertility can be studied with reference to age specific fertility rates (ASFRs) as well as age specific marital fertility rates (ASMFRs). In India, it is difficult to obtain adequate and reliable data on the annual number of birth by the age of the mother. Some surveys conducted by the National Sample Survey (NSS) and SRS, however, do provide information for the study of age pattern of fertility in India, which are presented in Table 6.

It is obvious from the figures of the table that the Indian fertility curve more or less conforms to the broad-peak type. Fertility remains fairly high during period 20 to 29 years of age both in urban and rural areas. Broadly speaking age specific fertility shows a low rate between 15-19 years, a sharp rise in the group 20 to 24 years with the peak being reached between 25 to 29 years. It continues to shrink with 30-34 age and tapers off in successive age group.

It should be noted that the shape of the ASFR-curve is determined, among other factors, by the female age at marriage, divorce and separation among women in the reproductive age, the incidence of widowhood, the extent of the use of birth control methods and the age pattern in the use of such methods.

The age specific marital fertility rates for rural and urban India are given in Table 7.

The rural as well as urban marital fertility in India exhibits a broad peak in the age group 20 to 29 with the maximum fertility in ages 20 to 24. Both in rural and urban India, substantial contributions to marital fertility continue until the age of 40.

Table 6. Age specific fertility rate in India from various sources from 1957 to 1978

Age group	NSS		SRS		Fertility Survey		Survey	
	1957/58 (rural)	*1960/61 (urban)*	*1968 (rural)*	*1969 (urban)*	*1972 (rural)*	*1972 (urban)*	*1978 (rural)*	*1978 (urban)*
10-14	0.5	0.9	—	—	—	—	—	—
15-19	144.7	105.0	109.4	97.8	97.5	52.2	72.7	41.9
20-24	266.2	244.7	251.4	261.9	273.5	220.6	237.7	192.1
25-29	238.9	218.6	272.6	266.6	283.4	247.3	240.7	190.5
30-34	191.9	168.9	224.3	226.9	272.2	173.4	167.9	133.4
35-39	120.7	110.7	172.3	158.3	151.2	108.2	115.0	70.0
40-44	48.5	41.5	81.6	77.1	82.7	43.3	52.3	24.1
45-49	17.8	9.6	39.2	35.5	32.7	13.0	24.9	6.8
General Fertility rate 10-49	136.1	128.2	—	—	—	—	—	—
15-49	—	—	176.9	173.7	174.0	134.0	137.0	104.0
Total Fertility rate	5.15	4.50	5.76	5.62	5.80	4.30	4.60	3.10

Table 7. Age specific marital fertility rates for rural and urban areas of India

Age	India 1972			
	Rural		Urban	
	ASMFR	*Percentage*	*ASMFR*	*Percentage*
15-19	211.5	15.4	220.6	18.2
20-24	312.9	22.8	312.6	25.8
25-29	302.8	22.1	284.3	23.5
30-34	248.8	18.1	201.2	16.6
35-39	170.1	12.4	123.7	10.2
40-44	94.5	6.9	52.2	4.3
45-49	32.5	2.3	15.5	1.4
General Marital Fertility rate	190.8	100.0	172.9	100.0

Source: Registrar General, India, Fertility Differentials in India, 1972 (New Delhi, 1976), pp. 5-6.

2. Rural-Urban Fertility

The National Sample Survey and the Sample Registration System have both consistently shown that the birth rate has tended to be

Table 8. Rural-urban differentials in the birth rate in India

National Sample Survey			*Sample Registration System*		
Round/Year	*Birth Rate*		*Year*	*Birth Rate*	
	Rural	*Urban*		*Rural*	*Urban*
17/1961-62	36.0	34.0	1968	39.0	—
18/1963-64	37.8	31.9	1969	38.8	32.8
19/1964-65	37.0	32.0	1970	38.9	29.7
20/1965-66	37.1	29.2	1971	38.9	30.1
21/1966-67	36.7	31.2	1972	38.0	30.2
			1973	35.9	28.9
			1974	35.9	28.4
			1975	36.7	28.5
			1976	35.8	28.4
			1977	34.3	27.8
			1978	34.7	27.8
			1979	34.4	28.0

Sources: (*a*) P.B. Brahma Sample Registration System (New Delhi, Office of the Registrar General, India), Appendix 1-4.

(*b*) New Delhi Office of the Registrar General, India, Sample Registration Bulletin, Vol. XV, No. 1, June 1981, p. 23.

lower in the urban areas than in the rural areas since 1960. The relevant data are shown in Table 8.

The lower urban marital fertility rate was demonstrated once again in 1978 from the Infant and Child Mortality Survey of 1979. According to this survey the general marital fertility rate for rural areas was 175.9 and that for urban areas was 147.9 while the total marital fertility rates were 5.6 and 4.7 respectively. The findings indicated the persistence of rural-urban differentials in marital fertility, with lower urban marital fertility at the national level, though it has been relatively a recent phenomenon emerging essentially after 1965.

Low urban fertility is caused by unbalanced sex-ratios, high living standards, economic insecurity and unemployment, social capillarity, occupational status, female employment, educational facilities and the availability of clinical aids towards family planning and so on, but there are no simple relationships.

The percentage of fourth or higher order births occurring in the large cities is around 30 compared with 40 for all-India. There is also the evidence of a higher extent of family planning practice in the cities.

Rural societies also have differing fertility levels. Just as in other parts of the world, in India, too, rural farm population is usually more fertile than the rural non-farm. Within the rural farm population owners and tenants have a larger number of children than do field labourers, and amongst the agricultural labour families, the landless labour families are even smaller in size; poverty in their case plays an important part in accentuating the process of multiplication.

A study on the fertility of currently married women in Greater Bombay in relation to their former residence has added a new dimension to the study of rural-urban differentials in fertility in India. This study has clearly shown that in Greater Bombay the non-migrants as well as migrants from other urban areas had lower fertility compared to migrants from rural areas.

Economic Status and Fertility

It has been observed in various fertility surveys in India that the total number of children born declines with an increase in per capita expenditure of the household. For instance, the National Sample Survey and the Mysore study have shown generally that fertility decreased with increase in per capita household expenditure. However, a detailed study of couples, on the basis of monthly income, shows that fertility is high among couples with lower income; it declines as income increases. Table 9 gives average number of children born alive to couples classified by income group.

Table 9. Average number of children born alive to couples classified by income group

Majumdar, D.N.		*Mukerjee, R.K.*		*Driver, E.D.*	
Below Rs. 50	4.43	Below Rs. 30	3.6	Below Rs. 500	4.6
Rs. 51-100	3.98	Rs. 30-75	3.2	Rs. 500-999	4.4
Rs. 101-200	4.18	Rs. 75-150	3.6	Rs. 1000-1499	4.8
Rs. 200 & above	6.18	Rs. 150-250	3.8	Rs. 1500-1999	3.8
		Rs. 500-1000	3.3	Rs. 2000 or more	4.6
		Rs. 1000 & above	3.9	All Income Groups	4.5
		All Income Groups	3.5		

Source: S.N. Agrawala. *India's Population Problems*, p. 129.

High per capita income of the household implies that the children and mother have better nourishment in the family. It also implies that medical care can be provided more easily and more often in case of sickness of the child which, in turn, prevents infant and childhood mortality. Once the couple is able to save the life of those children who are already born in the family, it does not need to go in for more and more births.

Fertility by Caste

There are a number of fertility studies which have some data, direct or indirect, on the fertility differentials by religion. Perhaps the most recent study which has bearing on fertility differentials by religion is the Fertility Survey conducted by the office of the Registrar General, India, in 1972 given in Table 10.

Table 10, General fertility rate by religion, India, 1972

Religion	*Rural*	*Urban*
Hindus	171.1	131.4
Muslims	191.5	150.8
Christians	136.6	109.6

The broad picture which has emerged from this table is that the fertility rate is higher for the Muslims as compared with the Hindus. It is not possible to do more than speculate on the reasons for this difference in fertility. However, it is said that the Muslims have higher fertility because of their greater toleration of widow remarriage. Another reason is that Muslim women do not follow as frequently the practice of going to their parents' house for confinement as do the Hindu women. As a consequence, the separation of the husband and the wife after confinement is of much shorter duration for the Muslims than for Hindus. The other cultural factors affecting the pattern of sex life also probably explain the higher fertility of Muslim women. Apart from the taboo on the sex relations for prolonged periods during lactation, Hindu tradition enjoins abstinence on a number of religious days. Another explanation which is given in this connection is that since a majority of the Muslims are poorer, more uneducated and tradition-bound than the Hindus, their fertility rate is higher.

A significant clue to the differences in fertility by religion is obtained by studying their mortality levels as indicated by the survival of children ever born. This involves the analysis of the average number of living children by religion. Table 11 presents the average number of living children per woman by present age and religion in Greater Bombay (1966). When standardised for the present age of the wife, the average number of living children shows much smaller variation from one religion to the other, except Zoroastrains. The uniformity in the average number of living children among the various religions arises because religions like Islam and others who exhibit higher fertility also have higher mortality in terms of the proportion of deaths among their children. Thus some degree of association is obvious between the levels of fertility and mortality among the religions. For explaining this phenomenon it may be argued that in the face of heavier mortality there is a greater need for higher reproduction felt by the subsystem, which develops ways and means, to promote higher fertility. Besides, higher fertility may lead to a fall in the levels of living, and in several ways may reduce the amount of infant and child care, thus increasing mortality among children.

Similar association between fertility and mortality was observed in another study in India by J.R. Rele in which social class with higher fertility also had higher mortality among children, so that the number of living children was about the same among the classes.

Education and Fertility

The relation between fertility and education has been the subject of investigation of a number of studies in India. Invariably all the studies have supported the view that a high level of formal education is ordinarily associated with low fertility. The Mysore population study revealed in Bangalore city the average number of children born to married illiterate women about the age of 45 was about 5.4, while that for women with high school or college education was 3.9. The National Sample Survey of 1960-61 conducted in urban areas also showed similar results. The number of children born alive to the women of completed maternity who were either illiterate or educated below primary standard or up to primary standard was 6.6. Corresponding figures for women with middle and high school education were 5.0 and 4.6, respectively. For women with

Table 11. Average number of children ever born per woman by per cent age and religion in Greater Bombay, 1966

Age of the woman	*Religion*					
	Hindu	*Muslim*	*Christian*	*Zoroastrian*	*Others*	*All religions*
Below 20	0.44	0.67	0.08	—	0.53	0.45
20—24	1.34	1.77	1.18	1.00	1.68	1.41
25—29	2.49	3.20	2.50	1.79	2.75	2.56
30—34	3.58	3.92	3.36	1.58	3.86	3.57
35—39	4.03	4.49	4.66	1.67	4.48	4.11
40—44	4.35	4.39	4.46	2.22	4.58	4.33
45+	4.75	5.32	4.55	2.40	5.11	4.64
All ages	3.04	3.06	3.39	2.03	3.17	3.07
Standardised average	3.06	3.50	3.04	1.60	3.36	3.07
Number of women	5656	785	712	147	572	7872

Source: J.R. Rele and Tara Kanitkar, "Fertility differentials by religion in Greater Bombay: role of explanatory variables, in Lado T. Ruzicka, ed., *The Economic and Social Supports for High Fertility* (Canberra, Department of Demography, Australian National University, 1977), p. 374.

university education it was as low as 2.0. Table 12 gives details of other studies.

Table 12. Total fertility by level of education

Mukerjee				*Driver*			
Wife		*Husband*		*Wife*		*Husband*	
Illiterate	3.5	Illiterate	3.5	Illiterate	4.7	Illiterate	5.0
Primary	3.4	Primary	3.3	Primary	4.3	Primary	4.3
Secondary	3.1	Secondary	3.2	Above Primary	3.4	Middle School	4.1
Technical	3.0	Technical	3.2	Total	4.5	High School	3.9
College	3.0	College	3.4			Marticulation	4.3
Post-graduate	2.5	Post-graduate	3.3			College	3.9
Private	3.7	Private	4.0			Total	4.5

Source: 1. Mukerjee, R.K., *Social Profiles of a Metropolis*, Bombay, pp. 163-164.

2. Driver, E.D., *Differential Fertility in Central India*, pp. 99-101.

The sixteenth round of NSS (1960/61) brought out an interesting relationship between the educational attainment of the wife and completed family size. It was observed that the completed family size was 6.10, 6.32 and 6.25 respectively for the illiterate, educated below primary level, and primarly passed women; in contrast, for those women who had passed the secondary level or were graduates, the completed family size was 4.25 and 2.62 respectively.

The studies conducted by J.R. Rele and Tara Kanitkar in two metropolitan cities, namely, Greater Bombay (1966) and Delhi (1969-70) have brought forth a distinct relationship between education of the wife and fertility. Data presented in Table 13 clearly indicate the negative association between the educational attainment of the wife and the number of children ever born in Greater Bombay. The nearly completed family size was 2.95, in the age group 40 and above for women in the educational category, matriculation and above. This was distinctly lower than that for women with lower educational attainment.

Similarly, a very striking inverse relationship between woman's education and fertility was also observed in the Delhi fertility survey. Really this is an healthy indication of the stage of declining fertility in the metropolitan cities in India.

There can be a number of reasons for a small family among the well-educated ladies; but two factors seem to be quite influencing. One reason may be that because the sense of responsibility towards the maintenance of family increases with a substantial degree of educational achievement. A large family may prove to be an hindrance in the fulfilment of this obligation. Secondly, because the educated women quite often opt for a career than for the domestic life, it is so natural for them to go in for a smaller family.

Table 13. Average number of children ever born per woman by present age and education, Greater Bombay, 1966

Age of the woman	*Education*			
	Illiterate and literate without formal education	*Primary or junior basic to matriculation*	*Matriculation and above*	*All educational attainments*
Below 20	0.59	0.40	0.13	0.45
20-24	1.72	1.24	0.76	1.41
25-29	2.84	2.62	1.53	2.56
30-34	3.91	3.65	2.26	3.57
35-39	4.52	4.13	2.49	4.11
40+	4.86	4.48	2.95	4.51
Average	3.41	3.01	1.95	3.07
	(3980)	(2905)	(979)	(7872)
Standardised average	3.39	3.07	1.90	3.07

Source: J.R. Rele and Tara Kanitkar, "Residence background and fertility in Greater Bombay", *Population Studies*, Vol. 28, No. 2, July 1974, p. 303.

The differentials in fertility could also arise due to the practice of family planning methods. It has been found that for all methods there is a positive association between educational attainment of

Table 14. Percentage of couples accepting various methods of contraception by education of wife, Greater Bombay, 1966

Education of wife	*Method of contraception*			
	Sterilization	*Loop*	*Other methods*	*All methods*
Illiterate	6.34	0.56	1.93	8.83
Literate without formal education	11.42	1.46	7.03	19.91
Primary passed up to matriculation	13.78	1.68	13.95	29.41
Matriculation passed with graduation	8.42	3.51	36.84	48.77
Graduate and above	4.33	3.36	60.58	68.27

Source: J.R. Rele and Tara Kanitkar, *Fertility and Family Planning in Greater Bombay* (Bombay, Popular Prakashan, 1980).

the wife and acceptance of contraception. The data on the practice of family planning by educational attainment for women of incomplete fertility are given in Table 14. It is obvious from the table that the association is more pronounced in acceptance of methods like condom, rhythm, coitus-interruptus, and diaphragm and jelly which are listed in the table under other methods.

The Operations Research Group (ORG) Survey of 1970 also showed a positive association between the educational attainment of husband and wife and the practice of family planning.

Occupation and Fertility

It has been found in some surveys in India that agricultural people have higher fertility than the trading and professional classes. For instance, Agrawala found that while cultivators and labourers gave birth to 7.4 children, those who were in service and profession had only 6.6 children. Driver found that while unskilled workers, agriculturists and artisans had highest fertility, the clerks had the lowest.

Summarizing the findings of several fertility studies in India we can conclude the fertility of those couples where the husband is in a white collar job, generally in a professional category or a manager, supervisor, administrative head, etc., of a firm or organization, is much lower than that of those couples where the husband is engaged in a blue collar job as unskilled or skilled labour or as a production process worker.

SELECT REFERENCES

As in previous chapter.

EXAMINATION QUESTIONS

1. Why is birth rate high in India? Explain fully. Did family planning policy help in reducing population in India?
2. Do the birth rates differ in different states in India?
3. Compare the birth rate in India with other countries. How can we bring down the birth rate in India?
4. What is meant by fertility rate? Trace the relation between education and fertility.
5. Write short notes on:
   (*a*) Fertility and effective age at marriage.
   (*b*) Economic standard and fertility.
   (*c*) Occupation and fertility.
6. Explain the reasons for the high birth rate in India.

23

Age at Marriage in India

Marriage and family are two important institutions which determine as well as are affected by demographic phenomena. Practically all births in India occur within the institution of marriage and the proportion of illegitimate births is negligible.

In India, marriage is universal. Everyone in India sonner or later, usually sooner gets married. Unmarried persons are looked down by the society. Marriage is not merely a necessary social institution but a quasi-religious duty. Among the Hindus, everybody must have at least one son otherwise the parents are supposed to be deprived of certain benefits in the other world after death. Marriage is perceived as an irrevocable union not dissoluble during the lifetime of the parties. Writing about Hindu marriage Das observed: "It is the most solemn affair in a man or woman's life, upon which depends his or her worldly land, spiritual welfare and final emancipation from bonds that tie him or her down to the earth. It is certainly not a thing to be donned or doffed at one's pleasure. It is an eternal bond that binds two souls together for ever and each suffers for other's lapses and derelictions. It is not a contract with them, but a sacrament and there is no breaking away or parting from the union."

In the matter of marriage, poverty does not come as a deterrent factor in India. Economic stability of the bridegroom has never been an important condition in contracting a marriage. Of course, the parents-in-law are anxious to see that the son-in-law is well employed; employment is not positive disqualification, since the resources of the joint family are available for the support of the newly married couple.

Besides universality of marriage in India, marriage age of both males and females is low. Eight out of 10 girls in India are married in most fertile period (*i.e.* between 15 and 20 years of age).

In the absence of a system of marriage registration in the country, no accurate calculations can be made regarding age pattern of marriage and marital status. However, with the help of available census data on marital status, and review of laws legislated in the past by various States or Central Government regarding age at marriage, it can safely be stated that universality of marriage and early age at which people marry are the two distinct features of India's marriage-pattern.

In 1891, the age at marriage among the males was 19.55 years, whereas among the females it was 12.54. It continued to increase till 1921, as would be evident from the table given below (Table 1):

Table 1. Mean age at marriage, 1891-1971

Year	*Male (in years)*	*Female (in years)*
1891	19.55	12.54
1901	20.01	13.14
1911	20.26	13.16
1921	20.69	13.67
1931	18.62	12.69
1941	18.91	14.69
1951	19.89	15.59
1961	21.6	15.9
1971	22.4	17.2

But after 1931, there has been a marked fall in the mean age at marriage of both sexes presumably due to the passing of the Child Marriage Restraint Act in 1929. The period between the passing the Act and its actual enforcement was utilized by the people to perform child marriages on a large scale, leading to a sharp decline in the average marriage age. However, after 1931 the female marriage age has tended to increase. It was 15.6 years in 1951, 15.9 years in 1961 and 17.2 in 1971. The average age of male marriage was 19.9 years in 1951, 21.6 years in 1961 and 22.4 years in 1971. It may be noted that between the period 1891 and 1951, the average age of male marriage was around 20 years. A direct question to women on age at effective marriage asked in the 17th Round of the NSS (1961-62) indicated the same average at marriage as 1961 census (15.9 years).

According to 1971 census in the age group 10-14 years about 8.7 million girls were enumerated as ever married. It is estimated that in the age group 15-18 years about 7.6 million girls were ever married. Thus 11.3 million girls below the age of 18 years were found to be married in the 1971 census. It is estimated from the Key Population Statistics based on 5 per cent sample data of 1971 census that about 10.9 million girls below the age of 18 years (2.73 millions in the age group 10-14 years and 8.14 million in the age group 15-18 years) were ever married. This clearly brings out that the Child Marriage Restraint Act is being widely violated and that the Act is not being enforced vigorously. However, those statistics reveal that there has been a slight raise (by 0.9 years) in the female mean age at marriage during the inter-census period of 1971-81.

Table 2 gives the relative frequency of marriage by age for persons married before age 45, estimated from one per cent sample. Age distribution of marriages thus obtained is shown in Fig. 1. The model age of marriages for males is 20-24 and for females 15-19 years,

Table 2. Age distribution of marriages, India, 1971 (Census synthetic cohort)

Age	*Distribution of marriage by age*	
	Males	*Females*
10-14	4.72	11.92
15-19	13.78	45.41
20-24	33.04	34.01
25-29	32.56	7.14
30-34	12.05	1.10
35-39	3.32	0.31
40-44	0.53	0.11

Source: Census of India, 1971, All India Census Tables (Estimated from one per cent sample), Series I, India, Part II, Special, pp. 118-19.

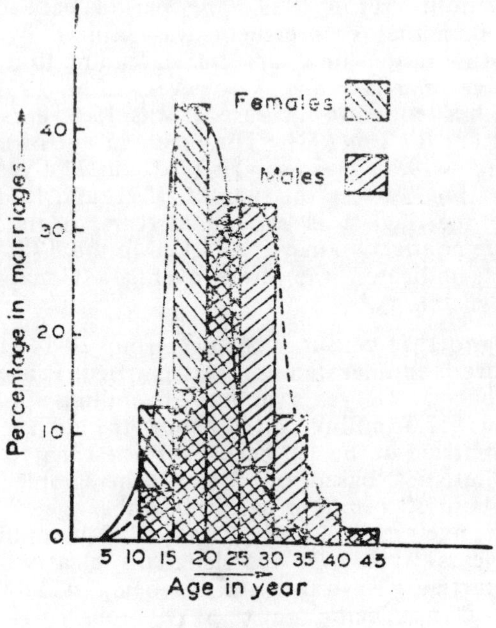

Fig. 1.

respectively. The averages for the two distributions are 24.78 years for males and 19.57 years for females, which are higher from those calculated by decade synthetic cohort method. The variances of male and female distributions are 32.56 and 18.85, respectively. This shows that females who marry on average around 20 years marry within a narrower age range than males who marry on average around 25 years. The difference between the ages of the spouses at aggregate level is around 5 years.

In India, age at marriage shows continuously an upward trend. Still the age at marriage is quite low in India compared even to other developing countries, and especially compared to the developed countries (Table 3).

Table 3. Mean age at marriage in selected countries

Countries	*Males*	*Females*
Norway	28.0	24.4
East Germany	27.4	24.7
France	26.0	22.6
Japan	25.8	23.0
Sri Lanka	26.1	20.0
Denmark	26.2	22.6
U.S.A.	22.8	20.3
India	22.2	17.2
Ireland	31.4	26.5
Switzerland	27.2	24.5

Rising age at marriage has been documented since the early twentieth century in Sri Lanka, Japan, South Korea, Taiwan, and the Philippines (see Figure 2).

In order to raise the age at marriage, in 1976, the Child Marriage Restraint Act was enacted, according to which the minimum age at marriage was fixed at 18 years for girls and 21 years for boys. In 1904, Infant Marriage Prevention Law, in Baroda State, defined the age at which marriage is permissible—twelve years for girls and sixteen years for boys. The Child Marriage Restraint Act, which took effect from 1 April 1930, provided penalties for solemnization of marriages of male children under 18 and of female children under 14 years of age. The Act was later amended in 1949 raising the minimum age of marriage of females to 15 years.

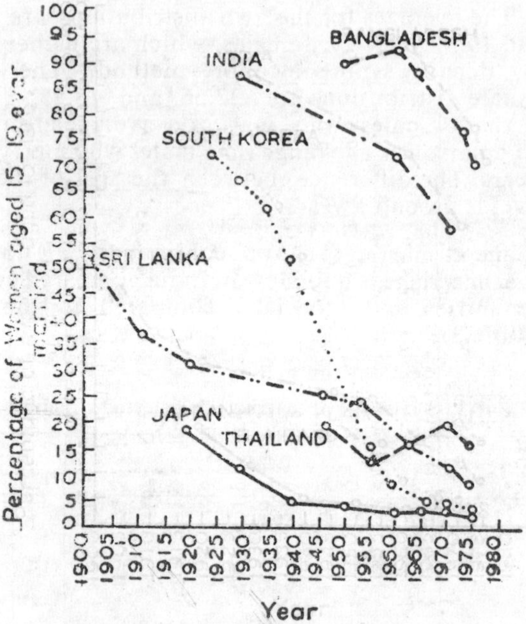

Fig. 2.

Regional Differences in the Average Marriage Age

There exist some regional variations in the age at marriage in India. Among the States, the medium age at marriage for woman in 1971 was lowest in Madhya Pradesh (15.2 years), followed by Rajasthan (15.4 years), U.P. (15.6 years), Bihar and Orissa (15.5 years), and A.P. (15.4 years); and relatively high in Assam (18.5 years), West Bengal (17.8 years), Karnataka (17.9 years), Punjab and Haryana (18.8 years) and Kerala (20.9 years) (for Appendix 1). It can be said that the States in south, north-west and east have higher mean ages at marriage. Low marriage ages are found in other States.

According to the 1981 Census, in Rajasthan, 64 per cent of the girls in the age group 15-19 were married. The comparable figure was 64 per cent in Bihar, 63 per cent in Madhya Pradesh and 61 per cent in Uttar Pradesh. Separate tabulations for rural areas are not yet available but obviously the proportion married would be much higher in the rural areas compared to the overall figure for the State as a whole.

In 1981, the mean age at marriage of females was 17.0 years in Rajasthan, 17.1 in Bihar, 17.2 in Madhya Pradesh, 17.6 in Andhra Pradesh and 18.3 in Uttar Pradesh. In contrast, it was 21.9 years in Kerala, 21.1 in Punjab and 20.3 in Tamil Nadu. According to the census estimates, the mean age at marriage has increased quite considerably between 1971 and 1981 in almost all States of India. In 1981, the all-India figure was 18.7 years but the prospects of raising the age at marriage in rural areas of Uttar Pradesh, Bihar, Madhya Pradesh and Rajasthan do not seem to be very bright, as things are.

Age at Marriage and Religion

Differences in the mean age at marriage among different religious groups are well marked in India. The estimates of average age at marriage for various religious communities at varied points of time until 1931 derived from census data on marital status show that in India the Christians have the highest mean age at marriage for both males as well as females, followed by Sikhs, Muslims and Hindus in that order (see Table 4). The average mean ages at marriage for the five decennial census points upto 1931 for Christian males and females were 23.9 and 17.2 years respectively, compared with 21.2 and 14.2 for Sikhs, 20.9 and 13.4 for Muslims and 19.4 and 12.5 years for Hindus.

Table 4. Differential nuptiality by religion: average age at marriage at different time periods

	Mean age at marriage of those married up to 1931		*Average age at marriage of those during 1930-1952*		*Age at marriage in 1972*	
	Males	*Females*	*Males*	*Females*	*Males*	*Females*
Hindus	19.4	12.5	19.6	14.2	22.0	16.3
Muslims	70.9	13.4	21.2	14.1	23.1	16.5
Sikhs	21.1	14.7	21.0	16.9	n.a.	n.a.
Christians	23.9	17.2	24.2	18.6	25.2	18.8

Sources: S.N. Agarwala, Age at Marriage in India, table 5.3, p. 136; Ajit Das Gupta, Couple Fertility, National Sample Survey Report, No. 7, p. 29. Obtained as weighted average of separate figures for rural and urban areas in S.R.S. Bulletin, Vol. X, No. 1, 1976, p. 15, table 4.

Note: n.a. —Data not available.

Marriage Age by Caste

Differences in the mean age at marriage by castes are also to be noticed in India. In 1901 the Census Commissioner of India estimated 2378 main sub-castes in India. The females of the depressed castes have lowest mean age at marriage. In some States like Karnataka, Tamil Nadu, etc. the females of the Brahmins have lowest mean age at marriage. In fact in many States the mean marriage ages of the Bania and Kshatriya females are nearly the same, and likewise Brahmin and Scheduled Caste females have very close marriage ages. The difference between the two pairs of castes is roughly one year.

Regional differences by caste generally follow the marked regional pattern except in the case of Brahmin females where the distinction becomes a little blurred. Caste classified data on marital status do not permit a more detailed analysis.

A survey in Delhi metropolitan areas also discloses wide differences in age at marriage between different castes and caste groups (see Table 5). According to the survey, there are large differences in the age at marriage of females between scheduled caste anp Khatri, Arora and Kayastha group of castes.

Table 5. Differential nuptiality by caste: average age at marriage of females in Delhi metropolitan area

Caste	*Average age at marriage (years)*
Brahmin	17.91
Bania	17.46
Khatri and Arora	18.05
Kayastha	18.91
Agriculturist castes (Jats, Gujars, Rajputs, etc.)	16.27
Functional castes	16.05
Scheduled castes	15.80

Source: Delhi Fertility Survey Report (Delhi, Demographic Research Centre, Institute of Economic Growth) (mimeo.), table 10.

Rural-Urban Differentials

As noted earlier, the age at marriage in India is gradually rising. However, the rising level has not been shared equally by rural and urban areas. The increase has been more marked in urban areas compared with the countryside (rural areas) resulting in substantial rural-urban differentials. It is clear from Table 6 that the mean ages at marriage of both males and females are substantially higher in urban than in rural areas in all the States in 1961 as well as in 1971.

The widening gap in the ages at marriage between the rural and urban areas is also confirmed by the data collected by sample surveys. The summary of the findings of these surveys presented in Table 7 clearly shows that the rural-urban differential in marriage age was small and marginal in the period prior to 1950 and that after 1950 the differential generally widened resulting in a substantial gap in the marriage age between urban and rural areas.

Table 6. Rural-urban differences: mean age at marriage of census synthetic cohorts in India, 1961 and 1971

State	Males				Females			
	1961		1971		1961		1971	
	Urban	Rural	Urban	Rural	Urban	Rural	Urban	Rural
Andhra Pradesh	23.27	21.67	24.02	22.11	16.64	15.12	17.95	15.94
Assam	25.42	24.87	26.70	24.87	19.12	18.52	20.02	18.21
Bihar	20.89	18.35	22.41	19.48	16.08	14.54	17.10	15.34
Gujarat	22.85	20.85	23.73	21.27	28.44	16.77	19.46	17.86
Jammu and Kashmir	23.52	21.74	25.39	22.79	17.06	15.89	19.84	17.25
Kerala	27.12	25.59	27.20	26.11	20.89	19.91	21.58	20.74
Madhya Pradesh	21.39	17.82	22.49	18.40	16.14	14.01	17.60	14.66
Maharashtra	24.06	21.17	24.61	23.37	18.16	15.10	19.44	16 56
Mysore	25.39	23.75	26.10	24.35	17.97	16.01	19.48	17.33
Orissa	23.10	21.52	24.03	24.46	17.03	16.45	17.42	17.15
Punjab and Haryana	23.20	21.11	23.87	21.82	19.00	17.21	20.28	18.33
Rajasthan	20.25	18.97	21.04	19.05	15.74	14.41	16.83	15.02
Tamil Nadu (Madras)	25.54	24.46	26.19	25.17	18.73	18.23	20.17	19.32
Uttar Pradesh	21.42	18.16	22.49	18.76	16.96	14.46	18.25	15.09
West Bengal	25.01	22.84	25.77	23.64	19.17	15.20	20.52	16.78
India	23.53	22.80	24.32	21.56	17.92	15.69	19.22	16 67

Source: R.P. Goyal, "Shifts in age at marriage in India between 1961 and 1971", Demography-India, Vol. IV, No. 2, 1975, p. 341, table 5.

Table 7. Rural-urban differences in age at marriage of males and females in urban and rural areas at various time points, 1950-1972

Period	*Males*		*Females*	
	Rural	*Urban*	*Rural*	*Urban*
1950	21.60	22.78	15.80	15.85
1960	21.82	23.50	16.60	16.95
1972	22.02	23.24	16.32	16.93

Note: Figures are based on NSS seventeenth round Report on couple fertility and all derived from B.N. Sarkar, Studies on age at marriage in India, p. 77, Bio-social Studies in India (Calcutta, Editions Indian, 1976), table 3.

Taken from SRS Bulletin, Vol. X, No. 1, 1979, p. 9, table 3.

Differences by Occupation

At the national level, some information on differences in marriage age by occupation and expenditure level are available for rural couples married after 1930 from the National Sample Survey data collected in 1951-52. The data from this survey indicate higher ages at marriage for males as well as females engaged in agricultural occupations compared with those engaged in other occupations. The average ages at marriage for males and females in agriculture were 19.6 and 14.2 years respectively, corresponding figures for other occupations being 21.3 and 15.0 years. Analysis of the average age at marriage by per capita monthly expenditure categories show that the average age at marriage in all expenditure categories is higher in the urban areas compared with rural areas (see Table 8). The analysis also shows that in rural areas, the average

Table 8. Differential nuptiality by income levels: average age at marriage of wives by per capita monthly expenditure: all India rural and urban couples

Per capita monthly expenditure (Rs.)	*Average age at marriage (years)*		
	Rural	*Urban*	*Combined*
0-10	14.0	14.2	14.0
11-20	13.4	14.4	13.6
21-30	13.4	15.1	13.7
31 and above	13.5	15.2	13.8
All	13.5	14.9	13.8

Source: Ajit Das Gupta, Couple Fertility, National Sample Survey Report No. 7, table 5, 11, p. 31.

Note: Combined figures are obtained as weighted average of separate figures for rural and urban areas.

age at marriage is highest for females in the lowest per capita expenditure category while in urban areas the average age increases with rising levels of per capita expenditure. The pattern obtaining in the rural areas is quite understandable in view of the social norms of rural people in favour of early marriage of females.

Differentials by Level of Education

In India, the level of educational attainment has also played an important role in determining the age at marriage. Available data confirm that the age at marriage has risen with increase in the level of education. For example, the Mysore Population Study (1951/52) shows that both in Bangalore City and in towns covered by the survey, the median ages at marriage of both men and women have witnessed a tendency to increase with the level of educational attainment (see Table 9). It is obvious from the figures of the table that the rise in the age at marriage is appreciably only upon the attainment of middle and higher level of education.

The results of the survey in the Delhi metropolitan area also indicate that improvement in education increases up the age at marriage (see Table 10).

Table 9. Differential nuptiality by education: median age at marriage by educational level in urban areas in Mysore State, 1951-52

Educational standard	*Men born during*		*Women born during*		
	1908-1917	*1918-1927*	*1908-1917*	*1918-1927*	*1928-1932*
Bangalore city:					
Illiterate	23.7	24.2	15.0	15.1	15.4
Literate	24.5	24.2	14.6	15.5	15.8
Middle school	24.4	24.0	16.1	16.2	16.8
High school	25.3	25.3	20.0	20.0	20.0
University	24.6	26.7	n.a.	n.a.	n.a.
Towns:					
Illiterate	24.7	23.2	14.5	15.2	15.2
Literate	23.5	24.3	14.9	14.5	15.0
Middle school	23.6	22.2	15.2	15.9	16.0

Source: Based on Mysore population study and obtained from Ashok Mitra, Indian Population, Vol. 1, pp. 340-41, table III.2.35 and III.2.36.

Note: n.a. —Data not available.

Table 10. Differential nuptiality by education: average age at marriage of females in Delhi metropolitan area

Educational level (years of schooling)	*Average age (years)*
Illiterate	16.05
1—3	16.50
4—7	16.80
8—9	17.56
10—13	19.35
14—15	21.13
16 and above	22.39

Source: Delhi Fertility Survey Report, Tables (Delhi, Demographic Research Centre, Institute of Economic Growth), (mimeo.).

Multivariate Analysis

Multivariate analysis has also been attempted to analyse inter-State differences in nuptiality patterns in terms of different socio-economic and demographic components. Malaker used six variables namely (*a*) percentage of males literate, (*b*) percentage of male workers in the age group 15-34, (*c*) percentage of male labour force in agriculture, (*d*) per capita income, (*e*) ratio of single males in the age group 15-44 to single females in the age group 10-39 and (*f*) percentage of population living in urban areas to explain inter-State variations in singular mean age at marriage of males. To account for inter-State variability in mean age at marriage of females he used four variables:(*a*) percentage of females literate, (*b*) percentage of female workers in the age group 15-34, (*c*) sex ratio of single males to single females obtained as in (*c*) above, and (*d*) percentage of population living in urban areas. The results of the analysis reflecting on (*a*) the level of correlations between the dependent and the explanatory variables and (*b*) the extent of variation in the dependent variable explained by the independent variables included are given in Table 11. The results clearly show that of the six variables considered three, namely, literacy, economic activity, and male labour force participation in agriculture are highly correlated to male nuptiality. While the relationships of the male mean age at marriage with the sex-ratio of the single and percentage of population living in urban areas are weak, that with the per capita income is also weak but somewhat stronger (Table 11).

In the case of females, the results show that of the four variables only literacy is highly correlated with nuptiality. Of the other three variables, economic activity and sex ratio some impact and urbanization no effect at all on female nuptiality.

Table 11. Nuptiality correlates: results of multiple regression analysis

Predictor	Singulate mean age at marriage		
	Zero order correlation coefficient	R	R
	A. Males		
Percentage male literate	0.6820[a]	0.682	0.4651
Sex ratio of singles	0.1050	0.751	0.5639
Percentage male worker	−0.5913[b]	0.770	0.5935
Per capita income	0.3416	0.781	0.6100
Percentage male labour force in agriculture	−0.6709[a]	0.783	0.6126
Percentage living in urban areas	−0.2690	0.783	0.6127
	B. Females		
Percentage female literate	0.8224[a]	0.822	0.6763
Sex ratio of singles	−0.3540	0.833	0.6941
Percentage female worker	−0.2622	0.837	0.7014
Percentage living in urban areas	0.1468	0.838	0.7022

Source: C.R. Malaker, Study of Indian Nuptiality, Ph. D. dissertation (Calcutta, Indian Statistical Institute, 1978), pp. 78-105.

Notes: (*a*) Significant at 1 per cent level.
(*b*) Significant at 5 per cent level.

Factors which Influence Age at Marriage

Many factors influence age at marriage and help in further increasing it.

(1) *Economic condition of the community.* It is usually observed that the rich try to delay the marriage of their children and wish to see them fully settled in life before their marriage is arranged.

(2) *Social condition.* In some societies it is socially desirable that the girl should be married at the earliest. Dowry system prevents the marriage of daughters in the case of poor people which causes delay. In some sections of society no girl is to be married till she is properly educated. In case where parents are unable or do not like to educate their children they wish to marry them as early as possible.

(3) *Level of employment.* In villages where all are treated to be engaged in agriculture, there is no question of delaying marriage on this account. On the contrary, in urban areas the marriages are delayed because it is considered most desirable that boys and girls should be suitably employed. Marriages are delayed in several cases to find a suitable employed partner.

(4) *Environment.* In some cases environments are such that the chances of the boys and girls getting spoiled are maximum. In such cases, the parents make haste to get their children married early.

Effects of Low Age of Marriage

The low age at marriage adversely affects the social and health status of women in three different ways: (1) Early marriage of females, especially to males of older age (generally a five-year difference) implies higher proportion of widows (the average age at widowhood is 35.2 for those getting widowed by age 45) and therefore, Indian society puts women at a great disadvantage; (2) Cohabitation and child-birth at immature age causes unfavourable physical effect; (3) Early marriage produces more children for at least three important demographic reasons. If women marry young (*i*) they are likely to have sexual intercourse frequently throughout their most fecund years; (*ii*) they begin having sexual intercourse at an earlier age and thus live through a longer period of exposure to conception; and (*iii*) they shorten the interval before the next generation is born and begin child-bearing. Each of these factors means more rapid population growth. Moreover, women who marry young tend to have less education and less opportunity to take on jobs or role other than motherhood. Bearing and raising children then become the major source of their status in the family and community. This lowers their incentive to limit family size.

Effects of Late Marriage on Fertility

It could be expected that the effect of an increase in the age at marriage on fertility would be to cut down the reproductive span. However, it is difficult to estimate the actual reduction in fertility occurring from a specified increase in the age at marriage without knowing what changes might occur in the family-building process on account of such an increase. A study carried out by the Regis-

Table 12. Average number of children born per married woman of completed fertility in different states by different marriage ages

Rural Marriage Age				*State*	*Urban Marriage Age*			
Below 18	*18-22*	*23 and over*	*All Ages*		*Below 18*	*18-22*	*23 and over*	*All Ages*
5.5	4.2	3.2	4.7	Jammu and Kashmir	5.2	4.2	3.7	4.9
5.7	5.2	4.4	5.5	Punjab	6.0	5.5	4.7	5.8
6.2	5.5	3.9	6.0	Kerala	6.2	5.5	4.0	5.8

Source: S.P. Jain, "Indian Fertility—Our Knowledge and Gaps", *Journal of Family Welfare*, Vol. X, No. 4, June 1964.

trar-General, India in 1961, on rural and urban samples in four selected States showed an association between postponement of marriage and reduction in the number of children born. Table 12 presents the data obtained.

Ryder estimatee that an increase in the mean age of child-bearing by 5 years can bring about 10 per cent reduction in annual birth rates over a period of 50 years. Prof. K. Venkatacharya in his study found that one live birth can be saved per married woman by raising her age at marriage from 15 years to 20 years which is about 16 per cent of the total fertility. However, by raising the age at marriage from 15 to 18, a 7 per cent reduction in total fertility can be achieved. His findings are given in Table 13.

Table 13. Reduction in total number of births by increasing age at marriage obtained on the basis of 21.00 simulated fertility histories

Age at Marriage	*Total No. of live births*	*Reduction in number of life births for women marrying at age x (x 15) compared to No. of live births for women marrying at age 15*	*Per cent Reduction*
15	6.47	—	—
16	6.44	.03	0.5
17	5.95	.52	8.0
18	6.04	.43	6.7
19	5.40	1.07	16.5
20	5.47	1.00	15.5

Source: Venkatacharya, "Impact of postponing marriages on India's birth rate", *Artha Vijnana*, Vol. XIII, No. 3, Sept. 1971, p. 340.

Although delayed marriage generally reduces the period of exposure to the risk of pregnancy, the decrease in child marriage might at the time give rise to a tendency to higher fertility, because in India and similar countries there appears to be evidence that early marriages have shown a lower completed fertility than later marriages. Very early marriages that are consummated at or even before puberty followed by early pregnancy, cause such physiological damages as to make further child-bearing difficult or even impossible. The objection seems to be valid, but evidence on this score is too scanty and contradictory to permit a firm conclusion. It is found that postponement of women's marriage at age well above puberty tends to decrease fertility. The fall in fertility becomes more precipitious only when the age of marriage is postponed beyond 20 years.

Fecundity before the age of 20 years is low and is characterised by what Ford calls as "adolescent sterility". Neonatal mortality is also shown to be high before the age of 19 years for mothers. In a study on Bengalee women's reproductive pattern, Talwar concludes that the median interval between the consummation and first birth varies from 6.36 years for age at consummation at 9 years to 1.96 years for age at consummation at 14 years, and 1.03 years for age at consummation at 20 years, and 0.89 year at 22 years. A number of other studies have also confirmed the feature of long interval between early age at effective marriage and first birth.

Though it has been established that females marrying at age 20 or later give birth to fewer children, but reasons because of which females marry late have lower fertility are not very clear. It has been observed in India that only the educated females marry late. Also, those females who are employed marry at a later age. Therefore, whether the age at marriage is an important determinant of fertility or education or employment, is not very clear. Probably, they act and react on one another. Even if we assume that age at marriage is a significant factor determining fertility, we are not very hopeful that it would substantially effect fertility rate in India. According to Dr. S.N. Agrawalal's estimate which is based on the data of the 1961 census, the average age at marriage of a female is 15.4 years in rural areas and 17.88 years in the urban areas. The terminal marriage age, by which bulk of girls get married, has remained unchanged at 25. There has been little change in the proportion marrying after 25 years. After 1931, there has been a substantial movement towards avoiding marriages at ages 10-14. This movement towards avoiding marriages with the result that such marriages were brought down to fairly small proportion in 1961. The pace of decline was slower in the rural areas whereas the proportion of marriage at 10-14 is still quite high. Though factors (such as impact of national family planning programme, improvement in literacy and urbanization) are operating in the urban areas independent of the law to raise the marriage age of girls, the age of marriage in India even now is quite low, especially in the rural part and has to rise substantially more before fertility rates are considerably effected. In some cases, however, such a rise in the age of Indian women at marriage might mean only that the interval between formal marriage and the 'Gauna' (which marks the shifting of wife to husband's home and before which consummation of marriage does not take place) was shortened. This would be specially likely to occur in those cases where marriage was postponed merely to comply with the law. Even if a rise in the marriage age is effected, fertility may not significantly be altered, for there is a great deal of sub-fecundity among girls under 20 years of age. Any changes in marriage frequency in that age group would have less impact on fertility than corresponding changes in a more mature group.

In a study of rural Uttar Pradesh, Saxena has shown that there are slight increases in fertility up of age at marriage of 17 years. The interval between age at effective marriage and first birth decreases with each year of increase in age at marriage. Based on his cohort analysis, Saxena reports that the reproductive span (being the average of the difference between first and last births) is reduced from about 25 years for marringe at less than 12 years to 23 years for marriage at the age of 16 years and above. Several studies show that in order to achieve substantial reduction in fertility, the age at marriage for females should be increased to more than 22 years.

Thus we conclude that as marriage pattern is rooted in the cultural milieu and assuming that marriage customs do not change rapidly, there would seem little reason to expect within the next few decades for any substantial change one way or the other. The only way to rise the age at marriage is through changes in the socio-economic factors that influence to help it low. This can come only with better education, employment or a general rise in the level of living beyond a certain minimum.

SELECT REFERENCES

1. Agrawala, S.N.: *Age at Marriage in India*, Kitab Mahal, 1968.
2. Coale, A.J.: *How a Population Ages or Grow Younger*, Ronald Freedman (Ed.) *Population, The Vital Revolution*, New York, 1964.
3. Dandekar, K.: "Why is the Proportion of Women in India's Population Declining?" *E.P.W.*, Vol. X, No. 42, Oct. 18, 1975.
4. India, Government of: *Census*, 1971, Part II.
5. Malakar, C.R.: Study of Indian Nuptiality, Ph. D. Dissertation.
6. Ross, A. John: *International Encyclopaedia of Population*, Free Press, New York.
7. Sinha, V.C.: *Dynamics of India's Population Growth, National.*
8. Yadav, S.S.: "Trends in Marriage Age of Girls in India", *Artha Vijnana*, No. 1.
9. Venkatcharya: "Impact of Postponing Marriages on India's Birth Rate", *Artha Vijnana*, Vol. XIII, No. 3, Sept. 1971, p. 340.

24

Widow Remarriage in India

High caste Hindu widows in India are socially prohibited from remarriage, because the Hindu religion eulogises ascetic virtues. Marriage after widowhood is contrary to this ideal. This restriction was imposed for 300 B.C. to A.D. 200. Manu the Hindu Law giver, decreed that a widow should never entertain the idea of remarriage. It stems from the view that marriage is a union of souls and not merely of bodies, and that the widow is going to join her husband at heaven after her death or in this world in her next birth.

Under the levirate system, the widow of an elder brother is married to his younger brother, and in his absence to a cousin. Marriage with an elder brother is not favoured.

At the time of the alliance, there is no formal marriage ceremony. It is called Kareva, not marriage. Kareva is a marriage of convenience whereby society provides protection to a widow and her children.

Restrictions on remarriage of widows were not imposed on lower caste Hindus because they were not required to lead a virtuous and ascetic life.

The problem of widowhood and widow remarriage is of considerable interest to demographers in country like India, where widowhood is a social phenomenon, because the ban on widow remarriages tends to remove a certain proportion of females of reproductive ages from contributing towards fertility.

The Indian censuses do not give information on widow remarriages, though they do provide information on current widows and widowers by age. Available data show that in 1911, the proportion of widows was 11 per cent of the total female population as against 3 per cent of widowers of the total male population; and 28 per cent of the widows were below 40 years and only 1.3 per cent under 15. In 1951, the proportion of widows and widowers was 12.8 and 5 per cent respectively of the total female and male population, and 57 per cent of the widows were below 44 and 0 6 per cent below 14 years.

Of course, with the decline in mortality, the percentage widowed in the population has declined steadily. The percentage of widowers has declined from around 5.7 in 1931-41, to 5.1 in 1941-51, to 4.1 in 1951-61 and to 3.1 in 1961-71, while the percentage of widows has declined from 15.1 in 1931-41, to 12.8 in 1941-51, to 11.3 in 1951-61 and to 9.1 in 1961-71.

Age at Widowhood

The census data give the mean widowhood age of those getting widowed by age 45, as 31 years in 1910-11, 29.8 years in 1911-21, 34.1 years in 1921-31, 28.8 years in 1931-41, 33.2 years in 1941-51, and 34.0 years in 1951-61. A decline in the mean widowhood age during 1911-21 could be because of the influenza epidemic which followed World War I, and in 1931-41, due to a large number of child widows following a rush for child marriage during 19.0-30. Recent increase in mean widowhood age is because of improved mortality. The sample data of 1971 census have brought out that the mean age at widowhood of those getting widowed by age 45 was 34.8 years in 1961-71.

Religion-wise Widowhood

The information in this regard is available only up to the period ending 1931. Available data show that the mean age at widowhood is highest for Christians followed by the Muslims, the Hindus, the Sikhs and the Jains. The mean age at widowhood for Hindus was 32.3 years, for Muslims 31.9 years, for Christians 32.5 years, for Sikhs 30.7 years, for Jains 29.3 years and for Buddhists 29.6 years. Thus it is clear that average age of widowhood of Christians and Muslims is very close while that of Hindus and the Sikhs is very near to each other. Similarly the average age of Buddhists and Jains is also very close.

Duration of Fertile Union

It begins with effective marriage and terminates with divorce or separation or death. Widowhood in India is either due to death, both accidental and natural. Husbands of some of the married girls die before 15 years of age and thus do not enter fertile period while there are others who spend most of their reproductive period without widowhood.

Widow Remarriage by Age

Table 1 gives the incidence of remarriage by age at widowhood.

It could be noted that the proportion of those getting remarried declines by age. Of those widow below the age of 15 years, nearly 90 to 100 per cent get remarried while very few are remarried after the age of 40. This is probably because a younger widow has greater opportunity and a longer time in which to get married.

Table 1. Percentage of widows getting remarried

Age at widow-hood	*Delhi (rural)*	*Rohtak (rural)*	*Mathura (rural)*	*Saharanpur*
Below 15	94.4	100.0	85.7	87.5
15-20	87.5	91.8	72.0	77.1
20-25	66.7	85.8	39.4	55.6
25-30	24.4	52.3	31.2	29.2
30-35	18.2	25.6	25.6	17.7
35-40	13.9	4.4	4.4	11.4
40-45	0.0	1.9	2.7	2.3
45+	0.0	0.7	1.9	1.1

Living Children and Widow Remarriage

A large majority of widows with no child and a substantial proportion of those with one living child at the time of widowhood are remarried. The chances of remarriage decline where the number of living children is large. Dandekar and Agrawala studies have proved this.

Table 2. Percentage of widows getting remarried by number of living children

Living children	*Delhi (rural)*	*Rohtak (rural)*	*Mathura (rural)*	*Western India (rural)*
0	72.7	75.7	49.3	61.1
1	42.9	28.4	30.2	26.9
2	23.9	24.3	9.4	14.2
3	16.7	8.6	4.2	—
4	17.9	8.2	2.2	—
5+	5.6	0.0	2.1	—

A large number of non-levirate widow remarriages are confined to widows with no children. Such remarriages with one or more children are very few. On the other hand 43.8 per cent levirate remarriages were among childless widows and 42 per cent among those with one or two children. Thus, the number of living children does not seem to exercise a restraint on levirate remarriages.

Widow Remarriages by Widowhood Duration

After how long should a widow remarry is another problem. Many factors influence this question.

There are social customs under which it is not permissible to remarry within a year or more of widowhood. Then there is the problem of levirate and non-levirate remarriage. In the case of levirate remarriage the boy is readily available. In the case of non-levirate remarriage the search for a suitable match takes time. It is linked with the age of widow, the number of her living children, social status of the family, features, outlook and nature of the widow and her own reputation as well as relations with the elders of the deceased family, etc. Thus, the period of widow remarriage varies to a great extent. The period differs from immediate remarriage, which of course is uncommon to 40 years. High caste people still avoid remarrying their widows.

It is noteworthy that in rural Delhi, 41 out of 50 levirate remarriage took place within a year of the widowhood. This is because of the prevailing custom that the remarriage or Kareva should take place on the first death anniversary of the husband.

It was found that some girls had been widowed before the performance of their gauna ceremony.

According to levirate remarriage, the remarriage was in the form of gauna ceremony with the new husband. This was celebrated when both the married partners were mature. In the case of non-levirate marriages, however, most of them were celebrated between 12 and 40 months of the widowhood.

Present Trends in India

With general social awakening and the spread of education and modern ideas, prejudices against widow remarriages are getting softened and, it is often asserted that as widow remarriages become more frequent, it would increase the overall levels of fertility in India. But there is no quantitative assessment of this trend. The Indian censuses do not give information on widow re-marriages, though they do on widowhood. Even if we take that the remarriage of widows is more frequent, there is no good reason to expect an appreciable rise in birth rate in India. The more frequent remarriage of widows would imply that the demand for young girls in the marriage market would decrease correspondingly. Declining trend in mortality implies that the frequency of loss of spouse in the reproductive ages will decrease. Taking all this into account, it would seem that the relaxation of the taboo in India against remarriage of widows cannot be expected to have any appreciable effect on future fertility, specially if the change proceeds slowly.

SELECT REFERENCES

As in previous chapter.

EXAMINATION QUESTIONS

1. Write an essay on widow remarriage in India.

25

Mortality (Death Rates), Trends and Differentials in India

Like the birth rate, death rate too is quite high in India. It is still a death-ridden country and we are fundamentally a death-stricken people, though of late, some improvements are visible in this direction.

The state of mortality can be indicated by (*a*) crude death rates, (*b*) the expectation of life and (*c*) the infant mortality. After Second World War, there has been very considerable improvement in all these respects in the population situation and they all point to one conclusion, namely, that mortality has been declining. In the table below available information for death rates is given.

Table 1. Estimated annual death rates in India, 1881-1981

Year	*Death per thousand population*
1881-1891	41.3
1891-1901	44.4
1901-1911	42.6
1911-1921	48.6
1921-1931	36.3
1931-1941	31.2
1941-1951	27.4
1951-1961	22.8
1961-1971	18.8
1971-1981	14.8

There are three distinct phases of mortality history in India; it was high and fluctuating up to 1921; it declined slowly at first during 1921-51, and rapidly thereafter. The period up to 1921 was characterized by fluctuations of the death rate around a very high level rate. In those days famines, epidemics and pestilences were fairly common. A conspicuous change occurred after 1921. With the technical know-how of the Western countries and the adoption of public health measures, control of communicable diseases and Malaria Eradication Programme, etc., there has been marked decline in mortality since

1921. With stable conditions, internecine strife and banditry disappeared. The only large scale famine of recent time was the Bengal Famine of 1943. Thus the death rate which started declining after 1921, shows that fatal diseases and epidemics were controlled through an increase in the medical and health facilities. Natural calamities like droughts and famines were also controlled through improvement in the transport system and irrigation facilities.

The comparatively rapid decline in death rate after 1951 could be explained by the overall socio-economic improvement and the progressive improvement in public health and medical services.

Table 2. Estimated death rates in 21 states of India, 1979

State	*Rural*	*Urban*	*Combined*
Northern Zone			
1. Haryana	11.0	8.7	10.6
2. Himachal Pradesh	10.4	5.6	10.1
3. Jammu & Kashmir	10.3	5.2	9.3
4. Punjab	10.3	8.3	9.9
5. Rajasthan	13.9	7.7	12.8
Western Zone			
6. Gujarat	13.8	10.9	13.1
7. Maharashtra	12.2	7.9	10.9
Southern Zone			
8. Andhra Pradesh	13.8	8.2	12.8
9. Kerala	6.9	6.5	6.8
10. Karnataka	11.8	6.6	10.4
11. Tamil Nadu	13.4	8.7	12.1
Eastern Zone			—
12. Assam	11.9	6.6	11.4
13. Bihar	13.3	9.5	13.0
14. Manipur	7.2	3.5	6.9
15. Meghalaya	13.2	6.4	12.1
16. Nagaland	8.2	—	—
17. Orissa	15.4	10.1	15.0
18. Tripura	10.8	7.4	10.5
19. West Bengal	n.a.	6.5	n.a.
Central Zone			
20. Madhya Pradesh	16.3	8.7	15.1
21. Uttar Pradesh	10.0	10.5	16.2
All India	13.9	8.4	12.8

Source: Registrar General of India, Sample Registration Bulletin, Vol. XV, No. 1, June 1981.

Since independence in 1947, the Indian economy has witnessed certain changes which are of a permanent nature and which have the potential of sustaining economic life at a higher level.

It is, thus, clear that the death rate in India has displayed a long downward trend, despite a step-by-step improvement in the reporting of deaths.

When we come to examine the figures of death rate State-wise, we find the position (Table 2).

A study of the death rate differentials in various states reveals that the extent of variation is wide. Among the major states, the death rate is found above the national average in Madhya Pradesh, Orissa, Rajasthan and Uttar Pradesh, the rates in Uttar Pradesh being generally above 20 per thousand. In contrast, Jammu and Kashmir, Karnataka, Kerala, Maharashtra, Punjab, Tamil Nadu and West Bengal had comparatively low death rates. Here, Kerala is the only State which has achieved a death rate of only 7.0 per thousand in 1978 and 6.8 in 1979.

It should be noted that death rates in urban areas are substantially lower than in rural areas in all States. The lower urban rates are often attributed to the relatively greater availability of medical public health, sanitation and drainage facilities in urban areas. But the deficiencies in the urban rates do not substantially affect the overall death rate, as the urban population constitutes only about 20 per cent of the total population of the country.

Another important feature which deserves attention is that Uttar Pradesh, Bihar, Orissa and Madhya Pradesh which together contain 40 per cent of India's population have very high rural death rates. Of these States, Uttar Pradesh which accounts for 16.2% of the country's population has a death rate of 16.2 per thousand. It could therefore be argued that further substantial reduction in the overall national death rate cannot be achieved unless there are concomitant declines in the death rates of these four States.

International Comparison

Though the death rate in India has declined, but it is still quite high in comparison with European countries. It is ever higher than in many countries of almost the same level of economic development such as Sri Lanka, Thailand etc. These differences show that there is still much scope for reduction in mortality. It is clear from the figures of Table 3 that Sri Lanka and Thailand have been able to achieve very low death rates comparable to those of the developed countries in spite of themselves being developing countries.

It should be remembered that the comparison of the Indian mortality level with those of developed countries serves little purpose except to set a target to be hoped for in the distant future. But comparison with the experience of other developing countries is of course more appropriate. Further the populations involved are much smaller in comparison with gigantic India. Though the obstacles in the way of bringing our mortality to the level reached by the more advanced countries of the world are serious, we have to strive hard to achieve this object. Reduction in the death rate will not be materially limited by comparatively developing state of our economy.

Table 3. Death rates in India and selected countries

Country	*Death rate*	*Year*
Bangladesh	20.5	1975
China	9.4	1975
India	14.2	1978
Indonesia	16.7	1975
Japan	6.1	1978
Nepal	22.5	1975
Pakistan	16.7	1975
Philippines	10.3	1975
Republic of Korea	9.4	1975
Sri Lanka	7.4	1977
Thailand	11.7	1975
United States of America	8.8	1978

Source: For India, see Sample Registration Bulletin, Vol. XIV, No. 2 (New Delhi, Registrar General's Office, December 1980).

Causes of High Death Rate in India

The figures regarding the incidence of death as a result of the various causes are highly deficient and they cannot be thoroughly relied upon because people in general are reluctant in giving the exact cause of death of the deceased. At present information is available only from hospitals, which are mostly located in urban areas; but efforts have been made to obtain some information about rural areas. A broad picture of the causes of death in the rural areas could be obtained from the data obtained in the Model Registration Scheme operated by the Registrar General since 1966. The percentage distribution of deaths by major causes groups for the years 1975 to 1979 is given in Table 4.

It is evident from the figures of the table that in all five years, the coughs group, or disorders of the respiratory system, accounted for about 21 per cent of deaths in rural India. The important diseases comprising this category are tuberculosis of the lungs, asthma, pneumonia and bronchitis.

Table 4. Percentage distribution of deaths by major cause group, rural India, 1975 to 1979

Major cause group prominent symptoms	*1975*	*1976*	*1977*	*1978*	*1979*
1. Accidents and injuries	4.6	5.1	4.3	4.9	4.6
2. Child-birth and pregnancy	1.0	1.1	1.1	1.0	1.1
3. Fevers	13.2	12.0	10.7	9.6	8.9
4. Digertive disorders	9.8	9.2	10.6	9.3	9.7
5. Coughs (disorders of respiratory system)	21.1	20.9	20.6	20.6	20.3
6. Disorders of the central nervous system	3.2	3.6	3.6	3.6	3.6
7. Diseases of circulatory system	7.0	8.5	8.1	9.0	9.3
8. Other clear symptoms	7.4	8.2	7.5	7.8	8.3
9. Causes peculiar to infancy	12.5	12.5	13·2	13.0	13.5
10. Senility	16.8	17.0	18.3	19.2	18.5
11. The rest	3.4	1.9	2.0	2.0	2.2
12. All causes	100.0	100.0	100.0	100.0	100.0

Source: Office of the Registrar General, Causes of Death, 1979: A Survey (New Delhi), table 3.

The second most important cause of death is senility which accounts for 18.5 per cent deaths in rural India. It should be noted that the proportion of deaths attributed to senility has been increasing from 16.8 per cent in 1975 to 18.5 per cent in 1979.

Causes peculiar to infancy constitute the third most important cause of death group in India accounting for about 13 per cent of the total deaths in 1978 and 1979. While the proportion of deaths attributed to diseases of the circulatory system has shown an increase over the years, the proportion of deaths due to 'fevers' has witnessed a gradual decline from 13.2 per cent in 1975 to 8.9 per cent in 1979.

As far as causes of mortality in urban India are concerned, time series information on them is not available. However, an analysis of deaths in major hospitals in urban areas in nine major states and three Union Territories in 1978 is presented in Table 5.

Some of the other important causes which are responsible for heavy mortality in India are as follows:

(*a*) *Malnutrition*. The most important single factor behind our death rate is malnurition. It is generally believed that nearly one-third of the population suffers from under-nutrition and another one-

Table 5. Proportionate distribution of deaths by major cause in India (urban areas), 1978

Major cause of death	*Proportion per 1000 deaths*	
	Males	*Females*
1. Infective and parasitic diseases	249	232
2. Neoplasms	40	38
3. Allergic disorders, all other endocrine, metabolic and blood diseases	42	55
4. Mental, psychoneurotic and personality disorders; diseases of nervous system and circulatory system	210	185
5. Diseases of the respiratory system	76	85
6. Diseases of the digestive system	64	42
7. Diseases of the genitourinary system and complications of pregnancy, childbirth and puerperium	15	41
8. Congenital malformations and certain disease of early infancy	84	97
9. Symptoms, senility and ill-defined conditions	135	143
10. Accidents, poisonings and violenee	85	82
11. All causes	1000	1000

Source: Office of Registrar General, India, Mortality Statistics of Causes of Death, 1978 (New Delhi), table 6.

third from malnutrition. This shows the broad magnitude of the quantitative and qualitative aspects of the food problems. Though it is easier to deal with nutritional diseases, it is much more difficult to deal with general malnutrition. Poverty is the basic cause of this and until the poverty of the masses is removed malnutrition will always remain.

(*b*) *Endemic and epidemic diseases.* A great variety of diseases are responsible for a large number of deaths in India. It has been said that India is a veritable paradise for microbes and one of the greatest cesspools of infection for plague, small-pox, cholera, leprosy, hookworm, influenza, typhoid and paratyphoid and bronchitis, etc., and those of a degenerative type associated with the ageing process.

It may be noted that improved public sanitation and medical science have reduced communicable diseases as a cause of death with startling rapidity. Specific medications for a variety of diseases and general antibiotics have done wonders in delaying mortality. Plague has practically disappeared from India. Malaria, which indirectly and directly used to cause so many deaths, has been greatly controlled. Cholera and small-pox do not cause a high proportion of deaths. In spite of progress made, people continue to suffer from a host of crippling diseases, which take a heavy toll of life and sap the vitality of those who somehow are able to survive their onslaught.

(*c*) *Lack of health and medical facilities.* Health facilities available in the country are an important determinant of the level of mortality. Medical and health services in India are poorly developed. There is acute scarcity of physicians, auxiliary health personnel and hospitals and clinics, particularly in the rural areas where most of the populace lives. How ill-equipped we are in the field of medical facilities in relation to our population is evident from the table below:

Table 6. Medical personnel, by type and hospitals, beds per 100,000 inhabitants in India

Year	*Physicians*	*Dentists*	*Nurses*	*Mid-wives*	*Hospital Beds*
1950-52	16.9	—	4.3	2.7	40
1957-59	19.2	0.9	6.5	7.8	45
1960	17.6	1.0	7.0	7.4	44
1962-63	17.7	1.2	8.9	10.9	50
1980	15.5	1.0	7.6	0.8	37

If we accept the figures as a rough characterization of the availability of the essential health facilities in India, it would appear that the physician population ratio remained stationary and the supply of dentists, nurses and mid-wives has increased somewhat more rapidly. In regard to hospital beds, the situation has improved slightly. But most of the hospitals have little or no facilities and wards are overcrowded. Consequently, infections quickly spread from one patient to another. Because of these and other conditions, the case-fatality ratio (that is, of the proportion of sick persons who die) is not high, giving weight to the popular belief that a hospital is "the place where one is bound to die". According to an authority on the Indian health situation, most infectious diseases hospitals in the country are "places of detention of persons dangerous to the community". Thus the shortage of personnel combined with insufficient number of hospitals, dispensaries, the quality of services rendered, shortage of food, low literacy, lack of proper health education facilities, unhygienic surroundings, unfavourable condition for work and rest, lack of legal implementations, etc.,—all contribute towards chronic morbidity in India.

(*d*) *Unfavourable environment and social factors.* The unfavourable environmental conditions also favour a high death rate in India.

In most parts of the country, the environmental sanitation is at a low level. Mahatma Gandhi observed "divorce between intelligence and labour has resulted in criminal negligence of the villages and so instead of having peaceful hamlets dotting the land, we have dung-heaps. The approach to many villages is not a refreshing experience; obviously, one would like to shut one's eyes and stuff one's nose, such is the surrounding dirt and offending smell." A more confined atmosphere, want of ventillation, absence of domestic and personal cleanliness, crowded insanitary dwellings, unhealthy diet, adulterated water and presence of filth add fuel to the fire and make people more susceptible to various infections. Consequently, high mortality follows. Social customs like the 'Purdah' system also produce adverse effects on health and play a larger role in morbidity and death.

All these factors tend to push the death rate higher in India.

Differentials in Mortality

The scarcity of reliable vital statistics in India is specially evident when one attempts to study differentials in mortality. This holds true for age and sex differentials in mortality and still more for urban-rural differentials and those related to econmic, social or occupational status.

1. Differentials by Religion

In India, the differentials in death rates have been studied in certain rounds of the National Sample Survey. Taking the data relating to 18th round (Feb. 1963-Jan. 1964), the differentials in death rate by religion are given in Table 7. Mortality in rural areas is highest among the Hindus and lowest among the Sikhs. However, in urban areas, the death rates for Hindus and Muslims are almost similar. Similarly, they are almost the same among the Christians and the Sikhs.

Table 7. Annual death rate by religion and rural-urban residence, India, 1963-64

(Rates per 1000 persons)

Household religion	*Rural*	*Urban*
1. Hinduism	12.85	8.10
2. Islam	10.62	8.28
2. Christianity	6.04	5.95
4. Sikhism	5.50	5.44
5. All	12.39	7.98

2. Age Differential

Age pattern of mortality reveals a rather disquieting feature. In the developing countries like India where modern death control has not been fully established, the age specific death rate curve is U-shaped, mortality being high in infancy and early childhood and also in the later years when senescence is a principal factor. In more advanced countries, the death rate curve is closer to J-shape, for their infant mortality has been sharply reduced.

The age specific death rates for India during 1970-1974 and 1978 are given in Table 8. It is clear from Table 8 that (*i*) the death rates are very high at the pre-school ages 0-4 but decline sharply in the next age group 5-14.

(*ii*) The death rates increase slowly during adult ages 15 to 39 years.

(*iii*) After age 39, the pace of increase accelerates with advancing age reaching substantially high level at ages 55 and above.

(*iv*) Between 1970-1972 and 1978, there has been a decline in the rates for most age groups both in urban and rural areas but this decline has been significant in respect of the younger age groups and in urban areas.

(*v*) The oveall death rate in 1978 was lower in comparison with 1970-1972 rate.

(*vi*) In both the periods, female rates are higher than the male rates at all ages up to 39 years.

The pattern then gets reversed and male mortality becomes higher than female mortality in the higher age groups. This is particularly true from age group 40 onward.

The higher mortality of the Indian female compared to that of the male is due to mainly two factors: the relatively low social status of the female with low education and employability, and her excessive child-bearing. In India, the social unpopularity of the female child and the woman's low status with low levels of education and employability are major contributory factors in the higher rate of mortality among females. "The aversion for females has been evident from a number of enquiries, conducted over the last 25 years, especially assessing the attitudes of parents towards children or to child-bearing. Attitudes towards sterilization or to family planning, given a certain composition of male and female children, prominently suggest the unpopularity of female children." The health survey conducted in rural areas reveals the same story.

The burden of excessive child-bearing, compared to those in the advanced countries, is also an important cause of the female's high mortality in India. In India, the total births in a year include only

Table 8. Age specific death rates by sex in India

Age group	India 1970-1972						India 1978					
	Rural		*Urban*		*All India*		*Rural*		*Urban*		*All India*	
	Males	*Females*	*Males*	*Females*	*Males*	*Females*	*Males*	*Females*	*Males*	*Females*	*Males*	*Females*
0-4	55.7	62.5	30.8	33.8	51.4	57.2	48.9	57.9	22.5	27.2	44.7	52.1
5-14	7.3	8.3	4.0	4.4	6.7	7.6	6.3	7.7	2.4	2.6	5.7	6.7
15-39	19.1	26.1	12.7	16.0	17.6	24.2	18.6	21.5	12.8	13.5	17.2	19.8
40-59	66.4	52.8	54.3	40.3	66.4	48.9	64.4	48.9	58.8	39.8	63.3	47.2
All ages	17.0	18.1	9.9	10.3	15.6	16.4	14.9	15.8	9.6	9.1	13.8	14.5

Source: India: Sample Registration Scheme.

40 per cent or so of the first and second order children; in advanced countries, there are today more than 70 per cent births of these two orders. Thus, Indian females experience higher risk of death than males partly as a result of frequent child-bearing and inadequate pre-natal and post-natal care of the mothers.

3. Infant Mortality

Of the high death rate in this country, there are some features intimately connected with the law of population which deserve consideration. Infant mortality is one of these. By infant mortality rate we mean the number of infants under the age of one year who die per 1000 live births in the course of a year.

In India, infant mortality is of special interest for several reasons:

(*i*) Infant mortality is one of the best indices for gauging the total health situation and the general well-being of a population.

(*ii*) A high level of infant mortality signifies wastage of effort and investment in rearing children.

(*iii*) Since it occurs early, it influences people's general outlook on life.

(*iv*) Expectation of life is greatly reduced by high levels of infant mortality.

(*v*) Infant deaths account for about 30 per cent of total deaths in the country.

Trends in Infant Mortality in India

It is unfortunate that reliable data are not available in our country to permit a systematic study of trends in infant mortality. We cannot place much reliance on date of civil registration as they suffered from gross underreporting of vital events. Estimates worked out by the Census Actuaries are available for the intercensal periods 1881 to 1971. For recent years SRS also provides estimates of infant mortality. Estimates from all these sources are utilized to obtain a rough idea about the trends in infant mortality in India. The figures in Table 9 portrays the trends in infant mortality in India.

Table 9 reveals that:

(*i*) There have been wide fluctuations in our infant mortality rates. The significant peaks observed in 1906-1911 and 1916-1921 are due to the severe malaria epidemic which was experienced over the whole of Northern India in 1908 and the influenza epidemic of 1918.

(*ii*) Since 1920, there has been a decline in infant mortality although there has been a peak during 1926-1931.

(*iii*) Despite these peaks and variations, a declining trend is observed since 1936 and by 1946-51 the infant mortality rate reached 134 per thousand.

(*iv*) The reduction in infant mortality rate has been more rapid after 1951. This is largely the result of an improvement of maternity services and better care of the children on the principles of hygiene and cleanliness. The improvement in literacy has also contributed to this factor. It has, however, to be noted that the civil registration data being deficient, the actual level of infant mortality is grossly under-estimated.

Table 9. Infant mortality rates in India

Period	*S. Chandrasekhar*	*Registrar General of India*	*Sample Registration Scheme*		
			Males	*Females*	*Both Sexes*
1901-1906	215				
1906-1911	228				
1911-1916	204				
1916-1921	219				
1921-1926	174				
1926-1931	178				
1931-1936	174				
1936-1941	161				
1941-1946	161				
1946-1951	134				
1951-1956	115				
1958		102			
1959		88			
1960		87			
1961		83			
1962		81			
1963		78			
1964		74			
1965					
1970			131	126	129
1971			129	129	129
1972			132	148	139
1973			132	135	134
1974			128	119	126
1975			140	140	140
1976			124	134	129
1977			126	135	130
1978			123	131	127

Source: S. Chandrasekhar: Infant Mortality in India 1901 to 1951. Sample Registration System.

For recent years, SRS provides more reliable estimates of infant mortality in India. The SRS data in Table 9 clearly indicates that though there has been violent fluctuations in infant mortality rates in the first half of the 1970s but since 1976 there appears to have been a gradual decline in these rates.

The figures in Table 10 presents the location of India in regard to infant mortality rate vis-a-vis the rest of world. The infant mortality rates of Japan, Hong Kong, Australia and the U.K. are very much smaller and are really not comparable to India. It is a matter of common observation that infant mortality is generally high in those countries in which the birth rate is high.

Table 10. Proportionate distribution of infant mortality by age of infants, India and selected countries and areas

Country	*Sex*	*Infant Mortality Rate*	*Proportion of infant deaths occurring within*		
			7 Days	*7-27 Days*	*28-264 Days*
1. Australia (1977)	M	14.0	58.9	10.0	31.0
	F	10.9	59.8	10.9	29.3
2. Hong Kong (1979)	M	12.9	59.6	10.9	29.5
	F	10.5	53.5	14.8	31.7
3. India (1978)	M	123.0	40.7	24.4	34.9
	F	131.0	34.4	22.0	43.6
4. Japan (1978)	M	9.3	55.4	12.8	31.8
	F	7.4	51.5	14.3	34.2
5. Malaysia (1977)	M	35.7	46.2	14.2	39.6
	F	27.7	42.9	15.8	41.3
6. Pakistan (1968)	M	131.3	32.9	22.1	45.0
	F	116.1	28.5	16.7	54.7
7. Philippines (1974)	M	65.1	34.5	16.1	49.4
	F	52.1	33.5	15.9	50.6
8. Sri Lanka (1977)	M	46.0	43.2	19.2	37.6
	F	38.6	40.0	18.6	41.4
9. United Kingdom	M	15.4	51.2	11.4	32.4
	F	12.0	54.5	12.4	33.1

Sources: (1) India: Sample Registration System.
(2) Other Countries: United Nations, 1979 Demographic Yearbook, Table 16.

The principal causes of infant mortality are malnutrition, pneumonia, diarrhoea, infections and parasitic diseases. A high level of infant mortality in India is mainly on account of persistence of exogenic causes arising from environmental and nutritional conditions. But these causes are largely controlled in advanced countries. The exogenic causes preponderate over endogenic in the developing countries like India, is well reflected in the percentage distribution of infant deaths according to the length of infant life as shown for different countries in Table 10. It has been observed that deaths in the first week of life are largely due to endogenic causes, and deaths after the first month of life, or in the post-neo-natal period occur due to exogenic factors. In the developing countries, percentage deaths claimed by this post-neo-natal period are more than 50, as against the corresponding figure of between 20 to 30 for the developed countries. The position as regards mortality during the first week is the reverse, in the advanced countries, this percentage ranges between 50 and 60; in most developing countries, it is between 25 and 40.

The Indian data also seem to suggest that in the neo-natal period and particularly during the first week of life, female infants have a better chance of survival than male infants, while the situation is reversed in the post-neonatal period.

The important causes of infant mortality in rural India for the years 1973, 1974, 1978 and 1979 as revealed by the Model Registration Scheme are given in Table 11. It is obvious from the table that the very broad group 'causes peculiar to infancy' account for over two-thirds of all infant deaths in India. Causes peculiar to infancy include prematurity, malposition, congenital malformation, birth

Table 11. Percentage distribution of infant deaths by broad cause, rural India, 1973, 1974, 1977, 1978 and 1979

Cause of Infant Death	*1973*	*1974*	*1977*	*1978*	*1979*
1. Accidents and injuries	0.4	0.5	0.5	0.6	0.5
2. Digestive disorders	4.9	5.4	2.6	3.7	3.3
3. Coughs (disorders of the respiratory system)	15.0	12.3	13.1	12.4	12.0
4. Fevers	9.6	9.7	6.0	5.1	4.7
5. Causes peculiar to infancy	58.2	59.2	69.0	67.8	69.2
6. Other clear symptoms	7.5	7.2	6.7	7,6	8.2
7. Diseases of the circulatory system	0.5	1.4	0.8	1.2	1.1
8. Disorders of the central nervous system	0.6	0.8	0.6	0.6	0.4
9. The rest	3.4	3.5	0.7	1.0	0.6
All causes	100.0	100.0	100.0	100.0	100.0

Source: Office of the Registrar General, Model Registration Unit, Causes of Death: A Survey for 1973, 1974, 1977, 1978 and 1979.

injury, cord infection, diarrhoea of new born, respiratory infection of new born, malnutrition and convulsions.

Maternal Mortality

Maternal deaths are those female deaths arising from deliveries and complications of pregnancy, child births and the puerperium. In India maternal mortality continues to be of great concern, whereas in Western countries deaths due to complications of child birth are few. According to the Registrar General's Office, the percentage of mortality associated with maternal deaths had declined from 1.5 per cent of all deaths in 1966 to 1.1 per cent in 1979.

The figures of Table 12 present the percentage distribution of maternal deaths by causes for all India for the period 1975 to 1979. It is clear from the table that anaemia and puerperal sepsis continue to be important causes of maternal deaths in India. Bleeding of pregnancy and puerperium appears to have been the most important cause of maternal mortality in 1979 while in 1978 toxaemia appears to be the most important cause and the proportion of deaths due to this cause has almost doubled between 1977 and 1978 accounting for over one-fifth of total maternal deaths in 1978.

Table 12. Percentage distribution of maternal deaths by cause, all India, 1975 to 1979

Cause	*1975*	*1976*	*1977*	*1978*	*1979*
Abortion	7.9	11.6	8.2	11.0	11.7
Toxaemia	6.7	10.4	11.2	21.2	16.1
Anaemia	20.7	22.1	15.9	14.6	15.0
Bleeding of pregnancy and puerperium	18.9	17.2	20.6	18.2	20.0
Malposition of child leading to death of mother	8.6	8.6	9.4	9.5	10.5
Puerperal sepsis	19.5	13.5	18.8	12.4	51.7
Non-classifiable	17.7	16.6	15.9	13.1	15.0
All causes	100.0	100.0	100.0	100.0	100.0

Source: Office of the Registrar General, India, Causes of Death, 1979: A Survey (New Delhi) Statement XVI, p. 32.

Expectation of Life at Birth

Life expectancy at birth is dependent on the incidence of mortality rate. Since the concept of 'expectation of life' is easily understandable and the figures are available, it can be used to determine the sex patterns of mortality in India. In India, life expectancy at birth of males is higher than the females, whereas in the Western countries the life expectancy of females is higher than that of males. One important factor depressing life expectancy of females is high level of maternal mortality. In Table 13, the figures of life expectancy for the last 30 years are given.

Table 13. Life expectancy at birth in India

(*in years*)

Period	*Males*	*Females*	*Overall*
1941-50	32 5	31.7	32.1
1951-60	41.9	40.6	41.2
1961-65	48.7	47.4	48.1
1965-70*	53.2	51.9	52.6
1976-80*	61.1	59.8	54.2

*Planning Commission (Projected).

Compared to figures of earlier decades, the average expectation of life of male and females has improved considerably. This is largely the result of an improvement of maternity services and greater care of women. But the present level of life expectancy in India does not compare favourably with the levels of the life expectancy obtaining in other countries of the World where females have longer span of life than males as is evident from Table 14.

It will be seen that expectation of life at birth is lower than that at subsequent early ages of life in India, Bangladesh, Iran and Pakistan. In case of Sri Lanka and Republic of Korea expectation of life at birth and expectation of life at age 5 are almost equal. In Australia, Japan, Hong Kong, Canada, Malaysia and Singapore expectation of life at birth is greater than expectation of life at age 5. In fact, in India, expectation of life increases up to age 3 and starts decreasing thereafter. Up to age 14, expectation of life continues to be above that at birth; it is only after age 15 that expectation of life starts having a lower value than at birth. These peculiar features are attributed to heavy childhood mortality.

PERSPECTIVES FOR FUTURE

Decline in mortality rates in India so far has been largely due to the manipulation of societal variables involving disease control measures, coupled with some improvement in other societal, household and individual variables. However, there is yet a long way to go before we achieve the mortality levels now existing in developed countries.

Table 14. Expectation of life at selected ages in India and other countries

Countries	Expectation of life at ages													
	0		5		10		20		30		40		60	
	M	*F*	*M*	*F*	*M*	*F*	*M*	*F*	*M*	*F*	*M*	*F*	*M*	*F*
1. Australia (1965-1967)	67.6	74.2	64.4	70.6	59.5	65.8	50.0	56.0	40.7	40.3	31.4	36.9	15.8	19.5
2. Bangladesh (1974)	45.8	46.6	54.4	54.2	50.5	50.3	42.5	42.2	35.4	35.1	28.1	27.7	14.4	14.1
3. Canada (1970-1972)	69.3	76.4	66.0	72.8	61.2	67.9	51.7	58.2	42.5	48.6	33.2	39.0	20.6	25.5
4. Hong Kong (1971)	67.4	75.0	64.3	71.6	59.5	66.8	49.8	57.0	40.4	47.4	31.3	38.0	22.8	29.0
5. India (1961-1970)	46.4	44.7	52.0	50.2	48.8	47.7	41.1	39.9	33.3	32.0	25.9	25.4	13.6	13.8
6. Iran (1973-1976)	57.6	57.4	63.4	65.0	59.1	60.9	49.7	51.6	40.4	42.6	31.4	33.7	16.1	17.9
7. Japan (1979)	73.4	78.9	69.3	74.6	64.4	69.7	54.7	59.8	45.2	50.1	35.7	40.4	18.5	22.1
8. Malaysia (1962)	66.2	71.4	64.2	69.0	59.5	64.3	50.0	54.7	40.8	45.2	31.7	36.1	16.4	19.0
9. Pakistan (1962)	53.7	48.8	60.8	54.8	57.0	51.7	47.8	42.9	39.2	35.4	30.8	27.7	15.6	15.5
10. Republic Korea (1970)	63.0	67.0	63.0	66.0	58.0	60.0	49.0	52.0	40.0	43.0	31.0	34.0	16.0	17.0
11. Singapore (1970)	65.1	70.0	62.0	66.6	57.1	61.1	47.5	52.0	38.2	42.4	28.8	32.9	12.9	15.6
12. Sri Lanka (1967)	64.8	66.9	65.0	66.8	60.5	62.4	51.2	53.0	42.2	44.0	33.2	35.0	17.0	17.8

M=Male, F=Female

Source: United Nations, 1979 Demographic Yearbook.

The targets set by the Government in its document "Health for All by A.D. 2000" are as shown in Table 15.

Table 15. Perspectives for future mortality rate

Mortality Index	National Averages				
	Present	1983	1990	1995	2000
Crude death rate	14.1	11	10.4	—	9.0
Infant mortality rate	129	—	80.90	—	Below 60
Peri-natal mortality rate	60-109	—	—	—	30-35
Pre-school (0-5) death rate	35-40	—	20-25	—	10
Maternal mortality rate	5-8	—	—	—	Below 2
Life expectancy	52.5 M	—	58.0 M	—	64 Yr
	51.6 F	—	57.7 F	—	

The present mortality of 14.2 per thousand is composed of:

Infants	4.3
1-4 years	2.5
5-9 years	0.7
10-59 years	3.2
60+	3.5

If the targets set for infant and child mortality are achieved, child mortality up to 5 years age will decline by 4 points. Another reduction by one point will be required to achieve the over-all target of mortality at the level of 9 per 1,000 by A.D. 2000; and this reduction may be achieved in other age groups through normal efforts.

The slow decline in mortality, especially infant and child mortality, in the last eight years (1970 to 1978) is a matter of concern.

Efforts will have to be concentrated in the future to achieve a faster reduction in mortality, especially infant and maternal mortality. A wider dissemination of health education would improve not only individual characteristics but household cleanliness and nutrition as well. It is necessary to educate the rural people to use the materials available at the village level in a more scientific way in order to obtain better benefits in terms of nutrition and disease prevention.

A hopeful sign is that government planning is now being focussed on the development of rural areas and the extension of health services to the rural masses. Nevertheless, the basic fact remains that socio-economic development is an essential requirement for improving the nutritional levels of the people and providing them with adequate public health and medical services, housing and education and ensuring an equitable distribution of income and employment opportunities. The importance of socio-economic development to mortality reduction in India is very well demonstrated by the fact that the death rate in the economically less developed states like Uttar Pradesh, Bihar, Madhya Pradesh and Orissa is higher than in other states and a substantial decline in overall national death rate is dependent on concomitant reduction in the death rates of these States.

EXAMINATION QUESTIONS

1. Analyse the trend of death rate in India and explain the causes for the decline in death rate during the recent years.
2. Trace the trend of death rate in India and explain the causes of high death rate.
3. High incidence of maternity and child mortality are responsible for high death rate in India. Elucidate.
4. Examine the trend in child mortality in India and point out the reasons for high child mortality.

26

The Composition of Population

In the composition of Indian population, it would be of interest to study the age composition and the sex composition.

The Age Composition or Age Structure

The age structure of a population is of major importance in demographic analysis. It can be mathematically determined by the levels of fertility, mortality and migration, or where the latter factor is negligible, by the first two alone. Conversely, given the age structure, the levels of fertility and mortality can be estimated under suitable assumptions.

The age composition (sometimes termed as age structure or age distribution) is one of the most basic characteristics of a population. One cannot proceed very far in the study of population growth or migration without examination of age composition. All aspects of individual or community life-social attitude, economic activities, political propensities, military service, mobility etc., are affected by the age. An examination of the age structure of a population is necessary for several reasons. It enables us to determine the proportion of the labour force in the total population. It is helpful in finding out how many children there are for whom educational facilities have to be provided. It indicates, in this age of social security, the approximate number of people who attain working age from year to year, as against the numbers who complete the working lives, so that an estimate may be made of net addition to the working force for which new occupations have to be created. The relative proportion of producers (represented by the working population) and consumers (including the old and infant dependent) determines the capacity of a community to save and consequently, the rate and volume of capital formation. Thus in a country where the proportion of the working population to the non-working dependents is large, the working population is under severe pressure not only to support their ownselves but their dependents as well. The "bottom heavy" age structure of population, due primarily to high birth rates and high mortality rates, requires the economy to devote a considerable part of its resources to the maintenance of children who die before reaching a productive age. Further, to understand the future trends in population growth it is necessary not only to know the crude rate of natural increase but also the age structure of the population, because the relative proportion of young to infants and old affects the marriage rates and correspondingly the fertility performances as well. So the variation in the proportion of young to infants and old affects the marriage rates and correspondingly the fertility performances as well. So the variation in the proportion of children to older people has led certain experts to propound theories whether the population of the country is of the progressive or the regressive type. The study of age structure of a country is also helpful in knowing how many old persons there are in the population for whom old-age pensions may have to be provided in a welfare State.

Causes of Errors in Indian Age Data

The Indian age structure is extremely inaccurate. Apart from ignorance and carelessness, there are many reasons which appear to operate towards the deliberate mis-statement of age at Census returns.

A unique cause of misstatement of age has been pointed out by Pandit Hari Kishan Kaul, the 1911 Census Superintendent of Punjab who noted:

"...an idea that telling one's correct age tends to reduce the span of life; and in the Niti Shastra it is laid down that man's age is one of the nine things which he must carefully conceal. A Hindu, therefore, who knows his age, will very often state it to be a few years more or less than it really is. It is suggested that the reason for this practice is that a man's age, coupled with the Rashi (sign of the Zodiac), which is usually indicated by his true name, would give his enemies an opportunity of setting the forces of black-magic against him. The explanation would also account for the common Hindu practice of concealing the true name and adopting a secondary one for actual use."

According to the 1921 Census Commissioner, age mis-reporting was also a phenomenon observed in respect of male adolescents. He noted:

"In the case of males the period of adolescence, 15 to 20, appears to be avoided, youths being either advanced to the ages of manhood or setback to childhood. The motive in this case is not clear, but may be an instinctive attempt to avoid the awkward category which receives neither the privileges of childhood nor the dignities of maturity."

Another important cause for the inaccuracy of the Indian age data is the deliberate misstatement of age. This is specially true of females, particularly young girls of marriageable age and older women. As noted by the 1891 Census Commissioner:

"...marriageable girls between 10 and 12 are returned in some areas as below 10 owing to the obloquy incurred by Hindu parents who have failed to marry them before puberty in accordance with the injunctions or at least the strong recommendations of the Smritis, whilst those between 12 and 14 are overstated at 18 or 20 and that there is no doubt habitual overstatement of age amongst the old of both sexes, especially women, where great age is considered a sort of distinction."

Digit preference of the tendency to state ones' age in numbers ending with a preferred digit has also been a major source of error in the Indian age returns.

A large number of people also do not attach much importance to age and have very vague notions regarding numbers.

A common practice which has affected all age returns is to reckon or estimate ages on the basis of well remembered local events such as famines, floods etc. A further source of error in Indian age returns arises from the practice of reckoning age from the time of conception and not from the date of birth.

In spite of the improvements in techniques and completeness of coverage, the inaccuracy of the age data continues to persist. However, there are evidences that the quality (as may be judged by the age ratio score and joint scores) of age statistics in India has been improving with successive censuses. Notwithstanding the various limitations, the census age data provides a fairly clear picture of the age structure of India's population for the last several decades.

Age Composition of India's Population

India has an age structure which is typical of the developing countries, with a very broad base and a tapering top. Such a structure is called 'pyramidical'. Table 1 gives the percentage distribution of the Indian Population by Age.

It will be clear from the table that as many as 42 per cent of the population of India are below the age of 15 years. The age composition worsened in 1971 as the percentage of children to total population increased from 41 in 1941 to 42 in 1971 for the country, that of the productive population (i.e. age group 15 to 60 years and over) has fallen from 59 to 58. It may be noted that the percentage of aged persons (i.e. 60 and over) also improved from 5.7 per cent to 6.0 per cent in 1971. This indicates a better expectation of life.

If we compare the proportions of population in different age groups in 1921 with those of 1971, population aged 0-14 has increased from 39.3 per cent in 1921 to 41.9 per cent in 1971 for males, and from 39 to 42.2 per cent in case of females for the same period. The age pyramid shown in Fig. 1. also depicts the same trend.

Table 1. Percentage distribution of population of each sex by broad age groups, India, 1911-71

Census Year	*Sex*	*Age Groups*			
		0-14	*15-44*	*45-59*	*60+*
1	*2*	*3*	*4*	*5*	*6*
1911	M	38.8	46.5	9.9	4.8
	F	38.1	46.9	9.4	5.6
1921	M	39.4	45.5	10.1	5.0
	F	39.0	46.0	9.5	5.5
1931	M	40.0	46.2	9.9	3.9
	F	40.1	46.4	9.4	4.1
1941	M	38.1	46.1	10.9	4.9
	F	38.4	46.1	10.6	4.9
1951	M	37.1	46.3	11.1	5.5
	F	37.9	45.7	10.6	5.8
1961	M	40.9	43.0	10.6	5.5
	F	41.2	43.3	9.7	5.8
1971	M	41.9	41.5	10.7	5.9
	F	41.9	42.4	9.7	6.0

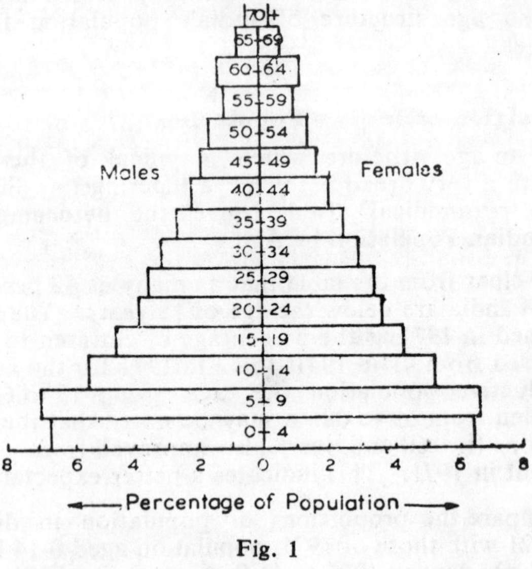

Fig. 1

Decline in infant mortality in the years to come will mean a further increase in the age group 0-14. "The predominantly young nature of our population implies that in the medium run, the sheer inertia of the system will lead to a substantial increase in the population size, even if we could assume that the current fertility levels were going to be very significantly reduced by some miraculous device."

The principal reasons for a higher child-population in India are:

(*i*) Decline in infant mortality rate.

(*ii*) Increase in birth rate due to reduction in maternal mortality and widow-remarrriage in early ages.

(*iii*) Declining trend in the length of lactation period.

(*iv*) Higher expectation of life at different ages.

(*v*) No marked change in low age at marriage to effect the birth rate.

A preponderance of children in the population is harmful for several reasons. Firstly, it reflects a high dependency ratio and a low working force participation. Secondly, a high proportion of children would call for a fairly high level of investment in social services including child-care, nutrition programme, school education, additional housing and ancillary services. Thus the high dependency ratio has an unfavourable effect on our ability to save and also limits the amount for directly productive investment. Finally, it poses most important problem before the country i.e., the problem of labour force explosion.

From the fact mentioned, it is abundantly clear that while our need to run fast is greater, our pace is likely to be inhibited because of high dependency ratio. We are beginning the race with a labour reserve, whose dimensions are very large.

Dependency Ratio

The presence of a large number of dependents sharply increases the 'dependency load' of the working population. Though the age divisions vary, the most common procedure is to compute the age dependency ratio as follows:

$$\textit{Dependency ratio} = \frac{P_{0-14} + P_{60}}{P_{15-59}} \times 100$$

The components of this measure may be calculated separately as child dependency and aged dependency ratios.

$$\textit{Child dependency ratio} = \frac{P_{0-14}}{P_{15-59}} \times 100$$

$$\textit{Aged dependency ratio} = \frac{P_{60}}{P_{15-59}} \times 100$$

It will be noted from Table 2 that during the two subsequent decades there was a substantial increase in the proportion of the

Table 2. Dependency ratio and index of aging, 1901-1971

Dependency Ratio			*Index of Aging**
Young	*Old*	*Overall*	
68.50	8.96	77.46	13.08
68.17	9.13	77.30	13.39
70.57	9.45	80.02	13.39
71.49	7.24	78.73	10.13
67.28	8.62	75.90	12.81
65.96	9.94	75.90	15.07
76.84	10.55	87.39	13.74
80.79	11.48	92.27	14.21

$$\text{*Index of aging} = \frac{\text{Percentage of population aged 60 and over}}{\text{Percentage of population aged 0-14}} \times 100$$

population in the younger age group (0-14 years) and a slight increase in the proportion of the older age group (60 years and over). Consequently, the overall dependency ratio recorded an increase to an all-time high of 92.3 in 1971. Thus India suffers from a heavy burden of dependency particularly at youg ages. It must, however, be noted that the true dependency load (ratio of non-workers to workers in the population) in India is very much higher than is indicated by the conventional dependency ratios, because not all persons of working age are actually at work.

Index of Aging and Median Age

In order to examine whether the population of India is growing, young, or old, two indexes viz, index of aging and median age of the population are computed for all census years from 1901 to 1971.

Table 3. Median ages of the population, 1901-1971

Census Year	*Median Age (in Years)*		
	Both sexes	*Males*	*Females*
1901	21.3	21.0	21.5
1911	21.2	21.2	21.3
1921	21.1	21.1	21.0
1931	19.9	20.1	19.7
1941	21.0	21.1	20.8
1951	21.1	21.2	20.8
1961	20.5	20.1	19.9
1971	19.1	19.1	19.1

As is evident from Table 2, the index of aging has shown fluctuations after the year 1921 and hence no definite trend in this index is ascertainable. But, a slight increase in its value is witnessed between 1961 and 1971 which may, perhaps, be due to the combined effect of the decline in fertility and mortality during the last decade.

It is obvious from the figures of Table 3 that the median age of the total population in 1901 was 21.3. It decreased gradually to 19.9 in 1931 and thereafter increased to 21.1 in 1971 and again registered a decline to 19.1 in 1971. This implies that exactly half of the population of India was below 19.1 years of age at the time of the 1971 census. This indicates that the population of India is becoming 'young'. The reduction in the median age of the Indian populations is largely due to the decline in mortality.

Age Composition of Population in States

Table 4 shows the distribution of population by broad age groups for each state in 1921-71. The proportion of persons under 15 years of age varied between 37.5 in Uttar Pradesh to 41.6 in Assam in 1921 and between 37.8 in Tamil Nadu and 46.7 in Assam according to the 1971 census as against the all-India percentage of 39.2 and 42 respectively. There is an increase in the percentage of population in both the young and old age groups (0-14 and 60+) between 1921-71 in all states except Jammu and Kashmir, Kerala and Tamil Nadu. In 1971 the proportion of population aged less than 15 years was slightly lower in Andhra Pradesh (40.5 per cent), Kerala (40.3 per cent), Maharashtra (41.3 per cent), Tamil Nadu (37.8 per cent) and Uttar Pradesh (41.8 per cent) than the corresponding proportion for India (42 per cent).

Comparison with Other Countries

Comparison of the age composition of population of various countries at the present time shows large differences, which are closely related to present levels and past trends of birth and death rates. The examples in Table 5 have been selected to illustrate representative patterns.

There are certain factors which differentiate the character of Indian age-composition from that of any Western country. They are (*i*) the low proportion of working population; (*ii*) The high birth-rate in India accompanied by a high infantile mortality; and (*iii*) the low expectation of life.

The U.N. publication on the Determinants of Population Trends observes: "Paradoxically, one of the chief obstacles to economic development is the manpower shortage which exists even in the so-called overpopulated countries. Owing to the age structure of the population there are not enough adults." Because of social customs only a small proportion of the adults is available for employment

Table 4. Percentage of age composition of population in states in India, 1921-71

(Percentage distribution of population by age)

States		1921			1961			1971		
		0-14	15-59	60+	0-14	15-59	60+	0-14	15-59	60+
		1	2	3	4	5	6	7	8	9
Andhra Pradesh	P	38.47	55.27	6.26	39.54	54.22	6.26	40.48	53.15	6.37
	M	38.18	55.73	6.09	29.52	54.37	6.09	—	—	—
	F	38.78	54.79	6.44	39.56	54.06	6.44	—	—	—
Assam	P	41.62	54.47	3.91	44.82	50.82	3.91	46.66	48.61	4.72
	M	41.09	54.90	4.01	42.70	52.65	4.01	—	—	—
	F	42.20	54.00	3.81	47.23	48.73	3.81	—	—	—
Bihar	P	39.70	55.29	5.01	42.31	52.05	5.61	42.58	51.51	5.90
	M	41.08	54.61	4.30	43.40	51.43	5.14	—	—	—
	F	38.35	55.94	5.71	41.20	52.68	6.09	—	—	—
M.P.	P	40.51	54.12	5.37	40.80	53.99	5.16	43.70	50.51	5.79
	M	40.88	54.31	4.81	40.93	54.42	4.60	—	—	—
	F	40.12	53.92	5.95	40.67	53.54	5.74	—	—	—
Jammu & Kashmir	P	41.21	52.55	6.24	40.62	54.11	5.07	42.88	51.55	5.57
	M	40.99	52.34	6.68	39.46	54.75	5.60	—	—	—
	F	41.45	52.79	5.76	41.94	53.39	4.47	—	—	—
Orissa	P	39.70	55.29	5.01	39.07	55.19	5.66	42.35	51.61	6.02
	M	41.08	54.61	4.30	39.30	55.47	5.15	—	—	—
	F	38.35	55.94	5.71	38.83	54.91	6.18	—	—	—
U.P.	P	37.46	57.12	5.43	40.48	53.19	6.29	41.85	51.38	6.77
	M	37.78	57.17	5.05	40.62	53.04	6.30	—	—	—
	F	37.10	57.05	5.85	40.32	53.37	6.27	—	—	—

		1	2	3	4	5	6	7	8	9
Karnataka	P	38.23	55.46	6.30	42.14	52.09	5.73	41.13	51.45	6.10
	M	37.48	56.18	6.34	41.49	52.85	5.63	—	—	—
	F	39.02	54.72	6.26	42.82	51.30	5.84	—	—	—
Kerala	P	42.39	53.44	4.18	42.63	51.51	5.84	40.26	53.51	6.22
	M	42.77	53.17	4.06	43.62	50.71	5.65	—	—	—
	F	42.00	53.71	4.29	41.66	52.30	6.02	—	—	—
Rajasthan	P	39.99	55.08	4.93	42.63	52.15	5.14	44.17	50.31	5.52
	M	39.95	55 49	4.56	42.59	52.32	5.01	—	—	—
	F	40.03	54.63	5.34	42.67	51.97	5.28	—	—	—
Tamil Nadu	P	37.94	56.20	5.86	37.60	56.79	5.60	37.77	56.48	5.74
	M	38.40	55.86	5.74	37.75	56.65	5.60	—	—	—
	F	37.48	56.54	5.98	37.46	56.94	5.60	—	—	—
West Bengal	P	40.02	55.32	4.17	40.92	54.05	5.01	42.90	51.56	5.30
	M	40.00	55.97	4.03	39.21	56.13	4.63	—	—	—
	F	40.04	55.66	4.31	42.86	51.67	5.49	—	—	—
Gujarat	P	39.36	55.77	4.87	42.87	52.15	4.94	42·58	51.51	5.90
	M	39.20	56.28	4.51	43.22	52·22	4.52	—	—	—
	F	39.53	55.20	5.26	42.51	52.07	5.39	—	—	—
Maharashtra	P	39.36	55.77	4.87	40.65	54.04	5.27	41.34	52.93	5.72
	M	39·20	56.29	4.51	40.18	54.77	5.01	—	—	—
	F	39.53	55.20	5.26	41.15	53.27	5.54	—	—	—
Punjab	P	40.25	53.15	6.60	43.55	49.84	6.65	43.30	49.96	6.73
	M	39.47	53.61	6.92	42.92	49.75	7.27	—	—	—
	F	41.20	52.60	6.20	44.27	49.95	5.73	—	—	—

which would contribute to economic development. It has to be remembered that a considerable proportion of the females belonging to the higher castes amongst the Hindus, as well as those under Purdah (both Hindus and Muslims) are precluded by the customs and institutions of the country from contribution to the production of wealth, except in so far as they perform services of mother and house-wives. To some extent, they also assist in farm operations and cottage handicrafts. At the most favourable estimate it would seem that the burden of supporting the entire population falls upon 40 per cent of the population.

Table 5. Age composition and dependence ratio, selected countries, 1969-74

Country	*Percentage of population in different age groups*			*Dependency ratio*
	0-14	*15-59*	*60+*	
Developed				
1. Australia	28.0	59.4	12.5	68.2
2. France	23.7	57.6	18.7	73.5
3. Japan	24.3	64.0	11.7	56.3
4. Sweden	20.7	58.3	21.0	71.6
5. United Kingdom	23.1	57.1	19.9	75.3
6. USA	24.5	60.5	15.0	65.2
Developing				
1. Ghana	46.9	47.7	5.3	109.5
2. India	40.1	54.6	5.3	83.2
3. Indonesia	44.0	51.5	4.5	94.0
4. Republic of Korea	38.6	56.0	5.5	78.7
5. Malaysia	42.1	52.4	5.5	90.8
6. Mexico	46.3	48.8	4.9	105.0
7. Pakistan	43.4	49.9	6.7	100.6
8. Zambia	46.5	49.3	4.2	102.6

We have seen in Table 5 that in India the burden of maintaining the young and the old people falls on smaller portion of the people than in developed countries. The last column of Table 5 represents the dependency ratio. It compares the proportion of a population which is in the relatively non-productive ages, under 15 years and over 60 years, with those of working age 15 to 59 years. From the data in Table for a few representative advanced and under-developed countries, what stands but is that the dependency ratio is distinctly higher in the under-developed countries than in the developed countries. In case of under-developed countries the dependents are mainly children.

India has a high dependency ratio because of the high proportion of children which lead to diversion of resources from capital formation to population maintenance and upbringing, etc. A heavy proportion of dependents acts as a serious drag on our production and improvement of living standards. Obviously the dependency ratio of a country greatly influences the proportion of the national income going into savings, investment, pensions, welfare and education. In reverse, it reflects the percentage of the population that is active in creating the wealth.

India has a smaller proportion in the working age-group because of the heavier mortality before the working age is reached. This indicates an enormous wastage of life in India. With a large proportion of younger generation or first age group, 0-14, it is but natural that India should have a very high death rate in the age group 0-14 to bring down the second age group to the 50 per cent average of Sundbarg. Infant mortality ratio is much higher in India. A high level of infant mortality signifies wastage of effort and investment in rearing up children. "Economically speaking, the under-developed countries suffer a considerable loss of investment, material and immaterial in upbringing and educational effort in respect of a substantial number of young people who never reach the prime of life. Even if the amount invested per capita is below the equivalent of the cost of education, clothing and food customary in western countries, the outlay lost in the aggregate is staggering."

Thus we can conclude that the 'bottom heavy' age structure of Indian population on the one hand reduce the chances of a larger 'take off' for investment due to the heavy dependency burden, and on the other hand, prevent the economically active population from repaying to the society adequately in terms of goods and services due to 'shorter span' of the productivity period.

According to the Seventh Plan, productive and non-productive consumers constituted 55 per cent and 45 per cent of India's population in 1980, and should change to 61 per cent and 39 per cent respectively by 1996. However, this optimism is not shared by all, at least for the immediate future. It is argued that with further decline in the death rate and with no change in the birth rate, the dependency ratio will rise. The problem in India is even worse because not all people in the working age group are gainfully employed. Consequently, the actual percentage of dependents is much higher.

SEX COMPOSITION

Importance of Sex Composition

Unquestionally the classification of population according to sex generally influences the form and/tempo of life in any community. The balance between the sexes is an important aspect of population structure. The proportions of men and women in total population of a society have vital bearings in so far as it affects the labour supply through marriage and fecundity. If the proportion of males is higher than that of females more workers will be available. With the exception of females of lower classes, women in India are precluded by the customs and institution of the country from contributing to the production of wealth. This reduces our national wealth to a great extent. Many economic and social relationships are closely related to the balance or disparity between numbers of males and females. The excess of males tends to lower the age of marriage for females since the number of females falls short of the number of the opposite sex. Early marriages lead to considerable disparity in age between husbands and wives. This difference in age tends to increase widowhood. The sex ratio which, in its own turn, may be affected by past fertility; mortality and migration plays an important part in determining birth and death rates in a community. India has got an adverse sex-ratio in the sense that females are outnumbered by males and this has got its own repercussions on the growth of population. In general the death rate among females, compared to that of males is low because of biological reasons, enabling females to resist diseases more effectively than males, as also the fact that males, more than females, are confronted with the strains and stresses of life. Consequently a population having a higher proportion of females may have a relatively lower death rate as compared with a population like India in which males preponderate. An adverse sex ratio (i.e. when the proportion of females is small) leads to the emergence of many social and moral evils like prostitution and V.D. impairing the moral of the workers.

Measurement of Sex Ratio

Sex composition may be studied with reference to the sex ratio which may be recorded in two different ways:

(a) *Masculinity proportion*: The simplest measure of sex composition of a population is the masculinity ratio defined as the percentage of males in the population. The formula for the masculinity proportion is:

$$\frac{P_m}{P_m+P_f} \times 100 \text{ or } \frac{P_m}{P_t} \times 100$$

(b) *Sex ratio*: This is the most widely used and principal measure of sex composition that has enjoyed the maximum use in analytical demography. It is usually defined as the number of females per 1000 males in a population, that is

$$\text{sex ratio} = \frac{P_f}{P_m} \times 1000$$

where P_m and P_f denote the population of males and females repectively and P_t denotes the total population.

Pattern of Sex Ratio in India

The population of India as at the Census of March 1981 was 68.4 crores of which 35.3 crores or 51.7 per cent were males and 33.05 crores or 41.3 per cent were females. At the Census of 1901, females numbered 11.7 crore persons as against 12.08 crore males. It will thus be seen that over a period of 80 years, the female population had increased by about 182 per cent compared with an increase of 193 per cent in the male population. In terms of absolute numbers, the gap between males and females had widened from about 3.4 million in 1901 to about 23 million in 1981. However, in the decade 1971-1981, the total females increased by 66 million compared with an increase of over 69 million in the male population. But in terms of growth, females registered a 25 per cent increase as against 24.4 per cent for males. This differential helped to arrest the long-term downward trend in the sex ratio (the number of females per 1,000 males) as will be seen from the figures of Table 6.

Table 6. Sex ratio (females per thousand males) in India, 1901-81

Census year	*Population (millions)*		*Sex Ratio*
	Males	*Females*	
1901	120.8	117.4	972
1911	128.4	123.7	964
1921	128.5	122.8	955
1931	142.9	135.8	950
1941	163.7	154.7	945
1951	185.5	175.6	946
1961	226.3	212.9	941
1971	284.0	264.1	930
1981	353.3	330.5	935

Table 6 depicts that the predominance of female deficiency has been a striking characteristic of our population throughout the whole of the regular census history. There were only 972 females for every

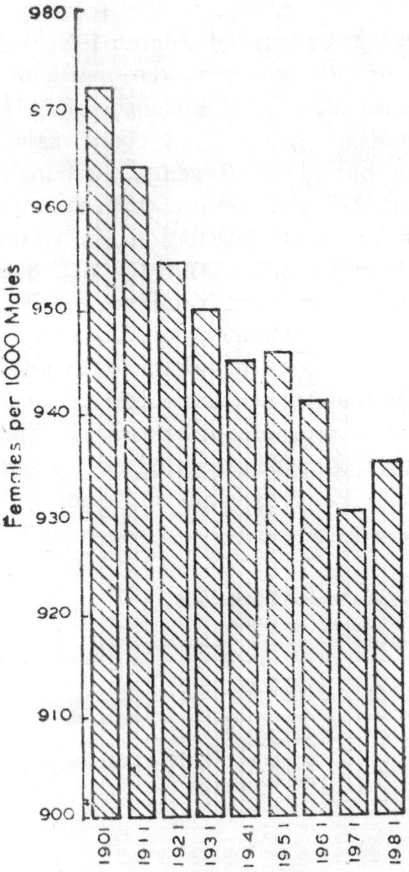

Fig. 2.

1000 males in 1901, as compared to 964 in 1911, 955 in 1921, 950 in 1931, 945 in 1951, 941 in 1961, 930 in 1971 and 935 in 1981. These figures show that there has been a steady fall in the proportion of females in all the successive Censuses, excepting the one of 1951 which showed but a small rise. The overall extent of decline comes to 40 points from 972 in 1901 to 930 in 1971. In short the sex composition of India's population (Table 6) shows a shortage of females per thousand males and this shortage has aggravated over time except that there is a reversal in the trend in 1981 (Fig. 2).

It may be mentioned that the sex ratio is different for different States in India. Table 7 presents figures relating to the sex ratio of States.

It is interesting to notice that certain States have had a fairly extended period where the sex ratio has been over one thousand, i.e., the sex ratio is in favour of females. In the case of Kerala the sex ratio has been throughout above 1,000 while in Manipur, Orissa, Tamil Nadu, Goa, Daman & Diu, Lakshadweep and Mizoram it has been above 1,000 for a considerable part of the period 1901 to 1981. On the other hand, the sex ratio has been constantly on the low side in comparison with other States and Union Territories in Haryana, Himachal Pradesh, Jammu and Kashmir, Punjab, Tripura, Andaman and Nicobar Islands, Chandigarh and Delhi. At this stage one would be reluctant to offer specific reasons for this phenomenon. In India the subject of 'surplus' men over larger part of the country and surplus women in others has not been made a matter of study and concern and its bearing on the population situation is not known. It has also not been established what effects this imbalance has produced or is producing. The high sex ratio of

Table 7. Provisional population sex ratio, 1901-81

Sl. No.	*India/State/ Union Territory*	*1901*	*1911*	*1921*	*1931*	*1941*	*1951*	*1961*	*1971*	*1981*
	India	972	964	955	950	945	946	941	930	935
	States									
1.	Andhra Pradesh	985	992	993	987	980	986	981	977	975
2.	Assam	919	915	896	874	875	868	869	896	900
3.	Bihar	1054	1044	1016	994	996	990	994	954	947
4.	Gujarat	954	946	944	945	941	952	940	934	942
5.	Haryana	867	835	844	844	869	871	868	867	877
6.	Himachal Pradesh	884	889	890	897	890	912	938	958	988
7.	Jammu and Kashmir	882	876	870	865	869	873	878	878	953
8.	Karnataka	983	981	969	965	960	966	959	957	963
9.	Kerala	1004	1003	1011	1022	1027	1028	1022	1016	1034
10.	Madhya Pradesh	990	986	974	973	970	967	953	941	941
11.	Maharashtra	978	966	950	947	949	941	936	930	939
12.	Manipur	1037	1029	1041	1065	1055	1036	1015	980	972
13.	Meghalaya	1036	1013	1000	971	966	949	937	942	956
14.	Nagaland	973	993	992	997	966	949	937	942	956
15.	Orissa	1037	1056	1086	1067	1053	1022	1001	988	982
16.	Punjab	832	780	799	815	836	844	854	865	886
17.	Rajasthan	905	908	896	907	906	921	908	911	921
18.	Sikkim	916	951	970	967	920	907	904	863	836
19.	Tamil Nadu	1044	1042	1029	1027	1012	1007	992	978	978
20.	Tripura	874	885	885	885	886	904	932	943	948
21.	Uttar Pradesh	937	915	909	904	907	910	909	879	886
22.	West Bengal	945	925	905	890	852	865	878	891	911

Union Territories									
1. Andaman & Nicobar Islands	318	352	303	495	574	625	617	644	761
2. Arunachal Pradesh	—	—	—	—	—	—	894	861	870
3. Chandigarh	771	720	743	751	763	781	652	749	770
4. Dadra & Nagar Haveli	960	967	940	911	925	946	963	1007	947
5. Delhi	862	793	733	722	715	768	785	801	810
6. Goa Daman & Diu	1085	1103	1122	1088	1083	1128	1071	989	981
7. Lakshadweep	1063	987	1027	994	1018	1043	1020	978	978
8. Mizoram	1113	1120	1109	1102	1069	1041	1009	946	936
9. Pondicherry	NA	1058	1053	NA	NA	1030	1013	989	985

women south of latitude 22 and low sex-ratio in the north, which has been an enduring feature of the social life of our people for an indefinitely long time, *prima facie* poses a problem of real consequence for population specialists to which earnest attention needs to be given.

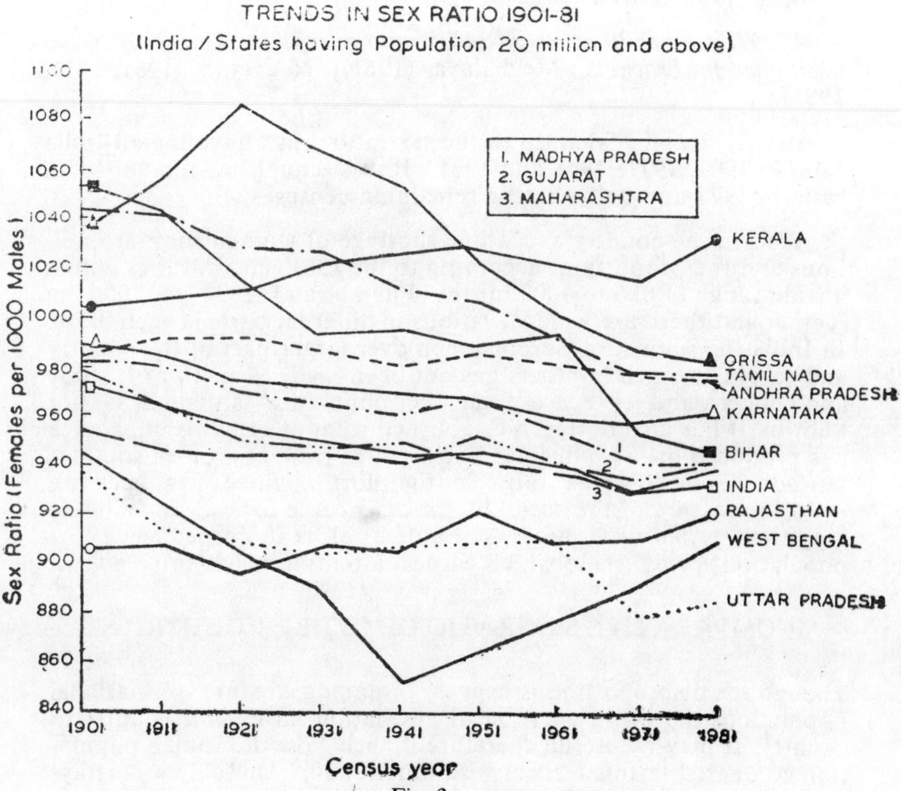

Fig. 3.

The State and Union Territories can be arranged on the basis of the behaviour of their sex ratio in the period 1901 to 1981 in relation to the all-India sex ratio on the basis of Information in Provisional Population—Table 7. On this basis the States and Union Territories would fall within the following groups:

1. *With sex ratio below all-India ratio during the period 1901 to 1981.* Assam, Haryana, Punjab, Rajasthan, Uttar Pradesh, West Bengal, Andaman and Nicobar Islands, Chandigarh and Delhi.

2. *With sex ratio above all-India ratio during the period 1901 to 1981*. Andhra Pradesh, Bihar, Karnataka, Kerala, Madhya Pradesh, Manipur, Orissa, Tamil Nadu, Goa, Daman & Diu, Lakshadweep, and Mizoram.

3. *With sex ratio below all-India ratio except in the census years mentioned in brackets*. Gujarat (1951, 1971, 1981), Himachal Pradesh (1971, 1981), Jammu and Kashmir (1981), Sikkim (1921, 1931) and Tripura (1971, 1981).

4. *With sex ratio above all-India ratio except in the census years mentioned in brackets*. Meghalaya (1961), Nagaland (1961, 1971, 1981).

In the case of Maharashtra the sex ratio was above the all-India ratio in 1901, 1911, 1941 and 1981. It was equal to the all-India ratio in 1971 and below in the remaining censuses.

Thus in the country as a whole shortage of women runs into millions and the proportion, according to the 1981 census, varies within a wide range of 886 to 1000 in the Punjab and 1034 to 1000 in Kerala and there are wide variations in different parts in each State. In India the subject of 'surplus' men over larger part of the country and surplus women in others has not been made a matter of study and concern and its bearing on the population situation is not known. It has also not been established what effects this imbalance has produced or is producing. The high sex ratio of women south of latitude 22 and low sex ratio in the north, which has been an enduring feature of the social life of our people for an indefinitely long time, *prima facie* poses a problem of real consequence for population specialists to which earnest attention needs to be given.

COMPARATIVE SEX RATIO OF OTHER COUNTRIES

Though sex disproportion is a very common feature of national populations the world over, but the deviation varies from country to country. It may be useful, therefore, to see how the Indian population compared in this respect with other countries. Table 8 portrays the sex ratio of selected countries.

The figures given in the table are self-explanatory and require no elucidation. However, it may be noted that in the emigrant countries such as Federal Republic of Germany, German Democratic Republic, France and U.K., the sex ratio is in favour of females, whereas in the immigrant countries such as Canada, Algeria and Venezuela it is in favour of males.

Table 8. Sex ratio in selected countries of the world

Country	*Census year*	*No. of females per 1000 males*
Canada	1971	998
Japan	1970	1037
German Democratic Republic	1971	1170
Federal Republic of Germany	1971	1101
Hungary	1970	1063
United Kingdom	1971	1057
Norway	1970	1011
Switzerland	1970	1029
USSR	1970	1170
Australia	1971	990
Nepal	1971	988
Pakistan	1972	885
Taiwan	1971	914
Israel	1972	990
Kuwait	1971	759
Argentina	1970	1014
Venezuela	1970	967
Morocco	1971	998
Algeria	1966	992
Uganda	1969	982
India	1971	930

Source: United Nations, Demographic Year Book, 1970, 1972, 1974 and 1976.

EXPLANATION OF INDIAN SEX RATIO

The puzzling phenomenon of the excess of males in India, in sharp contrast to the excess of females in most Western countries, has led to protracted discussion about the specific factors at work. There could be several reasons for masculinity in India.

(*i*) *Incomplete enumeration of women*. Sometimes it is said that the anomalous sex ratio of the Indian population is due, only or even largely, to sex selective enumeration or an omission of females in large proportion. This view is held by the Census Commissioner for 1891, 1911 and 1931. Evidence has not been found to support this contention. Prior to the sample verification check on the completeness of coverage undertaken after the 1951 Census, we had no direct evidence on this subject. The 1951 post-enumeration check estimated that the percentage (net) under-count in 1951 was higher among females than among males. However, the observed sex differentials in Census coverage do not make much difference to the observed masculinity of population in any zone of the country.

If this is assumed to be true that females are more under-counted than males, and is the only reason for low proportion of females, then the declining proportion of females since 1901 to 1971 in India should indicate that female under-count is increasing in magnitude since 1901. But to expect increase in female under-count with the advancement of social and cultural developments and with increasing census efficiency appears unconvincing.

A fairly impressive body of other indirect evidence also confirms the view that as far as one can judge, there is no basis for the hypothesis that the anomalous sex ratio in India is due to under-enumeration of females who are largely omitted.

(*ii*) *The excess of males at birth.* A higher masculinity at birth has also been classed as a cause for high overall excess of males over females in India. But recently the data of sex ratios of birth occurring in hospitals and health centres during 1948-58, collected by the Demographic Training and Research Centre, Bombay, have disapproved this hypothesis of a higher than normal masculinity at birth in India being responsible for the observed excess of males in the population. The excess of male child at birth is not the important cause of the male-dominant population of India. It is the difference in mortality rates of the two sexes which cause the male numbers in India to rise in comparison with female numbers.

(*iii*) *Female infanticide.* In past female infanticide was very common and various ways were used for killing the child. But at present there is no evidence to justify the assumption of widespread female infanticide except in such communities as Jats, Gujars, Khatris and Rajputs. There are tribes and classes of Rajputs in Jaipur and Gwalior States amongst whom the ratio of females to males is between 500 and 600 females per 1000 males. The Census Superintendent of Rajputana observed in 1931: "Deliberate infanticide seldom comes to light, but there is no doubt that unwanted female infants are often so neglected that death is the result." Thus female infanticide does exist in part of this vast country but it is of insignificant proportions hardly important to influence the general sex ratio. It does not explain the increasing margin between the number of the two sexes from census to census.

(*iv*) *Institution of early marriage and female neglect*: The higher mortality of the Indian females compared to that of the male is due to social rather than biological factors. The social unpopularity of the female child, early marriage, frequent maternity and poor nutrition (due to poverty) are responsible for the much higher female mortality in India. Early marriages subject girls to the risk of motherhood at a tender age when they are of weak constitution and physically immature. Their constitution is undermined and their vitality impaired by frequent births; and the result is a high rate of female mortality. In India the total births in a year include only 40 per cent or so of the first and second order children; in the advanced countries there are today more than 70 per cent births of these two orders. This has its impact on the death rate of the Indian female because she cannot bear the burden of excessive child-bearing. The burden of excessive child-bearing compared to in the advanced countries is, no doubt, the root cause of the female's high mortality. The hazards of death due to excessive child-bearing during the child-bearing ages is also manifest in the analysis of causes of death available from hospital data in urban Maharashtra, where deaths from puerperal trouble (i.e. concerning pregnancy, child-birth etc.) form 26 per cent of the total deaths in 1970 in the age group 15-49 years. Deaths from similar causes in the advanced countries constitute two to five per cent of total deaths. If the status of the female is raised, the excessive child-bearing may decline. Thus, raising the status of the female—by education and employment—may help the birth-control movement in India.

Not only are children born in a series of successive years by child mothers apt to be physically weaklings, but they are apt to be neglected if they are girls not through any lack of human sympathy, but on account of social customs of attitudes which make parents look upon girls as burden, while sons are looked upon not merely as means of support in later life but also as instrumental to the very preservation of life and the spiritual salvation of the father. The very name for son 'Putra' means one who saves his father's soul from the hell called 'Putra'. Without a son funeral rites cannot be performed and this naturally affects the desire for male issue. The aversion for females has been evident from a number of enquiries and health surveys conducted over the last 25 years. In 1957 in Bombay health surveys were conducted in six rural communities of six districts covering a rural population of 37,000. It was found that among non-adults (i.e. age-group below 15 years) there were 513 male non-adults ailing as compared to 730 females, in the year of the survey. Among the non-adults the percentage of males getting some medical treatment was much higher than the percentage of females.

On the basis of the discussions in the preceding sections it may be concluded that the important factors responsible for the excess of males in the total population appear to be the male-favoured sex ratio at birth, and the higher risks of deaths to which Indian women are exposed. The various arguments have been succinctly summed up by Mitra as follows:

"Even allowing for the argument that the differences between the male and female rates are so slight that they may be attributed wholly to defective age returns or computational errors, the fact remains that at each successive census the enumeration of females and their ages have, if anything, improved rather than worsened. Whatever the reason, the prospect of survival of females seems to have been ever so slightly better before 1921 than after. While the risk of male deaths at most ages seems to have steadily decreased especially after 1921, there has been no corresponding improvement in female deaths. In the first place, it is often contended, without much evidence of course, that masculinity at birth obtains to a greater extent in India than elsewhere. Secondly, girls in the first few years of their life still seem to suffer from greater neglect than boys, as a result of which nature's balancing action of taking away more boys than girls in the first years of life does not properly come into play, and the survival of girls never seems to draw even with that of boys. Thirdly, a heavy toll of female lives is taken in the earlier period of the reproductive age, that is, between the ages of 15 and 34. The toll is heavy that the difference between the male and female population grows remarkedly rapid and wide and this gap is never made up in middle or old age. What is more, proportionately greater deaths occur among females even between the ages 35 and 54 than is commonly believed. All these factors help to widen the male lead at birth with age, which one still modest expectation of life does not give much of a chance to narrow."

The decline in sex-ratio over times indicates that the risk of female lives at most ages has not improved upon the risk to male lives. This emphasizes the fact that demographically India has not entered the modern industrial age with its complementary characteristics of increasing risk of male lives and reduced risk of female lives. Whilst there has been an increasing pressure of population under present condition the decline in the number of female births may in the long run involve a declining population. The declining proportion of females to males which has been a feature characterising the few decades for which census figures are available might also suggest a trend towards lower national vitality which can only be explained in terms of malnutrition and general poverty.

Sex Ratio by Rural-Urban Residence

The sex ratio of the population by rural-urban residence for the various years is given in Table 9. It will be noted that in rural

Table 9. Sex ratio by rural-urban residence, 1901-1971

Census year	*Total population*	*Rural population*	*Urban population*
1901	972	979	910
1911	963	975	872
1921	955	980	846
1931	950	966	838
1941	945	965	831
1951	846	965	860
1961	941	963	845
1971	930	949	858

Source: Census of India 1971, General Population Table, Series 1, Part II-A (*i*) (New Delhi, Office of the Registrar General, 1975), p. 126.

areas the sex ratio has steadily decreased from 979 in 1901 to 949 in 1971, the highest decreased being recorded during 1961-1971.

The urban population also had recorded an decrease in the sex ratio from 910 in 1901 to 858 in 1971, though there have been fluctuations after 1941—increasing during 1941-1951, declining during 1951-1961 and again during 1961-1971. The highest decrease in the sex ratio for urban areas has been noticed during 1901-1911.

Sex Ratios by Religious Communities

Table 10 shows the sex ratios for the different religious communities in India for various census years since 1901.

It will be noted that in the case of Hindus who constitute the vast majority of the population, their sex ratio has been more or less equal to the national average in all census years; in other words, a more or less consistent increase in the sex ratio was recorded for the Hindus from 1901 to 1971.

The sex ratio for Muslim, which has been lower than that of the Hindus in all census years, steadily decreased until 1941, but increased substantially in 1951 and thereafter increased gradually.

The lowest sex ratio in all census years has been recorded for Sikhs.

The ratios for Christians and Buddhists have shown fluctuations over the years and in 1971 their sex ratios were higher than that of the Hindus.

According to the 1961 census, the Parsees and Jews had an excess of females over males and this feature was observed in 1971 as well.

SELECT REFERENCES

1. Clerk, J.I.: *Population Geography*. Also refer to (i) Coale, Ansley J.: How a Population ages or grows Younger. In Ronald Freedman (ed.), *Population: The Vital Revolution*, (ii) Petersen, William, *Population*. Smith, T. Lynn: *Fundamentals of Population Study*, United Nations Population Study No. 26. The Aging of Population and its Economic and Social Implications.
2. Trewartha, Glenn T.: *A Geography of Population.*
3. Desai, P.S.: *Size and Sex Composition of Population in India.*
4. Sivasubramaniam, S. and Rao, M.R.: *Inter-State Variation in Age, Working Force and Per Capita Income*. In Ashish Bose (ed.), *Pattern of Population Change in India 1951-61*.
5. Hopkins, W.A.B.: 'The Economics of an Aging Population', *Lloyds Bank Review*, January, 1963.
6. Alfred Bonne: *Studies in Economic Development.*
7. Spenglar, J.J.: Demographic Pattern in Williamson and Butterick.
8. Clarke, John J.: Population Geography. Also refer to (i) Smith, T. Lynn: *Fundamentals of Population Study*. Jastrzebaki, D.S. de: 'The Sex Ratio at

Table 10. Sex ratios of different religious communities, 1901-1971

Religion	*Census year*							
	1901	*1911*	*1921*	*1931*	*1941*	*1951*	*1961*	*1971*
Hindus	971	964	957	953	944	949	942	930
Muslims	939	922	912	903	903	938	935	922
Christians	939	931	935	952	959	992	989	986
Sikhs	767	739	756	984	811	851	849	858
Jains	928	940	932	942	930	927	924	940
Buddhists	948	950	934	935	939	917	981	962
Jews	948	955	933	937	961	823	1005	1010
Parsees	959	962	948	942	973	991	1038	
All religions	972	963	955	950	945	946	941	930

Sources: Census of India 1901 to 1941, Tables, Vol. I, Parts I and II (London, Her Majesty's Stationery Office); Census of India 1951, Religion and Livelihood Classes of Reorganized States, 1951, Paper No. 1 of 1959 (New Delhi, Office of the Regitrar General 1959), pp. 7-8; Census of India 1961, Socio-cultural Tables, Vol. 1, Part II C (i) (New Delhi, Office of the Registrar General, 1964), pp. 488-489; Census of India 1971, Social and Cultural Tables, Series 1, Part II-C (i) (New Delhi, Office of the Registrar General, 1976), pp. 92-93.

Birth', *Eugenics Review*, Vol. II, (ii) Thomlinson, Ralph: *Population Dynamics.*

9. Desai, P.B.: *Size and Sex Composition of Population in India and Pakistan and Regional Variations during 1901-61.*
10. Wattal, P.K.: *Population Problem in India—a Census Study.*
11. Sinha, V.C.: *Dynamics of India's Population Growth.*

EXAMINATION QUESTIONS

1. Comment on the decreasing proportion of woman to man in India. Explain its causes and its possible effects.
2. What are the causes of the maldistribution of sex ratio in India? How can the situation be remedied?
3. Explain the features of sex composition of Indian population on the basis of census data.
4. 'High dependency ratio in India is the main obstacle to capital formation in India.' Examine this state on the basis of age composition and suggest measures to reduce dependency ratio in the rural areas.
5. Write an essay on the age composition of India's population.

27

Migration in India

Today, the extent, causes and selectivity/differentials of migration are increasingly engaging the attention and concern of social scientists. Migratory movements exert a pervasive influence on the economic, political and demographic structure of both the sending and the receiving areas. The demographers' interests have included migration (a) as a key factor in population change; (b) as an inducing variable in population graphic areas; and (c) as an adjustive mechanism concomitant to growth and development. For these reasons, several studies of the internal migratory movement of the population in India have already been undertaken. But it is unfortunate that data related to migration in India are neither sufficient, nor homogeneous and clear cut. The definitions and concepts have been changing.

The census is the major source of data on internal migration in India. From 181 to 1981, the question on the place of birth was recorded in order to study the migration of the population. In 1881, the migration table depicted the distribution of the population by birth places especially outside the Indian empire which characterized the census of 1891 also. The 1901 census contained separate data about internal migration together with the data on general and detailed distribution of population by the birth places, the censuses of 1911 and 1921 extended the scope of migration enquiry by including a table on distribution of birth. In 1931, information on the place of birth was also related to city areas. Birth place data collected in 1951 census had not been tabulated for most of the states, as many territorial changes had occurred at that time.

For the first time in 1961 a comprehensive data on migration was collected in India. It was in 1961 that the birth place was classified as rural and urban as well as—(i) within the district enumeration; (ii) outside the district of enumeration but within the state of enumeration, (iii) outside the state of enumeration but within India; and (iv) outside India. Besides this, four types of data were collected—(i) movement from village to village, (ii) movement from village to city, (iii) movement from city to village and (iv) from city to outside.

Information on the 'duration of residence at the place of enumeration' was also collected for the first time in 1961.

In the 1971 census the scope was enlarged by including information on 'last residence' and 'duration of residence at the place of enumeration'. Accordingly, six tables were framed showing migrants characteristics according to birth place (Table D-I) and by place of last residence (Table D-II to D-IV). In this system, the 1971 census provides a considerable picture of movement of population and their demographic, socio-economic and educational characteristics. The 1981 census has included yet another question on 'reasons, for migrations.

We propose to examine the trends of migration in India and suggest implications for the future. Our inferences are based primarily on a detailed examination of the trends of internal migration during the period 1951-81, which has witnessed planned effort at economic development on an increasing scale.

Prior to analysing the pattern of migration in India, it would be more useful to examine the popular misconception about the immobility of Indian rural population.

Immobility of India's Population—Reality or Myth

It has often been said that population in India is more or less immobile i.e., most of them live, work and complete their allotted span of life in the place of their birth. In other words, it is alleged that in India migration within the country and outside it is -relatively speaking of hardly any consequence and that our population is, largely speaking, exceedingly stationary.

The migration statistics are being collected in the Indian Censuses since 1872 and in support of the thesis that mobility of India's population is very low, data from these reports, which are based on place of birth, have been cited. (Table 1).

The data in the Table 1 clearly indicate that in all decennial censuses since 1901, the proportion of persons enumerated in a state other than those of their birth have consistently been shown to be around 3 per cent. The 1981 Census did not show any change in this pattern. It was on the basis of these statistics that Kingsley Davis observed, quarter of a century ago, that the population of India "like that of most peasant regions is relatively immobile". The reason attributed by Davis for this immobility were economic, social and cultural. It is said that the rural population is comparatively non-migratory due to his close ties to his village origins by bonds of kinship, marriage customs, language and centuries of in-group living. The reorganisation

Table 1. Percentage of Population Living Outside State of Birth 1901-1981

Year	*Percentage*
1901	3.3
1911	3.6
1921	3.7
1931	3.6
1951	3.1
1961	3.3
1971	3.3
1981	3.2

of states in India, whose boundaries have been fixed primarily on linguistic considerations, has further been though to be a factor inhibiting the movement of people from one state to another. Only such events as great famines, floods or political upheavals (such as the partition with Pakistan) have been thought capable of driving the Indian peasant from his village to seek his fortune in strange environs.

It has also been advocated that the urbanization is not consistent with the Indian way of life with the corollary that the urban form of social organization ought to be kept suppressed and minimized to the greatest extent possible while trying to raise the standard of living. This view point is reflected in the frequent demand for decentralization of industry in India, i.e. bringing jobs to the people in the individual villages through cottage and small-scale industries.

A little reflection will show the shallowness of the thesis that Indian population is traditionally immobile and therefore unresponsive to economic changes and better opportunities, and so on.

Though the mobility figures derived from the earlier Indian censuses are indeed very low and indicate very limited mobility among India's population, but these statistics pertains only to inter-state and not to the total migration. But, in the Indian context intra-state migration is more important, in view of the fact that an Indian state equals in population size and area to many a country of the world. According to the 1971 Census, of the total internal migration, inter-state migration accounts for only 11.4 per cent, while the remaining 88.6 per cent is intra-state migration.

In the 1961 census, data were collected for the first time with reference to the exact place of enumeration. If we regard all persons who are born outside the place of enumeration (even if they are born in another district of the same state) as migrants, as should indeed the case, the percentage of migrants to total population in 1961 rises to 30.8 (from 3.31 which is the per cent of persons enumerated in a state different from the one in which they were born to total population). This shows that about one-third of the total population of India was involved in internal migration in 1961, which is quite a substantial amount. This also, to some extent, is an underestimate since it is based on place of birth statistics. Similarly in the 1971 census, 160.1 million persons were reported to be born outside the place of their enumeration and since the total population was 548.16 million, the percentage of migrants to total population was 29.21 which is again considerable by any standards.

Some of the empirical investigations also confirm that population of India is not as immobile as it has often been portrayed. A special study of National Sample Survey (NSS) on internal migration has revealed that 369 out of 1000 residents in the urban areas are migrants and this proportion is more than half in big cities. Similarly the socio-economic surveys of many Indian cities sponsored by the Research Programme Committee of Planning Commission has shown that the migrants constitute from 15 to 40 per cent of the population of various cities studied.

From the foregoing paragraphs, it is obvious that largely speaking population of India is not as immobile as it has often been said. It is quite possible that the great dominance of the village over the residential desire of the average Indian citizen (especially those feeling the pinch of population pressure the most) has been greatly exaggerated and that deficient statistics have perpetuated this bit of misinformation. Thus earlier thesis about the immobility of Indian people were based primarily on inadequate data and the new light shed by the 1961 census explodes the myth of an Indian's proverbial 'attachment to his locale'.

Though about one-third of India's population is involved in internal migration, but this mobility is in no way comparable to that found in the industrialised countries of the West. Nevertheless from the stand-point of a developing country, it is quite substantial. 'With increasing economic opportunities, rising expectations, social integration, developnent of transport and communication facilities the volume of migration in all directions is likely to increase tremendously in the foreseeable future.'

Patterns of Migration in India

In the 1971 census, 160.1 million persons (constituting 30.4 per cent of the total population) were enumerated at places other than their place of birth and were hence considered as migrants, whereas in the 1961 census, 135.3 million persons (or 33.0 per cent of the population) were counted as migrants by the same criterion. These figures imply that migration rate in India was lower during the 1960s in comparison to the 1950s. A reason for the same may be that in 1961 there were more survivors among persons who migrated to India as a result of country's partition in 1947 than they were in 1971.

Based on the place of birth (or last residence) and place of enumeration, migrants may be classified into the following four migration streams:

1. Rural to rural (known as rural turnover)
2. Rural to urban (known as rural push)
3. Urban to rural (known as push back, reverse or return migration)
4. Urban to urban (known as urban turnover).

Table 2 gives the distribution of internal migrants (on the basis of 'birth place' statistics) in different migration streams during the decades 1951-1961 and 1961-1971.

Table 2. Volume of Migrant Population by Types of Movement and their Sex Ratio (Females per 1000 Mal s)

(in millions)

Types of movement	*1961 Census*				*1971 Census*			
	Males	*Females*	*Total*	*Sex Ratio*	*Males*	*Females*	*Total*	*Sex Ratio*
Rural to Rural	23.5 (56.2)	75.6 (80.8)	99.11 (73.2)	3215	25.3 (52.8)	87.7 (78.2)	113.0 (70.6)	3252
Rural to Urban	10.6 (25.4)	9.0 (9.6)	19.6 (14.5)	851	12.4 (25.9)	11.3 (10.1)	23.7 (14.8)	906
Urban to Rural	1.19 (4.5)	2.9 (3.1)	4.8 (3.6)		2.9 (6.0)	5.0 (4.4)	7.9 (4.9)	1731
Urbרn to Urban	5.4 (12.9)	5.4 (5.8)	10.8 (8.0)		6.8 (14.2)	7.2 (6.4)	14.0 (8.8)	1074
Unclassified	0.4 (1.0)	0.6 (0.7)	1.0 (0.7)		0.5 (1.1)	1.0 (0.9)	1.5 (0.9)	
Total	41.8 (100)	93.5 (100)	153.3 (100)		47.9 (100)	112.2 (100)	160.1 (100)	

Note: Data in parentheses are percentages to the total.

Source: G.K. Mehrotra, Census of India 1971, Monograph No. 1 on Birth-place Migration in India, Statement, p. 32.

Table 2 reveals some important facts about the migration streams which can be stated as follows:

1. Rural to rural migration formed the dominant migration streams in both the censuses accounting for more than 70 per cent of the internal migrants. The strength of this stream, however, declined in 1971 in comparison to 1961, more so in the case of males, raising the sex ratio (females per thousand males) still further which was already more than three times.

2. Migration in the case of females is much higher compared with male according to both the 1961 and the 1971 censuses. According to the 1971 census, the total migrant population was 160.1 million out of which 112.2 million (i.e., 70 per cent) were females whereas in 1961 census, out of a total migrant population of 135.3 million, 93.5 million (i.e., 69.1 per cent) were females. This high proportion of female migration in rural areas was due to social reasons, namely prevalence of the system of patiarchal residence after marriage. This generate 'marriage' and 'associational' migration.

It should be noted that marriage migration and associational migration of females from rural to rural areas alone accounted for 56% of total migration in 1961 and 55% of total migration in 1971 (since according to figures of Table 2, out of 135 million migrants in 1961, 75.6 million were female rural to rural migrants and in 1971, out of 160.1 million total migrants, 87.7 million were rural to rural female migrants). Besides matrimonial reasons, migration of females is also owing to widowhood, desertation and abandonment. It has been observed in a report of the Government of India (1974) that the number of deserted woman is on gradual increase, leading to their migration in search of the means of livelihood.

3. Although rural to urban migration was about one-seventh of the total migration at the two time points, the sex ratio improved subtantially indicating greater urbanward migration of females during 1960s.

In this case male migration is also dominant than female migration. In 1971, 25.9% male migration was from rural areas to urban areas, while in 1961 this figure was only 25.4%. However, female migration was only 10.1% in 1971 and 9.6% in 1961.

The general assumption all the world over is that the rural poor, as a rule, migrate to urban centres to escape from poverty, hard life, monotony and in some cases repressive conditions, i.e., 'rural idiocy'. This applies to India as well in a significant measure. From the economic standpoint, in spite of a very impressive change in production which new technology has undoubtedly brought about in certain areas of the country, the rural scene as a whole remains exteremely depressing, while the acceleration of the rate of population growth has created even a more oppressive situation and the prospect is truly alarming.

The preponderance of male numbers in rural to urban migration lies in the fact that it is generally the male section of the population that is 'pushed out' from rural areas in search of employment and better opportunities and this phenomenon is found in most of the developing countries. Besides the value of Indian society are such that women are under great constraint in stirring out of home to make their living. Out-migration of female from village to town takes place either owing to marriage or owing to their dependence on the principal bread winner of family. Women usually do not out-migrate from the village to urban areas for the purpose of employment, though they sometimes take to jobs after they get settled there.

It should be noted that while in percentage terms male migration is more than female migration in rural to urban migration but the figures of Table 2 clearly reveals that in absolute numbers the difference is not much. Thus, against 10.6 million males who migrated from rural to urban areas the female migration was 9.0 million. In 1971, against 12.4 millon males, 11.3 million females migrated from rural to urban areas

4. It is noteworthy that migration from urban areas—urban to urban and urban to rural—was higher in the 1971 census than in the previous census. The data show that according to the 1961 census, the magnitude of urban to urban migration was 10.8 million which went up to 14.0 million in 1971, registering an increase from 8% to 8.8%. The main reason for increase in the urban to urban migration is a faster rate of growth of big cities, because bigger cities are in a better position to offer greater and more lucrative employment opportunities to in-migrants resulting from increasing concentration of services, location of both small and big industries and other cognate economic activities, than smaller ones. In short, the increase in this form of migration is due to strong pull forces operating in the large urban centres especially metropolitan centres which attract persons from urban areas of lower order.

Migration from urban to rural areas are reverse migration or push back migration. As far as magnitude is concerned, the least important is urban to rural migration. It was 7.9 million in 1971 and only 4.8 million in according to the 1961 census. In percentage term, its share was 3.6 in 1961 and 4.9 in 1971. This implies that the share of urban to rural migration is gradually increasing.

Marriage migrations are really the most important element in the reverse migrations and these are really not migrations at all but adherence to an old tradition whose survival is entirely due to the social inertia of our people. This form of migration is gradually increasing because of the fact that increasing unemployment and underemployment in urban areas and deteriorating living conditions in metropolitan centres (especially the mushroom growth of slums in such areas) are forcing back people from urban to rural areas. However, the real significance of these movements lies in their bringing with them an urban outlook and in some cases urban skills. Once, however, the migrants have acquired a taste for urban living, they rarely go back to the countryside.

5. The sex ratio improved in all the four streams pointing to greater mobility of females throughout.

The pattern of distribution between males and females is given in Table 3. It is interesting to note that in both the census years, the extent of female proponderance is indicated by their share in total migrants which was around 70 per cent. In 1971, rural to rural migration accounted for 78.9 per cent of total migration in the case of females. The corresponding figure in 1961 was 81.3 per cent. In the case of male, however, the share of rural to rural migration is not above 60 per cent in both the decades.

Table 3. Per Cent Share of Two Sexes in Different Migration Streams, India, 1961 and 1971

Migration Streams	*Per cent distribution in*					
	1961			*1971*		
	Male	*Female*	*Total*	*Male*	*Female*	*Total*
1. Rural to Rural	23.73	76.27	100	22.42	77.58	100.0
2. Urban to Rural	39.15	60.85	100	23.13	62.87	100.0
3. Rural to Urban	54.03	45.97	100	52.07	47.93	100.0
4. Urban to Urban	49.99	50.01	100	48.59	51.41	100.0

Source: Ashish Bose: *India's Urbanization 1901-2001*, p. 193.

The share of females in urban to urban migration was also higher than males. These migration streams are influenced more by social factors 'marriage migration' and 'return migration' rather than economic factor.

From the migration tables of the 1961 and 1971 censuses, migrants can further be classified into the following three categories roughly indicating of migration distance: (i) short-distance migration, (ii) medium-distance migration, and (iii) long-distance migration. Short-distance migration is generally taken to be intra-district migration (i.e., within the district), medium-distance migration is inter-district but intra-state migration, while long-distance migration is inter-state (*i.e.* from one state to another) migration. The combination of four migration streams of Table 1 with the above three distance factors gives rise to twelve streams. (Table 3).

In both 1961 and 1971, approximately two-thirds of the migrants were short-distance migrants and a little more than one-fifth were medium distance migrants. Long-distance migration has continued to contribute mere 10 to 11% of total migrants. However, as far as the volume of long-distance migration is concerned, it increased from 14.6 million in 1961 to 18.2 million in 1971. Thus the predominant form of migration is the short-distance one. This is the case more in respect of females than of males. Short-distance migration accounts for over 70 per cent of the female migration but over 50 per cent of the male migration. But the long-distance migration form nearly 20 per cent of the male and less than 10 per cent of the female migrants.

The bulk of female migration in the rural to rural stream in all the three distance categories was most probably due to the sytem of village exogamy in marriage in most parts of the country.

Between 1961 and 1971, there was a slight reduction in the proportion of medium-distance migrants of both sexes. But the relative importance of urban to urban stream of male migration is greater in 1971 as compared to 1961 in the categories of medium and long-distance migration but it is not true for short-distance migration.

It should be noted that in 1961 out of the total male migrants from rural to urban areas 16.58 were short-distance, 32.86 medium-distance and 41.72% long-distance migrants. In 1971, these percentages were 17.58, 33.11, 39.36 respectively. This gives the significant conclusion that about 40% rural to urban migrants have continued to be long distance migrants.

It is also important to note that whereas in intra-district and inter-district migration among males, rural to rural migration is most important, in inter-state migration rural to urban migration becomes most important. This is because of the fact that large urban centres especially metropolitan centres such as Bombay, Calcutta, Delhi and Madras attract people from far-flung rural areas. For example the metropolitan centres of Bombay and Calcutta have attracted continuous migration streams from the rural areas of Uttar Pradesh and Bihar.

It should also be noted as the distance increases, the sex ratio falls sharply in all the four migration streams and, among inter-state migrants, male migration becomes greater than female migration. The sex ratios in the urban to urban migration streams, however, are higher than rural to urban migration streams, probably reflecting greater amount of family migration in the urban to urban streams as well as some independent female migration for economic reasons.

Internal Migration in India and Some Ramifications

Study into migration process in India has thrown up some basic issues.

I. Measurement Aspect

In the census of 1971 two criteria were employed to measure migration. These were place of birth and place of residence criteria. According to place of birth statistics, an individual who is born in place '*x*' migrating to place '*y*' for a given period of time but goes back to the place of birth '*x*' is not treated as a migrant. On the contrary that person is treated as a migrant according to 'place of last residence' yardstick. Consequently the Registrar General and Census Commissioner, India, for 1971 census used the last residence statistics to estimate the migration stream. These statistics posed certain problems. For instance a person of foreign origin staying in India becomes an internal migrant by place of last residence. Thus if an Iranian student in India moves from Indore to Rewa, his movement becomes a case of internal migration instead of being temporary immigration. In contrast if, a person born in India, visits a foreign country and returns after some times, his movement falls under immigration according to place of last residence criterion. At the time of 1971 census, the number of immigrants by birth place statistics was 10.2 million while the last residence statistics put the number of immigrants at 8.5 million.

II. Classification Aspect

The 1971 census classified the location of an individual from three positions, viz. place of birth, place of last residence and thirdly place of enumeration. The immigration of an individual can be shown on three dimensional matrix as above. Generation of such a migration table is somewhat complicated, but it provides a great deal of additional information on the migrants. We can also study the migration pattern from place of birth to place of last residence and from the place of last residence to place of enumeration. However no attempt was made by the census organisation to generate such table from the 1971 census data. The 1981 census too, does not provide a three dimensional classification.

III. Comparability Aspect

Comparability of census results over time is an important aspect of a census study to help the study of changes taking place in society over time. This requires the generation of data at two or more points of time under the same classification schemes. However this norm has not been followed in the Indian census. The 1961 census migration tables were based on the place of last residence whereas the 1971 census tables were based on the place of last residence; which affected the comparability of data for two points of time.

Even in the same census provision should be made to make comparative analysis of the characteristics of the migrants and non-migrants at the city level. Unfortunately tables giving the distribution of of city population by education, age and marital status, etc., are not available for the city population. This lacuna should be overcome to provide comparative studies.

IV. Measurement of Net Rural to Urban Migration

Net rural to urban migration is necessary to understand the urbanisation process. In India the rural to rural migration stream constitutes more than 70 per cent of the total migration. It is therefore essential to understand the pattern of rural to rural, rural to urban and urban to rural migration at the intra-district, inter-district and inter-state levels. This provides a measure of urbanisation in the country.

V. Characteristics of Migrants

In data on the sex and marital status of the migrants can enable to understand (1) the pattern of age selectivity in migration, (2) quantum of marriage migration, (3) associational migration, (4) city migration, (5) migration for other reasons. Depending on the pattern of in migration to cities, they are classified as (1) regional, (2) national and (3) international.

The 1971 census provided for the first time the distribution of the migrants by sex, age and marital status. In addition it also provides information on the industrial classification of the migrant workers, educational attainment of the migrants to cities with a population of 100,000 and above and occupational classification of migrant workers.

VI. Migration and Economic Development

Nearly 45 per cent of the net domestic product is derived from agriculture and allied activities. Consequently, levels of internal migration will be governed by levels of agricultural productivity in different regions of the country as well as by the rate of growth of agricultural production. Regions with high agricultural productivity like Punjab, Haryana, etc., offer high agricultural wages and may, thus attract a larger number of migrants. Similarly districts in which large and medium scale industries have been established on account of development are likely to attract migrants in large number from other districts.

Backward districts with little transport and communication links with other districts are having intra-district migration. On the other hand districts with improved rail road facilities have greater inter-district and inter-state migration.

SELECT REFERENCES

1. Bose, Ashish: "Internal Migration in India, Pakistan, and Ceylon", In United Nations, World Population Conference, Belgrade, 1965.
2. Bose, Ashish, (ed.): *Patterns of Population Change*, Allied Publishers, New Delhi, 1967.
3. Bose, Ashish: *Urbanization in India: An Inventory of Source Materials*, Academic Books Ltd., New Delhi, 1970.
4. Mehrotra, G.K.: *Birth Place Migration in India*, Census of India, 1971, Special Monograph No. 1. Office of The Registrar General of India, Ministry of Home Affairs, New Delhi, 1974.
5. United Nations, Methods of Measuring Internal Migration, Manual VI, ST/SOA/Series A/47, New York, 1970.
6. Zachariah, K.C.: *A Historical Study of Internal Migration in the Indian Sub-Continent, 1901-1931*, Asia Publishing House, Bombay, 1964.
7. Zachariah, K.C.: *Migrants in Greater Bombay*, Demographic Training and Research Centre, Bombay, Research Monograph No. 5, Asia Publishing House, Bombay, 1968.

EXAMINATION QUESTIONS

1. **Analyse the recent trends in the rural-urban migration in India.**
2. **Write short notes on internal and international migration in India.**
3. **Explain the trend of our migration from villages to cities in India and state how can it be put to help in checking population growth.**
4. **Explain the socio-economic causes and consequences of outmigration from rural areas in India.**

28

Urbanization in India

The study of urbanization is assuming increasing importance all over the world and more so in the developing countries like India. Urbanization is the process by which villages turn into towns and towns develop into cities.

In India, the definition of an urban unit which was adopted in the 1971 census was continued in the 1981 census. In both the censuses an urban area is defined as follows:

(*a*) all places with a municipality, corporation, cantonment board or notified town area committee, etc. (*b*) all other places which satisfy the following criteria: (*i*) a minimum population of 5,000, (*ii*) at least 75 per cent of male working population engaged in non-agricultural pursuits; and (*iii*) a density of population of at least 400 persons per sq. km.

This definition of an urban area is arbitrary and is not the same as used in other countries. Therefore, for the purpose of a comparative study of urbanization process in various countries necessary adjustments should be made.

In 1961 census the definition of an urban unit was more or less similar to the one accepted at the last two censuses. Hence the data on rural-urban distribution made available by the last three. censuses are comparable. For earlier decades data are not strictly comparable and this fact has to be kept in mind while drawing inferences.

TRENDS IN URBANIZATION IN INDIA

It is obvious from the figures of Table 1 that the urban population in India during last 80 years has increased in three stages. Hence the trend of urbanization in India can very well be analysed under the following headings:

1. **Period of slow urbanization (1901-31)**

In India, the level of urbanization at the time of census conducted in 1901 was less than 11% which lazily creeped to the figure of 12 per cent in 1931. In 1901, there was a slight fall in the percentage of those living in urban areas. The main reason for this decline was the severity of plague in towns than in the rural areas, and a high urban death rate accompany the evacuation of some cities. The incidence of plague later on spread to all parts except the east and south; and its endemic nature in the towns of Madhya Bharat and Uttar Pradesh was great which drifted away the people to villages. Thus in the first thirty years of nineteenth century the urban population in India remained between 10.84% to 11.99%. In this phase, the growth of urban population was slow due to concentration of urban-based economic activities in a very few areas of the country. The areas in and around the major port-cities and a few mineral resource-based industrial towns gathered momentum slowly to attract population and began to develop as large townships. Even the distressing decade of 1911-21, which recorded −0.3% population growth could not deter the positive growth of urban population (8.26%; Table 1).

Table 1. Relative Growth of Urban and Rural Population

Year	*Population in millions*		*Percentage of total population*		*Percentage Increase in urban population during the decade*	*Total number of towns*	*Urban rural ratio*
	Rural	*Urban*	*Rural*	*Urban*			
1901	270.3	25.6	89.0	11.0	. .	1,834	1 : 8.1
1911	220.4	25.6	90.6	10.4	0.0	1,776	1 : 8.6
1921	216.6	27.7	88.7	11.3	+8.25	1,920	1 : 7.8
1931	237.8	33.0	87.8	12.2	+19.1	2,049	1 : 7.2
1941	265.5	43.6	85.9	14.1	+32.1	2,210	1 : 6.1
1951	288.2	61.6	82.4	17.6	+41.5	2,844	1 : 4.1
1961	347.2	77.6	81.7	18.3	+25.9	2,330	1 : 4.5
1971	421.9	107.0	79.8	20.2	+37.9	2,531	1 : 3.9
1981*	502.0	156.2	76.3	23.7	+46.0	3,245	1 : 3.2

*Excludes Assam and Jammu & Kashmir.

Re ources: Compiled from the data provided in Census of India 1981, Series 1, India, Paper 2 of 1981.

2. Period of medium urbanization (1931-61)

Since 1931, the process of urbanization has become more pronounced. As the process of industrialization began to create a new set of life-styles based on growth of towns and also the expansion of export-trade of raw materials and semi-finished commodities from major ports attracted more and more people towards urban areas. The rapid growth of urban population during 1931-41 (31.97%) indicates the beginning of the second phase of urbanization in India (Table 1). In short this change has been due partly to industrial development and partly to what Yeatts, Commissioner of 1941 Census called, "increasing appeal of city life to the ordinary middle class people, because for the first time accommodation within his means and to his taste has become available. The large number of newly built bunglows outside the city, renovation of the old buildings within the city walls, the large increase in educational institutions, increasing amenties of water supply, electric light and the city features of bus-service to and from the neighbouring areas, improvement in employment situation have meant an increase in numbers of people in the cities". Further, in 1930s, the fall in the agricultural prices pushed the peasants into the cities and plantations in search of jobs. There was an increased demand of industrial production during the Second World War and as a result urbanization received further push.

During 1931-41, the urban population increased by 32% as compared to an increase of 13.86% for the total population. In absolute figures, the urban population increased to 44.07 million from 31.34 million in 1931.

The effects of Second World War in furthering the industrial and service sector kept up the level of urbanisation during 1941-51 at a much higher level (41.43%, Table 1), than the preceding decade. The war attracted large numbers of people to industrial and service jobs, which increased substantially to meet war time needs of defence persons (about 20 million). From East and West Pakistan Sind people poured into cities and towns, especially into those metropolitan areas like New Delhi, Calcutta and Bombay, and those states lying close to the border areas. It has been estimated that the influx of displaced persons increased urban population by about 3 million.

During the decade, 1951 to 1961, the urban growth rate declined. It was only 26.4% as against 41.4% in the earlier decade. Dr. Bose attributes this fall due to definitional changes, though absolute figures increased from 62 million to 79 million. It is obvious from the figures of Table 1 that from 1911 to 1951 there was a continuous increase in the number of towns. However, during the decade 1951-61, the number of towns registered a marked decline from 3059 to 2699. This was the result of adopting a stricter definition of towns in the 1961 census. Some places which were classified as towns in 1951 were declassified in 1961. On account of this, the percentage increase of urban population declined to 26.4 which was considerably less than the previous decade. If definitional changes are eliminated, the growth rate in the decade 1951-61 will be found to be higher than 26.4% Ashish Bose has estimated that if the 1951 census definition is accepted by hypothetically including in the 1961 urban population the 1961 population of places which were urban in 1951 but eliminated in 1961 on account of stricter definition, the increase in urban population in the decade comes out to be 32.4% and not 26.4%. If, on the other hand, adjustment is undertaken by adopting the 1961 census definition to the 1951 census, the per cent increase in the decade 1951-61 works out to be 30.7%. Thus, in whatever way adjustments are carried out, the percentage increase comes out to be higher than given in Table 1.

We have seen that the absolute figures of urban population increased from 62 million to 79 million during the decade, 1951-61. These increases may have been due to the planned economic and industrial development consequent upon the launching of the First and the Second Plans. An additional reason for the small proportional increase in urban population is the very large increase in rural population (which increased from 299 million in 1951 to 370 million in 1961). The increase in rural population was owing to an increase in birth rate and a decrease in death rate. Migration contributed for a much smaller proportion of increase in urban population. Whereas, during 1941-51, about half the increase in urban population was due to migration, in 1951-61 less than one-fourth has been due to this factor.

Looking back over the history of eight decades of urbanization in India, we find that the growth of urban population has been very slow. We can blame the policy of foreigners for the slow progress of urbanization during this period as the country was under the yoke of slavery. But the independent India also does not narrate a very inspiring and encouraging Tale. The 1951-61 decade was marked by rapid strides in industrialization and it was generally expected that urbanization too would be rapid during this decade but the 1961 census data do not give and evidence of accelerating urbanization. The census authorities failed to give and convincing reason for this slow pace of urbanization in the context of rapid industrialization.

In his paper for the 1960 international seminar at Berkeley, Kingsley Davis posed the question, "Why has India's urbanization been so slow?" and proceeded to answer it as follows:

The answer, I suggest, "is the relative slowness of economic development in India. Although nobody knows the past Indian rate of economic development the evidence seems to indicate that it is not likely to have been rapid, compared to that of most other countries at roughly similar stages."

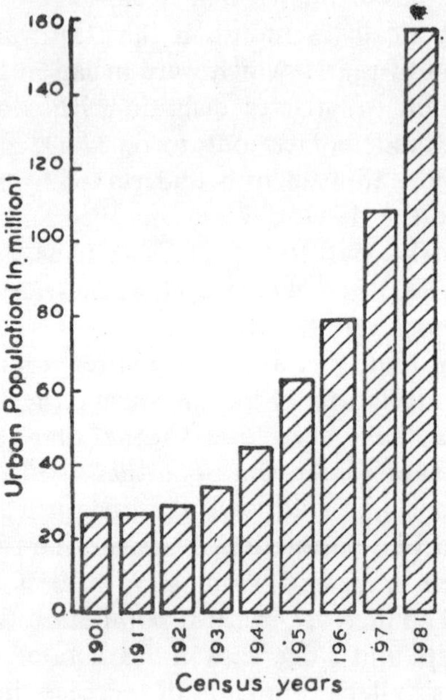

Fig. 1

3. Period of Rapid Urbanization (1961-81)

After 1961 urban population increased very rapidly. In 1971 the urban population was roughly 20 per cent of the total population of India—an increase of 2 per cent points over the 1961 figure cannot be regarded as an indication of a phenomenal increase in urban population. But in terms of absolute population size, there has been an increase of about 20 million in urban population of India during 1961-71 and the rate of growth of urban population has been of the order of 38.2 per cent which is quite high by any standard.

The findings of the census of 1981 have reinforced the trend that the pace of growth of the urban population is substantially higher than that of the rural pnpulation. The decennial growth rate for the period 1971-81 was 46.02 per cent urban as against 18.96 per cent rural, making an average of 24.43 per cent for the total. Stated in terms of percentage of urban population to the total, it was 23.73 in 1981.

Urban population increased from about 26 million in 1901 to 79 million in 1961—an increase of only 53 million in 60 years. But, thereafter, the absolute increase during the next two decades was of the order of 77 millions (1961-81). This indicates that programmes of industrialization did make an impact in terms of population absorption in urban areas, though this impact is not very discernible.

The process of urbanization during the 1971-81 decade turned out to be faster than that was expected by the Planning Commission. While the Sixth Plan had projected the level of urban population to be about 148 million in 1981, the 1981 census shows it to be about 156 million excluding Assam and Jammu and Kashmir.

Despite definitional changes the basic fact about urbanization has been that the process of urbanization has occurred since 1921. The gradual upward shift in favour of the urban population is evident right from 1921 onwards. The principal difference is that whereas the decadal shift in the percentage points between 1911-21 was marginal, being 0.94 in 1981 it was marked in that it was 3.5. Even during 1961-71 the shift was only 1.96 percentage points. The possibility that this trend may accelerate in the coming years cannot, therefore, be ruled out. Coupled as it is with the question of absolute numbers, with more than 49 million people having been added to the urban population during the seventies, one can forsee a situation in which, both in economic and in demographic terms, 'Urban' India would have a more significant role to play. The policy implications of such a shift have to be appreciated immediately because planning itself may have to be given a stronger urban bias.

Degree of urbanization in India—A comparison with some selected countries: While the increase in the proportion of the urban population for the country as a whole and particularly for the larger urban areas has been high, the overall rate of urbanization is still modest in world terms. Table 2 shows that India ranks quite low among the developed countries of the world in the degree of urbanization. The proportion of urban population to total population in 1980 was 65 per cent in USSR, 73 per cent in USA, 78 per cent in Japan, 89 per cent in Australia and 91 per cent in U.K. Compared to them, the Indian percentage of 22 pet cent in 1980 was too low. However, in terms of total urban population, India is well ahead of most of the developing countries and many developed countries such as Japan, U.K., Federal Republic of Germany, etc. In fact, 'next to USSR, USA and perhaps China, India, has the largest urban population in the world.

Again, in accordance with the pattern of population concentration in urban areas in developed countries, India also has the majority of its urban population concentrated in large urban centres. In

Table 2. Degree of Urbanization in some Selected Countries

	Uaban Population			
	As a percentage of total population		*Average annual growth rate*	
	1960	*1980*	*1960-70*	*1970-80*
Low income countries				
Bangladesh	5	11	6.3	6.1
India	18	22	3.3	3.3
China	NA	13	NA	3.1
Indonesia	15	20	3.6	4.0
Middle-income countries				
Egypt	38	45	3.3	2.8
Brazil	46	65	4.8	3.7
Yugoslavia	28	42	3.2	2.9
Israel	77	89	4.2	3.2
High-income countries				
U.K.	86	91	0.9	0.3
Japan	62	78	2.4	2.0
Australia	81	89	2.5	1.9
Canada	69	80	2.7	1.7
USA	67	73	1.7	1.5
USSR	49	65	2.8	2.2
Czechoslovakia	47	63	2.1	2.0
Iraq	43	72	6.2	5.4

Source: World Development Report, 1981.

1981, India had 216 cities, each having a population greater than one lakh and about 50% of total urban population was concentrated in them. In respect of the share of large cities in total urban population India is on par with such developed countries as the USA, the U.K., Garmany, and Japan. As we shall see later on, it is precisely on this account that large cities in India are plagued by a number of complex social and economic problems. The million cities in India are developing into a national metropolitan system with greater international links, and developing some of the traits of post-industrial structure. The two large agglomerations, Calcutta and Bombay, crossing 9 million and 7 million mark respectively join the group of the world's largest agglomerations in population size.

From the foregoing paragraphs it is clear that, in short, the urbanization process in India has the following important features:

1. In terms of the percentage of the total population, the level of urbanization is low.

2. In terms of absolute numbers, the level of urbanization is rather high in comparison with most of the developing countries and

Table 3. Urban Population in Different States of India 1951-1981

(*in millions*)

State	1951 Population	1951 % of total population	1961 Population	1961 % of total population	1971 Population	1971 % of total population	1981 Population	1981 % of total population	% in increase or decrease in 1951-61	% in increase or decrease in 1961-71	% in increase or decrease in 1971-81
1. Andhra Pradesh	5.42	17.42	6.27	17.44	8.40	19.31	12.46	23.25	15.68	33.92	48.26
2. Assam	0.41	4.64	0.79	7.69	1.33	8.87	NA	NA	121.95	66.80	NA
3. Bihar	2.63	6.78	3.91	8.42	5.63	10.00	8.70	12.46	48.67	43.95	54.40
4. Gujarat	4.43	27.24	5.32	25.77	7.50	28.08	10.56	31.08	20.09	41.00	40.82
5. Hareyana	NA	NA	1.31	17.26	1.77	17.66	2.88	21.96	NA	35.48	59.16
6. Himachal Pradesh	NA	NA	1.78	NA	2.42	6.99	0.33	7.72	NA	35.68	35.25
7. Jammu & Kashmir	0.46	14.11	0.59	16.66	0.86	18.59	NA	NA	28.26	44.65	NA
8. Kerala	1.83	13.51	2.55	15.11	3.47	16.24	4.47	18.78	39.34	35.72	37.63
9. Madhya Pradesh	3.13	12.01	4.63	14.29	6.79	16.29	10.59	20.31	47.92	46.63	56.07
10. Maharashtra	9.20	28.75	11.16	28.22	15.71	31.17	21.97	35.03	21.30	40.75	39.82
11. Manipur	NA	NA	0.07	NA	0.14	13.19	0.37	26.44	NA	108.95	163.77
12. Meghalaya	NA	NA	0.12	NA	0.15	14.55	0.24	18.03	NA	25.27	62.74
13. Mysore	4.45	22.94	5.27	22.33	7.12	24.33	10.71	28.92	18.43	35.23	5.39
14. Nagaland	NA	NA	0.02	5.40	0.05	9.95	0.12	15.54	NA	168.28	133.84
15. Orissa	0.59	4.03	1.11	6.32	1.84	8.41	3.11	11.82	88.14	66.30	68.29
16. Punjab	3.07	19.03	2.27	20.13	3.22	23.73	4.62	27.72	33.22	25.27	43.66
17. Rajasthan	2.96	18.53	3.28	16·28	4.54	17.63	7.14	20.93	10.81	38.47	57.15
18. Tamil Nadu	7.33	24.34	8.99	26.69	12.46	30.26	15.93	32.98	22.65	38.64	27.68
19. Tripura	NA	NA	0.10	NA	0.16	10.43	0.23	10.98	NA	57.64	38.51

20. Uttar Pradesh	8.63	13.65	9.48	12 85	12.39	14.02	19.97	18.01	9.85	30.68	61.22
21. West Bengal	6.28	23.88	8.54	24.45	10.97	24.75	14.43	26.49	35.99	28.41	31.61
22. Union Territories	1.61	NA	2.82	NA	NA	NA			75.16	NA	46.02
All India	62.44	17.29	78.93	7.97	09.04	9.91	5.62	23.73	26.43	38.22	

many developed countries.

3. The rate of population growth was higher in urban areas than in rural areas in each decade, except the first decade 1901-11.

4. From decade to decade the increase in population was shared unequally between males and females.

5. Instead of standing as a symptom of growth, as it was in the west, urbanization in India is an aspect of continued poverty. We shall elaborate this point later on.

State-wise Patterns of Growth

If we take up the process of urbanization from state to state we find a very surprising range of variation. This trend of variation in a planned economy and in a democratic country is unjustified and regrettable. Table 3 reveals that the urban population of the countries is very unevenly distributed.

The most urbanized state in India is Maharashtra where 35.03 per cent of its population is urban. It is closely followed by Tamil Nadu in which 32.98 per cent is urban. The only other state in which more than 30 per cent of the population is urban is Gujarat (31.08%). Karnataka, Punjab, Manipur and West Bengal are close to the 30 per cent mark.

The higher industrialization in the States of Maharashtra, Tamil Nadu, Gujarat, Karnataka, Punjab, Manipur and West Bengal has brought about greater concentration in the urban areas. Another important factor is the development of overseas trade on account of existence of important ports in those states. It is obvious that the more highly developed states like Maharashtra, Tamil Nadu, Gujarat and Punjab are also the states of greater urbanization.

The least urban states are Himachal Pradesh (7.7%), Tripura (11%) and Orissa (11.8%).

States of India may be classified into four categories by urbanization states on the basis of percentage growth in population as given in Table 4.

This classification of states by urbanization status with the help of Table indicates that there is absence of national policy of urbanization in India.

It is obvious from the figures of Table 4 that 54.27% of total urban population of the country resides in five states—Maharashtra, Uttar Pradesh, Tamil Nadu, West Bengal and Andhra Pradesh. This figure will accelerate to 99.10 per cent, if the urban population of Karnataka, Madhya Pradesh, Gujarat, Rajasthan, Delhi, Kerala, Punjab, Orissa, and Haryana is also included.

Table 4: Category of Urbanization (1981)

Category	*States*
1. Highly Urbanized (i.e. degree of urbanization more than 30%)	Maharashtra, Tamil Nadu and Gujarat
2. Medium but high (i.e. degree of urbanization varying from 20 to 30%)	Karnataka, Punjab, West Bengal, Manipur Andhra Pradesh, Haryana, Rajasthan and Madhya Pradesh
3. Medium but low (i.e. degree of urbanization varying from 15 to 20%)	Kerala, Meghalaya, Uttar Pradesh, Sikkim and Nagaland
4. Low urbanized (i.e. up to 15% only)	Bihar, Orissa, Tripura and Himachal Pradesh

As far the percentage of population in urban areas to total population of the state is concerned, the first position continues to be held by Maharashtra. Gujarat occupied the second place in 1951 but was pushed to the third place in 1961 by Tamil Nadu. In 1971 and 1981 also, Tamil Nadu continued to hold the second place while Gujarat was a close third.

Punjab witnessed a very marginal change in urbanization, between 1961 and 1981. In fact the people of Punjab living in villages are leading as comfortable life as the people of towns, hence there is no tendency to shift, from rural to urban sector.

West Bengal registered a decline over the decade 1961-71 and registered a very marginal increase in 1971-81. This is perhaps due to political disturbances in Bengal.

The states which show a significant change over the decade 1971-81 are also given in Table 3. It is interesting to note that the states which have shown the highest growth rates are also the ones which have an urban-rural composition which is less than the national average of 23.72 per cent. These include Orissa, Uttar Pradesh, Haryana, Rajasthan, Madhya Pradesh, Bihar and Andhra Pradesh. The first six states have traditionally been considered to be non-urban and rural oriented. Orissa Rajasthan, Madhya Pradesh, Bihar and Uttar Pradesh are also considered backward states. At the same time the more advanced and more highly urbanized states, such as Maharashtra, Gujarat, Punjab, Tamil Nadu and West Bengal have recorded an urban growth rate which is less than the national average of 46.20 per cent. One clearly noticeable growth pattern is that there is a slight tapering off the urban growth in the more urbanized states, and a sharp increase in the urban growth rate in the backward states.

Number and Size Class of Town: Intensity of Urabanization

The intensity of urbanization in India would be clear from an increase in the number of towns. In the census, towns have been divided into six classes according to different population size as follows:

TABLE 5: Size Class of Towns

Class	*Population*	*Category*
I	1 lakh and above	Metropolitan and large cities
II	50,000 to 99,999	
III	20,000 to 49,999	Medium towns
IV	10,000 to 19,999	
V	5,000 to 9,999	Small towns
VI	Less than 5,000	

Table 5 shows the number of towns and the total population contributed by each class and the proportion of the population of each class to the total population at each of eight censuses.

A careful study of Table 6 reveals that after a slight reduction in the first decade (1901-11), the number of towns composing the urban sector increased progressively in the course of four decades from 1834 in 1911 to 2844 in 1951. Ironically, the number of towns declined to 2531 in 1971. This is largely due to our rigorous definition adopted in each subsequent census. Ridiculing the very liberal definition of urban areas provided in certain census, the Census Commissioner (1971) points out that "in the pre-independence era, some princely states of India, in order to lay a claim to responsibility treated any village a lamp post as an urban centre." According to 1981 census the number of towns in India is 3245.

Table 6: Growth in Different Size Classes of Towns, 1901-1981

Year	*I*	*II*	*III*	*IV*	*V*	*VI*	*VII*
A—Number of Towns							
1901	24	42	135	393	750	490	1834
1911	23	39	142	364	743	495	1776
1921	28	45	153	370	741	583	1920
1931	33	54	193	439	806	524	2049
1941	47	77	246	505	931	404	2210
1951	74	95	330	621	1146	578	2844
1961	102	129	449	732	739	179	2430
1971	145	178	570	847	641	150	2531
1981	216	270	739	1048	742	230	3245

B—Total Urban Population in Lakhs							
1901	65.9	28.9	40.4	53.6	51.6	15.8	256.2
1911	69.6	26.8	42.3	50.8	49.4	17.0	255.9
1921	81.4	28.7	44.7	50.7	51.7	19.7	276.9
1931	100.0	39.4	56.0	59.6	56.5	17.4	328.9
1941	165.2	49.7	72.0	69.0	65.9	13.8	425.6
1951	273.1	61.3	97.3	85.0	80.4	19.2	616.3
1961	393.8	85.4	135.0	100.8	54.5	6.1	775.6
1971	601.2	120.2	174.5	119.8	48.9	4.9	1049.5
1981	942.9	181.9	224.1	148.6	56.4	7.9	1541.8
C—Per cent of Urban Population in each class							
1901	25.71	11.29	15.77	20.92	20.13	6.18	100.00
1911	27.19	10.49	16.52	19.85	19.31	6.64	100.00
1921	29.40	10.38	16.13	18.32	18.67	7.10	100.00
1931	30.60	11.95	16.98	18.07	17.13	5.27	100.00
1941	37.93	11.41	16.52	15.84	15.13	3.17	100.00
1951	44.31	9.95	15.79	13.79	13.04	3.12	100.00
1961	50.77	11.00	17.41	13.00	7.03	0.79	100.00
1971	56.21	11.24	16.32	11.20	4.57	0.46	100.00
1981	60.37	11.65	14.35	9.52	3.61	0.50	100.00

An inter-censal analysis of data show that, at all India level the proportion of people living in Class I towns has increased from 25.7 per cent in 1901 to 60.4 per cent in 1981. The relative proportion of urban population in Class II and Class III towns taken together has remained practically constant i.e., around 26.28 per cent during 1901-81. In case of small towns (Class IV, Class V and Class VI), the proportion of people living has declined sharply (47.23 per cent in 1901 to 19.63 per cent in 1981). This situation is depicted in the graph.

Figures of the table portray that there has been a significant rise in the number of Class I, Class II and Class III towns. The most spectacular rise is in the case of Class I towns whose number went up from 24 in 1901 to 216 in 1981. Therefore, over the period of 80 years (i.e., from 1901 to 1981) the number of Class I towns rose by 800 per cent. During the same period, the number of class II towns rose by 543%, Class III towns by 447%, Class IV towns by 168%. Against this, Class V and Class VI towns witnessed a decline of 1.06% and 53.06% respectively. The number of towns in the first three classes therefore registered an increase of about 600% over the period 1901-81.

Class I towns have been the seats of administrative and general economic activity. Industry, transport, trade and commerce, administrative and liberal services have been concentrated in these towns. This explains the increasing concentration of urban population in this size-class.

Moreover, towns at the margin in Class II have been jumping into Class I. This is evidenced by the fact that whereas there were only 74 towns in Class I in 1951, their number stood at 216 (nearly three times) in 1981. As a consequence, the total population of Class I towns increased from 273 lakhs in 1951 to 943 lakhs in 1981—an increase of 245 per cent.

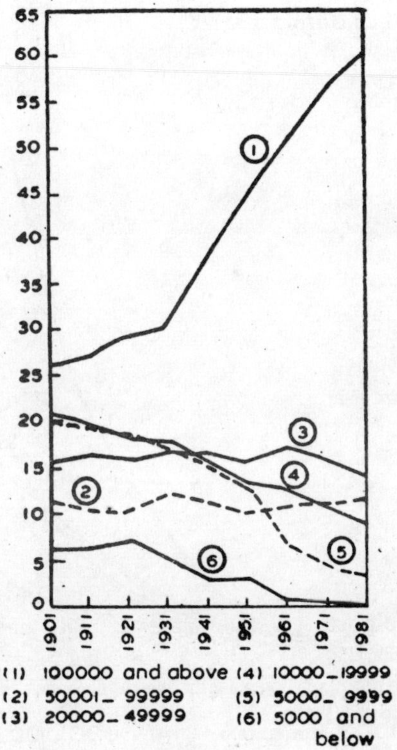

Fig 2.

Class II and Class III towns are those in a transitory stage. Their number as also their total population have increased in absolute terms, but as a relative proportion, the proportion of population in these two size categories has remained constant. The total number of class II towns increased from 95 in 1951 to 270 in 1981, and their total population from about 61 lakhs to 182 lakhs—a three-fold increase. The number of Class III towns increased from 330 in 1951 to 739 in 1981, and their total population increased from 97 lakhs in 1951 to 224 lakhs in 1981—an increase of about 130 per cent.

The proportion of urban population in Class IV, Class V and Class VI has shown a downward trend. The number of Class IV towns increased from 621 in 1951 to 1048 in 1981 and their total population increased from 85 lakhs to 149 lakhs an increase of only 75 per cent. As against it, the number of Class V towns declined from 1,146 in 1951 to 742 in 1981 and their total population declined from 80 lakhs to 56 lakhs during 1951-81. Ironically, the number of towns in Class VI declined from 578 in 1951 to merely 230 in 1981. The tctal population of Class VI towns also registered a sharp decline from 19.2 lakhs to 7.9 lakhs during 1951-81.

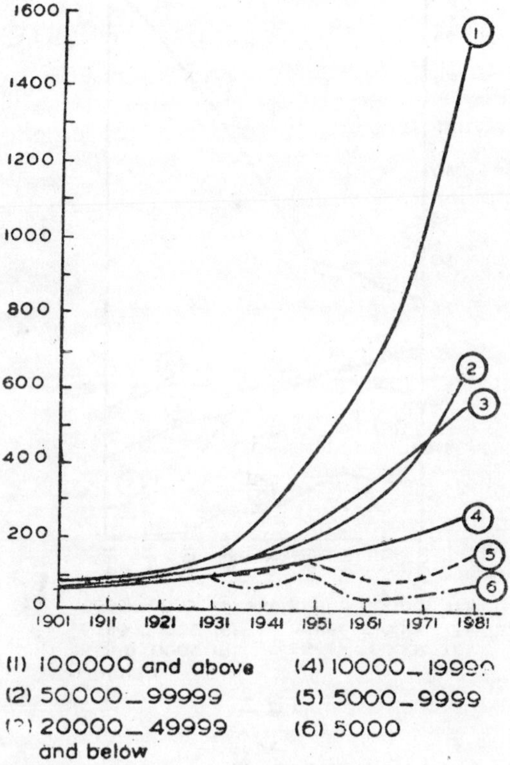

Fig. 3

State-wise data on variations in the proportion of urban population by different size classes of towns between 1951 and 1981 (Table 3) indicates that there was a high proportion of urban population living in the large cities of union territories and states like Jammu and Kashmir, Maharashtra, Uttar Pradesh and West Bengal. Except in

Bihar, in all other states there is a continuous growth in the proportion of urban population living in large cities. But, one can very see fluctuations among states, in case of proportion of people living in medium size towns. In Jammu & Kashmir, Maharashtra, Himachal Pradesh, Manipur Group and Union Territories, there was a declining trend in the proportion of population living in medium towns. The proportions of people living in small towns declined in all the states except in Manipur group, where it registered a sharp rise.

Thus the decay and decline of our small towns have been the features of our population for a number of decades, but they have been markedly accentuated in 1971-81. The persistent decline in the importance of small towns is an indication of the deterioration of economic conditions of small towns and the consequent movement of population towards big cities in search of better economic opportunities. This implies that these large centres are still expanding in industrial and commercial activity, claiming at the same time a larger share in construction activities, public amenities and transport services.

CONCENTRATION IN MILLION PLUS URBAN AGGLOMERATIONS

The 1971 census introduced the term Urban Agglomeration (hereafter referred to as UA) which is continued in the 1981 census. Very often large railway colonies, university campuses, port areas, military camps, etc., come up outside the statutory limits of the city or town but adjoining it. Such areas may not by themselves qualify to be treated as towns but if they formed a continuous spread with the adjoining town, it would only be realistic to treat them as urban. Such settlements have been termed as outgrowths (OG), and may cover a whole village, or part of a village. Two or more towns may also be contiguous to each other. Such towns together with their outgrowths have been treated as one urban unit and called 'Urban Agglomeration'. An urban agglomeration, therefore, constitutes:

(*a*) A city or town with contiguous outgrowth(s), the outgrowth being outside the statutory limits but falling within the boundaries of the adjoining village or villages; or

(*b*) Two or more adjoining towns with their outgrowth(s); or,

(*c*) A city with one or more adjoining towns with their outgrowths all of which form a continuous spread.

Table 7 reveals the growth of population in the million plus UAs over the decade 1971-81 and the increasing pressure of popula-

Table 7: Population of Large Cities with a Population of 1 million and above

	Population in lakhs		*Decennial growth of population (%)*
	1971	*1981*	
Calcutta	70.3	91.6	30.3
Greater Bombay	59.7	82.3	37.8
Delhi	36.5	57.1	56.6
Madras	31.7	42.8	34.9
Bangalore	16.5	29.1	76.2
Hyderabad	18.0	25.3	40.7
Ahmedabad	17.4	25.1	44.4
Kanpur	12.7	16.9	32.4
Pune	11.3	16.8	48.4
Nagpur*	9.3	13.0	39.5
Lucknow	8.2	10.1	23.7
Jaipur	6.3	10.0	57.8
Total	297.9	420.3	41.0

*Note: These towns were not included in the category of large cities with a population of 1 million and above.

tion on these metropolitan centres.

In 1971 census, 339 UAs' were recognized of which 87 belonged to class II (each having a population greater than one lakh), 57 UAs belonged to class II (each having population in the range 50,000 to 99,999), 86 UAs belonged to class III (each having population in the range 20,000 to 49,999), 56 UAs belonged to class IV (each having population in the range 10,000 to 19,999), 51 UAs belonged to class V (each having population in the range 5,000 to 9,999) and UAs belonged to class VI (each having population less than 5,000). The total population of the nine UAs was 193.13 lakhs in 1961 which constituted 24.5% of total urban population in that year. This proportion fell marginally to 22.7 in the 1971 census. This would reveal the fact that out of 339 UAs in India in 1971, more than one-fifth of the urban population was concentrated in merely nine UAs.

The UAs having population greater than 10 lakhs each were—Calcutta, Greater Bombay, Delhi, Madras, Hyderabad, Ahmedabad, Bangalore, Kanpur and Poona. Out of these 9 UAs excepting Poona all others had more than 10 lakhs persons living within the municipal carporation limits of the concerned UA. Thus there was 8 million plus cities and 9 million plus UAs in 1971. The number of million plus UAs rose to 12 in 1981. The new editions are Nagpur, Lucknow and Jaipur. Calcutta ranks first with a population of 92 lakhs, followed by Bombay with a population of 82 lakhs. The population of Delhi which was only 36.5 lakhs in 1971 jumped to 57.1 lakhs in 1981, showing an increase of about 57 per cent during the decade. The total population of these 12 large cities has aggregated to about 420 lakhs accounting for about 27 per cent of the total urban population. The overall decennial increase in the population of 12 metropolitan towns. works out to be 41 per cent during 1971-81 i.e. from 298 lakhs to 420 lakhs.

In the decade 1971-81 the most spectacular rise has been in the population of Bangalore UA which registered an increase of 76.2 per cent and thus rose to fifth position pushing down Hyderabad and Ahmedabad. The population of the four largest urban agglomerations—Calcutta, Bombay, Delhi and Madras—registered an increase of 30.4, 37.4, 43.3 and 35 per cent respectively in the decade 1971-81. Taken together, their population rose from 198.19 lakhs in 1971 to 268.74 lakhs in 1981 registering an increase of 36 per cent.

A healthy feature of urbanization during the last two decades (1961-81) is the establishment of new towns on a mass scale and some capital cities in India. Delhi with a lot of modifications and expansion, and Bhubaneshwar, Chandigarh and Gandhi Gram as entirely new planned capitals are our achievements during the last twenty years. New state capitals for Assam, Arunachal, Nagaland and Haryana, a twin capital at Bombay and the redevelopment of capital for Himachal Pradesh at Simla are on the cards.

The new Indian towns, planned and built under the pressure of rehabilitation, industrialization and administrative needs are as given below*:

(*i*) For rehabilitation of displaced persons: Faridabad, Nilokheri, Rajpura and Kalyani.

(*ii*) Administrative Capitals: Chandigarh, Bhubaneswar and Bilaspur.

(*iii*) Steel Towns: Rourkela, Bhilai, Durgapur and Bhadravati.

(*iv*) Other Industrial Towns: Chittaranjan, Nangal, Mithapur, Dandeli and Ranchi.

(*v*) Company Towns: Modinagar, Neyveli, Kagaznagar and Sindri.

(*vi*) Oil Town: Barauni.

(*vii*) Port Town: Kandla.

*Manickram, T.J. *et al.* : New Towns in India in United Nations Technical Assistance Programme, Public Administration Problems of New and Rapidly Growing Towns in Asia, New York, United Nations, 1962.

Apart from the above listed major new towns, some of the new towns have been located on the fringe of metropolitan cities, to relieve congestion in large cities.

Though most of the new towns have opened up most undeveloped regions and employment opportunities for thousand of landless labour, yet it is not early at this state to form a clear estimate of the probable impact of the new towns on their rural environs, because some of the effects oppose and tend to offset each other.

PROJECTIONS OF URBAN POPULATION: A.D. 2000

With regard to the future of urbanization in India, we may draw some inference based on our study so far. Several scholars, Indian as well as foreign, research organizations and institutions have tried to give an estimate of urban population of India. For example, projections have been made by the office of the Registrar-General, the Planning Commission, the Operations Research Group of Baroda, World Bank and individual scholars like Shri S. Raghavachari, J. P. Ambannavar, Robert Cassed and Tin Dyson. We shall discuss of these projections.

Shri S.R. Raghavachari in his paper 'Population Projections, 1976-2001' estimated that the urban population by 2001 would be approximately 169 million more than what it was in 1971, indicating 3.4 per cent geometric rate of growth on the average during the next 30 years. The following is the summary picture (Table 8).

Table 8: Raghavachari's Projections

(in millions)

	Urban	*Total*	*Per cent urban*
1981	150	618	22.5
1991	205	801	25.6
2001	278	945	29.4

His projection of urban population based on the ratio method using the logistic curve with the constraint that 90 per cent of the population would become urban by the year 2001, an increase of around 398 million between 1971 and 2001. Thus the future of urbanization in India will be disastrous, if not catastropic.

Prof. J.P. Ambannavar also attempted projections of total and urban population for this period. (See Table 9).

Table 9: Ambannavar's Projections

(in millions)

	Urban	*Total*	*Per cent urban*
1981	151	683	22.2
1991	210	839	25.1
2001	291	1003	29.0

Source: J.P. Ambannavar, *Population—Second India's Students*, Macmillan, Delhi, 1975. p. 74.

Thus according to Ambannavar by the turn of the century there will be approximately 291 million people in urban centres.

The 12 largest metropolitan centres, each with a population of one million plus, already have a population of about 50 million. By A.D. 2001, another six or seven cities will be added to the list. The magnetic strength and pull of the present metropolitan areas will continue to grow, leading consequently to selected megalopolitan areas with the concentration of enormous masses of people in ugly agglomerates. We envision five major megalopolitan areas with the projected population as shown in Table 10.

Table 10: Megalopolitan Areas with Projected Population

(in millions)

Megalopolitan areas	*Population in the year 2000*
1. Bombay, Ahmedabad, Poona	38.60
2. Calcutta	23.00
3. Madras, Bangalore	19.70
4. Delhi	19.00
5. Lucknow, Kanpur	10.00

URBANISATION AND DEVELOPMENT

The Sub-Committee on Population of National Planning Committee appointed by the Indian National Congress in 1938 recognised that "the growth of industrialisation would mean not only a redistribution of population as between town and country which has been proceeding silently but slowly in the last century—but also better alternative employment, so as to take off the burden on the soil of a disproportionately large population."

This was reiterated by the planning commission in the first Five Year Plan document.

In retrospect, the hope pinned on rapid industrialisation as a path of economic regeneration in India has not been matched by actual performance under the five year plans. The hope that urbanisation will usher in modernisation and social change also remained a distant dream. Mahatma Gandhi had underplayed both the role of industrialisation of western pattern and the role of urbanisation.

Gandhiji had a clear vision of the Indian society as he looked upon urbanisation as an evil as it was based on the exploitation of the villages and alien to the way of life based on nature.

During the British regime India was polarised into two segments viz. Anglostan and Hindustan. The municipalities played an ineffective role in urban development. Some of the constraints in urban development were:

(1) The planning commission is not required to look into the problem of local finance under the constitutional provisions.

(2) The needs of individual cities are not given proper cognizance by the planning commission under the planning process.

(3) The Department of Urban Development in the Central Ministry does some coordination work and the Town and Country Planning Organisations review master plans. However, there is no machinery to tackle urban problems on a national level as local self-government is regarded as a state subject.

(4) Urban problems are given least priority by the States and the Ministry of Local Self Government is considered unimportant. The tendency of State Govts. to supersede municipalities and corporations on political grounds makes confusion worse confounded.

(5) The municipal administration is incompetent to tackle the problems regarding housing, transport, environmental pollution etc. Besides, it has neither financial viability nor legal backing to face urban problems except in a limited sphere like use of land, zoning etc.

(6) Attempts have been made to overcome the urbanisation problems in a few cities through agencies like Calcutta Metropolitan Development Authority (CMDA), Delhi Development Authority DDA etc. But the overall position is far from satisfactory in our country.

Constitutional Aspects

The constitutional aspects of urban administration need careful study. This will help in specifying the role of big cities, intermediate cities and small towns. Besides, there is a need of an adequate administrative machinery to tackle the problems of urbanisation at the national level. Since urban development is a national issue the role of the Centre, the States and the local governments should be specified for implementing a progressive policy for urban development.

Wider Perspective

The outlook on urban problems remained confined to housing, slums and renewal so far. The problems in terms of pollution, environment, economic growth and social change received scant attention.

There is need for regarding the problems in their broader perspectives, to specify the role of cities in the international, national and municipal context.

The Sixth Five Year Plan laid special emphasis on the following aspects of urban development:

(*a*) Emphasis was given to slum development in place of slum improvement and slum renovation schemes were included in the minimum needs programme.

(*b*) Substantial funds were provided in the Central sector for Integrated Development of small and medium towns with a population of less than one lakh.

(*c*) Integrated urban development for metropoliton cities continued. Under it the development schemes under CMDA, State capital projects and Chandigarh received higher allotment.

(*d*) Under the scheme of development of national capital region counter magnet towns around Delhi received adequate financial assistance.

(*e*) Urban research was accorded much importance, as it was recognised that it can improve the formulation of policy in regard to urbanisation and urban development.

URBAN DEVELOPMENT POLICY

Towards a Comprehensive Strategy

We are still struggling to evolve a composite national urban strategy. Despite the claim to comprehensiveness of the national and state plans they have not placed sufficient stress on, or even lack, spatial thinking. The six national and state plans since 1951 may be said to be 'spaceless in outlook' as they have shown very little consideration to the location and distribution of investments and economic activities and their impact on urban and regional systems. The national and sub-national development endeavours do not seem to have been brought into a sharp 'spatial focus'. There is no settlement structure plans/physical development plans, as counterparts to our economic development plans. Questions or issues as to what scale or pattern of urbanisation, industrialisation, transportation and urban and regional development would best promote economic growth, social change and ecological balance have received little attention. The six successive national and state plans include programmes for the development and expansion of industries, as an important sector of economy. Nevertheless, there seems to be no realisation that industry 'power' transport and shelter operate and interact within the framework of single set of 'spatial coordinations'. There is hardly any appreciation of the fact that industries and other economic activities in combination produce a unified system of spatial economy, land use structure and circulation pattern. Consequently our national and sub-national plans seem to have overlooked some of the most crucial issues such as formulating an urbanization policy, identifying growth-poles, distributing investment, employment and new enterprises among major cities, medium size towns and small urban communities and so forth. Moreover, a disproportionate concentration of activities and people in large cities and the lack of any marked breakthrough in rural development reinforce the dualism in national economy and increase the socio-economic gulf between urban and rural settlements. A dismal picture is emerging, causing distortion in the rural and urban relations.

Given the rapid increase in the rate of urban population growth, it seems likely that there will be an accelerated increase in India's urban unemployment. This calls for the adoption of a comprehensive urban policy and effective steps to reduce the rate of population growth not only in the overcrowded cities but in the country as a whole. It is necessary to emphasize that urban problems cannot be solved without real progress in rural areas. Thus the issue is not which is to develop first, rural or urban areas, it is rather how to develop both in order to meet various national, regional and local needs. A large chunk of the rural population in India will continue to live in villages in the foreseeable future. Urbanization cannot absorb them because modern industries cannot employ so many people and the informal sector of the urban economy has its own limitations. The only way to raise the standard of living of the rural population, is, therefore, rural development, which in essence means increased productivity of agriculture and related activities and a more organic link between rural and urban functions.

Basic components of such an integrated and continuous approach would be:

1. Slowing metropolitan growth.
2. Urban development policies.
3. Promoting small towns and intermediate cities.
4. Rural development policies.

Now we will detail these components:

In order that the problems of metropolitan and large cities do not get further aggravated in future, it is certainly desirable to slow down primate city growth without resource misallocation and major losses in efficiency. Only that amount of population growth should be allowed which is required for the maintenance of their functions. Such growth rates can be achieved through the mechanism of channelling the economic activities towards the medium and small towns. Other steps for slowing primate city include taxes on urban wages, higher property taxes, higher metropolitan residential taxes, prohibition of new factories

Urban Development Policies

In the context of the urban crisis that India is facing today there is an urgent need to evolve a suitable strategy for the comprehensive development of the urban sector in consonance with the economic situation in the country and the available resources and expertise. Urban development policies would invariably try to do three essential tasks, namely: (*a*) arresting of deterioration in the physical form and the functions of the growing urban areas, (*b*) utilisation of the available social infrastructure facilities to the full and (*c*) proper programming and administration of urban functions by relating them to the size and the rate of growth of urban areas within the country.

The present congestion and over-urbanization problem of big metropolitan cities can be tackled by formulating and implementing programmes of slum clearance, urban renewal and control of land price Some of the policies in this regard are : (*i*) The slum development policy, (*ii*) Urban Housing Policy, (*iii*) Transportation policy, (*iv*) Pollution Control Measures and (*v*) Urban Administration.

The urban development policy should lay stress on the following:

(*i*) As to slums and squatter settlements are concerned, the policy should be to improve and rehabilitate them rather than go in for clearance and redevelopment. Long term solutions should aim at progressive elimination of the causes, e.g., by integrating economic development programme with regional, master and urban plans, to ensure more efficient utilisation of available resources in order to stop slum growth.

(*ii*) Housing programme should focus more on problems such as the acquisition and allocation of land, the provision of urban facilities and the strengthening of the housing finance system. At the same time, it is also very essential, that inputs for housing like steel, cement, aluminium, glass etc. should be available in the market without showing any erratic shortages. New technologies including prefabricated structure would have to be considered extensively and the input required for these provided in the national plan.

The high job potential of building and housing and urban facilities should be given careful attention.

(*iii*) Considering the resources available in a developing economy there is no doubt that top priority must be given to the needs of public transportation systems. The policy should be to move more people and not more cars.

Town and transportation planning must go hand in hand and the entire land-use planning must be linked to its effects on the transportation requirements.

With the bitter experience of the public sector, it is time now to think of de-nationalising certain sectors like transport, or allowing the private sector to compete with the public sector.

Advance in technology must be used both to increase the capacity and quality of existing transport system.

(*iv*) In order to create a healthy environment for the mental and physical growth of the inhabitants, widespread green belts and parks could be provided in newly built areas. In old areas, with the co-operation and consent of the inhabitants, decongestion programmes could be worked out. We should also see that all new industrial units should make provisions for pollution control devices in the project cost.

Pollution due to transport may be tackled by suitable design of combustion engines, catalytic treatment of exhaust gases, improving the quality of fuel, proper town planning and traffic planning.

(*v*) There appears to be need for having in a state different types of city development authorities having relationship to a hierarchy of settlements based on population size or their importance.

The Improvement Trusts and Urban Development agencies have, so far, depended heavily on financial assistance by state governments. It is imperative to provide for adequate finances for the city development authority so as to ensure its success.

Promoting Small Towns and Intermediate Cities

It is recognised that development of small town and intermediate cities as counter magnets for potential migrants to large cities, is an appropriate measure. The rationale for this approach is, that by orienting investments nearer to the locationally deprived poorer people in the stagnant rural areas, there are better chances that larger benefits of development would go to them. The small town acts as a powerful link between the rural settlement on the one hand and the urbanised city centres on the other with regard to the collection and distributtion of economic inputs and produces as well as provision of social services and amenities. A successful small town and intermediate city strategy requires the simultaneous implementation of several key elements. These include the following:

1. Economic development assistance should be geared to the economic structure prevailing in small town and intermediate cities. This implies an emphasis upon agro-processing industries, small scale industry and informal sector activities.
2. Policies to strengthen the support of urban centres to rural areas, such as improving marketing facilities for agricultural produce and the provision of agricultural extension services, should be developed.
3. Infrastructure bottlenecks should be relieved and public services expanded.
4. Decentralization of public facilities (such as universities, technical colleges, and routing Division of government departments) may be useful in strengthening the social structure of these cities.

What perhaps is more crucial is the integration of the growth of each town with respect to its hinterland where it may have a number of villages, large and small with different patterns of economic activity. Thus it will not be adequte, it is necessary to draw up a plan for the development of the town in relation to the projected development of its entire hinterland.

Another dimension of this integration is the linkage of the small town with the higher order towns and cities in the region. These linkages both forward and backward will help in the building up of economic development activities to higher levels. The form in which this integration has to be conceived will be in terms of flows of people, commodities and services within multi-directional spatial frame.

The Sixth Plan made a provision of Rs. 96 crores in the Central Sector for the centrally sponsored scheme of Integrated Development of small and medium towns with a population less than one lakh. It was expected to cover about 200 towns during the plan period. The proposed investment in these towns is housing, water supply and communication facilities. Facilities for education, health care and recreation will also be augmented. Pursuing the earlier policies in this respect, certain state governments—Bihar, Gujarat, Karnataka, Maharashtra, Punjab and West Bengal—have given various incentives for the development and promotion of medium and large industries in various towns and intermediate cities and for promoting ancillary industries around the established industrial locations like Jamshedpur, Ranchi, Bokaro, Sindri, etc.

Rural Development Policies

The urban and the rural sectors are two sides of the same coin, and hence require complementary development programmes. To the extent that rural development succeeds, urban development will also succeed.

As India is mainly an agricultural country and since the majority of the Indians live in villages, investments in rural development and rural industrialization is one of the best strategies to stop migration at the source. Under conditions of rapid population growth and agricultural stagnation, the flow of migration from rural to urban areas cannot be stemmed merely by restrictive policies. The best deterrent to migration in such a situation is accelerated rural development.

A rural development strategy might include the following elements:

1. Rural development policies should be framed in the context of a national development strategy, emphasizing rural-urban linkages.
2. Rural development programmes should not seek population retention alone. They should be primarily directed towards increasing agricultural and other rural production and efficiency, rural income and rural welfare, particularly among small producers. Regularization of land ownership claims, other needed inputs, and output prices policies geared to the needs of small holders should be of great help in absorbing rural labour and achieving rural development goals.
3. Adequate facilities should be provided for establishment of mini plants for manufacturing activities in rural areas, link mini-sugar plants, mini-cement plants, mini-spinning mills etc., as has been done in China to absorb the working force in the villages.
4. Rural development programmes like Twenty-Point Programme, Integrated Rural Development, etc., should be more effectively, efficiently and honestly managed so that greater economic benefits may accrue more and more to the less privileged section of the society. From the perspective of population distribution policies, the most important aspect of a successful rural development strategy is that it must be built upon its complementarities with small scale urban strategies because of the critical importance of improving rural accessibility to public services.

and of strengthening rural-urban linkages. A regional development strategy for rural regions requires policy-makers to combine agricultural development policies, rural development planning and a lower-order small town and intermediate city strategy.

In fact the whole development process should be so articulated that urbanization should promote rural development and rural development should back up urban development. Farms, villages, towns, cities and metropolises should have their specific functions to perform in relation to each other within the overall framework of regional planning. It is quite important that an equilibrium should be sought between the rural and urban communities, and within the urban areas, not the form of urban sprawl or slumps, but embodying a balanced interaction between various types of human settlements, independent functionally and yet supporting each other, to bring a coherent relationship between the town and the country...promote harmony and balance between man and man, and his environment. "It is hoped that the Seventh Five Year Plan which starts in April 1985, gives due importance to this strategy of rural-urban continuum".

SELECT REFERENCES

1. Bose, Asish (1970): *Urbanization in India*, Academic Books, New Delhi.
2. Desai, P.B. *et al*. (1969): *Regional Perspective of Industrial and Urban Growth—The Case of Kanpur*, MacMillan, Bombay.
3. Deshpande, C.D. (1976): *Trends in cities and towns of Western India (1961-71)*, Urbanization in Developing Countries, Ed. S.M. Alam and V.V. Pokshishevsky. Osmania University Press, Hyderabad, pp. 321-47.
4. Mitra, A. (1965): *Levels of Regional Development*, Census of India, I, Part I, A (i) and (ii), New Delhi.
5. Pathak, C.R. (1975): 'Spatial Variation in Urban Industrial Growth in India', *Indian Journal of Regional Science*, 7 (1), pp. 1-10.
6. Prakasarao, V.L.S. (1963): *Regional Planning*, Indian Statistical Institute, Calcutta.
7. Premi, M.K. (1981): *Role of Migration in the Urbanization Process in Third World Countries: A Case Study of India, Social Action*, Vol. 31, July-September 1981, pp. 291-310.
8. Raja, Moonis *et al.* (1979): *Spatial organization and urbanization in India: A case study of underdevelopment*, Rural Area Development Perspectives and Approaches, Ed. R.P. Misra and K.V. Sundaram. Sterling, pp. 333-377.
9. Tewari, V.K. (1976): 'Inter-State disparities in the level of industrialization and per capita total consumer expenditure in India', Golden Jubilee Volume, The Indian Geographical Society, Madras.

EXAMINATION QUESTIONS

1. Define urbanisation and bring out its importance.
2. Write an essay on the urbanisation planning in India.
3. What are the factors promoting urbanisation? Mention the main challenges of urbanisation in India.
4. Write a brief note on economic development and urbanisation.
5. Make a critical evaluation of urbanisation policy in India.

29

Occupational Structure of Indian Population

THE LABOUR FORCE

The total population of a country may be divided into two categories—the working and the non-working population. The economically active population or the working population or labour force is variously defined as:

(*i*) The population for working age: broadly speaking the adult population.

(*ii*) The working population: including men and women who are normally employed, but who may be temporarily unemployed.

(*iii*) The employed population: that is actually engaged in productive employment at a given time.

For international statistical purposes the second definition, that of the working population, is preferred by the United Nations, which includes employers, employees, the self-employed, unpaid family workers, domestic servants and members of the armed forces. The non-working population or inactive population is composed of children, retired persons, students, housewives, inmates of institutions, and those living on royalties, rents, pensions, dividends, etc.

The size of labour force in a country depends upon many factors such as age composition, life expectancy, definition of worker, availability of work, attitude towards work, etc. Since these factors are different in different countries, and show changes at different periods of time in the same country, the proportion of persons constituting the work force has differed in different countries and at different times in the same country. In most of the world, working population is about 35% to 40% of the total population of the country.

The proportion of a population that is economically active is an important factor which affects the entire stream of production. Various factors influence the proportions who are economically active, among them are age-structure, age of marriage, levels of income, average size of family and state of health. In young rapidly growing populations of under-developed countries the active population tends to be small and there is heavy young 'dependency' because of the high proportion of children. If the burden of dependents on the labour force is substantial its contribution to rising levels of savings and capital formation and consequently to more improved production would undeniably be insignificant. Figures relating to labour force are important in the sense that they indicate levels of employment already achieved. A rising labour force, particularly in under-developed countries like India where production and employment do not keep pace with it portends a challenging situation. This situation is specially noticeable in India where between 1966 and 1971, labour force increased by 2.3 crores. This rapid growth of labour creates a higher supply of labour than its demand leading to unemployment. The existence of population pressure makes it extremely difficult for an under-developed country like India to absorb the increase in labour force in gainful employment. Besides, the labour force data can be fully analysed to study the occupational structure of a country. The working population of an economy gets distributed in different professions according to the needs of the economy. Broadly speaking employment for the labour force may be in the primary, secondary, and the tertiary sectors of an economy.

Labour Force Participation Rates in India

Table 1 shows the trend of work force participation rate in India since the turn of the century.

Table 1. Work Force Participation Rate since 1901

(In Percentage)

Year	*Persons*	*Males*	*Females*
1901	46	61	32
1951	39	54	23
1961	43	57	28
1971	33	53	12
1981	33	52	14

Source: Census Reports.

The table reveals that the participation rate was only 33 per cent as per 1971 census as against 43 per cent of total population in 1961. This was due mainly to the fact that many of the housewives and students who were treated as workers on the basis of marginal contribution in 1961 census were not included in the 1971 census as workers. As a result the ratio of female workers in total female population got considerably reduced in 1971 census. As against 29% female workers in 1961 the 1971 census showed that only 12% were recorded as female workers. The 1981 data were more or less identical to the 1971 census figures which showed 33% work force. In 1981 the female participation showed a slight increase while male participation rate showed a slight fall.

Broad Features of Work Participation Rate

(1) India's social and economic backwardness is reflected in the work force participation rate. The work force participation in India is much lower than the participation rate in developed countries. Low participation rate in India can be attributed to the following reasons:

(*a*) Omission of unpaid family workers who actually work in the family farm in rural areas.

(*b*) Poor female participation in work force on account of peculiar social condition in the country. If proper adjustment is made for these factors, the work force participation rate in India may also approximate to that of developed countries. Curiously the pre-independence censuses placed the work force participation rate between 44 and 48 per cent.

(2) The work force participation rate is higher in rural areas in comparison to urban areas. In 1971 the rural participation was 34% and in 1981 it was 35% while it was 29% in urban areas in both the years. This can be attributed to the fact that in rural areas almost all adult members of family work in the field or in other family craft while this is not so in urban areas.

(3) As compared to male participation rate (53% in 1981) female participation rate is much less (14% in 1981). It is so because women belonging to upper class and other affluent sections do not generally work. Women belonging to economically weaker sections are required to work on account of economic compulsions. Female work force participation rate is higher in rural areas as compared to urban areas. This phenomenon has two interesting features:

(*a*) The work participation rate of female workers has increased from 12% in 1971 to 14% in 1981 which is a welcome trend.

(*b*) Among the various states the female work participation is not uniform. It is very high in the states of North-Eastern region, high in Andhra Pradesh, Maharashtra, Madhya Pradesh, Tamil Nadu and Karnataka low in states like Kerala, Haryana, Punjab, West Bengal etc.

Comparison with other Countries

In terms of labour-force participation rates, India does not compare favourably with some of the developed countries as can be seen in Table 2. The participation rate in Japan was 49 per cent, West Germany 48 per cent, England 46 per cent, Yugoslavia 45 per cent, and India 33 per cent. These figures are not strictly comparable because of differences in working age and definition of workers, etc. but these indicate broadly that participation rate in these countries is much higher than that of India.

Table 2. Labour Participation Rates in Selected Countries (1971)

Country	*Workers as percentage of total population*
Japan	49
W. Germany	48
U.K.	46
Yugoslavia	45
U.S.A.	40
India	33

This comparison focuses attention on two implications: First, that the number of dependents on the working population, or dependency ratio, is much larger in India than in other countries. Secondly, the low participation rate coupled with low productivity of the workers is responsible to a certain extent for the poverty of the country.

OCCUPATIONAL STRUCTURE

After having analysed the growth of labour force and its participation rates, it may now be instructive to study the employment of the working population in different occupations. In short, by occupational structure of a country we mean the distribution of labour force in different occupations for industries of that country. The broadest classification is possible in terms of sectors of an economy. These three sectors are:

1. **Primary Sector**

It relates to the production of primary goods. The goods are not primary because they are of primary importance but because they are primarily the first to develop in any economy and their products are essential or vital for human existence.

2. **Secondary Sector**

It includes all those activities that follow the primary, such as electric power and gas and construction. All those who are pursuing occupations that are dependent upon large scale manufacturing are to be included in this sector.

Mining is sometimes included under secondary sector. But properly speaking, it is a primary activity.

3. Tertiary Sector

It is the outcome of both the primary and secondary types of activity and, therefore, it is merely an adjunct to both these sectors. It includes storage, communication and services of all kinds.

We can, in most of the cases, classify the tertiary occupations as those which are the by-products of the primary and those which own their origin to the secondary sector.

Thus the term 'Occupational Structure' refers to division of working population in different occupations. Colin Clark argues that the rigidity or flexibility of the structure of production and the distribution of the working force in the primary, secondary and tertiary sectors constitutes an unmistakable indicator of the level of economic development attained by a country. It will be generally noticed that the more backward an economy is, the more population will depend upon agriculture and less on industry.

From the empirical evidence available, six broad conclusions may be drawn as regards economic growth and occupational structure:

1. The share of agriculture employment falls as economic development proceeds.
2. Real income per head is low in the countries in which the percentage of the total population engaged in primary production is high.
3. During the process of economic growth there is a general tendency for tertiary industries to expand more rapidly than the secondary industries.
4. A progressive fall in the proportion of workers in the primary sector has been invariably accompanied by a rise in productivity.
5. Agricultural productivity itself is higher in countries with a small percentage of agricultural workers than in countries with a high percentage.
6. The supply of services per head of population is a broad indicator of the standard of development attained by a country.

Occupational Structure in India

In the light of conclusions arrived at above we may now proceed to examine the occupation structure of India in order to highlight the recent shifts and their association with planned levels of economic development.

On the basis of census figures, estimates have been made about the broad pattern of our occupational structure since the turn of this century. Economic concept, definition and classification of productive and unproductive occupations differ so widely in various censuses that a comparative study of the economic data from the two censuses threatened to be abortive. Therefore, here we are drawing attention to broad trends only.

Table 3 indicates the trend of changes in occupational structure in India since the turn of this century.

Table 3. Occupational Distribution of Working Population in India

Occupation	*1911*	*1921*	*1951*	*1961*	*1971*	*1981*
Primary Sector (1+2+3)	71.8	76.0	72.1	72.3	72.1	66.7
1. Cultivators	50.6	54.4	50.0	52.8	43.3	41.5
2. Agricultural labourers	16.9	17.4	19.7	16.7	26.3	25.2
3. Livestock, forestry, fishing etc.	4.3	4.2	2.4	2.8	2.5	
Secondary Sector (4+5+6+7)	12.6	10.4	10.6	11.7	11.2	
4. Mining and quarrying	0.1	0.3	0.6	—	0.6	
5. Household industry	—	—	—	6.4	3.5	
6. Other than household industry	11.7*	9.3*	9.0*	4.2	5.9	33.3
7. Construction	0.8	0.8	1.0	1.1	1.2	
Tertiary Sector (8+9+10)	15.6	13.6	17.3	16.0	16.7	
8. Trade and commerce	6.0	5.8	5.3	4.0	5.6	
9. Transport, storage and communications	1.1	0.9	1.5	1.6	2.4	
10. Other services	8.5	6.9	10.5	10.4	8.7	
Total	100.00	100.0	100.0	100.0	100.0	100.0

Source: India Pocket Book of Economic Information 1972 and 1973.
*Pocket Book of Population Statistics, 1972, and Census of India 1981, paper 3.

The table highlights the stagnating character of the occupational structure, though the country has passed through two wars, a major depression, partition and three decades of planned industrialization. The stability of the occupational structure in a country where the total population is increasing rapidly means that the new population is being distributed among the available occupations practically according to the old pattern.

The 1981 census reveals the fact that the occupational structure of India is exactly that of an under-developed country in which a substantial proportion of the labour force is engaged in agriculture, and a very small proportion is found engaged in industry and services. In 1981 more than 70 per cent of the working population in India was engaged in agriculture and allied occupations and about 11 per cent of population was engaged in mining industry and construction. Tertiary occupations are taken up by nearly 17 per cent of people. This means that industries and services do not provide work even to one-third of the labour force.

Primary Employment

One of the important basic characteristics of Indian economy is that it is primary producing because agriculture contributes nearly half of national income and out of every ten persons employed in India, seven are engaged in agriculture. Economic growth in other countries has always been matched by a diminution in the numbers engaged in agriculture and by an increase in those engaged in secondary and tertiary employment. But the census figures of India for the last 80 years show that the percentage of workers engaged in agriculture has been nearly stationary.

The fact that the secondary and tertiary sectors have not been expanding sufficiently fast as to absorb the surplus labour working on land constitutes a big economic and social problem. The inevitable consequence of the relentless pressure exercised on land by this surplus population and lack of opportunities in smaller and smaller fragments, result in lower yields and giving rise to complex problems under tenancy reform. Thus over-crowding and the consequent pressure of population on land have led to sub-division and fragmentation of holdings, decline in the area of land per capita, disguised unemployment in agriculture and marginal productivity of labour which may be zero or even negative. The pressure of population on land has been so heavy that between 1901 and 1971 the area of cultivated land per cultivator has declined from 0.43 hectare to 0.36 hectare. The growth behaviour of the Indian economy during the two decades of planning has made us sceptical even about the capacity of the non-agricultural sector to absorb all the new entrants to the working force from within the sector itself. Prof. A.H. Khusro's elaborate calculations of the demand for labour in the non agricultural sector of the Indian economy and also the supply of labour from within the non-agricultural sector itself led him to the conclusion that industrialization and substantial increase in the national income would not involve any net transfer of under-employed agricultural workers to the non-agricultural sector of the Indian economy for 25 years (1951-76). As he put it, "... the non-agricultural sector of the Indian economy would be lucky if it had a state of near full employment by 1975." And indeed we do not seem to have been lucky.

The fact that the pressure on agriculture and allied pursuits during the period 1960-61 to 1970-71 has increased implies that alternative industries have not come up to provide employment for the rapidly growing population in the country. The impact of large-scale investment both in agriculture and industry over the first twenty years of planning failed to produce any significant impact on the occupational pattern. Mr. Priyatosh Maitra rightly said, "In Indian experience, employment multiplier seem to be small and, therefore, occupational structure remained almost static . . . limited employment horizons, resulting from a process of industrialisation devoid of 'built-in technological progress' effects, strengthen the hold of production techniques with built-in under-employment". Thus, changes in the industrial distribution of working force seem to run counter to the Clark-Fisher hypothesis that " . . . as time goes on and communities become more economically advanced, the numbers engaged in agriculture tend to decline relative to the numbers in manufacture, which in their turn decline relative to the numbers engaged in services."

Secondary Employment

In the secondary sector, the proportion of work force engaged has remained within the range of 10 per cent and 12.6 per cent. Till 1931 this proportion had continued to decline. For instance, the proportion was 12.6 per cent in 1901, 11.1 per cent in 1911, 10.5 per cent in 1921 and 10.2 per cent in 1951. This reflects the fact of destruction of indigenous industries. Thus on the whole, the percentage of work force engaged in secondary activities has been almost steady over the last 80 years. This only proves that even today industrialization has not made any significant dent in the occupational structure. As against the predominance of agriculture, the insignificance of industry and particularly of organised industry will be evident. The growing prosperity of the Indian large-scale industries has failed to create proportionate employment potential. While the capital formation, output and value added for all industries increased at an annual compound growth rate of over 15 per cent, the growth rate of total employment for all industries during 1959-70 had been a mere 3.6 per cent. However, the progress attained during the four plans shows that the country with sustained efforts during over the next few years, can successfully break out the shackles of a predominantly agrarian economy and put herself on the right road to modern industrial progress.

Tertiary Employment

A significant feature of the occupational pattern in India has been an uneven shift in the proportion of working force engaged in tertiary occupations. Up to 1931 tertiary activities show a decline but the subsequent decade records an improvement which level is maintained in 1951. The fall in proportion between 1951 and 1961 is believed to be due to differences in the definition of working force in the 1951 and 1961 censuses. The proportion in 1971 at 16.7 per cent was slightly higher. The fact that India has as high a percentage of tertiary employment itself does not mean much. If we accept the thesis that economic growth of a country is associated with a shift in working population from agriculture to industry and ultimately to tertiary (service) sector, then India is not positively on the path of economic development.

The outstanding fact of the economic situation is that at least since 1901 that is, for eighty years, the economic composition of our population has remained practically unchanged despite a conscious effort by the Government to alter it. The relative upsurge of the primary sector on the one hand and the stagnation in the other two sectors have produced a stage where surplus agricultural labour could not be effectively siphoned off from the primary sector. In other words in the context of a high rate of population growth the secondary and tertiary sectors have not grown rapidly enough to make an impact on the primary sector. Consequently, there is large scale under-employment and unemployment in the rural areas, and the problem of decreasing the proportion of population dependent on agriculture became relatively difficult, if not impossible.

Causes for the Failure

Failure of employment policy of the government is a basic cause for the rigidity in occupational pattern. The rural economy was not developed in a manner to (*a*) mobilise the idle rural labour and (*b*) to raise the producitivity of labour.

Firstly, poor organisation resulted in the failure of programmes to reduce rural unemployment and under-employment.

Secondly, little effort was made by the planners to create employment in non-agricultural vocations. Thirdly, the programmes of land reforms failed to create small owner holdings and did not diffuse the ownership among a large number of cultivators.

Government's help in the form of credit and subsidies for fertilizers did not benefit the poor peasantry. Rural development failed to remove poverty and the pattern of employment. The working population on land stood at 70% during 1951-71 period. But showed a slight fall thereafter and in 1981 it stood at 67%.

In the industrial sector emphasis was laid on heavy industries for which machinery and technical knowhow were imported. The small scale and cottage industries received low priority. Besides, luxury consumer durable industries also flourished. The highly capital intensive structure had very little employment multiplier which produced no effect on occupational structure.

P.C. Mahalanobis while advocating industrialisation also stated that 'In view of meagreness of capital resources there is no possibility in the short run, for creating much employment through the factory industries. Now consider the household or cottage industries. They require very little capital.'

With any given investment employment possibilities would be ten or fifteen or even twenty times greater in comparison with corresponding factory industries.

It is clear that India should adopt economic dualism. It should have heavy goods and defence industries. Simultaneously labour intensive techniques should be expanded to provide employment to the mass in the traditional sector.

High growth of labour force due to falling death rate and growing birth rate was a hindrance to changes in occupational structure. Fast increasing rural population swelled the rank of rural prolitariat which made it difficult to reduce the proportion of population dependent on agriculture. The Fifth Plan approach document admitted this fact in the following statement: 'At the present pace of industrialisation any mass scale transfer of labour force from agricultural to non-agricultural sector is ruled out. The growing labour force in agriculture has to be provided with fuller employment within agriculture. A redistribution land reform derives its basic rationale from this consideration.'

The main thrust of the investment policy so far was directed towards capital intensive industries and consumer durable goods industries. Besides, measures to reduce population were inadequate and ineffective. In the absence of concerted efforts to develop labour intensive technology in agriculture and industry on a vast scale, the occupational pattern remained more or less stagnant. By promotion of non-agricultural employment prospects alone can the occupational structure be changed. For this it is necessary to increase dependence on small scale industries and develop rural infrastructure. This along with population check can bring about the desired change in occupational pattern.

Symptoms of Change

Some indications of impending changes in occupational pattern are discernible in the Indian Economy:

1. The occupational structure of states like Kerala, West Bengal, Tamil Nadu and Maharashtra indicates a movement from the primary sector to the secondary and tertiary sectors.

2. The growth of banking, finance, trade, commerce etc. in the wake of industrialisation are providing employment as well as perpetrating a shift of occupation from primary to secondary and tertiary sectors. This is reflected in the growing urbanisation trend.

3. The pattern of economic growth since 1951 changed the relative significance of the three sectors Agriculture and related pursuits accounted for 52% of Gross National Product (GNP) in 1950 now account for only 34% of the GNP.

The corresponding shares of manufacturing and service sectors now account for 24.9% and 40% respectively. This altered pattern contradicts the static pattern of growth of the three sectors.

As V.K.R V. Rao puts it, 'It is this which constitutes both the problem and paradox of Indian economic development and has led to the controversy about the linkage between growth and employment.'

Changing the Occupational Structure in India

We have seen that the basic pattern of occupational distribution remains very nearly the same now as in 1911. Lack of any significant development in the industrial and non-agricultural activities in India is reflected by the very large proportion of the working force in the agricultural sector. The dependence of the country to such a large degree on agriculture is a serious evil in itself and diversity of occupation is badly needed.

In view of the massive size of India's population and consequently that of her labour force and the high rate of population growth, the increase in the labour force is likely to be the most serious limiting factor in bringing about structural changes in her economy, and the country will be faced at least for the next two decades, with a particular phenomenon of industrial growth without a significant rise in the ratio of the urban to the total population. Such structural stagnation can only inhibit economic growth. While we do not intend to belittle the importance of population control and family planning, we must point out that the size of the labour force over the next fifteen years will be independent of the current rate of population growth, in as much as all the potential entrants to the labour force during the next fifteen years have already been born. The remedy for the problem of structural stagnation during the next fifteen years does not, therefore, lie in family planning, though it can be argued that a lower rate of population growth may cut down consumption and increase the rate of saving and investment which will mean a higher rate of economic growth. And even at the end of the next fifteen years, on the assumption that the family planning movement succeeds, the proportion of the total population in the labour force will increase as a result of changes in the age structure of the population. This no doubt will be a desirable phenomenon in the sense that "age dependency" will decrease but it cannot be taken for granted that an increase in the proportion of the labour force will be conducive to economic growth. On the contrary, there is every possibility that "economic dependency" will increase in relation to the working population. This need not be a problem if the productivity per worker increases to such an extent that the increase in the income per worker will more than this happening seem to be meagre. However, the changes in occupational structure are not treated as independent goals to be pursued; these changes are in reality associated with economic development, and that too as a consequence and not as a cause of economic development. Of course, it is a wider issue involving the whole gamut of investment, employment, national income, etc.; a few more steps to expedite the desired shift in the occupational structure may be suggested.

Reduction in Primary Work Force

It is considered on all hands that a policy for achieving a growth-oriented occupational balance will necessarily have to involve a transfer of part of the working force from agriculture to secondary and tertiary activities. According to one rough estimate as many as 25 per cent agricultural workers are superfluous and their marginal productivity is almost zero. Their presence in agriculture in fact abstructs such desirable improvements as mechanization, consolidation of holdings, etc. One of the important goals of our long-term planning has, therefore, been to reduce the share of agriculture from the current level of 70 per cent to, say about 50 per cent within the next few decades There is no doubt that the process has to be extremely slow. Available data of changes in occupational structure in some of the countries of the world show that the target suggested for India is not in any way unrealistic. Russia, for example, was able to bring down the labour force depending on agriculture from 81.8 per cent in 1926 to 52.8 per cent in 1939, which means a decrease of 29 per cent within a period of 65 years.

In order to reduce the proportion of working force dependent on agriculture to around 5) per cent employment opportunities will have to be provided for the people who are to be weaned away from the dependence on agriculture, besides creating jobs for the already unemployed.

Improvement in Agricultural Productivity

Reduction in agricultural work force presupposes an increase of productivity in agriculture. In other words, increased agricultural productivity is a necessity for changing the occupational pattern in India. It has been marked in the economic history of many industrialized countries that prosperous and expanding agriculture formed the basis of expansion of manufacturing industries. The technological revolution in agriculture was indeed an essential foundation for Britain's industrial growth. The importance of technological revolution in agriculture as a pre-requisite for industrial change is one of the most important historical lessons for poor countries. Higher agricultural productivity reduces the number of persons required in agricultural operations to feed the total population of the country. Increased agricultural productivity, apart from increasing the savings available for investment in the economy helps overall economic growth by more adequately meeting the growing food requirements of the country, supplying the raw materials for industry, increasing the foreign exchange earnings through large exports and by releasing labour for employment in the growing industrial sector. In fact unless agriculture is modernized substantially, industrial expansion in most under-develeped countries is likely to proceed at a slow speed due to lack of purchasing power in the hands of the majority of population. Thus agricultural growth is a pre-condition for industrial expansion. With improvement in agriculture, rural sector itself undergoes a structural transformation. With the expansion of cash crops, the subsistence economy is converted into an exchange economy. A new pattern of agrarian relationships, new techniques and skills, new opportunities for entrepreneurial and organizational abilities appear on the scene. All this creates a 'climate' favourable for industrial growth and a substantial increase in tax revenue for social overhead capital.

A very comprehensive set of measures is called for to raise agricultural productivity in India calculated to improve all the factors employed in agriculture, viz., land-labour, capital and enterprise. Agricultural techniques must be improved; fertilizers and manures should be made available in ample quantity all over the country. Cheap modern tools and equipment should be designed and manufactured on a large scale. Liberal supplies of insecticides and pesticides should be distributed among the farmers free or at very cheap rates. Ample irrigation facilities must be provided through the extension of major and minor irrigation works. Adequate credit facilities at a reasonable cheap rate must be provided so that the farmer does not fall into the clutches of the money-lender. Farm units may have to be regrouped to form economical entities and to make them amenable to a use of scientific implements and improved techniques. The quality of man behind the plough should be improved through education, general and technical. Above all, administrative set up connected with agriculture should be streamlined and purged of corrupt elements. Many of these improvements are such that these will require a larger labour force. For example, with an increase in the irrigation facilities, the volume of work will increase considerably. According to one rough estimate with every acre put under artificial irrigation, the work to be done doubles. Thus with greater and proper use of fertilizers, intensive cultivation and better animal husbandry, the work to be done will increase to a very large extent. It has been estimated that rice cultivation by the Japanese method increases work by 40-50 per cent per acre.

Till recently increase in agricultural output has been handicapped by scarcity of land, fragmentation of holdings and primitive techniques. But in recent years, the use of modern better seeds, and agricultural mechanization have brought about a veritable agricultural revolution, more commonly called these days as the green revolution. In fact, it is not merely a "green revolution" but a "revolution of mind" on the part of millions of Indian farmers. For the first time in the history of Indian agriculture, the farmer has realised that farming is a business and not merely a way of life to which he must resign himself. Will the green revolution automatically bring about a change in the occupational structure by (*i*) meeting the growing food requirements of the country and supplying the raw materials for industry, and (*ii*) releasing labour for employment in the growing industrial sector? The answer to these questions will be affirmative, if there is simultaneous expansion in secondary and tertiary sectors so as to absorb the labour force thrown out of agriculture. "Agriculture improvements cannot go very far unless there is industrial development to take up the released manpower and to provide a solid technical base for the equipment and services essential for modernized agriculture." Necessarily, therefore, agricultural development should be properly linked together with industrialization so that there may be a welcome change in the occupational structure in India.

Expansion of Secondary and Tertiary Employment

It does not need much of reasoning now to make out a case for the sizable expansion of non-agricultural sector with a view to bringing about the desired shift in occupational structure. In England also the industrial revolution was preceded by an agricultural revolution as an essential element in development. In India too a similar development is taking place, but the problem is more difficult because of the relatively larger dimension of population and the alarmining rate at which it is increasing. In absolute figures, the Indian population increases by more than 30 million persons annually. This is the most serious handicap in bringing about favourable change in the occupational pattern in India. While the number of people seeking jobs is thus gigantic, the wherewithal to provide work in non-agricultural sectors is very inadequate. The rate of investment is very low and the techniques used are primitive. In view of these serious limitations, it is not feasible to expand industrial and service sectors so as to absorb all the job seekers and to draw off labourers from agriculture to an extent that the absolute number and proportion of workers decline in that sector. If, however, the labour force is drawn from agriculture without adequate provision for its absorption in non-agricultural sectors, then this will only add to open unemployment, involving large economic and social costs to the community. The non-agricultural sector is not in a position to absorb the influx of rural populations. The analogy of the advanced countries can fit in only when side by side with the agricultural development, there is rapid industrialization, absorbing the surplus agricultural labour of the rural areas of the country. Dr. V.K.R.V. Rao while talking about Rural Development and Urbanisation says that "Increase in agricultural production will not solve the problems of agricultural labourers, and their low level of income, nor will it necessarily provide for diversification of employment".

The importance of industry in the economic development has

been well realized and the process of industrialization is underway in different spheres. It is true that in the initial stages the contribution which industries make to the national output and employment will not be high, yet their presence dynamises the economy. Industrialization is thus code of economic development. Industrialization creates numerous and varied new employment opportunities which it may frequently be more realistic to consider as a process of addition rather than as one of substitution, the ultimate result being an increase in the proportion of non-agricultural employment. It has been the experience of the advanced countries that industrialization and its accompanying factors such as urbanization exercise a controlling influence on population growth and thus relieves the existing surplus agricultural manpower. We must not only quicken but also broaden the pace of industrial development by the establishment of basic and heavy industries.

Professor Gunnar Myrdal studies the spread effects of industrialization on employment and also its back-wash effects in terms of unemployment on the traditional sector. Myrdal, after a careful examination of the situation, observes: "The employment effects of industrialization cannot be expected to be very large for several decades ahead, that is until the region is much more industrialized. For a considerable time the net employment effects may even be negative. This dimension of the problem, as well as the wider consequences for labour utilization outside the modern sector is overlooked in the vision that sees industrialization as the remedy for "unemployment" and "underemployment". George Rosen, after studying the capital labour co-efficients in India's five major ndustries—cement, paper, iron and steel, sugar and textiles—reaches the same conclusion. To quote: "Investment in this sector has today probably one of the lowest direct employment expansion-effects, compared with an equal investment within other sectors of the economy".

What is the solution to the employment problem posed by this explosion of the labour force and the elasticity of industrial employment? Obviously, for absorbing all or at least a good proportion of the working force in non-agricultural occupations, reliance will have to be placed on small and cottage industries involving comparatively smaller capital investment. In other words, rural industrialization is the only alternative left to us for finding rewarding work for our fast growing lalour force in the villages.

The development of village industries would not only solve the problem of rural unemployment but also enable us to balance our occupational pattern. Revitalization of our rural areas in every way is the only answer to change favourably our occupational structure. We have to provide not only primary amenities such as good water, clean roads, electricity, education and health centres but also fuller gainful employment to the working population in the diversified rural economy, besides agriculture. Against the backdrop of this reality the development of village industries, therefore, assumes significance.

Rural industrialization should not rest on primitive technique. It would be better to switch over to intermediate techniques, till the process of industrialization gets a powerful momentum that the new entrants to labour force can be absorbed. For the period of high population growth potential, in which labour force is also expected to increase at an accelerated rate, it would be appropriate to adjust the choice of techniques consistent with the employment objective.

It is obvious that the utilization of labour force will continue to be the serious problem that it is today, really become much more serious with the extremely rapid growth of population. Our only hope lies in the development of an all-enveloping agro-industrial economy in which agriculture would continue to be the main stay of our national economy, even though with a diminishing proportion of labour force utilized by it, with an increasingly diversified economy at all levels. It will bring a modest but perceptible change in the occupational structure and will increase both agricultural and non-agricultural output. One feels happy that the attention of all leaders in various fields is drawn to this aspect of our economy. Our Late Prime Minister Smt. Indira Gandhi while inaugurating the 63rd session of the Indian Science Congress at Waltair, reminded the conference of what Gandhiji said: "If villages perish, India perishes too". She rightly observed: "Freedom and progress of India was synonymous with the self-economy of the villages". The development village industries would not only solve the problem of rural unemployment but also enable us to tap certain natural resources which are today lying unutilized and help as add to our national wealth.

SELECT REFERENCES

1. Census of India, 1981, Series 1, India, Paper 1 of 1981, Provisional Population Totals, New Delhi; Registrar General and Census Commissioner for India, 1981.
2. Census of India, 1981, Series 1, India, Paper 2 of 1981, Provisional Population Totals—Rural Urban Distribution, New Delhi; Registrar General and Census Commissioner for India, 1981.
3. Census of India, 1981, Series 1, India, Paper 3 of 1981, Provisional Population Totals—Workers and Non-Workers, New Delhi; Registrar General and Census Commissioner for India, 1981.
4. Gyan Chand: *Population in Perspective*, pp. 228-29.
5. Davis, Kingsley: *The Population of India and Pakistan*, 1968, reprint. New York; Russell & Russell, 1968, Chapters 4, 15-19, 21 and 22.
6. Ministry of Home Affairs, Office of the Registrar General and Census Commissioner, India, The Population of India, 1974, World Population Year, CICRED Series, New Delhi, 1974.

EXAMINATION QUESTIONS

1. What do you mean by occupational structure? Mention the features of occupational structure in India.
2. What is the strength of labour force in India. State the present occupationaly distribution of population in the country and suggest measures for its balanced distribution.
3. Major proportion of India's working population is engaged in agriculture. Examine this statement and explain the occupational structure of labour force in India.

30

Qualitative Aspects of Indian Population

'Man' being the citadel in the planning process development of the human resource has to be the essential concern of the planners.

Human resource comprises the men, women and children. Its development is the process of increasing knowledge, the skill and the capacities of all the people in the society. In economic terms, 'it could be described as the accumulation of human capital and its effective investment in the development of the economy'.

Although human resource development is usually equated with schooling or formal education, human resource development in its correct perspective has also other facets such as health, nutrition, housing, family and community welfare. It is in this totality and taking into account the total impact of all these factors on children, adults and the old people that a meaningful strategy for human resource development could be evolved. In short, development in human resources refers to these investments which are intented to develop the inner qualities of man. We may restrict investment in human capital to (*i*) education which includes general education and technical education and (*ii*) health, which includes health care services, medical education, nutrition and water supply. The importance of these items for improving the quality of human capital needs no stressing. Education helps in increasing the efficiency of the people and thereby the national income. Expenditure on items like health care, nutrition and water supply increase the physical and mental efficiency of the people and also improves the expection of life and thereby increase the economically active population.

Prof. V.K.R.V. Rao in 1966 as a member of the Planning Commission went a step further. He said "the development of human resources depends on what we do with the young, among human beings. It is the child and the youth who constitute the raw material for the talent which if properly developed ultimately helps in raising production. It is the kind of training we give them, and the attitude, skills etc., that this evokes among our youth that ultimately determines what kind of adults they will grow into in terms of skills, talents, techniques, attitudes, and all those other factors which together are responsible for the ability of the people to meet the needs of the society. From this it can be inferred that investment in children and youth development programme is something like investment in capital goods." A very relevant and telling slogan in our developing economy today is "to step up investment in the most precious commodity namely the talent wealth of our people and thus ensure the future of our nation. Thus, assessment of the economy is incomplete without considering the human resource." It is as if we have a map of resources which did not include a a mighty river and its tributaries. "The particular river . . . is fed by schooling, learning on the job, advances in health and the growing stock of information about the economy. Even at the micro level human asset plays a significant role."

In short, countries inadequate in human resources, despite massive imports of non-human capital, will remain underdeveloped as human capabilities do not stay abreast of physical capital and they do become limiting factors in economic growth. A diversified economy replaces brawn by brain, unskilled worker by skilled worker and 'labour-power' by 'manpower'.

Though the classical economists, like Adam Smith and Alfred Marshall had recognised the importance of human investment. Modern economists had neglected in their theory and practice of economic growth. Recently some economists like Prof. T.W. Schultz, Harbison, Simon Kuznets, and Dr. V.K.R.V. Rao, Mozes Abramovitz and a host of others have opened a new dimension in economic thinking to enthrone man as a productive source of production. Seen against this wider background, the term human capital, resumes its place as a useful and to some extent operative concept which has made it possible to focus economic analysis on a hitherto over neglected factor of growth and to underline the need to maintain a balance, to determine an optimum, between physical investment and the training of human beings. We can restore man to his due place in the economic system and the community without going to the length of reducing him to a machine. "Human resource is of paramount importance in a healthy growth of a country as the 'human factor is not merely a determinant of production'. The human being is also the object of production."

Efforts to increase the amount of capital per worker are called 'investment in capital goods' while the efforts to improve the quality of population are called 'human investment'. The optimum allocation between these two types of investments can be illustrated by the usual indifference curve type of analysis.

In diagram, IP_1, IP_2 and IP_3 are three iso-product curves. The curve IP_1 relates different amounts of fund for 'human investment' and

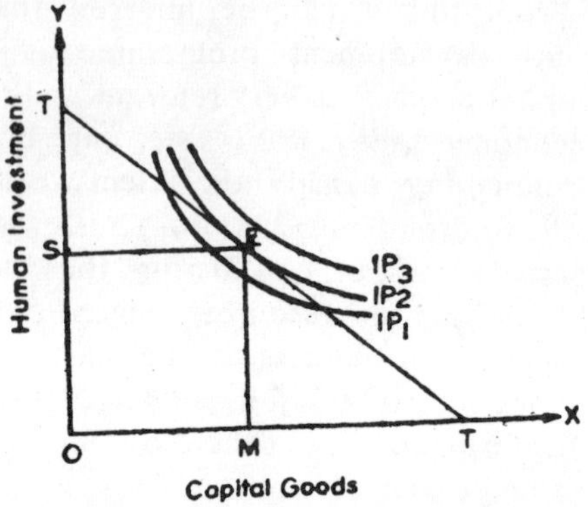

Fig. 1

different amounts of investment in capital goods required to produce a given quantity of product. Similarly IP_2 is the locus of combination of expenditures on the two types of investment that would result in greater quantity of product and so on. The given investment funds *OT*, output would be maximum only if *OM* were invested in capital goods and *OS* were allocated to 'human investment'.

Now we shall study the qualitative aspects of Indian population in detail in terms of 'health' and 'education'.

LEVEL OF HEALTH

The health of the people of India is shockingly poor. Statistics of positive health are difficult to obtain in India. Information in regard to morbidity is available only to a limited extent. We have, therefore, to rely on mortality statistics in assessing the state of public health. Even in regard to mortality statistics, causes of death particularly in villages and outlying areas, are not correctly recorded and people are generally recorded as having died of 'fever' which accompanies the disease in most cases. In urban areas some kind of health service is provided, but in rural areas, where more than 70 per cent of the people live, most primitive conditions prevail. A simple index of the health of a community is the life expectation of birth (age 0). Since the concept of expectation of life is easily understandable and the figures are available, we shall be using it to have a general idea about the level of health in India.

LIFE EXPECTANCY

The number of years for which people of a country expect to live at the time of birth is the average of life expectancy of that country. It depends mainly on the incidence of mortality rates and the age as the time of death. Thus, if the mortality rate is high and/or death occurs at an early age, the life expectancy will be low.

Till very recently, life expectancy in the country was very low. According to official estimates, the expectation of life at birth in 1901 was estimated at 23.6 for males and 24.0 for females. The corresponding estimates in 1970 were 47.10 and 45.60. Thus, during a course of seven decades, the rise in the expectation of life at birth was 100 per cent for males and 90 per cent for female s. Table reveals that at no age the rise prior to 1931 has been greater than after 1931. Moreover, the figures also bear that the gains at various ages during 1901-31 were only marginal in comparison to post-1931 period; at no age it was more than 15 per cent. This confirms the belief that during the former three decades of the current century the health conditions did not improve much. The information about life expectancy for the last 70 years in given in Table 1.

It is obvious from the table that the increase in the life expectancy has been very fast. This is indicative of a rise, however slight, in the standard of living. This reflects the steady improvement in the general health of the population. As there is a likelihood of further fall in the death rate and infant mortality rate, there is bound to be a further rise in life expectancy in the immediate future.

Although life expectancy in the country is rising fast and has almost doubled during the last 30 years, yet compared to many countries of the world, it is very low, as is evident from the Table 2.

It is interesting to note that in India both sexes have low span of life. A lower life expectancy is symbolic of backwardness. Shorter life expectancy does not mean merely that the people's life is cut short at an early age but it also adversely affects the interests of the country. The investments made in rearing up and educating people cannot bear full fruit because death occurs at an early age. Production and capital formation, too, suffer because people contribute to it for a shorter duration. Thus the country can reap full benefits from the investment made in people only if they live longer.

Life expectancy is dependent on the incidence of mortality rates which in turn depends on a large number of factors such as the occurrence of epidemics, the prevalence of disease, the level of disease, nutrition attained by the people of country, the condition of living,

Table 1. Expectation of Life 1901-70

Age in year	*Males*							*Females*						
	1901	*1911*	*1931*	*1951*	*1961*	*1971*	*1981*	*1901*	*1911*	*1931*	*1951*	*1961*	*1971*	*1981*
0	23.6	22.6	26.9	32.5	41.9	47.1	54.8	24.0	23.3	26.6	31.7	46.6	45.6	52.0
10	34.7	33.4	36.4	39.0	45.2	49.0		33.9	33.7	33.6	39.5	43.8	48.1	
20	28.6	27.5	29 6	33.0	27.0	40.2		28.6	28.0	27.1	32.9	35.6	39.7	
30	22.9	22.5	23.6	26.6	29.0	31.9		23.8	23.0	22.3	26.2	27.9	31.7	
40	17.9	18.0	18.6	20.5	22.1	24.7		29.1	18.5	18.2	21.1	22.4	24.7	
50	13.6	14.0	14.3	15.9	16.5	18.3		14.5	14.3	14.7	16.2	17.5	18.9	
60	9.5	10.0	10.3	10.1	11.8	13.0		10.0	10.1	10.8	11.3	13.0	13.4	

Source: 1. Saxena, G.B., *Indian Population in Transition*, pp. 103-13.
2. *Indian*, *1976*, p. 8.

Table 2. Expectation of Life at Birth in Some of the Selected Developed and Developing Countries of the World

(in years)

Name of the Country	*Year*	*Male*	*Females*
1. Australia	1965-65	67.6	74.2
2. France	1971	68.6	76.4
3. German Democratic Republic	1969-70	68.8	74.2
4. Japan	1974	71.2	76.3
5. Sweden	1971-75	72.1	77.6
6. USSR	1071-72	64	74
7. U.K.	1970-72	68.9	75.1
8. USA	1975	68.7	76.5
9. China	1970-75	59.9	63.3
10. Ghana	1960	37.1	NA
11. Hong Kong	1971	67.4	75.0
12. India	1961-70	46.4	44.7
13. Indonesia	1960	47.5	47.5
14. Sri Lanka	1967	64.8	66.9

care of women, infant mortality rates, etc. In comparison with the developed countries, the expectation of life in India is low on account of the high levels of death rates. Absence of a good and balanced diet and the existence of low levels of nutrition are also contributory factor in increasing the death rate in India. While poverty of the Indian people is at the root of this phenomenon of short life span, the discovery of wonder medicines to control epidemics like plague, cholera, influenza or small-pox, the general improvement in medical assistance, increase in the number of hospitals, doctors, nurses, midwives and better control of diseases have all helped to save life. In recent years, the public health measures taken under the various plans have further reduced death rate. In the last decades expectation of life has improved at the rate of about 0.5 per cent per year. This is a healthy trend and so it must continue till life expectation in India levels off with the advanced countries of the world.

Though the data of expectation of life of a country is useful index to characterize the health conditions in a country and their development, it is, however, important to keep in mind the limitations of these data when used for that purpose. They merely give an indication of the resultant of two component factors: the prevalence of diseases that can be fatal and the extent to which these diseases are not prevented from becoming fatal. Thus they are deficient measures of morbidity.

They tell nothing about many other important health deficiencies: Physical infirmities like blindness, incipient illness, and, more generally, physical and mental weaknesses caused by malnutrition, intestinal worms, and other infestations and diseases that are usually not fatal in themselves (though they may decrease resistance to other diseases, including fatal ones). It is conceivable that people live longer only to suffer debilitating conditions of ill health to a greater extent than before.

In every country there is a certain number of persons who are not able-bodied on account of some physical or mental infirmity. They are a burden to society. Their presence is an economic loss and indicates in the last analysis some defect in the social organism: poverty crime, vice, disease are all symptoms of a diseased body. It is necessary to consider the data connected with these defectives for ascertaining the causes that are responsible for them. The population of India is of a low quality because majority of the people inhabiting in India suffer from one or other infirmities. But the returns of infirmities have never been satisfactory in India. Feeble-minded persons are returned insane, many partially blind are returned as totally blind. Diseases like leprosy are likely to be concealed, particularly where the purdah system prevails.

EDUCATION

A distinction is usually made between levels of literacy which is the condition of literacy at a single point of time, and progress in literacy, which is the change in the condition over a period of time. The level of literacy is usually measured by the literacy rate, namely the number of literates expressed as a percentage of the total population. Table 3 presents progress of literacy rates in India.

In 1901 only 5.35 per cent of the total population was literate and amongst the females the literacy was as low as 0.69 per cent. Till 1931, the progress of literacy had been slow; the general literacy in that year was 9.50 per cent and the female literacy was only 2.9 per cent. The gap between female literacy and male literacy in 1931 was very vide, being 12.66 per cent.

In 1951, i.e., soon after we attained Independence the general literacy rate was 16.67 per cent. The female literacy rate was still very low being only 7.93 per cent and the male literacy also only 24.95 per cent.

According to the 1981 census, 36 per cent of the total Indian population were literate. Literacy among males (47 per cent) was

Table 3. Progress of Literacy Rates, 1901-1981 (All India)

Census Year	*Percentage of literate population to total population*	*Percentage of literate males to total males population*	*Percentage of literate females to total female population*
1901	5.35	9.83	0.69
1911	5.92	10.56	1.05
1921	7.16	12.21	1.81
1931	9.50	15.59	2.93
1951	16.67	15.59	7.93
1961	24.02	24.95	12.95
1971	29.34	39.51	18.44
1981	36.12	46.72	24.81

almost twice as high as among females (25 per cent). These figures reflect a considerable advance over the situation reported by the 1951 census, when 17 per cent of the total population (24 per cent of males and 8 per cent of females) were reported to be literate. In fact, these figures understate the extent of progress, because during this period the proportion of the population below age five increased. Despite the rise in the literacy rate and the total number of literates, the number of illiterates had increased (excluding Assam) from 37.23 crore in 1971 to 42.43 crore in 1981, due to an ever growing population.

STATE-WISE BREAK UP

There are marked inter-State differences in the levels of literacy both in 1971 and 1981, and despite the goals of narrowing of the disparities implicit in the development plans, there are indications of widening of disparities between States in male and female literacy, especially in the case of the latter. Differences in the male and female literacy rates in different States are brought out in Table 4.

If we analyse the data contained in the table, the following observations may, in particular, be noted:

1. In most of the States in India, female literacy rate lags behind male literacy and there has been little progress in bridging the gap between the sexes, although there have been gains in the literacy levels of each sex during 1971-81. The main reason that could be attributed to the low female literacy are the general poverty of the people and the traditional prejudice among the rural folks against

Table 4. Progress in Literacy in India and States, 1961-81

State/Union Territory	*Males literacy rates*			*Females literacy rates*		
	1961	*1971*	*1981*	*1961*	*1971*	*1981*
1. India	34.45	39.45	46.7	12.95	18.68	24.9
2. Andhra Pradesh	30.19	33.18	39.1	12.03	15.75	20.5
3. Assam	36.64	36.68	36.7	15.58	18.63	18.6
4. Bihar	29.83	30.64	37.8	6.90	8.72	13.6
5. Gujarat	41.13	46.11	54.5	19.10	24.75	32.3
6. Jammu & Kashmir	16.97	26.75	26.8	4.26	9.28	9.3
7. Kerala	54.97	66.62	74.0	38.90	54.31	64.5
8. Madhya Pradesh	27.03	32.70	39.4	6.73	10.92	15.5
9. Maharashtra	42.05	51.05	58.9	16.76	26.43	35.1
10. Karnataka	36.15	41.62	48.6	14.19	20.97	27.8
11. Nagaland	24.04	35.02	49.2	11.34	18.65	33.7
12. Orissa	34.68	38.29	46.9	8.65	13.22	21.1
13. Punjab	32.62	40.38	46.6	13.57	25.90	34.1
14. Rajasthan	23.71	28.74	35.8	5.84	8.46	11.3
15. Tamil Nadu	44.54	51.78	57.2	18.17	26.86	34.1
16. Uttar Pradesh	27.30	31.50	38.9	7.02	10.55	14.4
17. West Bengal	40.08	42.81	50.5	16.98	22.42	30.3
18. Manipur	45.12	46.04	53.3	15.93	19.53	30.7
19. Tripura	29.61	40.20	51.0	10.19	21.19	31.6
20. Andaman & Nicobar	42.43	51.64	58.4	19.37	31.11	41.8
21. Dadra & Nagar Haveli	14.71	22.15	36.2	4.05	7.84	16.8
22. Delhi	60.75	63.71	68.0	52.55	47.75	52.6
23. Goa, Daman & Diu	39.04	54.31	64.8	23.03	35.09	46.8
24. Lakshadweep	35.80	56.48	65.0	10.98	30.56	44.2
25. Pondicherry	50.29	57.29	64.0	24.64	34.62	44.3

sending girls to schools. The vacations in schools also do not synchronise with the heavy agricultural seasons of sowing and harvesting. The girls are, therefore, generally withdrawn in the middle of the term from the school to help in cultivation and to assist the overworked mothers at home.

2. A surprising feature of the data presented in the table is the fact that four States, namely, Assam, Bihar, West Bengal and Manipur have witnessed a higher rate of progress of female literacy than of male literacy. It is difficult to determine the factors which are responsible for the relative greater progress in female literacy in these States. It may, however, be noted that this phenomenon is observed in some of the border States that have been subject to a considerable influx of refugees.

3. According to the 1981 figures relating to male and female literacy State-wise, Kerala, recorded the highest literacy followed by Maharashtra, Tamil Nadu, Gujarat, West Bengal and Karnataka. The States in Sourthern and Western India have generally fared better in the advancement of literacy than the States of Northern, Eastern and Central India. In some instances like Orissa, Madhya Pradesh or Rajasthan, the inheritances of very low levels of development even at the time of independence may be held responsible for the poor progress in literacy in these States. One cannot give the same reason for West Bengal, Uttar Pradesh or Assam, which had a fairly well developed infrastructure even at the beginning of the decade. One of the factors responsible for the poor progress in literacy in the border States in the influx of refugees from Pakistan, who are invariably illiterate peasents.

4. Kerala topped the States in women's literacy also, the percentage being 64.48, Maharashtra with 35.08 and Punjab with 34.14 came second and third, respectively. Among the union territories, the first place was held again by Chandigarh with 59.30 per cent.

5. Number of persons enrolled in higher education as percentage of population in the age-group 20-24 was barely 8 per cent. This figure is quite high among low income countries, but when compared with advanced countries, it is only one-third to one-fourth of the total.

6. Table 5 gives the percentage distribution of the 1971 population by educational levels. If the "primary and above" level persons are considered to be literate in the true sense they formed only 27.3 per cent among males and 11.9 per cent among females. In the urban population these proportions were 45.9 per cent and 28.5 per cent, respectively.

Table 5. Percentage Distribution of Population by Educational Levels

Level of education	*Rural*		*Urban*		*Total*	
	Male	*Female*	*Male*	*Female*	*Male*	*Female*
1. Illiterates	66.2	86.8	38.7	57.9	60.5	81.3
2. Literate (without educational level)	11.4	5.2	15.4	13.6	12.2	6.8
3. Primary or junior basic	13.2	5.8	15.7	13.0	13.0	7.1
4. Middle	6.0	1.7	13.1	8.4	7.5	3.0
5. Matric or Higher Secondary	2.7	0.5	13.3	5.8	4.9	1.5
6. Non-technical diploma	0.2	n.	0.1	0.1	0.1	n.
7. Technical diploma	n.	n.	0.3	0.1	0.1	n.
8. Graduate and above	0.3	n.	3.4	1.1	1.0	0.3
Total	100.0	100.0	100.0	100.0	100.0	100.0

The proportion of males and females who have completed at least matriculation or higher secondary was only 6.1 per cent and 1.8 per cent, respectively. Most of these educated persons are found living in urban areas only.

The Problem

The problem of improving the quality of population is urgent and enormous in India. Despite this realisation by the India Economy planners, low priority was accorded to the growth of human capital in our plans. Table 6 shows the outlays under health and education in these plans.

It is evident from Table 6 that human resource development has remained a low priority area in Indian economic planning. The percentage expenditure on education of the public sector during the third plan was 6.9 per cent which declined to 2.6 per cent in the sixth plan. Similarly during the third plan, namely 2.6 per cent of the total expenditure was incurred on health and family planning which further dwindled to 1.9 per cent in the sixth plan.

The inadequacy and low stock of human resources in the Indian economy should be regarded both as a cause and result of poverty

Table 6: Outlays under Health and Education in Various Plans

	Plans						
	I	*II*	*III*	*Annual plan*	*IV*	*V*	*VI*
(*i*) Total public sector outlay (Rs. crores)	1960.0	4672.0	8576.0	6625.4	15782	39303	97500
(*ii*) Percentage of total outlay devoted to education	—	—	6.0	4.6	4.9	3.3	2.6
(*iii*) Percentage of total outlay devoted scientific research	7.6	5.9	0.8	0.7	0.8	1.1	0.9
(*iv*) Percentage of total outlay devoted to health	—	—	2.6	2.1	2.1	1.7	1.9
(*v*) Percentage of total outlay devoted to family planning.	5.0	4.8	0.3	1.1	1.8	1.3	1.0

Source: *Planning Commission.*

and backwardness. The relative meagre expenditure in India in education per head of population reflects largly the poverty of the country. As far as the government outlays on education as per cent of national income is concerned, India is investing nearly 3 per cent of her national income which is much less than what advanced Western countries are earmarking (refer Table 6). Till now, education has been a low priority area in the Indian economy. After the high priority

Table 7: Selected Indicators for Scientific and Technical Manpower and Expenditure on Research and Development

Country	*Year*	*Total stock of scientists & engineer per 10,000 population*	*Scientists & engineers engaged in R & D per 10,000 population*	*Expenditure on R & D as percentage of Gross National Product*	*Per capita expenditure on R & D (in U.S. Dollars)*	*Total Expenditure on education as percentage of Gross National Product*
U.K.	1972	—	13.8	2.1	58.79	- (1978)
India	1973	21.3	1.7	0.4	0.44	3.3
Canada	1973	280.9	6.9	1.2	90.44	7.6
USA	1974	75.2	24.8	2.3	158.05	6.3
Japan	1275	372.0	35.7	2.1	83.46	5.5
USSR	1975	372.5	48.1	4.8	63.08	7 6

areas like industry and agriculture had their required shares, whatever used to be left in the resource pot would be distributed among the low priority areas among which education also figured.

The other important indicators of human resource development are expenditure on Research and Development (R & D) and the state of scientific and technical manpower development. The per capita expenditure on R & D in India is merely $ 0.44 as against $ 158.5 in USA and $ 83.46 in Japan. Likewise the stock of scientists and engineers per 10,000 population in our country is about 1/18th of that in Japan or in U.S. Thus Indian population leaves much leeway for human resource development in comparison with advanced countries. (Table 7).

The following facts relating to the low standards of education and health in India *vis-a-vis* certain selected countries substantiate our argument (Table 8).

Table 8: Education and Health Indicators for a few Selected Countries

Name of countries	*Year*	*Population per bed*	*Doctor*	*Nurses*	*School Ratios*		
					First level	*Second level*	*Third level*
Japan	1974	100 (1975)	860	320	100	95	24.7
USA	1974	150 (1975)	610	160	—	—	—
U.K.	1974	120	750	270	116	76	16.2
Canada	1975	110 (1974)	580	130	117	64	34.6
USSR	1975	80	350	210	99	76	16.2
India	1978	1465	3730	5870	84	29	4.4

From the foregoing paragraphs it is evidently clear that human resource development has not been accorded the priority deserved, as basic resource of the country.

Dr. A.M. Nalla Gounden estimated the stock of human capital in India for 1950-51 and 1960-61 (refer Table 9). His estimates reveal that the stock of human capital increased from Rs. 4956 crores in 1950-51 to Rs. 7334 crores in 1960-61 signifying an increase of about 48 per cent during the decade. As against it, net physical capital formation increased by about 71 per cent during the decade 1951-61.

Thus, in India the physical capital is growing at a faster rate than human capital, where as "in the three developed countries human capital has increased faster than physical capital in Japan 3.3 times faster and in Germany 1.5 times faster. Both physical capital and human capital grew more or less at the same speed till 1930 in U.S.A. and Japan and till 1909 in Germany. The gap between the growth rate widened in later period." This fact is also supported by the study of P.R. Panchmukhi.

Table 9: Stock of Human Capital in India

(Rs. crores)

	At current prices	
	1960-61	1950-51
1. Literates	876.9	747.0
2. Primary	2894.5	1906.5
3. Matriculates	2098.4	1351.5
4. Technical diploma holders	39.4	31.9
5. Non-technical diploma holders	60.7	32.3
6. Degree holders	911.8	560.0
7. Technical degree holders	452.6	317.3
	7334.3	4956.5

Source: A.M. Nalla Gounden, *Education and Economic Development.*

According to his study in U.S.A. from the initial stages of development to 1956, the investment in education has increased much more rapidly than that in the formation of physical capital. Opposite has been the case in India where the physical investments have been increasing at a higher rate of 13.4 per cent per year as compared to the educational investments which are increasing at the rate of 9.5 per cent per year. Dr. H.N. Pandit's study reinforces the conclusion reached by Dr. Panchmukhi and Dr. Nalla Gounden that the rate of growth of physical capital has been faster than that of educational capital. His estimate reveals that whereas India was investing nearly 3.4 per cent of national domestic product in 1950-51, it went up to 7.38 per cent in 1965-66. As against it, gross physical capital formation as a proportion of national domestic product rose from 13.1 in 1950-51 to 17.93 per cent in 1965-66.

Thus in India, in the process of economic growth, great importance is attached to the addition of country's physical capital stock and the economy continues to lag woefully behind in the matter of 'human capital'.

Suggestions

We are living in era of rising expectations. Politicians and administrators have come to recognise the important role played by human resource in economic development. But mere recognition of the importance of human resource development is not enough. Proper steps must be taken to carry this out in actual practice.

The improvement in the quality of population can be divided into two categories:

(1) The improvement of quality of the existing population by improving the level of education and development of health services.

(2) The improvement of the inherited or biological quality of the population through scientific control of human breeding.

The Improvement in Quality of Existing Population

Some of the constructive suggestions are as follows:

(1) Education alone is not enough to bring about a rapid change; there must be opportunities to make use of education. Just as it is pointless to construct a steel mill unless there are factories to use the steel, iron and coal deposits to feed it, and skilled technicians to work it, so it is pointless to build a school system unless there are jobs for the people to go to, and capital equipment for them to work with. Only when there are improvements in other fields, investment in education will be fruitful.

Education can play an important role in economic development only when it is diffused throughout the community. Diffusion of education depends upon many factors like the presence of a continuum of communication among various socio-economic groups in the population. The presence or absence of mass communication media and adult education and extension programme, communications and transports facilities, the presence or non-economic motivation to acquire literacy and most important of all the existence of occupational opportunities. Unless we can enlist the sympathy and wholehearted co-operation of young educated people for taking up with an almost evangelical zeal the sacred task of teaching the three R's to their ignorant sisters and brothers in the villages, who look to them for help and guidance, no amount of appeals from our elders will enable us to eliminate mass illiteracy. Our Government, both at the Centre and the States, should encourage such services with monetary and other rewards and awards of special certificates of honour and merit.

Large investment in education is not likely to produce the type of manpower needed, if proper incentives are lacking, "Without a proper system of incentives for ability and performance the investment in education will be wasted from the standpoint of contributing to the country's progress." The obvious incentive is suitable wages and salaries. This will encourage people to study and acquire skills which will meet such serious shortages. Wages and salaries alone may not be sufficient incentives. The status of an occupation also is of equal importance. Thus without appropriate incentives, investment in education will contribute very little to accelerated development.

Since rapid industrialization is the prime objective of national planning in India a very high priority will have to be given to the teaching of science and technology. When a big programme of industrial and economic development is launched under the Five Year Plans, the demand for technical personnel for outstripped their supply. Only a phased programme of skill formation extending over several Five Year Plans can make India self-sufficient in the supply of technical personnel and thus remove the imbalance in the demand and supply of labour in various occupations. To achieve this goal, foreign assistance for the training of technical personnel, especially in newly established industries, is a *sine qua non*. Foreign collaboration is needed to train technical, managerial and administrative personnel at the top level. Moreover, there is also a great need for expanding technical colleges and schools at the lower level within the country, for the magnitude of demand of technical personnel at lower levels is enormous.

Adult illiteracy is very large in India. The average adult is not aware of the scientific and technical advances that have taken place in modern times. His knowledge of modern methods of production is woefully meagre. A programme of adult education aiming at increasing the efficiency and competence of rural people and stressing the importance of savings and limiting the size of the family, is of special urgency.

Every effort should be made to avoid waste of investment arising out of misallocated skills, educated unemployed and 'drop-outs'. No one denies that it costs money to train good professionals, scholars and scientists. And the country needs them. But if the country is to pay for their training, the country has a right to expect an adequate return.

Education must be related to economic growth, "Primary education should be designed to serve the needs of the countryside, secondary education should fulfil the dual role of preparing youngmen for vocations and university education should be available for all those who possess the fitness for it." Mere vocationalizing education would not provide the solution for the problem beseting us. For, though engineering and medical courses are vocational ones, we find many engineering and medical graduates unemployed. As Prof. K.V. Sivayya observed in his Presidential address at the 29th All India Commerce Conference held at Banaras Hindu University, Varanasi, "Vocational education is part of the wider problem of manpower planning. As it is, a large segment of higher education, including the sphere of commerce, is job oriented. But the output of the system is so large and haphazard that the economy is not able to absorb it." Hence respect for market forces is crucial and mushroom growth should be arrested to restore high academic standards. As such, all other reforms should coincide with selective admissions on the basis of a well conceived national manpower plan.

The policy conclusions that can be reached is this that the problem of reforming education in India is far from being merely a quantitative one of providing more schools; it is as much or more a problem of eliminating miseducation and large-scale waste of educational resources. What is needed is not simply an expansion of educational facilities and their re-apportioning to serve the various age groups, both sexes, and all social classes, but a more purposeful selection of the knowledge and skills taught, the attitudes implanted, and the learning methods employed.

The rapidly growing population has outstripped food supply, which is not only insufficient in quantity but also in quality. The diet of a vast majority of people in India is predominantly based on cereals and is deficient in such protective and energy-yielding foods as milk, fruits, leafy vegetables, potatoes, sweet potatoes, tapioca, eggs, fish, meat and processed protein-rich foods of vegetable origin. Thus looking at the behaviour of food output in relation to the demand for food may not seem very satisfactory in the context of the low levels of nutrition among the Indian masses.

It has been very strongly emphasized by the Public Health Commissioners for India that, "No preventive campaign against malaria, tuberculosis, or leprosy, no maternity relief or child welfare activities are likely to achieve any great success unless those responsible recognise the vital importance of the factor of defective nutrition and from the very start give it their most serious attention. Abundant supplies of quinine and the multiplication of TB hospitals, sanatoria, leprosy colonies, maternity and child-welfare centres are no doubt desirable, if not essential, but none of these go to the root of the matter. The first essentials for the prevention of diseases are a high standard of health, a better physique and a greater power of resistance to infection. This can only be attained if the food of the people is such as will give all the physiological and nutritional requirements of human frame." So says Dr. Megaw, "If the people of India were properly nourished, if they avoided living in the same room with persons who sneeze and cough, and if they took precautions to avoid swallowing infections with their food and drink, their average duration of life would be doubled and the quality improved.

Therefore, the first and the most essential fact is the improvement of the diet of the masses. For this purpose, the purchasing power of the masses should be increased but in the mean time such balance and nutritious diet should be evolved as is within the reach of the poorer and the middle-class people.

It is poverty of the people in India which accounts for both the insufficient quantity of food and its poor quality. The hunger can, of course, be eliminated only by raising the income levels of rural people and this is a function of economic growth and cannot be achieved in a year or two. In the meanwhile however, every effort needs be made to ensure that the real income of the low income groups does increase with an increase in national income. This can be done by assuring the supply of foodgrains to them at reasonable prices. In other words, the foodgrains distribution policy has to balance the needs of the rural sector and those of the urban sector.

The improvement of public hygiene and health condition is not merely a problem of acquiring the necessary financial material and human resources; it is also a problem of educating the masses. People must be taught to be more national and more concerned about their health. It is our impression that generally too little is done in regard to health education.

The new medical technology has been used to good advantage in recent decades to fight certain diseases that have been ravaging the country and they are largely responsible for the improvement in morbidity and mortality that has taken place. Further, progress will, however, increasingly depend on advances in popular cooperation, sanitation and hygiene, the provision of more and better hospitals, clinics, and health centres, and more and better trained medical personnel at all levels.

Limiting family size through voluntary adoption of family planning would greatly help to curb population growth. Without reduction in the rate of population increase, the cherished hopes of the people for better life are doomed to frustration. Even if bold efforts at mobilizing resources for intensifying both the production and productivity drive are made, the gaps between 'growth of population' and 'growth of investment' are not covered. An attempt to raise the standard of living and per capita income of the people of India without corresponding efforts to control their fertility would be a complete failure.

It should be noted that neither health nor education can be dealt with in isolation. To begin with, conditions of health and education are closely interdependent. On the one hand, a child's ability to take full advantage of the schooling provided him depends on his health, and an adult's ability to use the knowledge and skills he has a acquired depends on his mental and physical fitness. On the other hand, the extent to which health conditions can be improved depends on people's knowledge of and attitude towards hygiene. The improvement of public hygiene is largely a problem of educating the masses. People must be taught to be more rational and more concerned about their health. The relation of the health problem to education was recently stressed by a group of experts. Of the handicaps militating against rapid progress in health matters, perhaps the most outstanding is the very considerable amount of illiteracy which still prevails. The problem of literacy in our country is inextricably linked up with that of family planning, and unless the latter is solved in a satisfactory manner, the former is bound to remain insurmountable. Family planning and mass education especially in the rural areas must go *pari passu* and for the fulfilment of these two objectives, not only the spending of money by official and non-official organizations, for much of the money spent in these directions seems to have gone waste or at least failed to produce commensurate results, but the harnessing of youthful energies to the great task of making each rural family literate as well as conscious of the benefits of family planning and of the application of modern science and techniques to agriculture is absolutely necessary.

Science, health and education are closely interdependent, a proper co-ordination between them would be a desirable line of approach. Whatever strategy of investment in human resources is adopted, should be intimately related to the objectives of economic growth. There should be a proper synchronization of manpower availability with the growing needs of the economy. Human 'requirements and resources' must be properly balanced. Motivation for social and economic change should be inculcated inhuman beings. Investment in human resource would then prove fruitful and worthwhile.

II. The Improvement of the Inherited Quality of Population

The improvement in the biological quality of population be promoted to a greater extent through scientific control of human breeding.

Eugenists have advocated two ways of achieving improvement of mankind.

(*i*) Positive eugenics or constructive measures.

(*ii*) Negative eugenics or restrictive measures.

(*i*) *Positive eugenics.* It lays emphasis on the fact that genetically well endowed sub-population groups should be encouraged to reproduce. In other words, it refers to constructive measures which can improve the humanity by increasing the frequency of desirable traits.

This measure refers to the conservation of good germ plasm by dissemination among the people. Noble prize winner geneticist Muller has suggested that not only the number of children in a family of desirable traits should be increased, but that through artificial insemination outstanding men could serve as father and produce many more children with desirable traits. This method is adopted in animals and plants all over the world.

(1) Education.
(2) Prevention of germinal waste.
(3) Subsidizing the superior individuals.
(4) Regulation of immigration.
(5) Promoting genetic research.
(6) Enlarging individual opportunity.
(7) Improvement of environmental conditions.

Positive eugenics is based on the following assumptions. (1) Fertility among well endowed group is less. (2) Extraordinary intelligence is the result of family transition, not personal change.

Positive eugenics makes no distinction between biological and cultural progress.

(*ii*) *Negative eugenies*. This aspect lays stress on the necessity to prevent those sub-population with physical and mental deficiency from reproduction. Physically and mental handicaps include diseases like leporsey, yellow fever. venereal diseases like syphillis, gonerea. Besides physical and mental disorders includes, madness, deafness, muteness, paralysis, and mental deficiency. If is felt that such defects are transmitted to future generations. Therefore, a bar should be imposed on marriage and fertility in such cases.

In America many measures were taken to legalize the sterilization of persons showing one or more of the conditions-insanity, feeble mindedness, pauperism, epilepsy and criminality, inebriety, low mental and physical standard.

Davenport states that this is to "dry up the stream that feeds the torrent of defective and degenerate protoplasm." Negative eugenics also implies that the right of living for defective persons does not mean the right of reproduction. The betterment of human race may be brought about by restrictive measures such as:

(1) Discriminatory marriage laws.
(2) Sexual segregation of the defective.
(3) Developing eugenic sentiment through genetic advice.
(4) Defectives.
(5) Birth control.

(6) Genetic counselling.
(7) Control of immigration.

SELECT REFERENCES

1. Brierley, J.K.: *Biology and the Social Crisis*, Beinmann, London, 1967.
2. Davenport, Charles B.: *Heredity in Relation to Eugenics*, Henery Holt and Co., New York, 1911.
3. Dunn, L.C. and Dobzhansky: *Theodosius, Heredity Race and Saciety*, A Mentor Book, USA, 1952.
4. Denison, E.F.: "Education, Economic Growth and Gaps in Information", *Journal of Political Economy* (Supplement), Vol. 70, No. 5, Part 2, p. 127, Oct. 1962.
5. Harbison, F.H.: "Human Resources Development Planning in Modern Economies", *International Labour Review*, Vol. LXXXV, No. 5, May, 1962, p. 450.
6. Nalla Gounden, A.M.: *Education and Economic Development (1965)*, Unpublished Thesis
7. Panchmukhi, P.R.: "Educational Capital in India", *Indian Economic Journal*, Jan.-Mar., 1965.
8. Pandit, H.N.: "Cost and Financing of Education—Private and Social Participation", *Indian Educational Review*, July 1972, Vol. 7, No. 2.

EXAMINATION QUESTIONS

1. What does qualitative aspect of population mean? Write an essay on the qualitative aspect of India's population.
2. State the factors influencing qualitative aspects of population. Is it favourable in India?
3. What do you mean by life expectancy? Why is life expectancy low in India? Discuss the effect on the economy but an increase in average life expectancy.
4. Write a note on literacy in India. Do you agree with the view that human capital is the best form of capital which should be developed quickly?

31

Impact of Population Growth on Economic Development of India

Indisputably India is facing a population explosion of crisis dimensions. Every addition to the population, may be contended, is sure to result in untold tragedy to the existing population. Apart from causing enormous worry to planners, the population explosion washes away in its tidal wave whatever progress the plans have delivered to the country. "All efforts and sacrifices for ensuring planned development resulting in healthier, happier and wealthier society were being neutralised and would be further neutralised by the expanding ocean of population. It has caused other equally complex problems such as poverty, under-nourishment, unemployment and excessive fragmentation of land. The entire battle against poverty is thearted by the rapid increase in the population. S. Radhakrishnan aptly said, "The rapid increase of population in our country is one of the most disquieting problems with which we are faced. Despite the wide popularity and efficient organization of the Family Welfare Programme the population continues to grow at an alarming rate, thus striking at the very roots of planned development." It is precisely for this reason that an excessive growth of numbers has been viewed as an 'alarm signal' calling for an immediate corrective action. If population is not checked "our progress would be like writing on sand with the waves of population growth washing away all that we have written." Prime Minister of India Mrs. Indira Gandhi has rightly put it, "to plan when population growth's is unchecked is like building a house where the ground is constantly flooded."

In short, an excessively rapid growth of population in India imposes a heavy strain on our economy, it calls for large investments in new means of production and in social and economic infrastructures and tends to aggregate the existing scarcity of capital for development projects. The development process becomes all the more strenuous when a country's resources—natural and mineral—become increasingly scarce relative to the size of population and its consumption requirements.

The impact of rising population as a drag on economic resources in felt in a variety of ways.

I. Pressure of Population on Land

The continued increase of population, without any corresponding outlet in employment, has only intensified the pressure on the land. The density of population in India is already high and rising further as a consequence of the growing population. Density of population increased by about 31 per cent during 1971-81. Not only that the land-man ratio in general is bad, it is worse when we consider population in relation to agricultural land. This is but natural and the increase in population is much more than the increase in cultivated land.

No doubt in all these years some new land has been brought under cultivation. Nevertheless, per capita cultivable land has declined. Presently it is a little less than 0.3 hectare, as against 0.43 hectare in 1901. The pressure of population on land is reflected in steady increases in the number of agricultural labourers. As the family increases, sub-division of holdings leaves each member with a smaller holding which is much below the subsistence level and he accordingly turns into a labourer.

Like Malthus, protagonists of the theory that growing pressure of population on land would block development in this country, have little faith in the capabilities of mankind and the technological progress. Economists such as Kuznets. Spengler and Houthakker have convincingly dispelled all doubts about mankind's ability to cope with scarcity of natural resources. Specifically speaking about Indian situation, Subramaniam Swamy has crisply remarked, "In India. potential for enormous expansion in production exists. In agriculture, we are among the countries with the lowest yield per hectare. A ten-fold rise in yield per hectare would still not take us near the one attained in Japan. This implies that our lands could feed ten times more population at the level of technology presently available elsewhere in the world."

II. Population and Growth of National Income

During 1950-51 and 1978-79 (at 1970-71 prices) national income rose by 179 per cent but on account of a rise in population by about 78 per cent, per capita income rose by only 56 per cent. The annual average growth rate of national income works out to be 3.4 per cent (compound) and of per capita income to only 1.3 per cent. The cause of the big difference is the fast growing population of the country.

For some time past the country's population has been growing comparatively faster. As a result the per capita income rise has become still smaller in spite of the somewhat large rise in national income. What is the use of planning for economic development if per capita income of people does not increase?

III. Population and Food Supply

India's food crisis too is the result of population growth. In the process of economic development income elasticity of demand for food goes up. Heavy pressure of population on land has led to the low productivity of land and to make good the deficiency we are importing food from other countries which has been a constant strain on slender foreign exchange resource base. Our rising population has kept the per capita availability of cereals almost stable, imports of foodgrains have increased sizably, and productivity indices present a sad tale.

Between 1956 and 1982, net availability of foodgrains (cereals plus pulses) increased from 63 million tonnes to 117 million tonnes, signifying an increase of 81 per cent, but during the same period, population increased from 397 million to 704 million, i.e., by 74 per cent. Consequently, per capita domestic availability of foodgrains increased from 431 grams to 454 grams signifying a very small increase only. This very marginal increase in the per capita availability of foodgrain is to a great extent attributable to the rapid rise of population.

IV. Population and the Pressure on Social Overheads

Rising population increases the number of children and hence demands higher expenditure on education, medical care and housing etc. In other words, it requires colossal investment to build up a commensurate social overhead. India has to make up huge gaps of social amenities created by the swift swelling numbers. She is not able to feed, cloth and house to the existing population. But while she is attempting to do so more children are being born every year and the problem of feeding, clothing, housing, etc. becomes very difficult to solve.

Expenditure on education per pupil is estimated at Rs.98 per year. The population in the age group 5-14 being 25.6 million in 1971, increase in expenditure on education will work out to Rs.250 crores per year. Besides this, if we take into account the expenditure on university education that will have to be increased as a result of pressures of pupils from the secondary schools the total enhancement of expenditure on education will be still greater.

During the Fifth Plan Rs.30.67 billion were allocated for education, health and urban development. The Sixth Plan has made provision for Rs.25.24 billion for housing and urban development and Rs.39.22 billion for water supply and sanitation. This outlay does not include non-plan expenditure by the government and expenditure by the private sector. Expenditures on such a large scale impose a great burden on the limited resources of the country. If population growth could be reduced, some of these resources could then be diverted to other projects. Coale and Hoover have shown that if India could reduce its population growth by half between 1956 and 1981, the country could save as much as Rs.60-65 billion during the thirty-year period of 1956-86, from housing and education alone.

V. Population and Capital Formation

The most serious consequence of the fast growing population, from the point of view of economic growth, is that it reduces the country's capacity to save and invest. The increase in population invariably means a large proportion of children in the country. This implies a sudden rise in the consumption requirements of the country. We need more schools, more food especially baby food, more toys and so on. Thus a growing population results in a large scale and inevitable diversion of resources not only to consumption but to items of social overheads like education, health, housing, etc., so that the volume of capital formation suffers. It is known as a 'demographic investment' which would imply an investment sufficient to maintain a constant living standard of the growing population. We can distinguish it from the 'economic investment' which relates to investments for bringing about a rate of growth of national income higher than the rate of growth of population; so the per capita income rises and higher standard of living is attained. The pace and volume of the latter have naturally to be faster and greater than the simple 'demographic investment'. Thus if an economy is just embarking on 'demographic investment' it cannot achieve an improvement in living standards. How much a country actually should invest depends upon the rate of economic growth desired and its capital-output ratio. The rate of growth in per capita income can be obtained by subtracting the rate of population growth from the rate economic growth. The capital-output ratio indicates the amount of capital required to produce one unit of output. This ratio is about 3 : 1 for most developing countries such as India. This means that a country needs 3 units of capital to get one unit of output. The investment required to achieve a certain rate of economic growth can be estimated by multiplying the rate of the capital-output ratio. For instance, if a developing country with its population growing at 3 per cent a year desired its per capita income to increase at 2 per cent a year, it will have to grow at 5 per cent a year, and it will need to invest 15 per cent of its national income annual. On the other hand, at 1 per cent population growth a year, it will need to invest 9 per cent a year for getting the same increase in per capita income.

Table 1. Investment Required for Different Rates of Growth

Population Growth (%)	*Growth in per capita income*	*Growth of National Income* (%)	*Capital output ratio*	*Investment required* (%)
2 5	–	2.5	3 : 1	7.5
2.5	1.0	3.5	3 : 1	10.5
2.5	3.0	5.5	3 : 1	16.5
2.5	6.0	8.5	3 : 1	25.5
2.5	7.0	9.5	3 : 1	28.5

Using the above analysis, Table 1 gives the rates of investments which India must make to obtain different rates of growth in per capita income.

To keep the per capita income from falling India must invest 7.5 of its national income annually. The entire amount becomes demographic investment. An investment of 10.5 per cent will be required to obtain an annual increase of 1 per cent in per capita income. If India wants per capita income to rise at 3 per cent a year, so as to double it every 23 years, it must invest 16.9 per cent a year. And, if the aim is to double the per capita income in one decade, India must achieve a growth rate of 7 per cent a year in per capita income, and for that it must be prepared to invest as much as 28.5 a year.

Currently, savings as per cent of Gross Domestic Product at market prices are estimated to rise from 21.0 per cent in 1979-80 to 24.4 per cent in 1984-85. If these savings can actually be mobilised, India should be able to achieve an annual growth rate of nearly 6 per cent in per capita income by the end of the Sixth Plan.

VI. Population and the Burden of Unproductive Consumers

The existence of a relatively larger proportion of population in the lower age group and low life expectancy in India constitutes a drag on the productive effort of the economy. A high fertility rate in

India has saddled the economy with a large number of children who have to be fed without making any number of children who have to be fed without making any contribution to production. The greater the increase in population, the greater is the dependency ratio of non-workers to workers. The consumption requirements would naturally increase and they would affect the flow of savings adversely. Broadly speaking, children, old persons and a part of the population in the age group 15-59 which does not seek employment are included among non-productive consumers. The figures pertaining to these two categories as revealed in 1961 and 1981 censuses are given in Table 2. From the figures of working force given in Table 2, it is obvious that the ratio of working to non working population has deteriorated during 1961-81.

Table 2. Productive and Unproductive Consumers in India

	Total working population (productive consumers)		*Total non-working population (unproductive consumers)*	
	Million	*Per cent*	*Million*	*Per cent*
1961	183	43.0	256	57.0
1971	175	34.2	372	65.0
1981	220	37.6	464	62.4

A preponderance of children in the population is harmful for several reasons. Firstly it leads to a diversion of resources from capital formation to population maintenance. A high and increasing population of children increases the burden of the care of the young through nutrition, medical care, public health and education. But since mortality rate among children is higher, it means not only a diversion of resources but a wastage of resources as well. It has been estimated that the cost of rearing children who die before the age of 15 years is 22.5 per cent of national income in India as compared with 6.5 per cent in U.K. "Economically speaking, the underdeveloped countries suffer a considerable loss of investment-material and immaterial in up-bringing and educational efforts in respect of substantial number of young people who never reach the prime of life. Even if the amount invested per capita is below the equivalent of the cost of education, clothing and food customary in Western countries, the outlay lost in the aggregate is staggering. Besides the loss entailed by the economy on account of maintenance of children who die before reaching a productive age, the survivors' 'productive period' is shorter in poor countries than in the advanced countries.

It reduces the ratio of the labour force to the total population. Thus the bottom heavy age structure of population reinforced by a shorter life expectancy leaves an adverse impact on total and per capita output. Secondly, the dependence load represented by larger proportion of children is sought to be relieved by employing them at an early age and making them contribute what little they can to the family income. It amounts to a wasteful exploitation of children workers who may be forced into work at underdeveloped level of skill and stamina and may cause underemployment. The U.N. study on population makes the telling remark: "The position is rather than of peasants compelled by hunger to harvest their wheat every year before it has ripened."

According to the Sixth Plan, productive and non-productive consumers constituted 55 per cent and 45 per cent of India's population in 1980, and should change to 61 per cent 39 per cent, respectively by 1996. However, this optimism is not shared by all, at least for the immediate future. It is argued that with further decline in the death rate and with no change in the birth rate, the dependency ratio will rise. The problem in India is even worse because not all people in the working age group are gainfully employed. Consequently, the actual percentage of dependents is much higher.

In short, the low percentage of persons in the 'productive age' bracket in poor countries hampers their rate of economic growth. As argued by Coale and Hoover, "When mortality risks are reduced, high fertility becomes a burden by increasing the dependency ratio, by a diverting capital from uses that would raise per capita output, and in the long run by overwhelming any finite resources. Their studies of Mexico and India disclose that continued high fertility for the next three decades would result in very little addition to the labour force but would add appreciably to the population under 15 years of age. As the peace of economic development depends on conserving consumption to maximize investment, less of a given output can be devoted to investment when the ratio of dependents to producer is high. Thus high fertility promotes consumption at the expense of investment and economic growth. In contrast, with fewer dependents, more could be invested and more produced. Then, with fewer people to devide the output, investment could be maintained while adding to economic welfare and building up those forces that improve physical and psychological capacity to produce.

VII. Population and Unemployment

An important consequence of rapid rate of population growth

without a corresponding increase in the level of economic development is that there is a large-scale unemployment in urban areas and disguised unemployment in rural areas. For instance, the backlog of unemployment at the end of the Second Five Year Plan period was about 7 million and under employment was estimated to be 15-18 million. The committee of Experts on Unemployment (1973), estimated that the total number of unemployed in the country was 18.7 million in 1971. As revealed by the Sixth Plan (1980-85), the number of unemployed in 1980 was 20.7 million which represents 7.74 per cent of the total labour force. Massive additions to the labour force in rural areas is making unemployment problem more and more explosive and intractable. Prof. M.L. Dantwala had observed that the dark spot of the future is not food but the farmer himself. It is really a pity that the Government has not realised its full gravity and the revolutionary potential of the swelling ranks of the unemployed. The problem is becoming more and more acute and might reach explosive proportions in the not-too-distant future. It should be noted that unemployment will continue to increase if the population continues to grow at the alarming rate of 2.5 per cent per annum. The extremely accelerated rate of growth of population in India creates an urgent need for controlling it.

Conclusion

Thus, it becomes quite clear that India's galloping population is a cause of great alarm in the present phase of country's economic development. All developmental plans would flounder if we failed to stabilise the population or did not lower the rate of population growth substantially. The planners have given serious thought to the subject of checking the rise of population, but we see a growing spectacle of poverty, unemployment and low standard of living. The three good things-housing, food and clothing, that go to make a nation truly civilised are conspicuous by their absence in our country. Nothing to speak of the comforts and high standards, even the barest necessities of life are denied to millions of people in our country, despite vigorous planning. The population growth if allowed to go unchecked will bring in more hardships and misery. Hence, the paramount need for arresting the growth of population becomes compatible with our avowed aspiration of establishing a welfare state. Without reduction in the rate of population increase, the cherished hopes of the people for better life are doomed to frustration. Even if bold efforts at mobilising resources for intensifying both the production and productivity drive are made, the gaps between 'growth of population' and 'growth of investment' are not covered. According to Mrs. Sanjer, "An attempt to raise the standard of living and per capita income of the people of India without corresponding efforts to control their fertility would be complete failure." This calls for a suitable population policy to be pursued so as to unleash greater resources for real economic development, rather than fritter away the nation's wealth and output to feed the additional population.

By way of conclusion we can say that the 20-point programme launched by the Prime Minister Mrs. Indira Gandhi may be termed as 'The Path of Progress' for our vast republic. It is a programme for all round national development. Family Welfare is the main and concrete programme, virtually important to control the explosion of population, to eradicate chronic poverty, rampant unemployment prevalent in the country and thus pave the path of progress and prosperity. The programme must therefore be given special weightage for effective implementation.

SELECT REFERENCES

1. Agrawal, S.N.: *India's Population*, p. 98.
2. Bright Singh, D.: *Economic of Development*, Asia Publishing House, Bombay, 1962.
3. Coale, A.J. and Hoover, E.M.: *Population Growth and Economic Development in Low Income Countries*, Princeton, 1958, p. 232.
4. Gunnar, Myrdal: *Asian Drama*, Vol. II, Chapter 28, Part 6, pp. 1464-70.
5. Jain, S.P.: *Indian Population and Development*, New Delhi, NCERT, 1977, p. 180.
6. Sukhatme, P.V.: *Feeding India's Growing Millions*, London, A.P.H., 1965.

EXAMINATION QUESTIONS

1. Write an essay on the impact of population growth on economic development of India.
2. Write short notes:
   (*a*) Population and food supply;
   (*b*) Population and capital formation;
   (*c*) Population and unproductive consumer;
   (*d*) Population and unemployment.

32

Sources of Demographic Data in India

The main sources of demo graphic data in India are (*a*) Population Censuses, (*b*) Civil registration; (*c*) Sample Surveys; and (*d*) Family Welfare service statistics.

The coverage of population census is very comprehensive providing data on size, structure and growth of population. It does not, however, provide information on the annual growth of population and related variables. Information on fertility has been collected by including additional questions in the census. Analytical methods have been developed to find out decadal variation in vital rates. Fertility and mortality are worked out by reference to mid point of the decade. All these point towards the need for obtaining data through other sources for ascertaining short period changes in population growth, for projection as also for assessing the impact of family welfare.

In India the inhibiting factors like illiteracy, rural nature of population, inadequate registration etc. have handicapped the collection of vital statistics by traditional method. The registration data are deficient in coverage, content and completeness.

The National Sample Surveys (NSS) has provided basic data on the demographic situation. This is of retrospective nature which suffers from racial lapse.

Family Welfare statistics provide a cross sectional picture of demographic variables. All these methods are discussed below:

(A) Population and Housing Censuses

(*i*) History of Censuses

Though census was first held in India in 1872, it was spread over the period of 1867 to 1872. The first comprehensive census was held in 1881 throughout the country. The Canvasser method was adopted in all the censuses under which the enumerators elicited information from the heads of households.

House listing was not systematically done till 1961. In the census of 1961 a standard schedule was evolved to list the houses throughout the country.

The Census of India Act 1948 empowered the Central Government to appoint Census Commissioner and also to notify the data of census. Besides, it guarantees secrecy of information and also provides penalty for false information.

From 1951 onwards the Department of Registrar General of Census was established as a permanent and continuing organisation with a nucleus of permanent staff both at the centre and in the states. This department conducts population census, registration of births and deaths and undertakes surveys.

From 1961 onwards censuses have undergone radical changes in regard to scope, coverage and presentation.

(*ii*) **Coverage**

(*a*) *Population Census*

The items included in the censuses from 1872 to 1981 are given in Table 1.

In all censuses details of name, sex, age and religion were collected on a regular basis. Information on relation to head of household was introduced in 1951 while on marital status it was collected from 1881. Information on caste or class was discontinued from 1951 and later replaced by scheduled castes and tribes. The question of nationality was excluded in 1971. Information on mother tongue and other languages in common use were also collected. Information on infirmities was collected till 1931 and discontinued up to 1971. In the 1981 census information on physically handicapped was collected. In the 1971 census age at marriage was included in the census. Information on age at marriage, survival of children and number of children born alive by sex was collected in 1981 census. Information on literacy was collected regularly in all censuses from 1872 to 1981. To study migration, a question on place of birth was included from 1881. It was enlarged further in 1971 by including place of last residence, rural or urban, district, state, etc. In 1981 census information on reason for migration was obtained.

Information on economic activity was collected from 1872 onwards. Information on subsidiary occupation was collected from 1901 census. After 1951 the Income concept was dropped. In 1961 economie data was collected on work concept. In 1981 questions were formulated to find out whether a person has worked for more than six months or less than six months.

(*b*) *Housing Census*

Housing Census covered (*a*) the purpose for which the house is used, (*b*) if workshop or factory particulars of product,

Table 1. Items included in the censuses of India, 1872-1981

Items included in census schedule	*1872*	*1881*	*1891*	*1901*	*1911*	*1921*	*1931*	*1941*	*1951*	*1961*	*1971*	*1981*
I. Demographic and social characteristics												
Name	x	x	x	x	x	x	x	x	x	x	x	x
Relationship to head	—	—	—	—	—	—	—	—	x	x	x	x
Sex	x	x	x	x	x	x	x	x	x	x	x	x
Age	x	x	x	x	x	x	x	x	x	x	x	x
Marital status	—	x	x	x	x	x	x	x	x	x	x	x
Religion	x	x	x	x	x	x	x	x	x	x	x	x
Caste or class	x	x	x	x	x	x	x	x	a	a	a	a
Nationality	x	—	—	—	—	—	—	—	x	x	—	—
Mother tongue	—	—	—	—	—	—	x	x	x	x	x	x
Parent tongue	—	—	x	—	—	—	—	—	—	—	—	—
Language ordinarily used	—	—	—	x	—	x	—	—	—	—	—	—
Language ordinarily spoken in the household	—	—	—	—	x	—	—	—	—	—	—	—
Other languages	—	—	—	—	—	—	x	x	x	x	x	x
Infirmities	x	x	x	x	x	x	x	—	—	—	—	—
Number of children born to a married woman and children surviving	—	—	—	—	—	—	—	x	—	—	—	—
Age at birth of first child	—	—	—	—	—	—	—	x	—	—	—	—
For currently married women: age at marriage	—	—	—	—	—	—	—	—	—	—	x	—
any children in the last one year	—	—	—	—	—	—	—	—	—	—	x	—
For all ever-married women: age at marriage	—	—	—	—	—	—	—	—	—	—	—	x

number of children surviving	—	—	—	—	—	—	—	—	—	—	—	x
number of children ever born	—	—	—	—	—	—	—	—	—	—	—	x
II. Educational characteristics												
Able to read and write	x	—	—	—	—	—	—	x	—	—	—	—
Youths upto age 20 attending school/ college under private tuition	x	—	—	—	—	—	—	—	—	—	—	—
Under instruction	—	x	—	—	—	—	—	—	—	—	—	—
Not under instruction but able to read and write	—	x	—	—	—	—	—	—	—	—	—	—
Not under instruction and not able to read and write	—	x	—	—	—	—	—	—	—	—	—	—
Learning, knowing, illiterate	—	—	x	—	—	—	—	—	—	—	—	—
Literate or illiterate	—	—	—	x	x	x	x	—	x	x	x	x
Foreign language known	—	—	x	—	—	—	—	—	—	—	—	—
Know or does not know English	—	—	—	x	—	—	—	—	—	—	—	—
Whether literate in English	—	—	—	—	x	x	x	—	—	—	—	—
Educational level	—	—	—	—	—	—	—	x	x	x	x	x
Attending school/college	—	—	—	—	—	—	—	—	—	—	—	x
III. Migration characteristics												
Place of birth	—	x	x	x	x	x	x	x	x	x	x	x
Born rural/urban	—	—	—	—	—	—	—	—	—	x	x	x
Duration of residence	—	—	—	—	—	—	—	—	—	x	x	x
Place of last residence	—	—	—	—	—	—	—	—	—	—	x	x
Last residence rural/urban	—	—	—	—	—	—	—	—	—	—	x	x
Reasons for migration from place of last residence	—	—	—	—	—	—	—	—	—	—	—	x

Table 1 (*Continued*)

Items included in census schedule	*1872*	*1881*	*1891*	*1901*	*1911*	*1921*	*1931*	*1941*	*1951*	*1961*	*1971*	*1981*
						IV. Economic characteristics						
Principal occupation	x	x	x	x	x	x	x	x	x	x	x	x
Subsidiary occupation	—	—	—	x	x	x	x	x	x	x	x	x
Dependency (means of subsistence of earner/worker on whom dependent)	—	—	x	x	x	x	x	x	x	—	—	—
Industry	—	—	—	—	—	—	x	x	x	x	x	x
Class of worker	—	—	—	—	—	—	—	—	x	x	x	x
Non-worker	—	—	—	—	—	—	—	—	—	x	x	x
Seeking cr available for woik	—	—	—	—	—	—	—	—	—	—	—	x
						V. Other characteristics						
Are you in employment?												(1941 census)
Are you in search of employment? If yes, how long you have been in search of it												(1941 census)
Indigenous persons 'Assam, Manipur and Tripura'												(1951 census)
Are you an indigenous person of Assam?												
If so, state in the nearest *bigha*												
The land you own												
The land you have rented in cash or in kind from others												
Fertility (Bihar, Madhya Pradesh, Travancore-Cochin)												(1951 census)
Unemployment (Bombay, Saurashtra and Kutch, Vindhya Pradesh, Mysore, Punjab, PEPSU, Bilaspur, Delhi, Himachal Pradesh, Hyderabad)												(1951 census)
Area of land owned and cultivated (Orissa, West Bengal, Sikkim)												(1951 census)
Infirmities (Rajasthan, Ajmer)												(1951 census)

Note : [a]Scheduled castes and scheduled tribes only.

repair, number of workers, kind of fuel, whether machinery is used etc. (*c*) material of wall and roof (*d*) number of rooms occupied by household (*e*) whether lives in own or rented house (*f*) persons residing in household.

In 1961 the household schedule was introduced which collected information on economic activities of the households.

The district census handbook was introduced in 1951, which collected information of primary data down to village level. It covered items on historical background, physical features, agriculture, industry, education, vital statistics, banking etc.

Ancillary information was collected from 1961 ownards on village surveys, urban studies, ethnography and scientific personnel. Social economic changes due to planning, demographic, social, economic and ethnic behaviour of the villages have been depicted through village studies.

In 1961 a study was undertaken to ascertain the pattern of migration in eight cities of India with a population of 1 million or more. In 1971 census, special urban studies were conducted to collect information on physical, social and economic conditions of urban residents.

In 1961 an attempt was made to prepare ethnographic notes on scheduled castes, scheduled tribes, nomadic tribes etc. It was continued in 1971 census.

A study of scientific and technical personnel was undertaken in 1961 and continued in 1971 census also. The information included distribution of scientific and technical personnel by each branch type of activity, age, marital status, nature and sector of employment, total monthly income, tenure of employment and period of employment.

(*iii*) Tabulation

Prior to 1941 the "method of attraction by stokes or ticks" was used for tabulation purposes. From 1941 onwards processing was done by manually sorting out individual slips. Partial mechanisation of data was introduced in 1961 census. The use of electronic computer was used in the tabulation of data in 1971. The main tabulation avail in censuses is summarised in Table 2.

(B) Civil Registration

(*i*) History of Registration system:—

Registration of vital elements within an administrative machinery

Table 2. List of main census tabulations; 1872-1981

Items	1872	1881	1891	1901	1911	1921	1931	1941	1951	1961	1971	1981
1	2	3	4	5	6	7	8	9	10	11	12	13
Total Population												
Population (total)	×	×	×	×	×	×	×	×	×	×	×	×
Population by sex	×	×	×	×	×	×	×	×	×	×	×	×
Age												
Population by age groups and sex	×	×	×	×	×	×	×	×	×	×	×	×
Population by single year age and by sex	—	—	—	—	—	—	—	—	—	—	—	—
Marital status												
Population by marital status and by sex	—	×	×	×	×	×	×	×	×	×	×	×
Population by marital status, age groups and sex	—	×	×	×	×	×	×	×	×	×	×	×
Religion												
Population by religion and sex	×	×	×	×	×	×	×	—	×	×	×	×
Population by religion, age groups and sex	×	×	×	×	×	×	×	—	—	—	—	—
Literacy												
Population by literacy and sex	×	×	×	×	×	×	×	×	×	×	×	×
Population by literacy, age groups and sex	×	—	×	—	—	×	×	×	×	×	×	×
Education												
Population by educational level and sex	—	—	—	—	—	—	—	—	×	×	×	×
Population by educational level, age groups and sex	—	—	—	—	—	—	—	—	×	×	×	×

Attending school/college by completed level of education, age and sex	—	—	—	—	—	—	—	—	—	—	—	×
Nationality												
Population by nationality	×	—	—	—	—	—	—	—	×	×	—	—
Language												
Population by language spoken and by sex	—	×	×	×	×	×	×	—	×	×	×	×
Birth Place and Migration												
Population by birth place and sex	—	×	×	×	×	×	×	×	×	×	×	×
Migrants by place of last residence and duration of residence in the place of enumeration	—	—	—	—	—	—	—	—	—	×	×	×
Migrants by duration of residence, age groups and educational level	—	—	—	—	—	—	—	—	—	×	×	×
Migrants by industrial categories of workers and non-workers	—	—	—	—	—	—	—	—	—	×	×	—
Migrants by place of last residence, age groups, duration of residence and marital status	—	—	—	—	—	—	—	—	—	—	×	×
Migrants by place of last residence, duration of residence and reasons for migration	—	—	—	—	—	—	—	—	—	—	—	×

1	2	3	4	5	6	7	8	9	10	11	12	13
Occupation												
Workers by occupation	×	×	×	×	×	×	×	×	×	×	×	×
Workers by occupation and sex	—	×	×	×	×	×	×	×	×	×	×	×
Workers by occupation and age groups	—	—	×	—	—	—	—	—	—	×	×	×
Workers by occupation, level of education	—	—	—	—	—	—	—	—	—	×	×	×
Workers by occupation and religion	—	—	—	—	×	×	—	—	—	—	—	—
Workers by occupation and castes	—	—	—	×	×	×	×	—	—	—	—	×
Industry												
Workers by industrial categories and by sex	—	—	—	—	—	—	—	×	×	×	×	×
Workers by industrial categories by age groups, sex	—	—	—	—	—	—	—	—	—	×	×	×
Workers by industrial categories by sex and educational level	—	—	—	—	—	—	—	—	—	×	×	×
Non-workers												
Non-workers by sex, age groups and type of activity	—	—	—	—	—	—	—	—	—	×	×	×
Non-workers by sex and educational level	—	—	—	—	—	—	—	—	—	×	×	×
Persons seeking/available for work by age/sex and educational level	—	—	—	—	—	—	—	—	—	—	—	×

Housing and Establishment												
Census houses by type of wall and roof	—	—	—	—	—	—	—	—	—	×	×	—
Households by type of wall and roof or floor of the census house occupied	—	—	—	—	—	—	—	—	—	—	—	×
Census houses and the use to which they are put	—	—	—	—	—	—	—	—	—	×	×	×
Households by number of members and number of rooms occupied	—	—	—	—	—	—	—	—	—	×	×	×
Tenure status	—	—	—	—	—	—	—	—	—	×	×	×
Households by availability of electricity, toilet facilities and source of drinking water	—	—	—	—	—	—	—	—	—	—	—	×
Establishment by broad types	—	—	—	—	—	—	—	—	—	×	×	—
Establishments by size of employment	—	—	—	—	—	—	—	—	—	×	×	—

was in vogue in India since hundred years past. In the beginning only deaths were registered and the quality of statistics collected was highly deficient and incomplete. In 1868 the Govt. of India directed the Sanitary Commissioners to prepare a series of forms to collect vital statistics. Practically no attention was given to births. The Indian famine commission of 1880 laid emphasis on collecting vital statistics, throughout the country. The Commission recommended compulsory registration of births and deaths, monthly publication of vital statistics and analysis of the data collected.

In the year 1886, the Government of India enacted the births, deaths and marriage registrations Act, for the purpose of voluntary registration of births, deaths and marriage throughout the country. However, the Act remained a dead letter.

Several commissions and committees were set up for improving vital statistics like Bhore Committee in 1946, for proper collection of vital statistics. To give effect to this the collection of vital statistics was transferred to the Registrar General of India in 1960. In 1961 a committee of representatives of states and centre recommended (*a*) the enactment of a central law on vital statisties (*b*) tabulation of state headquarters and (*c*) uniform forms and registers. The third five year plan incorporated proposals for improving vital statistics at all levels. It was also proposed to strengthen the machinery for collecting vital statistics in State headquarters in municipalities and district registrar's offices and also for setting up mechanical tabulation units at state headquarters.

In 1969 a Central Registration of Births and Deaths Act was passed which provides for compulsory registration and issue of certificates. It also provides for obtaining certificates as to the cause of death and also gives statutory authority to the Registrar General to coordinate the civil registration work through out the country. The Act has now been enforced in practically all states and union territories.

(*ii*) System of Registration

The registration and compilation work of vital statistics are manned by staff deputed from various departments. In the rural areas the registration system falls into four categories, viz., Panchayats, Police, Health and Revenue. In the urban areas the municipal authorities are responsible for registration of vital events. The health officer is often the registrar in urban areas. In a few instances the executive officer is the registrar. Table 3 gives the registration machinery at the peripheral, district and headquarter level.

Table 3. Details of registration machinery

State/Union Territory	*Local registrar (rural areas)*	*District registrar*	*Chief registrar*
(1)	(2)	(3)	(4)
Panchayat agency			
Bihar	Panchayat Sewak	District Statistical Officer	Director of Statistics and Evaluation
Himachal Pradesh	Panchayat Secretary	Chief Medical Officer	Director of Health Services
Kerala	Executive Officer of Panchayats	District Panchayat Officer	Director of Panchayats
Maharashtra	Secretary of Village Panchayat	District Health Officer	Director of Health Services
Rajasthan	Village Level Workers/ Panchayat Sachiv	District Statistician/ Commissioner of Municipality	Director of Economics and Statistics
Uttar Pradesh	Gaon Sabha Pradhan	Deputy Chief Health Officer/ District Panchayat Raj Officer	Director of Medical and Health Services and Family Planning
Delhi	Panchayat Secretary		Director of Health Services
Goa, Daman and Diu	Panchayat Secretary	Collector/Civil Administrator	Director of Economics and Statistics and Evaluation
Police Agency			
Assam	Panchayat or Community Development Secretary	Civil Surgeon	Director of Health
Haryana	Thana Officer	Chief/Deputy Chief Medical Officer	Director of Health Services
Jammu and Kashmir	Thana Officer	District Medical Officer/ District Statistical Officer	Director of Health Services

(1)	(2)	(3)	(4)
Madhya Pradesh	Thana Officer	District Statistical Officer	Director of Economics and Statistics
Manipur	Thana Officer	District Medical Officer	Director of Health and Family Planning
Orissa	Thana Officer	Chief District Medical Officer	Director of Health and Family Planning
Punjab	Thana Officer	Civil Surgeon	Director of Health and Family Planning
Chandigarh	Thana Officer	Medical Officer of Health	Director of Health Services-cum-Deputy Secretary
Dadra and Nagar Haveli	Patel/Talati	Mamlatdar-cum-Survey and Settlement Officer	Secretary to Administrator
Health agency			
Tripura	Tehsildar/Medical Officer-in-Charge, Primary Health Centre	District Magistrate Collector	Director of Health Services
West Bengal	Sanitary Inspector/Medical Officer-in-Charge, Primary Health Centre	District Magistrate/Deputy Commissioner	Director of Health Services
Lakshadweep	Health Inspector	Deputy Director of Medical and Health Services	Director of Medical and Health Services
Revenue agency			
Tamil Nadu	Village Headman	Collector/District Revenue Officer	Additional Director of Health Services and Family Planning

Andaman and Nicobar	Tehsildar/Assistant Commissioner/	Deputy Commissioner	Director of Medical and Health Services
Arunachal Pradesh	Extra Assistant Commissioner/Circle Officer	Deputy Commissioner/ Additional Deputy Commissioner	Director of Health Services
Others			
Andhra Pradesh	Executive Officer of Panchayat/Village Munsif/Police Patel/ Mutta/Clerk/Patwari	District Medical and Health Services	Director of Public Health Family Planning and Drugs
Gujarat	Talati-cum-Panchayat Secretary/Forest Ranger	District Health Officer	Director of Health Services
Kernataka	Police Patel/Patel	Deputy Commissioner	Director of Economics and Statistics
Meghalaya	Block Development Officer	Civil Surgeon	Director of Health Services
Nagaland	Teacher-in-Charge of Government Lower Primary School	District Statistical Officer	Director of Economics and Statistics

Note: Wherever a thana officer (police) is the registrar, collection of information of vital events in the village is done by the chowkidars of the respective villages and periodically reported to the Thana officer. This system appears to be working well in Haryana and Punjab, but not so in Orissa, Jammu and Kashmir and Madhya Pradesh; perhaps the size of the thana is big. In Madhya Pradesh, the kotwar is the reporting official. He is a revenue man but is expected to report vital events to the thana officer. This apparently affects efficiency.

In Assam, Jammu and Kashmir, Maharashtra and Tamil Nadu, a formal notification of appointment of senior officials is awaited.

(*iii*) Coverage of Items

The items of information collected after revision of various forms under the registration of births and deaths Act 1969 are given below:

(*a*) *Births/Still Births*

(*i*) Characteristics of the event

- Date of registration
- Date of birth
- Sex
- Place of birth
- Order of live births
- Type of attention at delivery

(*ii*) Characteristics of mother and father

- Literacy
- Occupation
- Nationality
- Religion
- Age of mother at confinement

(*b*) *Deaths*

(*i*) Characteristics of the deceased

- Date of registration
- Date of death
- Place of death
- Cause of death
- Type of medical attention received

(*ii*) Characteristics of the deceased

- Age
- Sex
- Marital status
- Religion
- Nationality
- Occupation.

(*iv*) Tabulation

Before the 1969 Act data were compiled at the block and district level and sent to the state level head office. After the revision a tabulation plan was prescribed for compiling the data. The states bring out reports of the tabulated data. Besides, the Registrar General office brings out weekly and annual reports based on data received from the states.

(C) Sample Surveys

In India the following sampling techniques have been tried and tested: (1) Single and multiple round retrospective surveys, and (2) Dual record system.

In single round retrospective surveys vital statistics of sample households are collected generally for 12 months before the enquiry. This system suffers from the limitation that respondents cannot correctly recall the events happened in the household during the reference period. Often the results are underestimates. The errors over time and space are not of a consistent pattern and hence it is difficult to obtain valid estimates of births and deaths.

In the multi-round survey periodic observations on the same set of sample areas are made by repeated interview surveys and collecting other information. Experience suggests that multi-round surveys yield better results than single round surveys.

In the dual record system results obtained from two independent record of vital events are matched. The unmatched and partially matched events are reversified to get an unduplicated count of vital events. This method eliminates errors of duplication. It can lead to a qualitative assessment of the sources of difference in the two sets of records The system is self-evaluating as the event missed by either sub-system is detected while matching operation. It can be applied to an extensive list of topics.

(1) National Sample Survey

Information on demographic characteristics of Indian population was first collected in 1951 by the National Sample Survey (NSS) through single record round retrospective survey. During 1958-68 population surveys became an integral part of NSS rounds. However, they were discontinued afterwards. A comprehensive survey was conducted in the 28th round of NSS (1973-74) on population, family planning and morbidity which was repeated on a quinquinneal basis (5 years). NSS surveys provided data on size, composition and structure of population, birth-deaths, migrations, and marriages. The results of the various rounds have been published in various NSS reports as given in Table 4.

(2) Sample Registration System (SRS)

SRS provides information on fertility and mortality. Sample registration is an experiment in the dual reporting system with the object of providing reliable rates of vital statistics at the state and national level. The field investigation under SRS consists of continuous enumerations of births and deaths with the help of a local enumerator followed by an independent six monthly retrospective survey by a full time supervisor. The data from the two methods are

Table 4. Demographic data collected through NSS

Round	Survey period	*Type of data collected* Births-deaths	Historical fertility	Marriage	Migration	Morbidity
2	April-June 1951	—	×	—	—	—
4	April-September 1952	—	×	—	—	—
5	December 1952-February 1953	—	×	—	—	—
6	May-August 1953	—	×	—	—	—
7	October 1953-March 1955	×	—	×	—	×
8	July 1954-March 1955	×	—	×	—	×
9	May-November 1955	×	×	×	×	×
10	December 1955-May 1956	×	—	×	—	×
11	August 1956-January 1957	×	—	×	—	×
12	February-June 1957	×	—	×	×	×
13	September 1957-May 1958	×	—	×	×	×
14	July 1958-June 1959	×	—	—	×	—
15	July 1959-June 1960	×	—	—	×	—
16	July 1960-June 1961	×	—	—	—	—
17	September 1961-August 1962	×	×	—	—	×
18	February 1963-June 1964	×	×	—	×	—
19	July 1965-June 1966	×	×	—	×	—
20	July 1965-June 1966	×	—	—	×	—
21	July 1966-June 1967	×	—	—	×	—
22	July 1967-June 1968	×	—	—	×	—
23	July 1968-June 1969	×	—	—	×	—
24	October 1973-June 1974	×	×	—	×	×

matched. The unmatched and partially matched events are revesified to get unduplicated count of vital statistics. During the half yearly survey the population figures are updated.

(*i*) **Coverage of items**

Information collected under SRS covers the following :

(*a*) *Births*

(*i*) Particulars of the child

Place of birth
Date of birth
Live birth/still birth
Single/multiple births
Sex

(*ii*) Particulars of the mother

Mother's relation to head
Residential status
Present age
Religion

(*iii*) Other particulars

Type of attention at delivery
First information source

(*b*) *Deaths*

(*i*) Particulars of the deceased

Place of death
Date of death
Relationship to head
Residential status
Sex
Age at death
Marital status
Religion

(*ii*) Other particulars

Medical attention before death
First information source

(*ii*) **Sample Design and Sample Size**

In the rural areas the single stage stratified simple random sampling method with the village as the primary sampling unit was adopted with 1961 as the census frame. In the urban areas the design consisted of two stage stratified random sampling. The first stage units were the towns and the second stage units were census blocks. For rural areas the number of sample units was 150 for each state and in the urban areas it was 60-100 blocks which gives a total number of 3722 sample units. Out of this the urban units numbered 1300 covering total population of 3.6 million. Recently 1700 more sample units drawn from 1971 sample frame have been added to the existing units for improving the precision. The total number of sampling units now is 5422 covering a population of over 5 million.

(*iii*) Tabulation and Analysis

The vital statistics are regularly published. Fertility and mortality are brought out separately in the form of reports.

(*iv*) Family Welfare Service Statistics

Regular reporting of service statistics has been started from 1966-67 after the creation of the Ministry of Family Welfare. One of the sources of data is target couple registers which contains information on age of husband and wife, number of living children by age and sex, religion etc.

Besides, there are case cards for acceptors of IUD and sterilisation. The socio-economic characteristics of acceptors like religion, age of husband and wife, educational standard, number of living children and children born alive, etc. are collected. The data are published in the year book Family Welfare Programmes in India. It provides performance statistics on couples protected through different methods, number of births averted, characteristics of acceptors etc.

The Operations Research Group (ORG), Baroda conducted a survey on knowledge and practice of family planning methods on an all India basis in 1971. It covered about 25000 currently married individuals spread over 254 urban blocks and 704 rural centres all over India.

The data presented include

(a) Socio-economic and demographic characteristics of the couple;

(b) Attitudes towards family planning;

(c) Inter-personal communications;

(d) Awareness and knowledge of birth control methods;

(e) Awareness, knowledge and attitude towards Nirodh;

(f) Practice of family planning;

(g) Factors exhibiting association with practice.

The results are published in 'Family Planning Practices in India.'

33

Population Policy in India

After an analysis of the different aspects of India's population problem in the preceding chapters, there is now little to contest that India is on the verge of population explosion. Confronted with a burst of population growth, even the best laid plans for economic development are not able to achieve any satisfactory result. In order to stem the "explosion" of the human resource, a well thought out approach is called for. Two special reasons may be given on this score. First, the economic effects of alternative levels of fertility are not only very considerable, but also cumulative and progressive. Particularly as policy measures can only gradually affect fertility rates, it is imperative that they be initiated as early as possible. Secondly, with prevailing fertility rates, there is an extraordinarily large proportion of young people in the country, which implies that the breaking distance is large. Hence there is an urgent need for framing a positive population policy, aiming at a judicious control of the birth rate.

It is, indeed, surprising that in spite of the urgency of the problem, the Government of India was for a long time quite indifferent to it. The Population Policy of the Government of India passed through the following four phases:

1. The Period of Indifference
2. The Period of Neutrality (1947-1951)
3. The Period of Experimentation (1951-1961)
4. The beginning of the Policy of Control (from 1961 onwards).

The indifference and neutrality phases of the policy control were the direct outcome of the view that there is no harm if the country's population was rising. Gandhi's strong views that all means of fertility control other than avoidance of sexual intercourse, were immoral, combined with his economic views, led him early to deny that India was "overpopulated". The population problem in India was recognised as early as in 1951 and the family planning programme was started on an experimental basis in the fifties with a clinical approach to provide services to those who were so motivated. The infrastructure was created in 1961-62 by adopting the extensive approach for motivating the couples and making family planning services available near the homes of the people. But the programme really gained momentum in 1966 and today, it stands as a philosophy in action. The programme in its widest connotation includes family limitation and reasonable spacing of children, treatment of sterility, marriage counselling and guidance, family life education and others which contribute to the overall welfare of the family In short, family planning is an instrument of social transformation; it aims at creating better parents, healthier children, happier homes; it seeks to inject social responsibility into married life.

The scope of family planning is best explained by the following statement by Lydia Rapport, "One key concept is the regulation of fertility by preventing unwanted pregnancies, by spacing the number of children desired. This gives families a control over their reproductive functions and enlarges their capacity for choice and self-direction in individual and private family goals . . . . Family planning is also embedded in the Health Matrix and seeks to make an impact on foetal wastage, prematurity, maternal mortality and morbidity and child health. It is also rooted in concepts of social and psychologic well-being in its emphasis on strengthening the quality and stability of family life; thus it becomes a measure for positive mental health. Family planning objectives include not only conception control but also help with problems of infertility, although this dimension is underplayed in actual practice. Thus family planning deals with the promotion, postponement and prevention of conception.

History of Family Planning in India

The family planning movement in India from its very beginning in 1916 till the Government launched an official programme in 1951, was the result of the efforts of a number of social reformers, thinkers and voluntary organizations. In 1916 Shri Pyare Krishen Wattal published his book, "The Population Problem in India", advocating family limitation. Prof. Raghunath Dhondo Karve was the first to open a family planning clinic in India in 1925. The Neo-Malthusian League was formed in Madras a few years later. On June 11, 1930 the Mysore Government issued an order for setting up birth control clinics in the Victoria and Vani Vilas Hospitals in Bangalore and in the Krishnarajendra Hospital in Mysore. In 1932, the Senate of the Madras University accepted the proposals to give instructions on contraceptives and in the following year, the Government of Madras agreed to open Birth Control Clinics in the Presidency. In the same year, the All India Women's Conference at Lucknow passed a resolution recommending that "men and women should be instructed in methods of birth control in recognised clinics." The National Planning Committee, under the Chairmanship of Shri Jawaharlal Nehru, set up by the Indian National Congress in 1935, strongly supported family planning. At the invitation of the All India Women's Conference, Mrs. Margaret Sangar visited India during 1935-36 and stimulated interest in the country in family planning.

Dr. A.P. Pillai, a vigorous advocate for family planning conducted training courses in 1935. In 1939 the "Birth Control World-Wide" in Uttar Pradesh and Matru Sewa Sangh, Ujjain, in Madhya Pradesh opened birth control clinics. In 1940 Shri P.N. Sapru successfully moved a resolution in the Council of States for the establishment of birth control clinics. The Health Survey and Development Committee under the Chairmanship of Shri Joseph Bhore appointed in 1943 by the Government of India recommended provisions of birth control service, but mainly for health reasons.

The general governmental attitude towards birth control is reflected in the final report of the Famine Enquiry Commission (The Woodhead Commission) set up by the Government of India in 1943. The Commission stated that: "At the present time a deliberate state policy with the objective of encouraging the practice of birth control among the mass of population is impracticable. A fall in birth-rate will tend to follow rather than precede economic betterment. This was the situation just before the country became independent."

After independences, when the Congress Party came into power the vital role of population control in the overall planned development of national economy was fully recognised by the Government. In 1949, the Family Planning Association of India was formed in Bombay under the Presidentship of Shrimati Dhanvanthi Ram Rau and since its inception the Association has worked ceaselessly for greater family planning acceptance.

It is encouraging to note that the Planning Commission in India itself recognised in the beginning that a rapidly growing population can be a menace to economic development and advocated the need for family planning. The Government of India took a courageous stand on this question and displayed great foresight by adopting family planning as an integral part of its overall national development programme. In fact, India is credited to be the first country in the world to adopt family planning as a state policy.

FAMILY WELFARE (PLANNING) IN FIVE YEAR PLANS

First Plan (1951-56) and Family Planning

The first indication of the official attitude toward the population problem was contained in the First Plan which, *inter alia* stated that "there is no doubt that given a situation in which shortage of capital equipment rather than of labour is the main limiting factor in development, a rapidly growing population is apt to become more a source of embarrassment than of help to a programme for raising standards of living" And, it advocated the need for "reduction of the birth rate to the extent necessary to stabilize the population at a level consistent with the requirements of national economy." It directed that the family planning programmes in India should:

(1) obtain an accurate picture of factors which contribute to rapid increase of population;
(2) gain fuller understanding of humnn fertility and the means of regulating it;
(3) devise ways of educating the public, and
(4) make family planning advice and service an integral part of the services in hospitals.

Rs. 65 lakhs were allocated in the plan for family planning programme. During the First Plan period, 147 clinics were opened and 205 clinics, maintained by the State Governments, local bodies and voluntary organisations, were given grants by the Central Government. In this Plan more emphasis was laid on rhythm method. Still more attempts were made to provide the workers with educative materials and training so that they may take the message of family planning to the remote corners of the country.

Second Plan (1956-61) and Family Planning

The Second Five Year Plan retained the optimistic view of the First Plan about the rate of population growth and the possibility of slowing it down, but upgraded family planning to "a key factor of development and envisaged an extension of family planning advice and service through the establishment of a well-equipped organisation.

The Government was encouraged to lay additional emphasis on family planning in its Second Five Year Plan. The major activities emphasised in the Second Plan were: (*a*) use of mass communication media; (*b*) provision of clinical referred services, in urban and rural areas; (*c*) training of personnel; (*d*) provision of supplies; and (*e*) research.

In terms of organisation, posts of State Family Planning Officers were created in the States, and a Director of Family Planning was appointed at the Centre.

A sum of Rs. 497 lakhs was provided in the Second Five Year Plan for Family Planning Programme and out of which only Rs. 216 lakhs were spent. This means that less than 50 per cent of the amount allotted was spent.

A target of opening 2500 clinics—2000 in the rural and 500 in the urban areas—during the Second Plan period was fixed. Out of this target only 1502 clinics—1079 in rural and 423 in urban areas—were opened. In addition to these clinics, family planning services were provided at 1864 rural and 330 urban, medical and health centres.

Thus during the First and Second Five Year Plans (1951 61), family planning programme was taken up in a modest way with a clinical approach. The stress was mainly on research in the field of motivation, communication, demography, physiology of reproduction and on the extension of Central and State organisations in providing clinical services. But during the Second Plan period the planners' reliance on family planning clinics, in the Anglo-Saxon tradition, turned out to be a mistake; this was corrected in the Third Plan.

Third Plan (1961-66) and Family Planning

The programme for family planning in the Third Plan provided for: (*a*) education and motivation for family planning, (*b*) provisions of services, (*c*) training, (*d*) supplies, (*e*) communication and motivation research, (*f*) demographic research, and (*g*) medical and biological research.

A sum of Rs. 27 crores was provided in this Plan, but the actual expenditure incurred was Rs. 24.86 crores.

The clinical approach was supplemented by extension approach under which the messages, service and supplies of contraceptives were taken to the people. For effective planning and execution of the programme, a full-fledged department of Family Planning was created in 1966 in the Ministry of Health and Family Planning.

The family planning programme was intensified in the Third Plan in which in 1963 extension education in family planning was adopted. This was sought to be introduced on a nation-wide scale by creating an administrative apparatus similar to that of the Community Development Project and Agricultural Extension Service.

Period of Annual Plans (1966-69) and Family Planning

The period from 1966 to 1969 had been the period of annual plans. During this period Family Planning was given a crucial importance which is reflected from the budget allotment and the performance. Widespread public interest has been aroused in the magnitude of effort and organisation on the part of the Government.

Table 1 presents the expenditure on family planning and the total number of persons who have been sterilised under the family planning scheme during these years.

Table 1 Expenditure on Family Planning and Number of Persons Sterilized

Years	*Expenditure*	*(Rs. in Lakhs)*	*No. of Persons Sterilized*
	Budget Provisions	*Actual Expenditure*	
1966-67	2900.00	2303.41	9,24.612
1967-68	3100.00	2553.47	18,39,811
1968-69	3700.00	3051.45	16,64,817
1969-70	4200.00	4028.93	13,96,729

Fourth Plan (1969-74) and Family Planning

In the Fourth Plan the family planning programme was given high priority. A sum of Rs. 330 crores was provided (actual expenditure Rs. 284 crores) in the Fourth Plan for family planning It was contemplated that within 12 years, the birth rate would be brought down from 39 per thousand in 1969 to 25 per thousand by 1980-81. For the attainment of this target, emphasis was laid on (*i*) directing efforts to secure social acceptability for a small family, (*ii*) increasing the information and knowledge of the people about family planning devices, and (*iii*) making available the necessary devices and equipment for this purpose.

Some of the special steps taken during this plan deserve special mention, the first and the most important of this being the integration of family planning services with those of general health, maternal and child health services. The idea underlying this orientation was that if a single person could attend to the basic needs of the family in the fields of health, family planning and nutrition; he would be able to inspire more confidence among the members of the household and thus make the family planning programme more acceptable as one of the components of a family welfare programme.

Another significant feature of the Fourth Plan was the introduction of the Post-Partum Scheme which has produced commendable results in regard to tubectomy. The Medical Termination of Pregnancy Act, 1971 came into force with effect from 1st April 1972. Its implementation has also benefited the family planning programme indirectly. One of the spectacular features of the Fourth Plan was the organisation of mass vasectomy camps which attarcted a very large number of acceptors. The camp set up in Ernakulam District, Kerala, has won wide acclaim in India and abroad. The Fourth Plan had thus registered achievements in terms of strengthening the infrastructure, in providing supplies and services to larger sections of acceptors than ever in the past and in motivating the masses by properly educating them in favour of the small family norm. Notwithstanding all this, the overall levels of performance have been considerably below the targets. This was particularly due to lack of adequate number of trained doctors and other personnel and periodic shortages in the supply of contraceptives. Moreover, the constraints on financial resources which surfaced in the last year of the Plan have resulted in serious cu tailment of outlays which also has had its adverse effect on performance to a certain extent. If the entire performance in the Fourth Plan was to be summarised in terms of a single indicator, namely, the number of couples currently protected against conception the position would not appear very encouraging. In fact, out of a total of about 100 million couples, in the reproductive age group, that is, 15 to 45 years of age, only 16-17 million are estimated to have been protected against conception by the end of the plan period. On the basis of this level of performance, it is expected that the national birth rate has declined to about 35 per thousand population as against the target of 30 per thousand.

Fifth Plan (1974-79) and Family Planning

The time and target oriented approach to family planning introduced in the Fourth Plan was continued in the Fifth Plan. The Fifth Plan called for reducing the birth-rate to 30 per thousand by 1978-79 and to 25 per thousand by 1983-84. To achieve these goals the targets for the Fifth Plan included 18 million sterilisations, 5.9 million IUD insertions and 8.8 million users of conventional contraceptives by 1978-79. The Plan provided an outlay of Rs. 5.16 million for the implementation of the programme. Clearly, the Fifth Plan accorded a very high priority to controlling population growth and set an ambitious goal of reducing the birth rate from 36 per thousand to 30 per thousand over a five-year period. For achieving this goal, it was estimated that the proportion of couples protected against conception would have to increase from the current 16-17 per cent to 33 per cent by 1978-79. It was a monumental task but it was anticipated that the programme would launch a massive nation-wide family planning drive focussed primarily at the rural population for achieving this target.

There was a significant shift in the strategy of the Government under the Fifth Five Year Plan. In the first place, the Government decided to carry forward the family planning programme in an integrated manner along with health, maternity and child health care, and nutrition services at all levels. With this perspective, a decision was taken to convert vertical programme workers into multipurpose workers who were required to pay special attention to family planning work. Secondly, keeping in view the bold measures envisaged in the 1976 National Population Policy to restrict the rate of population growth. The New Population Policy marked a shift in the approach of the Government. While recommending from and bold steps to improve the tempo of the programme it approved of coercive methods The implementation of this policy had disastrous consequences for the future family planning programme.

The family planning programme took a dramatic twist during the national emergency. Taking advantage of the emergency and the willingness of several state governments to take drastic measures to curb population growth, the compulsory sterilisation approach became a major method for family planning, especially in certain northern states. The programme made spectacular progress during the emergency period and it achieved a total of 8.2 million sterilisations during 1976-77 as against the target of 4.3 million. The speeding up of the sterilisation programme was carried out through both coercive measures and the use of incentives, but the use of force became much more prevalent for achieving the targets. The feelings against compulsory sterilisation were so strong that it became a critical issue during the general election in 1977 and it is considered one of the major reasons for the defeat of Mrs. Gandhi's Government. In retrospect, compulsory sterilisation, in the way it was administered, seemed to have done more harm than good. It gave a major setback to the entire family planning programme, and whatever success the programme had achieved in creating a positive attitude towards family planning among the public was generally lost.

Soon after coming into power the Janata Government issued a revised population policy abdicating force, compulsion or coercive methods in family planning.

The return of Indira Gandhi and her party into power in 1980 brought the population problem into public focus once again. On assuming power the Gandhi Government expressed strong commitment to controlling population growth by reactivating the family planning programme and popularising it through education and persuasion, avoiding any form of coercion.

Family Planning under Sixth Plan

The mid-term appraisal of the Sixth Plan (1980-85) states that 'The 1981 census has revealed that the population of the century by March 1981 was higher by about 13.2 million than what has been assumed in the Plan document, on the basis of the Expert Committee. The 1981 census results also showed that the assumptions on which the Expert Committee has projected the population of the country had been over-optimistic and the demographic parameters at the beginning of the VI Plan such as the birth rate/death rate, annual growth rate were actually high.'

This disclosure forced the Health Ministry to revise the Family Planning targets. Firstly, the allocation towards family planning has been raised from Rs. 1010 crores to Rs. 1078 crores. Secondly, sterilisations target has been raised from 22 million to 24 million. The target of IUD insertions has been raised to 7.9 million and of CC and oral pill users has been raised to 11 million. A mid-term appraisal of the progress revealed that the achievement of sterilisations carried out was 8 8 million and that of IUD insertions achievement was 2.4 million by the end of March 1983. The Planning Commission stated that 'It has been possible to achieve only 36.7% of the Plan targets for sterilisations and 30 per cent of IUDs. The performance of the non-terminal methods like CC and OP was users is yet to register a significant increase. The percentage of effective protection of eligible couples against fertility at the end of 1982-83 was 25.9% against the target of 36.6% by the end of 1984-85.'

The total expenditure by the end of 1982-83 amounted to Rs. 620 crores and the balance left was Rs. 456 crores for the remaining two years. The provision for 1983-84 was Rs. 330 crores leaving only Rs. 126 crores for 1984-85. To overcome the shortfall in allocation, the Planning Commission emphasised the need for additional allocation to develop infrastructures in the form of post-partum centres and primary health centres. According to the Commission, 'Sterilisation is at present the mainstay of the programme constituting nearly 90% of the total number of couples effectively protected. Even in tubectomy it continues to be the predominant method.'

Besides sterilisation is the main method other non-terminal methods like IUDs, oral pills and condoms also should be encouraged. The programme should receive priority in the context of the findings of 1981 census.

Did the Family Planning Programme succeed in India?

Perhaps, India is the first country in the world where family planning programme has been launched as a Government sponsored movement. The initiative taken by the Government of India to propagate the programme among the masses and to promote awareness and use of it is unparallel in the annals of history. The entire programme is financed by the Government of India out of its own resources. The planners have given priority to those methods which reduce birth rate and create public awareness. Naturally, the question arises whether the programme has succeeded in India.

The following facts go to prove the success of the programme:

1. Creation of General Public Interest

Public approval of the programme has been brought to light by a study conducted by the Indian Institute of Public Opinion in 1969. The study showed that:

1. 72 per cent of the urban population prefer three or less than three issues while 66 per cent of the rural population prefer 3 or more than three children.

2. 85 per cent of the degree holders, and 79 per cent higher secondary certificate holders and 70 per-cent of those who have studied upto 8th class are in favour of three or less children.

3. 72 per cent of the population belonging to the age group of 21-35 years prefer less than three children and 65 per cent of the 36-59 age group also expressed similar opinion.

2. Target Achieved

The targets achieved since 1951 is an indication of the success of Family Planning. Out of 12.14 eligible couples whose wives belong to fertility age group of 15-44 years, 25.9 per cent couples have successfully averted child birth by recourse to any one of the accepted methods of family planning till 31st March 1983. The family welfare drive is estimated to have checked 547 lakh possible births.

3. Decline in Birth Rate

The continuous decrease in birth rate is a reflection of the success of family welfare measures. The birth rate during the 1951-61 period was 41.7 per thousand which declined to 39.9 during the 1961-71 period. The declining trend continued and the birth rate fell to 36.6 during the period 1971-76 and further to 32.9 during the period 1976-81. The projected figures of the Planning Commission for the periods 1981-86 and 1986-1991 are 29.5 and 27.0 respectively.

4. Population Projection

After the third five year plan special attention was given to family welfare research and investigation. Demographic research centres located in different states are engaged in demographic research. Similarly reproductive biological research and birth control research works are being carried by the Indian Council of Medical Research and the National Health and Family Planning Bureau.

India is also getting assistance from the World Health Organisation, UNICEF, United Nation's Family Welfare Assistance Fund etc. for Family Welfare Works.

5. Growth Rate

The decadal growth of population between 1961-71 was at an average rate of 2.48 per cent annually as against an anticipated growth rate 2 6 per cent annually. Thus, the .12 per cent fall in birth rate could be attributed to family welfare programmes. Similarly, the negligible increase in annual population growth rate of 0.02 per cent during the decade 1971-81 reflects the impact of family planning programme on birth rate.

6. Environment

Spread of family planning message has created an awareness among the people that the size of the family should be kept small. The creation of such an environment is a testimony to the success of family planning.

7. Legislation of Abortion

The popularity of family planning has made it incumbent on the Government to liberalise the rules regarding abortion and in some cases, abortion has been legalised.

8. Strong Organisational Structure

The Family Planning has strengthened its organisational structures. Many organisations like the family welfare board (1956). Establishment of special cell in the Central Health and Family Welfare Ministry (1966), changing the nomenclature of Central Health Ministry to Central Health and Family Welfare Ministry show the strong organisational structure of the family welfare programme.

Problems in the way of Family Planning in India

Family Planning had limited success in India on account of the multiple problems in implementing the programme. The main hurdles are as under:

1. Lack of Suitable Method

So far cheap, dependable and easily available means of family planning are not available in the country which the majority of people can use. All the methods recommended are normally based on foreign medical science which are very costly so that the people in general and more particularly those living in villages are not able to purchase them. Although loop is comparatively cheaper, its use has given rise to complaints like bleeding, body pain, etc. Besides, the contraceptives are not easily available at all places.

2. Lack of Public Co-operation

The family planning has failed to evoke satisfactory response from the public on account of illiteracy, ignorance, traditional outlook etc. People regard children as gift of God and they fight shy to interfere with the act of God. However, surveys conducted of late have shown that the public antipathy is gradually waning.

3. Housing Problems

Proper accommodation is not available to people in India and as a result it is difficult to employ chemical and mechanical devices of family planning due to lack of privacy.

4. Resistance on Social Grounds

Family welfare methods are opposed on the ground that girls will loose their virginity by adopting contraceptives when they are easily available. Access to contraceptives, it is feared, will lead to pre-nuptial sexual relations, prostitution, flesh trade etc. It is feared that public places may become centres of sex play and the purity of marriage will be destroyed.

5. Religious Opposition

Family planning is opposed by many on the ground that it will disturb the ratio between Hindus and non-Hindus, as the family planning programme is not popular among Muslims and Christians. However, this conception is not correct as Muslims too welcome this programme and make use of it. Studies conducted in Delhi show that the differences in the benefit derived out of family planning services are more due to socio-economic factors rather than due to religious reason. The Muslim population in Delhi is 5 per cent of the aggregate population whereas the proportion of Muslims who have benefited from family welfare programme is 14 per cent of the total beneficiaries. Similar conclusion has been obtained from studies conducted by the Institute of Economic Growth, Delhi University, in Bulandshahr and Mathura.

6. Lack of Publicity and Official Apathy

In a country like India with large population and vast area education, transport and communication are poorly developed. Consequently, wide publicity is required to carry the message of family planning to the masses so as to create public awareness. Efforts made in our country in this direction so far are not satisfactory. Even today in the rural areas people are ignorant about the need, importance and use of contraceptives. Besides the blame for the tardy progress of family planning is also due in a great measure to the lack of dedication, indifference and lack of self-confidence of the officials who are incharge of the programme.

7. Untrained and Inefficient Workers

Officials manning the family welfare programme suffer from inefficiency, inexperience, ignorance etc. The officials, by a large, are not trained. Shoddy handling of the programme has given rise to a lot of misgivings and apprehensions among the rural people towards the programme. The employees failed to convince and motivate the sceptical rural population. To fulfil the targets the officials have resorted to forced sterilisation which developed avertion and hostility towards the programme among the rural people.

8. Lack of Finance

To undertake the family planning programme on a massive scale require adequate resources which are lacking in our country. Consequently, we are facing difficulty in spreading the family welfare and health services on a wider scale. Resources constraint also pose problems in conducting research and training in family welfare.

9. Other Hindrances

(*a*) Officials in the family welfare centres could not provide proper guidance to the people, (*b*) Sufficient contraceptives are not produced in our country, (*c*) The country lacks adequate number of doctors and nurses to run the programme more particularly sterilisation and insertion of loop, (*d*) Many intellectuals oppose the programme as it will reduce the ratio of the intellectuals and the skilled workers because the programme is adopted more by the enlightened class.

Thus there are several constraints in the path of family welfare in India. Illiteracy is the fundamental obstacle in this respect. It is a matter of satisfaction that in recent years the programme has picked up a satisfactory tempo. However it is necessary to reinforce and consolidate the movement because to dream about economic progress without successful family planning will be a wild goose chase.

A Critique of the Family Welfare (Planning) Programme

Family welfare programme has won wide intellectual acceptance in India and it can play an important role in influencing the future course of fertility. It is true that achievements of the programme, in India, are far below the set goals but that should not be taken as an indication of its failure. The attitudes of persons cannot be changed overnight. Thus considering the complex nature of the problem in India, the achievement of the family welfare programme since 1966 in terms of creating awareness, dissemination of knowledge and acceptors of different family welfare methods have not been negligible. Several far reaching policy decisions such as initiating a national programme of family welfare, making funds available on demand basis, and creating a nationwide organisation to provide free and easy availability of many kinds of contraceptives and related services to every person in the country, have been taken within a relatively short period of time. However, Dr. Gyan Chand, Dr. Ashish Bose, Dr. S.N. Agrawal and Mr. D. Banerji have criticised the Government policy of family welfare.

1. The family welfare programme was started on an experimental basis in the fifties with a 'clinical approach' to provide services to those who are so motivated. This approach was modified in 1962-63 to the 'extension approach'. With this modification, emphasis was placed on the promotion among people of motivation in favour of family welfare acceptance and on the rendering of the services as near to their doorsteps as possible. Substantial additions were again made in the programme in the mid-sixties when intra-uterine device (IUD) was popularised. When this IUD programme failed, there came the "target-oriented time bound programme, and the adoption of the cafeteria-approach". The 'Cafeteria' provides a variety of contraceptive methods from which an acceptor can

freely choose the one that suits him best. When this also proved inadequate, recourse was taken, in the early seventies, to Mass Vasectomy Camps, which involved much more extensive and intensive use of the district administrative machinery along with much more enhanced 'incentives' and a massive publicity drive. Though India has been experimenting different approaches to family welfare programme from the 'clinic' approach to the extension approach followed by emphasis on the IUD, which in turn gave way to the target-oriented time bound programme coupled with the cafeteria approach, followed by the disastrous mass vasectomy camp approach, but the efforts so far made have failed to make any significant dent in the problem. The 'target-oriented time bound' approach prompted the family welfare staff to work in an indiscriminate manner. There were reports that administrative pressures were used to achieve health and family welfare targets. The result was that instead of projecting an image which reflected respect for the dignity of the individual by offering free choice of methods to the users and ensuring better health services, the family welfare workers in rural areas tended to give the impression of using pressure tactics to entice people to accept vasectomy or tubectomy. Partly this should also be attributed to the fear of the workers losing their jobs. Complaints began to be voiced that no help was received when complications were reported following IUD, vasectomy and tubectomy. All this was unfortunate since this resulted in a lack of rapport between the field workers and the villagers.

At a meeting of the Parliamentary Consultative Committee attached to the Ministry of Health and Family Welfare several members seemed to have expressed their concern over the excess committed in certain cases by the field staff in their over-enthusiasm for the success of the family welfare campaign.

Though an elaborate training infrastructure has been set up to prepare workers for manning the programme at different levels, but these training institutions have found it almost impossible to keep pace with the very rapid and not very rational alternatives in the programme. This has taken away the very purpose of the training and the whole process has degenerated into an agonizing and a very expensive ritual, involving considerable waste of our scarce resources. Frequent policy changes have also aggravated the situation by creating indecisiveness in the minds of those who have been entrusted with the work of implementing the programme at different levels.

2. In the present approach to family welfare in India, the term 'motivation' has been used in too loose a manner, without any reference at all to the complex processes which lead to the generation of motivation for small family norm in a community. The propaganda for family welfare has been only in terms of 'fewer children', some of the messages so communicated are (*a*) "Do Ya Teen

Bachche Bas", (*b*) "Do Ya Teen Bachche Hote Hain Ghar Main Achche", (*c*) 'Ham Do Hamare Do', (*d*) 'Chhota Pariwar Sukhi Pariwar' (*e*) 'Kam Santan Sukh Ka Praman'.

But, having fewer children does not automatically improve the economic lot of the family; at the most that may prevent it from being depressed further. Efforts were not made to spread birth control among the masses fully, integrated into the other policy programme to improve economic and living conditions in the country. "Programme for more houses, jobs, land, schools and hospitals are intrinsically more appealing than programmes for less babies." In our country, to majority of our people, life is a continuous, grim struggle for existence. They are being deprived of even the most elementary needs.

The poor and the landless labourers have not accepted family planning and are unlikely to do so readily because they have little hopes and aspirations to better their economic conditions and they perceive an additional child as tending to increase their income without adding to their cost. Because of their poor socio-economic conditions, these people are unlikely to get easily motivated and, therefore, time and efforts spent for the purpose will be economically unrewarding. It would be more result-yielding from the long term point of view if a conscious policy to improve their economic lot is following and efforts are made to distribute an additional 1 or 2 per cent of the GNP among those who are below poverty line.

In India, the family welfare programme has now been accepted as an integral part of comprehensive social and economic development. But there are reasons to believe that family welfare has not made the anticipated impact. The programme seems to be functioning more or less in isolation as one of the programmes in the Ministry of Health. It has not been effectively integrated even with the health programme, not to speak of the development programmes as a whole. According to Ashish Bose—"By hitching the family welfare wagon to the passenger train of public health and not to the express train of development, the plan blundered, and if family welfare has not succeeded in making a dent on the birth rate in spite of 15 years of trial and error, part of the blame must be shared by the Family Welfare Commission."

The inter-relationship of population growth and development efforts are many and varied. On the one hand, a high level of development, particularly in the countryside, serves not only as an effective check on rapid population growth but also creates the necessary climate for favourable response to family welfare programme. On the other hand, rapid growth of population creates many difficulties in the way of development. Our failure in the field of population can perhaps be traced to our strategy of welfare which has failed to make the right impact on the prevailing situation of unemployment and social inequalities. Dr. Bose writes: 'One of the myths of our family welfare programme in that reproductive behaviour in a country like India can be changed by propaganda and posters... . The people have been aroused and the "Garibi Hatao' slogan must be translated into action. People will demand positive steps and not negative slogans like "two or three children enough". So the efforts for education, a rise in living standards, the removal of glaring social and economic inequities and the efforts for the popularization, practice and substance of the small family norm are complimentary. They all hang together and have, therefore, to be co-ordinated.

3. Though family welfare is centrally sponsored and financed programme, its implementation, on the other hand, rests almost entirely with the States and their constituent parts—the districts, blocks and villages, as well as the towns and cities. This means that the programme strategies including pattern of services to be provided are decided by the Central Government. This has given rise to the concept of providing uniform pattern of services in different parts of the country. However, the official data on annual acceptor of different family welfare methods show a wide variation in the adoption and use of family welfare methods between States. If similar analyses are carried out by taking different geographic units such as districts within State and blocks within district as units of analysis we may also find wide variations in pattern of acceptance and use of family welfare methods between these units. If so, the desirability of providing a uniform pattern of services in different units is questionable and thus, needs further consideration. The situation in different parts of the country is different and the population situation in each area has its own specific feature, so the population policy based on the macro view of the country will not be very much meaningful. The local needs and circumstances must be identified for determining priorities and finalizing motivational strategies and adjustments according to the local requirements. Local resources must also be mobilized and efforts made to seek the co-operation of village personnel.

4. When in India goals of bringing down fertility have not been reached, this is often due to the fact that the administrative apparatus has been faltering. The official organization for promotion of family welfare in India is extensive and has necessary resources but it is almost completely bureaucratic in its methods of work and lacks drive and efficiency. Decisions of far-reaching importance are taken by committees in which generalist administrators, who are usually very busy, have little technical background. Such archaic and obviously inadequate ways of decision-making are responsible for quite a few of the present maladies of the family welfare programme. The distance is long between the bureaucracy in the capital and the individual families in the village or the urban slums. If the organization can be de-bureaucratized, a mass social drive developed and if voluntary work can enlist the support of the people

on a broad basis, the circumstances to all appearances are very favourable for the spread of contraception among the people.

It has aptly been remarked that "the shift in the emphasis on family welfare is towards an integrated approach to service, but the major problem in this integrated bureaucratic structure of the country and the fact that nothing moves at any level unless it is under the orders of an immediate superior. The jurisdiction of departmental authority is perhaps the major block to integration of any kind, both inter departmentally and between government and voluntary sectors. No programme can function in the field, however, well planned and financed, unless the human components who carry it out can do so as a team and not mindful of their territorial imperatives. A further problem is the fixed nature of government structure, the whole complex ramification of pay scales, leave transfers and above all status. The importance of the programme or the need for speed and intensity of action crumbles before the solid facade of official structure, and this is perhaps the most difficult task before us if we wish to deal with the problem of unwanted child, the irresponsible parent and the dinosaur threat of human extinction by the year 2000 under the weight of numbers.

An official programme of family welfare without the full cooperation of the people and their leaders cannot make any serious headway. The progress of family welfare in the western countries, Japan and the communist countries have been largely successful because the people themselves in one form or the other were drawn into the movement of family welfare and responded to it with full cooperation, because their approach values and motivations were completely changed. In India the conditions for realizing this objective have not been created unless the acceptance is voluntary and due to a definite change of attitude resulting from a long-term exposure to propaganda and unless it is the rasult of a decision taken after careful thought, psychological and social reactions after the operation will tend to take a negative colour.

Journals and booklets on family welfare concentrate more on photographs and accounts of seminars and conferences, rather than on field work and field experience. Family welfare must be for all people, not merely for family welfare circles.

5. The services created under the family welfare programme are very much under-utilized. Even from the very scanty, sketchy and often unreliable data that are available concerning utilization of the services, it is easily seen that only a very small fraction, often measuring less than 10 per cent of the capacity of institutions providing family welfare services, is utilized.

6. Some States have introduced measures of withdrawing educational concessions to families having more than a prescribed number (three) of children and of stopping the promotions and other facilities like maternity leave to the Government servants

having more (than three) children. Since having many children is the main cause of poverty, such measures would penalize the relatively poor and subsidize the relatively well-off. Such a result would not only violate rules of equity but would be detrimental to the health of the poor families, and so of the growing generation. The withdrawal of educational concessions, for instance, will deprive the families in the lower-income strata of perhaps their only chance of stepping on the ladder of progress. Those who are poor and indigent will thus be damned to even worse poverty without any hope of redemption. And if the line of thinking underlying these measures is carried to its bitter logical end, there will be no other alternative for controlling the growth of population, except compulsory sterilization of women, at least of those in the lower income group, after the prescribed number of children.

We fail to find in the population-policy movement and explicit discussion on long range goals, while these policies seem to promise a great deal in terms of population control, they confine attention to growth and size of population, leaving out its other attributes like age-sex structure, geographical distribution, racial composition, genetic quality, etc. Within this circumscribed area, they concentrate on the 'birth input' to the exclusion of mortality and migration. The family welfare bias further restricts the scope of action by its exclusive emphasis on modern contraception. According to Kingsley Davis, "A family planning orientation limits the aims of current population policy. Despite reference to 'population control' and 'fertility control', which presumably mean determination of demographic results by and for the nation as a whole, the movement gives control only to couples, and does this only if they use 'respectable' contraceptives."

SUGGESTIONS FOR IMPROVEMENT

No country can bring about quick results in the sphere of population control and family limitation. It is, therefore, of imperative necessity that sustained efforts be made over a considerable period of time to achieve positive results. The problem of 'birth control' through family limitation involves a number of problems and starts with the attitude of the community to adopt it. A discussion of these problems now follows.

Community Attitude

Even if family welfare is desperately needed in a country its ultimate success would depend upon the extent to which it is accepted by society. Family welfare is very closely linked with the emotional care of personality. It is deeply rooted into the social structure of every society through the institutions of family, marriage, religion, social norms and customs and codes of inter-personal social behaviour. Since family planning is affected by prevailing social beliefs and notions, there is a great possibility that a proper study of social attitudes would cast some light on areas which must be specially treated in the overall programme. In the last few years, special surveys on knowledge, attitude and practice (popularly known as KAP) of people have been conducted in different parts of the country to measure changes in knowledge, attitude and practice of family planning methods in different sections of population. These surveys do not indicate a mass aversion for family welfare as a method of increasing family happiness. Knowledge and use of contraceptives varied according to education, family income, superiority of professions, number of living children, age of wife, and level of urbanization. In order to be truly effective, the family welfare programme must take these attitudes into account and efforts must be concentrated either where response is too encouraging or where the malady is too consternating.

Motivation

Under the National Family Welfare Programme, eligible couples are motivated to accept small family norms. Although the Government has been making efforts to spread the message of family welfare, yet the motivation response is not adequate and is far from optimum.

It has been observed that though about 90 per cent of the eligible couples are aware of the Family Welfare Programme only 20 per cent of the eligible couples are practising family welfare methods. This wide gap between awareness and adoption calls for rethinking on Family Welfare Motivation Progrmme. As Keynes used to say in another context "You can take the horse to the river but you cannot make it drink".

Obviously, therefore, it is not enough to have availability of contraceptive materials and methods. People have to be motivated to take advantage of these facilities. This will require that (*i*) people should understand the relationship between small size families and family welfare especially in relation to their personal well being; (*ii*) married couples must have knowledge of modern methods that best suit their needs, (*iii*) supplies and services must be easily available, and (*iv*) physical and psychological barriers to the procurement of supplies and the use of services must be removed.

For the mass of the people acceptance of the small size family norm will mean a radical change in age-old attitudes, beliefs and values and a widespread diffusion of rational social attitudes. Thus the best motivating factor for the acceptance of family welfare is economic and social development. Reduction in fertility requires a shift in the social values directed towards the survival of society and the welfare and development of the individual. Such new interests are likely to develop during modernization which, invariably, is preceded or accompanied by declining mortality, widespread education, increased social mobility, a higher level of aspirations and such other processes Significant reduction in fertility occurred in western societies only after considerable changes had taken place in their social structure. Such changes may take several years in a developing country like India and during the period population might be more than double itself. Thus the process by which economic and social development creates a need for a small family norm is a slow process. It is, therefore, to be assisted and accelerated by special programme inputs like population education.

The problems of motivation for a small family norm are, therefore, intrinsically connected with the economic and social development. The family welfare programme, in isolation, is not best suited for the creation of this motivation. Rather it is effective in providing the knowledge and means to these couples who are already motivated or marginally motivated, while the goal of small family norm is set by the process of economic and social development. We do not have to depend mainly on the experience of developed countries, because problems of developing countries like India which are facing the task of economic development on the face of rapid population growth are unprecedented. Since the problem is new, it requires new strategy and new solutions. However, even in Asian countries where the decline in the birth rate is well on its way, such as in Japan, Taiwan, Hong Kong. Republic of Korea, Singapore, West Malaysia and Sri Lanka, a certain minimal level of economic development had already taken place before the onus of a sustained decline in the birth rate.

Thus provision of family welfare clinics and distribution of birth control devices are not by themselves a sufficient condition for fertility reduction. If there is demand for more children based on grounds of benefits (as in rural India where children begin to earn some income at an early age and do not cost much due to extremely low levels of living) families will be indifferent to the availability of birth control devices, no matter how effective they may be and how wide a propaganda campaign, the family welfare programme may launch. Parents must want to reduce family size, and only if they feel themselves better off in some sense by having smaller families, they can be reasonably expected to do so (aside from any issue surrounding the morality of the problem). This means if economic consideration strongly impinges on family size decisions, then policy measures designed to lower fertility rates can anticipate a high degree of success only when they strike directly at parents' basic economic motives for having children. The best way therefore of limiting the size of the family and thus the growth of population would be that, along with propaganda in favour of small size of the family attempts must be made to create economic conditions, where the benefits of smaller families are greater than the costs.

One of the reasons of the gap between awareness and practice of family welfare is that females have not been properly motivated under motivational endeavour compared to males. For this the motivation endeavour needs modification so that more attention is paid towards female motivation and persuasion. Women must now be involved not merely as acceptors of this or that contraceptive devices or as passive tools of policy, but must be active participants in shaping policies which will profoundly affect their lives. As long as women are not given the right by law to decide the number of children, they are prepared to bear, there is no chance of a real control of the population. In appealing to women, stress should be laid on grounds of better maternal and child health, whereas in appealing to men, stress should be laid on the importance of education, cost of rearing a child and maintaining a big family. The motivational barriers, such as the desire to have sons, the belief that contraceptive is against God's will and the notion that it leads to immorality, must be taken into account in designing further educational programmes.

The correlation between literacy and fertility is well known. The National Sample Survey (16th round) has shown that the number of children born per woman is 2.0 if the woman has passed intermediate and university examination, 4.6 if she is a matriculate, and 6.0 if she has school education. The obvious role of education thus seems to be the stimulation of critical thinking and development of a rational attitude towards child-bearing and child-rearing. A better standard of education by itself inculcates an aspiration for better things in life and stimulates the desire to take active steps to realize them. Poor standards of literacy create communication barriers. In a country like India where 70 per cent of the population cannot read and write, no programme of social change or of creating new norms can succeed wholly. Thus the spread of education particularly in rural areas in India is essential A strong case for expanding women's education can be made from the standpoint of family welfare.

The schemes that have been taken up under the minimum needs programme for promoting community welfare through integrated programmes of community health, medical care, nutrition and family welfare lend themselves for inclusion of adult literacy as a component. These programmes are then likely to bring about changes in the quality of life in our people.

If we want a large proportion of married couples to regularly practise effective contraceptive which require socio-culture changes of great magnitudes, we have to pay more attention to extension education. Extension-education approach presupposes that change comes from within and cannot be imposed on individuals by outside agencies. It is only when the decision for the change is made by the individuals themselves that any change is long lasting. The use of force or legal authority in bringing about change in behaviour does not go far. It may be a slow process as all such processes are but it is sure in its achievement and enduring in its results.

Fast and effective transmission of family planning messages to the Indian masses seems to hold the key to India's population problem. What Bogue has to say about the importance of communication in family welfare is worth recording. "We sincerely believe that communication with the masses about birth control has been the neglected area of family welfare programme all over the world. People must not only be made aware of the existence of such centres (family welfare clinics) but they must be stimulated to use them, or to visit private physicians or other sources of information to get help."

Communication is the process by which an individual transmits stimuli to modify the behaviour of other individuals. It must be understood that communication is more important than the educational total he employs to put across the message he chooses to convey. He has to decide on the choice of the media that are locally available. He has to clothe the message in the learner's language. He should get all his data for the message correctly and completely. The information should be related to the people concerned and their personal everyday life. They should feel that these are important for their family and community.

Efforts should be made to involve the people actively in the use of any method, especially in respect of mass communication. Therefore, use of these methods should be well planned beforehand and participation encouraged in as many ways as possible.

The family welfare movement must encourage individual drive among its personnel. It should push ahead in areas of high promise such as organisations covered by large industrial concerns, large government offices, commercial houses, public sector undertakings, where general development to some extent has already taken place and educational levels are higher. Fortunately some of our entrepreneurs and industrial managers are convinced advocates of population control. With the intention of involving workers and managements in the family welfare campaign, the worker's committee for family welfare set up over a year ago was recently reconstituted as a tripartite national committee on family welfare planning.

The family welfare organisation should give special attention to the most backward areas, where there is virtually no non official leadership. If we make the mistake of neglecting these areas, then no matter how good the achievements in the urban industrial areas, the national average will remain low. The birth control movement is so far confined to the upper slice—the educated, urbanised middle class and industrial working class has not spread to the villages, and it is in the villages, where 85 per cent of the babies are born. We should, therefore, give special attention to the backward areas.

The motivation has to be created in the rural areas where it has to overcome mounting resistance due to illiteracy and superstition among the masses. The persistence of a high level of birth rate in the rural areas is growing indication of the spread of poverty According to a socio-economic survey the mothers who have five or more children (63 per cent) belonged to the families with an income of less than Rs. 200 p.m. per family. Frequent and ill-spaced pregnancies invariably undermine the health of the mothers. A high birth rate with low standards of living and malnutrition may lead to a general deterioration of the health of the population and thereby help increasing the incidence of disease and infant mortality. Thus it is only among the poor that essential knowledge about planning their family must be communicated at the earliest possible. Right approach is to make the people aware of their social responsibility. as well as the advantage of having only one or two children which in turn helps their better health, as well as future birth.

Also important is the question of incentives. The incentives can boost up the performance of the programme particularly in poor, rural and illiterate sections of the society whom the demographers call as the "hard-core". It has been supported by a number of studies that the payment of incentives at present being made are low, relative to the return of birth prevention. Enhanced incentives might encourage many couples who would otherwise never go in for sterilization. If financial conditions prevent raising monetary incentives, special measures can be taken to raise funds from other sources, like, Lions Clubs, Rotary Clubs, Indian Red Cross Society. etc. The form and the nature of incentive seems to be of as much importance as the amount of incentive itself. Moreover, the form and amount of incentive should be planned in such a way as to satisfy several immediate needs of the acceptors.

It may be suggested that a person undergoing sterilization should be given a cash reward depending upon the economic status of the person. The lower economic status of the persons should be linked to a higher reward so as to induce more persons to go in for sterilization.

Social policy needs greater attention. The family welfare programme is conceived as a multi-disciplinary system. A number of related factors in terms of education, occupation, health, etc., are knit into this system. The progress of the programme thus is dependent upon the simultaneous progress in all the related areas. Age at marriage has already been increased in India. There are other areas such as investment in literacy, investment in strengthening the basic health structure resulting especially in the reduction of infant mortality; old age security, education and employment, peasant-proprietorship, location of industry, taxation, land-holding policy which cumulatively can affect people's attitudes.

FAMILY WELFARE METHODS

Contraception has played a dominant role in limiting the population levels of most western countries. Conception control involves all available methods for the prevention of conception. This includes a battery of techniques—behavioural, mechanical, chemical, physiological, and surgical. The behavioural methods encompass complete abstinence from sex, coitus interrupts, coitus sublimates, and the use of "the rhythm method"; the mechanical methods include the condom, the pessary, the diaphragm, and the intra-uterine device; the chemical methods include foam tablets, spermacidal jellies and the like; the physiological methods include the use of steriods, and other possible agents for controlling ovulation, possible anti-zygotic agents, and possible spermaticides or other agents for inducing male sterility; the surgical methods include ligation and vasectomy. Methods to prevent birth include, of course. all the methods of conception control, and, in addition, abortion—the prevention of births even if conception has occurred.

Government of India are committed to the use of all proven, safe and acceptable techniques of family welfare and control over reproduction and population growth. Following this policy encouragement has been given to the application of surgical methods, such as vasectomy and tubectomy as also the termination of pregnancy. Government have also supported programmes on mechanical preventive methods such as the use of condom and diaphragm and the use of intra-uterine devices. Table 2 gives the relative effectiveness of the contraceptives. Out of the 7 types of methods mentioned in the table, first 4 are for exclusive use of females (male sterilization is also exclusively used by male). The next two are exclusively used by males and the last though used by both is based on the menstrual cycle of the female.

An ideal contraceptive is one that is safe, easily administered, preferable by the individual himself or herself, reversible, with no side effects, not interfering with lactation, not expensive and not repetitive. A method that has all these attributes is yet to be discovered. The conventional contraceptives (diaphragm and jelly) have proved highly expensive and inconvenient in India .The intra-uterine contraceptive device (IUCD), which was inducted into the family planning programme in India in 1965, has not fared uniformly well and has become unpopular in recent years.

Table 2. Relative Effectiveness of Contraceptives

Method	*Effectiveness (per cent likely pregnancy in a year)*	*Possible side effects*	*Expertise required*
1. Sterilization (Male and Female)	0.003	None	Surgical
2. Oral Contraceptives	0.3	Weight gain, vomiting and nausea, epigastic discomfort	Prescribed and controlled by doctor
3. IUD	5	Infection, irregular bleeding, pain, backache, uterine perforation	Inserted by doctor and periodical check up
4. Chemical contraceptives (foam tablets, jelly and cream)	20	Minor irritations	Nil
5. Condom (Nirodh)	14	Allergic reaction, irritation	Nil
6. Withdrawal	18	Physiological	Nil
7. Rhythm	24	None	Doctor's advice may be required

Source: Sharma, V.P.C. and Singh, Nawal: "Family Planning Motivation and Education Programme", *Yojana*, 15 July, 1974, p. 23.

1. Provision of IUD must be made a part of the total health programme and the integration of family welfare with the general health services done at all service delivery levels.

2. IUDs should be inserted at family welfare planning centres which are adequately staffed, and equipped with necessary instruments, sterilization facilities and medicines.

3. The centres where there are facilities for IUD insertion must have adequate arrangements for follow-up of the acceptor.

4. Field workers should preferably belong to the local areas as field-workers who are culturally acceptable to the population whom they serve can function better.

5. Only the trained medical officer with experience in gynaecology should be allowed to perform the insertions The paramedical staff should not be allowed to perform the insertions.

6. A regular follow-up of the acceptors should be done and home visits made by the paramedical staff, in case women do not visit the clinic.

7. The feasibility of providing IUDs in a sterile package along with a sound and glove may be considered. This would be highly useful for centres which do not have adequate facilities for sterilization.

During the last few years there has been a very sharp increase in the usage of oral contraceptives (pills) in many countries. In some countries, of all women in the reproductive age group, over a third are already using pills as means of contraception. Recent information on the preferences for different methods of contraception in the developing areas is of interest. Table 3 illustrates the point that in most cases, oral contraceptives are overwhelmingly preferred to other methods.

Table 3. Per cent of Users of Different Methods of Contraception

Country	*Per cent of users of different methods of contraception in the total practising contraception*			
	Oral	*IUD*	*Sterilization*	*Other Methods*
Egypt	55	40	—	5
Hong Kong	46	12	10	32
Thailand	60	20	10	10
Mexico	79	9	—	12
Taiwan	7	60	15	18
Mauritius	60	11	—	29

Source: Varadarajan, S.: "Potential for the Development of Oral Contraceptives in India in Contraception and Population Planning", *Yojana*, p. 12.

Sterilization has come to occupy an important place in the armoury of family planning methods. Sterilization renders a person incapable of reproduction and the result is usually permanent. It can be carried on the male as well as on the female but the male operation of vasectomy is becoming popular and is comparatively easy to perform The fact that men's sterilization is revocable, that is, the sterilized men can, if necessary, be de-sterilized is also a point in favour of this method. The official policy in favour of its more extensive use is definitely right and commendable. For its success and popularity, it is necessary that competent doctors and nurses and good equipment are provided. The concentration should be made on the quality of the acceptors rather than the number. The acceptors should be below 35 years.

Intensive programmes for sterilization should be insisted upon (*a*) the population pockets in poverty zones where health, nutrition and balwadis services are already functioning with local participation, voluntary and state; (*b*) industrial belts of high density population; (*c*) urban slums and reconstituted slums, e.g., Madangir, Delhi; (*d*) coastal areas of Kerala and Orissa in fishing villages; (*e*) industrial belts of high density population; (*f*) cattle fare, 'country mela' where people congregate naturally. Staff to be engaged in intensive programmes should be recruited for known good work and care should be taken that sterilization operations are performed with extreme care. For sterilisation follow-up care is essential and vitally important.

The tubectomy operation in the post-partum period is one thing which has a very good success, because women coming for delivery or after miscarriage were found to be psychologically in a better receptive mind to accept advice on this. It is also easier to perform the operation after a delivery or involuntary or even voluntary abortion. The operation is to widen the scope for post-partum operations. To do that we must have a very big health programme providing facilities for delivery or post-abortion or post-miscarriage treatment under controlled conditions. 'By controlled condition' we mean nursing homes or in a hospital or in a place where 'Dais' come to the house for helping in the delivery but have had orientation in and knowledge of family planning.

Abortion has been given an increasingly important place in the programmes of birth control in many countries. In Japan, birth rate was reduced by 50 per cent in a decade by the use of abortion.

In India, Medical Termination of Pregnancy (MTP) Act was enforced from 1st April, 1972, to liberalize abortion. It was introduced as a health measure rather than family planning method. Medical termination of pregnancy or legalised abortion should be encouraged. MTP services by properly trained doctors should be made available more freely in urban as well as rural areas and this should be suitably publicized. The procedures for registration record keeping and reporting for MTP services should be simplified.

In conclusion, it may be emphasised that the development of new acceptable methods in the field of contraception can be naturally expected to take time to prove their safety and efficiency because of specially stringent requirements related to these agents. While efforts in this direction are maintained, priority allocation of resources and energy should be applied for more effective use of established methods by mass education, training, personnel and streamlining of distribution channels. In fact, the cafeteria approach will become far more rewarding if it is organized as a "package programme" consisting of condom, the loop or the pill for younger couples, abortion for women who conceive accidentally, an sterilization for those who do not wish to add to their families. It is obvious that in implementing the policy of birth control several measures will have to be undertaken in an integrated manner. There must be an expanded provision of clinic and distribution centres have been increasing in recent years but many of them are underworked for want of regular and adequate attendance. A mere installation of clinics is, therefore. not sufficient. The need to deploy a large staff of medical and paramedical personnel for carrying out the work of family planning is immediate and great.

Steps Towards a Rational Population Policy

Past experience of population growth in the world shows that there is correlation between high fertility and high infant mortality.

In developed countries like USA the mortality rate has been reduced to a low figure as 10 to 15 per thousand births. On the other hand in rural India infant mortality is as high as 136. Secondly, developed countries have well organised social security system. In urban India well to do sections in society are covered under social security schemes like provident fund, gratuity, old age pension life insurance etc. The rich classes possess large property which also provides security against life risks. Thus the motivation for small family exists for well to do sections. On the contrary the poor considers his son as the most important social security. Consequently the quest for sons results in having a large family. Hence it is necessary to motivate the poor for small family by providing employment guarantee schemes, old age pension etc.

Some experts in demography believe that socio-economic policies must integrate population and development goals. In this respect V.P. Pethe argues, 'The masses cannot be expected rationally and morally, to undergo hardships that may result from a small family under the current environment, unless the educated and well off classes also effectively demonstrate that they are willing to make sacrifices (in terms of reducing conspicuous consumption, sharing income and property benefits etc.) in the common commitment to economic development, social transformation and creating an egalitarian social order.'

Though development is the best contraceptive, the question naturally posed is that whether it would be desirable to wait. B.K. Banerjee states, 'Egalitarian distribution of income is a good toy to play with. But there is nothing visible even in the distant horizon, that portends its actualisation in the foreseeable future.' Banerjee raises the question: 'So how long could we wait for the egalitarian society to come? The population bomb is ticking away inexorably. By the turn of the century 700 million of the last census wi'l grow into 1082 million at an annual growth rate of 2.2% of which according to present levels, about 600 million will be sunk below the poverty line.' This reinforces the need of family planning to get precedence, as an independent programme, over programmes of development and equal distribution. However, a better socio-economic order is also a must. The Sixth Plan stated that 'It is almost axiomatic that economic development can in the long run bring about a fall in fertility rate.' At the same time it mentions that, 'Developing countries with large population cannot afford to wait for development to bring about a change in the attitude of couples to limit the size of families as the process of development itself is shifted by population growth.'

If the situation is allowed to drift it would not be possible to reduce birth rate to 25 per thousand with voluntary measures in the immediate future. This requires the building of a national consensus. The following facts should be kept in mind in this respect.

(*a*) More than half the population live below the poverty line and birth rate is high among this group steeped in ignorance and illiteracy. Voluntary methods are not effective with this group.

(*b*) The Government has the responsibility to promote the welfare of the weaker sections in a welfare state. Hence some degree of compulsion to reduce birth rate among the poorer sections is necessary. The only condition is that the compulsions should be sanctioned by the legislature and applied uniformly among all sections of the society.

(*c*) The Government can impose certain restrictions on different sections of community for reducing birth rate. Laws can be enacted to prescribe sterilisation, minimum age for marriage etc.

(*d*) Efforts should be made to bring down infant mortality rapidly to ensure the success of sterilisation programme.

(*e*) The one child family norm should be adopted in the country. China adopted this norm when the birth rate has been only 18 per thousand The Chinese government offers incentives like 12.5 per cent salary hike, priority in housing, preference in school admission and job, adult ration for the child etc. to achieve the norm. Those who refuse to accept the norm are taxed heavily. India has a birth rate of 33 per thousand and the need for one child norm is equally pressing.

No country can work miracles in controlling population. Hence for achieving positive results sustained efforts over a considerable period of time is necessary. The primary need is to arouse social consciousness. The motivation requires the transformation of social and psychological attitudes which requires a long period to materialise. Due to this reason the Committee on Family Planning stated, 'Family Planning is not a medical problem; it is a social and psychological problem.' A solution depends on the combined efforts of economists, doctors, biologists, psychiatrists, psychologists, sociologists, demographers, religious and political leaders etc.

NATIONAL POPULATION POLICY

The Government of India announced a long term policy in 1976 to reduce population growth and to ensure a balance between population and national resources. This policy has been recast on 28th April, 1977. The main features of the modified policy are as under:

1. Purely Voluntary

The family planning scheme shall be run speedily on a purely voluntary basis as part of a comprehensive family welfare programme which will include health education, child and maternal care, supplementary feeding programme for women etc.

2. Fixing Minimum Age of Marriage

In the new policy the minimum age of marraige has been raised to 18 for girls and 21 for boys. (Previously it was 14 and 18 respectively).

Any contravention of the law is deemed to be cognizable offence inviting conviction.

3. Representation

The strength of the Parliament and the legislative assemblies of the states will remain unchanged up to 2001 A.D. on the basis of the population of 1977. Hence no increase in the number of seats will be permitted on the basis of further increase in population.

4. Central Assistance

In future central assistance shall be provided to the states on the basis of the population figures of 1977. Of the aggregate plan assistance to the states by the Central Govt. 8% will be based on the progress achieved in the family planning. The Planning Commission is preparing the details of this assistance scheme. Those states which fail to fulfil the targets will have to face proportionate reduction in central assistance.

5. Sterilisation

The State Governments have been advised to enact legislation for sterilisation if they wish. Since administrative and medical facilities are inadequate in most part of the country, the Central Government does not wish to enact any law in this direction.

6. Expansion of Facilities in the Villages

Sterilisation facilities will be expanded in the rural areas and multi-media motivation strategy will be adopted to spread the message of family planning throughout the country-side by using all the available means of publicity.

6. Financial Assistance for Undergoing Sterilisation Operation

The monetary assistance for undergoing surgery (both vasectomy and tubectomy) has been raised to the following rates:

Family Planning Operations after two issues	:	Rs. 150
Operation after three issues	:	Rs. 100
Operation after four issues	:	Rs. 70

8. Contribution of Voluntary Organisations

For the success of this programme efforts will be made to obtain the help of voluntary organisations. It has also been decided that the grants provided by the Government for family planning to any organisation enjoying the approval and patronage of the Government or local bodies or Health Ministry, will be exempted from the purview or income tax.

9. Free Medical Aid

Any complication developing out of sterilisation operation will be treated free of cost and if it is necessary to desterilise, expert medical aid will also be provided freely.

10. Code of Conduct for the Government Employees

It is expected of the Government employees to accept the small family norm. This has been accordingly included in the Government servants conduct rules.

In this way the new population policy includes 'small family' and 'happy and prosperous future' concepts. The targets are likely to be achieved if the public cooperation is forthcoming as per expectations.

11. Wide Publicity

All available means of publicity will be used to popularise the message of family welfare throughout the nook and corner of the country with special emphasis on rural areas.

12. Citizen's Prestige

The Government attaches utmost importance to the prestige of the individual and his right to decide on the size of his family.

13. Group Motivation

In addition to individual motivation, the Government provides group incentives to make family planning a mass based movement in which a large number of people can participate.

14. Exemption for Donation Towards Family Planning

The Government has decided to give exemption from ineome tax to donors towards family planning. This donation can be given to any registered voluntary body approved by the Ministry of Family Welfare.

15. Population Education in the Curriculum

It is being considered to include population education subject in the curriculum of school education So that small family concept can be made popular. The Ministry of Education has been contacted to work out the modalities of this programme.

SELECT REFERENCES

1. Banerji, D.: *Family Planning in India: A Critique and a Perspective*, People's Publishing House, New Delhi, 1971.
2. Chandrasekhar, S.: *India's Population: Fact and Policy*, The John Day Co., New York, 1946.
3. Dubey, D.C. and Amita Burdhan: "Status of Women and Fertility in India", National Institute of Family Planning, Monograph Series No. 18, New Delhi.
4. Mamdani, Mahmood: "The Myth of Population Control", *Monthly Review Press*, New York, 1972.
5. Ministry of Health and Family Welfare, Health for All by A.D. 2000, Report of the Working Group, New Delhi, 1981.
6. Misra, B.D., Ali, Ashraf: Ruth Simmons and George Simmons, Organization for Change: *A Systems Analysis of Family Planning in Rural India*, Radiant Publishers, New Delhi, 1981.
7. Mitra, Ashok: India's Population: *Aspects of Quality and Control*, Vols: 1 and 2, Abhinav Publications, New Delhi, 1978.
8. Mukherjee, Ramkrishna: *Family and Planning in India*, Orient Longman, Calcutta, 1976.
9. Panandiker, V.A., Pai, R.N., Bishnoi and O.P. Sharma: *Family Planning under Emergency: Policy Implications of Incentives and Disincentives*, Radiant Publishers, New Delhi, 1978.
10. Sikmons, George B.: *The Indian Investment in Family Planning*, An Occasional Paper of the Population Council, New York, 1971.
11. Wyon, John, B. and Gordon, John E.: *The Khanna Study*, Harvard University Press, Mass, 1971.

EXAMINATION QUESTIONS

1. What are the main objectives of population policy in India? How far family planning can achieve these objectives?
2. Discuss the causes for rapid growth of population in India. In this context evaluate the population policy of the Government of India.
3. Give a critical assessment of the population policy of the Government of India.
4. Do you feel that family planning has dismally failed in India? Evaluate the problem and offer positive suggestions.
5. What are the main hurdles in the way of the success of family welfare/planning? Elucidate fully.

34

Population of World

GROWTH OF WORLD POPULATION

For proper study of the world population we can devide the world population growth into the following periods.

1. World population before 1650 (Ancient period)
2. World Population between 1650-1800 (Middle period)
3. World Population after 1800 (Modern period).

1. World Population Before 1950

As stated, it is impossible to make any quantitative assessment of the world population before 1650. So the method of backward projection was employed to estimate the ancient population. Many demographists estimate that 8000 years before Christ when human society was entering the agricultural stage the population of the world might have stayed at 50 lakhs. Gradually the number increased and at the time of Jesus Christ, it must have reached between 20 to 30 crores. The population of China by A.D. 156 might have been nearly 600 lakhs. Carr Saunders and Wilcox gave their independent projections for 1650.

UNO estimated world population for their period and the estimate is more or less nearer to the estimate of Carr Saunders. So the

Table 1. Estimates of World Population by Regions, 1650-1940

(Figures in millions)

World Region	*Carr Saunders estimates*				*United Nation estimates*			
	1650	*1750*	*1800*	*1850*	*1900*	*1920*	*1930*	*1940*
World Total	545	728	906	1171	1608	1834	2008	2216
Africa	100	95	90	95	120	136	165	177
Northern America	1	1	6	26	81	115	134	144
Latin America	12	11	19	33	63	92	110	132
Asia (except USSR)	327	475	597	741	915	997	1069	1173
Europe and Asiatic USSR	103	144	192	274	423	485	533	579
Oceania	2	2	2	2	6	9	10	11

projection of Carr Saunders that the world population was 545 million in 1650 can be accepted for all practical purposes.

2. World Population between 1650-1850

Information about the population this period is paltry. Some countries have population statistics based on census, but for many other countries it was guess work. Available evidence points to the fact that the since A.D. 1680 world population is maintaining its upward momentum. Birth rate during this period ranged between 35-55 per thousand but the system of agriculture improved. Machines were used in economic life. Between 1650 and 1750 the rate of increase in world population was 0.3 per cent while it was 0.45 between 1750-1800. Carr Saunders estimated the world population at 9096 lakhs in 1800 and puts the world population at 7280 lakhs in A.D. 1750. Wilcox estimated the world population at 6940 lakhs in 1750 and 9190 lakhs in 1800. Wilcox is estimates for these periods are slightly higher than the figures given by Carr Saunders. Curiously the estimates of Wilcox for 1600 at 4700 people is less than the data furnished by Carr Saunders which gives 5450 lakhs population for 1650.

3. World Population Since 1800

Modern period could be broken up into different sub-periods.

1. *World population between 1800-1900*. During this period public health facilities improved. The system of vaccination had also started. Treatment for many dreadful diseases were available. Means of transport and communications improved. Carr Saunders estimated that round about 1850 the world population rose at the rate of 0.65 per cent per year and reached 1171 million. Mortaility rate appreciably went down to 16 to 18 per thousand. Regionwise the annual increase was 0.50% in Europe, 0.44% in Asia and 0.18% in Africa.

2. *Population of the world between 1900-1931*. Between 1900-1930 death rates in many parts of the world had come down. Population declined slightly because developed countries took to family planning methods including abortion and infaniticide. Along with a fall in death rate to 10 to 13 per thousand, birth rate also went down. Region-wise, in countries like USA, Germany, Australia, U.K., France, Holland, etc., both birth and mortality rates shrunk. In countries like Spain, Portugal, Yugoslavia Bulgaria, Rumania, Japan, USSR, Egypt, Algeria, Poland, etc. death rate had been controlled but the birth rate remained high so the rate of population growth these countries was very high. Nearly 21 per cent of the

total world population lived in these countries.

In the third category comes such countries where both birth rates as well as mortality rates were high. The means of cultivation were ubiquitous and food shortage and starvation stalked the country side. About 59% of the world population lived in these countries. First World War accounted for a decline of 22.4 million people in world population.

3. *World population between 1930-1950.* After 1930 there was explosion in world population with declining death rate and increased birth rates. Diseases like Malaria, Plague, Cholera etc. have been contained. In under-developed countries birth rate continued to rise at an alarming rate of 2 to 3 per cent annually. The predictions of Malthus have been proved correct in these countries. In 1950 total world population was 2525 million as against 2015 million in 1930. The alarming feature of this period was that in the developing and under-developed countries, birth rate continued to be very high.

4. *World population between 1950-1980.* Table 2 indicates the broad features of population growth in world since 1950.

Table 2. Population Size and Rate of Increase for the World, More Developed Regions and Less Developed Regions, Medium Variant, 1950-1980, as assessed in 1980

Year	*World Population (million)*	*Rate of increase (percentage)*	*More developed region*		*Less developed regions*	
			Population (million)	*Rate of increase (percentage)*	*Population (million)*	*Rate of increase (Percentage)*
1950	2525	—	832	—	1693	—
1955	2757	1.76	887	1.28	1870	1.99
1960	3037	1.94	945	1.27	2092	2.25
1965	3354	1.99	1003	1.19	2351	2.33
1970	3695	1.94	1047	0.87	2648	2.38
1975	4067	1.91	1092	0.84	2974	2.32
1980	4432	1.72	1131	0.71	3301	2.08

Source: Results of the United Nations Demographic Estimates and Projections as assessed in 1980.

According to the United Nations world demographic estimates and projections as assessed in 1980, the total population of the world is estimated to be 4,432 million for 1980, with an annual rate of growth of 1.7 per cent. This rate appears to be in line with the gradual declining trend that began around the middle of the 1960s, when the world population was growing at an estimated rate of 2.0 per cent. In spite of this apparent abatement in the rate of population growth in the 1970's, the size of the annual addition to the existing world total has been increasing steadily to the current level of about 75 million per annum. This increment is the largest observed thus far and the size of annual increments is likely to increase further in the future. During the past three decades, from 1950 to 1980, the world population has increased by 1.9 billion i.e. from 2.5 billion to 4.4 billion, while 2.6 billion persons are expected to be added in the coming three decades, bringing the world total to billion by 2010.

One of the most prominent features of the recent demographic trends among the less developed regions is the increasing diversity in the rate of population growth. In the 1960s, differences in growth rates among regions were relatively small. Among the major areas, the highest rate was estimated for Latin America at 2.8 per cent during the period 1960-1965, closely followed by a rate of 2.5 per cent per annum for Africa. In Asia as a whole (excluding Japan), population growth was relatively slow in 1960-1965, with an annual rate of 2.2 per cent. This situation changed radically in the 1970s and the gap between the highest and the lowest growth rates widened. In Africa, the growth rate rose to 2.9 per cent during the period 1975-1980, mainly due to a decline in death rates, while East Asia (excluding Japan), due largely to the experience of China, had a dramatic decline in its growth rate from 1.9 per cent in 1960-1965 to 1.4 per cent in 1975-1980. In South Asia and Latin America, the growth rate has declined slightly.

The population of the more developed regions of the world, estimated at 1.131 million in 1980, or 26 per cent of the world total, has been growing at a low and declining rate since the 1950s, when the average annual growth rate was about 1.3 per cent. The rate subsequently declined to less than 1.0 per cent in the latter half of the 1960s and 0.7 per cent in the period 1975-1980.

Among the more developed regions, Europe appears to have the lowest rate of population increase. During the period 1975-1980, it grew at an annual rate of 0.4 per cent. As concerns the regions of Europe, Northern and Western Europe have practically reached a state of zero population growth, registering annual growth rates of 0.10 and 0.05 per cent, respectively. In contrast, the population of Eastern and Southern Europe both grew at an annual rate of 0.7 per cent in the period 1975-80, owing to moderately high birth rates of 17 and 16 per thousand, respectively. Outside Europe, the average

Table 3. Population Size and Rate of Increase by Major Area and Region Medium Variant, 1960-1980

	Population (Millions)				*Average annual rate of growth (percentage)*			
	1960	*1970*	*1975*	*1980*	*1960-1965*	*1970-1975*	*1975-1980*	*1980-1985*
World Total	3037	3695	4066	4432	1.99	1.91	1.73	1.70
More Developed Regions	945	1047	1093	1131	1.19	0.84	0.71	0.68
Less Developed Regions	2092	2648	2974	3301	2.33	2.32	2.09	2.04
Africa	275	355	407	470	2.48	2.73	2.90	3.00
Eastern Africa	77	100	115	134	2.63	2.76	2.94	3.09
Middle Africa	35	42	47	53	1.76	2.37	2.52	2.67
Southern Africa	20	25	29	33	2.43	2.61	2.75	2.87
Northern Africa	65	83	94	109	2.33	2.58	2.88	2.87
Western Africa	79	104	121	141	2.77	2.99	3.06	3.18
Latin America	216	283	322	364	2.80	2.54	2.45	2.38
Caribbean	20	25	28	31	2.27	2.06	1.84	1.82
Middle America	49	68	79	93	3.23	3.15	2.98	2.88
Temperate South America	31	36	38	41	1.66	1.33	1.33	1.29
Tropical South America	115	154	176	199	3.00	2.61	2.53	2.46
Northern America	199	226	236	248	1.94	1.96	1.38	1.24
East Asia	816	991	1096	1175	1.94	1.96	1.38	1.24
China	682	838	928	995	2.02	2.02	1.40	1.27
Japan	94	104	112	117	0.99	1.33	0.88	0.62
Other East Asia	40	51	57	63	2.78	2.21	2.05	1.92
South Asia	877	1116	1257	1404	2.40	2.36	2.22	2.17
Eastern South Asia	229	291	326	361	2.41	2.27	2.07	2.05
Middle South Asia	592	752	845	944	2.36	2.33	2.21	2.14
Western South Asia	56	74	85	98	2.76	2.94	2.84	2.89
Europe	425	459	474	484	0.91	0.63	0.40	0.34
Eastern Europe	97	103	106	110	0.68	0.55	0.71	0.61
Northern Europe	76	80	82	82	0.71	0.31	0.10	0.04
Southern Europe	118	128	134	139	0.87	0.98	0.72	0.61
Western Europe	135	148	152	153	1.23	0.56	0.05	0.04
Oceania	16	19	21	23	2.08	1.85	1.47	1.44
Australia-New Zealand	13	15	17	18	1.99	1.68	1.21	1.15
Melanesia	2	3	3	4	2.31	2.73	2.70	2.72
Micronesia-Polynesia	1	1	1	1	2.84	1.96	1.74	1.66
USSR	214	242	253	265	1.49	0.95	0.93	0.93

Source : Results of the United Nations estimates and projections as assessed in 1980.

annual rate of population increase for the period 1975-1980 was about 0.9 per cent for Northern America, Japan and the USSR, and 1.2 per cent for Australia and New Zealand. In all the more developed regions mentioned above, population is projected to grow at a similar, if not lower, rate in the near future.

Thus, the current demographic situation in the developing countries does not have historical precedents from they might take comfort. The considerably more rapid decline in mortality has created a greater imbalance than ever existed in the developed countries. This is the heart of "the population problem" in today's developing countries. Statistical evidences show that the pressure of population in developing countries of the world would increase in the next few years and the disparity in the distribution of population between the developed and underdeveloped countries would widen. In short, the burden of population would increase particularly in those areas which are already weighted down by it, and which are the least capable of bearing it.

Future Growth of Population in the World

There are different trends of population growth in different countries of the world at different times. So, it is difficult to forecast what would be the size of World Population especially at a distant data, except under certain assumptions. The past experience has also shown that population at any future year was always found to exceed or at least very substantially from the projected estimates.

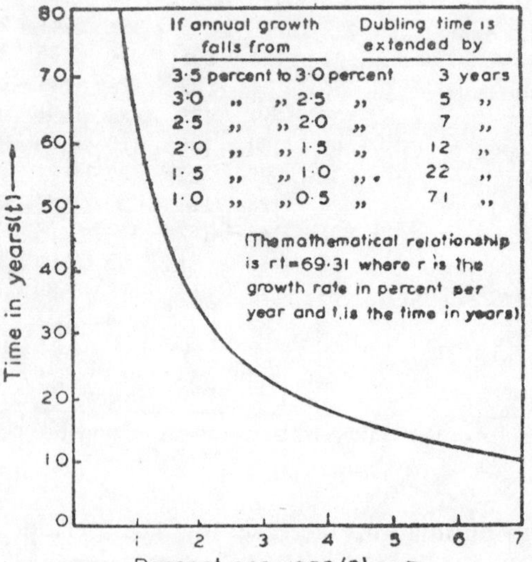

Fig. 1.

If the present rate of world population growth continue, it would take only 12.5 years to add one more billion to the world population; and on the sun rise of the first day of the next century, there will be at least 6.2 billion people on this planet, each sharing an average area of 0.02 sq. km. Nonetheless, the continuation of the present rate of growth of world population cannot be accurately forestalled. The global population, therefore, in the year 2000 would be lower than 6.2 billion, if the growth rate in some regions declined more dramatically than has happened in the past particularly in the last quarter of the present century.

Figure shows the relation between population growth rate and time in which population doubles.

The United Nations have tried to estimate the World Population from A.D. 1980 to 2000. The world population of 4.4 billion in 1980 will be likely increase to 6.1 billion by 2000 and 8.2 billion by 2025. It is obvious from the Table 4.

Due to the gap in the current growth rate between the more developed and the less developed regions, most future population growth is projected to occur in the latter regions. The less developed regions, with an average current growth rate of 2.1 per cent, are projected to continue to grow quite rapidly, at rates of 1.8 per cent during the period 1995-2000 and 1.1 per cent during 2020-2025. The more developed regions, on the other hand, are projected to experience a reduced growth rate from the current 0.7 to rates of 0.5 per cent per annum for the period 1995-2000 and 0.2 per cent for 2020-2025.

Among the less developed regions, Africa is projected to maintain the highest rate of population increase throughout the projection span, 2.9 per cent at the end of this century; and 1.9 per cent in the period 2020-2025.

Latin America is likely to have a faster pace of decline in growth rate than Africa: the current rate of 2.5 per cent per annum in Latin America is projected to decline to 2.0 per cent by 2000 and to 1.5 per cent by 2025. The population for Latin America is projected to be 566 million in 2000 and 865 million in 2025; these values are greater than the current 364 million by 55 per cent and 138 per cent, respectively.

On the other hand, Asia as a whole had a population of 2600 million in 1980 and comprised 58 per cent of the world total. That population is projected to grow to 3600 million in 2000 and to 4500 million in 2025.

Meantime, population growth in Northern America, Europe and

Table 4. Population Projections by Major Area and Region Medium Variant, 1980-2025, as Assessed in 1980

	Population (million)				*Average annual rate of growth (percentage)*			
	1980	*1990*	*2000*	*2025*	*1980-1985*	*1985-1990*	*1990-2000*	*2000-2025*
World Total	4826	5242	6119	8195	1.65	1.60	1.50	0.96
More Developed Regions	1170	1206	1272	1377	0.61	0.58	0.48	0.24
Less Developed Regions	3656	4036	4847	6818	1.98	1.89	1.77	1.10
Africa	566	655	853	1542	3.02	2.99	2.90	1.91
Eastern Africa	156	183	250	478	3.17	3.17	3.12	2.09
Middle Africa	61	70	91	162	2.74	2.75	2.72	1.90
Northern Africa	126	144	186	296	2.77	2.62	2.45	1.47
Southern Africa	38	44	58	101	2.87	2.82	2.71	1.76
Western Africa	166	195	267	505	3.23	3.20	3.13	2.01
Latin America	410	459	566	865	2.28	2.15	2.02	1.48
Caribbean	34	37	43	62	1.74	1.74	1.64	1.19
Middle America	107	122	156	242	2.72	2.51	2.31	1.43
Temperate South America	44	47	52	62	1.20	1.09	0.99	0.55
Tropical South America	226	254	315	498	2.36	2.23	2.10	1.66
Northern America	261	274	299	343	0.95	1.05	0.70	0.42
East Asia	1250	1327	1475	1712	1.20	1.09	1.02	0.38
China	1060	1128	1257	1469	1.24	1.13	1.05	0.39
Japan	120	123	129	131	0.49	0.48	0.49	−0.07
Other East Asia	70	76	88	111	1.76	1.54	1.35	0.60
South Asia	1565	1731	2075	2819	2.02	1.90	1.72	0.95
Eastern South Asia	400	440	520	688	1.91	1.77	1.58	0.88
Middle South Asia	1051	1160	1386	1867	1.98	1.87	1.70	0.90
Western South Asia	114	131	168	264	2.78	2.63	2.42	1.47
Europe	492	499	512	522	0.30	0.27	0.24	0.03
Eastern Europe	113	116	121	131	0.49	0.43	0.43	0.23
Northern Europe	82	82	83	81	0.03	0.05	0.02	−0.10
Southern Europe	143	147	154	161	0.53	0.46	0.40	0.12
Western Europe	153	154	155	150	0.07	0.08	0.05	−0.16
Oceania	25	26	30	36	1.36	1.29	1.19	0.61
Australia-New Zealand	19	20	22	25	1.05	0.99	0.93	0.35
Melanesia	4	5	6	9	2.63	2.46	2.18	1.37
Micronesia-Polynesia	2	2	2	2	1.52	1.30	1.10	0.34
USSR	278	290	310	355	0.84	0.70	0.64	0.50

Source : Results of the United Nations estimates and projections as assessed in 1980.

the USSR is projected to remain at or below the current modest rate throughout the projection span. Thus, for the more developed regions as a whole, including Australia, Japan and New Zealand, population is projected to grow from 1100 million in 1980 to 1300 million in 2000 and 1400 million in 2025. Consequently, the distribution of the global population by broad geographical areas will significantly change in favour of Africa, Latin America and South Asia. More specifically, by 2025 these areas will contribute to the world total 19, 11 and 34 per cent, respectively. These shares are larger than their 1980 shares, by 8.3 and 3 points, respectively. Conversely, East Asia and the rest of the world will contribute a reduced share of the total world population.

WORLD PATTERNS OF FERTILITY

Fertility varies greatly in time and space. For the world as a whole the estimated crude birth rate around 1980 was between 16-20 live births per thousand population. The highest levels of fertility, with birth rates of 20 per thousand and over are found in Latin America, Africa and in South-West and South-East Asia. At the other end of the scale, low fertility, with birth rates of less than 16 per

Table 5. Crude Birth Rates and Percentage of Change, in Selected Developed Countries and Less Developed Countries

Country	*Crude birth rate*		*Percentage change in crude birth rate*
	1950	*1978*	
A—Developed			
The Americas			
Canada	27.1	15.3	−43.5
United States	23.5	15.8	−32.8
Asia and the Pacific			
Australia	23.3	15.7	−32.6
Japan	28.2	14.2	−49.6
New Zealand	25.9	16.9	−34.7
Europe and the Soviet Union			
Denmark	18.7	12.2	−34.8
France	20.7	14.1	−31.9
Germany, East	16.9	14.0	−17.2
Germany, West	16.5	9.5	−42.4
Soviet Union	26.7	18.1	−32.2
Sweden	16.5	11.6	−29.7
Switzerland	18.1	11.3	−37.6
United Kingdom	16.5	12.3	−25.5

Country	Crude Birth rate 1965	1975 (or later)	Percentage change
B—Less Developed			
China	34	20	−41
India	43	36	−16
Brazil	42	33	−21
Bangladesh	48	48	—
Pakistan	47	47	—
Philippines	44	34	−23
Egypt	41	41	—
Burma	40	40	—

thousand, is almost confined to Europe. The less developed countries, on the other hand, apparently differ rather markedly in levels of fertility, a condition which would ordinarily be expected to indicate probable future change among them.

It would be clear from the foregoing paragraphs that there are three major trends in global fertility trends:

1. Persistent high fertility in numerous countries of Africa, Latin America and in South-West and South-East Asia (Fig. 1).
2. Recent Decline in fertility in Japan and some under-developed countries such as Argentina, Uruguay and Hong Kong, etc.
3. Long-term decline in fertility in many developed countries during the nineteenth and early twentieth centuries (Fig. 1).

World Pattern of Mortality

Broadly speaking, high mortality predominates in the developing realms and low mortality is the characteristic of developed regions. Countries with higher death rates are mainly in Southern Asia, Africa and parts of Latin America (with notable exceptions like Argentina, Chile, Venezuela and Uruguay). It should be borne in mind that relatively high death rates prevail in the developing regions in spite of the larger percentage of their people in the young age groups. Their age specific death rates are, therefore, higher than the crude death rates.

Moderate-to-low death rates are characteristic of all of the economically developed regions. In spite of the fact that the average population age is distinctly higher than in the traditional societies. Death rates in many West European countries including Great Britain are between 8 and 10 per thousand. The highest death rate was 10.7 in Austria and the lowest 5.3 in Poland and the Netherlands. Death rates below 10 per thousand are found in Australia, Canada, New Zealand and the USSR. These countries have been joined in recent years by Japan, Argentina, Uruguay and some other Latin American States as well as by a number of smaller countries .whose mortality has achieved extremely low levels; Bermuda 6.8 per thousand; Puerto Rico 6.7; Iceland 6.6; Taiwan 6.4; Hong Kong 5.9 and Signapore 5.9. In many of these small countries, the widening gap between fertility and mortality poses a severe problem of natural increase (Fig. 1).

The first phase of mortality decline occurred in the eighteenth, nineteenth and twentieth centuries in the advanced countries of Europe, North America and Australia. It began in the eighteenth century in Scandinavia and in the last quarter of the nineteenth century in most of the remaining countries of Western Europe. In contrast, many of the developing countries enjoyed no appreciable decline in mortality until the last two decades, but then the fall has been more spectaculars and sudden than the decline which took place in the industrialized countries of the West in the nineteenth century. For example, the fall in mortality rates which occurred in a decade (1940-50) in Britain, Guyana, Chile and Malaya is equivalent to the fall that took place in 62 years in Scandinavia and 30 years in Belgium. Some more examples of a sharp fall in mortality rates may be quoted:

1. Puerto Rico	Year	1900	30 per 1000
		1940	18 per 1000
		1955	7.6 per 1000
		1975	5.5 per 1000
2. Mexico	Year	1930	27 per 1000
		1954	17 per 1000
		1975	8.2 per 1000
3. Chile	Year	1945	19.3 per 1000
		1950	15.0 per 1000
		1975	9.5 per 1000
4. Ceylon	Year	1950	20 per 1000
		1958	10 per 1000
		1975	7.2 per 1000

Thus though the trend in mortality in the developing nations cannot be plotted as precisely as in the developed nations; but it is clear that a major reduction in mortality occurred in many countries of the developing regions in a very short period following the end of World War II. Further decline in the death rate in the very near future is inevitable, and it is going to have a revolutionary impact on the population situation in the developing countries.

The process of decline in death rates without any significant decline in birth rates in developing countries is in sharp contrast to the conditions which prevailed in the European countries in the early phase of their industrialization. The latter countries experienced a fall in their birth rates before there was a sharp decline in mortaliy. But, on the contrary, in the developing countries mortality is consistently declining since the Second World War while the birth rates are still high. The consequences are that developing countries are increasing their population at a rate double that of the North Western European countries in their early phase of development.

The question here for us to enquire is what causes an abrupt decline in the death rate in the developing countries. This steep fall of death rate is the result of provisions of better diet, pure drinking water, improved hospital facilities, better sanitation and, last but not least, the control by wonder medicine of several epidemics and other diseases which took a heavy toll of human life. In particular, improvement in medical knowledge and sanitation have been most important to controlling mortality from malaria, typhoid, typhus, cholera, dysentery and enteritis. And, while it took time for medical and sanitary progress in Europe and America, knowledge and techniques are now available for immediate transfer. For example, the dramatic post-war decline in mortality in Sri Lanka was in a large measure due to the vigorous anti-malaria campaign, improvements in curative and preventive medicine and in the economic situation. Equally important to the above factors is the establishment of international agencies which propagate the ideal of better health. In this context, one may remember the role played by WHO which spends millions of rupees in the developing countries for the provision of the basic health facilities to a large number of persons. At the initative of the international organizations like the WHO, most of the developing and developed countries have established parallel organizations in their own countries to reduce deaths.

The current decline in death rates in the developing areas has been especially marked for children, whose mortality rates have been influenced by the measures to control the epidemics. Death from famines has also been appreciably reduced as transportation and storage improvements enable relief from the impact of partial crop failures. Increased order and security and more frequent contact with Western concepts of the value of the human life have also helped to reduce mortality. But the decline in the death rates in the European countries was primarily the result of the economic development process itself. Industrialization brought about improvements in dectetic and these countries. But the rapid mortality declines experienced by the developing nations since the end of World War II, were independent of economic development. It was mainly the outcome of increasing use of the Western system of medicine and technique of death control.

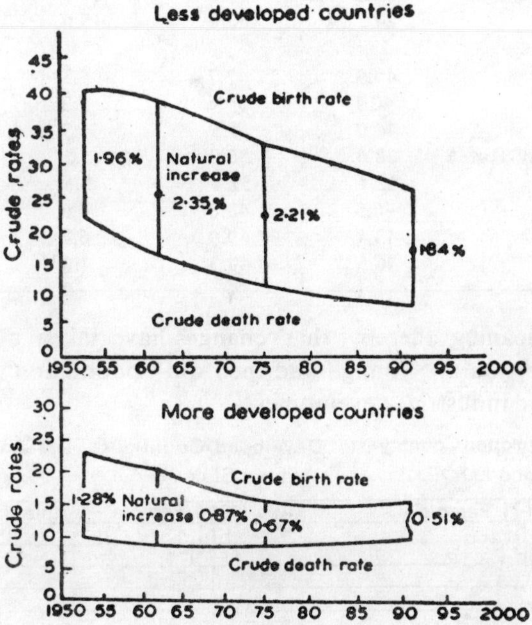

Fig. 2.

Age Structure of World Population

Comparison of the age composition of population of various countries at the present time shows large differences, which are closely related to present levels and past trends of birth and death rates. The examples in the table below have been selected to illustrate representative patterns.

From the study of Table 6, two conclusions can be drawn.

One, developing countries have greater proportion of "young" population; while the developed ones have more "old" population.

Second, the present day developed countries might have had large "younger" age-group in the pre-industrial era, that what they

Table 6. Age Composition and Dependency Ratio, Selected Countries, 1969-74

Country	*Per cent of population in different age groups*			*Dependency ratio*
	0-14	*15-59*	*60+*	
Developed				
1. Austrailia	28.0	59.5	12.5	68.2
2. France	23.7	57.6	18.7	73.5
3. Japan	24.3	64.0	11.7	56.3
4. Sweden	20.7	58.3	21.0	71.6
5. United Kingdom	23.1	57.1	19.9	75.3
6. USA	24.5	60.5	15.0	65.2
Developing				
1. Ghana	46.9	47.7	5.3	109.5
2. India	40.1	54.6	5.3	83.2
3. Indonesia	44.0	51.5	4.5	94.0
4. Republic of Korea	38.6	56.0	5.5	78.7
5. Malaysia	42.1	52.4	5.5	90.8
6. Mexico	46.3	48.8	4.9	105.8
7. Pakistan	43.4	49.9	6.7	100.6
8. Zambia	46.5	49.3	4.2	102.6

have today meaning thereby that changes have taken place in the of their proportion of "young" and the "old" population during the course of their industrial development.

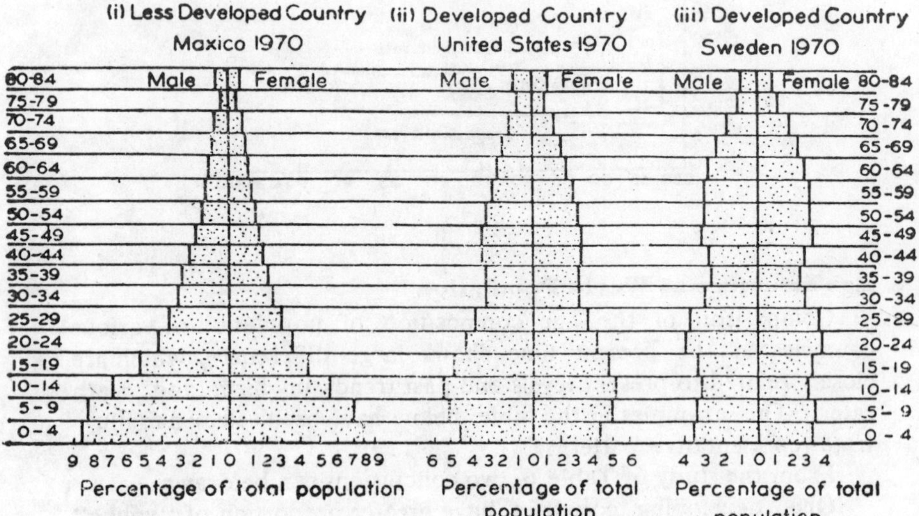

Age-Sex distribution in three countries

Fig. 3.

WORLD URBANIZATION

The most conspicuous feature of today's accelerated world population growth is its ever greater rapidity of urbanization. In many periods in history, population and cities have grown, but the tempo and dimensions of recent years have never been equalled.

It is estimated that nearly 3 per cent of the world population were living in towns of over 5000 population and 2.4 per cent in cities of 20,000 and over in 1800. The second figure (2.4) slightly less than doubled from 1800 to 1850 (4.3), more than doubled between 1850 and 1900 (9.2) per cent, more than doubled again (20.9) per cent in the first half of the twentieth century, and the rate of change from 1950 to 1960 was twice that of the preceding 50 years. In 1980 the proportion of the earth's population living in urban places of all size is estimated to have been about 41 per cent.

The distribution of world population as between developing and developed countries is presented in Table 7. The growth rates of population in these regions for the period 1920-50, 1950-80, 1980-2000 (Table 7); 1920-1980 and 1920-2000 are presented in Table 8. A study of these tables leads to the following conclusions.

Table 7. Distribution of World Population in Developed and Developing Countries

Year	*Per cent of total population in*		*Per cent of rural population in*		*Per cent of urban population in*	
	developed countries	*developing countries*	*developed countries*	*developing countries*	*developed countries*	*developing countries*
1920	36.2	63.8	27.5	72.5	72.2	27.8
1930	36.5	63.4	27.4	72.6	70.0	30.0
1940	35.8	64.2	25.3	74.7	67.5	32.5
1950	34.2	65.8	23.0	77.0	62.4	37.6
1960	32.7	67.3	20.4	79.6	56.6	43.4
1970	30.0	70.0	16.9	83.1	51.9	48.1
1980	27.0	73.0	13.7	86.5	46.2	53.8
1990	24.2	75.8	10.8	89.2	40.2	60.0
2000	21.7	78.3	8.8	91.2	34.0	66.0

Source: For a discussion of the characteristics of the spatial structure of modified under development see Chattopadhya and Moonis Raza (1975), "Regional Development: Analytical Framework and Indicators", *Indian Journal of Regional Science*, Vol. 7, No. 1.

Table 8. Growth Rates of Population in Developed and Developing Countries of the World: 1920-2000

Year	*Asia*	*Growth rates of population in* *developed countries*	*developing countries*	*World*
1920-1950	0.988	0.812	1.105	1.001
1950-1980	2.035	1.073	2.225	1.871
1980-2000	1.163	0.709	2.251	1.804
1920-1980	1.510	0.944	1.663	1.435
1920-2000	1.985	0.885	1.810	1.527

1. The proportion of the population living in developing countries has been continuously increasing since the beginning of the twentieth century. Nearly 73 per cent of the world population in 1980 was living in developing countries as compared to only 64 per cent in 1920. By the turn of the century this share is expected to go up to 78 per cent.

2. Not only does the share of population living in developing countries to the total world population continue to be very high but it is also increasing at a much faster rate as compared to the rest of the world. The total population in developed countries increased by 76 per cent between 1920 and 1980 in contrast to the developing countries, wherein the population more than doubled during this period. The differential has also been accelerating with time. While the growth rates of population in the developing countries was only slightly more than that of the developed countries for the period of 1920-1950, the corresponding ratio had gone up to more than double for the period 1950-1980. It has been projected that during the next two decades the population in the developing countries would grow at a rate of 2.25 per cent as compared to 0.709 for the developed countries.

3. Though experiencing only marginal increments in their levels of urbanization, the developing countries are undergoing massive urban growth. The average annual growth of their urban population between 1960 and 1980 was 4.39 per cent. This is in sharp contrast to the value of 2.1 per cent in the case of nine European countries for the period of the fastest growth of their urban population in the latter half of nineteenth century.

SELECT REFERENCES

1. Bogue, Donald J. : *Principles of Demography*, Wiley, New York, 1969.

2. Brown, L.R. : "World Population Trends; Sign of Hope, Sign of Stress", *Population Reports Series*, J.N. 13, 1977.
3. Brock. J.O.M. and Webb, J.W. : *A Geography of Mankind*, New York, 1973.
4. Coale, A.J. and Hoover, E.M. : *Population Growth and Economic Development in Low Income Countries*, Princeton, P.U. Press, 1945.
5. Carr-Saunders, A.M. : *World Population : Past Growth and Present Trends*, Frank Cars and Co., 1964, Chs. 2 and 3, pp. 17-45.
6. Cowgill, Donald, O. : "Transition theory as general population theory", in Thomas R. Ford and Gordon F. DeJong (eds). *Social Demography*, Prentice-Hall, pp. 627-32.
7. ECAFE Secretariate, "The Demographic Situation in the ECAFE Region" in United Nations, Population Strategy in Asia, Asian Population Study Series, No. 28, 1972, pp. 69-130.
8. Hauser, Philip M. : "World Population : Retrospect and prospect," in Rapid Population Growth : Consequences and Policy Implications: The Johns Hopkins Press, 1971, pp. 103-122.
9. Hauser, Phillip M. (ed). *The Population Dilemma*, Englewood Chiffs, Prentice-Hall, 1963.
10. United Nations, The Determinants and Consequences of Population Trends. New Summary of Findings on Interaction of Demographic, Economic and Social Factors, Volume I, 1973, Chapters 2 and 3, pp. 10-32.
11. Tomlison, Ralph, *Population Dynamics*, Random House, New York, 1965.
12. Thompson, Warren S. and Levis, David T. : *Population Problems*, Mc-Graw-Hill, New York.

35

Population of Japan

The demographic situation in Japan stems from an unique situation in which a highly developed economic system co-exists in total compatibility with a conservatives socio-cultural infrastructure.

Japan is the only Asian country which is counted among the developed countries of the world. Japan consists of four regions namely Hokkaido, Honshu, Shikaku and Kyushu which together encompass an area of 377,700 kilometers. As in India many ethnic groups reside in Japan among whom 60 per cent constitute. Malayan Mangolian, 30 per cent Chinese Mangolian Tungasian and 10 per cent Ayinu Palok sematic people. Most of the area are covered by mountains.

DEMOGRAPHIC BACKGROUND OF JAPAN

Systematic census in Japan was conducted for the first time in 1920 and so all previous estimates were mere quess work. It is estimated that between 1600 and 1850 A.D. the population of Japan was about 3 crores. During its initial stage Japan was an extremely poor country with a backward economy and high unemployment. Production and consumption was pitiably low and the people enjoyed a low standard of living. Under such circumstances its birth rate and death rate remained high which kept the population growth stable. Only after 1850 Japan entered the field of international trade which resulted in an increase in Population. Between 1912 and 1926 the population doubled and become about 60 million. In 1971 the population rose to 100 million and by the end of the twentith century it is likely to cross the 120 million mark. From the academic point of view the Japanese population can be divided and presented in the following order:

(1) *Japan's population between 1615-1860.* During this period Japan was ruled by the Tokugawa dynasty. The country was divided into small self-sufficient units. Foreigners were prohibited to enter Japan. The population stayed between 2.8 to 3 crores.

(2) *Japan's population between 1869-1912.* This period could be

considered as the priliminary stage of Japan's development. It was the period of Maiji rule in Japan when the population rose to 6 crores. During this period the country's agriculture, industry and trade prospered and consequently this poor country quickly rose to the rank of the developed countries.

(3) *Population of Japan between 1921-1926.* This period was the reigning period of Taisho, when the population increase at a rapid pace and reached the 6 crores mark, which was double the population of 1860. Between 1920 and 1925 Japan's population increased at an annual rate of 6.7 per cent. Death rate started decreasing after 1918.

(4) *Japan's population after 1930.* Since 1930 Japan's population registered continuous increase along with a dip in the death rate, which resulted in a net increase of 48 lakhs in the population between 1930 and 1935. However, the above trend received a slight set back between 1935 to 1940, when the overall increase in population showed a growth of 39 lakhs only. The period of 1920-40 falls into different phases of population growth the increase being 6.7 per cent during 1920-25, 7.9 per cent during 1920-30, 7.5 per cent during 1930-35 and 5.6 per cent during 1935-40. The declining trend in the population since 1935 created much concern to the Government which stood for a higher growth rate of population. The Japanese cabinet envolved a programme of action in 1947 which sought to raise the population to 10 crores by 1960. The population of Japan was 11.7 million in 1980.

In Japan population has been growing as depicted in following Table.

Table 1. Japan Population

Year	*Population in Crores*
1872	3.48
1878	3.62
1888	3.90
1898	4.29
1908	4.80
1918	5.47
1920	5.50
1930	6.45
1940	7.19
1950	8.32
1960	9.34
1962	9.52
1975	11.19
1980	11.69

Birth Rate in Japan

With a spectacular decline in fertility in Japan after the 'baby boom' of 1947-1949 and with a continuous and substantial drop in mortality since the end of the war, Japan has in a very short period undergone demographic changes similar to those which the nations of the West experienced from the mid-19th century to the 1930s.

The crude birth rate showed a gradual decline before the War, but was some 30 per thousand of population annually for the period 1941-1943. After rising to 33.34 per thousand of population during the post-war baby boom of 1947-1949, it dropped sharply to below 20 from 1955. While it fell to below 14 per thousand in 1966 (supposed to be an unluckly year in the Japanese zodaic calendar for girls to be born in), the crude birth rate showed a moderate increase to 19 per thousand in 1971-1973, since girls born during the post-war baby boom reached marriageable age in those years. Therefore, however, the crude birth rate began to decline again, and in 1981 had reached 13.0 per thousand of population, the lowest level ever recorded in Japan's demographic history.

Death Rate in Japan

The trend of the decline in mortality, both for males and females, is much more straightforward than that of fertility. In 1981-1982, Japan enjoyed probably the longest life expectancy in the world. The crude death rate was around 17 per thousand of population

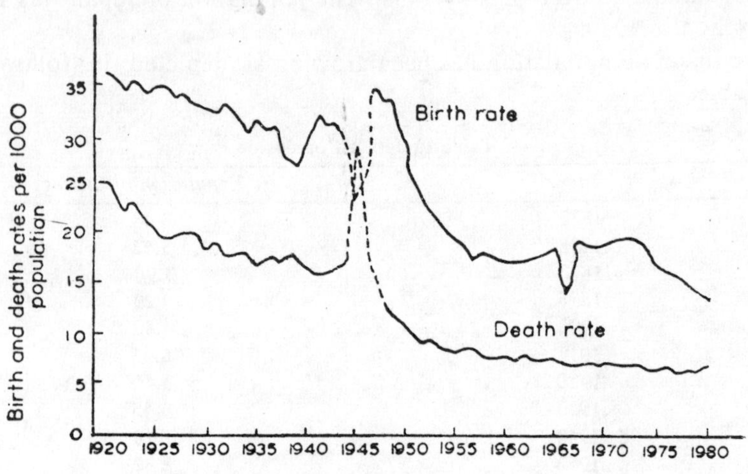

Birth and death rates in Japan, 1920-1980

Fig. 4.

during the 1930s, but it was lowered to 14.6 in post-war 1947 and has since been stabilized, being around 6 per thousand for the last five years.

The infant mortality rate has been below 100 per thousand live births since 1940. By 1950 it was 60, and this downward trend continued, until in 1981 it was 7.1, one of the lowest in the world. However, mortality for pre-school children and maternal mortality are still somewhat higher than in the Scandinavian countries and there is still room for improvement.

Density of Population in Japan

Unlike in other countries the distribution of Japan's population in uneven. In certain pockets of Japan the density of population is as high as 1800 persons per square kilometre while in some places it is very low. Tokyo is one of the most densely populated cities in the world. Average density of population in Japan is 314 per square kilometre in 1980 which could be considered significantly high. If we compare Japan's population density with the Asian countries it can be seen that similar high density of population could be seen only in Bengal, Jawa and Kerala. As compared to Japan's density of population of 314 per square kilometre 1960, India's density is 123 per square kilometre and Brazil's density only of 8 persons per square kilometre. Only 20 per cent of the 370 thousand square kilometre of Japan is useful for agricultural purposes. The pressure of population on land is seen to be even more significant when it is remembered that only 19 per cent of Japan's total area can be used for cultivation. High population density is not recent; it has been maintained through generations, and in fact, most Japanese commonly perceive their country as being overcrowded.

Urban-Rural Population in Japan

Urban population of Japan increase rapidly more particularly, since the Second World War. Today two-third of the Japanese population lives in cities. With the exception of Germany, no country witness such fast urbanisation process witnessed in Japan.

Table 2 gives the break up of the population in urban rural areas.

The Table 2 makes it clear that the population is gradually declining in Japan. The important population-related issues in Japan are the excessive concentration of population in the urban and metropolitan areas, notably in the Tokyo Metropolitan Area, and depopulation of the remote rural areas, and these continue to be among the nation's most critical population and development problems. Large governmental efforts have been made since the 1960s to rectify these imbalances by means of a series of development policies for the reasons. The recent slowing of population growth rate in the metropolitan areas, one very important cause of which is the deceleration of the rate of inflow of population into those areas, suggests that there will be a substantial closing of the gap in the future.

Table 2. Urban-Rural Areas

(in Crores)

Year	*Total population*	*Rural population*	*Urban population*
1891	0.38	—	0.38
1898	4.29	3.74	0.55
1913	5.13	4.24	0.89
1920	5.59	4.59	1.00
1930	6.45	4.92	1.53
1940	7.19	4.44	2.47
1950	8.32	3.65	5.93
1960	9.34	3.46	5.93
1970	10.87	3.84	6.13
1980	11.69	3.98	7.71

Age Structure

Despite the rapid post-war demographic transition, the age structure at first changed rather slowly. The proportion of the population under 15 years of age, which accounted for 35-36 per cent of the total population throughout the pre-war period and even until 1950, declined gradually until it was only 30 per cent in 1960. It then began to fall rapidly as the children born during the baby boom period reached their 15th birthday. In 1980, the percentage stood at 23.5. On the other hand, the proportion of the population aged 15-64 has risen gradually, from 60 per cent in 1980. The population aged 65 and over, who accounted for 5 per cent or the total population in 1950, increased to 7 per cent in 1970 and 9.1 per cent in 1980. With the percentage of young people being lower than that in the developing countries and the percentage of elderly people being lower than that in the western countries, Japan has a very larger proportion of its population of productiv age.

Figure 2 presents changes in the age structure of the population of Japan: 1960, 1980, and 2000.

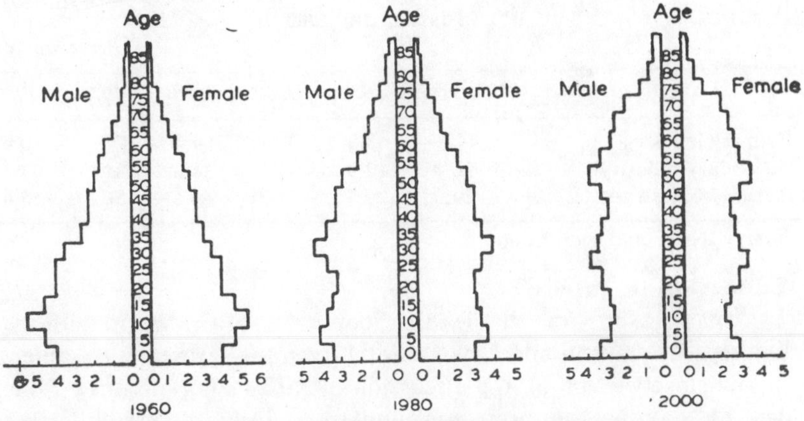

Changes in the age structure of the population of Japan: 1960, 1980, and 2000

Fig. 4.

Table 3. Population by Major Age Groups in Japan, 1920-1980 and 2000 (estimation)

(*Percentage*)

Year	*0-14 years*	*15-64 years*	*65 and over*
1920	36.5	58.3	5.3
1930	36.6	58.7	4.8
1940	36.1	59.2	4.7
1947	35.3	59.9	4.8
1960	30.0	64.2	5.7
1970	23.9	69.0	7.1
1980	23.5	67.4	9.0
2000	20.2	65.6	14.3

Source : National census data.

OCCUPATIONAL DISTRIBUTION OF POPULATION IN JAPAN

Industrialisation and economic development led to the increase of urban population and fall in rural population. Towards the end of 19th century nearly 75% of the population depended on agriculture and other primary industries. However from the beginning of the 20th century this percentage steadily came down.

The Table 4 gives the occupational distribution of population between 1940 to 1980.

Table 4. Distribution of the Economically Active Population in Japan, 1940-1980

(*Percentage*)

	1940	*1950*	*1960*	*1970*	*1975*	*1980*
Primary industry	44.3	48.3	32.6	19.4	13.9	10.9
Secondary industry	26.0	12.9	29.2	34.0	34.1	33.5
Tertiary industry	29.0	29.7	38.2	46.6	51.7	55.4

Source : National census data.

Education in Japan

Japan is one of the leading countries of the world with high literacy. Thompson and Lewis said, "Even the farmers were able to follow closely much of the discussion of Japan's population problem day by day in the press and indeed could hardly avoid doing so because of the large amount of space allotted to this topic in the papers and time allotted to it over the Radio." Illiteracy is totally wiped out of Japan. Education up to pre-university level is compulsory in Japan. Today education covers a wide range of fields and there is perfect coordination among them.

Internal and External Migration

Rural exodus to the cities continue unabated in Japan. Consequently the process of urbanization is proceeding at a tremendous pace. Hilly places are thinly populated. Till the third quarter of 19th century Japanese were not permitted to migrate to other countries nor were people of other countries permitted to enter Japan. After some time permission to migrate was granted. After the Sino-Japanese war, the people of Japan migrated to places like Korea, Manchuria and Formosa. By 1895, some 3 lakh people migrated to these places. By 1940 the number of people migrating to these places was 1.2 million. Other places like USA, Brazil, etc. also received large number of Japanese migrants. Japanese in America increased from 2.8 lakhs in 1930 to 6.29 lakhs in 1980. Today more than 20 lakhs Japanese are spread in different parts of the world.

Population Policy

The Government's involvement with fertility and the family in the policy area has mainly been in the health and welfare aspects. For a number of reasons the Government does not wish to adopt a policy that is pronatalist, preferring merely to create favourable living and environmental conditions which make it possible for young married couples to have children if they wish.

In 1948, the Eugenic Protection Law was passed, containing three major provisions: (1) family planning field workers were to be trained and deployed; (2) induced abortion was legalized for health reasons (a year later, the law was amended to include economic reasons); and (3) sterilization operations were legalized for health reasons. Before passage of the law, criminal abortions had been on the increase, and it was considered essential from the standpoint of maternal health to provide a channel for legalized, sanitary, safe abortion. The law did not constitute an explicit antinatalist policy. It was presented as a public health measure rather than a demographic one.

In 1952, the Ministry of Health and Welfare compiled a scheme for a national family planning programme. Technical guidance rather than general education in family planning was emphasized. Health centres, midwives, local community organizations, and voluntary workers all were mobilized. Since around 1960, however, the scope, coverage, and content of the national family planning programme have changed because of the rapid decline in the national birth rate and the accelerated diminution of family size.

During the 1960s, in discussing family planning, a positive approach, that is, having a few children rather than avoiding having children, was stressed. Birth control for population control gave way to family planning for individual health and well-being.

The Government has made determined efforts to ensure adequate social, economic and environmental conditions making it easier for a couple to have and rear children. These include the improvement of the quality of life, better housing conditions, provision of longer maternity leave, provision of better and more adequate nurseries, enhancement of the status of women, and creation of an attitude in society in general o. accepting and welcoming the return of a married women after having children to her previous place of work without serious loss of seniority, status or salary. With increasing gainful employment among married women, particularly in age group 20-35, emphasis has been placed on the creation of an employment structure in which child-bearing and child-rearing are not in conflict with a women's career and gainful employment.

SELECT REFERENCES

1. Japanese Organisation for International Cooperation in Family Planning: Bird's eye view of Population and Family Planning in Japan, Tokyo, March, 1980.
2. Muramatsu, Minoru: *Japan, Country Profiles*, New York; Population Council, March 1971.
3. Muramatsu, Minoru: and Toshio Kuroda. *"Japan" in Population Policy in Developed Countries*, edited by Bernard Berelson, pp. 704-730, New York; McGraw Hill, 1974.
4. Tecuber, Irene B.: *The Population of Japan*. Princeton, N.J., Princeton University Press, 1958.

EXAMINATION QUESTIONS

1. **Discuss the different aspect of the population of Japan and mention.**
2. **Assess the demographic state of Japan and explain the population policy of Japan.**
3. **Examine the demographic trends of Japan since the second world war.**

36

Population of China

When the People's Republic of China was officially proclaimed on 1 October 1949, it contained about one-fourth of the world's population. China still has by far the largest population of any country in the world, nearly twice as large as the combined totals for the United States and the Soviet Union.

During 1953 and 1954, the new Government conducted a national census, which reportedly disclosed a total population of 582,603,417 as on 30 June 1953. This figure was almost 100 million larger than previously cited totals and seems to have come as a surprise to the Chinese authorities. Subsequently, a total of 646,530,000 as of year-end 1957 was obtained from the national population registration system, a second census counted a total of 691,220,000 as of mid-year 1964, and a registration total of 982,550,000 was announced for year end 1980.

BIRTH AND DEATH RATE IN CHINA

Communist Government was first established in 1949 in China and the first census was held in 1953. Prior to that there were only isolated attempts to collect birth and death rate as for instance Prof. Ta Chen in 1942 made an unsuccessful attempt to collect figures on births and deaths in the running lake region.

Communist Government of China passed in 1952 the birth, death, registration law, which provides for the appointment of an official in each village for collecting the relevant information. In cities this work was entrusted to the police department. As per 1953 census of population birth rate was 37 per thousand and death rate was 17 per thousand. Between 1953 to 1957, both birth and mortality rates have come down in China. The position as in 1957 shows birth rate of 35 per thousand and mortality rate of 11 per thousand, yielding a natural growth rate of 23 people per thousand per annum. Dr. Chandrashekhar estimated that since 1965 the natural growth of Chinese population was 2 per cent annually, giving a net increase of

15 to 17 million people every year.

Birth and mortality rates and natural growth of population between 1952 and 1957 are depicted in Table 1.

Table 1. Birth Rate and Death Rate in China

Year	*Birth rate*	*Death rate*	*Natural growth rate birth death rate ratio*
1952	37	18.0	19.00
1953	37	17.0	20.00
1954	38	15.0	23.05
1955	35	12.4	22.60
1956	32	11.4	20.60
1957	34	11.0	23.00

Thus, fertility and natural increase remained high during the rest of the 1960s reaching a secondary peak toward the end of the decade. Fertility began to decline sharply after 1971, according to official sources, and by 1979 the birth rate was reported as 17.9 per thousand. The death rate was said to be around 7 per thousand in the middle 1970s and had declined further to 6.2 per thousand by 1979. In all probability, these figures are too low.

Official sources claim that the population growth rate peaked well above 3 per cent through the rest of the decade. The growth rate reportedly dropped sharply once more after 1971, mainly in response to the family planning effort, and by 1979 it was under 1.2 per cent. There are reasons to believe that the actual rate of growth is somewhat higher than the official figures indicate and that the target growth rates of 0.5 per cent by 1985 and 0 by the year 2000 are not realistic.

Life Expectancy

Average life expectancy for both sexes, estimated to have been about 32 years in 1949, has risen to 68.2 years. Whereas the breakdown by sex for the country as a whole is 66.9 for males and 69.5 for females, according to Government figures, life expectancy is reported to be somewhat higher in the major cities, as shown by the official figures of 69.5 for males and 72.3 for females in Beijing and 70.6 for males and 75.5 for females in Shanghai.

The Government considers levels and trends of mortality to be acceptable, given current economic and social circumstances. The Government notes that a significant decline in infant mortality, the elimination and control of the major infectious diseases, and the effective control of other infectious, parasitic, and endemic diseases have been the main factors behind the rise in life expectancy in China.

In enumerating its major health-related achievements during the past three decades, the Government has emphasized the establishment of a nation-wide medical and health services network, the launching of regular mass campaigns to improve sanitary conditions in rural and urban areas, and the development of a new medical science that incorporates both western and traditional Chinese medicine. The Government acknowledges, however, that a number of areas require improvement, reporting that "the rural areas are still lagging far behind in respect to sanitary conditions and medical attention", while "40 per cent of the nations health workers have not had a sound professional training".

Age at Marriage

In April 1950 the Communist Government enacted new legislation regarding marriage under which marriage was accepted as a social contract with provision for compulsory registration before marriage. The act also provides for compulsory health check up of both the bride and the bridegroom.

The new Marriage Law passed by the National People's Congress on 10 September 1980, which took effect as of 1 January 1981, raised the minimum ages to 20 for women and 22 for men.

The new marriage law also permits miniority areas to specify lower minimum ages for marriage in difference to local customs. Tibet, Ningxia, and other areas have enacted local variants of the marriage law setting the minimum ages at 18 for women and 20 for men. The reasons for the relaxation of marriage age restrictions at a time when the pressure to reduce the birth rate is being stepped up are not known, but known, but it is rumoured that the former regulations were extremely unpopular, had further alienated young people already frustrated by the lack of employment opportunities, and were contributing to a rise in extramarital sex and pregnancies in some urban areas.

DENSITY OF POPULATION

China is the third largest in total land area among the countries of the world, after the Soviet Union and Canada. It measures more than 5,000 kilometres (3,410 miles) from north to south. The population is very unevenly distributed. In much of the western two-thirds of the country the density is less than 10 persons per square kilometre (25.9 per square mile); the most intensively cultivated one-sixth of the country along the eastern coastal region has more than 500 persons per square kilometre (1295 per square mile). This differential reflects the differences in the carrying capacity of the land.

AGE COMPOSITION

It is difficult to pronounce authoritatively on the demographic composition of the Chinese on account of bias and inaccuracy. Here age counting is done on the traditional lines which suffers from errors. Whatever evidence that could be gleaned out of the available materials show that 41.1 per cent of the total population falls within the age range of 0-17, 45.4 per cent falls within 18-99 age range and the remaining 13.5 per cent population comes within the group of 50 years and over.

SEX COMPOSITION

Males outnumber females in China. As against 52 per cent male, the female population is only 48 per cent, thus more men are available per female. This low proportion of women is a distinct feature of the Chinese system from ancient time.

For every 100 females there are 107.7 males. Under the Chinese culture girls are not given much importance and durirg times of stresses and strains girls are abandoned. The following table presents the sex composition.

Table 2. Age-sex Composition

Age group (years)	*Sex ratio (Number of famels per 100 females)*
0-1	104.0
1-2	106.2
3-6	110.0
3-13	115.8
14-17	113.7
18-39	111.5
36-55	106.8
56 & above	66.7

From the table it is clear that the difference in ratio is less, in the 0-3 and 56 and above age group whereas it is more in the 7-13 age group.

URBAN AND RURAL DISTRIBUTION

The 1953 census indicated that China had 5,568 urban places, 9 of which had more than 1 million inhabitants; Beijing, Tianjin, Shenyang, Wuhan, Chongquing, Shanghai, Nanjing, Guangzhou, and Harbin. By 1960 the urban population had reportedly reached 131 million, about 19.8 per cent of the national total.

One Chinese source indicates that in 1979 China had only 3,400 cities and towns with a population of over 110 million, and another says that the urban population of over 110 million, and another says that the urban population had reached 129 million in 1979, or 13.2 per cent of the national total. These figures were obviously derived by different methods, and neither seems to be comparable with the figures for the 1950s.

China is unique among developing countries in that it has come into the modern age with a highly developed hierarchy of settlements, extending down to or even below the xian, or county level. The Government considers the distribution of population to be more or less appropriate, though requiring minor modification, since it is constantly seeking a more even distribution of productive forces, a reduced concentration of population and economic activity in the larger cities, and a narrowing of the gap between industry and agriculture.

The Government's present policy, which is linked to its emphasis on light industry and production of consumer goods, is to continue to develop small cities and towns with an upper limit of 200,000 inhabitants. At a national planning conference held in Beijing in 1980, the participants emphasized the need to develop three types of small urban centres; existing towns with populations of over 10,000, cities and towns in areas endowed with natural resources; and satellite towns around the major cities (although the Chinese have sometimes referred to these as "growth poles", those which have been developed have essentially been part of the expanding metropolitan fabric).

Although China certainly experienced some success in preventing the massive rural to urban migration that has occurred in most parts of the developing world, it is likely that its drive to achieve the four modernizations—which will involve the rationalization of agriculture (leading to the gradual and then more rapid release of agricultural labour from local agricultural activities), the consumption of ever larger quantities of high technology, the location of higher educational facilities in urban centres, and so forth will cause China's cities to be increasingly subject to the forces that have caused urbanization elsewhere.

Literacy

It is estimated that in 1949 about 85 per cent of Chinese adults were illiterate. A nation-wide literacy campaign was launched in 1953, but the effort was ill conceived and was subsequently criticized as a case of "blind adventurism". Another drive, aimed at culminating illiteracy within seven years, was initiated in 1955, but once again the programme was not well run, and in 1956 it was discovered that some of the graduates of literacy classes promptly lapsed into illiteracy again. During the Big Leap Forward of 1958, another campaign was mounted, and presently many provinces were claiming to have wiped out illiteracy. In 1978, a vice-minister of education said that China still had a fair amount of illiteracy and in 1979 it was said that there were still 100 million "young and able-bodied adults" who were illiterate or semi-literate.

INTERNATIONAL MIGRATION

The major immigration to China in recent years was the arrival of some 265,000 refugees between March 1978 and January 1980. Of this number, some 263,000 refugees fled across the border from Viet-nam during 1978; the remainder came from countries of first asylum in response to China's offer to accept 10,000 refugees from South-east Asia.

The Government of China has repeatedly denied that its workers are being sent abroad in order to ease unemployment "since the CCEC has only sent a few thousand abroad each year and this would not have any impact on employment in a country with a population of nearly one billion inhabitants".

Another change in China's international migration policy has been the imposition of strict controls on illegal emigration to Hong Kong. In 1979 the British Government exerted diplomatic pressure on China to curb illegal flows, and the Chinese Government complied, instituting strict penalties.

POPULATION POLICY

The Chinese Government embarked in 1979 on a vast experiment; the creation of a nation of one-child families. The one-child family translated into a reduction in the rate of natural increase to 5 per thousand by 1985 and to zero by the end of the century. The public's response appeared receptive. Of the 17 million births in 1978, half had represented the third or higher child in a family; the proportion fell to a quarter in 1979 and the rate of natural increase declined to 11.7 per thousand.

In 1980, the government announced to the National People's Congress (China's "Parliament") a precise formulation of the new population policy:

> Upon careful study, the State Council deems it necessary to launch a crash programme over the coming 20 or 30 years calling on each couple, except those in minority nationality areas, to have a single child, so that the rate of population growth may be brought under control as soon as possible. Our aim is to strive to limit the population to a maximum of 1,200 million by the end of this century.

The authorities believed that this stringent target had received an immediate and satisfactory response although in 1980 the recorded rate of natural increase actually rose to 12 per thousand. Not even the total exemption for minority nationalities proved sacrosanct, and by 1981 the entire nation, including many of the minorities was subject to the one-child policy.

SELECT REFERENCES

1. Aird, John S: "Fertility Decline in China", In Fertility Decline in the Less Developed Countries, edited by Nick Eberstadt, pp. 119-228. New York: Pragger, 1981.
2. Banister, Judith: *China's Pattern of Population Growth*, Stanford, Calif: Stanford University Press, Forthcoming.
3. Chen Muhua: "Birth Planning in China," *Family Planning Perspectives* 11 (6): 348-354, November/December 1979.
4. Dai Shiguang (S.K. Tai): "1953 Population Census of China", Paper presented in the anniversary lecture series of the Indian Statistical Institute, Calcutta, 20 December 1956.
5. Orleans, Leo A.: "China's Population Figures: Can the Contradictions Be Resolved ?" *Studies in Family Planning* 7(2): 52-57, February 1976.

6. United States, Library of Congress, Congressional Research Service. China's Population Policies and Population Data: Review and Update. Prepared for the Committee on Foreign Affairs, U.S. House of Representatives. Washington, D.C.: U.S. Government Printing Office, 1981.

EXAMINATION QUESTIONS

1. Write an essay on China's population problem.
2. Explain the demographic features of China.
3. Illustrate the population growth in China and explain the population policy of China.

37

Population of Sri Lanka

Location and Area

The island Republic of Sri Lanka (Ceylon) is situated in the Indian Ocean between the northern latitudes 5°′ 55′ and 9°′ 50′ and the eastern longitudes 79°′ 42′ and 81°′ 52′. It is separated from the Indian sub-continent by a narrow strip of shallow water, the Palk Strait.

Sri Lanka has an area of 25,332 square miles or 16,212,480 acres of which about 370 square miles or 236,700 acres comprise large inland waters..

Population Growth

Growth rates. The interesting feature about Sri Lanka's demographic situation is not so much the size of the population as the changes that have characterized the rates as well as the components of population growth over the past 100 years. Between 1871 and 1971, the country's population increased by about 10.3 million or by about 4.30 per cent. However, the population did not grow at a uniform rate throughout this period. The percentage increase as well as the average annual rates of growth, has shown appreciable variations from one intercensal period to another, as is evident from Table 1.

Growth factors. The growth of Sri Lanka's population over the years has been influenced by two factors, *viz.* natural increase (excess of births over deaths) and net migration (difference between the number of immigrants and emigrants). However, the relative importance of these two components has varied over time. This is illustrated by Table 2 which shows the proportionate contribution of natural increase and net migration to population growth during the various intercensal periods from 1871.

Table 1. Population of Sri Lanka in Census Years 1871 to 1971, Intercensal Increase, Percentage Increase and Average Annual Growth Rates

Year and date of population census	*Enumerated population*	*Intercensal increase*	*Percentage increase*	*Average annual growth rates (percentage)*
1871 March 27	2,400,380	—	—	—
1881 February 17	2,759,738	359,358	15.0	1.42
1891 February 26	3,007,789	248,051	9.0	0.86
1901 March 1	3,565,954	558,165	18.6	1.72
1911 March 10	4,106,350	540,396	15.2	1.42
1921 March 18	4,497,854	391,504	9.5	0.91
1931 February 26	5,306,863	809,009	18.0	1.68
1946 March 19	6,657,339	1,350,475	25.4	1.52
1953 March 20	8,097,895	1,440,556	21.6	2.84
1963 July 8	10,582,064	2,484,169	30.7	2.65
1971 October 9	12,689,897	2,107,833	19.9	2.20

Source: Government of Sri Lanka, *Census of Population 1971*, Vol. II. All Island Tables, Part I, General Characterics of the Population (Colombo, Departmnnt of Census and Statistics, 1975) Table 1.

Table 2. Intercensal Increase, Natural Increase and Migration Increase, Sri Lanka, 1871-1971

Period	*Total intercensal increase*	*Natural increase*		*Migration increase*	
		Number	*Percentage of total increase*	*Number*	*Percentage of total increase*
1871-1881	359,358	119,792	33.3	239,566	66.7
1881-1891	248,051	144,260	58.2	103,791	41.8
1891-1901	558,165	225,406	40.4	332,759	59.6
1901-1911	530,396	356,147	65.9	184,249	34.1
1911-1921	391,504	319,410	81.6	72,094	18.4
1921-1931	809,009	656,990	81.2	152,019	18.8
1931-1946	1350,476	1,280,916	94.8	69,650	5.2
1946-1953	1440,556	1,363,175	94.6	77,381	5.4
1953-1963	2484,169	2,513,248	101.2	−29,079	−1.2
1963-1971	2107,833	2,208,061	104.8	−100,228	−4.8

Source: A.G. Ransasinha, Census of Ceylon 1946, Vol. I, Part I, General Report (Colombo, Department of Census and Statistics, 1950), Table 5; H.E. Peries, Census of Ceylon 1953, Vol. I, General Report (Colombo, Department of Census and Statistics, 1957) Table 2; CICRED. The Population of Sri Lanka (Colombo, Department of Census and Statistics, 1974), Table 1.2 : Government of Sri Lanka. Census of Population 1971, Vol. II. All Island Tables, Part I, General Characteristics of the Population (Colombo, Department of Census and Statistics, 1975) Table 1.

It is clear from Table 2 that net migration contributed the greater share of the increase in the population between 1871 and 1901. Thereafter, natural increase has been the major determinant of population growth. Between 1901 and 1953, the contribution of migration has been gradually declining while that of natural increase has been gradually increasing. In recent years migration has had a negative effect on growth of Sri Lanka's population.

Natural increase. It was observed earlier that natural increase played a more significant role in the growth of Sri Lanka's population during the twentieth century. While in the first decade of the century, this factor accounted for about 66 per cent of the increase in the population, currently it appears to be the sole determinant of population trends in the country. This growing importance of the natural increase factor has been due to two reasons. In the first place, as noted earlier, the proportionate share of net migration gradually diminishing due to various economic and political developments. Secondly, the rate of natural increase itself has been increasing the birth rates and the death rates as is evident from Table 3.

Table 3. Average Decennial Birth Rates, Death Rates and Natural Increase Rates, 1871 to 1970

Period	*Birth rate (per thousand)*	*Death rate (per thousand)*	*Natural increase rate (percentage)*
1871-1880	27.4	22.7	0.47
1881-1890	29.4	24.3	0.51
1891-1900	34.4	27.6	0.68
1901-1910	38.1	28.8	0.93
1911-1920	37.6	30 4	0.72
1921-1930	39.8	26.5	1.33
1931-1940	36.8	23.0	1.38
1941-1950	37.7	17.1	2.06
1951-1960	37.3	10.4	2.69
1961-1970	32.7	8.2	2.45

Source: Computed from the date published in the Registrar-General's Reports on Vital Statistics.

Rural-Urban Distribution

Table 4 gives the rural-urban distribution of the population in all census years from 1871 to 1971.

It is evident from the table that while between 1871 and 1971, the total population increased by over 10 times, the proportion of urban population to total population has only a little more than doubled itself. About 22 per cent of the Sri Lanka's population today live in urban areas.

Table 4. Distribution of the Population by Urban and Rural Areas, Sri Lanka, in Census 1871 to 1971

Census year	*Total population*	*Urban population*	*Rural population*	*Percentage of urban*	*Percentage of rural*
1871	2,400,380	260,376	2,140,004	10.8	89.2
1881	2,759,738	281,065	2,478,673	10.2	89.8
1891	3,007,789	321,413	2,686,376	10.7	89.3
1901	3,565,954	414,025	3,151,929	11.6	88.4
1911	4,106,350	542,945	3,563,405	13.2	86.8
1921	4,498,606*	637,870	3,860,735	14.2	85.8
1931	5,306,863	737,272	4,569,591	13.9	86.1
1946	6,657,339	1,023,042	5,634,297	15.4	84.6
1953	8,097,895	1,239,133	6,858,762	15.3	84.7
1963	10,582,064	2,016,285	8,565,779	19.1	80.9
1971	12,689,897	2,848,116	9,841,781	22.4	77.6

Sources: A.G. Ranasinha, Census of Ceylon, 1946, Vol. I, Part II, Statistical Digest (Colombo, Department of Census and Statistics, 1950), Table 6*a*; H.E, Peries, Census of Ceylon, 1953, Vol. I, General Report (Colombo, Department of Census and Statistics, 1957), Tables 7 and 9; Government of Sri Lanka, Census of Population, 1971, Vol. II, All Island Tables, Part I, General Characteristics of the Population (Colombo, Department of Census and Statistics, 1975), Table 4.

Note : * Includes a miscellaneous population of 751 not distributed among the zones.

Population Density

The area of Sri Lank, including its inland water, is about 25,332 square miles. The enumerated population in 1971 was 12,689,897 persons. If the people of Sri Lanka were equally distributed over this area, there would have been 501 persons on every square mile in 1971 compared with about 95 persons in 1871. It has, however, to be noted that the over-all density figures are rather meaningless because of the heavy concentration of people in limited areas within the country (Table 5).

Urbanization

The numerical and percentage increase, as well as the average annual intercenal growth rates of both the urban and the total population as recorded at the various censuses of Sri Lanka during the 10 decades, 1871-1971, is given in Table 6. It will be observed

Table 5. Density of Population—Sri Lanka

Year	*Density of population (per square mile)*
1971	94.8
1881	108.9
1891	118.7
1901	140.8
1911	162.1
1921	177.6
1931	209.5
1946	262.8
1953	319.7
1963	417.7
1971	500.9

from the table that while the total population of the country increased by a little over five times, the urban population increased more than ten-fold during the 100 years. The proportion of urban population to total population, i.e., the level of urbanization, increased fluctuatingly from 10.8 per cent in 1871 to 15.3 per cent in 1953. Between 1953 and 1971, however, there was a remarkable growth in the urban population which more than doubled from 1.2 million to 2.8 million. The percentage increases as well as the average annual growth rates indicate that the largest increase in the urban population had taken place between 1953 and 1963. Except during three intercensal periods, 1871-1881, 1921-1931 and 1946-1953 the rates of growth of the urban population have been substantially higher than the rates of growth of the total population. Since 1953, growth rates of urban population have been a little less than twice the rate of growth of total population.

Sex Composition

The population of Sri Lanka classified by sex together with the masculinity proportion (percentage of males in the total population) and masculinity ratio (number of males per 100 females) for the various census years is shown in Table 7. It will be seen from the table that the males have outnumbered the females at all census counts, but the proportion of males in the total population has been declining almost continuously since 1871.

Table 6. Growth of the Total and Urban Population, Sri Lanka, 1871-1971

Census year	*Total population*	*Urban population*	*Percentage of urban*	*Percentage increase*		*Average annual growth rate (percentage)*	
				Total population	*Urban population*	*Total population*	*Urban population*
1871	2,400,380	260,376	10.8	—	—	—	—
1881	2,759,738	281,065	10.2	15.0	7.9	1.42	0.78
1891	3,007,789	321,413	10.7	9.0	14.4	0.86	1.35
1901	8,565,954	414,025	11.6	18.6	28.8	1.72	2.56
1911	4,106,350	542,945	13.2	15.2	31.1	1.42	2.74
1921	4,498,605	637,870	14.2	9.5	17.5	0.91	1.62
1931	5,306,871	737,272	13.9	18.0	15.6	1.68	1.47
1946	6,657,339	1,023,042	15.4	25.4	38.8	1.52	2.20
1953	8,097,895	1,239,133	15.3	21.6	21.1	2.84	2.77
1963	10,582,064	2,016,285	19.1	30.7	62.7	2.65	4.88
1971	12,689,897	2,848,116	22.4	19.9	41.3	2.20	4.23

Sources: A.G. Ranasinha, Census of Ceylon, 1946, Vol. I, Part II, Statistical Digest (Colombo, Department of Census and Statistics, 1950), Table 6*a*; H.E. Peries, Census of Ceylon, 1953, Vol. I, General Report (Colombo, Department of Census and Statistics, 1957), Appendix 3, Tables 7 and 9, Government of Sri Lanka, Census of Population, 1971, Vol. II, All Island Tables, Part I, General Characteristics of the Population (Colombo, Department of Census and Statistics, 1975), Table 4.

Table 7. Population Classified by Sex, and Masculinity Proportion and Masculinity Ratio Sri Lanka, 1871-1971

Census year	*Masculinity ratio*
1871	114.3
1881	113.9
1891	112.7
1901	113.6
1911	112.6
1921	112.5
1946	113.0
1953	111.5
1963	108.2
1971	106.1

Sources: A.G. Ranasinha, Census of Ceylon, 1946, Vol. I, Part II. Statistical Digest (Colombo, Department of Census and Statistics, 1950), Table 7; H.E. Peries, Census of Ceylon, 1953 Vol. I, Part I, General Report (Colombo, Department of Census and Statistics, 1957), Appendix 3, Table 16; Government of Sri Lanka, Census of Population 1971, Vol. II, All Island Tables, Part I General Characteristics of the Population (Colombo, Department of Census and Statistics, 1975), Table 3.

Distribution by Board Age Groups

The percentage distribution of the total population by four board age groups is summarized in Table 8.

Table 8. Percentage Distribution of the Total Population by Board Age Group, 1881-1971

Census	*Percentage distribution in age groups*				
year	*0-14*	*15-24*	*25-64*	*65 & over*	*All ages*
1881	43.7	20.3	33.8	2.2	100.0
1891	43.5	19.7	34.7	2.1	100.0
1901	42.2	20.8	35.6	1.4	100.0
1911	40.9	17.9	38.9	2.3	100.0
1921	39.4	19.0	39.2	2.4	100.0
1946	37.2	19.8	39.5	3.5	100.0
1953	39.7	18.3	38.6	2.5	100.0
1963	41.5	18.1	36.8	3.6	100.0
1971	39.0	20.7	36.1	4.2	100.0

Source: Ibid.

In 1881, children below 15 years formed nearly 44 per cent of the total population. This proportion has been gradually declining to about 37 per cent in 1946, and thereafter increased to 41.5 per cent in 1963. Since 1963, the proportion of children in the total population recorded a gradual decline to 39.0 in 1971 due largely to a fall in the birth rates during the 1960s. The percentage share of the 15-24 year age group has shown marked fluctuations between 1881 and 1971. The proportion which stood at 18.1 in 1963 had increased to 20.7 in 1971 due to the effect of the high birth rates of the late 1940s and early 1950s. Those aged 65 years and over have shown an appreciable increase in their proportionate share from 1.4 per cent in 1901 to 4.2 per cent of the total population in 1971. This increase has largely to be attributed to the increase in life expectancy during this period.

Other Features

(*a*) *Life expectancy*: The expectation of life has continuously increased in Sri Lanka with the progress made in checking diseases and improved medical facilities. Besides, fall in death rates has resulted in an increase in life expectation. The life expectation for 1972 is put at 68 years while the expectation was 60 in 1954. The figures for 1922 was 33 years for men and 31 years for women.

(*b*) *Literacy*: In Sri Lanka the percentage of literacy is higher as compared to other under developed countries. Besides the percentage of literates has been increasing continuously. In 1946 the percentage of literacy was 58 which rose to 72 in 1971, with 78 per cent among men and 64 per cent among women.

(*c*) *International migration immigration*: As a result of several restrictive measures adopted in 1948 and thereafter, international migration has ceased to make any significant contribution to population growth. The Government views the present level of immigration as satisfactory and desires to maintain immigration at its current level, which is not significant. In general, immigration is perceived as not desirable and is considered to be a possible constraint on the achievement of economic and social objectives. In addition, an aggeement was reached in 1964 between the Governments of Sri Lanka and India to repatriate to India 525,000 persons of Indian origin.

Emigration: In the past, emigration was negligible There is evidence, however, of a steady increase in emigration over the years. The pace of emigration is likely to hasten, primarily as a result of the progress in the repatriation of persons of Indian origin. The

Government considers the present level of emigration significant but satisfactory, contributing positively to social and economic objectives, although some problems do exist. On the one hand, emigration helps reduce surplus manpower in certain sectors of occupations; on the other hand, it produces shortages in manpower in certain sectors or occupations and leads to a loss of talent and innovative capacity. In 1974 a Cabinet Committee was set up to study Sri Lanka's "brain drain" and the problems posed by the emigration of qualified professional categories such as doctors and engineers. a compulsory period of service in government has been enforced.

Government's Overall Approach to Population Problems

Since 1965 successive Governments have supported programmed intervention as a means of modifying the rate of population growth. The present Government continues to emphasize the need to reduce Sri Lanka's birth rate. In an effort to modify the impact of fertility upon population growth, the Government is promoting women's education and employment in its economic and social policies to ensure the equitable distribution of the social product. The national family planning programme is considered to have as its objective both fertility limitation and the improvement of the health and welfare of mothers and children.

Successive Governments have considered the implications of rapid population growth in their various plans for economic and social development, but the frequent changes of government have made it difficult to formulate and implement development plans. As a result, there have been many interruptions in the process of formulating a clear population policy, even though population-associated problems have consistently been identified by each Government. In its Five-Year Development Plan for 1972-76, the Government drew attention to the implications of population growth for short-term and long-term economic development. This was also the first time that a Development Plan explicitly identified the priority implementation of fertility-modifying measures as an integral part of Sri Lanka's development strategy.

POPULATION PROJECTIONS

During the past three decades or so, there has been a growing interest in the probable size and composition of the furture population of Sri Lanka. This development has partly been due to the unprecendented increase in population which the country experienced during the years following in the Second World War. Partly, the increasing activities in the field of planning and development created a heavy demand for projections of the future populations. Also, the availability of adequate and fairly reliable data prompted several scholars and organizations to prepare independently a series of population projections for the country. The essential feature of the various population projection are summarized in Table 9.

Table 9. Important Features of the Various Population Projections for Sri Lanka

Year issued	*Author*	*Period covered*	*Number of projections*
1957	Sarkar	1951-1976	Two
1958	United Nations	1955-1980	Three
1957	Department of Census and Statistics	1955-1970	Two
1959	Selvaratnam	1956-1981	Three
1966	Department of Census and Statistics	1963-2003	Three
1966	Technical Working Group	1963-1978	Three
1969	Lesthaeghe and Chi	1963-1998	Three
1970	Selvaratnam, Wright and Jones	1968-1998	Three
1974	Department of Census and Statistics	1971-2001	Three
1174	Srivastava and Abeykoon	1971-1991	Four
1974	Frejka	1970-2150	Five

SELECT REFERENCES

1. Balakrishnan and Gunarenara: A review of demogrophic trends' in K.M. de Silva, ed., Sri Lanka : A Survey (Honolulu, University, Press of Hawaii, 1977).
2. Fernando, D.F.S.: Trends and differentials in fertility in population of Sri Lanka, Country Monograph series, No. 4 (Bangkok, ESCA).
3. Department of Census and Statistics, Sri Lanka : Population Census, 1971, Sri Lanka, General Report.
4. Nadarajah, T.: Trends and differentials in mortality, in population of Sri Lanka.
5. Wilson, P.: Economic Activity of the population, in population of Sri Lanka.

EXAMINATION QUESTIONS

1. Mention the main demographic features of Sri Lanka.
2. Compare and contrast the demographic features of India and Sri Lanka.
3. Evaluate the population projection of Sri Lanka.

38

Population of USSR

The Union of Soviet Socialist Republics (USSR), also known as the Soviet Union, has the largest area and the third largest population in the world. It covers an area of 2 crores 24 lakhs square kilometeres which is approximately equal to the combined are of north and south America put together. The length of Russia from north to south is 5000 km, and the distance from east to west is 10,000 km. Russia is the only country in the world which is spread in two continents of the world, i.e., Europe and Asia. Its area is 2.5 times more than USA, 7 times more than India, 60 times more than Japan and 90 times more than Great Britain.

So far 5 census enumerations were held in Russia, i.e. in 1897, 1926, 1939, 1959 and 1979. The Soviet Union has the third largest population in the world after China and India.

The population of the Soviet Union reached 271 million by the beginning of 1983. That means it has grown by 8.8 million or 3.3 per cent during the four years after the 1979 census. These statistics are given in a handbook recently brought out by the Political Literature Publishers, Moscow.

Carrying the results of a statistical survey, the book says that during 65 years of Soviet power the population of the USSR has grown 108 million. The number of men is growing more rapidly than women. In the period between 1970 and 1979, the number of men grew by 10 per cent and of women by eight per cent. But the fact remains that there are more women than men in the country.

The population figures might have been more impressive but for the consequences of the wars, says the book. During the Civil War and foreign intervention (1918-1920), 6.7 million people died. The Second World War took a heavy toll—20 million people were killed. This led to extreme demographic consequences. The country's population grew to its pre-war level only ten years after the victory over nazism. The consequences of war are still telling on population growth.

And yet, population growth rates in the USSR are higher than the average in many capitalist countries and much higher than in U.K., France, FRG, Sweden and Italy.

BIRTH AND DEATH RATES IN RUSSIA

Birth rate is rapidly sliding down in USSR During the last 60 years the birth rate must have slumped by 62 per cent. It has taken place in the face of the situation that the socialist countries have never felt the necessity of controlling population.

Table 1. Birth Rate in Russia

Year	*Birth rate per thousand*
1897	47.0
1913	47.0
1937	38.7
1950	26.7
1960	24.9
1965	18.4
1979	17.0

The means of family planning are produced only in Government. factories. The small size of Russian family is a reflection of the voluntary acceptance of small family norm by the Russian citizen in the face may economic constraints.

Over and above extensive education has made the people aware of the benefits of voluntary birth control. Apart from the birth rate, mortality rate also has been coming down. Mortaliy rate declined from 32 per thousand in 1897 to 6.5 per thousand in 1972.

Demographers in Russia have expressed the opinion that the fall in death rate in Russia in such a short span is unprecedented in the history of the world. Between 1913 to 1965 the fall in death rate was of the order of 75 per cent which is an all time record. For instance in 1913 the death rate per thousand in Great Britain was 14.2, in USA, 13.2, in France 19, and in Russia 30. The corresponding figures for 1963 was 12.1 for Great Britain, 9.6 for USA, 11.7 for France and only 7.2 for Russia which was the least.

The basic factors behind the success in bringing down the death rate in Russia was the unprecedented increase in health and medical facilities. In Russia health and medical facilities are within reach of one and all on the basis of social equality.

Table 2. Mortality Rate in USSR

Year	*Death rate per thousand*
1897	32
1913	30
1940	18.1
1952	8.4
1979	7.2

During the First and Second World War Russias. suffered heavily in terms of death rate. The population of the country which was 15.92 crores in 1913 registered a fall and reached 14.70 in 1926. Between 1949 and 1972 the net increase in population was 4 crores.

In terms of population growth the current trend in population-growth is 1.12 per cent.

RURAL AND URBAN POPULATION IN RUSSIA

Before the revolution, the number of cities with population of one lakh was 29. Rapid industrialisation initiated under the plans resulted in the springing up of many cities.

Now, three times as many people live in the town as in the country. There are over 2,000 cities and towns, and twenty new towns spring up every year. There are 272 cities with a population of over 100,000 and 21 cities with a population of one million or more.

The growth of the urban population at the expense of the rural population is continuing. The rural population is decreasing not only relatively but also in terms of absolute numbers—country dwellers are moving to towns and cities. On the one hand, expanding industry requires ever more manpower; on the other hand, the mechanisation of agricultural production and heightened productivity of labour make it possible for farmers to do more with less manpower. The population of the developing regions of Siberia and the Far East is growing rapidly. Table 3 indicates cities with a population of more than 1.5 million.

Table 3. Cities with a Population of more than 1.5 million

(*million people*)

Moscow	Leningard	Kiev	Tashkent	Kharkov
8.2	4.7	2.3	1.9	1.5

Density of Different Regions

Entire Soviet Russia falls into regions as follows:

(*i*) European Russia, (*ii*) Siberia, (*iii*) Cencasia, (*iv*) Central Asia. European Russia contains 3/4 of the total population (152.8 million), Trans Cancasia has 4.6 per cent (9.5 million), Siberia and far east 11.3 per cent (23.9 million).

Russia has a density of population of 10.4 persons per square kilometre. Moscow region has the highest density with 237 persons per square kilometre. Siberia's population rose by three times between 1897 and 1959. Cancasia's population remained more or less stationary. Central Asia consists mainly of desert region where the density range from 3 to 250 per square kilometre. Tashkant is the principal city of Central Asia.

AGE AND SEX

Women outnumber men in the Soviet Union. This phenomenon could be observed right from 1897 to the present day. In 1920, the population composed of 52 per cent females and 48 per cent males. This disparity further accentuated and by 1959 the ratio of female to male was 55 : 45.

The main reason of declining male population was the heavy male casualty during the war. In 1966 the female percentage was 59.4, while the male percentage was 40.6.

Age composition of the population shows that the population between 10-20 years is the lowest and between 20-40 is the highest. Low birth rates accounts for the low proportion between 10-20.

Age-Sex Pyramid,USSR

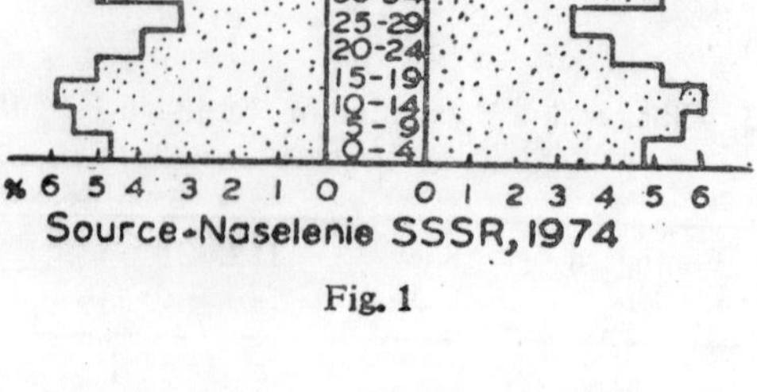

Source-Naselenie SSSR, 1974

Fig. 1

The 1897 census of the Russian empire revealed a smooth age-sex pyramid without gouges, typical of a country with fairly high fertility and mortality. The age-sex pyramid from the 1970 census (Figure 1) demonstrates the twentieth century changes in age-sex composition.

The male deficit at many ages has made it difficult for many women to marry and has certainly been an additional incentive to the Soviet Government to encourage the full employment of women. Also, the large differences in the sizes of adjacent cohorts makes social planning of age-related facilities such as schools very difficult.

Everywhere in the Soviet Union mortality has declined substantially from earlier levels. Table 4 shows expectations of life at birth by sex for 1938-39 through 1971-72. Along with a general long-term

Table 4. Expectation of Life at Birth, by Sex, Soviet Union, 1938-39—1971-72

Year	*Total*	*Male*	*Female*
1938-39	47	44	50
1958-59	69	67	72
1965-66	70	66	74
1970-71	70	65	74
1971-72	70	64	74

Source: Naselenie, USSR, 1973, p. 139.

Table 5. Characteristics of the Soviet Union and Selected Union Republics, 1979

Characteristics	*Soviet Union*	*Russian SSR*	*Estonian SSR*	*Armenian SSR*	*Uzbek SSR*
Population (thousands)	262,436	137,410	1,464	3,037	15,389
Crude birth rate	18.2	15.8	14.9	22.9	34.4
Crude death rate	10.1	10.8	12.3	5.6	7.0
Natural rate of increase	8.1	5.0	2.6	17.3	27.4
Growth rate per 1,000, 1970-79	9.0	5.1	8.5	22.0	29.5
Per cent Urban	62	69	70	66	41
People per Sq. km.	11.7	8.0	32.5	101.9	34.4
% Females aged 10 + with incomplete secondary schooling	60	61	60	69	61
% Workers who are women	51	53	54	46	43
Average family size	3.5	3.3	3.1	4.7	5.5

Sources: Narodone Kheziastvo, 1979, *Vestnik Statistiki*; 1980, Nos. 2, 6, 7 and 12.

improvement in living conditions, more increase in the mortality rate for older males has occurred since 1965-66. Increased mortality rates begin at age 30 and become more pronounced after age 50.

Selected characteristics for the total Soviet Union and four union republics for 1979 are shown in Table 5.

Quality of Life

The most general yardstick is the quality of life. In order to more clearly formulate this notion, experts of the Organisation of Economic Corporation and Development (OECD) worked out of a system of social indicators which are divided into eight categories, the first three being health, education and development of the personality, and employment.

Soviet society is being perfected in all aspects of this system, which is due to a steady rise in allocations to public health, education and other social and cultural spheres.

The average life expectancy in the USSR has been growing faster than elsewhere. Today it equals 70 years—more than two times that in Czarist Russia in the late 19th-early 20th centuries. Of course, this is by no means a limit. The same figure is much higher say, in Sweden which has not been at war since 1810. Soviet experts believe that the USSR can reach 80 years in the early 21st century. Breakthroughs in medicine, biology and genetics will play a prominent role in this regard.

At present 152 million Soviet people have a secondary (complete and incomplete) and higher education, which is nearly 10 times more than in 1939. Since than the USSR's population has gone up by only 40 per cent, which means that it changes qualitatively much more rapidly than quantitatively. The working people also improve their general educational standards, professional skills and competence.

Elementary education became compulsory for Soviet young people in the 1930s; eight-year education, in the 1950s; and secondary education (10 years), in the 1970s. Many sociologists suppose that a compulsory higher education will be introduced in the 21st century.

The problem of employment has long been solved in the USSR. Joblessness was done away with as far back as 1930. The closely connected rights to work and education, recorded in the Soviet Constitution, are ensured both *de jure* and *de facto*. These guarantees are being strengthehed along with the progress of Soviet society. Soviet people look confidently to the future and know that they will always be able to use their capabilities.

Though the population will cease to grow numerically, its qualitative changes and development have no limits. The USSR pays more and more attention to forecasting and analysing these problems.

FAMILY PLANNING

Soviet people have deep faith in the Marxist philosophy. Birth control and abortion are very popular here. However there is no compulsion towards family planning from the Government side. People are committed to be small family norm. Abortion was legalised in 1920 which however has been declared illegal from 1936. With effect from 1950 abortion was again given legal sanction.

Family planning policy of the Soviet Union is surrounded under a vail of secreacy. Birth rate is more manual labour class while it is less among educated class. Average annual increase in population is 1.2 per cent. The future possibility of further decline in growth rate cannot be ruled out.

Abortions have been a major form of fertility control in the Soviet Union. In 1958-59 there were approximately 85 abortions per thousand women aged 15-49 and in 1972 approximately 120. Survey questions on why women do not want more children elicited as frequent reasons lack of adequate living space, household members busy with work or studies, and no one available to stay home with the child.

SELECT REFERENCES

1. Arutiunian, Iu. V.: "Konkrento - Sotsiologicheskoe issledovanie nationalnikh otnoshenii" (A Concrete Sociological Study of Ethnic Relations). *Veprosy Filosofii* 12; 129-139, 1969.
2. Belova, V.: "Obsledovaniye mnenii o nailuchshem i ozhidaenom chisle detey v sem'e" (Survey of Attitudes of the Ideal and Intended Number of Children in the Family). *Vestnik Statistiki* 6: 23-24, 1971.
3. Coale, Ansley J., Barbara A. Anderson, and Erna Harm.: *Human Fertility in Russia since the Nineteenth Century*, Princeton, N.J.: Princeton University Press, 1978.
4. Heer, David M.: "Recent Developments in Soviet Population Policy." *Studies in Family Planning* 3(II): 257-264, November 1972.
5. Lewis, Robert A, Richard H. Rowland, and Ralph S. Clem.: Nationality and Population Change in Russia and the U.S.S.R. : An Evolution of Census Data, 1897-1970, New York : Praeger, 1976.
6. Narodnoe Khoziastvo (The Yearbook of the National Economy). Issued annually by the Central Statistical Bureau of the U.S.S.R., Moscow.
7. Vestink Statistiki (Statistical Herald). Issued Monthly since 1949 by the Central Statistical Bureau of the U.S.S.R., Moscow.
8. Weber, Cynthia, and Ann Goodman: "The Demographic Policy Debate in the USSR." *Population and Development Review* 7(2) : 279-295, June 1981.

EXAMINATION QUESTIONS

1. Explain briefly the demographic trends in the USSR and explain the population policy in USSR.
2. Soviet Union has no population problem. Examine this statement.

39

Population of United States of America

United States of America is a leading power among the affluent countries of the world. The United States of America is the fourth largest country of the world in population. Its approximately 230 million people occupy a land area of 3,540,023 square miles (9,168,660 square kilometres) divided into forty-eight contiguous states and the states of Hawaii, in the Pacific Ocean.

If we turn our attention to the demographic features of U.S.A., we can find that the population of the country was increasing just like any other country. However the rate of population growth was not similar to other countries. During the initial period of the 19th century, the rate of growth of propulation approximated 35% per year. The rapid increase in population witnessed between 1750-1850 was partly due to increased birth rate and partly due to the influx of immigrants. During the 160 years between 1820-1980, the number of immigrants was 54 million. The present population of America is put at 23 crores as compared to the 7.60 crores population in 1900. The following table gives the population of U.S.A. between 1750 and 1900.

Table 1. Population of U.S.A. between 1750-1900

Year	*Population in lakhs*
1750	11
1800	53
1850	232
1860	314
1870	386
1880	502
1890	630
1900	760

From the census figures of 1800, it is clear that the fall in birth rate was due to the disequilibrium in sex and the high age distribution. Urbanization started during this time, which led to the growth of rural people into urban complex. Evidence point to the popularization of contraceptives during the Eighteen-twenties.

The great depression of 1930 influenced the marriage rates and birth rates in U.S.A. Depression led to sharp fall in marriage rates with a corresponding decline in brith rates. After 1940 the birth rates started increasing. The fall in population between 1930-1940 could be attributed to the virtual stoppage of immigration. The increase in U.S.A.'s population between 1901-1970 could be gleaned through the table below:

Table 2. Population of U.S.A. between 1901-1980

Year (Decade)	*Population (crores)*	*Percentage rate of increase in the decade*	*Annual growth rate in percentage*
1901-10	9.2	2.10	2.10
1910-20	10.5	14.9	1.49
1921-30	12.3	16.1	1.61
1931-40	—	7.2	0.72
1941-50	15.1	14.5	1.45
1951-60	17.85	18.4	1.84
1961-70	21.00	17.00	1.70
1971-80	22.65	16.80	1.4

The rate of increase in population, in the U.S.A., which was 2.10 in the decade of 1901 to 1910, declined to 1.4 per cent in the 1970-81 decade.

Natural increase of population in the United States in the early 1980s is of the order of 0.7 per cent per year, which is quite high by the standards of most other industrialized countries. For example, the percentage of natural increase in France is 0.4, in West Germany 0.2, in the United Kingdom 0.1, in the Netherlands 0.4, in Poland 1.0, in Italy 0.2, and in the Soviet Union 0.8. If plausible levels of total net immigration are added to the U.S. levels of natural increase, then total annual population growth within the United States is probably 1.0 per cent or greater as of 1980.

Death Rate

U.S.A. is one of the most affluent countries of the world; and so its logical concomitant is a higher standard of living. Effort to provide medical, health and public services have been initiated much earlier as a result of which the general level of health is very high here. High standard of living, high income, universal education, etc. have resulted in continuous fall of death rate, as for instance the death rate which was 27-28 per thousand during 1600-1800 came down to 9-10 per thousand by 1980-81. However if we look into the death rate of the Negro and red Indian population it is clear that the death rate among them is pretty high, just as in the case of the birth rate.

During the nineteenth century, the available data suggest varying levels of mortality in different areas. Mortality records for Massachusetts indicate a rate of 27.8 per 1,000 white population in 1789, which dropped steadily to 17.3 per 1,000 around 1900. This indicates that the level of mortality among Negroes was much higher than that among the white population of Massachusetts. In addition, while the life expectancy at birth for white males was 44 years in Massachusetts and 46 in New Jersey, it was 40 or fewer in Philadelphia and the District of Columbia and only 34 in the cities of New York, Charleston, and New Orleans. The corresponding life expectancy for black males was even lower.

Data for the United States between 1890 and 1977 (See Table 3) demonstrate a continuing decline (interrupted only by the influenza epidemic of 1918-1919). These data show that (1) whites have experienced lower mortality than nonwhites, and in each racial group females have experienced lower mortality than males; and (2) before 1940 the adjusted rates were higher than the crude rates, while the reverse is true for the white population after 1940. This reversal is the result of the shift in the proportions of susceptiable age groups.

Trends in infant and maternal mortality are worthy of special mention. The infant mortality rate per 1,000 live births dropped in Massachusetts from 131.1 in 1851-1854 to 22.8 in 1950-1954. For the United States, national data became available in 1915 when the rate was about 100 per 1,000. The rate has since declined to about 13.8 in 1978. The maternal mortality rate also has dropped phenomenally during the twentieth century. From over 600 per 100,000 in 1978 (U.S. Bureau of the Census, 1980*b*).

Racial differentials in infant mortality rates have also diminished. In 1977, the overall infant mortality rate was 14.1 per 1,000 infants born that year, 12.3 for white infants and 21.7 for nonwhite. In 1960, the national figure was 26; 22.9 for white infants and 43.2 for nonwhite.

Table 3. Crude and Age-Adjusted Death Rates (Using U.S. Population, 1940, as Standard) by Race and Sex, United States, 1890-1977

Year	*Crude death rate*				*Adjusted death rate*			
	White		*Nonwhite*		*White*		*Nonwhite*	
	Males	*Females*	*Males*	*Females*	*Males*	*Females*	*Males*	*Females*
1890	20.2	18.0	31.6	28.3	23.8	20.9	40.0	34.2
1900	17.7	16.3	25.7	24.4	18.4	16.8	28.7	27.1
1910	15.4	13.6	22.3	21.0	15.7	14.4	24.8	23.2
1920	13.0	12.1	17.8	17.5	14.2	13.1	20.4	21.0
1930	11.7	9.3	17.4	15.3	12.8	10.6	21.0	19.2
1940	11.6	9.2	15.1	12.6	11.6	8.8	17.6	15.0
1950	10.9	8.0	12.1	9.9	9.6	6.5	13.6	10.9
1960	11.0	8.0	11.5	8.7	9.2	5.6	12.1	8.9
1970	10.0	8.1	11.2	7.8	8.9	5.0	12.3	7.7
1977*	9.9	7.8	9.6	6·7	8.0	4.4	10.7	6.4

*Figures for 1977 were calculated from U.S. Bureau of the Census, 1980 Table 1, and from U.S. National Centre for Health Statistics, 1980, Part A, Table 1-2, and Part B, Table 7-3.

Source. Omran, 1980, Table 2.

Birth Rate

American birth rates rose to dizzy heights during the 1660-1800 period. The main reason for the above phenomenon was the availability of land and other resources in plenty. There was no shortage of wealth and food grains. During the initial stages joint family system was in vogue. Due to religious and cultural traditions artificial means of family planning were vehemently opposed. Society faced shortage of factors, to overcome which early marriage and too much children were considered feasible. The birth rate during the period of 1660-1800 remained round about 55 per thousand population. But this trend was not maintained in later years. Birth rate began to go down drastically and by 1950 the birth rate went down to 24 per thousand population. During the depression period of 1930-35 the birth rate declined to 18 per thousand population. The actual birth rate in 1980 was 15 per thousand.

These data are used in Fig. 1 to approximate fertility trends in the United States. It is unlikely that the birth rate was much higher than 55 per 1,000 in the early part of the century, even for the under privileged. A downward trend became visible throughout most of the first half of the twentieth century, reaching 19.7 per 1,000 among whites and 28.4 among nonwhites in 1945. For both groups, the rates then increased with a peak in the 1950s (due to the baby boom) and then declined again in the 1960s.

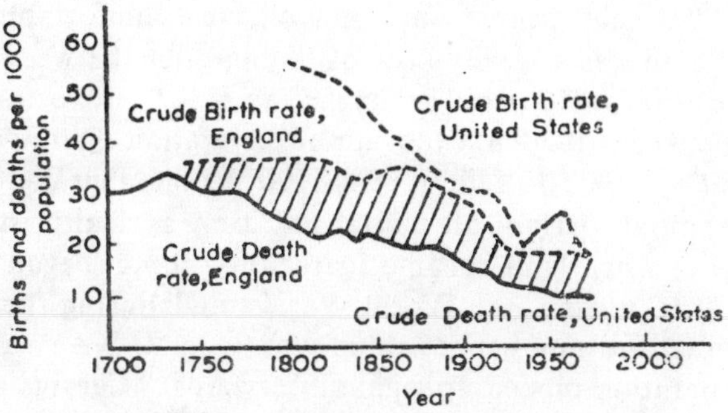

Mortality and fertility transition in the United States and England

Fig. 1

Life expectancy at birth for the total population in 1977 reached a record high of 73.2 years—a continuation of a general upward trend over the past several decades, as shown in Figure 2. Recent gains in life expectancy have been greater for females than for males.

Racial differentials in death rates and life expectancy that are characteristic of the United States have narrowed somewhat in the last decade. Expectation of life at birth for nonwhites in 1977 was 64.6 for males and 73.1 for females compared to 70.0 and 77.7, respectively for whites. Increases in life expectancy from 1940 to 1977 for nonwhites were approximately 12 years for males and 18 for females, while the increase for white males was 7 years, and for white females 10 years. The difference in life expectancy between the total white population and all other races in 1977 was 5 years.

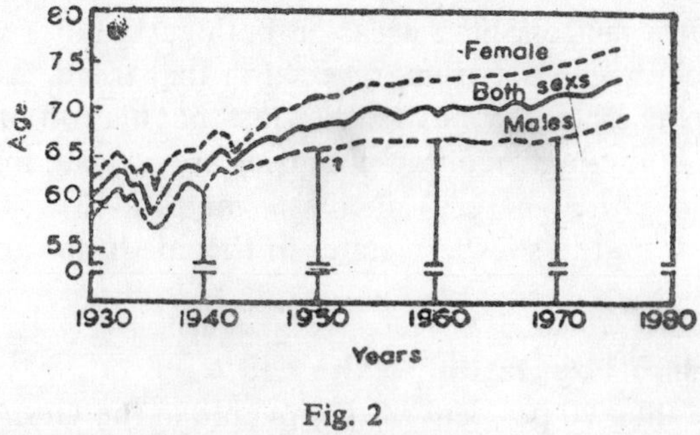

Fig. 2

Immigration

Today people from the nook and corner of the world make bee line to the U.S.A. to settle there. Employment prospects are very bright in U.S.A. and people can hope to have a comfortable standard of living. There was a steady flow of immigration between 1610 and 1914. In 1610 only 210 people migrated to U.S.A. It rose to 84,800 in 1960. Between 1830-40, the annual migration figure was 60,000 people. During 1901-10 about 8,80,000 people migrated to U.S.A. During the initial period of migration, only agriculturist migrated to U.S.A., but when land became scarce the people began to settle in cities. It is during the World War Ist and during the period of depression that the number of immigrants to U.S.A. came down. However migration picked up again afterwards. Migrants are drawn from the western as well as the eastern countries. Of late more and more restructions are imposed on the immigrants so that the native population gets full employment. Only limited categories of skilled workers are permitted to enter the country.

In 1980, the number of legal immigrants and refugees was of the order of 800,000. In addition, an unknown but evidently large number of persons enter the United States illegally. (Given the clandestine nature of this flow, no accurate data are available.) The number of emigrants from the United States has been systematically underestimated: it is probably at least 100,000 per year—nearly three times the figure employed in Census Bureau estimates and projections. Overall, there are likely to be as many as 1 million net immigrants to the United States each year.

About 18 per cent of the U.S. population changes residence every year, although many of these moves are of short distance. The major flow in this century was from the farm to the cities and from the south to the north. In 1900, 60 per cent of the population were on farms or in small towns. By 1970, that figure had declined to 26 per cent in a long, solid trend towards urbanization that created large, virtually unbroken metropolitan areas on both east and west coasts. The 1970s brought an apparent reversal of that trend. The largest metropolitan areas especially have either lost population or stopped growing, and the non-metropolitan countries are registering population gains from either natural increase, migration, or both. The earlier net flow from the southern states to the north has also reversed direction.

Rural and Urban Population in the U.S.A.

Today more than 70 per cent of the people in the U.S.A. lives in urban complex and the remaining 30 per cent in villages. Areas with 50,000 or less population are classified under the rural group. Till 1790 New York was the only city in America where more than 5 per cent of the entire population of U.S.A. was living and the rest of the population was living in rural areas. But since this period industrialization took place on a large scale which led to the influx of villagers to the cities. By 1920 the proportion of urban and rural population became equal. But the flow of population towards the cities continued unabated. But 1960 the percentage urban population outnumbered the rural population to the ratio of 70 : 30. Thus in 1960 the urban population in U.S.A. was 12.53 crores and the remaining rural population. Migration from rural area constituted the main single factor for the growing urbanization in the U.S.A.

The term urban in U.S.A. means urbanized area. As stated by Thompson and Lewis "The unbanised area can be characterised as the physical city as distinguished from both the legal city and the metropolitan community. In general unbanised areas represent the thickly settled urban core of the (larger) standard metropolitan areas."

In U.S.A. there are about 30 cities with population of 10 lakhs or more. New York with a population of 114 lakhs is the most thickly populated city. Some of the other cities are Los Angles, Chicago, San Francisco, etc.

Sex Ratio

Sex ratio is the number of males per hundred females which is worked out by dividing the total number of males by the total number of females and multiplying the product by 100. Till 1940, the ratio of male was higher than female. This was due to the fact that most of the immigrants were male. But the immigrants became land owners in later years and undertook agriculture on large scale. This along with the declining fear from red Indians encouraged the settlers to bring their wife and families into America. Consequently the proportion of women started rising very rapidly. By 1950 the ratio of females outnumbered the men. Among Negroes the number of women always remained higher than men. According to the U.S. Bureau of Census Report the sex ratio in U.S.A. has been given in Table 4.

From the Table 4 it becomes abundantly clear that till 1940 the proportion of male remained higher than female population and afterwards the proportion of men started declining. Among other nonwhites the proportion of male remained high till 1920 but afterwards the proportion of females rose in comparison to males. At present the proportion of females shows increase over the male population.

Table 4. Sex Ratio in U.S.A.

Year	Number of males per hundred females			
	All classes	White	Negro	Other nonwhite
1860	104.7	105.3	99.6	26.8
1900	104.4	104.9	98.6	185.2
1920	104.0	104.4	99.2	156.6
1950	98.6	99.0	94.3	131.7
1960	97.0	97.3	93.3	111.5
1965	97.4	na	na	na
1981	93.8	na.	na	na

Age Composition

In U.S.A. the composition of population shows that the maximum population amounting to 56 per cent belongs to the 15-59 age group, 31.10 per cent population belong to 0-14 age group and 13.21 per cent population falls in the age group 60 years and above.

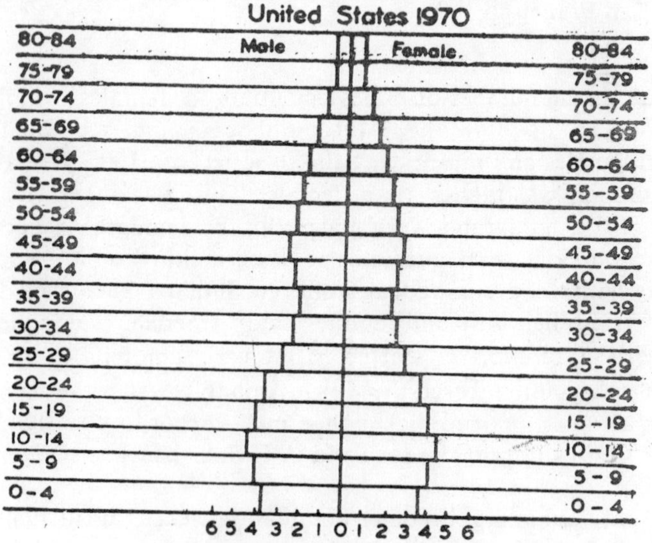

Fig. 3

The aging of the United States population has brought about a 2.4 per cent increase in the population aged 65 and over in the short period from 1975 to 1978. The age group from 5 to 17 declined during that period by 1.6 per cent, and the group under 5 years declined by 1.1 per cent. The median age of the population was 29.6 in 1978.

The population pyramids presented in Fig. 3 provided striking evidence of the variations in age distribution that can occur. The population of Sweden in 1970 had an age structure visibly older than that of the United States in 1970 and was in marked contrast to the very young population of Mexico in that year. Comparative analysis of the demographic rates that have prevailed in these three populations shows fertility differences to be the factor most responsible for these variations in age structure.

Marital Status

As per 1960 census, 25.1 per cent of U.S.A.'s male population were unmarried, 5.7 per cent were either divorced or widowers and the remaining 69.1 per cent were married. Of the female population 19.1 per cent were unmarried and 15.9 per cent divorced and the remaining 65.9 per cent were married. 90 to 95 per cent population of 35 years and above were married. Recently the phenomenon of early marriage is discernible. Between 1965-70 of every 3 persons belonging to the 14-24 year age group 2 were found to be married. Married women outnumber the men population. The number of windows is more than widowers which indicates higher life span among women.

The 1980 census showed that 2 out 3 belonging to 14 to 24 age group were married.

Marital disruption is also in an upward trend. There were about 92 divorced persons per 1,000 intact marriages in 1979, a 96 per cent increase from 1970. Remarriage rates are high, but there has been a marked increase in single-person households and in the proportion of families headed by women. Nearly one child in five was living with only one parent in 1979.

Age at Marriage

Age at marriage in the United States has been increasing since the 1960s to an average in 1979 of 22.1 years for women and 24.4 years for men. Some reasons offered for this change are the rising educational attainment that tends to delay marriage; economic uncertainty and high unemployment; and ideological changes regarding arly marriage and even the need to marry. An additional cause might be the increase in the number of couples living together outside of marriage, a number that was estimated at 1.3 million in 1979. Never-married women aged 25 to 29 increased by more than 100 per cent from 1960 to 1979.

Education

U.S.A. has cent per cent literacy level among the whites. Few among the negros and other non-whites are illiterate. Between 1965-70 it was observed that every year nearly 4.1 million children below 6 years newly entered educational institutions. The government makes elaborate arrangement like schools teachers and equipments to facilitate large intake of students. The number of college going students was 3.7 million per year between 1965-70.

Occupatienal Structure

U.S.A. today is a developed, wealthy commercially and industrially advanced country of the world. Occupational pattern shows that the vast majority are engaged in industry, trade finance and services. Agriculturists constitute less than 7 per cent of the population. The American economic transformation is a story of agrarian economy becoming an industrial country.

Classifications commonly used to depict the labour force and occupational characteristics of a population are shown in Table 5.

Population Policy

The United States does not have an explicit policy regarding the growth and distribution of the population. As in many other countries, however, there are policies and programmes on various social and economic subjects that together amount to a population policy.

United States population policy has been characterized by three broad perspectives.

1. In principle all persons are guaranteed access to family planning services and abortion, both through legislative mandate and judicial requirement. In fact such access applies only to methods of family planning; there is a continuing controversy over government support for abortion.

2. Massive investment in reduction of the mortality rate is made through expenditures in the areas of medical services and preventive health. There is considerable domestic debate as to the advisability of current policies regarding health care, but the magnitude of the investment cannot be doubted.

3. Policy with regard to immigration and refugees is apparently incoherent. The United States has a long tradition of openness to

Table 5. Percentage Distribution of Employed Persons, by Occupation and Race, 1960-1975[1]

Occupation	*White*					*Black and other*				
	1960	*1970*	*1973*	*1974*	*1975*	*1960*	*1970*	*1973*	*1974*	*1975*
Total employed (thousands)	58,850	70,182	75,278	76,620	75,713	6,927	8,415	9,131	9,316	9,070
Per cent	100.00	100.00	100.0	100.00	100.00	100.00	100.00	100.00	100 00	100,00
White-collar workers	46.6	50.8	49.9	50.6	51.7	16.1	27.9	31.1	32.0	34.2
Blue-collar workers	36.2	34.5	34.7	34.0	32.4	40.1	42.2	40.8	40.2	37.4
Service industries	9.9	10.7	11.7	11.8	12.3	31.7	26.0	25.4	25.1	25.8
Farm workers	7.4	4.0	3.7	3.6	3.6	12.1	3.9	2.8	2.7	2.6

[1]Covers persons 16 years old and over, Annual figures are monthly averages, 1973-1975 not comparable with prior years because of reclassification of census oecupation.

Sour ce: U.S. Bureau of the Census, 1976, p. 373.

immigration, but in the past decade the country has proved to be politically and administratively incapable of enforcing its own laws regarding such flows. The issue is a controversial and emotional one in domestic politics.

In the 1960s family planning became a legitimate part of regular medical services. The approximately 5,000 public and non-profit family planning clinics in the United States in 1980 were largely subsidized by various federal and state financing authorities. About three-fourths of the funds for organized family planning programmes in 1977 came from federal source.

In 1977, more than 4.2 million women went to public and non-profit clinics for family planning services. Most of them had low or marginal incomes, and about 1.3 million were adolescents. The pill and surgical sterilization were the main methods used. Approximately 1.4 million abortions (or 27.5 per 1000 women of reproductive age) were performed in the United States in 1978.

SELECT REFERENCES

1. Bogue, Donald J. and Wilson H. Grabill: *The Population of the United States*, The Free Press of Glencoe, New York, 1959.
2. Bowley, A.L.: "Estimates of the Working Population of Certain Countries in 1931 and 1941", submitted to the preparatory committee for the International Economic Conference. League of Nations, Geneva, 1926.
3. Federal Security Agency: "Man and His Years : An Account of the First National Conference on Aging", Health Publications Institute, Raleigh, N.C., 1951.
4. Hagood, Margaret J. and Jacob S. Siegel: "Projections of the Regional Distribution of the Population of the United States to 1975", *Agricultural Economics Research*, Vol. 3, No. 2, pp. 41-52, 1951.
5. Reed, Lowell J.: "Population Growth and Forecasts", Annals of the American Academy of Political Social Science, Vol. 188, pp. 159-166, 1936.
6. Terborgh, George: *The Bogey of Economic Maturity*, Machinery and Allied Products Institute, Chicago, 1945.
7. Thompson, Warren S.L.: "The Economic Consequences of Slow Population Growth in the United States", Proceedings, 1939 Ohio Conference of Statisticians on Business Research, Ohio State University, Columbus Ohio, pp. 3-11, 1940.
8. Thompson, Warren S.L.: "Future Population Growth and Real Estate Values". *Journal of Real Estate Appraisers*, Vol. 3, pp. 33-41, 1934.
9. Thompson, Warren S.L. and P. Whelpton: "Counting Tomorrow's Customers; How will America's Growth Affect Your Business?", *Nation's Business*, Vol. 17; pp. 41-42, 154-155, February, 1929.
10. United States: Commission on Population Growth and American Future. Population and the American Future. Washington, D.C. : U.S. Govern-

ment Printing Office, 1972, New York: New American Library (Signet) 1972.

11. United States: National Centre for Health Statistics, Monthly Vital Statistics Report 28(1), supplement, 11 May 1979. (United States, NCHS, 1967).
12. Vital Statistics of the United States. Issued annually by the U.S. National Centre for Health Statistics, Hyattsyilie, Md.

EXAMINATION QUESTIONS

1. Write a descriptive essay on the population of U.S.A.
2. Discuss the main demographic features of U.S.A.
3. Immigration was the primary reason for unprecedented growth of U.S. population from 19th century to 1930. Explain this statement and point out the various factors responsible for population growth.
4. Mention the causes responsible for the decline in the birth rate in U.S.A. Evaluate the population control policy of U.S. Government.

40

Population of Great Britain

Great Britain was one of the leading powers of the world till the Second World War. Numerically its strength was not large. The tendency to population growth could also be witnessed here just as in other countries of the world.

POPULATION GROWTH

The population growth in Great Britain falls into four parts:

1. Population Growth between 1800-1850

In 1901 the first census enumeration was held in Great Britain giving a population of 10 million. The population *inter alia*, included long number of migrants children constituted 35 per cent of the total population. System of registration was not in vogue during that period which makes it difficult to assess the birth and death rates. Subsequent census reveals that the annual increase in birth rate was 35 per thousand and death rate 22 per thousand. Death rate declined appreciably after 1940 with the result that the population showed large spurt. Agriculture was the mainstay of the people. Considerable proportion of the people worked in factories under deplorable conditions.

2. Population Growth between 1851-1900

This period witnessed remarkable technological growth. Population quadrapuled during this period. Improved medical facilities resulted in sharp fall in death rate. Nearly one million Britishers migrated to U.S.A. as immigrants. In the wake of prosperity women were conscious of limit in the family size. Spread of education also created consciousness among the masses to limit their numbers.

Age composition altered with the retardation of population growth. Children below 15 years constituted 3.2 per cent of the total population while those aged 60 years and above formed 5 per cent of the population.

3. Population Growth between 1901-1930

One of the salient feature of this period was the First World War which was responsible for large number of deaths of young man and women. The war also gave a momentum to migration. Age and sex composition in Britain also underwent sea change. The annual rate of population growth declined because the World War I took a heavy toll of births as well as death in England.

Economic depression and the resulting unemployment accentuated the desire to limit the famlly size. Postponement of marriage in several cases influenced fertility rate which reduced the growth rate of population. Improvement in the living standard of the people through the application of science to health problems also brought down death rate drastically. The total population above sixty years constituted 9 per cent during this period. Britain during this period had low birth rates and low death rates, both under a large measure of volundary control.

4. Population Growth between 1930 to Present Day

The Second World War, considerably influenced population growth in the United Kingdom. The aerial bombing of civilian population was begun early in the war. The United Kingdom suffered heavily from such bombing both early in the war and again near its close. Besides in the forward areas great many soldiers had to lay down their life, especially the youth. Rough estimates put it that nearly three lakh people of British origin ware either killed or wounded. Economic and trade position deteriorated with the result that people

Table 1. Total Population in Great Britain

(*in million*)

Year	*Population*
1950	50.29
1970	55.42
1979	55.84
1980	56.05

became keen to limit their family size. When the living standards of the people increased between 1950-60, then population growth rate in the country also increased. The percentage of married couples went up and more and more people began to feel interested in marriage. Birth rate of the children also increased. Large number of people from countries like, India, Pakistan, etc., migrated to Great Britain. Table 1 gives the population of Great Britain between 1950-80.

Density of Population

The average density of population in U.K. is 226 per square km. With the exception of Belgium, Netherlands and West Germany this is the highest density of population recorded for any country in Europe.

Northern England and South Wales are the centres of the densest population, because these are the industrial areas. Recently population in Southern England, particularly in the suburbs of London, has increased with great rapidity. Lancashire, Staffordshire, Durham, Glamorgan, and Warwickshire, have more than 600 people per square km. The industrial activities of these regions attracted people from other parts of the country.

Birth Rate

In England authoritative evidence of birth rate is lacking for want of registration figures till 1970. However available evidence indicates a rise in birth rate till 1870 followed by a 50 per cent fall between 1871-1935 and afterwards the birth rate further declined. In 1980 the crude birth rate in England was 12.3 whereas it was 16.5 in 1950.

As regards illegal abortion, the rate has been gradually coming down. It was 18 per thousand during 1861-65 for women between 15-45; which declined during subsequent period and reached 5.6 per cent during 1936-40. However of late, the rate of illegal abortion has picked up and the figure for 1971-81 stood at 21 per thousand.

Death Rate

Table 2 shows that during the last thirty years death rate in

Table 2. Crude Death Rate and Infant Mortality Rate

Years	*Death rate*	*Infant mortality rate*
1950	11.8	32.2
1960	11.5	22.6
1970	11.8	18.3
1980	11.9	12.4

Great Britain has stababilized at about 12 per thousand. No significant changes are to be expected in the next thirty years unless the difficult problems of the residual killing diseases (e.g., cancer) are solved.

In Great Britain infant mortality rate has declined remarkably since 1950, and it is really stabilized at a low level. Rapid declined in the rate is largely the result of improvement in the social environment, but the continuing decline in lower rates is probably because of increasing professional supervision of pregnancy and birth, and rising proportions of hospital deliveries. It is presumed that the present rates at over 12 per thousand will tend to fall still further.

Marriage and Divorce

The age of women at marriage has long been treated as an important determinant in fertility because it affects the length of exposure—to the risk of pregnancy. This factor is now less important than modern reliable contraception and the widespread norm of the two-child and three-child family. United Kingdom has witnessed a marked decline in marriage in recent years, from 470,000 in 1970 to 416,000 in 1979. The cause of this decline is the increasing numbers of young men and women who choose to cohabit, sometimes quite permanently, without marriage: many of these couples have children and many actually marry at quite a late stage of bringing them up.

An important feature of Great Britain's nuptiality is the increase in divorce since 1960. It is now found that in the United Kingdom about 20 to 25 per cent of present marriages will terminate in divorce. The number of divorces in United Kingdom was 398,000 in 1965 which increased to 152,700 in 1977-78. In general, the divorce rate is higher in towns than in rural areas, owing to different social attitudes as well as economic conditions.

Pattern of Households

England and Wales have witnessed a great increase in the numbers of households, owing to more marriages, earlier marriages and smaller families. They have risen from just below 8 million in 1911 to 16,503,000 in 1971. By 1971, some 9,542,000 of all private households had no child under age 15, and 3,554,000 had only one child. Nearly one in seven contained only one person; this does not imply that all such persons are living entirely alone, but it is indicative of family fragmentation.

Age Composition

Great Britain has a narrow base age pyramid implying a small proportion of young population with a significantly broader top. The age structure of Great Britain's population with nearly 23.1 per cent below 15 years of age and 15 per cent being of age 60 years and above has remained almost stable over the last two decades.

Projection of Population

Various projection on the likely population at the turn of the century have been made from time to time. Royal Commission on population and Government Actuary's department also have made attempts in this direction. But the authors of "Pears Encyclopaedia" are of the view that, "Predictions of future trends is difficult. . . . In the near future the population will certainly continue to rise slowly as improving medical services raise the average length of life and as the gap between the generation shortens". However, the present population situation of Great Britain suggests a continuing trend towards low fertility and low mortality, with high marriage rates and small family size, including some increase in childless women. It is probable that all European countries with the exception of West and East Germany will have larger population in the year 2000 than in 1975. Developments after 2000 will increasingly depend on fertility trends over next two or three decades and the way they affect the age structures. According to the United Nations projection, the population of Great Britain in the year 2000 would be about 57,525 thousands whereas in 1979 it was 55,840 thousands.

Table 3 sets out some estimates of broad age groupings and shows the expected trend towards a smaller proportion of children and young people and some increase in the elderly with less marked changes in the adolescent and adult population, the economically active age groups.

Table 3. Population Projections of Great Britain by the Age Group

	Age groups		
	Below 15	*15-64*	*65+*
1975	22.5	63.5	14.0
2000	22.0	63.8	14,2